PIONEERS IN CRIMINOLOGY

PUBLICATION NO. 121 IN THE
PATTERSON SMITH SERIES IN
CRIMINOLOGY, LAW ENFORCEMENT, AND SOCIAL PROBLEMS

A listing of publications in the SERIES *will be found at rear of volume*

PUBLICATION No. 121: PATTERSON SMITH REPRINT SERIES IN
CRIMINOLOGY, LAW ENFORCEMENT, AND SOCIAL PROBLEMS

PIONEERS

IN

CRIMINOLOGY

EDITED AND INTRODUCED

BY

HERMANN MANNHEIM

SECOND EDITION ENLARGED

MONTCLAIR, NEW JERSEY

PATTERSON SMITH

1972

Second edition published 1972 by
Patterson Smith Publishing Corporation
Montclair, New Jersey 07042

Library of Congress Cataloging in Publication Data

Mannheim, Hermann, 1889–   ed.
    Pioneers in criminology. 2d ed. enlarged.
    (Patterson Smith series in criminology, law
enforcement, and social problems. Publication
no. 121)
    Includes bibliographical references.
    1. Criminologists. I. Title
HV6025.M322   1972   364'.092'2 [B]   78-108238
              ISBN 0-87585-121-5

This book is printed on
permanent/durable paper

CONTENTS

PREFACE TO THE SECOND EDITION

THE first edition of *Pioneers in Criminology* was published in 1960. The book quickly became established throughout the world as a widely used and quoted standard work on the history of criminology and penology. It is very satisfying, therefore, that it has now been possible to enlarge the work and issue a second edition. The thanks of the Editor are due to the former Editor-in-Chief of the *Journal of Criminal Law, Criminology and Police Science,* Professor Fred E. Inbau of the Northwestern University School of Law, Chicago, Illinois, and to the Patterson Smith Publishing Corporation, Montclair, New Jersey, whose interest and joint efforts have made this a reality.[1]

Six new essays have been added to the original collection: two on American pioneers, Edward Livingston and John Henry Wigmore; two on Frenchmen, Arnould Bonneville de Marsangy and Charles Lucas; and one each on an Englishman, William Douglas Morrison, and a German, Karl Roeder.[2] It might be argued by critics that some of these newcomers were comparatively minor figures in the history of our subject. This may be true if they are considered against the background of such famous innovators as Beccaria, Bentham, Lombroso or Ferri, men whose writings had a world-wide appeal and initiated ideas and movements of first-rate importance to the progress of criminology. On the other hand, not all of those included in the first edition were men of such stature, and the inclusion of a few relatively minor figures can be of distinct value, not only to the historian but also to those penologists and politicians in many countries who, having to make practical decisions, are interested in the intricate pros and cons in the evolution

---

[1] In my original Preface I mentioned the great and lasting contributions made to criminological literature in general and to the "Pioneers" articles in particular by Professor Robert H. Gault. His "unbroken record of half a century of successful editorial work" can, I wrote, "have very few parallels in the history of publishing." Now it is my sad duty to report his death at the ripe age of 96 years. Among the many monuments he is leaving behind, his work for the "Pioneers" will not be forgotten.

The death of two of our contributors, Mr. Justice Barry and Professor Millar, has also to be recorded.

[2] The selection has again been in line with the general policy to include in *Pioneers in Criminology* only essays previously published in the *Journal.* Another large volume might profitably be devoted by future editors to such outstanding historical figures as John Howard, Sir Samuel Romilly, Adolphe Quételet, and, to mention only a few more recent names, to Sigmund Freud, Franz von Liszt, Etienne de Greeff, Edwin H. Sutherland and Clifford Shaw.

of progressive ideas. The newcomers to the present series, for example, have made significant contributions to the literature in the areas of the abolition of capital punishment and its alternatives; parole and indeterminate sentences; constructive work with pay for prisoners; the establishment of a legal basis for the relationship between the prisoner and the state; state compensation for the victim of violent crime; and, last but not least, the awareness that crime may sometimes be due to the inhumanity and class bias of the criminal law and the penal system. Where, on the other hand, they fought for ideas which are now regarded as retrogressive, such as overly harsh treatment of all those sentenced to life imprisonment for murder or solitary confinement for all long-term prisoners, we must understand these ideas in their contemporary setting and realize that these concepts often were an improvement over the prevailing practices. In the field of methodology, too, it is of interest to see that, long before the coming of the Positive School, some of our pioneers, especially Livingston, made use of empirical techniques of research, such as case histories, questionnaires, and statistical tables. Field-work methods such as visits of observation to penal institutions, of course, had already been employed by John Howard before they were contemplated by Livingston.

To take up another point, the study of some of the additional essays may remind readers of the discussion in our Introduction to the first edition of the problem, "men or movements." Here again it is obvious that certain ideas, notably parole and the indeterminate sentence, have at certain moments of history been "in the air" and "only waiting for somebody to take them up." Whether the idea of parole was first mooted, as English-speaking penologists are inclined to think, by Maconochie and Crofton, or, as French experts tend to assume, by Bonneville de Marsangy, will probably never be decided to the general satisfaction of all those interested in the history of the matter. As André Normandeau writes: "The innovations of history are often created independently and almost simultaneously." Moreover, even if the idea was "in the air" simultaneously in several countries, the expression which it found in legislative thought was far from uniform.

Whereas fewer than one-half of the seventeen pioneers represented in the first edition were lawyers and nearly as many were members of the medical profession, the professional distribution among the newcomers is different: with the exception of the theologian Morrison, they are all jurists and administrators. Some of them, Livingston, Bonneville and Roeder, were greatly interested in legal philosophy and legislative reform, which latter they tried to place on a sound scientific basis within the limits and possibilities provided by the tools of scientific knowledge available at the time. Characteristic of this is, for example, Bonneville's dictum, quoted by Normandeau, that the study of innovations in penal reform should be based on "comparative legislation and statistics" because this makes it "difficult for serious authors to go astray, since the first shows them the state of laws, and the second, the state of facts." This is admirable as far as it goes, if only we bear in mind that the "facts" produced by statistics can often be accepted only with a good many reservations and that the really crucial arguments in deciding on important pieces of law reform frequently are based, subconsciously at least, not on the study of comparative legislation nor on that of comparative statistics but on deep-rooted emotional and political motivations.

A special word may be warranted with regard to John Henry Wigmore, the eminent authority on the law of evidence, because of his outstanding services in connection with the founding of the *Journal of Criminal Law and Criminology,* as it was then called. As is generally known, it was under the auspices of the *Journal* that this series of "Pioneers" was conceived and published, but it may not be equally remembered now, after the lapse of sixty years, that the preparatory work required to bring the *Journal* into existence was done, as pointed out in Professor Millar's essay, mainly by Wigmore. Moreover, as he was also the "prime mover and architect" in the establishment of the American Institute of Criminal Law and Criminology, which in turn produced the Modern Criminal Science Series, it is fitting that he should be honored not only as a great jurist but also as a pioneer in criminology.

In 1960 a fairly substantial section of my Introduction was devoted to a critical appraisal of Professor Jeffery's concluding chapter. He has now supplied a postscript in which he discusses what he considers to be American trends in criminology during the 1960s. In it he also comments on some of the points which I had made in my Introduction and elsewhere. While some of his material is interesting as reflecting views recently expressed by American courts and writers I regret to say that I do not throughout find it easy to reach a common basis with him. My position towards Jeffery's criticisms of Positivism and of myself is still difficult to define in a few sentences. As I wrote in 1960 (p. 9), "Much as we might disagree with some of his views, it is greatly to his credit that he forces us to reconsider the whole relationship between Positivism and Criminology." As far as my own writings are concerned, Jeffery now, as in his 1960 contribution, criticises certain points made in my *Group Problems in Crime and Punishment*,[3] but he does not appear to have considered the relevant sections of my *Comparative Criminology*.[4] It would be too tedious to deal here with all the points of difference between us or to repeat once more that I am not a positivist, not even a "neo" one. I will rather confine myself to a few brief remarks on more specific points.

First, there is the position of the sociology of the criminal law— is its study the task of criminology or of the sociology of law in general? Jeffery is in favor of the first, whereas I would prefer the second. However, this is a problem on which one should not be too dogmatic. In *Group Problems* I have discussed at some length all its aspects (pp. 250–71), and I would have wished that Jeffery had considered my arguments instead of merely saying that they remind him of Ferri. And he might also have taken into account the reservation expressed in my Introduction (p. 33): "it may be argued, however, that it does not greatly matter who has to undertake that study if only it is done by somebody. The essential point of difference lies elsewhere: while the task defined by Jeffery is important, it can be no more a substitute for the study of the individual criminal than vice versa. Both are equally indispensable."

Jeffery further criticises my view that "criminology must be made independent of criminal law," and adds, "This position, which is basic to positivism, has been rejected in American criminology in the 1960s." Here, I am afraid, I can find little room for a compromise. However, even here I have always made the important reservation that criminologists should never ignore the criminal law and that no behavior should be called a "crime" which is not a crime in law.[5] We have now the useful term "deviance" for such forms of behavior. I make no attempt here to decide how far Jeffery's contention is correct that the independence of criminology

[3] 1955; 2nd ed., Montclair, N.J., 1971.
[4] Boston, 1965.
[5] *Comparative Criminology*, Chaps. I and II, especially pp. 14ff. and 34.

from the criminal law—always understood with the above reservations—has been rejected in American criminology of the 1960s, but even if it were correct this in itself would provide no sufficient proof that the view he attacks is wrong. In scientific discussions it is the strength of the arguments that matters, not the size of the battalions drawn up on opposing sides. If Jeffery had extended his survey beyond the frontiers of American criminology he might perhaps have become less sure of his position.[6]

One final point: Jeffery wishes to build up a "third school" of criminology that "transcends both the Classical and Positive Schools." I share this wish. It is not of recent origin, and in my sixty years on the job I have seen many such attempts. Jeffery thinks that in my Introduction I regarded the movement of Social Defence as presenting such a "third school", but if he had carefully read what I wrote there (p. 35) he might have had some doubts on my attitude. He then suggests reform of the environment for the "third school" of the future. If he were to read the relevant chapters of *Comparative Criminology*,[7] he might discover that our views on this subject are perhaps not as far apart as he seems to think—Positivism or no Positivism! Let us free ourselves of all these unnecessary slogans and tackle the really vital matters. And on this relatively happy note I close this discussion and leave it to the editor of the Third Edition—whoever he may be—to carry on in due course, not on "positivist" or "anti-positivist" but on positive and constructive lines!

HERMANN MANNHEIM.

London, July 1972

---

[6] See, for example, one of the best recent German texts, H. Göppinger, *Kriminologie*, Munich, 1971, pp. 12–14.
[7] Especially Part IV, Chaps. XIX–XXIII.

PREFACE TO THE FIRST EDITION

I⸀ has been a great pleasure to accept the invitation extended to me by Professor Robert H. Gault, Editor-in-Chief of the American *Journal of Criminal Law, Criminology and Police Science*, and his Editorial Board to assume the Editorship of a volume reproducing their series "Pioneers in Criminology" which was then nearing completion. I regard it as an honour done not only to me personally, but to European criminology as a whole. Coming at the present time, it is also a gesture of some historical significance. The "National Conference of Criminal Law and Criminology," held at Northwestern University, Chicago, fifty-one years ago in June 1909, proved to be an important landmark in the history of criminology. The American Institute of Criminal Law and Criminology was then created, and its *Journal*, now completing its fiftieth volume, was founded under its original title of *Journal of Criminal Law and Criminology*, with Robert H. Gault assuming the Editorship one year later. Surely, such an unbroken record of half a century of successful editorial work can have very few parallels in the history of publishing.

At the same Conference it was resolved " that important treatises on criminology in foreign languages be made readily accessible in the English language," and accordingly a committee of five was appointed to select such treatises and to arrange for their translation and publication. Among the members of this Committee we find such distinguished names as Dean Roscoe Pound and Dean John H. Wigmore. The achievements of the Committee are known to every criminologist. In their *Modern Criminal Science Series*, within the short period between the years 1911 and 1917, English translations were published of nine of the principal works of the leading European criminologists of the time: C. Bernaldo de Quirós, Hans Gross, Cesare Lombroso, Gabriel Tarde, Raymond Saleilles, Gustav Aschaffenburg, Raffaele Garofalo, Willem A. Bonger and Enrico Ferri. The stimulating effect which these publications had on criminological thought in the United States and the encouragement they gave to European scholars can hardly be overrated. With only two exceptions the same authors are also represented in the present volume. In addition, we have now five pioneers of British descent, Bentham, Haviland, Maconochie, Maudsley and Goring; one Spaniard, Montero; one Italian, Beccaria; one Frenchman, Durkheim. Only two Americans, Ray and Doe, have been included, which may be regarded as an under-representation, but it is also a consequence of the fact that American criminology began to develop comparatively late. On the other hand, it is in keeping with its rapid growth in recent decades that twelve of our contributors are Americans. There are also six non-Americans among them, representing Australia, Austria, Great Britain, Western Germany, the Netherlands and the Spanish-speaking world.

Unavoidably in any such symposium, the contributions show certain differences in approach, in the technique of presentation, in length and fullness of the bibliographical documentation, and in many other ways. The Editor, while trying to reduce technical differences, has not thought it advisable to interfere too drastically with the freedom accorded to individual contributors.

In the following, the chapters on individual pioneers have been reproduced in chronological order, *i.e.*, according to the dates of birth. Any other classification, as shown in Professor Jeffery's concluding chapter and in the Introduction, might have been controversial and of doubtful value since most of our pioneers could easily be classified under various headings.

Naturally, any such selection of " pioneers " will be open to criticisms from many quarters. Some of them have been anticipated in the Introduction. Time and space did not permit to make the present volume more comprehensive, but it is the hope of the Editor that, if this venture should be favourably received, the existing gaps may be filled in a second volume.

Acknowledgments have to be made to Northwestern University School of Law, Chicago, as the owners of the *Journal of Criminal Law, Criminology and Police Science* and to The Williams &

Wilkins Co., Baltimore, for permission to reprint the contributions which have appeared in the *Journal*. More specific references to these sources can be found in the appropriate places of this volume. The thanks of the Editor are also due to Professor Robert H. Gault, to his successor, Professor Claude R. Sowle of Northwestern University, and to Messrs. Stevens & Sons, Limited, for their invaluable help.

HERMANN MANNHEIM.

THE LONDON SCHOOL OF ECONOMICS AND POLITICAL SCIENCE
(UNIVERSITY OF LONDON).

March 1960.

NOTE ON THE EDITOR

Dr. HERMANN MANNHEIM was born of German nationality and studied law at various German universities, taking his degree of Dr.juris in 1912 and qualifying as an assistant judge soon afterwards. In the First World War he became a judge of courts-martial. He was appointed a judge in the criminal courts of Berlin in 1923, and was later promoted to a judgeship of the Kammergericht; also in 1923 he was made a lecturer in the Law Faculty of Berlin University, of which he was to become professor. When Hitler came to power he was dismissed from his professorial post; the following year he emigrated to the United Kingdom (acquiring British citizenship in 1940). There he became a lecturer and then a reader (associate professor) in criminology at the London School of Economics and Political Science, where he established criminology as an academic discipline. Since his retirement in 1955 he has concentrated on editing and writing.

Dr. Mannheim is a Vice-President of the Institute for the Study and Treatment of Delinquency (in London), and of the British Society of Criminology, which he founded with Edward Glover; he is also a co-founder of the *British Journal of Criminology;* for several years he was a member of the Council and President of the Scientific Commission of the International Society of Criminology (in Paris). He holds honorary doctorates from the universities of Utrecht and Wales, is an Officer of the Order of the British Empire, and has been awarded the Grand Cross of the Order of Merit of the German Federal Republic and the Golden Beccaria Medal of the German Society of Criminology. His publications include *The Dilemma of Penal Reform* (1939), *Social Aspects of Crime in England between the Wars* (1940), *War and Crime* (1941), *Young Offenders* (with A. M. Carr-Saunders and E. C. Rhodes) (1942), *Criminal Justice and Social Reconstruction* (1946), *Juvenile Delinquency in an English*

Middletown (1948; reprinted 1971), *Prediction Methods in relation to Borstal Training* (with Leslie T. Wilkins) (1955), *Group Problems in Crime and Punishment* (1955; 2nd edition 1971), *Deutsche Strafrechtsreform in englischer Sicht* (1960), *Comparative Criminology: A Text Book* (1965), and numerous articles and reviews in periodicals, notably in the *British Journal of Criminology*. He also served as an editor of the International Library of Criminology.

PIONEERS IN CRIMINOLOGY

1

INTRODUCTION

The place of our pioneers in the history of criminology—Men or Movements ?

It is not without significance that this volume is called not *Pioneer Criminologists*, but *Pioneers in Criminology*. In fact, many of those included may not have regarded themselves as criminologists at all, but rather as lawyers, psychiatrists, sociologists, administrators or architects, who happened to be interested in crime and criminals. The appearance of a separate profession of criminologists, theoretical and practical, is a comparatively recent development, and even nowadays the foundations of this calling are far from secure. With some slight over-simplification it might well be said that most criminologists are still inclined to think of themselves in terms of the discipline in which they took their first university examinations, and for those who courageously insist on calling themselves criminologists the label " kings without a country " has not yet lost its adhesive strength. Should we, perhaps, following the well-known definition of criminals as being individuals who " conceive of themselves as criminals," call criminologists only those who are such in their own estimation? Or would not these views lead to regrettable losses to both the criminal classes and the criminological profession? This is particularly likely to happen in view of the fact that until the middle of the last century writers and men of action interested in problems of crime and punishment would hardly have thought of calling themselves criminologists, nor would they have been so described by others.

The term " criminology " was, according to Bonger, first used by the French anthropologist Topinard, whose principal work appeared in 1879. For writers of the eighteenth and early nineteenth centuries, whose main interest was in the punishment or treatment rather than in the scientific analysis and observation of crime and criminals, the description " penologist " and, still better, " penal reformer " would have been more appropriate. In his

Introduction to Bernaldo De Quiros's *Modern Theories of Criminality*, W. W. Smithers wrote, and not without reason: " The science of criminology is a secondary evolutional consequence of the study of penology. The early writers who from humanitarian impulses condemned the severities attending the administration of criminal law . . . had no thought of creating a new science." And in the Preface to the English translation of Beccaria's famous book the author is, very properly, called " a philosopher who introduced humanity into the legal codes of the Continent." [1] Humanity, not science! Beccaria, it is true, did include in his treatise a chapter " Of the Sciences " which begins: " Would you prevent crime? Let liberty be attended with knowledge," but what he meant had but little to do with scientific knowledge in the modern sense. Jeremy Bentham was both a great humanist and a scholar of genius, but his scientific work was almost exclusively concerned with the reform of English law and of the English penal system, and he had no understanding of criminological problems in the narrower sense of the term. Maconochie, who was a practical administrator and had an instinctive understanding of the personality of the criminal, miles apart from Beccaria's and Bentham's purely theoretical approach to penal matters, nevertheless shared with them their rather one-sided predilection for the penological side of the subject. This was natural enough since, in spite of the beginning of statistical studies of crime in the 1830s, even the most primitive tools of criminological research were still lacking at his time.

Looking at the principal inclinations and qualifications and at the official status of our pioneers we find that eight of them—Beccaria, Bentham, Ferri, Garofalo, Montero, Tarde, Gross and Doe—were lawyers; five—Ray, Maudsley, Lombroso, Goring and Aschaffenburg—were members of the medical profession, most of them psychiatrists; two—Durkheim and Bonger—were sociologists; one—Maconochie—was a naval officer and geographer; and one—Haviland—an architect. In some cases, however, such a classification would appear to be over-simplified and hardly reveal the real position. Tarde, for example, was a sociologist at least as much as he was a lawyer; he was a professor of modern philosophy at the

[1] Preface to *An Essay on Crimes and Punishments.* Translated from the Italian of Marquis Beccaria with the Commentary by Voltaire, translated from the French. The 5th ed., revised and corrected, London, 1804.

Collège de France and also did distinguished work on criminal statistics; Bonger, the sociologist, on the other hand, had also been a student of law. Beccaria became a professor of political economy soon after writing his treatise; Durkheim's chair was one of philosophy; Ferri was a passionate politician.

The aggregate life span of our pioneers covers more than two hundred years, ranging from the year 1738, when Beccaria was born, to 1944 when Aschaffenburg died. Chronologically, only one of them, Beccaria, is entirely an eighteenth-century figure. Bentham and Haviland belong to both the eighteenth and the nineteenth centuries, Ray and Doe entirely to the latter; and all the others had their feet in both the nineteenth and twentieth centuries. Chronologically, too, it is interesting to observe that two of the most momentous events in the history of criminology occurred in the sixties and seventies of the eighteenth and nineteenth centuries: the publication of Beccaria's *Dei Delitti e Delle Pene* in 1764 and Lombroso's *L'uomo Delinquente* in 1876. Are we to expect similar bombshells in the coming two decades, and from which direction are they likely to come?

Chronological reflections apart, it is far from easy to determine the exact place occupied by each one of our pioneers in the history of criminology and of the social sciences in general. This is all the more so since, as already indicated, they differ profoundly in the range of their abilities and interests as well as in the extent and intensity of their contacts with our discipline. Some of them, for example, Bentham, Tarde and Ferri, cover, if not the whole field, at least large sections of it; others, in particular Haviland and Doe, touch only the fringe. If we take two near-contemporaries, Beccaria and Bentham, we find that the former's contributions to criminological thought were almost exclusively confined to one book, whereas the latter, favoured not only with greater ability but also with a much longer life span, has to his credit a whole library of penological works. When looking at Beccaria's work we are in some ways reminded of the far greater figure of his compatriot Niccolo Machiavelli of two and a half centuries before. Each of these two men is remembered and has become world-famous chiefly through one slim book, written on the spur of the moment within the short time of six or nine months. Neither of them anticipated the full impact of his work on future generations, and *mutatis mutandis* what has been said of Machiavelli is also true of Beccaria: " Had he been a shrewd and profound historian Machiavelli would merely have written a masterpiece. As it was, he was a very bad historian, and he thereby became a universal influence. . . . Certainly, he gave to posterity far more than he directly intended." [2] Here, however, the similarity between these two men ends; whereas Machiavelli, in addition to *Il Principe*, produced several historical works of great value, notably his *Discorsi* and his *History of Florence*, Beccaria's other writings, mostly on non-penological topics, are rightly forgotten,[3] although Coleman Phillipson regards his lectures on political economy, " considering the date of their composition," as a remarkable production.[4]

What is it that makes a man a " pioneer "? Is it the objective value of his work or rather its effect, its impact on posterity? " Bonger," writes Professor van Bemmelen in the present volume, " was certainly a great man. Not one of the greatest in history, but his publications had great effect. It was due to him that criminology in Holland became a separate field of science." Here the main emphasis is placed on the effect of Bonger's work, although van Bemmelen gives all due credit to the intrinsic value of Bonger's writings, too. Most likely both are needed, intrinsic value and external success. Without a certain measure of lasting success the achievements of an individual would soon pass into oblivion and, except for a few specialists, nobody would know enough about him to proclaim his fame. Achievement, real merit, is also required, however, to furnish the material for the historian's work. Nevertheless, it all remains a question of degree, and some of our pioneers are no doubt more distinguished by their success than by their real achievements in the fields of criminology and penal reform.

Moreover, what do we mean by " value " and " success " when dealing with historical processes? And how far can we expect an individual worker, single-handed, to influence historical developments? Has he, to be regarded as successful, to discover striking new facts or to formulate a new criminological " law "; to be responsible for major changes in penal policy; to produce a new

[2] Federico Chabod, *Machiavelli and the Renaissance* (English ed., 1958, London), p. 120; Friedrich Meinecke, *Die Idee der Staatsräson* (München and Berlin, 1924), p. 187.

[3] *Opere diverse del Marchese Cesare Beccaria Bonesana*, Patrizio Milanese (2 vols., Napoli, 1770); *Le Consulte Amministrative inedite di Cesare Beccaria a cura di C. A. Vianello* (Milano, 1943).

[4] Coleman Phillipson, *Three Criminal Law Reformers* (1923; reprinted Montclair, N.J., 1970), p. 21.

and better understanding on the part of society of crime and criminals and of the true functions of the penal system? Is it at all justifiable or even possible to write the history of criminology around the lives and the work of, say, a few dozen great figures and their respective "Schools," or should we rather concentrate on the history of ideas? Men or Movements? We are here confronted with one of the fundamental and most controversial problems in the philosophy of history. "Historically significant developments can be treated either as the history of individuals, or of groups as individual media of historical actions, or as history of contents, of impersonal, material or ideal objects. The history of art can be written as the history of artists or as that of styles, of forms of expression . . . as a matter of principle there is always the possibility to start either from the subject or from the contents." [5] Actually, this tolerant view has often been ignored. On the one hand, there are the extreme hero-worshippers such as Carlyle, Treitschke or Nietzsche who, proclaiming the "religion of the great man," dominated the scene in the late nineteenth century. If they would have their way altogether, history would be reduced to mere biography. There are, on the other hand, the equally extreme worshippers of the crowd, of mass movements, those who, with Marx, believe that impersonal, mainly material, forces determine the course of history and that the individual is nothing but their tool.[6] From this point of view, if even Julius Caesar was nothing but the incarnation of the "*Weltgeist*," [7] such comparatively minor figures as Beccaria or Lombroso could only be regarded as inflated dummies, thrown up by the waves of the Age of Enlightenment or that of Evolution. This interpretation might be particularly tempting in the case of Beccaria, whose indebtedness to the great French philosophers was so strong that his book has often been claimed as their spiritual property. Between the more extreme theories, however, we find a great variety of intermediate views with innumerable shades and qualifications. "The outbreak of the second Punic War," wrote one of the great late nineteenth-century historians,[8] "was the result of a decision taken by Hannibal, that

---

[5] Georg Simmel, *Die Probleme der Geschichtsphilosophie* (5th ed., 1923, München und Leipzig), p. 65. (Editor's translation.)
[6] Simmel, p. 207 *et seq.*
[7] Alfred Heuss, *Theodor Mommsen und das 19. Jahrhundert* (Kiel, 1958), p. 79.
[8] Eduard Meyer, *Zur Theorie und Methodik der Geschichte* (Halle, 1902), pp. 16 and 50 *et seq.* (Editor's translation), and the criticism of his views by Max Weber, *Gesammelte Aufsätze zur Wissenschaftslehre* (Tübingen, 1922), pp. 215 and 266 *et seq.*

of the Seven Years' War of a decision by Frederick the Great, and that of the 1866 War was due to a move by Bismarck. They could have decided differently; other men would have done so, and the course of history would have been a different one "; but, he adds, whether those wars could have been avoided is a question which nobody can answer. Nowadays, it is more intriguing to speculate whether the Bolshevist Revolution would not have happened without Lenin's return to Russia. Criminologists might ask whether the course of events in their field of study would have been radically changed if, say, Beccaria, Bentham, Lombroso or Ferri had not lived, or at least not published, their major works. To give an answer one would have to write a detailed history of the past two hundred years of our subject, and even then one would probably have to admit failure. A recent writer, Philip Bagby, who postulates that " new ideas are produced by the culture and not by individuals " is nevertheless willing to admit that " occasionally individuals do affect culture "; this happens, he thinks, mainly by way of invention and discovery, but even here in most cases " a number of different people have been working on the same problem." [9]   One thing seems to be certain, *i.e.*, that we have become rather sceptical of the idea of " historical inevitability " [10] and of grandiose and brilliant schemes such as Comte's, Spengler's, Toynbee's or Sorokin's. While it is entirely permissible, therefore, or indeed essential to stress that at certain stages of criminological history certain ideas and theories seemed to have been " in the air " and only waiting for somebody to take them up, we shall never be able to say with any degree of certainty that, because of the immanent force of circumstances at the critical time, even without the appearance of this or that great man, without the additional and unique stimulus emanating from him, the history of criminology would have taken the same course. Lombroso was no doubt, as Professor Wolfgang points out, deeply indebted to the anthropological studies of Gall, Broca, to Darwin, Virchow and many others.   Nevertheless, without his unbounded, though often uncritical, enthusiasm crimino-anthropology would hardly have gained the hold it had upon many minds in many European countries for nearly a hundred years.   And but for Enrico Ferri's fanatical

[9] Philip Bagby, *Culture and History : Prolegomena to the Comparative Study of Civilizations* (London-New York-Toronto, 1958), p. 151 *et seq.*
[10] Against this idea, see Isaiah Berlin, *Historical Inevitability* (Auguste Comte Memorial Trust Lecture No. 1, London, 1954), esp. p. 69 *et seq.*

eloquence and the " phenomenal success of his South American lecture tour " (Sellin) the lasting influence which the anthropological School achieved in that continent would hardly be explicable.[11]

Interestingly enough, at least one of those represented in the present series, Willem Bonger, seems to have been fully aware of this problem of the great man *versus* mass movements. As van Bemmelen points out, Bonger, a socialist in politics and a sociological environmentalist in his scientific work, was opposed to Carlyle's concept of the great man, but even he was not able to follow the opposite line of thought right through to the end.

Whichever of these views we accept, the personalities of the men with whom we are here dealing cannot be ignored. Even those who regard ideas and movements as all-important will wish to know how and why certain men were chosen as their instruments. How much, then, do we learn from the following sketches about the persons behind the books and why they became interested in this particular subject? Might at least some of these men have undergone childhood experiences of the unhappy nature commonly regarded as criminogenic and might they have taken to the study of crime because of an early acquired feeling of fellowship with the offender and sympathy for the outcast? In the case of Beccaria we hear that he was a rebel against the authority of his father and his school and that, as John Howard before and Alexander Maconochie after him, he had some personal experience of imprisonment, though of a non-penal character. Many of Bentham's biographers have commented upon his mental precocity, coupled with retarded physical growth; upon the tormenting effect of the ghost stories inflicted on him by servants; upon the premature death of his mother, leaving him with a hectoring and unimaginative father and an unloved step-mother.[12] On the other hand, although Ferri, coming from a poor family, had a " somewhat perturbed education," his early history, turbulent as it was, seems to be a typical success story; and in most of the biographical sketches in this book there are no indications of any serious childhood troubles. Dorado Montero seems to be another of the few exceptions; his early accident which left him crippled is regarded by Dr. Lopez-Rey as a factor undoubtedly influencing his already reserved and not very

---

[11] On this see the detailed study by Günter Blau, *Gefährlichkeitsbegriff und sichernde Massregeln im iberoamerikanischen Strafrecht* (Bonn, 1951).

[12] Coleman Phillipson, *op. cit.*, p. 109 *et seq.*

sociable character. Maudsley's childhood, too, is described as drab
and " a succession of sombre and dreary years." The fullest search
for an explanation comes from van Bemmelen, who tentatively
refers to Bonger's " *Mutterbindung* " and his dislike of the somewhat narrowly religious atmosphere in his home. In more comprehensive biographies similar features might have been discovered
in other cases as well, but at present the material is often lacking
even for speculations.

Both Ferri and Bonger were ardent socialists, and their criminological views were strongly influenced by their political creed, but
whereas Bonger remained true to himself until the bitter end, the
same cannot be said of Ferri whose personality displayed a variety
of colours far exceeding the scope offered by any single party. In
the lives of our other pioneers party politics seems to have played
no decisive part, and it is a moot point how far a criminological
and, in particular, a penological, or indeed any scientific system
depends on the political views of its author. True scholars are not
often willing to toe the line of any political party programme.

One of the pitfalls occasionally encountered in biographical
writings has been avoided in the present series, *i.e.*, the danger that
the biographer might become so enamoured of his hero as to lose
his critical faculty. Without exception, these sketches, sympathetic
and appreciative as they are, try to give objective and well-balanced
views.

Does this selection present a coherent and complete picture of
the development of criminological thought as a whole over a period
of some hundred and fifty years, and does this development show
a line of unbroken progress or rather a zig-zag course? Are the
issues which occupied, and in a few instances almost obsessed, the
minds of these pioneers still live issues to us? How far can we
honestly claim that they are still topical and not merely venerable
museum pieces? And where they are still topical how far can we
say that the solutions recommended are the ones we would approve
of today? Have we made any further progress since the last of our
pioneers published their contributions? In the over-simplified
terminology of the " Schools " we might say our volume shows the
progress from the Classical School of Beccaria to the Positivist
School of Lombroso and Ferri and from there to the Sociological
School of Tarde and Durkheim. But is such a simplification admis-
sible? And would the displacement of the ideas of the Classical

School by those of the Positivists and eventually by the Sociological School be universally accepted as " progress "? To some considerable extent, our answers to these questions will depend upon our preconceived ideas and value judgments. While to many readers any history of recent criminological thought without a chapter on Freud will appear like Hamlet without the Prince, others might welcome this omission, and a few might even argue that Freud was not a pioneer in criminology. In European legal-sociological quarters the absence of the founders of the International Association of Penal Law, in particular of Franz von Liszt and Adolphe Prins, may be regretted. For such and other reasons, no completeness whatever can be claimed for the present volume.

While it will have to be left to the reader to form his own judgment on the queries posed above, an attempt might here be made to clarify certain important issues raised in Professor Jeffery's stimulating chapter, entitled " The Historical Development of Criminology," which concludes the symposium.

The meaning of Positivism in the history of social science

There are in the following chapters many references, laudatory, critical or neutral to Positivism, but nowhere in recent criminological literature—perhaps with the exception of some of Professor Jerome Hall's writings—has the positivist controversy been given so much prominence as in Jeffery's contribution. Much as we might disagree with some of his views, it is greatly to his credit that he forces us to reconsider the whole relationship between Positivism and Criminology.

What does Positivism mean? What are its achievements and its weaknesses? What has been its place in the history of criminology? Who is a positivist? How can we define its role in the writings of our pioneers?

Already the work of Auguste Comte, the father of Positivism, shows certain ambiguities and inconsistencies. The terms Positivism and positivist, wrote John Stuart Mill in what was probably the first penetrating analysis of Comte in the English language,[13] are " ill-fitted to take roots in English soil," and are " as usual, better known

13 John Stuart Mill, *Auguste Comte and Positivism* (London, 1865), pp. 2 *et seq.*, 9, 51. On the different definitions of Positivism, see also Richard von Mises, *Positivism* (Cambridge, Mass., 1951), p. 1 *et seq.*; and on the changes in Comte's views, Vilfredo Pareto, *The Mind and Society* (Vol. I, London, 1935), § 284 *et seq.*

through the enemies of that mode of thinking than through its
friends." The term " positive," he complains, " is not always used
by M. Comte in the same meaning." Small wonder, then, that
controversies as to the very meaning of Positivism have persisted up
to the present day. Moreover, there is general agreement that there
are several different branches of it, such as, in particular, philosophical and logical, scientific, legal, historical and sociological
Positivism, which, though closely interrelated, are by no means
identical.

Even so, a list of the principal features of positivist thought
might perhaps usefully be drawn up which, with the exceptions
indicated below, will be fairly universally acceptable. Some of these
characteristics have a special significance for this, others for that,
discipline, but altogether they comprise what is commonly understood by Positivism.[14]

(a) There is, first, Comte's distinction of social statics and social
dynamics and his famous law of the three stages through which
human thinking has to pass: from the theological or fictive to the
metaphysical or abstract state, and from there to the scientific or
positive state. Positivism, while according to Comte by no means
identical with atheism,[15] repudiates anything metaphysical and
speculative; and, although this is controversial,[16] it denies freedom
of will as commonly understood.

(b) Positivism insists on a clear-cut divorce of science and law
from morals.

(c) It proclaims the priority of science and believes in the
existence of invariable social laws. It tries to transform history, for
example, from an art into a science akin to the natural sciences.[17]
It establishes a hierarchy of the various scientific disciplines according to their generality and complexity, beginning with mathematics
and ending with sociology as the most specific and complex of all.
Psychology, on the other hand, is given no place in Comte's system.

---

[14] One of the clearest critical expositions of Comte's system has been given by Morris
Ginsberg, "On the Diversity of Morals" (*Essays in Sociology and Social Philosophy*,
Vol. I, London, 1956), Chap. XIII. Also Vol. II, *Reason and Unreason in Society*
(London, 2nd impr. 1956), Chap. XII.

[15] Auguste Comte, *A General View of Positivism*, 1848 (Engl. transl. London, 1880),
p. 33.

[16] According to Ginsberg, "neither Comte nor Durkheim can be fairly regarded as
determinists. Consistently or not they are both moralists . . ." (Morris Ginsberg,
"Social Change," *British Journal of Sociology*, Vol. IX, No. 3 (September 1958),
p. 207).

[17] Erich Rothacker, *Einleitung in die Geisteswissenschaften* (Tübingen, 2nd ed., 1930),
Chap. V, " *Der Positivismus.*"

(d) On the other hand, it emphasises the essential unity of scientific method, whether applied to the social or to the natural sciences. This point, however, is again controversial.[18]

(e) Scientific methods are to be based upon observations of facts, experimentation, quantitative rather than qualitative research, the distinction of stages and periods, the working out of types and of historical laws of succession and evolution.

(f) As a theory of society, interested in civilisations, social laws, stages and types, Positivism is, on the whole, apt to neglect the study of the individual. Man exists mainly as a member of society, whereas " the intuitive methods of metaphysics could never advance with any consistency beyond the sphere of the individual." According to Comte the highest moral value of Positivism is " social sympathy." The " cult of the masses " became the centre of interest especially to positivist historians. On the other hand, Comte himself also advocated the " commemoration of great men." [19]

(g) Some doubts seem to have arisen as to the positivist attitude to the concepts of causality and prediction. To give but two illustrations, while a modern criminologist accuses Positivism of trying to promote a conception of crime in terms of mere causation,[20] Comte himself writes: " The true Positive spirit consists in substituting the study of the invariable Laws of phenomena for that of their so-called causes, whether proximate or primary; in a word, in studying the *How* instead of the *Why* " [21]—the search for causes he believed to be " beyond our reach," a dictum which may explain the historian Marc Bloch's complaint: " In vain positivism claimed to eliminate the idea of cause from science." [22] With regard to prediction, A. N. Whitehead stated that " Positivistic science is solely concerned with observed fact, and must hazard no conjecture as to the future. If observed fact be all we know, then there is no other knowledge. There is no probability as to the future within the doctrine of Positivism." [23] This, however, is not the prevailing interpretation which rather regards " *voir pour prevoir* " as one of the objects of Positivism: " The knowledge most needed was foreknowledge " [24];

18 On this, see Karl R. Popper, *The Poverty of Historicism* (London, 1957), p. 130 *et seq.* Ginsberg, however (*Social Change*, p. 206), disputes that in Comte's view social facts are similar in nature to the facts dealt with by the physical sciences.
19 Comte, *op. cit.* pp. 68–69, 75.
20 H. Bianchi, *Position and Subject-Matter of Criminology* (Amsterdam, 1956), p. 124.
21 Comte, *op. cit.* p. 34.
22 Marc Bloch, *The Historian's Craft* (Engl. transl. Manchester, 1954), p. 190.
23 A. N. Whitehead, *Adventures of Ideas* (London, Pelican ed., 1942), p. 124.
24 Ginsberg, *op. cit.* Vol. I, p. 213; J. S. Mill, *op. cit.* p. 6.

and in fact Comte used his system of stages and his other laws for purposes of prediction.

It will now be our task, first, briefly to indicate the main achievements and weaknesses of Positivism in the general field of scientific thought and, secondly, to outline its role in the history of criminology, with special reference to the pioneers here represented.

Comte's doctrine was over-ambitious; to him and some of his followers it took the place of a religious creed and was intended to solve all conceivable problems of mankind. In Mill's words, he " never allows of open questions." His conception of sociology was all-embracing. His law of the three stages, thought-provoking and to some extent even correct as it is, has long been discarded as a universally valid philosophy of history. Determinism, having been somewhat knocked about in the natural sciences, is now rather on the defensive in the world of the social sciences, too, and the idea of human responsibility has consequently regained some of its former strength. The doctrine of the separation of law and science from morals and other value judgments has, more perhaps than any other feature of the positivist system, been a source of confusion in legal science and in sociology. If it is taken to mean that what is and what ought to be should always be kept clearly apart in our thoughts, nobody is likely to disagree with it as an ideal of legal and scientific technique, but it is now generally realised that our views of what is are in fact greatly coloured by our views of what ought to be, and vice versa. If, however, the meaning be that value judgments should be altogether ignored and excluded from scientific research or that the lawyer's only concern should be the positive law regardless of any considerations of " natural " justice, such a doctrine would be altogether out of tune with the prevailing sentiments of our age.[25] It is now more fully understood than fifty years ago not only that, consciously or unconsciously, our views of the facts and of the positive law are influenced by our moral ideas but also that, in social research as well as in legislation and in the

[25] The literature on the place of value judgments in social research is very extensive; only the following references can here be given: Arnold M. Rose, *Theory and Method in the Social Sciences* (Minneapolis, 1954), Section II, and the present writer's review of it in *The British Journal of Delinquency*, Vol. VII, No. 2 (October 1956), p. 154 *et seq.*; Gunnar Myrdal, *Value in Social Theory* (London, 1958), esp. Chap. VII. On legal Positivism now in particular H. L. A. Hart, " Positivism and the Separation of Law and Morals," and Lon L. Fuller, " Positivism and Fidelity to Law—A Reply to Professor Hart," Harv.L.R., Vol. 71, No. 4 (February 1958); Jerome Hall, *Studies in Jurisprudence and Criminal Theory* (New York, 1958), p. 31 *et seq.*

administration of the positive law, we are under an obligation to pay attention to the moral values of our society. As to the positivist belief in the priority and the unlimited possibilities and resources of science, at least in the field of social sciences we have become much more sceptical than were our predecessors; and while Julian Huxley's word " The only cure for the insufficiency of science is more science " is equally applicable to our field as it is to the natural sciences, we have now discovered that even more and better science is not likely to solve all our problems. Positivism is on firmer ground when it claims that scientific research should begin with the observation of facts, instead of mere speculation, and there is some truth in J. S. Mill's contention : " There never can have been a period in any science when it was not in some degree positive, since it always professed to draw conclusions from experience and observation." [26] However, before it can make systematic use of its observations, scientific research has to know what the object and purpose of these observations are going to be; it has to make a corresponding selection and it has to have a specific hypothesis and a specific problem. Equally important is the positivist emphasis on the need for experimentation and prediction, but while " piece-meal experiments " and predictions are possible and often indispensable in the social sciences,[27] they are perhaps even more difficult here than in the natural sciences, partly because of the existence of strong moral factors sometimes incompatible with the use of such techniques and partly because of the special difficulties of predicting human behaviour. Quantitative methods, too, are indispensable to the social sciences, and much of our recent progress would have been inconceivable without more refined statistical techniques. Nor should it be forgotten that closer scrutiny has shown the gap between quantitative and qualitative, intuitive, impressionistic, methods to be smaller than is often believed. This does not prove, however, that the latter can be dispensed with; on the contrary, the closest co-operation and a constant process of give and take are needed.[28] Nor should we be justified in concluding that there is no real difference in the methods used by the natural and the social

[26] J. S. Mill, *op. cit.* p. 51.
[27] See Karl R. Popper, *op. cit.* pp. 83 *et seq.*, 93 *et seq.*, 121.
[28] Popper, pp. 24 and 143; H. Mannheim and Leslie T. Wilkins, *Prediction Methods in relation to Borstal Training* (London, H.M.S.O., 1955), p. 36 *et seq.*; Paul E. Meehl, *Clinical v. Statistical Prediction* (Minnesota and London, 2nd impr. 1956), and the reviews in *The British Journal of Delinquency*, Vol. VII, No. 4 (April 1957), pp. 320-321.

sciences. Even Popper, who advocates the doctrine of the fundamental unity of methods, admits the existence of such differences;
and, as Ginsberg has pointed out, social facts, owing to their greater
complexity and variability and to the pressure of subtle, irrational
and largely uncontrollable mental factors, are less likely to be
repeated in identical fashion [29]; all of which necessitates different
techniques of research.

Even this brief and superficial survey will have shown that
Positivism cannot be summed up in a few words. It has become a
slogan which means many different things to different people, and
some writers use it as a term of mere invective which can be thrown
in an opponent's face instead of an argument. On the other hand,
even bitter opponents such as Whitehead occasionally admit our
debt to the movement initiated by Comte. What is true beyond
doubt is that, strictly speaking, " it has never been acted on. It can
never be acted on." [30] Neither Comte himself nor his followers
were able to carry their doctrines of the strict separation of science
and morals, of the complete banishment of speculation, and many
others right through to their logical end. And after all, his theory,
far from being entirely original, was in many respects a revival of
eighteenth-century beliefs in the omnipotence of science and the
inevitability of progress.[31] Nevertheless, with all these shortcomings, " Positivism," writes a great humanist, Gilbert Murray,
perhaps slightly too sympathetically, " remains a great coherent
statement . . . of certain permanent and all-important truths. One
reason why Comte seems so often to have been superseded is that
he often anticipated later thought or knowledge " and, particularly
significant to this volume, " pioneers are always superseded. Otherwise they would not be pioneers " [32]—just as in the practical field
it has rightly been said that it is the fate of reformers to be forgotten
once they have succeeded.[33]

The place of the Positive School in international criminology

To the student of criminology most of what has just been said
about Positivism in general will appear strikingly relevant. Here

[29] Ginsberg, *Social Change, loc. cit.* p. 220 *et seq.*
[30] Whitehead, *op. cit.* p. 124.
[31] W. H. Walsh, *An Introduction to Philosophy of History* (London, 5th impr. 1958),
      p. 155.
[32] Gilbert Murray, *Stoic, Christian and Humanist* (London, 2nd ed., 1950), p. 154.
[33] C. K. Allen, *Legal Duties* (Oxford, 1931), p. 120, with reference to Bentham.

it is as true as elsewhere that Positivism has many different meanings, that it assumes different shades in the writings of criminologists generally labelled as " positivists "; and some of the latter may be positivists in one respect but not in another. All this, as will be shown below, makes it often difficult to say with certainty whether the label has been rightly attached to this or that of our pioneers. It also makes it rather hazardous to pronounce any general statements about alleged positivist doctrines. It is with all these reservations in mind that the following remarks may be offered,[34] and if, for convenience' sake, we should occasionally attribute to " positivists " in general views actually held only by some of them the reader will appreciate our reasons. In parenthesis it should be added that the relations between general and criminological Positivism have been very much in the nature of a one-way traffic as but little attention has been paid to the efforts of the Italian School by positivists working in other fields of science.

First, historically, positivists must have regarded the work of the Classical School, with its abstract notions of crime, its neglect of the criminal as an individual human being, and its attempt to produce a correspondingly abstract equation between crime and punishment, as truly representative of the metaphysical stage in the development of criminology. While that School might have been useful in helping to overcome the previous theological stage, now, with the appearance of Lombroso, it was thought that the time had arrived to replace it by something radically new. Ferri, while acknowledging the debt of Positivism to the Classical School, nevertheless insisted that something much more drastic than mere reform, that a complete Copernican transformation of criminal justice was needed. " The historical mission of that school consisted in a reduction of punishment. . . . We now follow up the practical and scientific mission of the classic school with a still more noble and fruitful mission by adding to the problem of the diminution of penalties the problem of the diminution of crimes." By sticking to the obsolete conceptions of free will, guilt and responsibility, he argued, Beccaria and his followers had been able to make but little progress since the days of the *Digests* and the Middle Ages. Their work was sentimental rather than scientific.[35] Now, as Sellin points

[34] See also the summary of the main points of the Positivist doctrine in Marc Ancel, *La Défense sociale nouvelle* (Paris, 1954), p. 58 *et seq.*
[35] Enrico Ferri, *The Positive School of Criminology* (1901, Engl. transl. Chicago, 1908), pp. 9, 23 and 96; *Criminal Sociology* (abridged Engl. ed., London, 1895), p. xvii.

out below, Ferri insisted that moral responsibility was to give way
to the idea of social and legal responsibility; punishment had to be
replaced by morally neutral sanctions to be used in accordance with
the dangerousness of the offender, and the phantom of a just
equation between crime and punishment had to yield to a realistic
relation between the personality of the offender and his treatment
needs. The nature of the crime committed was of a very secondary
significance only. Scientific methods of observation, experiment
and measurement—" we must build upon measurements and upon
measurements only," wrote another of our pioneers, Goring, several
years later [36]—had to be employed to establish the facts of crime,
measurements of body and mind in the case of the individual and
statistics in the social sphere. Such methods would help to establish
criminological " laws," modelled after the laws of natural science,
such as Ferri's often-quoted " law of criminal saturation," according
to which "just as in a given volume of water, at a given temperature, we find the solution of a fixed quantity of any chemical
substance, not an atom more or less, so in a given social environment, in certain defined physical conditions of the individual, we
find the commission of a fixed number of crimes." [37] From this,
Ferri concluded that the deterrent effect of punishment had been
greatly overrated. As in medicine, prevention—more important
than punishment or even cure, but entirely ignored by the Classical
School—and a scientifically planned system were needed. Such a
system should be based on detailed classification of criminals
according to types and on a great variety of measures of security
either in the place of or in addition to ordinary penalties—measures
designed in accordance with the characteristics and the dangerousness (*état dangereux*) of the individual criminal instead of moral
guilt and culminating in indefinite segregation for the most serious
cases. Protection of society was to be the keyword instead of
retribution; and deterrence and reformation had to take second
place. In their impact on the individual offender such protective
measures were not necessarily meant to be more lenient; they might
well be more severe than the traditional penalties of the Classical
School.

[36] See my article, " Lombroso and his Place in modern Criminology." reprinted in *Group
Problems in Crime and Punishment* (2nd ed., Montclair, N.J., 1971), p. 73 *et seq.*
[37] Ferri, *Criminal Sociology*, p. 76 *et seq.*

Thus reduced to the barest outlines, this programme of the Positive School seems to be nothing but the logical application to the subject of crime and punishment of the doctrines of Comte and his followers. Actually, however, although nineteenth-century positivist criminologists did perhaps not foresee the full consequences of their activities, there was bound to be a vast difference in kind between a purely theoretical system such as Comte's and the attempt to translate his grandiose abstractions into the small coin of practical legislation and administration or even of criminological research. Here, not only ideas were at stake, but also the fate of countless human beings. Not surprisingly, therefore, the teachings of Positivist Criminology and its practical applications have been the subject of bitter controversy ever since the days of its founders, and some of the repercussions of this struggle can be seen in the present volume, notably in Jeffery's contribution. The impact on criminology of Positivism has, of course, been of very different intensity in different countries, relatively insignificant in the Anglo-American world,[38] strongest in Italy and some South American countries; somewhat weaker in France, Germany, Spain and the rest of Europe. In France, this lack of success was due not only to Tarde's and Durkheim's sociological studies but also to the work of Lacassagne and Manouvrier, who could fight Lombroso on his own ground, anthropology and medicine. In England, in spite of the positivistic bent[39] of her nineteenth-century philosophy and sociology, theoretical Positivism met with little interest in the field of criminology, and even the determined efforts of Havelock Ellis to popularise the work of Lombroso had only very limited appeal. Goring, who is sometimes believed to have been in disagreement with the latter's methods rather than with his findings (see Professor Driver's chapter), nevertheless reached the final conclusion that " there is no

[38] See, *e.g.*, Arthur E. Fink, *Causes of Crime* (Philadelphia, 1938), pp. 113 and 244; Barnes and Teeters, *New Horizons in Criminology* (New York, 1943), p. 165. For other brief discussions of the Positive School in American textbooks, see Nathaniel F. Cantor, *Crime and Society* (New York, 1939), pp. 206–219; Donald R. Taft, *Criminology* (New York, 3rd ed., 1956), p. 78 *et seq.* References are often limited to specific aspects of the work of individual positivists. Slightly fuller and more systematic is the recent discussion in George B. Vold, *Theoretical Criminology* (New York, 1958), Chap. 3.

[39] With reference to late nineteenth-century England, Noel Annan writes in his recent Hobhouse Memorial Lecture, *The Curious Strength of Positivism in English Political Thought* (London, 1959), p. 10: " In England, though weakened by the challenge of Idealism, the old-fashioned positivism remained curiously strong because it had won a spectacular and celebrated battle in the sixties and seventies." On the other hand, he regards the " concern with morality " as one of the reasons why Positivism maintained its strength for so long in England (p. 15).

such thing as a physical criminal type." And it seems equally doubtful how far the other famous figures of modern English criminology, Henry Maudsley, Cyril Burt and Norwood East, could reasonably be labelled as positivists. Altogether, the English mind, with its practical rather than theoretical bias, has been more interested in penological questions of treatment than in the criminological and philosophical issues of causation and responsibility. Lombroso's anthropological studies were fully and often very critically discussed, and occasionally—as Dr. Scott suggests in the case of Maudsley's views on epilepsy—some of the former's theories may have left their mark. Little or no attention, however, was paid to the more general aspects of positivist doctrines, and the word " Positivism " appears but rarely or not at all in the English criminological literature of the late nineteenth and early twentieth centuries.[40] This does not mean to say that positivist ideas have not been prominent in English criminal and other legislation of the past fifty years. Only two illustrations can here be given. In the Criminal Justice Act, 1948, s. 21, the legislator has, without any theoretical qualms and probably even without being aware of any but the purely practical implications of the change, transformed the previous " double-track " system of preventive detention, based on the classical distinction between punishment and measures of security, into a " single-track " system which abandons that distinction. In theory, this is of course pure Positivism. In practice, however, the Court of Criminal Appeal has repeatedly refused to impose long sentences of preventive detention or corrective training in cases where the offence was only of a comparatively minor nature; and it has also to be stressed that under the Act of 1948 such sentences are not indeterminate, but their length has to be fixed by the courts. The second illustration may be taken from the Mental Health Act, 1959, which proposes not only a similar single-track system for certain categories of mentally ill, psychopathic, or subnormal offenders (s. 60), but also compulsory hospital detention and treatment without judicial control for such persons who, while not found guilty of an offence, are regarded as showing symptoms of an " *état dangereux* " (s. 26). This, too, is " Positivism."

In Spain, the eminent lawyer and criminologist Dorado Montero was not only in sympathy with certain positivist doctrines, but, in

---

[40] See, *e.g.*, Sir Norwood East, *Society and the Criminal* (London, 1949), Chap. VI; and the same, *The Adolescent Criminal* (London, 1942), pp. 30 *et seq.*, 167 *et seq.*

the words of Dr. Lopez-Rey, influenced by Comte himself rather than by the Italian positivists he even went beyond them. Montero, who tried to combine determinism and free will; who rejected the doctrine of the born criminal; who stressed the psychological and moral elements in crime and the need for a more humane and essentially psychological and religious penal treatment; who favoured the abolition of the principle *nulla poena sine lege* and of legal definitions of individual offences—seems to be too unorthodox to qualify as a member of any of the traditional " Schools." In the words of a present-day Spanish criminalist, Professor Juan del Rosal, " his originality reaches the utopian," [41] which does not prevent another eminent Spaniard, Jiménez de Asúa, calling him the " real master of Spanish criminal science." [42]

Even more complex and hardly capable of being pressed into the strait-jacket of any convenient formula have been developments in Germany over the past three-quarters of a century. Certainly, Professor Jerome Hall's statement,[43] supported by no references to German or other sources, that " the Positivism of the last century . . . found its warmest advocates among German and Italian criminalists " is a misleading over-simplification of the complicated history of German criminal law and criminological thought. Already twenty years before Goring, Lombroso's doctrine of the born criminal had been refuted by the Berlin prison doctor Adolf Baer; and still earlier, in 1889, the most influential and representative German criminalist of his age, Franz von Liszt, strongly protested against certain attempts to enlist him as a follower of the Italian School.[44] However, it was not only Liszt, primarily a lawyer and a penologist, who was opposed to Lombroso's teachings. As indicated by Professor von Hentig, the psychiatrist Aschaffenburg, too, although scrupulously fair to Lombroso and greatly impressed by Ferri's Draft Code of 1921, remained critical of at least some of their methods, results and practical recommendations. Nevertheless, under the influence of Kretschmer's typological

[41] On Montero see, in addition to Lopez-Rey's chapter, Günter Blau, *op. cit.* pp. 36 and 65; and *Zeitschrift für die gesamte Strafrechtswissenschaft, Sonderheft* (1957), p. 88; Juan del Rosal, the same journal, Vol. 67 (1954), pp. 148–149.

[42] Jiménez de Asúa in the same journal, Vol. 70 (1958), p. 499.

[43] Jerome Hall, *General Principles of Criminal Law* (Indianapolis, 1947), p. 287.

[44] See Adolf Baer, *Der Verbrecher in anthropologischer Beziehung* (Leipzig, 1893); Franz von Liszt, *Strafrechtliche Aufsätze und Vorträge* (Berlin, 1905), Vol. I, p. 302 *et seq.*; II, p. 436 *et seq.* Also Gerhard Daniel, *Zeitschrift für die gesamte Strafrechtswissenschaft*, Vol. 50 (1930), p. 475 *et seq.*

studies he was inclined to accept a modified and modernised version of Lombroso's theories; and in harmony with the prevailing views of the natural scientists of his time he was also a firm determinist.[45] It is true, moreover, that on various points, notably in their emphasis on the criminal rather than on his crime, and on the need for criminological-sociological studies modelled on the lines of the natural sciences, Liszt and most other members of the *Union internationale de droit pénal (Internationale Kriminalistische Vereinigung,* IKV) shared the positivist outlook [46]; but on other, equally important and more practical, issues their attitudes underwent significant changes in the course of time. This applies in particular to such crucial questions as the indeterminate sentence and the relationship between punishment and measures of security, where even the progressive Draft Code, Gustav Radbruch's of 1922, tried to steer a middle course.[47] The famous " *Schulenstreit* " (struggle between the Classical and the Sociological Schools), which seemed to have come to a peaceful solution in 1902 when the work on the new Penal Code began in earnest, was resumed in 1925 through the formation of a new Society pledged to resist any drastic deviations from the ideals of the Classical School.[48] As a consequence of this revival and the subsequent coming of National Socialism, German criminology became more and more opposed to such positivist tenets as the negation of free will, guilt and responsibility and to the complete replacement of punishment by measures of security, while on the other hand, under the influence of the crimino-biological school, the individual criminal was studied on lines not basically different from those of the positivists.[49] The new Western German Draft Code of 1956–58, while retaining the ideas of guilt and responsibility and, at least in principle, separating penalties from measures of security, tries to rethink the work of previous generations in the light of changed conditions and the recent progress of criminological methods.[50]

45 See Gustav Aschaffenburg, *Crime and its Repression* (American ed., 1919, reprinted 1968; third German ed., 1923), pp. 190 *et seq.*, 219 *et seq.*, 229 *et seq.*, 272 *et seq.*; in *Handwörterbuch der Kriminologie,* Vol. I (Berlin-Leipzig, 1933), p. 834; and in *Zeitschrift für die gesamte Strafrechtswissenschaft,* Vol. 44 (1924), p. 15 *et seq.*
46 For a critical analysis of von Liszt's system, see Paul Bockelmann, *Studien zum Täterstrafrecht* (Berlin, Vol. I, 1939; Vol. II, 1940).
47 See Gustav Radbruch's *Entwurf eines Allgemeinen Deutschen Strafgesetzbuches* 1922 (Tübingen, 1952), pp. xxi *et seq.* and 58 *et seq.*
48 See Max Hagemann, *Handwörterbuch der Kriminologie* (Berlin-Leipzig, 1934), p. 243.
49 See my *Group Problems in Crime and Punishment* (2nd ed., Montclair, N.J., 1971), p. 75 *et seq.*
50 See *Entwurf eines Allgemeinen Teils eines Strafgesetzbuchs . . . mit Begründung* (Bonn, 1958), *Begründung*, p. 1 *et seq.*

Of considerable interest to historians of the Positivist School of criminology should be the state of affairs in South American countries where, as already indicated, Ferri's influence was very strong in the early decades of the present century. It would be dangerous, however, to apply one single formula to the somewhat bewildering variety of systems and ideas, all the more as we are here confronted with at least twenty independent legislations. The present writer has to rely mainly on the detailed analysis presented by Dr. Günter Blau and on Professor Jiménez de Asúa's regular reports on South American literature and legislation, supplemented by the study of some of the more important Penal Codes, of occasional reports to international Congresses and, on the peno-logical side, of Negley K. Teeters's book, *Penology from Panama to Cape Horn*.[51] The impression gained from these sources is not altogether unequivocal. On the one hand, the almost exclusive, not to say obsessive, interest in anthropological-biological inter-pretations of crime at the expense of sociological studies and the emphasis on positivist conceptions such as " *peligrosidad* " (*estado peligroso, état dangereux, pericolosità* and *temibilità*) and " social protection " stand out very clearly. Significantly enough, the Cuban Code of 1936 is called not Penal Code, but Code of Social Defence. The German writer Blau and the Frenchman Herzog both agree that Italian Positivism has for fifty years been the dominant force in South American criminal law and criminology. On the other hand, one of the most distinguished authorities on the subject, Jiménez de Asúa, maintains [52] that " no South American Penal Code is any more inspired by Positivism which has become out of date in philo-sophy and entirely obsolete in criminal science." The truth may be that Positivism, while dominating much of the voluminous criminological literature, has not been carried to its logical conclu-sions in any of the many, often only short-lived, Draft Codes and actual legislations of the South American republics. This has been

---

[51] Günter Blau, *op. cit.* (note 36, above); de Asúa, *Zeitschrift für die gesamte Strafrechts-wissenschaft*, Vol. 66 (1954), p. 449 *et seq.*; Vol. 68 (1956), p. 295 *et seq.*; Vol. 69 (1957), p. 114 *et seq. Das Argentinische Strafgesetzbuch* (German transl., Berlin, 1957, and Introduction by Heinz Mattes); *Das Cubanische Gesetzbuch der Sozialen Verteidi-gung* (German transl. and Introduction, Berlin, 1957, by Günter Blau); Jacques Bernard Herzog, " *Le problème de l'état dangereux en Amerique latin*," *Deuxième Cours International de Criminologie*, Conférences publiées par Jean Pinatel (Paris, 1954), p. 514 *et seq.*; Negley K. Teeters, *Penology from Panama to Cape Horn* (Philadelphia, 1946).

[52] Jiménez de Asúa, *Zeitschrift für die gesamte Strafrechtswissenschaft*, Vol. 66 (1954), p. 450.

due in part to the prevailing lack of unanimity as to the actual meaning of Positivism, in part to the ambivalent theoretical attitude of many leading criminologists, to changes in the political climate, the influence of the Catholic Church (especially underlined by Blau), and possibly also to the awareness that the actual penal systems of their countries were too underdeveloped to make any consistent application of the positivist doctrines feasible in actual practice. There seems to be a strange incongruity between theory and practice; and just as, according to Teeters, South American penitentiaries are called *Panópticos*, although built on the lines of John Haviland's Eastern Penitentiary,[53] similarly some of the Penal Codes appear under positivist labels such as "Social Defence" without being much different from other modern Codes. Actually, there are considerable differences from country to country, from Draft to Draft, and from Code to Code.[54] Even the Argentine Code of 1921, however, passed when Ferri's popularity was at its height, provides the indeterminate sentence not as a general principle but only for certain categories of offenders; its measures of security merely supplement the penalties instead of replacing them; it contains the traditional definitions of individual offences; and there are no preventive measures in it for pre-delictual dangerousness (*estado peligroso sin delitto*).[55] The Cuban Code of 1936, too, retains the principle *nulla poena sine lege*, the "dual-track system," the concept of guilt, the distinction between penalties and measures of security; but it permits the imposition of such measures in certain cases of "pre-delictual dangerousness" (arts. 48B, 48c and 580), which is a far-reaching concession to positivist ideas and even more extreme than Ferri's own Draft Code.[56]

Positivist tendencies are present in Denmark and even more in Sweden, largely under the influence of the eminent Swedish psychiatrist Olof Kinberg, whose book, *Basic Principles of Criminology*, contains some of the most penetrating discussions of positivist philosophy.[57] With his strong opposition to the ideas of free will, moral responsibility and just retribution, with his emphasis not on the crime committed but on the individual criminal and on the psychiatric classification of the concept of *l'état dangereux*, to which

---

53 Teeters, *op. cit.* p. 8. The whole of his first chapter is illuminating.
54 See, in particular, the analysis by Blau, *op. cit.*, p. 34 *et seq.*
55 See the details in Mattes (note 51, above).
56 Blau, *op. cit.* pp. 52, 88.
57 Olof Kinberg, *Basic Problems of Criminology* (Copenhagen, 1935).

latter he has devoted several important studies,[58] Kinberg has to be regarded as an outspoken representative of Positivism, although deviating from its orthodox teachings in certain questions of responsibility. Recent Swedish penal policy follows similar lines in abandoning the concept of punishment and replacing it by the neutral term " sanctions," and in adopting a purely biological definition of mental abnormality.[59] While the Danish Penal Code of 1930 does not go so far as to abolish penalties in favour of sanctions, this step has been taken in the Danish Criminal Code of 1954 for Greenland which, although it has accepted the principle of " no measures without law," knows neither criminal responsibility nor penalties and thereby comes very near to positivist ideas.[60] From Denmark, however, we hear that Danish criminal courts are disinclined to impose detention for indeterminate periods on psychopathic offenders unless it seems justified because of the seriousness of the crime committed.

Individual differences within the Positive School. Positivists and non-positivists among our pioneers

Important differences regarding adherence to positivist principles can be observed, however, not only between the various countries but also between the writings of individual authors; and this applies to the pioneers in the present volume, too. As indicated above, perhaps with the only exception of Beccaria, most of them were positivists in some respect but not in others; some of them consciously and enthusiastically, others talking Positivism much as Molière's Monsieur Jourdain was talking prose without knowing it.

---

58 Olof Kinberg, " *Le Droit de Punir,*" *Theoria,* Vol. XIV (1948), Part II, p. 124 *et seq.*; " Will a Concept of Imputability be of practical Use in a Penal System founded on empirical Psychology? "—*The British Journal of Medical Psychology,* Vol. XIX (1941–43), p. 124 *et seq.*; " *Les situations psychologiques précriminelles révélatrices des caractères de l'état dangereux,*" *Theoria,* Vol. XVI (1950), p. 185 *et seq.*; " *l'étude psychiatrique des situations precriminelles* " in *Premier cours international de Criminologie,* edited by Georges Heuyer and Jean Pinatel (Paris, 1933), p. 173 *et seq.*

59 See Thorsten Sellin, *The Protective Code. A Swedish Proposal* (Stockholm, 1957), pp. 9–10; Gösta Rylander, " The Treatment of Mentally Abnormal Offenders in Sweden," *British Journal of Delinquency,* Vol. V, No. 4 (April 1955), p. 262 *et seq.*; H. H. Heldmann in *Materialien zur Strafrechtsreform,* Vol. 2, Part I (Bonn, 1954), pp. 346–350.

60 On Denmark, see Knud Waaben's Introduction to the English edition of the Criminal Code (Copenhagen, 1958); Stephan Hurwitz in *Internationales Colloquium über Kriminologie und Strafrechtsreform* (Freiburg, 1958), pp. 85 *et seq.,* 92–93; Franz Marcus, Introduction to the German edition of the Greenland Criminal Code (*Sammlung Ausserdeutscher Strafgesetzbücher,* No. 68 (Berlin, 1955)); the same, *Zeitschrift für die gesamte Strafrechtswissenschaft,* Vol. 67, No. 2 (1955), p. 323 *et seq.*

Only a few illustrations of such differences can here be given. Bentham was regarded by Ferri as a member of the Classical School, though " with a more positive bend of mind than others." [61] Actually, although he derived his principle of the greatest happiness of the greatest number from the classicist Beccaria; although he paid but little attention to the individual, and over-estimated the deterrent effect of punishment—Bentham was a positivist in his whole utilitarian philosophy, his rejection of retributory punishment, his suggestion that one might well punish an innocent person if this should be a deterrent to others, his emphasis on prevention, his passion for classification, interference, regulation and control. [62] Maconochie was in favour of the indeterminate sentence long before its adoption by the positivists, [63] but, in Mr. Justice Barry's view, he would not have approved of certain modern developments in this field; he was against retributive punishment, but his whole system " rested upon the notion of freedom of the will and the doctrine of moral responsibility." [64] Even within the inner circle of the Positivist School numerous differences, inconsistencies and deviations from their own programme can be observed, some of them minor ones and unavoidable, others of major importance and bound to undermine in the minds of some critics the belief in the existence of a sound scientific " system." Lombroso himself, as shown in Professor Wolfgang's chapter, changed his views from time to time and worked much more intuitively than on rigidly scientific lines, [65] and Ferri's classifications of the various criminal types differed from those of Lombroso. Again, as Professor Allen points out, " Garofalo found the emphasis of Lombroso's theories inadequate for his purposes," and it has been doubted—not without reason—whether Garofalo's ideas with their emphasis on such moral factors as pity and probity can altogether be fitted into the positivist system. [66] Moreover, it was a truly " formidable task " (Allen) to reconcile the moralising basis of his conception of crime with his positivist rejection of free will, and also to make his theory of " natural crime " acceptable to the legal positivists and the evolutionists in his own

[61] Ferri, *The Positive School*, p. 26.
[62] Leon Radzinowicz, *History of English Criminal Law*, Vol. III (London, 1956), pp. 434–435.
[63] Marc Ancel, *The Indeterminate Sentence*, United Nations (New York, 1954), p. 12.
[64] John Vincent Barry, *Alexander Maconochie* (Melbourne, 1958), p. 237 *et seq*.
[65] See also my *Group Problems in Crime and Punishment*, p. 72; Aschaffenburg, *Handwörterbuch der Kriminologie*, p. 834.
[66] Blau, *Gefährlichkeitsbegriff*, p. 43.

camp.[67]   Whereas Garofalo wanted to retain the death penalty, Ferri regarded it as obsolete.   The question of whether poverty causes crime and, more generally speaking, the compatibility of Positivism and socialism became, in the words of Tarde,[68] " the favourite battle ground of the two rival factions of the Positivist School, the socialist faction and the orthodox faction," and Ferri needed all the fertility and versatility of his genius to produce a face-saving formula.   In particular on such subjects as socialism and religion there was a profound difference of opinion between him and Garofalo.[69]   On the subject of " pre-delictual dangerousness," we have already referred to the discrepancy between the positivist doctrine that the actual commission of a crime is not an essential symptom of dangerousness and Ferri's reluctance to introduce pre-delictual sanctions in his Draft Code.   In recent years, even orthodox positivists such as Grispigni, realising the precariousness of a diagnosis of " pre-delinquency " with the inadequate scientific tools of today, have advised against any such sanctions.[70]   Modern legislation, too, has, as a rule, renounced them, and the few exceptions such as some of the American Psychopathic Sex Offenders Laws have been fairly universally disapproved.[71]   Whatever scientific progress has been made of late in predicting delinquency in non-delinquents is intended for objects outside the penal system.

Were Hans Gross and Bonger positivists? Yes and no. If there has ever been a criminologist interested in the observation of facts and the application of the methods used by the natural sciences, not only for his favourite subject, criminalistics, but also for criminal anthropology and psychology, it was Hans Gross.   " One of the most important tasks of his *Journal* was to report on observations " (Grassberger).   On the other hand, he strongly opposed Lombroso, his methods, his statistics and his " nihilism." [72]   Bonger, for his part, was a " historic-materialistic Marxist " (van Bemmelen) and a determinist; he insisted on the application of scientific, especially statistical, techniques in criminology instead of metaphysical and

[67] See Professor Allen's quotation from Tarde, *Penal Philosophy*, p. 72
[68] Gabriel Tarde, *Penal Philosophy* (1912; reprinted Montclair, N.J., 1968), pp. 388 and 74; also C. Bernaldo de Quirós, *Modern Theories of Criminality* (London, 1911), p. 67 *et seq.*
[69] Enrico Ferri, *Socialism and Positive Science* (Engl. transl. London, 1905).
[70] Filippo Grispigni in *Deuxième cours international de Criminologie* (see note 51, above), p. 59.
[71] See my *Group Problems in Crime and Punishment*, p. 205 *et seq.*
[72] Hans Gross, *Handbuch für Untersuchungsrichter* (München-Berlin-Leipzig, 7th ed., 1922), Vol. I, p. 153 *et seq.*

religious conceptions. At the same time he, too, was an anti-positivist in his rejection of the anthropological foundations of the Lombrosian School.

Tarde and Durkheim are probably the two most strongly anti-positivist writers in our series. This does not mean, however, that they have been entirely consistent in their attitudes. Tarde acquired a highly honoured place in nineteenth-century Continental criminology largely as a brilliant critic of the Lombrosian School and through his theory of imitation. Professor Wilson Vine rightly deplores the neglect of his work in English-speaking countries. Even as the precursor of Sutherland's theory of differential association he has by no means received all the credit due to him.[73] There is no need to recapitulate the points where Tarde was opposed to Positivism—he missed no opportunity of attacking it and its principal exponents.[74] He was critical not only of their anthropological doctrines but also of their utilitarianism and their poor view of the deterrent value of punishment. On the other hand, he did believe in the value of scientific techniques in criminology and in the possibility of sociological and criminological laws. His theory of responsibility, ably discussed by Professors Gault[75] and Wilson Vine, is an interesting and original attempt to salvage the idea of moral responsibility by making it independent of free will and basing it instead on the psychological and sociological factors of " personal identity " and " social similarity." In doing so, he arrives at some sort of compromise between the absolute moral responsibility of the Classical and the absolute irresponsibility of the Positivist School. He rejects the positivist distinction between moral and social responsibility because the former, he argues, is part of the latter.[76]

The case of Durkheim is even more doubtful. Durkheim himself did not want to be called a positivist. Historically, however, Comte's Positivism was " a point of departure " for him and " in a sense he continued Comte's work, although he was critical of him at various points " (Professor Lunden). In what direction did he

[73] Compare the scanty references to his work in Sutherland–Cressey, *Principles of Criminology* (Philadelphia, 5th ed., 1955), pp. 56 and 291. Equally brief, but slightly more laudatory, George B. Vold, *Theoretical Criminology*, p. 188.
[74] For a case where his attacks seem to have been based on some misunderstanding, see Veli Verkko, *Homicides and Suicides in Finland and their Dependence on National Character* (Copenhagen, 1951), Chap. XV.
[75] Robert H. Gault's Introduction to Tarde, *Penal Philosophy*.
[76] See, *e.g.*, *Penal Philosophy*, pp. 155 and 184, and the whole of Chaps. III and IV.

proceed from this starting-point? His method of scientific inquiry has been called positive because of his insistence that theories, ethical or sociological, were not capable of being established *a priori*, but had to be derived from the facts [77]; and several writers have classified him as a positivist in other respects, too. In his later stages, he moved more and more away from Positivism and arrived at a position where, as Talcott Parsons has well said, his "idealism" alienated the positivists, whereas the elements of "Positivism" which he could not entirely shake off alienated the idealists.[78] Positivist was his tendency to treat sociology as a natural science, opposed to metaphysics; to classify and to search for sociological and criminological laws and for causal explanations. He greatly disliked psychological explanations, and the "*verstehende*" psychology did not yet exist for him. Moreover, for some of his most distinguished work, especially in his *Suicide*, he used statistical techniques, with great ingenuity though of course without the refinements of modern statistics; and he was altogether deeply interested in problems of methodology. He was not a positivist, however, in his anti-utilitarian attitude, in his endeavour to "infuse morality into the society of his time," [79] and above all, in his views on the functions of crime and punishment in society. It is indeed strange to see how widely these views have been ignored in criminological literature. Whereas Durkheim's conception of anomie and his book on suicide have received well-deserved recognition, the same cannot be said of his functional theory of crime and punishment; and its sympathetic discussion in the present volume by Professors Lunden and Jeffery is, therefore, particularly welcome.[80]

To sum up this part of our analysis, to the work of most of our pioneers the profound words of a great Swiss poet, Conrad Ferdinand Meyer, may well be applied: "*Ich bin kein ausgeklügelt Buch, Ich bin ein Mensch mit seinem Widerspruch*" (I am not an artfully contrived book, I am a human being with all his inconsistencies). In less poetic language, criminologists, too, can expect

---

[77] Morris Ginsberg, *Essays in Sociology and Moral Philosophy*, Vol. I, Chap. IV, p. 41.
[78] Talcott Parsons, *The Structure of Social Action* (1st ed., New York and London, 1937), p. 74. Chaps. VIII to XI contain a penetrating analysis of the evolution of Durkheim's thought. See also Harry Alpert, *Emile Durkheim and his Sociology* (New York, 1939), especially pp. 25, 79 *et seq.*, 83 *et seq.*, 97, 109, 114, 124.
[79] Kurt H. Wolff, *The American Journal of Sociology*, Vol. LXIII (May 1958), p. 596.
[80] Durkheim's functionalism has recently been criticised by Arnold M. Rose in *The Institutions of Advanced Societies*, edited by Rose (Minneapolis, 1958), p. 17. See also the detailed analysis of functionalism in Robert K. Merton, *Social Theory and Social Structure* (rev. and enlarged ed., Glencoe, 1957), Chap. 1.

to be judged not merely as members of this or that " School," but as individuals, and it is in this sense that our previous remarks on " men or movements " seem to be pertinent.

As indicated in our preface, the present selection makes no claim to present a complete history of the last two hundred years of criminology. Not only pioneers who are still alive or died only after the last world war have here been omitted; there is also no representative of the important statistical-sociological school of the early nineteenth century, beginning with Quételet and A. M. Guerry [81] and of the Central European legal-sociological school gathered around the founders of the *Union internationale de droit pénal*.[82] If, with such reservations and with the over-simplifications unavoidable in any such sketches, we try to trace certain basic developments in the history of our discipline we find that, although the wheel has certainly not turned full circle, there has at least been the usual zig-zag course. Neither the Classical School nor Positivism have won the final and decisive battle, but modern criminology could not exist without either of them. History has shown that the human mind is equally disinclined to dispense with certain of the fundamental, not to say eternal, truths of the Classicists as it is to disown the real achievements of Positivism and that, consequently, there is a need for an eclectic system of criminology. The future can belong to neither of the two extremes. " Third Schools " are usually dull and have a bad reputation among doctrinaires, but the practical criminologist will give them their rightful place. It is here that we disagree with Professor Jeffery's spirited attack on Positivism. As the analysis of the work of our Pioneers will have shown, there are very few " pure " positivists even among those customarily counted as members of that School, and, on the other hand, there are very few, if any, anti-positivists who do not share its views in some important aspects and make no use of positivist methods. Generalisations are therefore dangerous, and there is an urgent need for concessions from all sides. There is also a strong need to understand the shortcomings of each successive School in the light of the weaknesses of its predecessors. If, for example, the positivists went to the extremes of determinism, this

---

[81] On Quételet, see especially J. M. van Bemmelen, " The Constancy of Crime," *British Journal of Delinquency*, Vol. II, No. 3 (January 1952), p. 208 *et seq.*; on Guerry, see Terence Morris, *The Criminal Area* (London, 1957), p. 44 *et seq.* and Barnes-Teeters, *New Horizon in Criminology* (New York, 1943), p. 138.
[82] See above, p. 9.

was merely their answer to the equally extreme formula of indeterminism used by the classicists.

The critics of Positivism and the possibility of a " Third School "

In the light of these observations it is now my task as editor of this symposium briefly to define my attitude to the challenge thrown out in Professor Jeffery's concluding chapter on " The Historical Development of Criminology." While this is not the place for an exhaustive comment on all his points, at least some of the most important differences between us, as well as the main area of agreement, will have to be outlined. First and foremost, having stressed throughout the whole of this Introduction that unwarranted generalisations should be avoided, I am bound to disagree with many of Jeffery's statements referring to " the " positivists and " the " psychiatrists, and with his identification of the positivist and " the " criminologist. Some of his strictures, it is true, seem to refer only to American criminology, but most of their implications are of a fairly universal nature and should therefore be treated in a broader context. " The criminologist," he writes, " seeks the answer to crime in the behaviour of the offender rather than in the criminal law. . . . The question ' why and how people commit crimes ' is an important one; however, a theory of behaviour is not a theory of crime." According to him, " the main characteristic of Positivism is its attempt to answer the riddle of criminality by means of scientific studies of the *individual offender*." The use of scientific methods, he thinks, is only one of the major characteristics of Positivism, as " scientific studies can be made of crime and criminal law as well as of the criminal." The criminologist is, however, " not interested in studying law and society " because of his " reform orientation. There is no way in which knowledge of law and society can be used to reform the criminal." Modern criminology, he goes on to say, " views punishment always in the context of what it means to the individual offender, never in terms of what it means to society. . . . The Positive School was opposed to the position taken by Durkheim, that is, it focused attention on the act and not on the meaning of a violation to the social group." While we can agree with some of these statements we have to object to others. There is no need for us to repeat what has already been said above about the glaring weaknesses and excesses of certain teachings of the Positivist School; unless we are very careful, there is no doubt a certain danger that some of them might gain the upper hand. This applies, in the first place, to various doctrinal problems concerning determinism, guilt and responsibility, strict liability, the objects of punishment, the relation between penalties and measures of security, and the protection of society against dangerous and potential criminals. It applies, secondly, to the separation of facts and values and to the use of statistical techniques in criminology. The thoughtful remarks of such writers as Herbert A. Bloch on the need for quantitative studies of the " neo-positivist " type to be integrated into a wider theoretical framework on the Durkheim model [83] and Sorokin's outspoken criticism of the prevailing " Quantophrenia " seem to deserve our full attention. [84] With rare exceptions, such as the Psychopathic Sex Offenders Laws, however, it can be said of our positivist dogs of today that their bark is worse than their bite. Even where the legislator follows a radical positivist line, the courts have not seldom been disinclined to follow suit. Judicial practice and legislative theory have occasionally proved to be two entirely different matters. To the theorist and to the law-giver, who is often also a mere theorist in this field, it may appear easy to carry certain radical ideas right to their logical conclusion, such as, for example, the dogma that it is not the crime but only the criminal that matters. The judge, however, who is face to face with the individual offender and also aware of his own short-comings, may find it an almost superhuman task to judge the " total personality " instead of a single act. This is one of the reasons why preventive detention has encountered serious difficulties in its practical application, notably in Britain and Germany. [85]

Professor Jeffery is inclined to blame the Positivist School at the same time for neglecting the interests of the state and the victim in favour of the individual offender and, vice versa, of neglecting those of the individual in favour of the state; for being too lenient and, at the same time, over-severe. Which of these two charges is justified? Although apparently contradictory, they may, of course, both be well founded in some respects, while unjustified in others.

[83] Herbert A. Bloch, *American Sociological Review*, Vol. 23, No. 6 (December 1958), pp. 756–757.

[84] Pitirim A. Sorokin, *Fads and Foibles in Modern Sociology and related Sciences* (Chicago, 1956).

[85] On Germany, see the illuminating article by Eduard Dreher, " *Liegt die Sicherungs-verwahrung im Sterben ?* " ("Is preventive Detention dying? "), *Deutsche Richter-zeitung*, Vol. 35 (March 1957), p. 51 *et seq.*

Individualisation of punishment and treatment, if taken seriously, may imply the greatest severity as well as the greatest leniency. On the other hand, the " right proportion " between crime and punishment, that apparently so simple ideal of the Classical School, is clearly unattainable except in a purely formal sense.

There are, moreover, the charges levelled by Jeffery at the psychiatrists as a body. Already in 1937, Lindesmith and Levin had, in their brilliant but slightly unbalanced attack on " The Lombrosian Myth," tried to explain the rise of Lombrosianism in terms of what they regarded as a " ' seizure of power,' so to speak, by the medical profession." [86] Although they, and to some extent Jeffery, too, are careful to call this phenomenon and others of which they equally disapprove " primarily an American product," these are largely ideas and problems of an international character which have to be treated as such. While the present writer holds no brief for the psychiatric profession in general, or for American psychiatrists in particular, he is bound to say that, as far as his personal knowledge goes, psychiatrists are usually most reluctant to assume responsibility for legal decisions. When the English Mental Health Act of 1959 was debated, the strongest criticism in the House of Commons and outside came from psychiatrists who refused to accept the sole responsibility for compulsory detention of mentally ill persons in mental hospitals.[87] To take one of the most famous of the psychiatrists in the present series, Henry Maudsley, his dictum, quoted by Scott, that " the good of society is a larger interest than the good of the individual . . . it is he who must suffer in the larger interest of society " does hardly fit into Jeffery's picture of " the " psychiatrist who, in the interest of the individual offender, desires to " abolish certain basic concepts such as responsibility, guilt and punishment." " Not for him [Maudsley] was the equation of all criminality with mental illness . . . ," writes Scott, and " he was very pessimistic about the prospect of treating criminals successfully." " Medical men," Maudsley urged, " should discard the notion of insanity in the abstract, and leave off talking of it as if it were something definite or constant which annulled all responsibility." In all this, he has not remained a lonely voice

[86] Lindesmith and Levin, *American Journal of Sociology*, Vol. XLII (1936–37), p. 653 *et seq.*; and against them, Thorsten Sellin, p. 897.
[87] *Hansard* of January 26, 1959, cols. 755–756, 780–784; Peter Scott, *British Journal of Delinquency*, Vol. IX, No. 4.

crying in the wilderness. On the contrary, modern Continental psychiatry, too, with certain exceptions, shows a tendency towards greater emphasis on human freedom of choice and the use of value judgments [88]; and one of the most representative living psycho-analysts has recently expressed himself very strongly against the misconception that Freudians wish to deny the significance of the idea of guilt.[89] How, indeed, could a psychological theory to which we owe the discovery of that new category, the " criminal from a sense of guilt, and from a need of punishment," be guilty of an error that would undermine its very foundations?[90]

However, Maudsley did address himself not only to his fellow psychiatrists; as Dr. Scott reports, he also appealed to the lawyers " to renounce unreservedly their discredited test of disabling mental disease." The M'Naghten test, he thought, was based " on wrong observation and bad psychology." This test, discredited already in the eyes of Isaac Ray and Maudsley, has become even more so in the intervening decades, and this in spite of various efforts to rehabilitate it. Jeffery maintains that the Rules are intended not as a scientific statement but as a matter of policy, and that the psychia-trist when finding them unacceptable assumes the role of policy-maker, which he is not supposed to play. " The sociologist has decided he could not act as both scientist and policy-maker, and perhaps the psychiatrist will find it necessary to make a similar distinction between science and policy." Does this not ignore the fundamental difference between the position of the sociologist, who is concerned with the subject mainly as a theorist, and that of the psychiatrist, who is called upon to give his opinion in practical cases concerning the fate of individual human beings? If the psychiatrist finds that he is faced with questions which he not only regards as unscientific but to which he can honestly give no reasonable answer, he has either to withdraw from the case altogether [91] or to try to interpret the question in such a way as to make it more reasonable. This does not mean an attempt to establish the dictatorship of the

[88] Hans-Heinrich Jescheck, *Das Menschenbild unserer Zeit und die Strafrechtsreform* (Tübingen, 1957), p. 17; C. F. Wendt, *Monatsschrift für Kriminologie und Strafrechts-reform*, Vol. 40, No. 7–8, p. 201; Sorokin, *op. cit.*, p. 285 *et seq.*

[89] Edward Glover, *British Journal of Delinquency*, Vol. IX (January 1959), p. 229, and now in his *The Roots of Crime* (London, 1960), p. 302 *et passim.*

[90] Out of an extensive literature, see Kate Friedlander, *The Psycho-Analytical Approach to Juvenile Delinquency* (London, 1947), pp. 149–150; J. C. Flügel, *Man, Morals and Society* (London, 1945), pp. 143 *et seq.*, 208 *et seq.*

[91] This was actually done by a few eminent German psychiatrists; see my *Group Problems*, pp. 283–284.

psychiatrist, but it does mean that the lawyer, who is in certain cases dependent upon the psychiatrist's co-operation, would be unwise to ignore the growing consensus of opinion in favour of abolishing the M'Naghten Rules. It was one of the legal Pioneers in the present series, Charles Doe, who, probably as the first member of the judiciary, recognised what Mr. Justice Frankfurter, nearly a century later, called the " sham " nature of the M'Naghten Rules (see Chief Justice Kenison). Meanwhile, modern Continental and American legislative efforts and court practice have shown that less out-of-date definitions of mental abnormality and irresponsibility can be found without delivering criminal justice entirely to the mercies of the psychiatrist.[92] The whole dispute is, of course, only part of the much wider problem of the place of the expert in the administration of criminal justice with which I have dealt at some length elsewhere.[93]

As indicated earlier on in our discussion of Durkheim's work, we are in agreement with Jeffery's view that it would be a grave mistake exclusively to concentrate on the study and treatment of the individual offender and to neglect the study of society and of the criminal law and their attitude to crime and punishment. " No evaluation of the personality of the individual criminal," Jeffery writes, " is going to substitute for a sociological analysis of law." This is very true, although we are still inclined to think that such a sociological analysis of the law and of the attitude of society to crime and punishment may be the task of the sociology of the criminal law rather than that of criminology.[94] This is perhaps the reason why some criminologists are " not interested in studying law "; the further statement that they are " not interested in studying society " does probably less than justice to most of them. It may be argued, however, that it does not greatly matter who has to undertake that study if only it is done by somebody. The essential point of difference lies elsewhere: while the task defined by Jeffery is important, it can be no more a substitute for the study of the individual criminal than vice versa. Both are equally indispensable. Neither of them can " answer the riddle of criminality " in isolation. And here it can hardly be disputed that most of the advances made in the present century in our understanding of crime and in

---

[92] See Henry Weihofen, *The Urge to Punish* (London, 1957).
[93] *Criminal Justice and Social Reconstruction*, p. 219 *et seq.*
[94] See *Group Problems*, p. 264 *et seq.*

the treatment of criminals have been due neither to the Classical
School nor to the early nineteenth-century sociologists, but to the
great upheaval caused by the Positivists. Franz von Liszt's word is
still true that " the Italians stirred us up . . . somewhat rudely and
with unnecessary noise, but with lasting success." [95] Some of these
innovations such as the indeterminate sentence and the treatment
tribunal are still, rightly, controversial [96]; others, such as probation,
suspended sentences, pre-sentence inquiries and psychiatric treatment, preventive detention and parole, have come to stay, and even
the most extreme Classicist would hardly wish to abolish them. Let
us be careful, therefore, not to throw out the baby criminology
with the positivist bath water, and let us beware of slogans,
positivist or otherwise.

With regard to the application of scientific methods in the study
of crime and its treatment, to which Jeffery seems to have no
fundamental objections, this, too, is indispensable unless we wish
to put the clock back by more than a century, but we have to see to
it that statistical techniques should not run away with us, that they
should not immerse us in a flood of useless correlations and in the
process destroy that precious and delicate plant, intuition. This
need not happen since, as we have said in another connection, the
conflict between intuitive and statistical methods, if sensibly applied,
is more apparent than real and they are, to some extent, working
on similar lines.[97] Statistical techniques have to be used not only
in criminological studies and in order to assess the effect of the
various measures of dealing with crime, but also to ascertain the
reaction of the various social groups in the community to different
types of crime and different legal provisions and penalties. In fact,
the study of those aspects of the problem in which Jeffery is particularly interested requires statistical research as well as intuitive understanding. Let us criminologists beware that what Noel Annan has
written with reference to his subject, political science, should not,
mutatis mutandis, apply to us: " we are still trying to produce ore
from mines which have for long been worked out, namely, the old
concepts of state, society, will, rights, consent, obligation; and we
have turned our back on the social studies and methods of analysis

[95] *Group Problems*, p. 71.
[96] The present writer has recommended the establishment of treatment tribunals only " as
a second best "; see *Criminal Justice and Social Reconstruction*, p. 227.
[97] Hermann Mannheim and Leslie T. Wilkins, *Prediction Methods in relation to Borstal
Training* (London, 1955), p. 36 *et seq.*

which alone would restore some value and new meaning to those concepts." [98]

With Positivism largely discredited and the Classical School too static and sterile to guide further progress our eyes might well turn to the latest movement in our field as a potential twentieth-century " Third School." Judge Marc Ancel has given us a clear exposition of the points of difference between Positivism and that new movement, Social Defence, of which he is one of the most eminent and moderate representatives. The *" Défense sociale,"* he writes,[99] could come into existence only after the *" révolte positiviste,"* but although positivists, in particular Ferri, incessantly use the term " social defence," they give it a different meaning. According to Ancel, the main differences are: (1) Social Defence is not deterministic; (2) it disapproves of a rigid classification of offenders into types and stresses the uniqueness of human personality; (3) it believes in the importance of moral values; (4) it appreciates the duty of society towards the criminal, tries to establish an equilibrium between him and society and refuses to employ measures of security against him as mere administrative tools; (5) while fully utilising the resources of modern science, it refuses to be dominated by it and replaces the outmoded *" scientisme "* of the positivists by a modern system of *" politique criminelle."* Unfortunately, the *" Défense sociale "* has so far spoken with too many different voices; if the voices of such moderate leaders as Marc Ancel and Jean Graven should in future prevail, the foundation of a real " Third School " might eventually emerge from the present Babel.[100] Even then, however, no single " School " is likely to resolve all the contradictions and dilemmas inherent in the penal problem, and at least for a period of transition such as ours it might be wiser to dispense with all attempts to draw up grandiose paper schemes and programmes and to concentrate on more tangible objects.

HERMANN MANNHEIM.

[98] Noel Annan, *op. cit.* (note 39, above), p. 21.

[99] Marc Ancel, *La Défense sociale nouvelle* (Paris, 1954), pp. 57 *et seq.*, 101 *et seq.*, 164; see also the equally moderate views of another prominent member of the Society for Social Defence, Professor Jean Graven-Geneva, in the *Revue internationale de défense sociale*, Vol. XI, No. 3/4 (July–December 1957) (also in German in the *Internationales Colloquium über Kriminologie und Strafrechtsreform* (Freiburg, 1957), p. 48 *et seq.*).

[100] See *Group Problems*, pp. 208–209. This chapter was written before the publication of Marc Ancel's book. On the many dissensions within the " *Défense sociale*," see the critical assessment of its aims by Erwin Frey, *Bulletin* of the *Société Internationale de Criminologie* (Année 1956, 2e Semestre), p. 119 *et seq.*, and the following discussion. Certain extremist tendencies seem to have not been entirely absent from the discussions of the Vth Congress of Social Defence in Stockholm, August 1958; see the report by Jescheck in the *Zeitschrift für die gesamte Strafrechtswissenschaft*, Vol. 70, No. 4 (1958), p. 203 *et seq.*

2

CESARE BECCARIA
1738–1794

ONE seeks in vain for any clues in Cesare Beccaria's childhood and adolescence which would be even slightly suggestive of the renowned essay on penal reform that he was to write—an essay which showered upon him the acclaim and plaudits of some of the best minds in the world in which he lived. As a matter of fact, Beccaria in his early years did little more than to demonstrate that he was just ordinary intellectually and not too much interested in nor concerned with scholarly pursuits. It is true that he showed some flair for mathematics, but in general, his scholastic activities could hardly be considered predictive of the authorship of *Dei delitti e delle pene*.

Earlier years

Milan was the birth-place of Cesare Bonesana, Marquis of Beccaria, and the date of his birth was March 15, 1738. He died on November 28, 1794. Both his father and mother were members of the aristocracy and amongst his ancestors were persons who had achieved distinction in various fields of endeavour. Beccaria received his early schooling at the Jesuit College in Parma and later studied law at the University of Pavia. He was graduated from the University of Pavia in 1758. The years he spent under the tutelage of the Jesuits at Parma were, by his own admission and evaluation, unprofitable. He rebelled against the authoritarian methods of instruction, and the inflexible and dogmatic demeanour of his teachers tended to make the subject-matter taught unstimulating and uninspiring. For a period he found mathematics attractive; this subject too, however, soon failed to intrigue him further. The years he spent exposed to what was then considered the essentials of an education of an aristocrat failed to produce in Beccaria a modicum of enthusiasm for scholarship. All that these years

* Reproduced from *The Journal of Criminal Law, Criminology and Police Science*, Vol. 46, No. 4, November–December 1955.

seemed to create in the frustrated young man was lethargy and discontent. These drab and stifling educational experiences may have played, however, an important part in the creation of Beccaria's essay on penal reform. Perhaps we are merely speculating when we suggest that the nature of Beccaria's formal education directly contributed to the formulation of the arguments against the *status quo* so forcibly recorded in his essay. It does seem, however, that in his tightly knit and succinct indictment of the prevailing penal practices one can discern protestations against unrewarding and detestable early educational experiences.

With his formal education completed Beccaria returned to Milan and shortly after developed an interest in philosophical works. This interest was apparently kindled by Montesquieu's *Lettres persanes*. In this satire on the religious and political institutions of Montesquieu's world Beccaria found that something which he had so sorely missed before. The interest thus aroused led him to read and to digest the philosophical writings of others and especially those of the French Encyclopedists. In addition to philosophy he also began to read extensively of literature. Beccaria's interest in penology and crime was, however, aroused by his friendly association with two stimulating and intellectually keen brothers, Pietro and Alessandro Verri. These two men, Pietro, a distinguished Italian economist, and Alessandro, a creative writer of note, attracted to them a group of young men dedicated to the study and discussion of literary and philosophical subjects. It is to membership in this group of brilliant young men, that met for study in the Verri home, that Beccaria owes the incentive and the encouragement which eventually resulted in the essay on penal reform. The environment provided by the intellectually stimulating discussions which followed the serious study of the many social problems of the day aroused in Beccaria an intense and fervent desire to question many aspects of eighteenth-century society. He found in Pietro Verri and in other members of the group the spark needed to set in motion his creative powers.

Beccaria's first published work appeared in 1762 and was entitled: *Del disordine e de' rimedi delle monete nello stato di Milano nell' anno 1762*. This monograph, of practically no current significance, dealt with the plight and needed remedies for the monetary system of the State of Milan. It is, however, in many respects quite original and provocative and does demonstrate that Beccaria possessed the ability to write clearly and forcibly.

His famous essay

Although Beccaria seemed to have at last found the intellectual interests, which he had never acquired during his formative years, amongst his imaginative and scholarly friends, he was by no means consumed by an eagerness to write. As his friend and mentor Pietro Verri recounted, Beccaria tended to be lazy and easily discouraged. He needed prodding and even had to be given assignments upon which to work. It was such an assignment, given to him by Verri, that eventually culminated in the essay *Dei delitti e delle pene*. Beccaria, so the story goes, knew nothing of penology when he undertook to deal with the subject. Fortunately, however, Alessandro Verri, who held the office of Protector of Prisoners, was able to give Beccaria the help and the suggestions he needed. Work was begun on the essay in March 1763 and the manuscript was completed in January 1764. It was first published anonymously in July 1764 when Beccaria was barely a little more than twenty-six years of age. The essay was an immediate success, acclaimed by almost all who read it. However, not all who read it agreed with Beccaria. The fact that the essay was at first published anonymously suggests that its contents were designed to undermine many if not all of the cherished beliefs of those in position to determine the fate of those accused and convicted of crime. The essay was a tightly reasoned devastating attack upon the prevailing systems for the administration of criminal justice. As such it aroused the hostility and resistance of those who stood to gain by the perpetuation of the barbaric and archaic penological institutions of the day.

In order to appreciate the reason Beccaria's brief essay, *Dei delitti e delle pene*, created such excitement, enthusiasm and controversy one needs to recall the state of the criminal law in continental Europe at the time the essay first appeared.

The existent criminal law of eighteenth-century Europe was, in general, repressive, uncertain and barbaric. Its administration permitted and encouraged incredibly arbitrary and abusive practices. The agents of the criminal law, prosecutors and judges, were allowed tremendous latitude in dealing with persons accused and convicted of crime, and corruption was rampant throughout continental Europe.

Fantastic as it may now seem to many now living in certain parts of the world, the criminal law of eighteenth-century Europe vested in public officials the power to deprive persons of their freedom, property and life without regard for any of the principles which are now embodied in the phrase " due process of law." Secret accusations were in vogue and persons were imprisoned on the flimsiest of evidence. Torture, ingenious and horrible, was employed to wrench confessions from the recalcitrant. Judges were permitted to exercise unlimited discretion in punishing those convicted of crime. The sentences imposed were arbitrary, inconsistent and depended upon the status and power of the convicted. Punishments inflicted upon the more unfortunate of the offenders were extremely severe. A great array of crimes were punished by death not infrequently preceded by inhuman atrocities. Equality before the law as a principle of justice was practically non-existent, but rather the treatment accorded persons depended solely upon the station in life of the offender and upon the power that he and his friends could exercise over the agents of the law. In practice, no distinction was made between the accused and the convicted. Both were detained in the same institution and subjected to the same horrors of incarceration. This same practice prevailed in regard to the convicted young and old, the murderer and the bankrupt, first offenders and hardened criminals, men and women. All such categories of persons were promiscuously thrown together free to intermingle and interact.

This was the status of the criminal law and it is against this backdrop of abuses, vagaries, cruelties and irrationalities that we must place Beccaria's treatise in order to appreciate its human and revolutionary character. Many other enlightened humanitarians had, before Beccaria, protested against the prevailing customs; it was, however, left to Beccaria to make the most succinct and effective plea for the reform of the criminal law.

As one reads the first pages of *Dei delitti e delle pene*, one finds the roots of Beccaria's thought and general intellectual orientation. Although well versed in the writings of the French Encyclopedists, the essential reformative characteristics of his treatise on penology stem from his study of the works of Montesquieu and his acceptance of the contract theory of society so ably presented by Rousseau.

Thus, in the closing paragraph of the introduction to his treatise, Beccaria, after having briefly noted the deplorable state of the criminal law and of the administration of justice, writes that : " The immortal Montesquieu had but briefly considered this matter; and the truth, which is indivisible, has prompted me to follow in the steps of this great man. Thinking men, for whom I write, will know, however, how to distinguish between that which is his and that which is mine. I will consider myself fortunate, if, like him, I can obtain the secret thanks of the obscure and peaceful disciples of reason and inspire that gentle sentiment with which all sensitive persons respond to whosoever pleads the cause of humanity." [1]   In these words Beccaria not only pays credit to Montesquieu as a source of many of his own ideas but also suggests that his treatise is primarily intended to stimulate action designed to bring about a sweeping reform in European criminal law.

The social contract theory of the state phase of Beccaria's thinking is revealed in the opening paragraph of Chapter I of his essay. Thus, he writes: "Laws are the conditions whereby free and independent men unite to form society. Weary of living in a state of war, and of enjoying a freedom rendered useless by the uncertainty of its perpetuation, men willingly sacrifice a part of this freedom in order to enjoy that which is left in security and tranquillity. The sum of all of the portions of the freedom surrendered by each individual constitutes the sovereignty of a nation, deposited in and to be administered by a legitimate sovereign. It was not, however, alone sufficient to create this depository of freedom, it was also essential to defend this sovereignty from private usurpation of every man who would want not only that portion of the sovereignty that he individually had contributed but also that which had been contributed by all others. . . . It is because of this that punishments were established to deal with those who transgress against the laws." [2]   Thus, we note that the basis of punishment lies, according to Beccaria, in the necessity to restrain men from encroaching upon the freedom of one another defined and established by the terms (laws) of a social contract.

The social contract theory of the state is the major premise of Beccaria's penological syllogism and if one grants the tenability of this basic proposition, the rest of Beccaria's argument is not only logical but also compellingly persuasive.

The right to punish transgressors is an essential consequence of

[1] *Dei delitti e delle pene* (6th ed., 1776), pp. 12–13. This translation and others that follow are not literal, but are, rather, attempts to put Beccaria's words in present-day English.
[2] *Op. cit.* pp. 13–14.

the nature and scope of the contractual relations of men in society. It, the right to punish, must exist and be exercised if men are to be prevented from disrupting their orderly social existence. But Beccaria, following Montesquieu, warns that every punishment which is not founded upon absolute necessity is tyrannical. Punishment is legitimate only when it is employed by the Sovereign to defend the sovereignty of all against the depredation of any single individual. The right to punish should be exercised only by the Sovereign when it is necessary to defend the liberty and rights of all the people.

Having set forth this basic principle Beccaria then proceeds to suggest that if it is accepted certain consequences inevitably follow. First, he declares that punishment for crime is established only by law and the power to enact penal laws can only be vested in the " Legislator," who represents all members of a society. No magistrate, who is himself a member of society, can with any justification inflict upon another any penalty not ordained by law. Nor can any magistrate, regardless of circumstances, either increase or decrease, or change in any fashion, the punishment prescribed by law. It is the " Legislator " that determines the penalties, and it is the duty of magistrates to inflict such penalties exactly as they have been prescribed.

The second consequence following the acceptance of the principle is that the laws of a society apply equally to all members of society regardless of their station. This, Beccaria indicates, stems from the contractual nature of society. Exceptions to this all-binding principle cannot be tolerated since to do so would in effect result in encouraging the development of anarchy.

Further, the Sovereign can enact laws which are general in scope and in applicability, binding upon all members of society. He cannot, however, judge whether any specific person has violated the terms of the social contract. If he should attempt to play such a role, it would divide society into two parts; one part represented by the Sovereign who would be the accuser and affirm that a violation of the terms of the contract had occurred, and the other part consisting of the accused, who in turn would deny that a violation of contract had actually taken place. It is therefore necessary, Beccaria suggests, that a third party be given the duty of determining whether in fact a violation had occurred. In short, a magistrate is needed to resolve the issue from whose findings of the fact no appeal should be permitted and which consist of a simple negation or affirmation of the fact.

A third consequence deduced from Beccaria's major premise centres upon the severity of punishment. Beccaria states, if it can be demonstrated that severe punishment, although not in itself contrary to public welfare, is useless in the prevention of crime, such severe punishment is contrary to enlightened reason and justice.

Further, since judges or magistrates are not legislators, they have no right or authority to interpret penal laws. This is the function of the Sovereign who represents all members of a society. The task of judges consists in determining whether a person has or has not acted contrary to law. And in doing so, judges should conduct the inquiry by adhering strictly to the rules of logic. Decisions should be in the form of a syllogism wherein the law constitutes the major premise and the action of the individual whether it be or not be in conformity with the law, the minor premise. To punish or not to punish, or to grant freedom, should be the conclusion. For judges to go beyond the limits circumscribed by the rules of syllogistic reasoning results in usurpation of the power of legislators and in the introduction of ambiguity and uncertainty into the judicial process. Judges should never be permitted to interpret the laws but should confine their work to the application of laws. The inequities that may arise from a policy of strict application of penal laws cannot, according to Beccaria, be compared in their untoward effect with the inequities that are the results of a policy which permits judges to interpret them. Such a policy produces intolerable conditions wherein persons are placed at the mercy of the whimsical and venal emotions of magistrates. The power to remedy the untoward effects of existent laws should be vested in legislators and not in judges. It is only under such a governmental system that it is possible to obtain the maximum security for the life, property and freedom of persons.

To insure that judges keep within their proper and prescribed sphere of action is not enough. Beccaria declares that laws, penal and otherwise, must be written in a language so as to render them completely understandable to the people. Obscurantism in the law paves the way for interpretation and despotism. " The more widely known and widely understood is a code of laws the lesser the number of crimes, because, and undoubtedly, ignorance of the laws and the uncertainty of the consequences of transgressions of laws facilitates the expression of human passions." [3]   By implication a society without writing can never attain a fixed form of government in which power to govern is vested in the whole and not in any single part of this whole, and in which the laws are not subject to alteration or subversion in the interest of the few.

Up to this point we have tried to outline in brief the essential and central ideas of Beccaria's treatise.   These basic propositions constitute the major motifs of his argument and, if one grants Beccaria their tenability, the remainder of his essay is an exposition of their logical implications.   The structure he erected on these foundations will be found to be a devastating and logically reasoned assault upon the shortcomings and inhuman inconsistencies of the criminal and penal law of his day.

Why and how punish ?

Why should crimes be punished?   How should crimes be punished?   These are the important questions to which Beccaria next devotes attention.   Again, briefly, he declares that the necessity for punishment of crimes is inherent in the compact consummated when men agreed to live together.   Men are by nature self-seeking and motivated to gain all that they can from one another.   These self-centred individualists must, however, be kept within bounds if the society they willingly created is to endure.   It is therefore necessary to find a method to achieve this end and punishment is that method.   To Beccaria, the primary purpose of punishment is to insure the continued existence of society.   Furthermore, the amount and nature of punishment inflicted against transgressors should vary in proportion to the degree to which an act of an individual endangers the existence of society.   It is, Beccaria believes, in the common interest of all members of society that crimes should not be committed and that crimes should be prevented.   It becomes necessary, therefore, to provide legislators with means to achieve these objectives.   The goals or objectives can be attained by the enlightened utilisation of punishment, which should be inflicted in measures commensurate with the effects of the crime upon society.   It follows that the more threatening the crime is to societal welfare and existence, the more severe the punishment inflicted should be.

[3] *Op. cit.* p. 28.

The only measure of the seriousness of crimes is the amount of harm done to society.

Beccaria next turns his attention to a classification of crimes. Three categories of crimes are noted, based on varying degrees of injury done to society by their perpetrators. The first category consists of crimes considered to be most injurious to society. Such crimes as high treason, or acts of an individual against the state or its representatives, are considered by Beccaria to be most serious since such crimes threaten the existence of all members of society. Second in seriousness and in importance are crimes that injure the security and property of individuals. The third category of crimes are those that are disruptive of public peace and tranquillity, such as riots, rabble rousing, inciting disorder, etc. These categories of crimes, as indicated, are considered to represent different degrees of harm to society and to its members and, as such, should carry different penalties whose severity would differ as the seriousness of the crime differs.

The essential end of punishment is not, says Beccaria, to torment offenders nor to undo a crime already committed. It is rather to prevent offenders from doing further harm to society and to prevent others from committing crimes. Punishment is thus looked upon as an educative process and the types of punishments selected and how they are imposed should always be done so as to make the greatest impact and the most enduring impression upon all members of society, while inflicting the least pain on the body of the offender.

To be effective as a deterrent to crime, punishment should be both prompt and inevitable, applied to all alike for similar crimes. It is not cruelty nor severity, Beccaria believes, that renders punishment an effective deterrent, but rather its certainty. To this end Beccaria suggests that the accused should be tried as speedily as possible in order to reduce to a minimum the time that elapses between the commission of the crime and its punishment. This, Beccaria declares, will produce a more lasting effect and tend to strengthen the association between crime and punishment. He further believes that the sought-for connection between crime and punishment can be made more impressive where it is possible to make the punishment analogous to the crime. It is for this reason that Beccaria questions the utility of punishing lesser crimes in the obscurity of prisons.

It is the strength of the association of crime and punishment that

Beccaria believes to be the most effective deterrent. It is not the severity of punishment but rather its certainty that leaves a lasting impression on the minds of men. He contends, therefore, that punishments that are severe, cruel and inhuman do not prevent crime. As a matter of fact he argues that extremely severe penalties actually encourage persons to commit crimes. Thus, he states: " The certainty of punishment, even though it [punishment] be moderate, will always make a stronger impression than the fear of one more severe if it is accompanied by the hope that one may escape that punishment, because men are more frightened by an evil which is inevitable even though minor in nature. Further, if the punishment be too severe for a crime men will be led to commit further crimes in order to escape punishment for the crime." [4] He suggests that history indicates the existence of an association between inhuman and violent punishments and the most atrocious and bloody of crimes, for the legislators and offenders were both motivated by the same ferocious spirit. " As punishment becomes more cruel and more severe, the minds of men . . . grow more hardened and calloused. . . . In order to insure that a penalty will produce the desired effect it is sufficient to provide that the *evil* attendant the penalty exceeds the *good* expected of the crime." [5] In every calculation of the excess of evil over good, it is necessary to include the certainty of the penalty and the denial of the expected advantage produced by the crime. Anything that goes beyond is superfluous and is therefore tyrannical.

The death penalty

The death penalty is next considered by Beccaria and he argues that it is neither legitimate nor necessary. He proposes that men in forming the social compact did not deposit with the Sovereign their right to life. To have done so would have been illogical since the primary reason for the creation of society was better to insure the right of men to live. Life is the greatest of all human good and no man willingly gives to another man the authority to deprive him of his life.

If, as Beccaria has contended, the only reasonable basis of punishment is its effectiveness as a deterrent of crime then the death penalty must be considered useless. The death of an offender is a

[4] *Op. cit.* p. 113.   [5] *Op. cit.* p. 114.

passing spectacle leaving no enduring impression upon those who witness the execution. Penalties which are continued over a period of time and which are known to be continuous are, according to Beccaria, much more efficacious than penalties which are merely momentary. Capital punishment, even though it be inflicted in a most cruel fashion, cannot be made lasting beyond a certain point— the victim eventually dies, and though spectators are shocked and revolted by the spectacle, the fear aroused in them is only passing in its effect. It is the anticipation of continued suffering and terror that is the more efficient as a method of deterrence. But even then Beccaria warns that the severity of punishment should be just enough to prevent others from committing crimes rather than to torment the criminal.

The death penalty is unreasonable on another score. The execution of an individual though it may be authorised by law is an act of violence and barbarity. It represents an injustice in that it renders an act legitimate in payment for an equivalent act of violence. Its infliction is no more than homicide even though it is in repayment of homicide. It constitutes an act of ferocity intended to curb ferocity.

Administration of justice

Beccaria next devotes attention to a consideration of several of the procedural phases of the administration of criminal justice. He is outspoken regarding many of the abuses residing in the pre-conviction practices of his day. To Beccaria the use of torture to extract confessions from offenders is intolerable and should never be permitted. No one, he insists, has the right to maltreat or punish an individual until after he has been convicted. The utilisation of torture before and during the trial of an accused is looked upon as an infamous test of the truth and a completely barbaric custom. He contends that no one is a criminal until he is found guilty of having committed a crime; consequently, to punish a person before he has been duly found guilty is to impose upon that person punishment which goes far beyond any reasonable limit. The employment of torture makes pain and suffering, rather than established evidence, the test of truth.

Beccaria is also unalterably opposed to the utilisation of secret accusations. Where such practices exist they constitute proof of the weakness of government, and render men false and treacherous. No one can effectively defend himself against secret accusers and Beccaria believes that the practice cannot be justified on any count. Beccaria strongly believes in public accusations followed by a public trial of the accused to determine the falsity or validity of the accuser and the accusation. All trials, he insists, should be public and every man should be tried by his peers. Differences in rank or station should be disregarded when the life, liberty and fortune of an individual is in question. On such matters class differences should not be the basis upon which the guilt or innocence of a citizen is decided. Beccaria does, however, suggest that in crimes involving the offence of one citizen against another one-half of those who try the case should be peers of the accused and one-half be peers of the person offended. It is through this means that Beccaria hopes to achieve that impartiality necessary to a fair trial. The accused should also be given the right to exclude, up to a point, a number of judges whose impartiality he has reason to question.

Prevention of crime

" It is better to prevent crimes, than to punish them." [6] This Beccaria believes to be the basic character of good legislation which in actual practice means leading men to the attainment of maximum happiness and minimum misery. How would you then prevent crimes? First, enact laws that are clear and simple and let them apply equally to all men. These laws must be for all and not in favour of, nor against, any class or any segment of society. They should also be feared, but the law alone must be feared and not men, for the fear of men, Beccaria argues, is a source of crime. The laws should also be certain so as to render the consequences of crime not problematical but rather inevitable. It should be the primary interest of magistrates to insure the observance of laws rather than to punish their violation.

Would you prevent crime? Beccaria again asks. Then reward virtue—make virtue a desired goal of men. But more than this is needed to prevent crime. Every effort should be made to increase and extend knowledge, since Beccaria believes that human liberty should be accompanied by enlightenment. The most effective method for the prevention of crime is a perfect system of education.

[6] *Op. cit.* p. 188.

Dei delitti e delle pene ends with the following admonition: "So that any punishment be not an act of violence of one or of many against another, it is essential that it be public, prompt, necessary, minimal in severity as possible under given circumstances, proportional to the crime, and prescribed by the laws."[7]

Conclusion

The above briefly discussed essentials of Beccaria's penal philosophy made a tremendous impact upon the enlightened and kindred minds of his day. His book, as already noted, was an immediate success in most of Europe. The acclaim it received was not because its contents were exclusively original, as a matter of fact many of the reforms Beccaria advocated had been proposed by others, but rather because it constituted the first successful attempt to present a consistent and logically constructed penological system—a system to be substituted for the confusing, uncertain, abusive and inhuman practices inherent in the criminal law and penal system of his world. His brief treatise was in many respects propagandistic and a well-reasoned attack on the prevailing customs. It called for sweeping reforms in all phases of the administration of criminal justice. The book, easily read and exceptionally lacking in the usual trappings of pedantry, was most opportune and formulated in a convincing fashion the hopes and desires of a great many vigorous and outspoken reformers of his day. It had the power to rally to the cause it pleaded the energies and efforts of most of the enlightened minds of eighteenth-century Europe. Beccaria's slim but potent book was a success primarily because it advocated changes deemed desirable and supported by public opinion. It appeared at a moment marked by a growing revolt against despotism and absolutism—it was the product of an era given to the serious questioning of the sanctity and utility of prevailing social institutions. There are reasons for believing that the essay would have failed to impress or to have attracted but passing attention had it not appeared when it did. Europe was ready for it in 1764 and what Beccaria said in it was employed to assault and eventually destroy many of the customs and traditions of eighteenth-century society by the protagonists of a new order. Chief amongst these was the brilliant and able Voltaire,

[7] *Op. cit.* p. 205.

who, perhaps more than anyone else, prepared the way for the implementation of the reforms that Beccaria proposed.

Without such perspective the present-day reader of Beccaria's essay is quite apt to see little that is new or striking in the essay, since what Beccaria proposed and so ably argued for in 1764 has been in great part achieved in the modern world. We must, however, remember that it was Beccaria's rapier-like thrusts at the barbarism and inhumanity of the penology of his day that played a tremendously significant role in bringing about the present-day penal practices. It is not an exaggeration to regard Beccaria's work as being of primary importance in paving the way for penal reform for approximately the last two centuries. The reader will find proposed in his essay practically all of the important reforms in the administration of criminal justice and in penology which have been achieved in the civilised world since 1764.

With the publication of *Dei delitti e delle pene* Beccaria's literary productivity comes rather abruptly to an end. After a visit to Paris in 1766, he was appointed Professor of Political Economy in the Palatine School of Milan in 1768, and held this post for only two years. The lectures he delivered on political economy were collected and published (1804) ten years after his death and represent his only other major published creative work.

ELIO MONACHESI.

SELECTED BIBLIOGRAPHY

By Beccaria

BECCARIA, CESARE. *Dei delitti e delle pene.* (6th ed.), Harlem, 1776. An Essay on Crime and Punishments. (Translated from the Italian with the commentary by Voltaire.) (5th ed.), London, 1804.

About Beccaria

CANTÙ, CESARE. *Beccaria e il diritto penale.* Florence, 1862.

LANDRY, EUGENIO. *Cesare Beccaria, Scritti e lettere inediti raccolti ed illustrati da Eugenio Landry.* Milan, 1910.

MAESTRO, MARCELLO T. *Voltaire and Beccaria as Reformers of Criminal Law.* New York, 1942.

PHILLIPSON, COLEMAN. *Three Criminal Law Reformers: Beccaria, Bentham, Romilly.* 1923; reprinted Montclair, N.J., 1970.

NOTE ON THE CONTRIBUTOR

Dr. ELIO MONACHESI was, until his death in 1971, Professor and Chairman of the Department of Sociology at the University of Minnesota, with which he was connected throughout his academic career, except for two years' research in Boston and in Italy under the auspices of the Social Science Research Council. He co-authored *The Rehabilitation of Children* (with E. M. H. Baylor, 1939), *Elements of Sociology* (with Don Martindale, 1951), and *Analyzing and Predicting Juvenile Delinquency with the M.M.P.I.* (with Starke R. Hathaway, 1953).

3

JEREMY BENTHAM
1748–1832

They say he cherished men,
Their happiness, and then
Calmly assumed one could
Devise cures for their good
Believing all men the same
And happiness their aim

He reckoned right and wrong
By felicity—lifelong
And by such artless measure
As the quality of pleasure
For pain he had a plan
Absurd old gentleman.[1]

JEREMY BENTHAM was an eccentric personality, an incredibly prolific writer, a thinker who had the colossal temerity to attempt to catalogue and to label all varieties of human behaviour and the motivations giving rise to them. With this information in hand, as he pointed out with disarming simplicity, he believed that he could select the precisely proper procedures to control human actions and direct them into desirable channels.

It is periodically fashionable to resurrect an old philosopher, such as Bentham, dust him off, and present him as the author of contemporaneously significant prose. This is probably a function of the vested interest the researcher acquires in his subject. In some cases, undoubtedly, a writer actually has been unduly neglected.

Such is not the case, however, with Bentham. A very large part of Bentham's thought is badly dated. Reading his works may not arouse the froth that drove Karl Marx to immortalise Bentham (in a certain way, at least) with the bombastic assertion that " in no time and in no country has the most homespun commonplace ever strutted about in so self-satisfied a way." [2] But neither will it likely impress the present-day criminologist with its immediate relevance, particularly in the sphere of criminological theory.

* Reproduced from *The Journal of Criminal Law, Criminology and Police Science*, Vol. 46, No. 2, July–August 1955.

[1] Helen Bevington, " A Bomb for Jeremy Bentham," in *Nineteen Million Elephants and Other Poems* (Boston: Houghton Mifflin, 1950), p. 33. Reprinted by permission of Miss Bevington.

[2] Karl Marx, *Capital: A Critique of Capitalistic Production* (New York: Modern Library, n.d.), p. 668. Marx applied a further epithet to Bentham which has since become a Soviet *cliché*. " Bentham," he wrote, " is a genius of bourgeoise stupidity."

With the above in mind, then, the direction of the present paper can be labelled. No attempt will be made to detail all of Bentham's major postulations, but only those will be treated which appear to have interest or value for contemporary times. This will lead to a skewed portrait of Bentham's production. Often minor points will be taken out of context if the remainder of the context is not presently relevant. Thus, for instance, an elaborate reproduction of Bentham's catalogue of types of crimes would appear meaningless now; yet, within this catalogue there is an occasional differentiation which has today the germ of a neat analytical separation.

This paper will discuss: first, Bentham's life and times; secondly, his theories of criminality; and thirdly, his unique contribution to penology—the Panopticon prison design.

Bentham's life and times

All sources comment on Bentham's extreme precocity, both intellectual and artistic. This precocity combined with a retarded physical growth during his early years to give rise to a badly unbalanced developmental pattern. One can further note briefly the few Freudian-tinted remarks that biographers have placed on the record.[3]

Bentham's relationship with women, for instance, was very unusual. His mother died when he was eleven and Bentham did not get along well with his stepmother. He never married and is said to have formed a close romantic attachment with only one woman in his life; indeed, it is reported that at the age of fifty-seven he proposed to this lady but was rejected.

Bentham did not get along easily with other persons. " He shrank from the world in which he was easily browbeaten to the study in which he could reign supreme," one writer notes,[4]

[3] The standard biography of Bentham is considered to be that by his executor, John Bowring, *The Works of Jeremy Bentham* (Edinburgh: Tait, 1843), Vols. I and XI. This work is used extensively and often exclusively in later studies for biographical information on Bentham.

Everett, however, maintains that Bowring (" who had in some way wriggled his way into the old man's esteem ") wrote a " hasty and inaccurate Life." (Charles Warren Everett, Editor's Introduction, in Jeremy Bentham, *The Limits of Jurisprudence Defined* (New York: Columbia University Press, 1945), p. 28.) Everett's own work, *The Education of Jeremy Bentham* (New York: Columbia University Press, 1931), is an interesting source containing much new information on Bentham's life as gleaned from the voluminous unpublished Bentham papers stored in the University College and the British Museum in London.

[4] Leslie Stephen, *The English Utilitarians* (New York: G. P. Putnam's, 1900), Vol. I, p. 175.

providing background explanation, perhaps, for one of the most telling criticisms of Bentham's work on crime—its total failure to consider criminals as human beings, as live, complicated, variegated personalities.

Sir Norwood East neatly puts a finger on this shortcoming: " It is interesting to note," East points out, " that in the index to the text of Bentham's volume on *The Theory of Legislation* reference is made to crime, offences, and criminality, but none to criminals or offenders. In fact, although [Bentham's] school was seriously concerned with abolishing injustices and the vindictiveness of punishment, and believed that the function of punishment was solely deterrent, it paid little attention to the individuality of the offender." [5]

It is likely that Bentham's need for neat catalogues—catalogues which could be stated with specific details and without the diverse elements inevitably occurring when the human being *per se* is considered, accounts for the philosopher's concentration on crime in the abstract. His was arm-chair criminology, in which a keen, rather pedantic mind inductively derived sweeping principles of human behaviour and supported them sometimes with historical citations and, more often, with constructed examples. The advantage was that the trivia of empirical *minutiae* did not obstruct far-ranging insight; the disadvantage, that the reality of empirical truth was not allowed to infiltrate into mental machinations.

Bentham, of course, was intensely influenced by the times in which he worked. Against these times he towers as a giant, fearlessly challenging the assumptions of criminal law. Phillipson characterises the criminal codes of Bentham's time as " a mass of incongruities, absurdities, contradictions and barbarities " and notes further that:

There had been a capricious, unsystematic accumulation of statutes aimed at the same crime for which earlier provisions were allowed to remain unrepealed. Different penalties existed for the same offences. Different forms of indictment were necessary for crimes which were similar fundamentally, but varied in certain minor particulars. Thus, in the case of receiving stolen goods, several laws were applicable; but one referred exclusively to pewter-pots, another was confined to precious metals; and neither could be used as against receivers of horses or banknotes. . . .

There was no consistency, no harmony, no method whatever in the legislation. The law was in theory one thing, and in practice it was often another.

[5] Norwood East, *Society and the Criminal* (Springfield, Ill.: C. C. Thomas, 1951), p. 98.

The infliction of punishments was to a large extent left to the arbitrary and capricious discretion of the judge . . . so that from circuit to circuit practices varied to an extraordinary degree, sometimes being marked by ferocious violence, at other times by unpardonable weakness.   The punishments threatened by law could not be more rigorous.   The spasmodic prescription of measures of extreme severity and ferocity was evidently thought to be an effective panacea for the preventing or curing of the country's criminal ills. Many laws were laid down whose violation was actually disregarded.   The somewhat indiscriminate classification of crimes into felonies and mis- demeanours, the outworn technical rules respecting " benefit of clergy " were fertile sources of abuse, evasion and injustice.   Innocent persons were liable to become the victims of an irrationally applied law; the guilty could cherish a hope of impunity—and very frequently were their hopes fulfilled.[6]

It was against this chaotic background—a background, inci- dentally, that finds some echoes in contemporary conditions—that Bentham did his work.   He attempted to arrange affairs into a harmonious unity, and brought to bear on illegal behaviour a multi- plicity of analytical concepts such as felicity calculus, greatest happiness, pain and pleasure, and utility.

Bentham's theories of crime

Bentham undertook the gigantic task of expounding a compre- hensive code of ethics, but believed that such an undertaking alone was sterile—too non-utilitarian—and he therefore put great emphasis on the practical problem of eliminating or at least decreasing crime. He was in this sense aiming at a system of social control; a method of checking human behaviour according to a general ethical prin- ciple.   The ethical principle was utilitarianism: An act is not to be judged by an irrational system of absolutes but by a supposedly verifiable principle.   The principle—one that had been enunciated by a long line of thinkers prior to Bentham [7]—was that of " the greatest happiness for the greatest number " or simply " the greatest happiness."

An act, Bentham said, possesses utility " if it tends to produce benefit, advantage, pleasure, good or happiness (all this in the present case comes to the same thing) or (which again comes to the same thing) to prevent the happening of mischief, pain, evil or

---

[6] Coleman Phillipson, *Three Criminal Law Reformers: Beccaria, Bentham, Romilly* (1923; reprinted Montclair, N.J.: Patterson Smith, 1970), pp. 166–168.

[7] For a detailed discussion of the background of the concept, see " The Principle of Utility and Bentham's Place in its History," in David Baumgardt, *Bentham and the Ethics of Today* (Princeton: Princeton University Press, 1952), pp. 33–60.

unhappiness to the party whose interest is considered." [8] To measure the "goodness" or "badness" of an act Bentham introduced the pseudo-mathematical concept of felicity calculus. In his writings, however, statements of felicity calculus invariably deteriorate into long-winded attempts to explain verbally the method of arithmetically arriving at the quantitative weights to be attached to various items of behaviour. But the actual carrying out of the operation is not undertaken nor are the ultimate implications of such a procedure considered.

Bentham was certainly aware of the infinite ramifications of any given act—criminal or non-criminal—but this did not deter him from the claim that these ramifications could be tagged and weighed within his conceptual framework. At one point, for instance, Bentham notes that the single honking of a goose some thousand years previous undoubtedly had significant effects on every aspect of life today, and he even attempts to name some of these effects and to rate their importance. The presumptuousness of such an effort appears incomprehensible to humbler minds, particularly since Bentham had no criteria but his own feelings for determining the ultimate utility of an act and of the endless waves that it sets into motion.

Bentham's basic concern with "happiness" rather than with "utility" again reflects his dedication to practical affairs. He was thinking, one commentator declares, "of the . . . welfare . . . of the community as composed of individuals" rather than being "merely concerned with barren speculative theory." [9] It is the failure to lay a sound theoretical foundation, however, that has undermined the lasting value of Bentham's work.

Bentham, nonetheless, possessed an extremely fertile mind and it turned its attention on many problems which later thinkers have often not solved but only avoided. These are some of the criminological concepts that form segments of Bentham's work:

Motivation

The influence of psychiatric theory on the interpretation of criminal action has primarily been in terms of a concentration on

---

[8] Jeremy Bentham, *An Introduction to the Principles of Morals and Legislation* (edited by Laurence J. Lafleur) (New York: Hafner, 1948), p. 2.

[9] William L. Davidson, *Political Thought in England : The Utilitarians from Bentham to J. S. Mill* (New York: Henry Holt, 1916), pp. 48–49.

the motives underlying human behaviour. Human beings, we now believe, attempt to satisfy their needs in a number of ways, some legal and some illegal (social definitions), but the thesis that some needs are universal has had extensive implications for criminological theory.

In contrast to the seeming sophistication of the present psychiatric stress on motivation, Bentham's efforts appear rather juvenile. He was unaware, reasonably enough, of the unconscious genesis of human behaviour. Bentham believed that all men pursued their ends deliberately, after rational consideration of the divergent elements involved. Persons today, on the other hand, as Larrabee points out, " have been made [aware], as Bentham never was, of the more insidious dangers of deceiving themselves. . . . Bentham . . . was much too sure that he was always on the side of the angels, and that his opponents were plagued by evil motives rather than by apathy and ignorance." [10]

Motives—or " springs of action " as Bentham labels them,[11] using a term from mechanics to suit his so-called dynamic morality [12]—refer to " anything that can contribute to give birth to or even to prevent, any kind of action." Beyond the definition, Bentham's exposition is more interminable than illuminating. His exhaustive list of motives can be well summarised with the not-undeserved sarcasm it drew from a contemporary reviewer:

" In multiplying these distinctions and divisions . . . Mr. Bentham appears to bear resemblance . . . to one of the old scholastic doctors, who substituted classification for reasoning, and looked upon the ten categories as the most useful of all human inventions," the critic wrote. " Though much acuteness and industry may be displayed in finding them out, the discovery is just as unprofitable to science as the enumeration of the dissyllables in the decalogue would be to theology." [13]

Sophistical as they are, the tables of motives are stage setters for

---

[10] Harold A. Larrabee, Editor's Preface, in Jeremy Bentham, *Handbook of Political Fallacies* (Baltimore: Johns Hopkins Press, 1952), p. ix.

[11] Bentham's writings on motives can be found in various sections of *An Introduction to the Principles of Morals and Legislation*, and in *A Table of the Springs of Action*, which is reprinted in Bowring, *Works*, Vol. I, pp. 195–219.

[12] Elie Halévy, *The Growth of Philosophic Radicalism* (translated from the French by Mary Morris) (New York: Macmillan, 1928), p. 459. The best bibliography of Bentham's works has been compiled by Everett and appears in this volume, pp. 522–546.

[13] Francis Jeffrey, *Contributions to the Edinburgh Review* (London: Longman, Brown, Green and Longman, 1855), pp. 619–620. The original appeared in the *Edinburgh Review* of April 1804.

the future elaboration of Bentham's theory. For basically, he avows, all human action is reducible to one simple formula of motivation: The pursuit of pleasure and the concomitant avoidance of pain.

"Motive necessarily refers to action," Bentham writes. "Pleasure, pain, or other events prompt the action." And, "It follows, therefore, immediately and incontestably, that there is no such thing as any sort of motive that is in itself a bad one." It is only the consequence of the motive that can be bad because of its effect on others, because of its ultimate influence.

Bentham does point out, amusingly, a criminal court lesson in semantics as he proceeds through his labyrinth of motive delineation. He calls attention to the ethical valuation that is deeply rooted in the language of motivation and notes the preponderance of defamatory words in contrast to praiseworthy denominations and even more so in contrast to neutrally toned designations. The love of wealth, for example, possesses a large number of derogatory names such as " avarice, covetousness, rapacity, niggardliness " and only a few relatively appreciative labels such as " frugality." But the motive, regardless of the connotation of the word chosen to tag it, remains precisely the same.

Bentham flirts continuously in his discourse on motivation with one of the most important tenets of criminological theory; namely, that criminal behaviour is generally learned behaviour. But he actually never comes to intimate grips with the idea. He deserves considerable credit, nonetheless, for his adherence to a theory of social (*i.e.*, pleasure pursuit) causation of crime rather than a concept of biological, climatic or other non-social causation.

The problem of why certain persons pursue criminal patterns in their quest of happiness while others do not is not considered deeply by Bentham. His only answer would seem to be that the external given situation is such that, without adequate deterrence (pain), any person in the situation would act in a criminal manner. This fails to take cognisance of the variations in the individuals facing the given situation. It is not the individuals who vary, Bentham believes, but the situations which are different. Bentham could easily incorporate stereotyped acts in his theory. But he avoids examples which are, to him, promiscuous variations of clear-cut, readily understandable behaviour. And his understanding and interpretation of behaviour is always in terms of his own perception of what seems reasonable in a given context.

Put another way: It appears to be futile to attempt to determine how much pain (punishment) can effectively deter homicide, even after homicide is broken down into innumerable analytical categories in terms of exact amounts of premeditation and precise particles of malice aforethought. A general, statistical answer can be given to the question, but the basic fact that evaded Bentham is that there are some individuals who simply do not conceive of homicide as one of a number of solutions to whatever problem presses them, while others turn to homicide immediately as representing the only possible solution.

Mitchell has adequately summarised the shortcomings of Bentham's work on motivation. " The real reason we find this concept artificial," he notes, " is that we have another stock of ideas about behaviour with which Bentham's views are incompatible." [14]

Social control

It is obvious that all persons might derive considerable pleasure from uncontrolled orgies of criminal behaviour if there were no checks—no pains—attached to this behaviour. These checks, or *sanctions* as Bentham designated them, may be set up by legislation, and they serve to bring the individual's pursuit of his own happiness in line with the best interests of the society as a whole.

The bold assumption is further made that the gain of individual happiness by a person in the society inevitably contributes to the total happiness of the society as a whole. As Sorokin has pointed out, Bentham does not take into account the basic idea that what gives happiness to the greatest number of human beings does not necessarily bring the maximum of happiness to some individuals; and what gives the most happiness to some persons does not necessarily give the maximum happiness to all.[15]

Bentham clearly recognised that any legal sanction must be acceptable to the majority of the people before it will be effective. He was aware of other items of social control too, items oftentimes more effective than the legislated don'ts. He called the sanctions physical, political, moral (or popular) and religious. Everett

[14] Wesley C. Mitchell, " Bentham's Felicific Calculus," *Political Science Quarterly*, 33 (June 1918), p. 183.
[15] Pitirim A. Sorokin, *Society, Culture, and Personality: Their Structure and Dynamics* (New York: Harper, 1947), p. 575.

illustrates their operation and differentiation with a case of drunkenness:

> If a man suffers from a headache as a result of drunkenness, that may be styled a punishment of the physical sanction; if he is fined or imprisoned by the sentence of a magistrate, it is a punishment of the political sanction; if his neighbours refused to associate with him on account of dislike for his moral character, that is a punishment of the moral sanction; if a Mohammedan, he may suffer from the fear of God's displeasure for having violated a precept of the Koran, and is thus punished by the religious sanction.[16]

Bentham advocated social engineering primarily in the realm of political sanctions, since this is the most malleable area in the pleasure-pain equation. He dismissed any idea of recourse to traditional or natural law ("nonsense on stilts" he caustically labelled the latter).

Deterrence and punishment

The nature of conduct could be evaluated, Bentham believed, by considering its consequences. Present criminologists, on the other hand, would probably say that the consequences of an act (and this is particularly true in the sociolegal handling of juvenile delinquents) are not nearly as important as the personality and the attitudes of the offender. Though the law would not pose the question, the criminologist should: What difference in terms of the offender does it make whether a bullet, intended to kill, proves lethal or merely injures slightly?

Bentham made very worth-while advances in the rationalising of criminal jurisprudence by insisting that the function of law should not be to achieve vengeance for a criminal act, but to prevent the commission of the act. That he did not clearly understand the connection between laws and their effect on deterring crime is not surprising. We still do not adequately comprehend the complexities of this relationship, and our laws still are a mosaic of disjointed ideas without empirically founded substance.

On capital punishment, for instance, Bentham pointed out that afflictive executions, as he calls executions in which extraordinary brutality is used to carry out the killing, are not satisfactory punishments because they produce more pain than is necessary for the purpose. In general, Bentham's reasoning on capital punishment

---

[16] Everett, *The Education of Jeremy Bentham*, p. 190.

is very keen. Consider, for example, his arguments against extensive capital punishment statutes when public opinion does not
support them. In such cases, he notes, the following occurs:

1. It makes perjury appear meritorious, by founding it on
   humanity;
2. It produces contempt for the laws, by rendering it notorious
   that they are not executed;
3. It renders convictions arbitrary and pardons necessary. . . .
   [And] all these causes of uncertainty in criminal procedure
   are so many encouragements to malefactors.[17]

Punishment is considered an evil, but a necessary evil to prevent
greater evils being inflicted on the society and thus diminishing
happiness. Bentham presumably does not consider the possibility
that an outlawed act might actually serve to increase human happiness; the dilemma so brilliantly portrayed by Dostoevsky in *Crime
and Punishment* in which a murder is defined, with considerable
justification, as a social good by its perpetrator and thus morally
justifiable.

The application of the principle of utility to criminal behaviour
produced, among other things, one valuable insight that today is still
not totally incorporated into criminal jurisprudence. An offence,
Bentham reasoned, must be productive of evil (unhappiness: pain);
otherwise it is not an offence. Thus Bentham's measuring stick of
criminal behaviour represents a neat distinguishing instrument
between acts which a society may consider meretricious and those
which it should label as criminal.

Bentham in this vein declaims against what he calls " imaginary
offences "—" acts which produce no real evil, but which prejudice,
mistake, or the ascetic influence have caused to be regarded as
offences." To illustrate his point, Bentham points to the case of
vestal virgins who were buried alive for unchastity. Many commentators on the criminal codes today, with Professor Kinsey in the
vanguard, would undoubtedly echo a fervent agreement with the

---

[17] Jeremy Bentham, *The Rationale of Punishment* (translated from the French by Richard
Smith) (London: Robert Heward, 1830), pp. 196–197. This book has an odd printing
history that is not atypical of Bentham's works. It first formed the second volume of
Théorie des Peines et des Récompenses (Londres, 1811) and represented the initial publication of a Bentham manuscript which had been translated into French by Etienne
Dumont. The material for the English edition was drawn primarily from the Dumont
work and is thus a translation of Bentham back into his native language.

Bentham distinction between imaginary and real offences, particularly with the position that " offences which originate in the sexual appetite, when there is neither violence, fraud, nor interference with the rights of others, and also offences against one's self, may be arranged under this head." [18]

There is another capsule of advice in Bentham's discussion of remedies—means short of incarceration for preventing crime—that is of relevance to contemporary events. " Never use a preventive means of a nature to do more evil than the offence to be prevented," Bentham cautions. It is a lesson that still must be learned.

Bentham is at his logical nadir when he attempts to impose his felicity calculus on criminal jurisprudence in an effort to state the amount of punishment necessary to deter various acts. His moral arithmetic falls short of reasonableness; it is, as the poem at the outset of this discussion suggests, " an artless measure." Man is not, to employ the words of two commentators on Bentham's work, " a human calculating machine." [19] Bentham's theory of criminal behaviour, to mention another criticism, is unduly individualistic, intellectualistic and voluntaristic, and " assumes freedom of will in a manner which gives little or no possibility of further investigation of crime or of efforts to prevent crime." [20]

But Bentham's penology—in contrast to his theories of criminal jurisprudence—often reaches a summit that present-day climbers are still scrambling to attain. It is short on positive suggestions, but it is strikingly sophisticated in its criticisms of illogical punishment. Penology is not the heart of Bentham's work but, to this writer, his pronouncements on the subject constitute the most lasting segment of his extensive publications in criminology.[21]

Bentham is particularly adept at analysing the various types of punishment in terms of their pragmatic usefulness to the society. The aims of punishment, he avers, are to prevent recidivism and to deter others from the commission of similar offences. Here, Bentham cannot separate the two goals in a workable fashion (and

[18] Jeremy Bentham, *Theory of Legislation* (translated from the French of Etienne Dumont by R. Hildreth) (London: Kegan Paul, 1905), pp. 245–246.

[19] Harry Elmer Barnes and Howard Becker, *Social Thought from Lore to Science* (Boston: D. C. Heath, 1938), Vol. I, p. 259.

[20] Edwin H. Sutherland, *Principles of Criminology* (revised by Donald R. Cressey), 5th ed. (Philadelphia: Lippincott, 1955), p. 53.

[21] This judgment, it might be said, is shared by at least one Benthamite. Atkinson has written that " no part . . . is more luminous, or possesses greater living interest, than the author's enunciation of the general principles of punishment." Charles Milner Atkinson, *Jeremy Bentham: His Life and Work* (London: Methuen, 1905), p. 139.

he is certainly not alone in this). He has no logical answer, for instance, to the problem of the murderer who commits a single offence and then no longer, by statistical probability, represents a threat to the society. In Bentham's theory of utility, for any offence that can be regarded as an isolated incident, the like of which will never recur, punishment is considered useless because it adds a further pain to an original one without purpose.

Punishment should not be an act of anger, resentment or vengeance. These types of punishment are berated: (1) Where the punishment is groundless, since there is no offence because consent has been given, or where the evil is more than compensated for by an attendant good, such as in justifiable homicide; (2) Where the punishment is inefficacious because it has no power to affect the will, such as in cases of nonage, insanity, or under circumstances where the act appears to be absolutely involuntary; (3) Where the punishment is unprofitable because the evil of punishment exceeds that of the offence. It would be wise, Bentham notes in this connection, to pardon an offender who is protected by a foreign state whose goodwill it is essential to obtain; and (4) Where the punishment is needless because the end may be obtained as effectually at a cheaper price " by instruction, for instance, by informing the understanding. . . ." [22]

Also enunciated are two principles which still have not obtained adequate recognition: first, the general concept that the less certain the punishment the more severe it must be if it is to have any possibility of deterrence; and second, that overtly equivalent punishments are not really equivalent because of the variations among the offenders. A fine to the rich man may be a mild punishment, while the same fine to the poor man may impose severe hardships.

Bentham's notes on imprisonment also have a contemporary ring: " An ordinary prison is a school in which wickedness is taught by surer means than can ever be employed for the inculcation of virtue. . . . United by a common interest, the prisoners assist each other in throwing off the yoke of shame. . . . Upon the ruins of honour is built a new honour, composed of falsehood, fearlessness under disgrace, forgetfulness of the future, and hostility." [23]

Bentham also devotes considerable attention to a philosophy of crime prevention along the lines that today underlie the theory of

[22] Bentham, *Rationale of Punishment*, pp. 23–26.
[23] Bowring, *Works*, Vol. I (" Principles of Penal Law," Pt. II).

delinquency control. He notes that the problem can be approached both by making it impossible for a person to acquire knowledge necessary to commit an offence or by redirecting the will to commit the offence. The pre-delinquent may then be acted upon both physically and psychologically. One can, for instance, prohibit the sale of instruments used in counterfeiting, and one can also work to change the course of dangerous desires, to channel inclinations towards amusements compatible with public interest, and to arrange it so that a given desire may be satisfied without injury to the society. In a more general fashion Bentham advocates attention to " the culture of honour, the employment of the impulse of religion, and the use to be made of the power of instruction and education." [24]

Bentham, however, misses the mark badly in his understanding of criminal motivation when he proposes reciprocal punishments of the type that fit the crimes' motivations. Fines should be levelled against those motivated by avarice; those who commit offences because of idleness should be assigned compulsory labour. Here, in philosophically compounding a felony, Bentham displays a basic misunderstanding of the roots of crime. We now believe that motivation must be treated rather than attacked. We seek to ascertain why the man was idle. Bentham, a dynamo of activity himself, would answer in terms of his own feelings. It would be a perverse trait—laziness. In this sense, Bentham's criminology becomes highly subjective. [25]

The Panopticon prison

The much-maligned scheme for a utopian prison, Bentham's ill-fated Panopticon plan, represents the philosopher's most tangible contribution to penology. [26] It is a story of eccentricity in action. To Bentham's credit it must be remembered that imprisonment represented a rather novel form of treatment during this period. Capital punishment, fines, pillory, transportation and assignment to prison hulks constituted the usual method of disposing of convicted felons. [27]

[24] Bowring, *Works*, Vol. I ("Principles of Penal Law," Pt. III).
[25] For an excellent discussion of this point, see Leon Radzinowicz, *A History of English Criminal Law and Its Administration from 1750 : Vol. 1, The Movement for Reform, 1750–1833* (London, 1948; New York: Macmillan, 1948), pp. 370–377.
[26] The major points of Bentham's work on the Panopticon can be culled from Bowring, *Works*, Vol. I, pp. 498–503; Vol. IV, pp. 37–248; and Vol. XI, pp. 96–170.
[27] An excellent description of these conditions can be found in Sidney and Beatrice Webb, *English Prisons Under Local Government* (New York: Longmans, Green, 1922).

There were two intriguing facets to the Panopticon plan. One concerns the unusual architectural pattern for the prison, and the other the method of running the institution.

Architecturally, the Panopticon was to be a circular building with a glass roof and containing cells on every storey of the circumference. It was to be so arranged that every cell could be visible from a central point. The omniscient prison inspector would be kept from the sight of the prisoners by a system of blinds " unless . . . he thinks fit to show himself."

The philosophy behind the proposed prison operation was admirable, but the precise method of carrying it out often shows more vivid imagination than practical knowledge. The pivotal figure in the prison was to be the manager who would employ the convicts in contract labour. The manager would derive a proportion of the money earned by the prisoners. Meanwhile, he would be financially liable if felons once under his charge subsequently committed offences. Further, if more than a specified number of prisoners were to die in a given period, the manager would have to pay a certain sum to the government. These fines were to provide incentive for high-minded supervision of the Panopticon population. The manager would care for the prisoners because he would be " forced to do for his own interest anything that he was not inclined to do for them."

The prison was to be placed near the centre of the city so that it would be a visible reminder of the fruits of crime. Within the Panopticon, idleness would be eliminated and the prisoners would be taught profitable trades. There would be a segregation policy by classes of offender, and religious services were to be adjusted to the special needs and tastes of the inmates. Finally, there is some anticipation of today's pre-release units. Bentham bewails the fact that prisoners are transferred directly from the prison into society and he recommends an intermediate stage in this process.

Bentham was convinced that the Panopticon would produce all of the following admirable results: " Morals reformed, health preserved, industry invigorated, instruction diffused, public burdens lightened, economy seated as it were upon a rock, the Gordian knot of the poor laws not cut but untied."

The Panopticon idea was something of a monomania with Bentham; its abortive history occupies a large proportion of his time, correspondence and thoughts. His travail in attempting to have a

Panopticon built by the British Government need not be detailed here. The episode reflects to the high credit of the various committees of Parliament that reviewed the scheme and rejected it so that in England, to use one writer's term, the "monstrosity" was never built.[28] From Bentham's viewpoint, the Panopticon represents a prolonged case study in extraordinary frustration.

There was some little diffusion of the Panopticon idea outside of England. In France, for instance, the National Assembly had Bentham's work printed for study, but the project never went any further.[29] Other efforts were made to have it adopted in Ireland. A committee reported adversely upon it in New York in 1811.[30]

Two Panopticon-type prisons actually were constructed in the United States. The Western State Penitentiary which opened at Pittsburgh in 1826 was modelled to some extent on Bentham's plan. But the prison, "wholly unsuited for anything but a fortress," was ordered rebuilt in 1833.[31]

In addition, from 1926–35, Illinois constructed the Stateville prison, six miles from Joliet, upon the Panopticon plan. After four of the circular cell houses were built and occupied their impracticability was so obvious that it was decided to change to a more conventional plan in completing the institution.[32] The construction drew from a noted prison architect the comment that it was "the most awful receptacle of gloom ever devised and put together with good stone and brick and mortar."[33]

One of the major drawbacks at Stateville has been aptly described by a former inmate of the institution:

I stood in the cell looking out through the bars, which were panelled with glass. In the centre of the house was a tower of tubular steel. On top of it was a round porchlike affair with large oblong openings. Through these openings the guard kept constant watch on the cells surrounding him.

I remembered what Carl had said: "They figured they were smart building them that way. They figured they could watch every inmate in the

[28] Harry Elmer Barnes and Negley K. Teeters, *New Horizons in Criminology*, 2nd ed. (New York: Prentice-Hall, 1951), p. 388.

[29] Elmer Louis Kayser, *The Grand Social Enterprise: A Study of Jeremy Bentham in His Relation to Liberal Nationalism* (New York: Columbia University Press, 1932), p. 89.

[30] Frederick Howard Wines, *Punishment and Reformation* (New York: Crowell, 1910), p. 146.

[31] Harry Elmer Barnes, *The Evolution of Penology in Pennsylvania: A Study in American Social History* (1927; reprinted Montclair, N.J.: Patterson Smith, 1968), pp. 138–141.

[32] *Handbook of American Prisons and Reformatories* (edited by William B. Cox, F. Lowell Bixby and William T. Root), 4th ed. (New York: Osborne Association, 1933), Vol. I, p. 145.

[33] Alfred Hopkins, *Prisons and Prison Building* (New York: Architectural Book Publishing Co., 1930), p. 43.

house with only one screw in the tower. What they didn't figure is that the cons know all the time where the screw is, too." [34]

Conclusion

A summing-up of Bentham's contributions to criminology need not concern itself overlong with detailed criticism. Many of the weak points in his theory have been pointed out in the foregoing paragraphs. On the positive side, a backward look clearly shows Bentham standing as a towering landmark along the road of criminology. Whatever its shortcomings, the positivistic school, in which the name of Cesare Beccaria, in particular, is associated with that of Bentham, focused a penetrating light on illegal behaviour and strenuously attempted to illuminate the avenues leading towards control of such behaviour.

Bentham attacked, and in innumerable ways succeeded in reforming, what Phillipson has described as " the caprice, the barbarity, the inconsistency, the blundering aimlessness, the arbitrary attitude, the indiscriminate excessive punishments, . . . the disastrous jail system, and the other evils, all conspiring to make criminal law and penal administration nothing less than a consummate national folly." [35] The practical results, rather than the theoretical heritage he left behind, stand as major monuments to Bentham. He was not a great philosopher, but he was a great reformer.

Reference might be made to just a small number of the reforms suggested by Bentham which have either partially or wholly been enacted into law since his time: There was the mitigation of the severity of criminal punishment; the abolition of transportation; the adoption of a prison philosophy stressing example and reformation; removal of certain defects in jury systems; substitution of an effectual means of appropriating and realising a debtor's property for the practice of imprisonment; abolition of usury laws; abolition of law taxes and fees in courts of justice; removal of the exclusionary laws in evidence.[36] Bentham's " untiring attacks " on the complacency of lawyers in the face of judicial injustice are credited by Frank with the " elimination of some of the worst features of judicial

[34] Paul Warren, *Next Time Is for Life* (New York: Dell, 1953), p. 139.
[35] Phillipson, *Three Criminal Law Reformers*, p. 191.
[36] The list is adapted from Hilda G. Lundin, " The Influence of Jeremy Bentham on English Democratic Development," in *University of Iowa Studies in the Social Sciences*, Vol. III, No. 3 (1920), p. 82.

practice."[37] "He found the practice of law an Augean stable," another writer notes. "He turned the river into it, . . . sweeping away mound after mound of its rubbish."[38]

Maine's panegyric on Bentham is widely quoted: "I do not know of a single law reform effected since Bentham's time which cannot be traced to his influence,"[39] he wrote. In a sense this is the highest tribute that can be raised to Bentham, for it underscores the practical utility of his achievements rather than the theoretical wisdom of his philosophy.

GILBERT GEIS.

SELECTED BIBLIOGRAPHY

By Bentham

The most thorough bibliography of Bentham's voluminous work appears on pp. 522-546 of Eli Halévy, *The Growth of Philosophic Radicalism*, 1928. Other Bentham manuscripts, however, are constantly being printed, while works previously published are reissued with new introductions and interpretations. The simplest procedure in locating this material is to consult the bound index volumes of Library of Congress cards or the Library of the British Museum.

About Bentham

The leading studies include these:

ATKINSON, CHARLES MILNER. *Jeremy Bentham : His Life and Work.* 1905.
BOWRING, SIR JOHN. *The Works of Jeremy Bentham.* Vols. 1 and 2. 1843.
EVERETT, CHARLES EDWARD. *The Education of Jeremy Bentham.* 1931.
KEETON, GEORGE W. and SCHWARZENBERGER, GEORG (eds.). *Jeremy Bentham and the Law.* 1948.
PHILLIPSON, COLEMAN. *Three Criminal Law Reformers : Beccaria, Bentham, Romilly.* 1923; reprinted Montclair, N.J., 1970.
RADZINOWICZ, LEON. *A History of English Criminal Law.* (London, Vol. I, 1948, pp. 355-393; Vol. III, 1956, pp. 431-441.)

---

[37] Jerome Frank, *Courts on Trial : Myth and Reality in American Justice* (Princeton: Princeton University Press, 1950), p. 91. One of the few humorous remarks in Bentham's works, which are notoriously deficient in humour, is typical of his scorn for the legal profession. "Only the lawyer," he wrote sarcastically, "escapes punishment for his ignorance of the law."

[38] John Stuart Mill, *Mill on Bentham and Coleridge* (London: Chatto & Windus, 1950), p. 75. The essay originally appeared in Mill's *Dissertations and Discussions* (1838), Vol. I, pp. 330-392.

[39] Henry James Sumner Maine, *Lectures on the Early History of Institutions* (New York: Henry Holt, 1875), p. 397.

NOTE ON THE CONTRIBUTOR

Dr. GILBERT GEIS is Professor of Sociology at California State College, Los Angeles. In 1964–65 he was a Fellow in Law and Sociology at Harvard Law School, and in 1969–70 Visiting Professor at the School of Criminal Justice of the State University of New York at Albany. He was an adviser to the President's Committee on Narcotic and Drug Abuse, and consultant to the President's Commission on Law Enforcement and Administration of Justice, the National Commission on Causes and Prevention of Violence, and the Joint Commission on Correctional Manpower. His publications include *Man, Crime, and Society* (with Herbert Bloch: 1st edition 1962, 2d edition 1970), *The Longest Way Home* (with William Bittle, 1964), *Juvenile Gangs* (1966), and, as editor, *White-Collar Criminal* (1968).

4

EDWARD LIVINGSTON
1764-1836

In the literature of criminology, the names of Beccaria, Bentham, Maconochie, Haviland, Lombroso, Tarde, Garofalo, and Ferri are familiar. In contrast, Edward Livingston has been largely ignored or misrepresented. Called by William Tallack America's greatest penologist,[1] and considered to have been the first legal genius of modern times,[2] this son of parents who participated in the American Revolution grew up to write a system of criminal jurisprudence for the State of Louisiana and subsequently served as Secretary of State and Minister to France under Andrew Jackson.

His place in the history of criminology and penology

The exclusion of Livingston from most contemporary criminological literature gains interest when we understand that he is neither an obscure nor an insignificant figure in the history of American criminal jurisprudence. From the beginning he received widespread recognition. In addition to Sir Henry Maine and William Tallack, such contemporaries as Thomas Jefferson and Beaumont and Tocqueville recognized his abilities and praised his production.[3] Throughout the years scholars have maintained an interest in him. Carleton Hunt and Eugene Smith published articles on him at the turn of the century; Charles and Mary Beard made favorable reference to him in the 1920s.[4] Finally the height

---

* Reproduced from *The Journal of Criminal Law, Criminology and Police Science*, Vol. 54, No. 3, September 1963.
1 William Tallack, *Penological and Preventive Principles* (London, 1889), p. 117.
2 This phrase is attributed to Sir Henry Maine: see Charles Havens Hunt, *Life of Edward Livingston* (New York, 1864), p. 278, n. 31.
3 Negley K. Teeters and John D. Shearer, *The Prison at Philadelphia: Cherry Hill* (New York, 1957), p. 25; Gustave de Beaumont and Alexis de Tocqueville, *On the Penitentiary System in the United States and Its Application in France*, trans. Francis Lieber (Philadelphia, 1833), p. xii.
4 Carleton Hunt, "Life and Services of Edward Livingston," *American Lawyer*, Vol. 12 (1904), p. 154, and "Edward Livingston and the Law of Louisiana," *Law Notes*, Vol. 7 (1903), p. 88; Eugene Smith, "Edward Livingston and His Criminal Code," *Journal of Social Science*, Vol. 39 (1901), pp. 27–28, and "Edward Livingston and the Louisiana Codes," *Columbia Law Review*, Vol. 2 (1902), p. 24; Charles Beard and Mary Beard, *The Rise of American Civilization* (New York, 1949), p. 561.

of academic and professional interest was shown in 1936, when an Edward Livingston Centennial was held in New Orleans, October 27–30, 1936, featuring lectures by Dean Roscoe Pound, and a series of articles were published in honor of Livingston in the *Tulane Law Review* and other journals.[5] Yet in spite of this widespread interest and extensive literature, a review of modern works in the field of criminology and penology shows that only two studies make reference to him. In the earlier study he is correctly judged as an opposer of the death penalty, a supporter of solitary confinement without flogging or other forms of brutality, an advocate of productive work for due pay for prison inmates, and a supporter of the separation of those imprisoned before trial from those already found guilty. In the later study, he is simply and mistakenly referred to as a follower of the phrenologist Combe.[6]

Livingston deserves greater recognition and understanding on the part of criminologists. His influence on the origin and early development of the penitentiary system in Louisiana suggests it, and the quality of his ideas, considering his place in history, requires it.

Historically Livingston's life-span most closely coincided with those of Cesare Beccaria and Jeremy Bentham. Beccaria was a much admired intellectual progenitor. Bentham was a contemporary, and Livingston corresponded with him.

As would be expected, Livingston has been compared with these thinkers. Jerome Hall has correctly noted that in Livingston's writings there is a shift from Beccaria's reliance on abstract principles and a marked tendency to use empirical methods. Eugene Smith and later Paul Brosman have acknowledged that while Livingston was indebted to Jeremy Bentham, he reached a broader and higher plane of thought.[7] The importance of these comparisons is not that they show Livingston's intellectual debts but that they bring us, through Livingston, to the heart of an issue of the Enlightenment which is very much alive today; namely, the respective merits of the "rational" and "positive" orientations.

[5] E.g., Paul Brosman, "Edward Livingston and Spousal Testimony in Louisiana," *Tulane Law Review,* Vol. 11 (1937), p. 243; Mitchell Franklin, "Concerning the Historical Importance of Edward Livingston," *ibid.,* p. 212; Rufus C. Harris, "The Edward Livingston Centennial," *ibid.,* Vol. 11 (1936), p. 1; Jerome Hall, "Edward Livingston and His Louisiana Penal Code," *American Bar Association Journal,* Vol. 22 (1936), p. 191.

[6] Teeters and Shearer, *The Prison at Philadelphia,* pp. 24–25; Richard R. Korn and L. W. McCorkle, *Criminology and Penology* (New York, 1959), p. 213.

[7] Hall, "Edward Livingston and His Louisiana Penal Code," p. 195; Smith, "Edward Livingston and His Criminal Code," p. 35; Brosman, "Edward Livingston and Spousal Testimony in Louisiana," p. 256.

It is generally agreed that Beccaria is a member of the "Classical" school of penology. Even Mannheim, who questions the validity of classifying thinkers into schools, places Beccaria—but only Beccaria —in the Classical school. Bentham on the other hand has received contradictory treatment. Clarence Ray Jeffery combines Bentham with Beccaria to construct the Classical school, while Mannheim places Bentham in the Positivist school of Lombroso and Ferri.[8]

It is axiomatic that these writers were in the main tradition of the Enlightenment. Beccaria's indebtedness to the French philosophers, especially Montesquieu and Rousseau, is so great that his book has often been claimed as their spiritual property. Bentham in turn admits a direct debt to Beccaria, for one, in the development of his principle of utility; "Before it was mine," he wrote, "it was M. Beccaria's."[9] As inheritors of the Enlightenment, Beccaria and Bentham expressed, respectively, the two main spirits of that age: the "rational" and the "positive" spirits. And while it is correct to state that each placed greater emphasis on one, it is incorrect to imply—by the separation of these spirits into "schools"—that the mind of the Enlightenment ever considered these two "spirits" in conflict. In fact, as Cassirer points out, a major goal of the Enlightenment was to create a synthesis of the two "spirits." "One should not seek order, law, and 'reason' as a rule that may be grasped and expressed prior to the phenomena, as there *a priori;* one should rather discover such regularity in the phenomena themselves, as the form of their immanent connection."[10] Thus universals remain the proper goal of inquiry, but a significant methodological shift has occurred in that *a priori* universals have changed into universals grounded in human experience.[11]

The writers who compose the movement referred to as "the American Enlightenment"[12] also inherited this synthesis of the "rational" and "positive" spirits and expressed them in their writings. Jefferson—as a single example—believed that every man was born with a moral sense or instinct. This instinct did not provide men with immediate or intuitive knowledge of good or evil, rather it

[8] Hermann Mannheim, *supra,* p. 8; Clarence Ray Jeffery, *infra,* pp. 459–460.
[9] Mannheim, *supra,* p. 5; Elio Monachesi, *supra,* p. 39; David Baumgardt, *Bentham and the Ethics of Today* (Princeton, 1952), p. 37.
[10] Ernst Cassirer, *The Philosophy of the Enlightenment* (Princeton, 1951), pp. 8, 9.
[11] *Ibid.,* chap. 5.
[12] Including, for example, Benjamin Franklin, Thomas Jefferson, Thomas Paine, and Benjamin Rush. See Joseph Leon Blau, *Men and Movements in American Philosophy* (New York, 1952).

allowed men to judge acts correctly in relation to the specific conditions of the environment. "Men," he wrote, "living in different countries under different circumstances, different habits and regimens, may have different utilities; the same act, therefore, may be useful, and consequently virtuous in one country which is injurious and vicious in another differently circumstanced." Obviously the underlying assumption is that man is inherently reasonable and basically good. Defects in human beings, evils and perversions, are capable of being corrected through education and the use of reason. Yet in its specific expressions virtue can vary, can be determined by the conditions of its environment.[13]

Edward Livingston is a direct descendant of the great movements of European and American Enlightenment. Within the confines of his immediate family, he came into contact with those ideas of social contract and the rights of man that played such an important part in developing the American Revolution. His grandfather was an extreme advocate of an American revolution and predicted that it would occur within the grandchildren's lifetime. Edward's brother, Robert Livingston, served with Jefferson, Franklin, Sherman, and Adams as the committee selected by Congress to prepare the Declaration of Independence.[14] Later, in 1782, Robert Livingston along with George Washington and Robert Morris arranged for Thomas Paine to "receive a salary of eight hundred dollars a year, no trivial sum in those days, to write in the cause of liberty."[15]

From the European movement of the Enlightenment, Edward Livingston acknowledged, in addition to Beccaria and Bentham, intellectual debts to Francis Bacon and the encyclopaedists Voltaire, Condorcet, and Diderot.[16] He undoubtedly was familiar with Edmund Burke, Thomas Hobbes, Grotius, Rousseau, and others, but the quality and extent of their influence is difficult to determine, mainly because Livingston's ideas are expressed in a single work, which was commissioned.[17] Furthermore, at its completion the

---

[13] *Ibid.*, pp. 48–49.
[14] Hunt, *Life of Edward Livingston*, pp. 20–21.
[15] Blau, *Men and Movements*, p. 55.
[16] Edward Livingston, *The Complete Works of Edward Livingston on Criminal Jurisprudence* (1873; reprinted Montclair, N.J., 1968), Vol. I, pp. 31, 116, 155, 207.
[17] Acts of the General Assembly of Louisiana, February 10, 1820, and March 21, 1822, authorized a code of criminal law for Louisiana. See Livingston, *Complete Works*, Vol. I, pp. 1–4. There was strong opposition to Livingston's proposals, and his codes were never enacted. Subsequently, Livingston's work was published in two volumes, the first composed of introductory remarks to the codes, and the second containing Livingston's proposed codes themselves. It is to these volumes that this article has reference.

original draft of this work, along with most of his notes, was destroyed in a fire, and Livingston was required to rewrite his entire work, mainly from memory and a few remaining notes.[18]

His theory of man and society

Within the limitations of this single work Livingston articulates a theory of man and society which, in spite of obvious identities with prevailing Enlightenment theories, shows a degree of sophistication and awareness not expressed in criminological literature until Durkheim and Tarde, in the 1880s, published attacks on the Lombrosian theory.[19] Livingston, first, rejects all prevailing theories of "social contract." He does not accept the Hobbesian state of nature composed of selfish men continually warring with one another.[20] Similarly he rejects the peaceful state of nature theory as expressed by Grotius (1583–1645), Locke (1632–1704), and subsequently drawn in idyllic terms by Rousseau (1712–1778). Livingston considers the argument meaningless. Man, he argues, has always lived in a state of society. Societies are found wherever men are found and must have come into existence as soon as the number of the species was sufficiently multiplied to produce them.[21] Thus society is a natural and inevitable product of human existence. And, logically, the main function of society is the preservation of the life of its members.[22] This is in no way an original statement. The similar doctrine of inalienable rights was a major theme of the French philosophers of the Enlightenment. And as Cassirer points out, John Locke's theory of social contract held that:

All such contractual ties are rather preceded by original ties which can neither be created by a contract nor entirely annulled by it. There are natural rights of man which existed before all foundations of social and political organization; and in view of these the real function and purpose of the state consists in admitting such rights into its order and in preserving and guar-

18 William Bass Hatcher, *Edward Livingston: Jeffersonian Republican and Jacksonian Democrat* (Baton Rouge, 1940), p. 263.

19 Margaret S. Wilson Vine, *infra*, p. 292; Walter A. Lunden, *infra*, p. 385.

20 On this point, Livingston takes an important step away from Beccaria. Beccaria's entire system is predicated on the Hobbesian theory of social contract. To Beccaria crime is a result of man's inherent nature, which is self-seeking and which therefore leads him into conflict with society. Punishment functions to control this self-seeking nature and thereby to preserve society. See Monachesi, *supra*, pp. 36–50.

21 Livingston, *Complete Works*, Vol. I, pp. 192–193. While Livingston, because of other interests, failed to make the next logical step from this premise, he has nevertheless brought us to the threshold: namely, that societies will vary according to the size of their populations.

22 *Ibid.*, p. 533.

anteeing them thereby. Locke counts the right of personal freedom and the
right of property among these fundamental rights.[23]

But in Livingston we find a more extreme position, for Livingston, completely unhindered by the contract theory, is free virtually
to drop the theme of preservation and right of property and focus
on the preservation and rights of man. This position is unquestionably consistent with the more "radical" American Enlightenment.
As Thomas Jefferson wrote, "The freedom and happiness of man
are the sole objects of all legitimate governments. And God forbid
that we should ever be twenty years without a revolution." [24] In
Livingston the theme of human rights and the preservation of life
becomes a thread that unites such uncommon items as his opposition to the death penalty and his insistence that society is responsible for its beggars, paupers, vagrants, and criminals.

If Livingston sees man as potentially reasonable and inherently
good and virtuous, how then does he explain the not infrequent
acts of evil? That some men differ from the majority so significantly as to comprise a different class of being—the view of Lombroso, to whom criminals were of atavistic or degenerative origin
—is completely excluded by Livingston's acceptance of Hobbes'
theory of human equality.[25] To Livingston, criminals—no matter
how depraved and degraded—are still men, men capable (in our
modern terms) of rehabilitation to the point of successful function
in society. Livingston writes that the "error . . . lies in considering them as beings of a nature so inferior as to be incapable of
elevation, and so bad as to make any amelioration impossible." [26]

His criticism of existing legal systems and his analysis of criminal behavior

Rejecting the theory that defective humans are the source of
criminality, Livingston turns his attention to the existing legal system. Again in the spirit of Voltaire and Diderot, he blames much
criminal conduct upon inhuman laws, and upon the jurist who

[23] Cassirer, *Philosophy of the Enlightenment*, p. 250.
[24] Blau, *Men and Movements*, p. 49.
[25] Hobbes wrote: "Nature hath made men so equal in the faculties of the body and mind;
as that though there be found one man sometimes manifestly stronger in body, or of
quicker mind than another; yet when all is reckoned together, the difference between
man, and man, is not so considerable, as that one man can thereupon claim to himself
any benefit, to which another may not pretend." Thomas Hobbes, *Leviathan* (London,
1946), p. 80.
[26] Livingston, *Complete Works*, Vol. I, p. 563.

would make use of such laws for his own ends.[27] To Livingston laws generally have been oppressive and have supported "class" interests. He writes: "Everywhere, with but few exceptions, the interest of the many has, from the earliest ages, been sacrificed to the power of the few. Everywhere penal laws have been framed to support this power."[28] Livingston is especially bitter about the role law has played under the English common-law system. The English had "seen their fellow subjects hanged for constructive felonies; quartered for constructive treasons; and roasted alive for constructive heresies."[29]

From this criticism of legal systems Livingston moves to an analysis of criminal behavior as behavior learned by the individual during maturation from a defective family environment and through association. Here Livingston steps right out of nineteenth-century criminological thinking directly into a main tenet of twentieth-century criminological theory; namely, that crime is normal learned behavior. Beccaria, tied to his Hobbesian social contract theory, couldn't approach it. Bentham, it is said, flirted continuously with the idea, but never really came to grips with it. However, Lombroso, it is argued, expressed the germ of the normal learned behavior theory in defining his third category of "occasional criminals," which he called "habitual criminals"; these criminals, he maintained, were the product of defective education and training, which evoked primitive tendencies.[30] They were, he observed, drawn into crime mainly through associations.

Livingston quite clearly states the main ideas of the "crime as normal learned behavior" theory, arguing that deviant behavior among children is produced by defective rearing in which the child is improperly taught. He writes:

> The moral sense is, in childhood, produced by instruction only, and the force of example, and . . . with the children who are generally the objects of criminal procedure, instruction has either been totally wanting, or both that and example have been of a nature to pervert, not form, a sense of right. . . .

---

27 *Ibid.*, pp. 115–118.
28 *Ibid.*, p. 54. This statement and others lead Mitchell Franklin to view Livingston as anticipating Marx. He states: "Edward Livingston's ideological conceptions are definitely historical conceptions reflecting the bourgeois social bases that then existed. Livingston, however, represented the material conditions of several advanced liberal countries, in such a way that he was enabled to create an ideology different from any that actually prevailed; and perhaps he almost reached the threshold of socialism." Franklin, "Concerning the Historical Importance of Edward Livingston," p. 172.
29 Livingston, *Complete Works*, Vol. I, p. 13.
30 George B. Vold, *Theoretical Criminology* (New York, 1958); Gilbert Geis, *supra*, p. 57; Marvin E. Wolfgang, *infra*, p. 253.

Either they have parents who entirely neglect the task, or abuse the power given to them by nature, and confirmed by the laws of society.

These children, devoid of true family relations,

are thrown friendless and unprotected into the most contaminating associations, where morality, religion and temperance are spoken of only to be derided, and the restraints of law are studied only to be evaded.[31]

Thus a defective environment during the formative period combined with subsequent associations whose standards of behavior differ grossly from those of society are the natural conditions that breed criminal behavior.

In considering the conditions underlying adult criminal behavior, Livingston develops the important social dimension of the "dispossessed"; these are the unemployed, the paupers, the mendicants, the idle in general. Mitchell Franklin claims that "from the relatively advanced methods of production in England and America he [Livingston] found the free working class and other dispossessed groups, and thus discovered unemployment."[32]

The motives for criminal behavior for this class need not have originated in the defective environment of the formation period, but arise out of the wants and needs created by a defective adult social environment. Livingston unequivocally states that such conditions as idleness, unemployment, pauperism, etc., create needs which send the greatest numbers to our prisons.[33]

Of even greater interest than his analysis of causation is Livingston's refusal to leave his analysis at that level. He recognized that explanations of motives of criminal behavior do not tell how the methods of criminal behavior are acquired, and he knew that such methods are normally learned through association with the criminally sophisticated. Hatcher states that in Livingston's view, "the criminal ranks drew their recruits from those who were unable to

---

[31] Livingston, *Complete Works*, Vol. I, pp. 572–573. Here Livingston's emphasis on association clearly antedates the focus that led to Sutherland's formulation of the "differential association" theory. Livingston's views that human character is formed in early childhood mainly by the conditions of the environment were antedated by the writings of Robert Owen. Owen's experience as an owner-manager of a Scottish textile mill allowed him to become intimately acquainted with the effects of a brutalizing factory environment on children. In 1813 he published *A New View of Society*, in which he argued that the antisocial child behaves as he does due to physical hardships and emotional disturbances. Owen's position was that these delinquents had to be helped, not punished; society owes that obligation to itself as well as the individual. See Jacob Bronowski and Bruce Mazlish, *The Western Intellectual Tradition* (New York, 1960), pp. 450–471.

[32] Franklin, "Concerning the Historical Importance of Edward Livingston," p. 173.

[33] Livingston, *Complete Works*, Vol. I, p. 528.

secure employment or who were able to work but refused to do so."[34] The following is an example of Livingston's observations in this regard:

> The bridewell of a large city is the place in which those representatives of human nature, in its most degraded shape, are assembled; brought into close contact, so that no art of fraud, no means of depredation, no shift to avoid detection, known to one, may be hid from the other; where those who have escaped received the applause due to their dexterity, and he who has suffered, glories in the constancy with which he has endured his punishment, and resisted the attempts to reform him. Here, he who can "commit the oldest crime the newest sort of way," is hailed as a genius of superior order, and having no interest to secure the exclusive use of the discovery, he freely imparts it to his less instructed companions.[35]

His interest in empirical research

An immediate impression gained from Livingston's observation on the bridewell is of its empirical quality. This "positivist spirit" runs as a recognizable theme throughout his study. Jerome Hall notes that in collecting notes and preparing his study Livingston sent out circular letters or questionnaires, developed statistical tables, and constructed "partial mortality tables showing the number of persons committed for trial, tried, convicted, discharged or acquitted." He also "proposed to engage in field work by devoting a few months of the summer to a personal examination of the different institutions of the kind (penal) in the Atlantic states."[36] Furthermore, he made use of case-history materials, of which the following are examples:

> D.B.L.—Aged fifteen years, born in New York, committed from the police, on suspicion of having stolen a shawl. He was brought up in the vicinity of Bancker Street, and for some months played the tambourine in those receptacles of vice and misery, the dancing-houses of Corlears Hook. . . .
>
> L.S.—Aged about sixteen years, born in Ireland; his parents emigrated to this country about eight years ago. His father has since died. His education was entirely neglected by his parents, and the choice of his companions left exclusively to himself. He has worked at several mechanical branches of business, to none of which his restless disposition could attach itself. He was committed to the Refuge in March, 1825, from the police office, for stealing a copper kettle.[37]

[34] Hatcher, *Edward Livingston*, p. 277. See also Livingston, *Complete Works*, Vol. I, pp. 528–540.
[35] Livingston, *Complete Works*, Vol. I, p. 538.
[36] Hall, "Edward Livingston and His Louisiana Penal Code," p. 195.
[37] Livingston, *Complete Works*, Vol. I, p. 578.

Livingston's analysis of crime and criminal behavior was unsystematic and incompletely expressed; but it was subservient to his more ambitious goal of providing a "plan of jurisprudence, combining the prevention of crime with the reformation of the criminal . . . on such a scale as would embrace all the different stages and departments of criminal procedure." [38] In achieving these ends Livingston proposed a wide range of reforms.

His ideas on penal reform

To correct injustices originating from vague, outmoded, and inhumane laws administered by self-seeking judges, Livingston turns to and asserts great confidence in the general public, when this public is properly informed and educated. To Livingston, "publicity is an object of such importance in free government, that it not only ought to be permitted, but must be secured by a species of compulsion. The people must be forced to know what their servants are doing, or they will, like other masters, submit to imposition, rather than take the trouble of inquiring into the state of their affairs." Equally, for education, Livingston held that "religious, moral, and scientific instruction must be not only provided but enforced, in order to stamp on the minds of the people that character, that public feeling, and those manners, without which laws are but vain restraints." [39]

He, therefore, made such specific suggestions as that laws be written in a language comprehensible to the public, and in his own case, he submitted his code to men not familiar with legal terminology, and had them to mark each word not completely understood. "The words so marked were, in the body of the work, always printed in a peculiar character, to show that they were the subject of explanation in a separate place, the Book of Definitions; and each word thus marked received all necessary attention in that book." [40]

He was a strong advocate of the jury system, suggested legislation that would make trial by jury mandatory, and recommended that judges be restricted to the law, and the statement of evidence only when requested by the jury.[41] Livingston supported his stand

[38] *Ibid.,* p. 525.
[39] *Ibid.,* pp. 15, 587.
[40] Hunt, *Life of Edward Livingston,* p. 264.
[41] Hall, "Edward Livingston and His Louisiana Penal Code," p. 196.

with the statement that "by our constitution the right of a trial by jury is secured to the accused, but it is not exclusively established. This, however, may be done by law, and there are many strong reasons in its favour, that it has been thought proper to insert in the code, a precise declaration, that in all criminal prosecutions, the trial by jury is a privilege which cannot be renounced." [42]

For those individuals who either violated laws, or for whom a high probability for criminal behavior existed (paupers, mendicants, etc.), Livingston proposed a complex machinery that contained a house of detention, a penitentiary, a house of refuge and industry, and a school of reform all under the centralized supervision of five inspectors.[43] The school of reform was a juvenile training school for all youths under the age of eighteen and over the age of six who were sentenced to any term less than life imprisonment. All youthful vagrants, beggars, etc., within these age limits would also be placed in the school of reform for instruction and training.

Livingston conceived that the major function of the school of reform was to teach youths essential skills so that they could successfully seek and meet the conditions of employment following their release. To achieve these ends he proposed that fully qualified teachers be placed in charge of the apprenticeship program. He also introduced a type of indeterminate sentence, in that youths would be discharged after they had successfully completed their apprenticeship even though they had not yet served out their full sentence.[44] But he felt that a minimum of two years was required for a successful apprenticeship and, therefore, specified that no apprentice could be discharged before that time. Judgment of whether a youth had achieved a successful apprenticeship was made by the warden and required final approval by the five-man board of inspectors.[45]

For those with a high probability of turning to criminal acts (ex-convicts newly released, vagrants, beggars, unemployed), Livingston devised the house of refuge and industry, for he believed that society owed to the discharged convict and the dispossessed in general the opportunity to utilize skills necessary for their support.

[42] Livingston, *Complete Works*, Vol. I, pp. 15–16.
[43] Hatcher, *Edward Livingston*, p. 278.
[44] Alexander Maconochie (1787–1860), who was superintendent of the British penal colony, Norfolk Island, from 1840 to 1844, is considered the originator of the movement that led to the indeterminate sentence. Maconochie, who published his articles on penal reform after his recall from Norfolk Island in 1844, expressed many ideas that are almost identical with Livingston's. See John Vincent Barry, *infra*, pp. 84–106.
[45] Livingston, *Complete Works*, Vol. II, pp. 577–584.

In the house of refuge and industry, Livingston writes, "the discharged convict may find employment and substance, and receive such wages as will enable him to remove from the scenes of his past crimes, place him above temptation, confirm him in his newly-acquired habits of industry, and cause him safely to pass the dangerous and trying period between the acquisition of his liberty and restoration to the confidence of society." [46] Likewise, the unemployed, vagrants, beggars and other dispossessed, would be placed in houses of industry and refuge where they would be given employment. Obviously, Livingston strongly felt that society had a basic obligation to its members, and providing them with the basic necessities of life was one of the foremost.

Livingston conceived the house of detention as holding all those with short sentences who did not require penal incarceration, those arrested and awaiting trial, and even those needed as witnesses who might not freely present themselves. In order to avoid "vicious associations" Livingston proposed that these houses be divided into separate departments for those held for investigation, those charged with crimes, and those serving sentences. He considered a further subdivision between those awaiting trial for misdemeanor crimes and those awaiting felony trial. [47]

The penitentiary itself was the subject of Livingston's most intense interest and study. As previously stated, he approached his task in a highly empirical manner, making studies and securing statistics and information from other states and from Europe. He was particularly interested in the penitentiary systems of Massachusetts, New York, and Pennsylvania. [48] He concluded from his study of the Pennsylvania "experiment" that "while the numbers were not too great to admit of seclusion, offenses diminished; and when it was no longer practicable, they increased." [49] This and other considerations led him to hold that seclusion with labor would successfully diminish offenses. But Livingston adds qualifications to his system which prevent his being classified as a simple proponent of solitary confinement.

In viewing the penitentiary as a system of reformation as well as punishment, Livingston proposed that education and employment

[46] *Ibid.*, pp. 564–566. See also Hatcher, *Edward Livingston*, p. 281.
[47] *Ibid.*, pp. 541–543.
[48] Hall, "Edward Livingston and His Louisiana Penal Code," p. 195; Hatcher, *Edward Livingston*, pp. 279–280.
[49] Livingston, *Complete Works*, Vol. I, p. 513.

training be made available to inmates so that they could develop skills which would allow them, through the aid of the houses of refuge and industry, to make a successful readjustment to society. But he did not propose to make education and training available to all inmates; those with life sentences would be denied these privileges, and those who showed no interest in "reforming" would not only be denied these privileges but would also be required to exist under the extreme deprivations of solitary confinement.[50]

For those who manifested a desire to reform, Livingston planned such bonuses as a better diet, partial relief from solitude, and the right to visitors at stated intervals. When the prisoner manifested his interest in reforming by good conduct and participation in limited programs, for a period of time usually covering six months or longer, he could then commence employment training. Then, after a relatively long period of probation, he might be permitted to work outside the penitentiary. On discharge he would receive a portion of the proceeds of his labors and a certificate of good conduct, industry, and skill in the trade learned or practiced while in prison. All privileges would be suspended for misbehavior.[51]

Livingston opposed the death penalty, but for those convicted of the normally capital offenses he did not offer privileges; nor did he conceive that they should ever return to society. Instead, he felt their punishment should provide an example to the public. Hunt wrote that Livingston recommended "imprisonment for life in a solitary cell, to be painted black without and within, and bearing a conspicuous outer inscription, in distinct white letters, setting forth the culprit's name and his offence, with its circumstances." This inscription would be:

His food is bread of the coarsest kind; his drink is water, mingled with his tears: he is dead to the world; this cell is his grave; his existence is prolonged that he may remember his crime, and repent it, and that the continuance of his punishment may deter others from the indulgence of hatred, avarice, sensuality, and the passions which lead to the crime he has committed. When the Almighty, in His due time, shall exercise towards him that dispensation which he himself arrogantly and wickedly usurped towards another, his body is to be dissected, and his soul will abide that judgement which Divine Justice shall decree.[52]

[50] It is of interest to note that Erving Goffman analyzes "total institutions" as privilege-deprivational systems. See the two articles by Goffman in Donald R. Cressey (ed.), The Prison: Studies in Institutional Organization and Change (New York, 1961), pp. 15–67, 68–106.
[51] Livingston, Complete Works, Vol. I, pp. 526–528.
[52] Hunt, Life of Edward Livingston, p. 266; Livingston, Complete Works, Vol. II, p. 573.

Recognizing this function of punishment, Livingston antedates Durkheim's position that a wrongdoer is punished so that the act will be judged as abhorrent in the minds of all men, thus maintaining the moral ideals of the society.[53]

Livingston's comprehensive code was never made law, and he subsequently left Louisiana to reenter national politics. Still his influence on the Louisiana penitentiary system can be seen. Louisiana did build an urban-industrial penitentiary which incorporated the ideas prevalent in existing northern systems, and to supervise the system it appointed a five-man Board of Control, whose statements on penal philosophy frequently echoed the ideas of Livingston. The subsequent development of Louisiana's penal system grossly violated Livingston's philosophy, but this constitutes the subject of another study.

Joseph Mouledoux.

BIBLIOGRAPHY

By Livingston

The Complete Works of Edward Livingston on Criminal Jurisprudence (2 volumes). 1873; reprinted Montclair, N.J., 1968.

About Livingston

Brosman, Paul. "Edward Livingston and Spousal Testimony in Louisiana." *Tulane Law Review*, Vol. 11 (1937).

Franklin, Mitchell. "Concerning the Historical Importance of Edward Livingston." *Tulane Law Review*, Vol. 11 (1937).

Hall, Jerome. "Edward Livingston and His Louisiana Penal Code." *American Bar Association Journal*, Vol. 22 (1936).

Harris, Rufus C. "The Edward Livingston Centennial." *Tulane Law Review*, Vol. 11 (1936).

Hatcher, William Bass. *Edward Livingston: Jeffersonian Republican and Jacksonian Democrat*. Baton Rouge, 1940.

Hunt, Carleton. "Life and Services of Edward Livingston." *American Lawyer*, Vol. 12 (1904).

—— "Edward Livingston and the Law of Louisiana." *Law Notes*, Vol. 7 (1903).

Hunt, Charles Havens. *Life of Edward Livingston*. New York, 1864.

Smith, Eugene. "Edward Livingston and His Criminal Code." *Journal of Social Science*, Vol. 39 (1901).

—— "Edward Livingston and the Louisiana Codes." *Columbia Law Review*, Vol. 2 (1902).

[53] Lunden, *infra*, pp. 390–391.

NOTE ON THE CONTRIBUTOR

Joseph Mouledoux is Associate Professor of Sociology at Sir George Williams University, Montreal. Until 1961 he was Assistant Director of Classification in charge of the Admission and Orientation Unit of the Louisiana State Penitentiary. His publications include: "Organizational Goals and Structural Change: A Study of the Organization of a Prison Social System," *Social Forces,* 1963, and "Political Crime and the Negro Revolution" in Clinard and Quinney's *Criminal Behavior Systems,* 1967.

5

ALEXANDER MACONOCHIE

1787–1860

The injustice to Maconochie

It is a commonplace that mankind remembers admiringly its oppressors rather than its benefactors, but the promptness with which pioneers in humanitarian movements are forgotten or undervalued by their successors in the field in which they have laboured is sometimes rather startling. The fate of Captain Alexander Maconochie, R.N., K.H.,[1] supplies an instance. Although he was a pioneer in the field of penal reform, indefatigable in his labours in that cause and foremost among the formulators of the principles on which modern penal administration in British and American communities rests, he was not, until 1958, the subject of a biography, nor until recently has there been any readily accessible account of his theories or his work. It is usual to find acknowledgment in sound modern works on criminology[2] of the importance of his conceptions and his practices, but copies of his pamphlets, and of publications about the time of his death which describe his greatness of character and tenacity of purpose, are not easy to come by.[3] Yet

* Reproduced from *The Journal of Criminal Law, Criminology and Police Science*, Vol. 47, No. 2, July–August 1956.

[1] K.H. is the abbreviation for Knight of the Royal Hanoverian Guelphic Order, an honour which did not carry the designation " Sir." Maconochie was awarded the distinction in 1836. It has not been awarded since the death of William IV in 1837.

[2] See Albert Morris, *Criminology* (1938), p. 370; Barnes and Teeters, *New Horizons in Criminology* (1951), pp. 519–520; M. Grünhut, *Penal Reform* (1948), pp. 76–80; L. Fox, *English Prison and Borstal Systems* (1952), pp. 41–42, 46, 149; Norval Morris, *The Habitual Criminal* (1951), p. 21; E. H. Sutherland, *Principles of Criminology* (4th ed., 1947), pp. 418, 450–451, 514; Walter Reckless, *The Crime Problem* (1955), p. 473; Sheldon and Eleanor Glueck, *500 Criminal Careers* (1930), p. 14 *et seq.*; Edward Lindsey, *Historical Sketch of Indeterminate Sentence* (1952–56), 16 *American Criminal Law and Criminology Journal*, p. 9, whose information about Maconochie is taken from Wines, *Punishment and Reformation*, Chap. X; UN publication, *The Indeterminate Sentence*, p. 12; W. Y. Tsao, *Rational Approach to Crime and Punishment* (Taipei, 1955), pp. 87–88.

[3] M. D. Hill, *Our Exemplars* (1861), which contains an autobiographical fragment finished by another hand, possibly Florence Davenport Hill; Obituary, *Friend of the People* (November 17, 1860); Rosamond and Florence Davenport Hill, *Memoir of Matthew Davenport Hill* (1878), p. 184ff.; *Meliora* No. 13 (1861); Mary Carpenter, *Our Convicts* (1864, reprinted 1969), Vol. 1, p. 95ff.; Bishop Ullathorne, *On the Management of Criminals* (1866); W. L. Clay, *The Prison Chaplain* (1861, reprinted 1969), p. 246ff.

it is beyond question that the principles which he formulated in 1837, when he was living in Hobart in Van Diemen's Land, as Tasmania was then called, and which he applied at Norfolk Island between 1840 and 1844, were the foundation of Sir Walter Crofton's Irish Prison System. Crofton's methods influenced the thinking of Enoch Wines and Theodore Dwight, of the New York Prison Association, very greatly. Zebulon Brockway recognised in his later years that there were forerunners in the field he had made his own, but he seems to have been unaware that the origin and development of his ideas owed a good deal to others. It is plain, though, that he must have known of the investigations of Warden Hubbell, and of Wines and Dwight into the Irish system, which led to the recommendation for its adoption made by Wines and Dwight to the New York legislature in 1867.[4] Thus Maconochie's principles had their influence upon the founding of Elmira and upon the Cincinnati Declaration of 1870 and they now flourish vigorously in the Borstal system in England and in the California Institution for Men at Chino and the Federal Institution at Seagoville, Texas, and in all penal institutions which apply the concepts of modern penology.

Essentially, Maconochie's principles rested upon insights which are obvious now, but which in 1837 were revolutionary in their impact upon the English Convict System. The labours of John Howard had shown the urgent need for penal reform, and had pointed eloquently to the direction it must take. William Eden, later Lord Auckland, had stressed the social unacceptability of vindictive justice, and had proclaimed that " public utility is the measure of human punishment." [5] Wagnitz had argued that whilst the security of the state may be the principal object of criminal law, that very security would also be promoted by reforming the criminal.[6] Paley and Whately had adumbrated the central idea of task instead of time sentences which Maconochie believed he had discovered for himself. But it was Maconochie who investigated the debasing brutalities of the convict transportation system and presented a coherent and revolutionary plan of penal reform, which embodied not only a philosophical justification for reform, but also the practical measures by which it could be achieved. The insights which came to him in Van Diemen's Land were that cruel and

---

[4] See Z. R. Brockway, *Fifty Years of Prison Service* (1912, reprinted 1969), pp. 126–135; F. H. Wines, *Punishment and Reformation,* pp. 196n., 199n.
[5] *Principles of Penal Law* (1771).
[6] Quoted, M. Grünhut, *Penal Reform* (1948, reprinted 1972), p. 39.

brutal punishments debase not only the victim, but also the society which employs them; and that from the standpoint of mere utility, to say nothing of religious and ethical considerations, the object of secondary punishment (as imprisonment was called by the controversialists in those days, death being the primary punishment) should be to reform the offender so that he should leave prison capable of useful citizenship, and a better man than when he entered the prison gates. These are the fundamentals of modern penal philosophy, and they still are the touchstone by which the social worth of a penal system is to be determined. His great merit is that once these ideas took hold of him, he gave the rest of his life, his fortune, and his very considerable talents to gaining their acceptance, and to devising the penal machinery that would carry them into effect.

But the injustice to Maconochie goes further than a denial, until recently, of an adequate presentation of his philosophy and his labours. The historiographers [7] who have written of him have not only failed to understand the worth of the man and his immense importance in reducing the sum of avoidable human misery; in disregard of the irrefutable evidence, they have presented him as a crank and a failure. Calumnies and derisive legends are the price exacted from all sincere reformers by conservative contemporaries, but it is, or should be, the business of the historian to dispel them and to put the record straight.

Maconochie's early life

Alexander Maconochie [8] was born on February 11, 1787, at Edinburgh, of good Scots family. His father was by profession a writer, as attorneys were called in Scotland, and was cashier and agent for the first Duke of Douglas. He acted as one of the lawyers for the successful claimant in the lengthy litigation (it lasted eight years) known to history as the Douglas Cause, and later succeeded Adam Smith, the economist, as a Commissioner of the Board of Customs for Scotland. He died when Alexander was eight or nine years old, and the upbringing of the boy was undertaken by his

---

[7] *Cf.* John West, *History of Tasmania* (1852), Vol. 2, pp. 263–304; H. D. Traill, *Life of Sir John Franklin* (1896), Chaps. XIII, XIV, XV; K. Fitzpatrick, *Sir John Franklin in Tasmania, 1837–1843* (1949), *passim*; Frank Clune, *Martin Cash, The Last of the Tasmanian Bushrangers* (1955), pp. 279–280. This list could be lengthened by other references.

[8] The spelling of his surname varied; when in the Navy, it was spelt M'Konochie, but in 1832, when secretary of the Royal Geographical Society, he adopted the present spelling and used it thereafter.

kinsman, Allan Maconochie, Lord Meadowbank, who was one of the most brilliantly universal intellects of his time.

Alexander was destined for the law, but he wanted to join the Navy, and in 1803, being then aged sixteen, he became a first-class volunteer, and in March 1804 a midshipman. He was connected by family ties with a distinguished sailor, the Hon. Alexander Inglis Cochrane, a younger son of the eighth Earl of Dundonald, and he saw a great deal of active service, in the course of which he was twice wounded. Studious by nature, he was especially interested in languages and was proficient in Latin, Greek, French and Spanish. In 1810 he was captured by the French when the vessel on which he was serving as a Lieutenant was wrecked in a violent storm, and he remained a prisoner of war until Napoleon's abdication. It is probable that this experience, which he had in common with two other contemporary penal reformers, Obermaier of Bavaria and Montesinos of Spain, made him the readier to see the evils of the convict system when he first directed his mind to penal questions in Van Diemen's Land in 1837.

When he was repatriated in 1814, he rejoined the British Navy and commanded vessels in the Anglo-American War, seeing service at the taking of Washington and the battle of New Orleans. He was twice mentioned in dispatches. In 1815 he was paid off, being then a commander in the Royal Navy and entitled by courtesy to the title of Captain. He was on naval reserve from then until he was retired, in 1855, with the rank of Captain. There can be no question that in his naval career he achieved success and distinction.

He went to live on a farm near his native Edinburgh and occupied himself by pursuing studies in what he called " Ethical or Political Geography," a field of inquiry that is now covered by geopolitics and ecology. Two publications resulted from these studies. Both were concerned with the Pacific, which then figured little in British calculations, and both showed considerable power of thought and remarkable prescience.

On April 10, 1822, when aged thirty-four, he married Mary Hutton Browne, who was twenty-seven. There were seven children of the union, three daughters and four sons. One of the daughters died at birth.

About the year 1829 he moved with his family to London, where he renewed old friendships with distinguished naval men, amongst whom were Sir John Barrow, Sir John Franklin and

Admiral Beaufort. With these gentlemen and others he was instrumental in forming the London Geographical Society which, because
of the interest and patronage of William IV, immediately became
known as the Royal Geographical Society. Maconochie was its first
secretary, and he held that position until he resigned in 1836 to go
to Van Diemen's Land. In accepting his resignation, the Council
of the Society recorded their appreciation of Maconochie's " sound
judgment, even temper and untiring zeal."

In 1833 Maconochie was appointed the first Professor of
Geography in University College, London, a position he held until
he left for Van Diemen's Land.

The island prison—Tasmania

Sir John Franklin, a gallant naval officer and famous Arctic
explorer, was appointed in 1836 to succeed Sir George Arthur as
Lieutenant-Governor of Van Diemen's Land, as the beautiful island
of Tasmania, pendant to the Australian continent, was known
officially until the middle of the nineteenth century. In the view of
the English authorities, Van Diemen's Land was an island prison,
and it was administered accordingly. Franklin asked Maconochie,
then in his forty-ninth year, to accompany him as his private secretary. It is clear that in accepting this position Maconochie did so on
the understanding that he would be given an appointment in the
Australian Colonies more suited to his standing and acknowledged
abilities. He had turned his mind to the question of colonial self-
government, and had written a paper before he left England which
showed a liberal understanding of the problem, but he had not
taken any interest in the controversy concerning the disposition of
Great Britain's criminals. When the American War of Independence ended, Britain had to find another place to which to
transport her felons, and the penal settlement of New South Wales
was brought into being by the landing at Sydney of Captain Arthur
Phillip and his soldiers, and the felons, male and female, of the
First Fleet, on January 26, 1788. Norfolk Island was settled for the
same purpose in March of the same year, and Van Diemen's Land
in 1803. By the 1830s the critics of transportation as a secondary
punishment had the backing of informed English opinion, and it is
strange that Maconochie should have stood outside the controversy,
but the evidence is convincing that he did so until he arrived in

Tasmania in 1837. This circumstance is important, for it has been the habit of his historiographer critics to present him, falsely, as a man who arrived in Tasmania with his mind fully made up that the convict system as it existed was bad, and that it should be supplanted by a fantastic system of his own devising.

Before he left London he was asked by the Society for the Improvement of Prison Discipline to obtain answers to a questionnaire concerning the penal system in Van Diemen's Land. He informed the governmental authorities of this request, and with their concurrence set about obtaining the desired information. His investigations soon convinced him of the iniquities of the system, and the report he submitted to Governor Franklin led to the compilation of a series of official rejoinders which furnish a vivid picture of the penal administration and the complacent attitude of officials who controlled it. Two very powerful officials in Hobart, the main settlement of Van Diemen's Land, were John Montagu, the Colonial Secretary, and Matthew Forster, the Chief Police Magistrate. They set about creating a breach between the new Lieutenant-Governor and his private secretary. Franklin was a gallant officer, but he was hopelessly unequipped to detect the duplicity of the officials on whom he relied for the running of the administration. His wife was a woman of remarkable ability and unusual character, and there is more than a little reason to think that she exercised considerable influence over her husband in his official decisions. The story is too long and involved to be told here, but soon it was obvious that only an excuse was needed for Franklin to dismiss Maconochie. This was found when the arrival of English newspapers revealed that a report by Maconochie which Franklin had sent on, unread, with a dispatch concerning the convict system, had been given to the Molesworth Committee which was then investigating transportation, and had been released for publication. Maconochie's criticisms of the local settlers, and his outright condemnation of the system it was Franklin's duty to enforce, were thus made public, and his dismissal was probably unavoidable, but coming as it did from an old comrade in arms, it was a bitter blow, and it meant the end of his hopes of obtaining a position of any importance in the colonial administration.

Maconochie and his family continued to reside in Hobart, and in 1838 he published *Thoughts on Convict Management*, followed in 1839 by *Supplement to Thoughts on Convict Management* and in the same year by *General Views regarding the Social System of Convict Management*. Although he was to publish many pamphlets subsequently, the essential features of his proposals are to be found in these first publications.

His "apparatus" for prison administration and prison discipline

Maconochie shared with two remarkable Quakers, James Backhouse and George Washington Walker, who were in Van Diemen's Land in 1837, the fundamental conceptions on which he based his proposals, and his discussions with them had much to do with the formation of his ideas.

He sought to define his attitude in anticipation of the opposition he realised his proposals would excite. " I am no sentimentalist," he wrote in his report in 1837. " I most fully subscribe to the right claimed by society to make examples of those who break its laws, that others may feel constrained to respect and obey them. But the individuals thus sacrificed to what is, at best, but a high political expediency (for vengeance belongs to another) have their claims on us also, claims only the more sacred because they are helpless in our hands, and thus helpless, we condemn them from our own advantage. We have no right to cast them away altogether. Even their physical suffering should be in moderation, and the moral pain which we must and ought to inflict with it should be carefully framed so as, if possible, to reform, and not necessarily to pervert them. The iron should enter both soul and body, but not so as utterly to sear and harden them. Another world should be thought of, even by the sternest temporal legislator; and it is frightful to think of the responsibility otherwise attached to him."

In his essay, *Crime and Punishment* (1846), he set out his fundamental proposition. " It is by no means intended . . . to advocate lenity to criminals. This, when injudiciously extended, injures rather than benefits them, and greater, or at least more certain, rather than less, severity would be desirable for them. But it should be made parental, not vindictive, and severity seeking to raise even while it chastens. There is no lesson more important in social science, nor more wanting at present in penal science, nor to which the perfection of both will be found more directly to tend, than that the common interest is the interest of each and all, not of any section merely; that when beyond all question individuals are sacrificed, the public also indirectly suffer." " What is wanted, then, in our conflict with crime is to give due importance to the object of reforming our criminals and to study every means by which we can make severity subservient to that end." " We must make our whole arrangements in arrest of crime prospective, rather than retrospective—preventive rather than merely remedial."

Later in the same work he wrote: " The proper object of prison discipline is to prepare men for discharge; the first object of prison discipline should be to reform prisoners, and then prepare them to separate with advantage both to themselves and to society after their discharge." In a set of regulations he prepared in 1840 he commenced with the statement: " The object of the New System of Prison Discipline is besides inflicting a suitable punishment on men for their past offences, to train them to return to society, honest, useful and trustworthy members of it, and care must be taken in all its arrangement that this object be strictly kept in view, and that no other be preferred to it."

This being the object, the problem was to find means to achieve it. The " apparatus," as he called it, which Maconochie devised for this purpose involved five ideas, each of them novel in prison administration at that time. They were:

(i) sentences should not be for imprisonment for a period of time, but for the performance of a determined and specified quantity of labour; in brief, time sentences should be abolished, and task sentences substituted;

(ii) the quantity of labour a prisoner must perform should be expressed in a number of marks which he must earn, by improvement in conduct, frugality of living, and habits of industry, before he can be released;

(iii) whilst in prison a prisoner should earn everything he receives; all else should be added to his debt of marks;

(iv) when qualified by discipline to do so he should work in association with a small number of other prisoners, forming a group of six or seven, and the whole group should be answerable for the conduct and labour of each member of it;

(v) in the final stage, a prisoner, whilst still obliged to earn his daily tally of marks, should be given a proprietary interest in his own labour and be subject to a less rigorous discipline in order to prepare him for release into society.

In 1839 the British Government offered Maconochie, who was still residing in Hobart, the position of Superintendent of Norfolk Island. The plan was that newly transported convicts should go direct to Norfolk Island and that Maconochie should try out his system on this material. Norfolk Island was quite unsuitable for the experiment, and Maconochie said so, but, there being no alternative, he accepted the appointment.

It was intended by the British authorities that only the newly transported prisoners, about 700 in number, should be on the island, but there were already there over 900 doubly and trebly convicted prisoners who were regarded as the dregs of the convict system, irreconcilable and irreclaimable.[9] They were men transported from England who, after completing their term of punishment in Australia, had been convicted again, and they had been sent to Norfolk Island because it was a place of terror, *un enfer sur terre*, as it was called by one of the Canadian political prisoners of 1838, whose unhappy fate it was to be transported to New South Wales. It was the presence of these outcasts, however, that gave his work on Norfolk Island especial significance in the science of penology.

The application of these principles at Norfolk Island

Bishop Ullathorne,[10] who had extensive experience of the convict system, observed: " The brief writings of Captain Maconochie abound in the best maxims for men who have to deal with prisoners, and an admirable little manual might be drawn up from them." This is as true now as it was when it was uttered in 1866. Maconochie's memoranda, written after his appointment, but before he took up his duties, and his reports during the four years he was in charge of Norfolk Island, contain ideas and suggestions, as well as full descriptions of his methods, which should be of considerable interest to penal administrators at this day. At a time when the official view of penal discipline was that it should terrify by its

---

[9] It is difficult to ascertain precisely the number of convicts under Maconochie at Norfolk Island. He said he had " 2,000 men cooped up in a nutshell. Two-thirds were the refuse of both penal colonies," *i.e.*, doubly convicted felons from New South Wales and Tasmania. In March 1843 he had 593 newly transported convicts and 876 doubly convicted men, but a number had been discharged between his arrival in 1840 and Governor Sir George Gipps' visit in 1843, when these figures were ascertained by Gipps.

[10] Ullathorne, William Bernard (1806–89), Benedictine, Vicar-General of New South Wales, 1832–40; R.C. Bishop of Birmingham and later titular Archbishop of Cabasa; author of many works, including *The Horrors of Transportation Briefly Unfolded*; supported the abolition of transportation.

harshness, he conceived the notion that music and literature and improved education were useful adjuncts in a prison, and what is more remarkable, he put his ideas into effect.

Just how his system was applied in Norfolk Island is well described in a work published in the year after his death.[11]

" The mark system rests on four chief principles. Instead of a time-sentence it inflicts a labour-sentence, thus setting the convicts to earn back their freedom by the sweat of their brows; it teaches self-denial, by enabling them to purchase a speedier termination to their slavery by the social qualities, and makes the prisoners themselves coadjutors in the preservation of discipline, by giving them an interest in each other's good behaviour; and lastly, it prepares them for restoration to society, by gradually relaxing the restraints on their conduct and training their powers of self-governance. To carry out his principles, Captain Maconochie treated the convict as a labourer, with marks for wages, and required him to earn a certain number as the condition of his discharge. These marks had an alternative value; they could either purchase extra food, or the deduction of so many days from the sentence. He fixed on ten marks as a fair day's wages, the men being paid by piecework, and not by time; and for every ten marks he saved, the convict shortened his term by a day. At the stores he purchased daily his necessary supplies, paying for them in marks. The rations were served out at three rates; the coarsest and cheapest cost three, the next four, the best five marks per diem. The abstemious felon might thus save seven marks, and even the self-indulgent five, each day, for the purchase of his liberty; and as extra marks were allowed for over-work and hard work, it was possible to hoard at the rate of eight or ten a day. The marks, too, furnished the means of disciplinary punishment, a proportionate fine being the penalty for every act of misconduct. And while, by this machinery of marks, Captain Maconochie trained his convicts to self-denial and industry, he secured his other objects by different means. He divided the convicts' sentences into three periods. During the first—the penal stage—the men worked under sharp, stringent discipline. At the conclusion of this, they were allowed to form themselves into companies of six each (being left to themselves to choose their own companions), and they then entered the social stage; in this, the six

---

[11] Rev. W. L. Clay, *The Prison Chaplain*, pp. 247–248.

had a common fund of marks, into which the daily earnings of each were paid, and from which the food and fines of each were deducted. They were thus made responsible for each other's conduct, and moreover, by this means, Captain Maconochie, who well knew the intense selfishness of criminals, hoped to implant kindly and social feelings. In the last, the 'individualised' stage, the parties were broken up, and though every man was still kept to penal labour to earn his tale of marks, he was in other respects free. He had his own hut and garden, and, if he wished, he might have a piggery and poultry yard; for the Captain, by giving the probationer property and rights of his own, hoped to teach him respect for those of other people."

Norfolk Island is the largest of a group of islands about 900 miles east-north-east of Sydney. It is not quite five miles long, with a median breadth of two and one-half miles, and is in area about 9,000 acres. It is a natural paradise, but for almost seventy years, except during Maconochie's régime, and a period of disuse from 1813 to 1826, it was defiled by the most appalling brutalities.

These were perpetrated under the guise of penal discipline. The gallows stood permanently ready as a visible reminder to unhappy wretches of the fate that might soon be theirs; for years at a time men worked and ate and slept in irons; the lash or the cat-o'-nine-tails were in habitual use, and the gag, solitary confinement and the pepper mill were constantly employed as punishments calculated to subjugate creatures made sub-human by deliberate policy. Any manifestation of resentment was classed as insolence, as was the contradiction by a prisoner of the evidence of an official. Subservience, the despot's substitute for respect, was insisted upon, and even the private soldier was entitled to require the outward marks of servility from the convicts. When Dr. Ullathorne, a Catholic priest, went to the island in 1834, to bring the consolations of religion to men sentenced to death for their part in a rising against the authorities, the men who were reprieved wept with sorrow that they had to go on living, and those doomed to die fell on their knees and thanked God for the release that was to be theirs.[12]

When Maconochie arrived there on March 6, 1840, the prison buildings were inadequate and overcrowded. Sir George Gipps was the Governor of New South Wales, and Maconochie was subject to

---

[12] *Autobiography of Archbishop Ullathorne* (1891), p. 100.

his control. Gipps considered that the newly arrived convicts should be kept separate from the " old hands," as the doubly convicted prisoners were called, and when Maconochie, because of the practical impossibility of doing anything else, allowed them to mingle, so that all were subject to the same system, he was sternly rebuked. This rebuke was given wide publicity in the colonies, and did much to injure his authority and to expose him to ridicule. Furthermore, the stories of his methods, which contrasted fantastically with the brutalities with which the colonists were familiar, were widely circulated to make him an object of derision. New South Wales had determined to be no longer a dumping place for overseas criminals, and transportation to that colony ended in 1840, though it continued to Tasmania until 1853, and to Western Australia until 1868. " Bushrangers," as criminals turned highwaymen were known, had terrified the free settlers, and local opposition to the release to the mainland of convicts from Norfolk Island was so strong that it is doubtful if Gipps could, as a matter of practical politics, have honoured Maconochie's proposal that " old hands " who had earned their tally of marks should be released.

Be that as it may, Maconochie was never given the free hand or the full authority which he understood would be his when he accepted the appointment, and his four years were marked by disappointment and frustration arising from official indifference and hostility.

Nevertheless, under his rule, the dreaded penal settlement lost its brutalising characteristics, and took on an appearance not dissimilar from a modern open institution. He dismantled the gallows and removed the protective bars from his own house. He weeded out the abandoned characters—the undeterrables and those incapable of reformation—and allowed working gangs of sawyers, woodcutters and similar parties to camp out at the site of their labours. He abolished the obligation to cringe before officials, bidding prisoners, in his own phrase, " to stand up like men, whomsoever they addressed." He held his court in public, frequently acquitting, and he refused to accept anonymous denunciations as a basis for conviction and punishment. He checked petty tyrannies by inferior officers. He built two churches for the men and read the lesson at divine service himself. He established schools and encouraged reading sessions and distributed prizes. The lash and irons were little used. He walked unarmed among the convicts with his family. He permitted prisoners to use knives and forks—previously they ate their food with their fingers—and to have their own cooking utensils. He allowed first-class prisoners to wear garments other than convict clothing, and he established a band with instruments and music which cost the authorities £103 15s., a not inconsiderable sum in those days. Plots were allotted to parties of men upon the mutual association principle, and each party was permitted to keep portion of the produce that it raised, either for the men's own use, or for sale at fixed prices to the commissariat. Far in advance of his time, he allowed the men to grow and use tobacco, not, as he said, " to encourage its consumption, but to legalise an indulgence which it is impossible to prevent." In honour of the young Queen's birthday, on May 25, 1840, he allowed his charges a holiday and they were permitted without restraint to attend various amusements—a dinner at which they were given a small quantity of rum and lemonade to drink the Queen's health, sports at which they engaged in their national games, and theatrical performances in which the characters were played by the convicts. The day was unmarred by any abuse of liberty, but when an account of it reached Sydney, and later London, authority, long accustomed to connect the notion of crime and punishment with guilt and misery, was so violently shocked that the decision to recall him waited only on the choice of a successor.

It has been the custom to present Maconochie's period on Norfolk Island as one in which mutiny and murder prevailed because of the fatuities of a visionary idealist. This presentation has no foundation in fact; order was maintained throughout his period of command, and when Governor Gipps visited the island unexpectedly in March 1843, he found " good order everywhere to prevail, and the demeanour of prisoners to be respectful and quiet," and the stories he had heard of increased crime on the island " exaggerated and over-coloured." [13] It is true that some convicts tried to seize the brig, the *Governor Phillip*, in June 1842, and a soldier was drowned whilst swimming ashore. Five convicts were killed in the unsuccessful attempt and four of the survivors were later tried in Sydney and executed for their part in this affair, but there was no official suggestion that Maconochie was to blame, and no ground for thinking so.

[13] Dispatch, April 1, 1843, Gipps to Lord Stanley, *Historical Records of Australia*, 1st series, Vol. 22, p. 623.

Maconochie himself claimed that he " maintained perfect order and tranquillity "; that he found the island " a turbulent, brutal hell, and left it a peaceful well-ordered community," and all the evidence shows his claim to be completely true.

But the constant calumnies, and the hostility of officialdom to ideas that were in direct contradiction of assumptions it accepted as unquestionable, finally led to his recall in February 1844. He was replaced by Major Childs, an incompetent who sought to carry out instructions to restore the previous evil methods in place of Maconochie's reforms. This led, on July 1, 1846, to a revolt by some of the convicts, and four of the penal staff were murdered. After a mockery of a trial, twelve prisoners were hanged in two batches on the one day in the presence of the other convicts, drawn up to observe the spectacle, and under a new Commandant, John Price, Norfolk Island became again a place of terror and brutality as dreadful as in its worst days. It was finally abandoned as a penal colony in 1856.

Today it is an aphorism of penology that men are sent to prison, not to be punished, but as a punishment. Maconochie anticipated this approach. In a pamphlet, *On Reformatory Discipline*, published in 1851, he wrote: " It may be said that I . . . overlooked, or even sacrificed the great object—that of punishment—for which the prisoners were sent on the island but, as I still conceive, not so. I carried into effect the full letter and spirit of the law, and merely did not indulge in excesses beyond it. Every man's sentence was to imprisonment and hard labour; the island was his prison; and each was required to do his full daily government task before bestowing his time on either his garden or education. What I really did spare was the unnecessary humiliation which it is the fashion to impose on prisoners besides, and which I believe does more moral injury than all other incidents of ordinary prison life put together. It crushes the weak, unnecessarily irritates the strong, indisposes all to submission and reform, and is, in truth, neither intended by ' the law ' nor consistent with the professions made by law-givers when framing it."

The testimony of the Bishop Ullathorne and of Bishop Willson, and of other witnesses, is specific that Maconochie succeeded beyond all reasonable expectations during his command of Norfolk Island. During that period, and at the time of his departure, about 1,450 prisoners were discharged, and the percentage of reconvictions was

less than 3 per cent. Of 920 "old hands," supposedly irreclaim-
ables, only twenty were known to be reconvicted. It was a proud
boast, as well as evidence of sound reformation, for a former convict
to be able to say he was "one of Captain Maconochie's men."

Governor of Birmingham Borough Prison

Maconochie returned to England in 1844 determined to campaign for penal reform. He became associated in that cause with a
very remarkable man, Matthew Davenport Hill, q.c., who was the
Recorder of Birmingham and a highly successful and able barrister.
Hill devoted himself to humanitarian labours throughout his life;
he was the founder of probation in England. Maconochie wrote a
number of pamphlets, among them a valuable essay called *Crime
and Punishment*, and was indefatigable in his efforts for reform.

In 1849, largely through the efforts of M. D. Hill, he was
appointed Governor of the new Birmingham Borough Prison. He
was never allowed a proper legal basis to enable him to put his
system into effect, however, and in October 1851 he was dismissed
from his position by the visiting justices, in whom control of the
prison was vested, because of their opposition to what was said to
be the leniency of his methods, although other unsupportable
reasons were given for their action. He was succeeded by the
Deputy Governor, an ex-naval officer named Austin. Austin's
discipline was based on cruelty and terror, and after three young
inmates had taken their own lives, public indignation forced the
appointment of a Royal Commission to inquire into the management of the prison. The shocking disclosures at that inquiry are
told in Charles Reade's novel, *It's Never Too Late to Mend*. Austin
resigned, but the findings of the Commission led to his being
charged with assault on one of the prisoners who had committed
suicide, and he was sentenced to three months' imprisonment.

Maconochie's good faith and humanitarian purposes were conceded by the Commissioners, but they found that although he was
guiltless of the cruelties which occurred under Austin's governorship, he had used methods not sanctioned by law for the purpose of
disciplining some intractable inmates. Maconochie claimed in his
pamphlets that his system had been successful, and his figures go
far to substantiate this, and M. D. Hill and prominent citizens of
Birmingham made him a public presentation as a mark of their

confidence. But the criticism of the Commissioners seems just, that Maconochie " was led in the pursuit of his objects [of promoting the reformation of the prisoners and the well-being of society] to sanction the infliction of punishments which were not warranted by the law, and the employment of which was the more to be regretted, inasmuch as such a course is apt to lead to the use, in the hands of persons not restrained by the same benevolent feelings, of practices equally illegal and more objectionable, from their greater frequency and their general severity."

Maconochie's health failed him after his dismissal, and he was never employed again in penal work. But he continued in his labours for reform by his pamphlets, by giving evidence before committees of inquiry and by participating in the work of voluntary bodies with similar aims. These activities were extensive, for we tend now to forget how vigorous was the movement for penal reform, both in England and the U.S.A., during the nineteenth century, as we do also the quality and disinterestedness of the persons associated with it.

Maconochie's final years were clouded by sorrow. His eldest daughter died in 1855, and in the previous year his youngest son sustained fatal wounds in the charge of the Heavy Brigade at Balaclava. Illness reduced him to a shadow of his former self, and on October 25, 1860, he died at Morden, Surrey, being then aged seventy-three.

Prison reform since Maconochie

As has been mentioned, one of Maconochie's disciples was Walter Crofton, who became Chairman of the Board of Directors of the Irish Prisons. Crofton and his colleagues, avowedly under the inspiration of Maconochie's ideas, attracted world attention for the excellence of their system. It rested on the following principles:

(1) Reward—by making all advantages, including ultimate release, dependent on industry and good conduct, as shown by a record kept from day to day.

(2) Individual influence—exercised by the governor, schoolmaster and chaplain, in prisons in which the inmates were not allowed to exceed a number which could be personally known to the governor and his assistants. These numbers were about 300 in ordinary prisons, and 100 in intermediate prisons.

(3) Gradual approximation to freedom—in every successive stage of discipline the prisoner was less and less under restraint until in the last stage—the intermediate prison—he was half at liberty.

(4) Strict supervision after discharge—and certain revocation of ticket of leave on any appearance of a relapse.

So long as this system was under the control of devoted men its success was remarkable, and it influenced penal administration for good throughout the world.

But the Irish experiment apart, it is doubtful whether until recently the reformatory system has been given a fair trial. Legislatures have rarely been generous with funds, public opinion has been usually indifferent and often hostile, and what is of greater importance, men truly dedicated to the difficult and discouraging task of reforming unpromising human material are not in generous supply. Every correctional institution is in the final analysis a reflection of its warden or superintendent, for the tone of an institution and the attitude of its staff will depend in large measure upon the extent of his dedication to his work. Maconochie perceived this truth: " a good system in a bad gaol," he observed, " is as much better than a bad system in a good gaol, as a good commanding officer is better for the discipline of a regiment than a good barrack."

The range of Maconochie's proposals is remarkable. He advocated prison farms; schools, and especially industrial schools, for children; segregation of different classes of offenders and a proper system of classification; and the limitation of the use of the bastille-type prison with its masonry, bolts, locks and bars to essential custodial purposes, and the use of " less and less secure but more and more cheerful quarters." The science of finger-printing had not been discovered in his day, but he was conscious of the need to identify recidivists, and proposed that each convicted person should receive " a small private brand (as between the toes or elsewhere) which shall be invisible, but yet identify cases of second conviction in any part of the world." Prison work, he thought, required something of the missionary spirit, and he urged that prison staff should be properly trained, employed on a civil service basis, and imbued with the realisation that it was their vocation to reform their charges. Giving evidence before the Committee of 1856, he said that whilst society could not then do without the protection of capital punishment, he considered that it would not be able long to retain it, and he suggested instead a sentence of civil death. After very adequate experience, for he had on occasions resorted to the lash, he thought that " it was only rarely that corporal punishment operated beneficially," and that the power of inflicting it hardened and corrupted those to whom it was entrusted. Solitary confinement was not a proper disciplinary measure, for " it is vain to talk of ignorant, inert and corrupt minds profiting by their own unassisted reflections." Stripes and all methods of degradation tending to destroy self-respect should be avoided: " there is no greater mistake in the whole compass of existing penal discipline (fertile as it is in such) than the studied imposition of degradation as a portion of punishment."

Maconochie recognised that the complete separation of the sexes inevitably involved undesirable consequences. He proposed that prisoners should be permitted to have their wives and families live with them on Norfolk Island, being debited in return for this indulgence with a large number of marks (2,000) which they would have to earn before they would be entitled to release. The Governor, Sir George Gipps, observed drily that " Women have never yet been sent to Norfolk Island, and the universal impression is that it would be highly dangerous to have them there (not less on account of the male convicts, than of the troops who guard them)."

The humane and resourceful qualities of his mind are well illustrated by the case of Charles Anderson, the man who had been chained to a rock in Sydney Harbour. Anderson as a youth had a good record of naval service, during which he received a severe head wound at the battle of Navarino. In the course of a street riot in a Devonshire seaport, some shops were broken into, and Anderson, then aged eighteen, was convicted of participation and sentenced to seven years' transportation. He was sent to Goat Island in Sydney Harbour, and because of ill-treatment he absconded. Recaptured, he received 100 lashes and, on being returned to Goat Island, another 100, and was ordered to wear irons for twelve months. During that twelve months he received in all 1,200 lashes for the most trivial offences, such as looking up from his work. He escaped again, and this time was sentenced to 200 lashes, to which 100 more lashes were later added by a sentence which directed as well that he be chained to a rock for two years. He was put in irons, and attached to the rock by a chain twenty-one feet long. A hollow in the rock served him for a bed, and at night a wooden lid, perforated with holes for air, was put over him and locked into position. His food was pushed into his eating vessel on a pole. Other prisoners were forbidden to speak or approach him under penalty of 100 lashes. His wounds became maggot-infested, but he was refused water with which to bathe them. He remained in this state for several weeks, when the Governor, Sir Richard Bourke, heard of his treatment, and had him released and sent to the lime works at Macquarie Harbour, one of the most dreaded places of punishment, where work involved carrying lime in baskets, on backs already lacerated by the " cat," through the sea for the purpose of loading it into vessels. He escaped again, but was recaptured, given 200 lashes, and returned to his gang. Goaded beyond endurance by the overseer, he killed him, and on conviction was sentenced to death. This sentence was commuted to imprisonment in chains for life, to be served at Norfolk Island.

Maconochie found him there when he became Superintendent, and despite his record for violence, which now included an additional ten convictions for violent assaults since his arrival on the island, the new Superintendent sought to restore him to his senses. Anderson was then twenty-four years of age, although the years of brutality made him appear a middle-aged, broken man. Maconochie put him in charge of some unruly bullocks and ordered that no one should interfere with him. This bold form of occupational therapy was successful, and Anderson and the bullocks grew tractable together. Maconochie next erected a signal station on the highest point in the island, and put Anderson in charge of it. Anderson lived there, taking great pride in his garden and meticulously discharging his duties as lookout and signalman. When Sir George Gipps, on his visit to the island in 1843, saw Anderson " tripping along in his trim sailor dress full of importance, with his telescope under his arm," he asked: " What smart little fellow may that be? " and to his astonishment was told: " That is the man who was chained to the rock in Sydney Harbour." Ultimately, Anderson lost his reason completely, and died in a lunatic asylum in Sydney, but his devotion to Maconochie persisted to the end.

" The Indeterminate Sentence "

In the UN monograph, *The Indeterminate Sentence*, Maconochie is said to have been the originator of the whole movement leading to the indeterminate sentence. This statement is unquestionably correct, but I am disposed to think that he would have been startled by some modern developments. He was a firm believer in the rights of the individual, and it is highly unlikely that he would have found himself in sympathy with the arbitrary powers entrusted to tribunals such as Adult and Youth Authorities and Parole Boards. It was of the essence of Maconochie's system that a prisoner should learn self-discipline, for he saw, rightly, that crime is usually the product of a surrender to self-regarding impulses in disregard of the social obligations that should have restrained the offender. The prima facie proof that he had learned self-mastery was the discharge of his debt to society by hard work and frugal living, undertaken for the purpose of regaining his liberty. But under his system it was fundamental that, within the limits of his status, a prisoner should be in control of his own destiny, and that his freedom should be attainable when he had satisfied a debt, expressed intelligibly to him in marks, by efforts which carried a fixed reward. Similarly, the system fixed in marks the penalties for indiscipline which were added to the original debt and had to be cancelled by his own efforts. One of his aims was to eliminate caprice or unfairness on the part of the authorities in the valuation of a prisoner's labour and behaviour and in the imposition of penalties; he had seen too many instances of the abuse of power in Van Diemen's Land. When he gave evidence before the English Select Committee in 1856, he said: " I do not object to (sentences for) minima of time. I think, on the contrary, that minima of time prevent abuse, and prevent a man getting off too easily, . . . but I would never adopt maxima of time. I am quite certain that maxima of time are excessively injurious." He then expounded his proposals in their final shape; he would no longer treat marks as wages as he had previously advocated; he would, instead, treat them as certificates of daily conduct, awarded in such fashion that caprice should not influence them. He contemplated that marks should be affixed daily by various gaol officials, acting separately, for various aspects of a prisoner's conduct and labour. In this way he considered that the dangers of abuse of discretion would be lessened.

Whether or not this proposal was practicable is immaterial; its significance is that it shows clearly his desire to confine official discretion within narrow limits in assessing a prisoner's progress towards release. The greatest merit any system can have is to be nearly independent, for its operation, of the vagaries of the human beings who exercise power under it. Maconochie's emphasis was always upon the desirability of a prisoner's knowing where he stood, and what he had to do to gain his liberty. I do not think he would have cared for a system where the time of release depends, not upon a prisoner's own efforts, but on a tribunal's estimate of the significance of those efforts, and of various other considerations which may not be known or disclosed to him. Maconochie would probably have found himself in agreement with the view Sir Lionel Fox has expressed [14]:

" If the date of his release is entirely vague, and dependent on the decision of some Board or Committee which will be taken on grounds that are never likely to commend themselves to a disappointed prisoner even if he understand them, he will be in a state of constant unrest, always ' sweating on the next Board ' instead of concentrating on the job in hand, and thrown into a fury of resentment whenever A is lucky and B is not, whether B be himself or one of his friends. This does not make for ' a happy prison.' Nor is it certain that either the prison staff or a Board— with or without the advice of psychiatrists—on the basis of past records and of behaviour in prison conditions, could make enough good guesses about the behaviour of prisoners after release to justify a system of selective discharge in the face of these disadvantages."

Conclusion

It is impossible within the scope of this article to present an adequate picture of Maconochie, the penal scientist, the reformer and the very gallant gentleman, but the judgment of some of his able contemporaries, who knew the man and the nobleness of his character, may be offered by way of conclusion.

At the presentation at Birmingham in 1851, after his dismissal from the governorship of the prison, Matthew Davenport Hill addressed him thus: " We feel that by your writings, and by the experiments which you have instituted, the science of prison discipline has been much advanced. . . . Years must probably elapse, and many trials must yet be made before a perfect system can be devised; but we feel that no future explorer will act wisely, who

[14] Fox, *English Prison and Borstal Systems*, p. 306.

does not make himself acquainted with the charts you have laid down before he sails on his voyage of discovery."

" I believe," said Bishop Ullathorne in 1866, " that the name of its [the Mark System's] inventor, Captain Maconochie, is destined to a future celebrity side by side with John Howard. . . . There stands the leading principle, destined after no long time to enter into all other systems of reformatory punishment."

And of the man himself, let the anonymous writer [15] of his obituary speak:

" At the time when it was our privilege to become acquainted with Captain Maconochie—now several years ago—his hair was already snowy white, and his general appearance betokened premature old age, the consequence, doubtless, of hard service in tropical climates during his early years, and of the bitter disappointments of his later life, under which probably he must have succumbed, but for his singularly buoyant and sanguine disposition. In his demeanour were combined the frank cordiality of a sailor with the refinement and courtesy of high breeding and the nobler attributes of a sincere Christian. It was his genuineness of character, his entire forgetfulness of self, his gentleness of manner—the overflow of a loving heart which, combined with great mental powers and earnest piety, gave Captain Maconochie that marvellous ascendancy over the most abandoned of men which the narratives of his residence at Norfolk Island reveal. This wondrous influence is rarely granted, but when we recognise it in a Demetz, a Montesinos, a Howard, an Elizabeth Fry, a Sarah Martin, or a Maconochie, let us reverence it as one of the most precious gifts of the Almighty, and fitly honour those of His servants whom He has been pleased thus to endow."

The centenary of Maconochie's death falls in 1960, and the occasion should not be allowed to pass unnoticed. It is far from easy to obtain the pamphlets in which he set out his philosophy and his proposals, and some of his most interesting contributions to penal science, the reports he made when Superintendent of Norfolk Island, are buried in the volumes of the English Parliamentary Papers, a series which is not readily available outside the great libraries, to American and Continental scholars and students. A memorial of a kind that would have pleased Alexander Maconochie would be a volume reprinting the more important of his pamphlets,

---

[15] In the journal, *Friend of the People*, November 17, 1860. Probably Florence Davenport Hill.

and some of his reports from Norfolk Island. Such a volume would serve a dual purpose; it would commemorate a pioneer of great significance in the development of penology, and it would make available to criminologists, for use in the solving of still intractable problems, the authentic record, not only of his worth as a penal administrator, but also of the humane wisdom that inspired and directed his labours.

JOHN VINCENT BARRY.

BIBLIOGRAPHY

BARRY, JOHN VINCENT. *Alexander Maconochie of Norfolk Island. A Study of a Pioneer in Penal Reform.* (Oxford University Press, Melbourne and London, 1958.)

This full-length biography of Maconochie gives an account of Maconochie's life, of his administration on Norfolk Island, of his governorship of Birmingham Prison, and of his theories and practices. It has a bibliography which contains a full list of Maconochie's writings and also a list of publications containing biographical and other information concerning him, with thirteen plates and a map of the major Australian penal settlements and of Norfolk Island. Among the plates are reproductions of a portrait in oils and a bust of Maconochie.

NOTE ON THE CONTRIBUTOR

The Hon. Mr. Justice JOHN VINCENT BARRY was a judge of the Supreme Court of Victoria, Chairman of the Department of Criminology of the University of Melbourne, Victoria, Australia, and Chairman of the Parole Board of Victoria. In 1955, as recipient of a grant from the Carnegie Corporation of New York, he spent six months in the U.S.A. and Canada, and three months in Great Britain and Europe, during which he investigated developments in criminology and penology, and attended two International Congresses. He is the author of *Alexander Maconochie of Norfolk Island* (1958). He died in 1969.

6

JOHN HAVILAND
1792–1852

In a cherry orchard on the northern outskirts of Philadelphia construction was begun in 1821 on John Haviland's Eastern State Penitentiary. It was to be the first large-scale experiment ever attempted with the newly emerging Pennsylvania System of solitary confinement day and night with work in the cells. Even before it was half completed, the Eastern Penitentiary became a *cause célèbre* among reformers and the object of world-wide interest and investigation. For the remainder of the nineteenth century this prison, along with others designed by the same architect, became the model for almost all the newly developing centralised prison systems in Europe and South America, and later in Asia. Much has been written about the Pennsylvania System, which had a brief and stormy career in America but has enjoyed more prestige on the Continent. However, almost nothing is known about the architect of this system, a man who must be ranked as the most important architect of any period in prison building. The object of this article is to bring together some of the previously unavailable information on Haviland's personal life, the historical antecedents of his influential plans, their progressive development out of his early associations with the Philadelphia reformers, and his effect upon penology, particularly during the nineteenth century.

Haviland was born on December 15, 1792, in Somerset, in the south-west of England. After showing some aptitude for mathematics and art, he was sent by his family to London to study under the well-known architect, James Elmes. Although neither Haviland nor Elmes apparently ever was responsible for prisons in England, Elmes published a small pamphlet on prison planning in 1817 in which he revealed a careful reading of John Howard's

* This chapter represents an expanded version of the original article published in *The Journal of Criminal Law, Criminology and Police Science*, Vol. 45, No. 5, January–February 1955.

works and a general interest in prison reform, which he may have passed on to his pupil. Following the pattern of many talented young men of that period, Haviland left England in 1815 to visit St. Petersburg and the court of Alexander I. He had originally intended to enter the Imperial Engineers and had made the trip at the invitation of the Minister of Marine, Count Morduinoff,[1] who was also an uncle by marriage. It is not clear just what made Haviland decide not to remain in Russia. However, while at the court he met Sir George von Sonntag, a former Philadelphian, who was currently both an admiral and a general in the Czar's military establishment, and it may have been he who urged the young architect to embark for the United States. At any rate, Haviland arrived in Philadelphia in 1816, armed with letters of introduction to President Monroe and others, written by von Sonntag and John Quincy Adams, then United States Minister to Russia.

Haviland immediately opened a school of architectural drawing and began to get commissions for churches, public buildings and private residences. In 1821 the legislature of Pennsylvania authorised a new penitentiary to be built in Philadelphia, and Haviland's plans won the competition. However, there was considerable dissension among the Building Commissioners for the new prison, and it was not until 1823 that he was appointed official architect and his entire plan approved. He continued to supervise construction of the prison which went on intermittently until 1836.

The Eastern Penitentiary, which came to be known as Cherry Hill, became famous and controversial even as it was being erected, and lifted Haviland from relative obscurity to international renown. During the 1830s he became a veritable commuting architect-contractor. Busy with the large-scale construction at Cherry Hill as well as with many important public and private buildings in the Philadelphia area and a new naval asylum at what is now Portsmouth, Virginia, Haviland soon found himself travelling to Pittsburgh, Trenton and New York City as well. Almost from the beginning, the unusual circle of cells which composed the Western Penitentiary at Pittsburgh, erected by Haviland's rival, William

---

[1] Morduinoff was an intimate of John Howard and was at his bedside when he died of jail fever in the Crimea. Undoubtedly, Haviland heard much of the great reformer during his Russian visit and in his personal papers can be found copied eulogies of Howard and a description of his funeral (*Haviland Papers*, MSS. in the University of Pennsylvania Library).

Strickland, had proved unworkable,[2] and in the early 1830s Haviland was engaged to tear down the interior of this prison and reconstruct it along the lines of his Eastern Penitentiary. He was at the same time superintending the construction of a court building and detention centre in New York City, which later came to be known as the " Tombs " because of its heavy Egyptian style—the name persisting even in subsequent structures. On his trips to New York Haviland would stop at Trenton where he was building a new state prison. During the same decade Haviland designed state penitentiaries in Rhode Island and Missouri and a county jail and court house in Newark, New Jersey. He also submitted plans for the District of Columbia prison and state prisons for Arkansas and Louisiana, but these designs were never used.

By 1839 Haviland had no important projects to occupy him, and among his papers we find letters to officials in England, France and Mexico offering his services for various prison-building projects. His dissatisfaction with his adopted homeland seen in these letters was undoubtedly short-lived. By the following year he again found himself busy building prisons. Certain counties in Pennsylvania had been authorised by law to construct their own penitentiaries, and following the lead of Philadelphia County, one after another of the more populous and wealthy counties decided to replace unsafe jails with new county penitentiaries. In 1840 the prison at Harrisburg was begun under Haviland, in 1846 the one at Reading, and his last prison was begun in 1849 at Lancaster and completed just before his death.

Not much is known concerning Haviland's family life. Shortly after his arrival in Philadelphia he had married a sister of General von Sonntag. There were three children, a daughter, Mary, and two sons, John, Jr., and Edward. John studied law and later emigrated to England. Edward, also, was admitted to the Bar but later turned to architecture, designing several county prisons in the style made famous by his father.[3]

[2] For details of some of the enormous difficulties incident to running this peculiar institution, see, for example, " Report of the Commissioners of the Western Penitentiary," in *Journal of the House of Representatives* (Pennsylvania, 1829–30), Vol. II, pp. 634–641; and Eugene E. Doll, " Trial and Error at Allegheny," *Pennsylvania Magazine of History and Biography*, LXXXI (January 1957), 3–27.

[3] This similarity has led to considerable confusion and the two prisons completed in 1855 by Edward for York and Cumberland counties have variously been credited to his father and to a brother of John Haviland living in America. A description of these prisons, as well as a letter written by the architect in which he discusses his debt to his father, can be found in *Pennsylvania Journal of Prison Discipline*, Vol. X, No. 2 (April 1855), pp. 57–93.

On March 28, 1852, Haviland died suddenly of apoplexy at his home in Philadelphia and was buried in the family vault at St. Andrew's Church in that city.

Haviland's task

This bare recital of the facts of Haviland's life contributes little to an understanding of the reasons for his influence and fame during this period. For this we must turn back to a more detailed consideration of the circumstances surrounding the building of the Eastern Penitentiary and the influence it had on subsequent prison construction.

Beginning with the advanced Quaker penal code instituted by William Penn in 1682 which declared the reform of the offender to be more important than his punishment, the colony of Pennsylvania had always shown an interest in the problem of the lawbreaker. Although Penn's code was repealed after his death, humanitarian thought and advanced European ideas combined to make Philadelphia in Revolutionary times the centre of prison reform agitation. Imprisonment became the penalty for more and more offences instead of death or mutilation. In 1790 the famous Walnut Street Jail came under joint county and state control and a decade of advanced penal administration was launched. A " Penitentiary House " was constructed in the yard of the prison to house sixteen prisoners in solitary confinement, presumably the worst offenders among the prisoners. The Philadelphia Society for Alleviating the Miseries of Public Prisons, as well as many prominent citizens such as Benjamin Rush and Benjamin Franklin, constantly urged the state legislature to relieve the overcrowding at Walnut Street by the construction of state penitentiaries. As the result of these efforts and complaints from the western counties who had to bear the expense of transporting prisoners to Philadelphia, the Western Penitentiary was authorised and in 1818, near Pittsburgh, construction began on a prison to provide solitary confinement day and night without labour. In March of 1821 Cherry Hill was authorised by the legislature for housing prisoners from the eastern half of the state.

What sort of prison did the reformers want to be built in Philadelphia? As the result of experience at Walnut Street and early trials at Pittsburgh, the religious beliefs of the Quakers, and the new humanitarian philosophy so much in the air in Europe and America, the idea of reformation was coming to be regarded as more important than punishment. Men and women, convicts and detainees had been separated at Walnut Street. But for the new prisons each man was to have a separate cell. Every effort was to be made to avoid contacts among the prisoners because the Quaker reformers were well aware of the ill effects of such mingling among inmates and their continuing friendships once released. For the criminal already imprisoned, isolation from his fellow men was to prevent harmful corruption, protect his good resolutions, and give him ample opportunity to ponder on his mistakes and make his peace with God. If this were not effective, once the man was released the memory of this complete and awful isolation would be sufficiently terrifying to deter him from further crimes. Likewise, the prospect of solitary confinement plus the grim and forbidding appearance of the prison itself would serve as a powerful deterrent to the potential offender on the outside. Solitary confinement day and night became, then, the Quaker solution to the problem of rehabilitation as well as the deterrence of potential law-breakers.

Whether or not the prisoners should be compelled or allowed to work during their confinement was still a disputed point when the first Western Penitentiary was opened, and prisoners were not provided with work. But increasing difficulties with inmates who became physically and mentally ill, as well as the high costs of maintenance which resulted from complete solitary confinement without work, eventually forced a change of policy. By the time the first prisoners were admitted to the Eastern Penitentiary in 1829, legislation had provided that prisoners must work in their cells. The Pennsylvania System, as it came to be known, was becoming fully articulated at this point.

The Eastern Penitentiary Act of 1821 authorised construction of a prison to house 250 in solitary confinement. (Later supplementary legislation provided for more cells, more than doubling this initial capacity.) It was to be constructed on the Pittsburgh plan " subject to such alterations and improvements as the said commissioners . . . with the approbation of the Governor, approve and direct, *provided always, that the principle of the solitary confinement of the prisoners be preserved and maintained.*" [4]

[4] Thomas B. McElwee, *A Concise History of the Eastern Penitentiary* (Philadelphia: Neall & Massey, 1835), Vol. I, p. 144.

The new state prison at Pittsburgh had been operating too short
a time to provide any valuable experience upon which Haviland
could draw when he designed Cherry Hill. As an architect his task
therefore was to plan a building for the first large-scale experiment
in a new kind of penal treatment. Some of the problems could be
anticipated with ease, others could not. The main job was to create
cell blocks where prisoners could be kept completely isolated from
one another in surroundings which would not be injurious to
their health but would prove secure from escape, the whole of
which would have to be easily accessible to constant inspection
by guards.

Haviland chose a peculiar radial type of layout for the prison,
consisting of a central hub with seven wings converging on it and
connected to the centre building by covered passage ways. It is
this most obvious and perhaps spectacular aspect of Haviland's plan,
easily recognisable in later prisons modelled after Cherry Hill,
which is usually regarded as his great and original contribution to
prison construction. This is not quite accurate, as we shall see in a
closer examination of prison design before and after Haviland.

Evolution of the radial plan

Within the limits of this paper it is not possible to trace the
gradual development of the radial plan on the Continent prior to its
introduction into the United States by Haviland. However, a few
details must be given here for purposes of perspective. The fifty
years from about 1775 to 1825, particularly in England, saw a great
many local prisons constructed for pre-trial detention and short-
sentence offenders. At first these local jails were simply strong
buildings with a series of large rooms. However, the appalling
conditions of filth, suffering and promiscuous mingling of all types
of prisoners without proper supervision, which were common in
most of these institutions, were made known to the public through
the writings of John Howard and later reformers, and forced a re-
examination of the whole process of penal treatment. The actual
prison structure itself, for the first time, was considered important,
not only in preserving the health of the prisoners but also in
affording opportunities for their effective supervision.

The great preoccupation which reformers of this period showed
with proper surveillance of prisoners by guards (and guards by their

superiors) led to the development of several highly characteristic and original forms of prison layouts, which might be regarded merely as whimsical architectural curiosities were it not for the fact that they became so common and had a direct influence on the more sophisticated prison structures which were to follow. These forms tended to be either circular or semicircular; polygonal; or radial, that is, some variant of a cross, star or fan shape. The circular prison plan was first proposed systematically by the great English law reformer, Jeremy Bentham, when he published in 1791 his proposals for a *Panopticon House*.[5] This vast circular structure of cast iron and glass, which Aldous Huxley once termed a " totalitarian housing project," was never erected, but the idea was partially carried out in much altered form in the Edinburgh House of Correction, the Lancaster Female Prison at Kirkdale (which is still in use), and in numerous little crescent-shaped county jails built in both England and Ireland between 1790 and 1830, and in Spain much later.[6] Although no true *Panopticons* appeared in Britain, three were erected in Holland in the 1880s, several at the Illinois Penitentiary near Joliet and at Cuba's large penal colony on the Isle of Pines, the latter prisons constructed in the twentieth century.

The polygonal plan, first seen in the famous *Maison de force* at Ghent and consisting eventually of eight trapezoidal sections around an octagonal inner structure, was seldom imitated. The disastrous variation of this plan found in the great Millbank Prison, erected in London between 1813 and 1821, was never copied.

Although cross-shaped structures were not new to institutional architecture,[7] the end of the eighteenth century saw for the first time many little British county jails erected whose buildings were arranged so that the governor or keeper could visually supervise the prison. Usually his house was located in the centre of the prison so that from his windows he could look out on to yards and sometimes into the dayrooms located at the near ends of the cell wings a few feet away. Probably the first radial jail whose plan permitted

---

[5] See Bentham, *Panopticon or Inspection House* (London: T. Payne, 1791); *Panopticon Postscript*, published the same year; and his *Works*, edited by Sir John Bowring (Edinburgh: Tait, 1843), especially Vols. IV, X and XI. See above, p. 63 (Ed.).

[6] See, for example, the 50th and 51st *Report of Inspectors-General of the Prisons of Ireland*, which contain a series of plans of these county institutions.

[7] For example, Joseph Furttenbach in his *Architectura Civilis* (1628) and *Architectura Universalis* (1635) published plans for hospitals, arsenals, schools and lazarettos, all in a cross form.

visual inspection of corridors from a central vantage point, however, was the Suffolk County Jail at Ipswich, erected by the English architect, William Blackburn, who built a score of radial prisons in varying designs during his brief and promising career.[8] Mental hospitals also engaged in a vast building programme during this period, and some of these also were built along radial lines, with the wings often joined to the centre building.[9] A " Lunatic Asylum " plan, published in London in 1814 when Haviland was in that city studying architecture, clearly indicates that the radial plan was almost fully developed at that time, and makes the inspiration for Haviland's designs quite obvious.[10] Model plans of prisons published in the following several years show the same six- or seven-wing radiating pattern, although usually the wings were separate from the centre building. The centre structure was usually devoted to cells, service facilities, or more often a combination of governor's quarters and chapel. The opportunities for actual observation of prisoners in such arrangements was extremely limited, in spite of the great importance attached to such visual inspection by the prison reform groups and their formal espousal and promotion of the radial plan.

Haviland builds a prison

In Haviland's originally submitted designs, the arrangement of the prison then was largely an adaptation of the most approved type of plans which were being publicised by the prison reform groups in his native country during his architectural novitiate. His original plans for the Eastern Penitentiary called for an elaborate front

[8] An idea of the layouts of the early English prisons can be got from several sources: the richest in plans and diagrams is a pamphlet issued by the London Society for the Improvement of Prison Discipline in 1826, entitled *Remarks on the Form and Construction of Prisons With Appropriate Designs* (London: J. & A. Arch). Good prose descriptions of prisons of this period are contained in James Neild, *State of the Prisons in England, Scotland and Wales* (London: John Nichols & Son, 1812). The first-cited work gives considerable evidence, bearing out conclusions from other sources, to indicate the distinctive role of the little-known Blackburn in developing radial prison forms. See especially p. 17.

[9] See, for example, the Glasgow Hospital pictured in William Stark, *Remarks on Public Hospitals for the Cure of Mental Derangement* (Edinburgh: James Ballantyne, 1807); and John Foulston, *Public Buildings Erected in the West of England* (London: J. Williams, 1838), plates 105 and 106, following p. 74.

[10] The hospital plan appears in Hans Pfeiffer, " Neuzeitliche Gefängnisbauten und ihre Geschichte," *Blätter für Gefängniskunde*, LXV (1934), Zweites Sonderheft, p. 58, which is taken from a plate appearing in H. A. Adam, *Über Geisteskrankheit in alter und neuer Zeit* (Ansbach: C. Brügel & Sohn, n.d.), p. 29. Its resemblance to the Eastern Penitentiary, and especially to what must have been the initial designs, is quite striking.

building to house administrative offices and quarters for the staff. This structure was designed in a heavy Gothic style complete with iron portcullis and an eighty-foot belltower. Originally the central rotunda was to house cells, a laundry, bakehouse, and, below, a series of dungeons each with a private entrance from the floor above and a fireplace.[11] Fortunately, by the time construction was begun, the architect decided to make an open inspection hall of this centre building, a nerve centre for the prison from which vantage point guards could view all the corridors of the prison. The first three cell blocks constructed were single storey, each containing about forty large cells. Entry to the cells was not from the cell-house corridor but from the outside of the buildings, through the twenty-foot-long exercise yards which were attached to each cell. Every cell contained a flush toilet, water tap, a bunk on chains against the wall and equipment for the prisoner's work activities. The remaining four cell blocks of Haviland's design were two storeys in height and access to cells was by means of double doors opening into the corridors, the previous arrangement having soon been found too inconvenient.[12]

Although it is the Eastern Penitentiary which became the point of controversy in the struggle of rival penal systems and the prison most mentioned in penological writings, three Haviland prisons have been important in influencing subsequent designs. The reconstructed Western Penitentiary at Pittsburgh and the New Jersey state prison at Trenton were both erected in the 1830s on plans different from Cherry Hill. Pittsburgh was in the form of a " V " with an inspection room in the hub. The Trenton plan, although not all its wings were built at the time, consisted of five wings radiating from an inspection room in a half-circle radial pattern. It was the Trenton plan, which embodied improvements over the original Cherry Hill buildings such as detached exercise yards, cell

---

[11] *Haviland Papers*, MSS., University of Pennsylvania Library. This early description appears in a Journal Book kept by the architect (labelled No. 1 in the collection) under an entry dated July 2, 1821.

[12] An early version of the plan appears in an engraving in George W. Smith, *A View and Description of the Eastern Penitentiary of Pennsylvania* (Philadelphia: C. G. Childs, Engraver, 1830), frontispiece; and in McElwee, *op. cit.* frontispiece. A bird's-eye view of this version is in *Description of Haviland's Design for the New Penitentiary now Erecting Near Philadelphia* (Philadelphia: Robert Desilver, 1824), end of pamphlet. Most plans which have been published are idealised, symmetrical versions of Cherry Hill. The one which most closely resembles the actual prison in 1836 is that contained in Frédéric Demetz and G. Abel Blouet, *Rapports sur les pénitenciers des États-Unis* (Paris: Imprimerie Royale, 1837), Part II, plate 23, opposite p. 61.

doors into the corridors and two-storey wings, which was most widely imitated.[13]

The imitators

What were the consequences of Haviland's prisons? This question must be answered separately with reference to the United States and the rest of the world. From the beginning, Cherry Hill had become the tangible symbol of the emergent Pennsylvania System of solitary confinement. This highly controversial method of treatment was inextricably linked with the physical structure which Haviland had created. In the few prisons which he designed outside Pennsylvania brief attempts were made to carry out the system of continual solitary treatment but these experiments were abandoned within a few years. Only in its parent state was the Pennsylvania System retained for any number of years in the United States. It was its arch rival, the Auburn System, consisting of solitary confinement at night and congregate work in silence during the day, which was to be adopted almost universally in North America. And with it, the Auburn cell block was widely copied— inside cells, back to back on tiers, and only large enough to house a bunk and toilet bucket. It is this lengthy rectangular type of cell block which has become standard in most United States prison plants. In a few institutions Auburn-type blocks radiate from a central rotunda, as exemplified in the reformatories built in Michigan, Ohio, Pennsylvania, Indiana and New Jersey, and in the more recently constructed United States Disciplinary Barracks at Fort Leavenworth, Kansas, built in the 1930s.

Although Haviland's prisons never were a direct major influence on American prison architecture, it is one of those strange tricks of history and cultural diffusion that the radial plan, originally developed in English and Continental prisons, was not widely recognised or accepted for large-scale prisons until it had first been transplanted to America by Haviland and then reintroduced to

13 The style of the prison was a heavy Egyptoid instead of the Gothic of Cherry Hill. This was not imitated elsewhere.

The original Haviland plan appears in Demetz and Blouet, *op. cit.* plate 31, p. 68, and in Edouard Ducpétiaux, *Du progrès de l'état actuel de la réforme pénitentiaire* (Bruxelles: Société Belge de Librairie, 1838), Vol. III, plate 15.

The only known printed plan of Haviland's Pittsburgh institution is in William Crawford, *Report on the Penitentiaries of the United States* (1835; reprinted Montclair, N.J.: Patterson Smith, 1969), plate 4, opposite p. 15 of the Appendix.

European reformers by the many observers and commissioners sent here by various governments. Soon after the first three cell blocks were finished at the Eastern Penitentiary, the Governments of Great Britain, France, Prussia, Russia, Belgium and several other nations began sending representatives to evaluate the rival American experiments, and particularly Cherry Hill. Almost without exception their reports favoured the latter, and it seems safe to assume that the high quality of the architecture which Haviland linked with the system was one of the more important factors in its widespread acceptance throughout the rest of the world.

Following Sir William Crawford's visit and elaborate report on the American penitentiaries, which favoured Cherry Hill, Haviland submitted model plans to the British Government which were substantially those of the Trenton prison.[14] On the basis of these plans and with some modifications, the Model Prison, later known as Pentonville, was completed in 1842 and was destined to become the most copied prison in the world. In Britain itself new prisons were built or reconstructed at a rapid rate following the erection of Pentonville, all except the very small being radial in layout, and all adopting the Pentonville cell-house details.[15] At least thirty radial structures were erected during the remaining years of the century, the largest of which were in the characteristic four- or five-wing pattern of Trenton or Pentonville. Similar radial prisons were built in other parts of the Empire such as Egypt, Australia, Malta, Burma and Canada.

This pattern of building was duplicated in other European countries where political instability, inadequate government finances or wars did not interfere with the progress of prison reform. In Germany, following official visits by Dr. Nicolaus Julius to America and Frederick William IV to Pentonville, a new model prison was

[14] There is some indication that Haviland regarded Trenton as an improvement over Cherry Hill and he once described it as his prison "most worthy of copying," according to a letter written to the French commissioners, Demetz and Blouet (*Haviland Papers*, Journal No. 3).

[15] Estimates of the number of prisons and cells patterned after Pentonville vary, depending on the time the estimate was made and the type of institution included. An 1867 source sets the number of prisons at 145, with over 24,000 cells (Great Britain, Colonial Office, *Prison Discipline in the Colonies. Digest and Summary of Information Respecting Prisons in the Colonies*, p. 65).

An idea of the pace of construction can be derived from the statement of an early chairman of the Prison Commissioners that, within six years after the Model Prison was erected, fifty-four new prisons, with a total of 11,000 cells, were constructed after its general design (Edmund F. DuCane, *The Punishment and Prevention of Crime* (London: Macmillan & Co., 1885), p. 56).

begun in the Moabit district of Berlin in 1844 on the Pentonville design. Shortly afterwards prisons were erected at Münster and Ratibor on cross plans. The Moabit and Ratibor plans became the two basic patterns for almost all subsequent nineteenth-century prison building in most of the German states.[16] Although a number of prisons, especially for long-term offenders, were located in old fortresses, over forty radial prisons were erected in Germany before 1910.

Belgium, perhaps more than any other European country, completely replaced its old prisons in the last half of the nineteenth century, largely through the untiring efforts of one man, Edouard Ducpétiaux. A devotee of the Pennsylvania System and a student of English prisons, he made certain that most of the establishments erected during his long administration were radial in form. Some like Antwerp, Audenarde and Charleroi, were " V "-shaped like the second Pittsburgh prison, others were in an " X " form, such as the great prison at Forest near Brussels. Still others, like Louvain and St. Giles, consisted of five or six wings radiating from a central rotunda. Only three of the over twenty new prisons erected in this country were not radial in the true sense.

Beginning with Vitoria prison in 1859, Spain began to build new provincial prisons which have, down to the present day, consistently been erected on the radial plan. The great " model prisons " in Madrid (1877) and Valencia (1887) were directly patterned after Pentonville, and Barcelona was built in a six-wing radial form. An eight-wing full-circle radial provincial prison is partially completed at the present time in Carabanchel, a suburb of Madrid.[17] Altogether, over forty major prisons have been erected on the radial plan in Spain.

In the smaller countries of Western Europe, where but a few large prisons were erected, these were almost always patterned after Cherry Hill and Pentonville. The large prisons in Holland, Switzerland, the Scandinavian countries and Finland, Portugal,

---

[16] Plans for most of these prisons can be found in Karl Krohne and R. Uber, *Die Strafanstalten und Gefängnisse in Preussen* (Berlin: Carl Heymann, 1901), Atlas, and a supplemental Atlas brought out in 1909.

[17] Photographs of the construction of this modern example of the Cherry Hill plan appear in the annual reports of the Dirección General de Prisiones. See, for example, *La obra penitenciaria durante el año 1950*, p. 272; the *Memoria* for 1952, pp. 153 and 163 *et seq.*; and also in the 1955 *Memoria*, pp. 199–201.

Austria and especially Hungary follow this pattern.[18] In France, Russia and Italy, political unrest, repeated financial problems and available confiscated church properties resulted in few prisons being erected aside from detention or short-term institutions. These, however, were almost invariably faithful to the Pentonville layout as can be seen in the large prisons of Mazas and Santé in Paris and Orléans in the provinces; in Italy at San Vittore in Milan, Regina Coeli in Rome and the detention prisons at Piacenza and Turin; or in Russia in the city prison at Piotrokow (Petrokof) and the great Viborg prison in St. Petersburg. A few long-term institutions were erected in these countries and in the familiar layouts—Civita Vecchia near Rome and Palermo, for example; or the Russian provincial prisons at Grodno, Lomja, Staraïa-Roussia, all based on model plans put forth by the prison administration and usually in a two- or three-wing pattern such as is found primarily in Belgium.[19]

The various countries of Latin America have, with one or two exceptions, built few large central prisons until recent years. These early structures, usually erected in or near the capital, were almost always radial, reflecting either direct North American or British and Continental influences. Argentina showed the greatest activity in nineteenth-century prison building: the first of the new prisons, located at Buenos Aires (1872), was a classic five-wing radial. Others were erected on variations of this design.

One of the first effects which accompanied Westernisation of Japan was the advent of prison reform. Shikueya Ohara, a jurist and under-director of the prison administration, visited British colonial prisons and sent officials to America and Europe. The result was the enthusiastic adoption of cellular confinement and the acceptance of the radial prison plan as part of official policy.[20] The first of the new prisons, Miyagi (1879), was designed by an English architect and consisted of six wings arranged very much like Louvain prison in Belgium.[21] Over thirty-three radial prisons were

[18] An excellent picture of Hungarian prisons can be obtained from a single source, which contains many plans and photographs: Étienne de Megyery, *Les institutions pénitentiaires de la Hongrie* (Budapest: Ministère Royal Hongrois de la Justice, 1905).
[19] These model plans were published by the government about 1860: Administration Générale des Prisons, *Recueil des projets de bâtiments pénitentiaires* (n.d.). Many model plans were published during this period in Russia but few ever eventuated in prisons.
[20] In 1883 a disastrous fire at Hiroshima prison caused a temporary shift of policy to isolated parallel blocks, but after five years this was abandoned as too inconvenient, and radial plans were again used.
[21] The writer is indebted to the Japanese Ministry of Justice, and especially Mr. Fujitaro Kusunoki, architect of the Bureau of Correction, for these details as well as a series of

erected in Japan until very recent years, the most common plan being based on Pentonville, as at Tokyo (1879), or occasionally five- or six-wing full-circle radial designs, as at Gifu and Hakodate, opened in 1931. More true radial prisons were erected in Japan than in any other country, and only Belgium has rivalled her in the consistency of its architecture.

Reform came later in China and the first new prison was built in Peking in 1909 by a Japanese architect. Like many new prison structures put up in the following ten years, it consisted of a complicated array of three .Trenton-type radial layouts, a three-wing " T " form, and shop buildings.[22]

Generally, by the end of the nineteenth century, most prison construction in Europe had ceased and new forms, such as the so-called " telephone pole " plan developed at Fresnes, the great provincial prison outside Paris, and small open colonies, were superseding the classic radial prison. In spite of this fact, radial forms still persist: the United States Disciplinary Barracks at Fort Leavenworth and the new Madrid prison have been mentioned. A new minimum-security housing unit at Washington State Prison was completed in 1954 and consists of six wings and an observation hub.[23] Two proposed institutions, one in California and the other in Colorado, are variations of the radial plan, as are most of the new provincial prisons now being erected in Spain.

Haviland's contributions

This brief review of prison building before and after Cherry Hill brings out two important facts: first, we must conclude that Haviland, often regarded as the innovator of radial prison design, brought with him from his home country the most recent experiences and ideas for this type of prison arrangement which had

plans and data on other Japanese prisons. Details of only a few of these prisons have appeared in European language sources. Some material can be found, however, in Carl Krauss, " Das Straf- und Gefängniswesen in Japan," *Blätter für Gefängniskunde*, XXX (1893), 165–204; and Georg Crusen, *Das heutige japanische Gefängniswesen* (Tokio: Druck Der Hobunsha, 1902); and in Christophe Eckenstein, " Regard sur le système pénitentiaire japonais," *Revue internationale de criminologie et police technique*, IX (January–March 1955), 28–40.

22 The plans for this and many other Chinese prisons can be found in *Chinese Prisons*, published by the Commission on Extraterritoriality, Peking, 1925. Further details on the Peking prison appear in China, Ministry of Justice, *The First Peking Prison*, translated by Chen chi, Chou tsuei chi, Lin shu ning and Woo tsing yu, Peking, 1916.

23 Photographs appear in Bob Karolevitz, " New Thinking in Prison Construction," *Pacific Architect and Builder*, LXIII (June 1957), 21–22.

been developing in Europe since at least 1780; secondly, that in spite of its origins, it was not until the construction of Cherry Hill that the radial plan received widespread and articulate approval and adoption in large-scale prison construction. What then has been Haviland's contribution?

Perhaps Haviland, more than any other prison architect before or after him, was aware of what functions the prison building was expected to serve and how these could best be accomplished architecturally. Up to that time any architect who had designed successful theatres or state houses was felt competent to design a successful prison as well—an attitude which has not completely disappeared. The dismal failures of some of these efforts and Haviland's notable successes did much to change these notions. For example, the many details which Haviland was careful to incorporate in his prison—such as the floor paving stones being joined at points which were inaccessible to a prisoner and the entire prison and yards visible from a central tower—made it remarkably secure in comparison with structures of that period. In fact after over 130 years, the original buildings, little altered except for additions, are still being used to house maximum-security prisoners in Pennsylvania. Haviland also gave much attention to the vexing problem of communication among the prisoners, one which subsequently proved to be insoluble on a large-scale basis. He initiated the first large-scale use of flush toilets in America to obviate the contact which would otherwise have resulted from convicts emptying toilet buckets or being escorted to central privies. The problem of communication through the heating system proved more difficult. After considerable experimentation with hot-air ducts and various arrangements of water pipes, the architect was satisfied before he had completed Cherry Hill that such contacts had been reduced to a minimum.

Because the success of the Pennsylvania System relied more heavily than others on the construction and design of the cell itself, due to the fact that the prisoner spent his entire sentence there, Haviland gave considerable attention to providing adequate light, warmth and ventilation, and sufficient space for exercise and work. Some important innovations in design were made also to facilitate communication among the prison staff, as well as to improve their surveillance of prisoners. This was particularly true of his use of the central rotunda, apparently for the first time, as a sort of communications hub and nerve centre of the prison, an idea which has been carried out in many prisons in the United States as well as in Europe, regardless of their plan.

In Cherry Hill the architect had succeeded in incorporating and combining many technical developments, and in so doing set standards of space, plumbing and ventilation which were seldom equalled in prisons during the ensuing seventy-five years. Compared with the penitentiaries of their day, the prisons of Haviland were overwhelmingly superior, both technically and stylistically. Because of the widespread imitation of the Eastern and New Jersey penitentiaries, particularly in Europe, Haviland's great service to penology would seem to be not in publicising the radial plan, which might or might not have caught on otherwise, but in establishing high standards of construction, standards which were to have an influence on almost all of the prison construction of the nineteenth century, and even down to the present time in some instances.

A word should be said concerning the style of Haviland's prisons because some modern criminologists have heaped abuse on Cherry Hill and the other penitentiaries of that period for establishing the "fortress school" of prison architecture, suggested by the heavy and forbidding Gothic which accents security and the punitive nature of imprisonment. It should be kept in mind, however, that far from being oblivious to the effects of such a style, Haviland and his contemporaries found it admirably suited to the atmosphere which the reformers sought to create. Haviland's teacher, James Elmes, in commenting on the design of the newly built Newgate prison in London, wrote: " without doubt the most appropriate and correct design in the metropolis or perhaps in Europe; for no one viewing this edifice can possibly mistake it for anything but a gaol, the openings as small as convenient, and the whole external aspect made as gloomy and melancholy as possible." [24] And the Building Commissioners of Cherry Hill went on record as saying that: " the exterior of a solitary prison should exhibit as much as possible great strength and convey to the mind a cheerless blank indicative of the misery which awaits the unhappy being who enters within its walls." [25] In the context of such a philosophy then, Haviland's

---

[24] James Elmes, *Hints for the Improvement of Prisons* (London: W. Bulmer & Co., 1817), pp. 14–15.
[25] *Book of Minutes of the Building Commissioners*, bound MSS. volume in archives of Eastern Penitentiary, Philadelphia, p. 115.

choice of the heavy and gloomy Gothic and Egyptoid styles used at Philadelphia and at Trenton seems to have been entirely appropriate. Such choices cannot be criticised in the light of a changed, enlightened point of view concerning rehabilitative treatment which developed many years later.

It might be noted parenthetically that the restrained Gothic façade of Haviland's Eastern Penitentiary has come in for much praise from architects and art historians. A present-day critic writes that the prison " comes nearer to being a work of art than any other building of its kind. . . ." [26] This simple style became much more elaborate and corrupted in latter-day examples, which found themselves the targets for criticism by those who regarded their appearance as too ornate for a prison and thus inappropriate and anything but a deterrent. It is extremely doubtful if stylistic factors were of much importance in motivating either prisoners or the so-called " criminal classes " from which they were recruited, however.

The prison structure and rehabilitation

Even with this cursory view of early prison construction, particularly John Haviland's, it must be evident that the prison structure admirably fitted the penal philosophy of that day. What kind of building would have been better suited to keep men away from their fellow men during the entire sentence? What style could have been better calculated to deter the potential law-breaker by its forbidding external appearance and make the prisoner think twice before committing new crimes once released? What sort of cell layout would have been better suited to the degree of maximum surveillance of men continually locked in their cells?

Modern penal philosophy rejects some, but not all, of these early Quaker theories of crime control as being naïve, oversimplified and certainly not in keeping with our present knowledge of human nature contributed by the various behaviour sciences. What about our current prison structures? How closely do they reflect modern penal philosophy? With a few notable exceptions, most present-day institutions show little basic deviation from the early patterns of prison construction established at Philadelphia, Pentonville and Auburn over a century ago. This is partly because some of the prison structures were built during an early period and for economic reasons must continue to be used.[27] But it is also true that the traditional cell block and prison layout with minor variations has dominated prison construction right down to the present day, with very few exceptions. The great gulf between modern penal philosophy, on the one hand, and our prison buildings, on the other, a condition which seems not to have been present in the prison building of the early nineteenth century, can only partly be explained in terms of the inertia of tradition. Certain significant factors then operative no longer are. In the first half of the nineteenth century prison reform was a problem which drew to it the keenest intellects, the most influential leaders of the community. Prison reform was in the air. No effort—financial, legislative or philanthropic—was too great to apply towards a solution of the newly " discovered " problem of the criminal and his reformation. Today prison reform finds itself in the backwaters of society's problems, receiving little attention from community leaders except for brief periods following riots or scandals.

In addition, the formula of treatment in the 1800s was simple: keep men completely secluded so they can repent their sins and avoid contamination from fellow prisoners; teach them industry by compelling them to work and virtue by supplying them with religious instruction; and make the whole thing so unpleasant that, should all else fail, they will be deterred from further crime out of sheer hedonism. Such a philosophy busy civic leaders, state legislators and practical architects could understand and translate into their own areas of action without much difficulty. But modern penal philosophy is characterised by inconsistencies of an Alice-in-Wonderland magnitude, tortuous by-ways of psycho-analytic theory and sociological statistics and a massive complexity made necessary by our ever-increasing body of knowledge about human behaviour. This has reached the point where all but the highly specialised " expert " find the field almost inaccessible.

If modern prisons are ill adapted to modern penal philosophy, does it really make any difference? How important is the physical structure anyway in limiting or encouraging the type of programme

---

[27] James V. Bennett has stated that only twelve of the 152 state penal establishments in the United States are less than fifty years old (_Annals, American Academy of Political and Social Science_, Vol. 293 (May 1954), p. 13). Only two have been built in England since the turn of the century and other national prison systems show similar patterns, with the exception of Spain and South American states.

which can be carried out inside its walls? This is a difficult question to answer with empirical evidence. Many prison administrators feel that bars, walls and other maximum-security trappings definitely structure the spirit and determine the attitudes of both guards and inmates. It is obvious that the conventional prison allows little opportunity for classification, graded release using degrees of security, special treatment for certain classes of offenders, education, industrial activities and other measures deemed essential by modern penologists. Above all, the great size of the average American prison, of no great moment under earlier penal philosophies, makes present-day programmes of differentiated treatment almost impossible. There is no doubt that progressive and intelligent leadership can do much to offset the harmful effects of an outmoded prison plant, and it is certainly true that a well-designed structure is no guarantee of the presence of the more intangible elements of rehabilitation. But it seems safe to assume that a prison system whose architecture is based upon a careful thinking through of the aims of modern correction can do much to keep these aims alive and effective. Perhaps it is not too much to ask that modern-day architects make as great an effort as did John Haviland to build prison structures in harmony with a treatment philosophy. One can only hope they will approach his success.

NORMAN B. JOHNSTON.

BIBLIOGRAPHY

The following references have been divided into three sections: those which deal with prison construction prior to John Haviland, those which contain material on Haviland or his prisons, and finally those which describe the post-Haviland prison buildings. No attempt has been made to be inclusive, but rather to select a few sources which give a general view of the period under consideration, or in some cases, a more detailed account of one area.

I. Prison Building before Haviland

BIFFI, SERAFINO. *Sulle antiche carceri di Milano.* (Milano: Bernardoni di C. Rebeschini, 1884. 371 pp. + 12 plates.)

CRAWFORD, WILLIAM. *Report on the Penitentiaries of the United States.* (1835. Reprinted Montclair, N.J.: Patterson Smith, 1969. xvii + 56 + 229 pp. + 18 plates.)

HOWARD, JOHN. *The State of the Prisons in England and Wales.* (4th ed. 1792. Reprinted Montclair, N.J.: Patterson Smith, 1972, as Vol. 1 of *Prisons and Lazarettos.* xxix + 540 pp. + 22 plates.)

JULIUS, NIKOLOUS H. *Leçons sur les prisons.* Translated from the German by H. LAGARMITTE. Vol. II. (Paris: F. G. Levrault, 1831. 502 pp. + 4 plates.)

MAYHEW, HENRY and BINNY, JOHN. *The Criminal Prisons of London.* (London: Griffin, Bohn & Co., 1862. xii + 634 pp.)

NEILD, JAMES. *State of the Prisons in England, Scotland and Wales.* (London: John Nichols & Son, 1812. lxiv + 643 pp.)

ORRIDGE, JOHN. *Description of the Gaol at Bury St. Edmunds to Which Are Added Designs for a Prison Made at the Request of T. F. Buxton, Esq., M.P., for the Emperor of Russia.* (London: Rodwell & Martin, 1819. ix + 37 pp. + 5 plates.)

PFEIFFER, HANS. "Neuzeitliche Gefängnisbauten und ihre Geschichte," *Blätter für Gefängniskunde,* LXV (1934), Zweites Sonderheft, xi + 182 pp.

SAGRA, RAMON DE LA. *Atlas carcelario.* (Madrid: Colegio Nacional de Sordomudos, 1843. 104 pp.)

SOCIETY FOR THE IMPROVEMENT OF PRISON DISCIPLINE, AND FOR THE REFORMATION OF JUVENILE OFFENDERS. *Remarks on the Form and Construction of Prisons with Appropriate Designs.* (London: J. & A. Arch, 1826. vii + 72 pp.)

—— *Rules Proposed for the Government of Gaols, Houses of Correction and Penitentiaries, to Which Are Added Plans of Prisons on Improved Principles.* (London: T. Bensley, 1820. vii + 65 pp.)

WIESELGREN, SIGFRID. *Die Entwickelung des Gefängniswesens in Schweden.* (Stockholm: P. A. Norstedt & Söner. 1900. 93 pp. + plates.)

II. Haviland and his Prisons

DEMETZ, FRÉDERIC AUGUSTE and BLOUET, G. ABEL. *Rapports sur les pénitenciers des États-Unis.* (Paris: Imprimerie Royale, 1837. 144 + 115 pp.)

ELMES, JAMES. *Hints for the Improvement of Prisons.* (London: W. Bulmer & Co., 1817. 28 pp.)

Haviland Papers, University of Pennsylvania Library, on loan from Archaeological and Natural History Society, The Castle, Taunton. 26 vols. of correspondence, records and ledger books in MSS.

JACKSON, JOSEPH. *Early Philadelphia Architects and Engineers.* (Philadelphia: privately printed, 1923. xii + 285 pp.)

McELWEE, THOMAS B. *A Concise History of Eastern Penitentiary of Pennsylvania together with a Detailed Statement of the Proceedings of the Committee Appointed by the Legislature, December 6, 1834.* 2 vols. (Philadelphia: Neall & Massey, 1835.)

"Minute Book, Board of Trustees of Penitentiary." Bound copy covering 1829–40. Archives Pennsylvania State Library, Harrisburg.

Teeters, Negley K. and Shearer, John D. *The Prison at Philadelphia: Cherry Hill.* (New York: Temple University Publications by Columbia University Press, 1957. 249 pp.)

Vaux, Richard. *Brief Sketch of the Origin and History of the State Penitentiary for the Eastern District of Pennsylvania at Philadelphia.* (Philadelphia: McLaughlin Bros., 1872. 143 pp.)

Vaux, Roberts. *Notices on the Original and Successive Efforts to Improve the Discipline of the Prison at Philadelphia.* (Philadelphia: Kimber and Sharpless, 1826. 76 pp.)

III. Post-Haviland Prisons

China. Commission on Extraterritoriality. *Chinese Prisons.* (Peking: 1925. 130 pp.)

France. Ministère de l'Intérieur. *Instruction et programme pour la construction des maisons d'arrêt et de justice: atlas de plans de prisons cellulaires.* (Paris: Août 1841. 65 pp. + 25 plates.)

—— *Plans des établissements pénitentiaires de France.* (Mélun: Imprimerie Administrative, 1895. 95 plates.)

Gernet, M. N. *Istoria tsarskoï tiurmy.* 3 vols. (Moscow: State Editorship of Judicial Literature, 1951–52.)

Great Britain. Sir Joshua Jebb. *Report of the Surveyor-General of Prisons on the Construction, Ventilation and Details of Pentonville Prison, 1844.* (London: Wm. Clowes & Sons for H.M.S.O., 1844. 30 pp. + 22 plates.)

—— *Second Report of the Surveyor-General of Prisons.* (London: H.M.S.O., 1847. 149 pp.)

Hopkins, Alfred. *Prisons and Prison Building.* (New York: Architectural Book Publishing Co., 1930. x + 140 pp.)

Krohne, Karl and Uber, R. *Die Strafanstalten und Gefängnisse in Preussen.* Anstalten in der Verwaltung des Ministeriums des Inneren. (Berlin: Carl Heymann, 1901. 431 pp. Atlas with 103 plates.)

—— *Nachtrag* [supplement] 1909. 48 pp. Atlas with 20 plates.

Landauer, Theodor von and Schmitt, Eduard. "Gefangenhäuser," *Handbuch der Architektur* (Stuttgart: A. Kröner, 1900), IV Teil, Halbband 7, Kapitel 2, pp. 340–456.

Lemos Britto, José. *Os penitenciarios do Brasil.* 3 vols. (Rio de Janeiro: Imprensa Nacional, 1924–26.)

Litchfield, Clarence B. "Correctional Institutions," *Forms and Functions of 20th Century Architecture.* Edited by Talbot Hamlin. Vol. III. (New York: Columbia University Press, 1952. xlix + 931 pp.)

Mayhew, Henry and Binny, John. *The Criminal Prisons of London.* (London: Griffin, Bohn & Co., 1862. xii + 634 pp.)

Megyery, Étienne de. *Les institutions pénitentiaires de la Hongrie.* (Budapest: Ministère Royal Hongrois de la Justice, 1905. 634 pp.)

RUSSIA. ADMINISTRATION GÉNÉRALE DES PRISONS. *Recueil des projets de bâtiments pénitentiaires.* (Imprimé par ordre de la Direction Générale des
Prisons, n.d. 10 pp. + 49 plates.)

STEVENS, JEAN BAPTISTE. *De la construction des prisons cellulaires en Belgique.*
(Bruxelles: Librairie C. Muquardt, 1874. 45 pp. + 4 plates.)

UNITED STATES DEPARTMENT OF JUSTICE, BUREAU OF PRISONS. *Handbook of
Correctional Institution Design and Construction.* (Leavenworth,
Kansas: United States Bureau of Prisons, 1949. 317 pp.)

WIESELGREN, SIGFRID. *Die Entwickelung des Gefängniswesens in Schweden.*
(Stockholm: P. A. Norstedt & Söner, 1900. 93 pp. + plates.)

NOTE ON THE CONTRIBUTOR

Dr. NORMAN B. JOHNSTON is Professor and Chairman of the Department of Sociology at Beaver College in Philadelphia. Until 1951 he
was a sociologist with the Illinois Penitentiary System, and he has
extensively visited European prison systems. For the past several
years he has been engaged in research on prison architecture, particularly of the nineteenth century, and has served as architectural consultant in new correctional construction. He is co-editor of *The
Sociology of Crime and Delinquency* and *The Sociology of Punishment and Correction.*

7

ARNOULD BONNEVILLE
DE MARSANGY
1802–1894

ARNOULD BONNEVILLE DE MARSANGY was an influential voice in the field of criminal legislative reforms in the France of the mid-nineteenth century. Jurist by profession, his innovative ideas on many criminological problems led the *Encyclopedia of the Social Sciences*[1] to include him as a reformer and a social scientist.

Born in Mons, Belgium, of French parents, in March 1802, Bonneville was a descendant of an ancient noble family. He studied law in Paris, and had a distinguished career as prosecutor, president judge at Versailles and imperial councillor at Paris.

Bonneville mainly directed his thinking and research to the institutions "complementary to" the penitentiary system. Bonneville elaborated his ideas most notably in his *Essay on the Institutions Complementary to the Penitentiary System,* published in 1847, in which he discussed topics such as reparation by criminals, the pardoning power, parole, after-care services and rehabilitation. His influence is shown by the fact that this book was distributed by the French Government to the members of both Chambers as an official document. Bonneville's other major work, *Of the Amelioration of the Criminal Law,* published in two volumes, in 1855 and 1864, extended his ideas in the same framework.

He always tried to push a new reform under the cloak of a legislative and *de facto* past or present precedent, in foreign legislations or, most often, in the French criminal law and institutions. His study of innovations was based, as he himself once indicated, on "comparative legislation and statistics," because in this way it is "difficult for serious authors to go astray, since the first shows them

* Reproduced from *The Journal of Criminal Law, Criminology and Police Science,* Vol. 60, No. 1, March 1969.
[1] *Encyclopedia of the Social Sciences* (New York, 1930), Vol. II, pp. 637–638.

the state of laws, and the second, the state of facts."[2]   His books, like his articles in journals, have not the well-integrated logic and sophistication of treatises on penal law and institutions, but consist rather of small essays and monographs.

Bonneville's ideas, which seem particularly worthy of retaining our attention, because they are a part of the modern criminological picture, can be joined to three key concepts: the parole system and the indeterminate sentence, victim compensation, and the penal registry plan to identify recidivists.

Parole and indeterminate sentences

Bonneville delineated a parole system, which he called "preparatory liberation" or "conditional release," *as early as 1846,* when he delivered a discourse on the topic at the opening session of the Civil Tribunal at Reims.   He defined parole as "a sort of middle term between an absolute pardon and the execution of the entire sentence; the right conceded to the administration by the judiciary to release provisionally under certain conditions, and after a sufficient period of expiatory suffering, a convict who appears to be reformed, reserving the right to return him to the prison if there is any well-founded complaint against him."   Parole was seen as "a powerful incentive to self-reformation" and as a system which had the "advantage of testing and maintaining, for a certain period of time and in the ordinary tempo of life, the good behavior of discharged convicts; of facilitating, thus, their moral rehabilitation and their re-classification in society; finally, it would be a notable source of economy for the State."[3]

Bonneville's parole system was in fact divided into two stages, a "quasi-release" and the "conditional release" *per se.*   In the first phase, industrial or agricultural work would be performed.   Either the prisoners would reside in a State industrial complex or a State farm, or they would work for private individuals.   Convicts working on the open market during the day would, obviously, sleep in prison at night.   Bonneville's intention was to prepare convicts for the competition of free labor and to facilitate their re-classification. In the second phase, parole would involve, like our own contemporary system, a supervision by parole officers providing guidance, aid and control of the offenders.

---

[2] Arnould Bonneville de Marsangy, *De l'amélioration de la loi criminelle* (Paris, 1864), Vol. II, p. xvii.

[3] Arnould Bonneville de Marsangy, *Traité des diverses institutions complémentaires du régime pénitentiaire* (Paris, 1847), pp. 202–203.

Bonneville was very preoccupied at the same time with the problem of recidivism, so that, having devised a system of parole, he immediately devised a mirror-image system for fighting recidivism. This means was the infliction of "supplementary detention"[4] on convicts who were not reformed when their sentences ended. If we think of Bonneville's parole system in connection with his system of supplementary detention, in a framework of a minimum of time served before being released and a maximum of "time-to-serve-in-addition" (which minimum and maximum he discussed in his work), and in the perspective of a large gap in-between left to the discretion of administrative authorities, we have here one of the first formulations of the principle of the indeterminate sentence— more clearly stated than in the prior discussions of it by Paley, Whately and others at the turn of the nineteenth century.[5]

A historical note is interesting at this point. In America and England Maconochie and Crofton are usually claimed as the originators of the parole system.[6] Europeans on the other hand often recognize Bonneville as the father of parole. De Quirós mentions that Frenchmen claim Bonneville as its inventor.[7] Vidal strongly maintains this point of view.[8] European legislation on parole seems to have been influenced primarily by Bonneville. Thus, the general rapporteur of the project of the Portuguese Penal Code, which instituted Parole in that country, wrote a letter to Bonneville, dated July 4, 1859, in which he recognized that "the Commission has introduced in its penal reform all the improvements that your works have indicated. It confesses as much to you. It sees in this a tribute by Portugal to your efforts."[9]

The innovations of history are often created independently and almost simultaneously. This seems to be the case with the origins of parole, especially in view of the slowness of communications at that time. In fact, Maconochie developed his scheme in the years 1840–1844 as governor of Norfolk Island, a famous penal colony east of Australia, whereas Bonneville's ideas came out in the years 1846– 1847. Our knowledge of the slowness of communications at the

---

[4] *Ibid.,* pp. 242–247.

[5] See Edward Lindsey, "Historical Sketch of the Indeterminate Sentence and Parole," *Journal of Criminal Law and Criminology,* Vol. 16 (1925–1926), pp. 9–126; Thorsten Sellin, "Paley on the Time Sentence," *ibid.,* Vol. 22 (1931–1932), pp. 264–266.

[6] John Vincent Barry, *supra,* pp. 84–106, in particular pp. 102–104; Max Grünhut, *Penal Reform* (1948; reprinted Montclair, N.J., 1972), p. 84.

[7] Bernaldo de Quirós, *Las nuevas teorias de la criminalidad* (Havana, 1946), p. 167.

[8] Georges Vidal, *Cours de droit criminel et de science pénitentiaire,* 2nd ed. (Paris, 1910), p. 686.

[9] Bonneville, *De l'amélioration de la loi criminelle,* Vol. II, p. vii.

time, especially in a field of activity such as this, leaves us with the impression that Bonneville really did not know about Maconochie's proposal. As to Crofton's Irish system, established during 1854–1862, it seems to have been based on refinements of Maconochie's system alone, although Bonneville's propositions about parole were quite extensively known throughout Europe by the time.

At any rate, some countries, like Portugal, have been influenced by Bonneville's ideas, and others, like Great Britain, probably derived their system from the Australian experience. In America, it is interesting to recall that the celebrated First National Prison Congress at Cincinnati in 1870 (precursor of the International Penal and Penitentiary Prison Congress held for the first time in London in 1872) paid its regards to Bonneville, Crofton and Maconochie for their contributions to the parole system, and that Enoch Cobb Wines, the initiator of both congresses and an ardent promoter of parole in the United States, had himself, in 1867, translated the first address of Bonneville on the topic.[10]   Dr. Wines was also one of the leaders responsible for the creation of the New York Reformatory at Elmira, opened in 1876, and for putting into its program the first parole system in the United States based on indeterminate sentences.

Victim compensation

Reparation or restitution by an individual offender to the person he has victimized is an old idea which, viewed as a civil matter exclusively (as it had been—and still is—conceptualized), was by now little more than an empty principle, so that reparation has disappeared from daily judicial practice.   The propositions of Bonneville in this matter, directly responsive to the radical thinking of the Italian Positivist School, favored a limited mingling of criminal and civil procedures in cases of reparation in order to satisfy efficiently a personal injury.   Bonneville stressed the element of public responsibility.   He thus proposed, for example, that the amount of restitution by the offender to the victim should be decided "ex officio" in the criminal court and that the obligation to repay the victim as prescribed should be a "criminal obligation" just as it is when restitution is due to the State.

The importance attached by Bonneville to the fate of the victims

---

[10] Arnould Bonneville de Marsangy, "Preparatory Liberation," trans. Enoch C. Wines, in *Report of the Prison Association of New York, 1867*, pp. 165–178.

and public responsibility towards them led him, moreover, to advance the idea of a State victim-compensation plan. Bonneville thus wrote that reparation was, in principle,

one of the indispensable elements of *public security*. Now, if it is true that there is no real social security without reparation, the conclusion is that this reparation must take place, cost what it will, and as one of the sine qua non conditions of the social contract; and that, in consequence, society must rigorously impose it on the culprit, at the same time and under the same justification that it imposes punishment on him; however, by the same token, we must conclude that if there is no known culprit, *society itself must assume the responsibility for reparation.* . . . It would be easy to show, with arguments of an irresistible logic, that, when the authors of a crime are unknown or when the condemned persons are insolvent, the State should repair the harm done to the victim.[11]

We must admit that such plans for victim-compensation by the State[12] as those of New Zealand (1963), Great Britain (1964) and California (1965), at least for crimes of personal violence, come in their general formulations close to Bonneville's approach, more than one hundred years after. . . .

Sutherland rightly recognizes Bonneville's historical achievement in the field of victim reparation and compensation.[13]

Penal registry plan

Bonneville is overtly recognized as the father of the penal registry plan commonly called "casiers judiciaires." The Twelfth International Penal and Penitentiary Congress, held at The Hague in 1950, devoted a full session to the topic, paying its due regards to an institution which had originated in France a century before, in 1850, two years after Bonneville had imagined it.

The problem underlying the proposal was as follows. Since the beginning of the nineteenth century, recidivism as defined by law was a ground for increasing the maximum duration of a sentence and an important factor in determining the type, the duration and the character of punishment and security measures. In order to

---

[11] Bonneville, *Traité des diverses institutions complémentaires,* p. 6.
[12] Robert D. Childres, "Compensation for Criminally Inflicted Personal Injury," *New York University Law Review,* Vol. 39 (1964), p. 444; James E. Culhane, "California Enacts Legislation to Aid Victims of Criminal Violence," *Stanford Law Review,* Vol. 18 (1965), p. 266; and Marvin E. Wolfgang, "Victim Compensation in Crimes of Personal Violence," *Minnesota Law Review,* Vol. 50 (1965), p. 223. A survey of current and recent legislation all over the world in this area is provided by Stephen Schafer, *Compensation and Restitution to Victims of Crime* (2nd ed., Montclair, N.J., 1970).
[13] Edwin H. Sutherland, *Principles of Criminology,* 4th ed. (Philadelphia, 1947), p. 576.

form a considered opinion about the accused, it was necessary to know if he had been previously convicted. Bonneville's idea was, thus, to develop a reliable and complete record of all previous convictions of an offender. Bonneville's simple but practical solution [14] suggested the assembling of all the reports of sentences imposed on a given individual by having such reports sent to the clerk of court in the district of his birthplace. The proposed system would create at each district tribunal a "mobile card-index cabinet" where, henceforth, certificates of final sentences pronounced anytime and anywhere against people born in a district would be centralized and classified there in alphabetical order. Such a penal register could easily and promptly answer an inquiry by the prosecuting authorities.

Established in France in 1850, the system was widely copied later in most European countries and exchanges of information between countries began. It is still commonly used today in Europe, although the system was never tried in Anglo-Saxon countries, where, especially in the United States, a preference for a fingerprint system, centralized in the Federal Bureau of Investigation, has been shown.

Bonneville's ideas on this matter may, however, have been at the origin of some modern American works in criminology, such as the Gluecks' prediction studies. Marc Ancel, for one, thinks so. He writes:

> Perhaps, it should be recalled that Bonneville de Marsangy was not just the inventor of the criminal record (casier judiciaire). Very well informed and much in advance of his time, he sought to draw up a systematic record of the previous convictions of accused persons simply because he was interested in the general problem of crime and the repetition of offences. He was perhaps the first to show clearly that an individual's present behavior, correctly interpreted, may be the pointer to his future conduct. In this respect, Bonneville de Marsangy can be claimed as a precursor of doctrines such as those of the preventive treatment of crime and those underlying the concept of preventive measures (mesures de sûreté). He could even be claimed as the ancestor of the ideas which inspire contemporary research into the foreseeability of conduct, exemplified by the prediction tables that are advocated in particular by S. and E. Glueck.[15]

Bonneville and modern criminology

As Jeffery put it, "if we understand the pioneers, then we can better understand the current issues in criminology. . . . Twentieth-

---

[14] Arnould Bonneville de Marsangy, *De la localisation au greffe de l'arrondissement natal des renseignements judiciaires concernant chaque condamné* (Versailles, November 5, 1848).

[15] Marc Ancel, *Social Defence* (London, 1965), pp. 39–40.

century criminology is a product of the theories of the eighteenth and nineteenth centuries." [16]

The name of Bonneville may be linked with the modern principle of the "individualization of punishment." His advanced ideas may better be understood if we recall that he was living in the middle of the nineteenth century, when the impact of the Classical School and Beccarian ideas about the fitting of the punishment to the "crime" was still at a high peak, having been embodied in the French Codes of 1791 and 1808. That punishment should be fitted to the "criminal" and not to the "crime," and that the criminal should not be punished essentially for what he has done but for what he is, were ideas at the source of Bonneville's thinking in criminological matters. It is evidenced by his proposals for parole, indeterminate sentences and victim reparation and compensation.

Thus, it is not surprising to see Ferri linking the name and the works of Bonneville with the two main and fundamental criteria of the System of Social Defense elaborated at the turn of this century by the Italian Positive School of Lombroso, Ferri and Garofalo, *i.e.* "segregation for an indeterminate period" [17] (parole and indeterminate sentences) and "reparation in damages" [18] (victim compensation). Ferri wrote: "I see that as early as 1847 Bonneville de Marsangy, with admirable common sense, stating that the private damage caused by crime was almost never paid, made . . . remarkable proposals." [19]

In addition to this recognition of Bonneville as a precursor by the Positivistic System of Social Defense, what has been called the New Social Defense or what Mannheim calls "The Third School" [20] of the mid-twentieth century, exemplified by Judge Marc Ancel, also claims Bonneville as one of the forerunners of this "new" movement, together with John Howard and Elizabeth Fry in England, Charles Lucas in France and Ducpétiaux in Belgium.[21]

The Italian as well as the New schools of Social Defense both stress the need to understand crime as a social and individual phenomenon, the need to prevent its commission or repetition and the need for asking oneself what attitude is to be adopted towards the criminal, beyond imposing the legal penalty. Ferri, however, went

[16] Clarence Ray Jeffery, *infra*, p. 458.
[17] Enrico Ferri, *Criminal Sociology* (Boston, 1917), pp. 502–509, esp. p. 505.
[18] *Ibid.*, pp. 509–515.
[19] *Ibid.*, p. 512.
[20] Hermann Mannheim, *supra*, p. 35.
[21] Ancel, *Social Defence*, p. 39.

so far as to maintain that, criminal law as such having allegedly failed, the field should be left open to medical and social action of a preventive nature in which the lawyers would have no place. As Ancel puts it: "The imperialistic monopoly of the criminal law was thus to be succeeded by a criminological imperialism, ill defined and probably all the more dangerous, preoccupied solely with practical efficacy." [22] The New Social Defense, on the other hand, took a moderate position, viewing the process of resocialization as one which can take place only by way of an ever-increasing humanization of the "new" criminal law. In its confrontation with the large and new field of social sciences, the New school has sought to preserve the "balance" between criminal law and criminology.

There is not the slightest doubt in our mind that, if Bonneville de Marsangy was living today and could see the development of the behavioral sciences as we know it, he would react favorably towards the moderate view which tries to make the best use of both criminal law and criminology, without according superiority to the one or the other.

André Normandeau.

BIBLIOGRAPHY

By Bonneville

BOOKS

De la liberté, de l'instruction, du travail et de la morale, comme bases du bonheur public (Paris, 1837).

Du sentiment du devoir chez les magistrats (Paris, 1838).

De la répression des plaideurs de mauvaise foi (Paris, 1843).

De la récidive, ou des moyens les plus efficaces pour constater, rechercher et reprimer les rechutes dans toute infraction à la loi pénale (2 volumes) (Paris, 1844).

Traité des diverses institutions complémentaires de régime pénitentiaire (Paris, 1847).

De l'amélioration de la loi criminelle, en vue d'une justice plus prompte, plus efficace, plus généreuse et plus moralisante (Paris, 1855–1864). (A third volume was written, but the author refused to publish it: *Traité analytique de la réforme du droit pénal et pénitentiaire,* 1874.)

De la moralité comparée de la femme et de l'homme (Paris, 1862).

PUBLISHED OFFICIAL MEMORANDA

"Mémoire sur l'enregistrement des traités de cession des offices ministériels au droit de 2%" (Saint-Amand, January 3, 1832).

[22] *Ibid.*, pp. 106–107.

"De la libération préparatoire des condamnés amendés" (Reims, November 3, 1846). Translated in *Report of the Prison Association of New York, 1867*, pp. 165–178.

"De la localisation au greffe de l'arrondissement natal des renseignements judiciaires concernant chaque condamné: Les casiers judiciaires" (Versailles, November 5, 1848).

ARTICLES

"Réparation civile en matière criminelle," *Revue pénitentiaire*, Vol. 4 (1847), pp. 444–463.

"De la répression pénale," *Revue contemporaine*, 2nd ser., Vol. 58 (1867), pp. 64–92.

"De la détention pénale," *Revue contemporaine*, 2nd ser., Vol. 58 (1867), pp. 240–279.

"Examiner la question de la libération conditionnelle des condamnés (amendés), abstraction faite du système irlandais," *Actes du Congrés Pénitentiaire International de Stockholm*, Vol. 1 (1878), pp. 283–289.

Bonneville also wrote many articles in a daily law newspaper called *Gazette des Tribunaux*.

ARTICLES PUBLISHED IN THE UNITED STATES

"On the Prisons of France," *Twenty-Third Annual Report of the Prison Association of New York* (Albany, N.Y., 1868), pp. 141–157.

"On the Mode of Preventive Detention," *ibid.*, pp. 158–164.

"Preparatory Liberation," *ibid.*, pp. 165–178.

"Criminal Registers in France," *Twenty-Fourth Annual Report of the Prison Association of New York* (Albany, N.Y., 1869), pp. 546–554.

"Criminal Registers as a Means of Knowing the Antecedents (criminal biography) of Persons Charged with Crime or Trespass," *Transactions of the National Congress on Penitentiary and Reformatory Discipline, Cincinnati, Ohio, 1870* (Albany, N.Y., 1871), pp. 232–243.

"Analytical Outline of a Scheme of Penal and Penitentiary Reform," *Transactions of the Third National Prison Reform Congress, St. Louis, Missouri, 1874*, pp. 643–673.

"Draft a Prison System," in *Transactions of the Fourth National Prison Congress, New York, N.Y., 1876*, pp. 218–232.

For the Note on this Contributor see p. 157.

8

CHARLES LUCAS

1803–1889

CHARLES (JEAN-MARIE) LUCAS was a well-known Parisian barrister, prison administrator and publicist, whose public influence in France and abroad in the field of penal reform was primarily important in the second and third quarters of the nineteenth century.

Born in Saint-Brieux (Brittany), near the shore of the English Channel and approximately 250 miles from Paris, on May 9, 1803, Lucas went to Paris for his college and university studies and received his degree in law in 1825.

A single event was to determine the final profile of his lifetime career. In effect, public competitions were opened in 1826, one by Count de Sellon of Geneva and another by the Society of Christian Morality of Paris, on the subject of the legitimacy and the efficacy of the death penalty. Lucas, as a youthful abolitionist, wrote a major essay on the topic and submitted it independently to both competitions. Both prizes were awarded to Lucas, whose work received careful attention by the press. The prizes ensured that Lucas would become a prominent figure in political and intellectual as well as in the more specialized penal reform circles. The work was published in 1827.[1] From that moment, Lucas's major endeavors were to deal mainly with criminological problems, especially in the field of penology. He was to try all his life to find an efficient replacement for the death penalty.

From 1828 to 1830, he published a three-volume work on *The Penitentiary System in Europe and the United States.* He sent this work to the members of the Chambers of Deputies and Peers with two special petitions demanding the introduction of the "penitentiary system" in France. This so-called penitentiary system referred at the time to the idealized version of the regime at the Walnut Street

* Reproduced from *The Journal of Criminal Law, Criminology and Police Science*, Vol. 61, No. 2, June 1970.
[1] Charles Lucas, *Du système pénal et du système répressif en général, de la peine de mort en particulier* (Paris, 1827).

Jail in Philadelphia. (The Duke of La Rochefoucauld Liancourt
had visited this jail in 1793 and published a small book on it in
1796.[2]) The prestigious French Academy awarded Lucas the Mon-
thyon Prize for his work, and his book was also publicly praised in
the Chambers' precincts. His case was good. The Chamber of
Deputies unanimously asked the government in November 1830 to
call Lucas to an administrative office where he could help in the
execution of penal reform.

As inspector general of French prisons, a job he would hold until
his retirement in 1865, Lucas had a direct contact with the practical
penal reality. On the basis of this empirical knowledge and of his
reading of the literature on prisons coming from the United States
(he never himself came to this country), he wrote his major book
in 1836 to 1838, another three-volume work[3] about prison reform
wherein he took a definite position against what is known as the
Philadelphia system of prison discipline and in favor of a revised
version of the Auburn system of prison discipline.

This work assured his fame in France and elsewhere. What has
been called in Europe the "penitentiary science" was born. It consisted of a systematic study and elaboration of the "best" prison
system to adopt. For many decades to come, Lucas was to assume
leadership of the movement. The *Grande Encyclopédie* of 1880
called him in fact the "creator of the penitentiary science," and the
International Penal Congresses of Stockholm (1878) and Rome
(1885) recognized Lucas as the "Dean of penitentiary reform
and master to all of us." On that international plane, we may
add, incidentally, that Lucas was a correspondent member at one
time or another of the Prison Societies of Paris, London, Dublin,
Philadelphia, Boston, and New York, as well as of the National
Institute for the Advancement of Sciences (Washington).[4]

As an active member of the famous French Academy of Moral
and Political Sciences for fifty years, Lucas read hundreds of papers
which were in most cases published in book form later on. All in
all, his work covers nearly forty volumes. It is thus impossible to

---

2 F. A. F. de La Rochefoucauld Liancourt, *Des prisons de Philadelphie* (Philadelphia,
1796). An English edition was published at the same time. The French version was reissued several times in France between 1796 and 1830.
3 Charles Lucas, *De la réforme des prisons ou de la théorie de l'emprisonnement* (Paris,
1836–1838).
4 The interested reader is referred to two memorial articles about Charles Lucas: Alphonse
Bérenger, *Mémoires de l'Académie des Sciences Morales et Politiques de l'Institut de
France*, Vol. 18 (1894), pp. 483–525; and Jules Simon, *ibid.*, Vol. 19 (1896), pp. 57–90.

present Lucas's ideas in terms of the common perspective provided by the bibliographical succession of even his major writings. It seems preferable here to present his substantial thoughts in terms of six unit-ideas: (1) the prison system, (2) the death penalty, (3) juvenile institutions, (4) transportation, (5) war, and (6) causation.

The first idea is the most important because the question of the "best" system of imprisonment was at the core of a large humanitarian movement in the nineteenth century and forms an important chapter in the "social history" of this century.

The prison system

The *ancien régime* (before 1789) used imprisonment primarily as a means of holding the suspected delinquent or the accused before trial or the convicted before sentence and execution, but not as a method of punishment *per se*. This latter idea came with the Enlightenment and the rational and humanitarian thinking of people like Beccaria, Montesquieu, Rousseau, Diderot, Voltaire, Howard, Bentham, and Romilly.[5]

The first half of the nineteenth century was to be the carrier of their ideas and was to become the cradle of the four major types of prison systems, which, when reduced to their most simple elements, are the following: (a) the "congregate" prison, where prisoners live, work, eat and sleep in common, and are allowed to talk; (b) the "absolute solitary confinement," identified originally with the Walnut Street Jail, where prisoners live in an individual cell night and day without working; (c) the "relative solitary confinement," identified with the Eastern State Penitentiary in Philadelphia (variously labeled also cellular, Pennsylvania, or Cherry Hill), where prisoners live in an individual cell night and day but are allowed to work; and finally (d) the so-called "silent" or "Auburn" system where prisoners work and eat in common but in silence during the day, though they sleep in individual cells at night.

The first prisons in France were patterned on the congregate type, with all the promiscuity involved in these circumstances. Following the French Revolution of 1789, members of the Constituent

[5] The few scattered institutional antecedents have been described in some articles by Thorsten Sellin: "Filippo Franci: a Precursor of Modern Penology," *Journal of Criminal Law and Criminology*, Vol. 17 (1926), p. 104; "Prison Reform in Belgium," *ibid.*, Vol. 17 (1926), p. 264; "Dom Jean Mabillon: A Prison Reformer of the 17th Century," *ibid.*, Vol. 17 (1927), p. 581; "The House of Correction for Boys in the Hospices of St. Michael in Rome," *ibid.*, Vol. 20 (1930), p. 533; "The Historical Background of Our Prisons," *Annals*, Vol. 81 (1931), p. 1. See also his book: *Pioneering in Penology: The Amsterdam Houses of Correction in the 16th and 17th Centuries* (Philadelphia, 1944).

Assembly proposed bills to reform prisons, some in favor of the solitary confinement system, some in favor of the silent system. These bills never passed, however, because of political upheavals. Another attempt to install solitary confinement in French prisons was made in 1814 by Louis XVIII. The turmoil of the Hundred Days of Napoleon prevented the execution of the law. The second major attempt by France to reform its prisons thus also failed. A Royal Society of Prisons was then created, in 1819, in order to improve penal institutions. Just at the time when the Society's work was to lead to a major reform, it was dissolved by the July Revolution of 1830.[6]

The following years, however, were to be the most fruitful. The period 1830–1848, in effect, was probably the most active time of discussions on prison reform that has ever existed, at least in France, if not everywhere. A publicist of the time wrote, indeed, that "there is no question, not even a political question, which has engendered a greater amount of publications. . . . It seems that one cannot die without having done, with his testament, a little brochure on the penitentiary system." [7] And Lucas was to write himself, ironically, that "the penitentiary reform question one day became fashionable and required only some wit, without the necessity of any practical knowledge; so that, in a nation as gifted with wit as ours, an innumerable amount of writings were and are written which will constitute in a very short while a course in penitentiary literature." [8]

The main point of the debate by then was focused on the efficacy of the solitary confinement system as exemplified in Philadelphia, versus the silent system used in Auburn.

Alexis de Tocqueville and Gustave de Beaumont were the first and most noted of the supporters of the separate discipline. In 1831 these young magistrates persuaded the minister of the interior to commission them to visit the United States and report on the prisons there. During their tour of this country, they discovered a storm raging in American prison circles as to the value of the disciplines used in its two leading prisons. Auburn officials tried to convince the French commissioners that France should adopt the silent

---

[6] A fine historical penological sketch of this French period, as well as up to 1850, is found in Thorsten Sellin's Introduction to an abridged edition of Gustave de Beaumont and Alexis de Tocqueville, *On the Penitentiary System in the United States* (1964), p. xv. See also John H. Cary, "France Looks to Pennsylvania," *Pennsylvania Magazine of History and Biography*, Vol. 82 (1958), p. 186.

[7] Louis M. Moreau-Christophe, "Défense du projet de lois sur les prisons," *Revue Pénitentiaire*, Vol. 3 (1846), p. 400.

[8] Quoted in Jean Pinatel, "La Vie et l'œuvre de Charles Lucas," *Revue Internationale de Droit Pénal*, Vol. 18 (1947), p. 126.

system, since separating each convict during his entire confinement made madmen of many of the prisoners at Philadelphia. On the other hand, the officials at Eastern State Penitentiary argued that the Auburn system was too lax, and that the solitude of their own system actually reformed the convicts by giving them an opportunity to meditate on their crimes and, by their gaining an "inner light" —one of the central tenets of Quaker theology—to correct their evil dispositions. In the official reports of their trip to America, published in 1833,[9] Tocqueville and Beaumont tried to remain nonpartisan and to avoid committing themselves to the support of either of the American prison disciplines. Actually, they did believe that the Philadelphia institution did more to reform convicts. It was thus but a short time after this that Tocqueville and Beaumont, because of severe criticism of separate confinement in France, were defending the Pennsylvania prison in the Chamber of Deputies and creating in the European mind an image of it as the most important penal institution in the Western Hemisphere.

The report of Tocqueville and Beaumont set the stage for the struggle over adoption of the separate system. Other writers and reformers took their cue and entered the fight, some in support of and others in opposition to individual confinement. Tocqueville was undoubtedly the leader of the partisans of the Philadelphia system. Their opponents sided with Charles Lucas, who was giving his allegiance to the Auburn system.

Lucas was already one of the most distinguished of all French penal reformers when he published in 1836-1838 his *Reform of Prisons or Theory of Imprisonment*. His humanitarian position was clearly stated from the beginning. Punishment should not be the aim but merely an instrument of penal policy. The true object ought to be the protection of society, and the means to this end were the prevention of crime and reformation of the criminal. Reformation, in this context, was understood as turning the obnoxious and troublesome into tolerable, acceptable, and, if possible, useful citizens. Lucas's motto, stated in the introduction to the book, was significant in regard to his general approach. He wrote in a sociological vein where society was held liable for the criminals in its wake: "It is time that human justice washes its hands in front of God and men

---

[9] Gustave de Beaumont and Alexis de Tocqueville, *On the Penitentiary System in the United States*, trans. Francis Lieber (Philadelphia, 1833). See also George W. Pierson, *Tocqueville and Beaumont in America* (New York, 1938).

of the terrible reproach to the effect that it contributes to increase rather than to diminish the stain of crime." [10] His philosophy of punishment was in fact a philosophy of social rehabilitation when he said, "Society finds the criminal. This is a first healing. However, the criminal is in fact a sick person in a social sense who must be healed not by medical cures but by social cures." [11] So that, by healing criminals, we heal society itself. For Lucas, thus, education was to represent the instrument *par excellence* of a penitentiary system; the aim of such education was to repair the failure of social education. Prisons were, in a sense, schools. By the same token, and well before the Italian school, Lucas turned the attention of lawyers and criminologists "from the crime to the criminal," as the old cliché has it. As Lucas put it:

Legislators have forgotten the actors and focused only on the acts. . . . Such codes are based on false and vicious presumptions. . . . False, because in reality the degree of perversity of a crime changes with each actor since the intentionality is different. . . . Vicious, because reformation is more or less rapid according to this degree of perversity; thus the length of punishment should be proportionate to the actor's perversity and not to his violation as such, because, for two offenders having committed the same crime, a certain amount of corrective detention will be necessary for one and another amount for the other. But when punishment is proportionate to the criminal act only, we are opened each day to detain a reformed man and to release an unregenerated man. Repressive justice should then be focused on agents and not on acts.[12]

Lucas's method of study, finally, was scientific and comparative. "The important study," he wrote, "is the one related to man, his nature, his penchants, to the factors which maintain him in the right track or alienate him from it as well as those which may help to bring him back to it after the fall. The stability of the social body demands from the legislator, nowadays, that element which has long been absent but is now prevalent in the medical approach to the human body, i.e. *science*." [13] And reflecting more specifically on his work, he added: "There are two languages in Society, one is science and is concerned with the finding of truth, the other is teaching and is a way to get the masses to understand what has been discovered rigorously by science. I hope that my language pertains

[10] Lucas, *De la réforme des prisons*, Vol. I.
[11] *Ibid.*, p. 25.
[12] Lucas, *Du système pénal*, pp. 276, 281–282.
[13] Lucas, *De la réforme des prisons*, p. lxxv.

to the first one." [14]   As to his comparative method, Lucas was quick
to study the penal legislations and their practical outputs in terms of
penal institutions of several countries. It is in this sense that the
American penitentiary system was highly praised by Lucas. "Why
not supplement," he wrote to the Chambers, "our lack of knowledge
by the abundance of their researches? On what basis could we
disdain the evidence of their experience, and trust only ours?" [15]

Lucas's practical solutions, again well in advance of his time,
were in the realm of a progressive prison system and the use of the
indeterminate sentence and parole, although this terminology was
not used by him and appeared on the "penological verbal market"
only several decades after.

These modern ideas were delineated by Lucas, for example, as
early as 1827, when he proposed a system of minimum and maximum sentences, in which the judge would consider extenuating
circumstances (which means in fact a consideration of the actor
rather than, or in addition to, the act). Five such categories of
sentence were recommended: up to five years of imprisonment, 5 to
10, 10 to 15, 15 to 20, and 20 to 25. However, once the criminal
was in prison, a discretionary power over each prisoner's time to
serve was allowed by Lucas to a disciplinary board, and eventually
to what we could call today a parole board, whose function was to
reclassify each prisoner according to his moral improvement. In
this fashion, the court sentence was to become, in fact, wholly indeterminate. Thus, a prisoner condemned to 20 to 25 years of
imprisonment could be reclassified in the next lower category after
two years, in a lower one again after another year, and then, after
two and a half years, in the 5-to-10-year category, in which he would
become eligible for parole which he could achieve, let us say, after
six months. Condemned originally to 20 to 25 years, this individual
could win his freedom in only six years, if rapid signs of regeneration could be detected by the board. Another prisoner with the
same 20 to 25 years sentence, however, could stay ten years in the
same category, and be only at the 10 to 15 years stage after 25 years
of imprisonment. As Lucas put it:

> In the first instance, justice would have ascertained the perversity of the
> criminal in an exaggerated negative way; in the second, in an exaggerated
> positive way. But the control of experience in prison would repair these

[14] *Ibid.,* p. 29.
[15] Charles Lucas, *Du système pénitentiaire en Europe et aux Etats-Unis* (Paris, 1828–1830),
Vol. I, p. xiii.

errors, one of which would have unduly extended the captivity of a man who was not dangerous any more, and the other would have given back to society a man still dangerous.[16]

Lucas later reduced these five categories to three, which he called "categories of moralities," consisting of a class of exceptions or punishments, a class of trials or testing, and a class of rewards or permissions. But this "moral screening" was essentially a reformulation of the very same principle imbedded in his progressive system of five categories.

This idea of classification was coupled with one stressing the further different disciplinary regime in each category, with a progressive liberalization of the rules. The last stage would even be accompanied by relatively free walks of the prisoner in the city or the village in order to reconnect, little by little, the culprit with the community. This very same classificatory idea led him also, obviously, to stress the need for separate institutions for adults and juveniles, and for males and females. (We may mention here, even if it is not directly relevant, that Lucas knew the difficulties he would encounter from the inside in order to implement his scheme. Using the old image of the congregate prisons as training schools which breed crime and grant Ph.D.s in criminal know-how, Lucas, as a forerunner of the sociology of prison organization, talked about the underground structure of the prison society with its professors and teachers of vices, the inmate's hierarchy of power, and the prisoners' peculiar dialects, rules, politics, policing and penalties or rewards, etc.[17] Lucas made here the well-known distinction between what he called "social criminality," *i.e.,* the ordinary criminality which grows outside prison walls, and "scholarly or erudite criminality" which is formed in prison. One of his solutions to the problem was the establishment by the government of a special educational institute devoted to the training of professional correctional administrators and personnel.) [18]

But what physical setting could "best" implement these ideas of penitentiary reforms? Lucas, as well as his contemporaries, had the two main models already well described by Tocqueville and Beaumont: the Philadelphia and the Auburn systems.[19] Tocqueville and

---

[16] Lucas, *Du système pénal*, p. 308.
[17] *Ibid.*, pp. 282–283.
[18] Lucas, *Du système pénitentiaire*, p. lxxix.
[19] See the following studies on the subject: Harry Elmer Barnes, *The Repression of Crime: Studies in Historical Penology* (1926; reprinted Montclair, N.J., 1969); Harry Elmer

his followers had sided with the Philadelphia system; Lucas and his sided with a revised Auburn system.

Lucas believed that life in common during the day was absolutely essential to the preservation of the mental and physical faculties of man. Man was born sociable and total solitude, like that of the Philadelphia system, was a state against nature. Man was bound to live in society, and it was among members of this society that he had to learn to behave in a proper social way. As he put it: "Solitary confinement cannot be for a long-termer the right preparation for the social milieu from which he stemmed and to which he must return when he is set free from prison." [20] Lucas would have permitted the use of separate confinement, but only for those awaiting trial, for those sentenced to two years or less, and as an extraordinary punishment for incorrigibles and convicts who violated prison regulations. And, even in the case of persons sentenced to two years or less, if the term was served in solitary, Lucas recommended an automatic reduction in sentence to a maximum of one year. He also felt that prisoners subjected to this discipline should be allowed to speak to each other, to families, and to friends, with permission, and to attend chapel services together. As for the bulk of prisoners living under the silent Auburn system, he would never allow the use of corporal punishment or the whip, as it was done in Auburn to enforce the rule of silence. He would enforce this rule by the threat of an increase of the time to serve in prison since his system provided for an indeterminate sentence.

Lucas, in addition to his argument of sociability, put forth three main objections to the Philadelphia system: (a) it increased expenses in construction and operation; (b) it increased the rates of physical and mental disabilities; and (c) it increased the rates of recidivists.

Tocqueville and the champions of the Philadelphia system agreed with the first point. However, they ingeniously argued that the danger of riots and escapes in prisons with the silent discipline was

Barnes, *The Evolution of Penology in Pennsylvania: A Study in American Social History* (1927; reprinted Montclair, N.J., 1968); Negley K. Teeters, *The Cradle of the Penitentiary: The Walnut Street Jail at Philadelphia, 1773–1835* (Philadelphia, 1955); Negley K. Teeters and John D. Shearer, *The Prison at Philadelphia: Cherry Hill* (New York, 1957); Le Roy De Puy, "The Walnut Street Prison: Pennsylvania's First Penitentiary," *Pennsylvania History,* Vol. 18 (1951), p. 130; Le Roy De Puy, "The Triumph of The Pennsylvania System as a State's Penitentiary," *Pennsylvania History,* Vol. 21 (1954), p. 128; John H. Cary, "France Looks to Pennsylvania," *Pennsylvania Magazine of History and Biography,* Vol. 82 (1958), p. 186.
20 Lucas, *De la réforme des prisons,* Vol. III, p. 484.

much greater than in institutions on the Pennsylvania plan. This raised personnel costs to ensure security, thereby offsetting the difference in construction and operation expenses. As for the rates of disabilities and recidivists, this matter could be discussed only on the basis of the statistics given by the American administrators and partisans of each system. Obviously, two difficulties were involved here in assessing the validity and reliability of these statistics. First, the factual statistics collected were scarce. Second, the collection, organization and presentation of these statistics were often done by each group with the explicit *a priori* purpose of proving a point in opposition to one another—thus biasing these official statistics. In fact, the same set of statistics was sometimes turned upside down by one group to prove exactly the reverse of the position taken by the other group on the basis of this very same set of statistics. In the United States, the Boston Prison Discipline Society, headed by Louis Dwight, was prominent in the use of statistics in this fashion to defend the Auburn system, whereas the Philadelphia Society for Alleviating the Miseries of Public Prisons proceeded to do the opposite.[21] The usefulness of these statistics was certainly not increased in France when Lucas and his friends relied on the statistics published by the Boston Society whereas Tocqueville's group relied on the Philadelphia Society's publications. In fact, what has been said by Barnes about the unfairness and dishonesty (or perhaps it was only plain naïveté) of the American belligerents could be applied to the French antagonists:

> A careful examination of the polemic pamphlets of both parties cannot fail to impress an impartial reader with the fact that neither was qualified to cast the first stone. Both were fiercely partisan and both were disgracefully unscrupulous in their use of statistics designed to support their cause or damage that of their opponents.[22]

Be that as it may, the supporters of the Pennsylvania system in France were making headway, despite the strong opposition of Lucas and those of his party. An administrative decree in 1841 outlined a program for individual separation by day and night. But the advocates of the Philadelphia system, feeling that a legislative act would be more permanent and authoritative than an administrative

[21] *Reports of the Prison Discipline Society of Boston* (1826–1854; reprinted Montclair, N.J., 1972); *The Pennsylvania Journal of Prison Discipline and Philanthropy* (Philadelphia, 1845–   ).
[22] Harry Elmer Barnes, "The Historical Origin of the Prison System in America," *Journal of Criminal Law and Criminology*, Vol. 12 (1921), p. 58.

circular, supported legislation from 1843 to 1848 in the Chambers
of Deputies and Peers in this direction. A bill providing for the
creation of a system of prisons on the Auburn plan had already been
proposed in 1840. It was defeated. This time, in 1843, the supporters of a bill for the introduction of the Pennsylvania discipline
in French prisons were larger than ever in prestige as well as in
numbers. They had strong batteries firing rounds in defense of the
separate system. Tocqueville himself introduced the bill on July 5.
However, because of the opposition Lucas was able to muster, and
because of certain different points of view among the Philadelphia
partisans themselves as to the appropriate length of the separate
confinement (from a maximum of ten years to a full term of the
sentence), the debates lasted for five years. As finally accepted, for
presentation to a final vote, the bill provided for isolation by day and
night for the entire length of a prison sentence.[23]

But, once again, political revolution was to interfere with social
reform. The bill was on the point of being voted when the Revolution of February, 1848, overthrew the government which had sponsored it.

Not all was yet lost for the supporters of the separate system. An
administrative decree in 1849 confirmed the one of 1841 and ordered
both the continuation of work already begun and the construction
of new departmental prisons on the separate discipline plan. Thus,
by the end of 1851, despite the legislative defeats of Tocqueville and
his group, forty-seven departmental prisons had been established on
the solitary plan and fifteen more were in the process of construction. In this sense, Lucas seemed to have lost the battle.

However, Louis Napoleon effectively brought the Second Republic to an end by his *coup d'état* of December 2, 1851. Again
politics wiped out the victories achieved by Tocqueville's group.
The previous decrees were abrogated, the congregate system was
fully reinstalled, and a system of transportation to the colonies was
instituted in 1854.

Under Napoleon III's totalitarian tendencies, the entire prison
reform movement was effectively suppressed for more than twenty
years.

By the time France underwent another revolutionary change in
government in 1870, Tocqueville had died and Lucas was almost the

[23] See details in Paul Cuche, *Traité de science et de législation pénitentiaires* (Paris, 1905);
Georges Vidal, *Cours de droit criminel et de science pénitentiaire*, 2nd ed. (Paris, 1910).

only prominent figure in the field to hand on the tradition of prison reform to a new group of men who were to be active during the Third Republic. As a result it was a moderate, compromise plan of Lucas's, rather than the full separate system, which was embodied in the famous prison reform law of June 5, 1875. Only offenders sentenced to one year and one day or less were to be confined in the "solitary" prisons. The Auburn discipline would be used for all the other inmates.

Lucas had won a great victory, which crowned his life's work. But he had been fortunate in that politics, more than anything else, had killed the penal reforms of the Philadelphia supporters. In a socio-historical perspective, the relationship of the penal reform movement to France's political history, illustrating the close relationship of a nation's political development and its social and cultural history, is of significance today for a study of social reform strategies in a world where politics still has the final word.

The death penalty

The main theme of Lucas's first book in 1827 was the death penalty, on which he took a firm abolitionist viewpoint. He attached great importance to the problem all his life and never abandoned a personal predilection for it. In fact, he used to say that he had been interested in prison reform only inasmuch as he had been looking for a "replacement penalty" for the death penalty.

The work of 1827 was devoted principally to an examination of the legitimacy and efficacy of the death penalty. On the philosophical level, he was defending the idea of the inviolability of human life, save for self-defense. Traditional viewpoints pertaining to the spirit of Christianity, the natural rights of man and the rights of society to punish, were used in an elegant fashion by Lucas. On the practical level, however, Lucas was bolder. In a Beccarian style, he maintained three fundamental principles: (a) that the efficacy of penalties depends on the certainty and proximity of repression; (b) that the certainty is in inverse relationship with the severity of penalties; and (c) that, in this perspective, the death penalty was, of all penalties, the least repressive. Lucas then proceeded to prove these assertions by statistical data related to the number of indictments and accused, acquittals, condemnations and commutations, for capital crimes in France for the years 1825 and 1826. If, by chance, the offender was arrested, there was a fifty percent chance that he would be acquitted. Condemned, he had again a fifty percent chance that death would not be pronounced in his case. Even if condemned to death, he had a twenty percent chance of being pardoned. All in all, a capital offender had less than one chance out of ten to die under the guillotine. How could the death penalty be effective and deterrent in such a state of affairs?

His interest in the question led Lucas to study the legislations in almost every country in the world, to write special petitions to the Chambers of Deputies and Peers of France as well as to the leaders of other countries. It is astonishing that so many European countries have abolished the death penalty whereas France still has it in 1970.

Juvenile institutions

Lucas's theory of the necessity for the individualization of treatment was bound to focus its attention on juvenile delinquents because it was obvious to him (as it still is to us today) that to combat criminality at its roots was the best safeguard for the future.

Lucas began by insisting that juveniles should be separated from adult inmates. As early as 1828–30, he proposed the creation of "schools of reform" for juveniles. His petitions to the Chambers at the time explicitly called for the establishment of such special institutions for juveniles under a discipline of the Auburn type. A strong emphasis on education was the main feature of his proposal. A specific project to this effect was proposed by Lucas in 1831 to a special State Committee. In addition to his earlier general scheme, Lucas stressed the necessity for a complementary post-prison institution, called "patronage," for juveniles. This *patronage* was to be equivalent, broadly speaking, to a "house of refuge" or, in modern terminology, a "halfway house." Lucas founded, with Alphonse Bérenger, the first society of *patronage* in Paris in 1833.

In 1832, the Paris institution for juvenile delinquents, La Petite Roquette, had been intended to embody in its system of treatment many of Lucas's ideas. However, the system came to be modeled on the Pennsylvania system, and Lucas rejected it as obviously uneducational and unrehabilitative.

While waiting for governmental action, private institutions for juveniles began to proliferate. Lucas organized one of the first in

Bordeaux in 1834. The same year, he wrote a brochure in which he suggested the establishment of "agricultural colonies" and coined his well-known slogan: "The regeneration of the child by the land, and the land by the child." This stimulus led Frédéric Auguste Demetz and Lucas to some practical endeavors. They became the founders, and for many years the heads, of agricultural colonies, Demetz at Mettray in 1839 and Lucas at Val d'Yèvre in 1843. These establishments had accommodation for 500 to 700 young offenders who were admitted when under sixteen. A family system was predominant. The institution consisted of various houses, each the home of a family of thirty to fifty inmates. The congregate system was used at Mettray, but the Auburn system at Val d'Yèvre, although the cells here looked much more like rooms than anything else. The importance of a new type of personnel as a prerequisite for constructive work was recognized as essential. Teachers were especially trained for educational and social work. The agricultural work gave ample opportunity for healthy employment. It was, in fact, a real educational system, based on moral persuasion rather than on force, with the object of making the juvenile capable of self-control and self-support. Discharged boys were placed under the supervision of a patron, and often the institution remained in touch with the boy's employer.

A law in August 1850 about the education and patronage of young inmates established Lucas's, Bérenger's, and Demetz's work in this domain. And, in 1872, the State bought Lucas's institution at Val d'Yèvre, and special institutions for young offenders became even more numerous under the leadership of the government.

Transportation

Lucas was preoccupied all his life with the unification of all criminal sentences into one consistent sanction: imprisonment. The time element was to be the central factor in aggravating or mitigating a punishment according to the moral aim in view. It is in this perspective that Lucas, as early as 1827, took a strong stand (a) against the "bagnes" (these hulks or shore prisons that had succeeded the French penal galleys), and (b) against transportation and colonization. He attacked particularly the then extensive English system of transportation to Australia as inhuman and inefficient. As he put it: "Societies must absorb their criminality and must not try to throw it out arbitrarily on an unknown land."[24]

The "bagnes" were indeed replaced in 1854, but by transportation to the colonies, and not by imprisonment as wished by Lucas. The transportation system was even extended in 1885. It was to disappear only during World War II, when imprisonment then became the general and uniform punishment in France . . . more than a century after Lucas's suggestion.

Causation

Causation of crime as viewed by Lucas was related to misery and lack of education—to a lack in "civilization," as he put it. In a little study of criminality in France, in 1827, Lucas started from an analysis of the French criminal statistics for 1825 and 1826, and divided France into two groups, the "Bright France" and the "Obscure France," according to their intellectual and material resources, using indices like the number of book stores, the level of education, or the amount of taxes paid. "Bright" was identified with "civilized." He examined in these two Frances the crimes against property and the crimes against the person. He found fewer crimes against the person in the "Bright France" but more crimes against property. He thought it was significant in view of the fact that crimes against the person were more immoral. He concluded: "Thus, we have proven, with mathematical rigor, this great truth that, with civilization, our persons are more secure. Even our property is, because the relative increase of this type of crime among civilized people, compared with others, is simply the result of the multiplicity for evil in the former since they are richer."[25] In a similar vein, and using extensively the available statistics for a series of years and from many places (France, England, Pennsylvania, Geneva, and Spain), Lucas tried to prove the moral influence of civilized nations on the decrease in criminality. His conclusion was as before: personal crimes diminish proportionately as civilization increases and even property crimes do so, in a way.[26] His thesis was clear: the increase in well-being, work and business, in short the whole advance of material prosperity, brings with it a proportional increase in the number of crimes. The theory is to the effect that there is a

[24] Lucas, *Du système pénal*, p. 336.
[25] *Ibid.*, p. xxxiv.
[26] Lucas, *Du système pénitentiaire*.

proportion between evil activity (crime) and honest activity (commerce, industry, and affairs). It rests upon the principle that when the latter increases, there necessarily is a stimulation to the former, so that the increase in crime would be merely an apparent increase if it were exactly in proportion to the progress of honest activity. If we admit this premise, that an increase in the number of crimes that is exactly proportionate to the increase in material progress is without importance, signifying in reality that crime is stationary, then it follows that an increase in crime proportionately less than the increase in prosperity really means that crime has diminished. We might therefore find in a given period double the number of crimes of the preceding period, and at the same time be obliged to recognize a "real" diminution in criminality. Lucas wrote:

> Civilization, which is merely the progress of liberty, widens the abuse of liberty, precisely because it extends its use. To obtain an exact notion of the morality of civilization, we must, instead of contrasting liberty and civilization, place on one side of the balance the use, and on the other the abuse of liberty. Let us establish the rule that the morality of civilization is to be judged by comparing the use with the abuse.[27]

This principle once posited, he sees little ground for alarm in the larger number of certain classes of offenses appearing in France, as compared with Spain:

> We are not called upon to give especial credit to a poverty-stricken and ignorant people because of the small number of harmful acts occurring in their midst. This fact is due to the lack of occasion for inflicting harm; to nothing else than an animal-like ignorance. The greater number of such acts occurring among civilized peoples is merely the result of a larger development of human freedom.[28]

War

Lucas, notwithstanding the onset of blindness in 1863, never gave up his activism in the cause of penal reform. The contrary indeed is true. However, he did find, in addition to his old interests, a new one. He became, after the Franco-German War of 1870–1871, an "apostle of international law." But this new role was not so far away from his role as a penal reformer. It was in complete harmony with his whole life and work. In effect, he started his study

27 *Ibid.*, p. xiv.
28 *Ibid.*

of the death-penalty problem by investigating society's right to punish. The problems of prison and war stemmed from the same starting-point, *i.e.,* the question of self-defense. He wrote:

> What is a reform relative to the abolition of the death penalty if it does not acknowledge the principle that, in the criminal penalty as in war, we must respect, with regard to the culprit as well as to the disarmed warrior, human life, save in the case of self-defense? And what is a penitentiary reform if it is not only a purely defensive right which consists in neutralizing the disarmed culprit by privation of liberty, but also a duty to work so as to rehabilitate the criminal in order to curb recidivism? Thus, in penal sanction as in war, we do not proceed against the law, which is based on the respect for life and for man's freedom; but we must, on the contrary, sanctify this respect by proclaiming the principles of life's inviolability and of man's freedom, save in the case of self-defense.[29]

On the occasion of the First International Penitentiary Congress, held in London, in 1872, Lucas concluded that two complementary congresses, logical consequences of the Penitentiary Congress, were necessary: one to work for the abolition of the death penalty; the other for the abolition of a war civilization and the renewal of a peaceful Christian civilization. He focused on the idea of a "mediator" between nations, somewhat similar to a United Nations organization.

Lucas did not only talk on the subject. He was active in promoting a French organization for peace and an International Institute for the Rights of Man, and wrote to political leaders such as Gladstone, the future Prime Minister of England, and Rutherford B. Hayes, President of the United States.

Conclusion

Modern penology has always tended to favor a penitentiary regime largely based on scientific selection of convicts. It has been dominated by the notions of individualization and progressiveness. When this conception is based on a more general doctrine where the supremacy of the prison as a mode of execution of punishment is stressed, we see immediately how Lucas fits perfectly well in the contemporary penological scheme.

In effect, let us only recall here some of the major concepts developed by Lucas, often quite in advance of his time and all initially developed in the few years between 1827 and 1838 when he

[29] Quoted in Pinatel, "La Vie et l'œuvre de Charles Lucas," pp. 130–131.

wrote his three leading books: the importance of the criminal as an individual and actor over the crime and the act; classification (by necessity based on a social and personality study of the offender, however rough such a study would have been in Lucas's time); indeterminate sentence; parole; special institutions and care for juveniles; halfway houses; etc. These concepts are also at the very heart of the modern conception, without any doubt, and can be encapsulated by the two more encompassing ideas which Marc Ancel, the leader of the New School of Social Defense in Europe, has stressed in his recent book: "a rational penal policy aimed at the systematic *resocialization* of the offender," and "an ever-increasing *humanization* of the new criminal law." [30]

It is thus not surprising at all to hear Ancel claiming the name and works of Lucas as a challenging figure in the field of criminal law and criminology, and as a pioneer in the movement of the New Social Defense which tries to achieve a balance between criminal law and criminology without any imperialism of one over the other so as to eliminate any "cold war atmosphere." As Ancel puts it:

> If time allowed, it might . . . be possible to seek in the doctrinal writings of the nineteenth century, underneath the thick shell constituted by the legalistic theory of classical criminal law, the first rather fugitive and cloistered glimpses of theories of social defense. In this connexion . . . there was the important movement in favor of the *individualization* of penalties which was to make a significant and notable contribution to the legislative developments of the nineteenth century. . . . The prison reform movement which emerged in the last years of the eighteenth century with the work of John Howard and Elizabeth Fry in England, leading to the "penitentiary school" of the mid-nineteenth century associated with the names of Charles Lucas, Bonneville de Marsangy, and Ducpétiaux, revealed the possibilities and the advantages of the re-education of offenders.[31]

And elsewhere: "when the United Nations, in 1958, adopted the *minima rules* on the treatment of inmates, prepared by the International Penal and Penitentiary Commission, they were joining the great tradition of John Howard, Elizabeth Fry, Charles Lucas and Bonneville de Marsangy. . . ." [32]

We may put a final point to our investigation by quoting a very sensitive thought that Lucas expressed near the end of his life and which should inspire in us the energy to follow his path and, at the

---

[30] Marc Ancel, *Social Defence,* pp. 24–25.
[31] *Ibid.,* pp. 38–40.
[32] Marc Ancel, "La Défense sociale nouvelle," *Revue de Science Criminelle et de Droit Pénal Comparé,* Vol. 14, p. 201.

same time, the modesty of self-limitation. On November 6, 1875, at the Institute, he said:

Fifty years of studies is a lot in the lifetime of a man. But, it is so little for finding a solution to the problem of penitentiary education when we think that, for 2000 years, people have discussed the role of education in the family and in the State. I have no illusions, and the only objective I may aspire to is to bring a very modest stone to the building of this great movement of penitentiary education which will develop only gradually in the course of the years, thanks to the persevering work of science, the accumulated data carried by experience, and the continued action of time.[33]

ANDRÉ NORMANDEAU.

BIBLIOGRAPHY

By Lucas

Du système pénal et du système répressif en général, de la peine de mort en particulier (Paris, 1827).

Du système pénitentiaire en Europe et aux Etats-Unis (3 volumes) (Paris, 1828–1830).

Recueil des débats des assemblées législatives de la France sur la question de la peine de mort (Paris, 1831).

De la réforme des prisons ou de la théorie de l'emprisonnement (3 volumes) (Paris, 1836–1838).

Des moyens et des conditions de la réforme pénitentiaire en France (Paris, 1848).

Le Droit de légitime défense dans la pénalité et dans la guerre (Paris, 1873).

La Civilisation de la guerre (Paris, 1881).

De l'état anormal en France de la répression en matière de crimes capitaux et des moyens d'y remédier (Paris, 1885).

Lucas also wrote hundreds of pamphlets, memoirs and articles. Many of them have been published in the *Proceedings* of the Académie des Sciences Morales et Politiques, of which Lucas was a member for more than fifty years (1833–1889). We take the liberty of referring the reader to this primary source.

General

AYLIES, SÉVERIN. *Du système pénitentiaire et de ses conditions fondamentales* (Paris, 1837).

BÉRENGER, ALPHONSE. *Des moyens propres à généraliser en France le système pénitentiaire* (Paris, 1837).

BLOUET, GUILLAUME ABEL, and DEMETZ, FRÉDÉRIC AUGUSTE. *Rapports à M. le comte de Montalivet . . . sur les pénitenciers aux Etats-Unis* (Paris, 1837).

[33] Quoted in Pinatel, "La Vie et l'œuvre de Charles Lucas," p. 154.

BLOUET, GUILLAUME ABEL. *Projet de prison cellulaire* (Paris, 1843).

DEMETZ, FRÉDÉRIC AUGUSTE. *Résumé des questions pénitentiaires* (Paris, 1847).

DUCPÉTIAUX, EDOUARD. *Du progrès et de l'état actuel de la réforme péniten-tiaire et des institutions préventives aux Etats-Unis, en France, en Suisse, en Angleterre et en Belgique* (3 volumes) (Bruxelles, 1837–1838).

FAUCHER, LÉON. *De la réforme des prisons* (Paris, 1838).

FOUCHER, VICTOR. *Sur la réforme des prisons* (Rennes, 1838).

LA ROCHEFOUCAULD LIANCOURT, FRÉDÉRIC GAËTAN DE. *Documents relatifs au système pénitentiaire* (Paris, 1844).

MOREAU-CHRISTOPHE, LOUIS M. *Rapport à M. le comte de Montalivet . . . sur les prisons de l'Angleterre, de l'Ecosse, de la Hollande, de la Belgique et de la Suisse* (Paris, 1836).

—— *De l'état actuel des prisons en France, considéré dans ses rapports avec la théorie pénale du Code* (Paris, 1838).

—— *De la mortalité et de la folie dans le régime pénitentiaire* (Paris, 1839).

VARRENTRAPP, GEORG. *De l'emprisonnement individuel* (Paris, 1844).

Revue Pénitentiaire et des Institutions Préventives, edited by L. Moreau-Christophe from 1843 to 1847.

NOTE ON THE CONTRIBUTOR

Dr. ANDRÉ NORMANDEAU received his Ph.D. in Sociology from the University of Pennsylvania in 1968, and is now Chairman of the Department of Criminology at the University of Montreal. He is the author of *The Public Looks at Crime and Corrections in Quebec* (with E. Fattah, 1969) and *Attitude Surveys on Crime in Montreal* (1969), and, with D. Szabo, the editor of *Deviance and Criminality* (1970) and *The Cost of Crime and Crime Control* (1971). He has also published extensively on crime statistics, shoplifting, and violence, in professional journals throughout the world.

9

KARL ROEDER

1806–1879

KARL DAVID AUGUST ROEDER was born on June 23, 1806, in Darmstadt, Germany, into an officer's family. In 1822 he entered the University of Göttingen and later continued to Heidelberg. After his law studies he worked for a couple of years in the public service of his native state, Hessen, but returned to his studies. In 1830 he earned his doctor's degree at the University of Giessen with a dissertation *De usuris in futuris acceptis.* He taught a private course on the theory of criminal law, but was prohibited from lecturing in political science, as his theories were considered revolutionary. He became "Dozent" of criminal law at Heidelberg in 1839 after having written another book on criminal law in the same year, *Commentatio de questione an poena malum esse debeat,* and in 1842 he returned to Heidelberg University for the rest of his life. In 1879 he was appointed honorary professor. His main inspiration came from the German philosopher Karl Christian Friedrich Krause (1781–1832), whose *System der Rechtsphilosophie* he finally brought out in 1874. In the preface Roeder relates that although he heard Krause lecture only once he still (more than forty years later) remembered the deep impression the lecture had made upon all those present. As early as 1837 he started his writing on political theory, legal philosophy, and criminal law, which continued without interruption to his death. After some years, however, he specialized in penology and became the main propagandist in his generation of the Pennsylvania system of prison discipline in Germany. He had very lively relations with legal philosophers and penologists abroad, and participated in several international congresses. He was also

* Reproduced from *The Journal of Criminal Law, Criminology and Police Science*, Vol. 59, No. 2, June 1968. This article originally appeared in German, in the *Zeitschrift für die gesamte Strafrechtswissenschaft* (Vol. 73, pp. 107–129). The footnotes and bibliography that were provided there have been restored in this volume.

a member of several societies for prison reform. Roeder died in Heidelberg on December 20, 1879.[1]

His philosophical interests and general legal theories

In order to explain Roeder's philosophical starting-point, a few words on Krause will be necessary. The latter was a kind of academic nomad, who for thirty years moved from one German university to another, without ever getting a definite appointment, and in constant economic distress. He was a prolific writer on many subjects, but his main subject was philosophy. In the latter field he was inspired by Schelling and Fichte, but he worked out a system of his own. The main idea is advancement on one analytical way from human self-consciousness to the absolute, and on one synthetical way via rational theology, psychology, natural philosophy and anthropology to religious philosophy. On the next level follow the "formal sciences," mathematics, logic, aesthetics, ethics and law. The uppermost level in his system is represented by the philosophy of history. Because of his personal, rather complicated terminology his system is difficult to grasp. Besides Roeder he found some disciples in Belgium and Spain.

In his introduction to Krause's *System der Rechtsphilosophie* Roeder paints a lively picture of the present bad state of the prison question and suggests that the solution should be sought in Krause's writings.[2]

In the book itself Krause criticizes the school of repression and argues for reformation through educative measures as the only possible way to influence the criminal through changing his spirit. He found the causes of crime not in an evil will, but in lack of education, need, overpowering urges or madness. His program against crime included the destruction of the inner foundations of evil in the mind of the offender, the abolition of external conditions of evil and unjust character, the influence upon the mind of the offender through rational reasons in order to make him mend his ways and application of sufficient force on behalf of the state to keep evil designs from becoming realized. A basic idea is also that the right

---

[1] *Allgemeine deutsche Biographie* (Leipzig, 1881), Vol. LV, pp. 590–591; Enciclopedia universal ilustrada europeo-americana, Vol. LI, p. 1326.

[2] Karl Roeder, Preface to *Das System der Rechtsphilosophie,* by K. C. F. Krause (Leipzig, 1874), p. xii.

to punish is only a right to educate, which is the same towards children and adults. The lectures that founded the basis of the book were originally given during the beginning of the century, and Krause hailed the American penitentiary system as the only hope for the future.[3]

The discussion of Roeder's theories will be divided into three parts: the first and shortest on general legal theories, the second on theories of criminal law, and the third and most important on penal questions.

Roeder's main ideas on general legal questions are embodied in his *Grundzüge des Naturrechts oder der Rechtsphilosophie,* which originally appeared in 1846, but was completely rewritten in a new edition in 1860–63. His basic ideas were in great part based upon the old theories of natural law, and his starting-point is that the realization of justice must not depend upon the character and strength of the individual will, but that it is an unalienable right of the society that the will of a law-breaker must not be realized.[4] In another connection he characterizes justice as primarily a social and external relation between different human beings, but also as an internal relation between the same human beings, a relation that is rational, inclusive and individual.[5] It is also evident from all of his writings that he was a definite adherent of the theory of free will.

His theory of criminal law and punishment

The next section is a report of Roeder's theories of criminal law. Although he wrote a large number of books on the subject during his life, there seems to be no special growth or change of his ideas— we find the same theories in his earliest as in his last books. He also often used the same material in arguing his case, and covered the same grounds, although some of his books were written as scientific treatises and others were aimed at the general enlightened public.

In his preface to *Die herrschenden Grundlehren von Verbrechen und Strafe,* published in 1867, he states that the book is based upon a series of lectures given in 1830–31, and that he had worked on them more or less continuously since then, but that it had been no use to publish them, as long as Anselm Feuerbach's theory of punishment

[3] Krause, *System der Rechtsphilosophie,* pp. 312–318, 534.
[4] Karl Roeder, *Grundzüge des Naturrechts oder der Rechtsphilosophie,* 2nd ed. (Leipzig and Heidelberg, 1860–1863), Vol. II, p. 164.
[5] Francisco Giner de los Rios, "Carlos Roeder," *Revista General de Legislación y Jurisprudéncia,* Vol. 56, p. 133.

as a psychic force still reigned in Germany. Now he intended, however, to describe and disprove all other theories of punishment than
the corrective one, and thus prove that this was the only possible
one. He also, he said, expected to be either refuted and proved
wrong, or recognized if he was right. Roeder then runs through
all known or imaginable theories of punishment and disproves them,
one after another. As he hardly started from an impartial position,
there is no use trying to criticize him in detail, because he succeeds to
his own satisfaction to prove what he already believed in. His
discussion becomes more important, when he reaches the theory of
reformation. Here, he sees in punishment the reasonable and necessary measure to help a citizen, whose will is unjustly directed, to
self-determination, because (and to the extent that) the disharmony
that stems from this wrong will disturbs the harmony of the whole
reasonable organism of the state. This defined object of punishment is based upon a chain of reasoning with the following links.
Justice is the concept of the fulfilment of human destiny through the
free will of creating conditions. It must be realized independently
of faulty or disturbed wills. If a man's will has become immoral in
an externally visible way and intends to destroy the social order, this
becomes intolerable for society. As far as the individual through
this character of his will has proved himself incapable of good use
of his full external freedom, he must lose his right to use this freedom, i.e., must be considered incapable of using it and in need of
after-education. Every legal procedure against a law-breaker has
the necessary stamp of a guardianship, and all measures that are
found necessary because of his act must be used against him, no
matter how unpleasant and painful they may seem to him personally. Only the theory of reformation is good both for the state
and its individual offending members, and thus it solves the forced
conflict of the present criminal law. Nothing can create such
respect for the state and its laws in the eyes of the criminal and the
whole world as a general opinion of the inner justice of a punishment, that looks not to an immoral repaying of evil with evil, but
with good. Under such conditions the victim of the crime will
forgive and forget the offender, and the latter will regain his self-
esteem and also the confidence of his fellow-citizens, and thus the
path back to the free society is cleared to him. Roeder also attempts
to refute the criticisms against his theory by running through all of
them, and concludes his review with the pious hope that he has

persuaded the thinking reader of the deficiencies of the present criminal law and of the only possible way to reach humanity and justice in the future.[6]

He expresses the same ideas in a different way in *Grundzüge des Naturrechts,* where he states that if the original lack in the will of the criminal reveals itself in an illegal act, it is not enough to repair the damage done through the act. For a real reinstatement of the legal position it is necessary to heal the will of the criminal through what we call punishment. But in doing so, it is always necessary to remember that the criminal is also a human being, who must not lose his human rights. Consequently he cannot be treated as a wild animal or mad dog. Only such measures that are fit to wake up his human qualities and influence him to a change may be used. He must, however, be considered as morally and legally a minor, who, while being punished, still has a right to an opportunity to change his will for the better. The only useful measure to produce this is a strict regime of guardianship and after-education, adapted to the condition of moral illness in the individual case. If the criminal has shown himself unworthy of his external freedom through misusing it, this freedom must be limited in several ways. The just punishment must never lose its character of education, which is already recognized for juvenile delinquents. The difference between punishment and other educational measures is that the former is much more difficult to apply. The common factor for all criminals is lack of moral resistance. In our days the previous misunderstanding has disappeared that punishment is an evil, and it has been generally understood that it is only intended to procure the true good of the criminal and that its true character is beneficent. Through true repentance and reformation the criminal is reconciled to himself, God, and the world. In this way he pays his moral debt and restores the confidence to his morally reborn self.[7]

A contemporary friend, disciple and commentator of Roeder in Spain, Francisco Giner, gives the following concentrated description of the concept of punishment according to Roeder: restriction of the liberty of the individual in order to keep him away from the elements that had contributed to his downfall, educational discipline of his habits and medical treatment of inferior subjects. It is of no importance, he says, if the criminal, because of the state

[6] Karl Roeder, *Die herrschenden Grundlehren von Verbrechen und Strafe in ihren inneren Widersprüchen* (Wiesbaden, 1867), pp. 97, 106–107, 113, 119–138.
[7] Roeder, *Grundzüge des Naturrechts,* Vol. II, pp. 163–174.

of his individual will, considers this punishment as an evil. The serving of a prison sentence must be seen as a beneficent and regenerating treatment.[8]

The same concepts about the necessity of a guardianship for the criminal, as in any other abnormal individual state, have been expressed in another way:

> . . . not only in its restrictive sense of decreasing the criminal's exterior freedom, so as to diminish the stimulus and the opportunities that cause him to persist in his condition, to relapse, and to grow worse; but also, in its positive sense—which is always the first—of protecting the development of his freedom, . . . the regeneration of his conscience, the restoration of the sense of justice in his soul, and his energy and strength in the realization of his deeds.[9]

Propagandist of solitary confinement

Before going over to Roeder's most important contributions—as propagandist of the Pennsylvania system of solitary confinement in Germany and the rest of Europe—it is necessary to describe how the idea traveled across the Atlantic.

The origin and growth of this system in the United States, its characteristic traits, and the fight between it and the Auburn system are so well known that it seems superfluous to use any space for a closer description of it.[10] Let it suffice to say that the idea of solitary prison confinement as a punishment, intended to produce an inner reformation, is a very old one and can be found as far back as in Plato.[11] It is also well known that a great number of foreign visitors, especially from Europe, came to Philadelphia and other places with prisons based on that system in order to study and report upon them to their governments or to interested organizations. An extensive literature on the subject exists and consequently only the most prominent of these visitors will be mentioned. One of the most important visits was made in 1831 by two Frenchmen, Gustave de Beaumont and Alexis de Tocqueville, who wrote a calm and judicious report contrasting the two systems, which was first published in 1833.[12] It evoked great interest and was trans-

8 Giner, "Carlos Roeder," pp. 145–148.
9 C. Bernaldo de Quirós, *Modern Theories of Criminality* (Boston, 1911), pp. 126–127.
10 See for example Harry Elmer Barnes, *The Repression of Crime* (1926; reprinted Montclair, N.J., 1969), pp. 112–115 and chapter 4.
11 Benjamin Jowett (transl.), *The Dialogues of Plato* (New York, 1901), pp. 420–421.
12 Gustave de Beaumont and Alexis de Tocqueville, *Du système pénitentiaire aux Etats-Unis*, 3rd ed. (Paris, 1845), pp. 180–203, in particular p. 185.

lated into English the same year by Francis Lieber under the title *On the Penitentiary System in the United States,* with an additional essay by the translator strongly arguing the case for the Pennsylvania system. A German, and more impartial, translation was also published in the same year by Nicolaus Heinrich Julius under the title *Amerikas Besserungssystem.* When the English edition had appeared, Julius found it necessary to write an article, *Das amerikanische Besserungssystem,* in his journal *Jahrbücher der Straf- und Besserungsanstalten,* in which he reported upon Lieber's English translation and its additional essay. The French report appeared in its third edition in 1845 together with a *Rapport sur le projet de réforme des prisons etc.* by Tocqueville, who in the years since the publication of the first edition had changed his original impartial opinion and now presented a strong recommendation of the Pennsylvania system.[13] Another important visitor was the English philanthropist William Crawford in 1832. He also became a strong adherent of the Pennsylvania system, and his laudatory report[14] contributed to the decision to design Pentonville Prison (completed in 1842) as an English "model prison," along the lines of the Eastern Penitentiary in Philadelphia.

A strong link between the United States and Germany in this field was Francis Lieber, who had emigrated to America from Germany in 1827 for political reasons, becoming professor of political science in 1835 at South Carolina College and in 1857 at Columbia College. Like most other great men of that day his interests and his authorship were very wide. Lieber met Beaumont and Tocqueville in 1831 and visited the Eastern Penitentiary in the same year. He then became a decided adherent of the Pennsylvania system and completed his prison studies by visiting all the penitentiaries in the eastern states. Lieber had a highly personal reason for recommending the solitary system; in 1819 and in 1824 he himself had spent a total of ten months in solitary confinement in Germany because of his political activities. He had, however, been able to receive visits from his friends, and became so deeply influenced by this experience that he considered it advantageous. His translation of the French report on the American prison systems has already been mentioned. In 1835 he wrote to the Prussian

---

[13] *Ibid.,* pp. 373–436, in particular pp. 391–393.
[14] William Crawford, *Report on the Penitentiaries of the United States* (1835; reprinted Montclair, N.J., 1969).

Minister of Justice Karl von Kamptz and suggested the establishing of a penitentiary on the solitary plan near Bonn "as a moral clinicum for criminalists and government officers in general." In 1838 he published his most important writings in the field of penology, a term which, by the way, was invented by him and used for the first time in the book in question, *A Popular Essay on subjects of penal law and on uninterrupted solitary confinement.* The book was intended as a contribution to the discussion on the merits of the Pennsylvania system. When carefully enumerating its much-vaunted advantages he found that they amounted to nineteen, while the disadvantages came to only four. Lieber had occasion to continue his propaganda for the system in 1844 when he visited Prussia and met King Frederick William IV, to whom he strongly argued its advantages. A chair of penology for Lieber, combined with a post as prison inspector, was also suggested at the same occasion, but did not materialize. During the same trip to Europe Lieber also visited his correspondent of several years' standing, K. J. A. Mittermaier, the famous professor of criminal law at Heidelberg, which was also Roeder's university.[15]

The man who probably had contributed most to the spread of knowledge of the Pennsylvania system in Germany was Nicolaus Heinrich Julius (1783-1862). He was trained as a doctor, and had held posts as poorhouse doctor in Hamburg, thus becoming interested in prisons. Following in the footsteps of John Howard he traveled around Europe to study prisons. Upon his return to Berlin in 1827 he gave twelve public lectures on prison questions.[16] The lectures were published in 1828 as *Vorlesungen über die Gefängniskunde* and dedicated to Frederick William, who was then still crown prince. A French edition was published in 1831 as *Leçons sur les prisons.* He also exerted a strong influence through his *Jahrbücher,* which he published in ten volumes in 1829-33. He traveled to the United States to study prisons in 1834-36, during which time he visited Philadelphia. He went as an adherent of the Auburn system but came back a pronounced believer in the Pennsylvania system. His experiences during the years in the United

---

[15] Frank Freidel, *Francis Lieber, Nineteenth Century Liberal* (Baton Rouge, 1947), pp. 96–98, 101, 216–218; T. S. Perry (ed.), *The Life and Letters of Francis Lieber* (Boston, 1882), pp. 105, 186–187; Francis Lieber, *A Popular Essay on Subjects of Penal Law and on Uninterrupted Solitary Confinement* (Philadelphia, 1838), pp. 6, 61–67.

[16] *Allgemeine deutsche Biographie,* Vol. XIV, pp. 686–689. This biography says nothing of the professorship at Berlin that is attributed to him by Barnes and Teeters.

States were recorded in his *Nordamerikas sittliche Zustände,* where he also gives his reasons for preferring the Pennsylvania system and argues for its speedy introduction into Germany.[17] From 1840 to 1849 he held a semi-official post as prison inspector of Prussia without connection with the administration but based upon a personal appointment by the Cabinet. He continued working for prison reform by publishing *Jahrbücher der Gefängniskunde und Besserungsanstalten* in eleven volumes from 1842 to 1849.

Finally, another German author in this field should at least be mentioned, as Roeder refers to him several times: G. M. Obermaier (1789–1885), a Bavarian prison official. In his books *Anleitung zur vollkommenen Besserung der Verbrecher* (1835) and *Die amerikanischen Poenitentiarsysteme* (1837), he criticized both the Auburn and the Pennsylvania systems and argued for a system of his own that would avoid the disadvantages of both of them.

As a result of all these influences Germany, still divided into a great number of small states, got its first solitary prison in Insterburg in Prussia in 1832.[18] King Frederick William, who took a strong interest in prison questions, visited Pentonville some time around 1840. His favorable impressions contributed to his decision in 1842 to override the opinion of the administration and introduce the Pennsylvania system into Prussian prisons. This decision was realized in 1849 with the new Moabit prison in Berlin.[19] Lieber's visit to the King in 1844 was probably also of some importance in the same general direction.

The spread of the Pennsylvania system over Europe and its lasting impressions there are so well-known that they need be mentioned only in passing.

These were the influences that aroused an interest in penology in Roeder—and led him to that definite opinion of the superiority of the Pennsylvania system in which he never seemed to vary. Over and over again he expressed in his various books the reasons for the supremacy of solitary confinement. The same reasons and the same steps in his logical reasoning were restated in more or less

---

[17] Nicolaus Heinrich Julius, *Nordamerikas sittliche Zustände* (Leipzig, 1839), Vol. II, pp. 254ff., 369ff.

[18] *Handwörterbuch der Kriminologie* (Berlin and Leipzig, 1936), Vol. I, p. 545. Grünhut states that the first cellular prison in Germany was the one at Dreibergen in Mecklenburg (1839): the first year of imprisonment there was spent in solitary confinement (Max Grünhut, *Penal Reform* (1948; reprinted Montclair, N.J., 1972)).

[19] Franz von Holtzendorff and Eugen von Jagemann (eds.), *Handbuch des Gefängniswesens* (Hamburg, 1888), Vol. I, p. 124.

detail, depending upon the size of the book in question. Only three of his books will be mentioned in this connection.

The first is *Die Verbesserung des Gefängniswesens mittelst der Einzelhaft,* written in 1855 at the wish of the Prussian Government for use in official discussions on prison reforms. It is based mainly upon experiences from the Bruchsal Prison in Baden. The advantages of the solitary system are given as the possibility of influencing the inner life through awakening and developing the thinking, feeling and will; the very strong influence upon the spiritual development of the prisoner through educative measures; the possibility of individualizing the treatment; and the changed relationships between personnel and prisoners. Among these educative measures were counted church and school in prison, the influence of talks with warden and visitors, and finally the reading of good books. When discussing the purported weakening of the prisoner's intellectual abilities under the Pennsylvania system, Roeder heatedly denied that this happened and pointed to the many laudatory reports from visitors to Philadelphia as proof of the opposite. On the other hand he strongly criticized attempts to change the solitary prison system into a system of complete isolation, and proposed that dark cells or temporary isolation should be used only as measures for enforcing internal discipline.[20]

A much more detailed treatment of all these questions was given in his next book,[21] where he makes a basic demand in order to justify solitary confinement, viz, that the state must recognize its duty as the guardian of a criminal, who has lost his liberty because of a criminal act, not to let him suffer spiritual or bodily need. Roeder also tries a diplomatic approach in order to catch the adherents of the old strict theories through pointing out that the solitary system is in many respects harder than the old common prisons. Finally, he stated the conditions that work in prison must fulfill: it must not damage the health of the prisoner, but should, if possible, strengthen his body and soul and give him a good future; and only in the last place might the choice of work be determined by economic considerations.

In *Besserungsstrafe und Besserungsstrafanstalten als Rechtsforderung* Roeder characterizes imprisonment, especially the solitary

---

[20] Karl Roeder, *Die Verbesserung des Gefängniswesens mittelst der Einzelhaft* (Prague, 1856), pp. 16–25.
[21] Karl Roeder, *Der Strafvollzug im Geist des Rechts* (Leipzig and Heidelberg, 1863), pp. 68, 95–96, 313–323.

system, as suddenly tearing wild men loose from their urges and their previous barren ways amongst bad company and overwhelming temptations, placing them in good surroundings and relating them to a totally opposite moral way of life, which gradually becomes a second nature. In the last part of the book he once more runs through the reasons for the Pennsylvania system, traces its spread through Europe, points to the small German state of Baden as a pattern for the whole world in this respect, and gives a good description of the prison conditions in many other small German states.[22]

Roeder also made active contributions to the propaganda for the Pennsylvania system by participating in congresses and corresponding with international organizations or friends and colleagues in other countries. Thus he participated in the First International Penitentiary Congress in Frankfurt am Main in 1846, although he does not seem to have taken part in the discussions. President of the Congress was Mittermaier, and among the participants were many internationally known penologists and prison administrators, like Ducpétiaux, Louis Dwight (the champion of the Auburn system), Julius, Moreau-Christophe and Obermaier. The latter was the dominating member of the congress. Several resolutions in favor of the general use of solitary confinement were adopted practically unanimously. As this congress had settled the question which prison system should be introduced in Europe, the next congress, in Brussels in 1847, limited itself mostly to questions of prison architecture. Roeder attended this congress, too, but, according to the proceedings, he only took part in the discussions on one small point, where he argued in favor of small prisons and played down the economic viewpoints. In a later article in a professional journal which contained his contribution to the congress, Roeder polemized against some persons who had participated in the discussions on more general questions.[23]

Roeder also tries to give some important conditions that must be fulfilled if the Pennsylvania system was to live up to the expectations. Among them are that the institution must be managed in a true reformative spirit, that it must not contain more than three hundred prisoners, that the prisoners shall work for the prison

[22] Karl Roeder, *Besserungsstrafe und Besserungsstrafanstalten als Rechtsforderung* (Leipzig and Heidelberg, 1864), pp. 44, 170–185.
[23] Karl Roeder, "Zur Verständigung über das Verhältnis der Einzelhaft zur Strafgesetzgebung," *Archiv des Kriminalrechts* 1850, pp. 412–453, in particular pp. 418–419.

itself and not for contractors, and that all unnecessary penal or judicial aggravations of the punishment must be abolished. The solitary system should also be used for all categories of prisoners, even during the pretrial stage, because of its general beneficent influence. The only other types of punishment for which there is any use besides the solitary system, are temporary banishment, fines and loss of the right to occupy certain important positions. As a consequence of the reformative influence of the Pennsylvania system he also argued strongly for not only a reduction by at least one-third of the length of the sentence, but also for an indeterminate sentence, so that the court might once more go over the case and change the length of the punishment according to the more or less complete reformation of the prisoner during the first part of his stay in prison. The reasons given for this proposal seem to be the same as have been given in the more modern discussion on indeterminate sentences. Roeder was, however, prepared to make a few exceptions to the all-embracing character of the solitary system, for children and young persons under fourteen years of age, very old people, invalids, and mental defectives—but they must not be kept together with other prisoners, and should immediately be transferred to specialized institutions for these various categories.[24]

The Third Congress, dedicated to Charities, Correction and Philanthropy, was also held in Frankfurt, but not until 1857 because of the political upheavals of the intervening years. One of the three sections was dedicated to penal reform and one of the three subjects in this section was the cellular imprisonment system. Roeder attended this Congress and participated very actively in the discussions of the section. He protested against the official designation of three objects of punishment, expiation, deterrence and reformation, and recognized only the last one. He suggested the possibility of special rules for political prisoners and offenders who were not real criminals. He spoke of the beneficent influence of work and education. He also argued that there must be no exception from the rules of complete solitary confinement other than for ill or dying prisoners, or for children under twelve years of age, and he wanted to adjourn the discussion of conditional release. Generally, he found himself in the minority on all points.[25]

[24] Roeder, *Strafvollzug im Geist des Rechts*, pp. 97–110, 118–120.
[25] *Congrès International de Bienfaisance de Francfort-sur-le-Mein, session de 1857* (Frankfurt, 1858), pp. 37, 396–399, 372–377, 401–403, 408, 413. The Congress still expressed itself in favor of the Pennsylvania system.

Besides this participation in Congresses, Roeder was active in prison discussions and belonged to the leading group among those teachers of criminal law who had great influence on penology around the turn of the century.[26] That he evidently sometimes could lose his temper a little on these questions is indicated by a quotation from *Die Verbesserung des Gefängniswesens,* where, in mentioning a temporary minor change in the English adaptation of the Pennsylvania system, which he evidently considered as heresy, he said: "these changes have been made since the head of the prison system became a Mr. Jebb, an engineer (!) and by the way quite well-meaning and personally known to me."[27] The poor Sir Joshua Jebb seems to have had somewhat better qualifications than Roeder's words indicate. He had started as an officer in the Royal Engineers, where he had reached the rank of first captain, when in 1837 he became surveyor-general of prisons in order to serve as technical adviser to the Home Office on the construction of prisons. In 1842 he became a commissioner of Pentonville Prison, which he had helped to construct, in 1844 inspector-general of military prisons, and in 1850 chairman of the board of convict prisons.

Roeder believed that he had at least contributed to some extent to the Prussian King's decisions on prison issues through *Die Verbesserung des Gefängniswesens.*[28] His contributions have also been noted by at least one German penologist, who has pointed to his importance in spreading the theory of reformation.[29]

Among the results of the writings of Roeder and others was the building of the first new German prison along the lines of the true Pennsylvania system, Bruchsal in Baden, ready in 1848 but not put into use until 1851 because of legal obstacles.[30] A whole literature grew up around this prison, to which both officials, visitors, and a couple of prisoners contributed. Two other later milestones on the road to victory of the Pennsylvania system in Germany were the resolution of the German Congress of Jurists in 1869, demanding the solitary system as the regular way of serving a prison sentence, and the German Criminal Code of 1871, in which the solitary system became the rule at least during the first three years of a prison sentence. And as late as 1889 the distinguished penologist Krohne

[26] *Handwörterbuch der Kriminologie,* p. 550.
[27] Roeder, *Verbesserung des Gefängniswesens,* p. 31.
[28] Roeder, *Besserungsstrafe,* p. 188n.
[29] N. Hermann Kriegsmann, *Einführung in die Gefängniskunde* (Heidelberg, 1912), p. 61.
[30] K. Krohne, *Lehrbuch der Gefängniskunde* (Stuttgart, 1889), pp. 171–173.

spoke in favor of the solitary system.[31]   That this idea had not lost
all of its original impact much later on is indicated by the fact that
both the Sixth International Penal and Penitentiary Congress in
Brussels in 1910 and the Tenth Congress in Prague in 1930 seemed
to consider it still important.

Roeder had a rather strong influence in Spain.   A particular
factor that contributed to his importance there was the fact that his
teacher Krause had influenced several Spanish philosophers and
professors of criminal law, who were at least partly interested in
penology.[32]   The most important and influential of these men was
Francisco Giner de los Rios, who on several occasions expressed
ideas on the character of crime and punishment similar to Roeder's.
He also spoke of social education as a function and duty of the
government.[33]   Several of Roeder's works were also translated into
Spanish by Giner or Romero Giron.   Thus his *Grundzüge des
Naturrechts* was translated as *Principios de derecho natural.*   In
1873 Roeder wrote an original work in Spanish, *Necesaria reforma
del sistema penal español,* where he argued for a complete reform
of the Spanish penal system patterned after the Pennsylvania one.
Probably because of the interest that this and his earlier books had
evoked, he was that year commissioned by the Spanish Minister of
Justice to write some authoritative reports on penal reform.[34]   One of
these was published as an appendix to the translation that appeared
in 1877 of his *Die herrschenden Grundlehren* under the title *Las
doctrinas fundamentales reinantes.*   The appendix was called *Reforma del sistema penal español mediante al regimen celuar,* and
contains nothing that is not mentioned already.

Finally, in 1885, another book of Roeder's appeared: *La idea del
derecho.*   Through this literature and through his correspondence
with Giner and others Roeder had a marked influence on the growth
of the so-called correctionalist school in Spain during the latter part
of the last century.[35]   One of those who became influenced by him

31 *Ibid.,* p. 250.
32 De Quirós, *Modern Theories,* p. 127n; Giner, "Carlos Roeder," *op. cit.* note 5, pp. 134–
136, 152; C. Bernaldo de Quirós, Preface to *Naturaleza e función del derecho,* by Pedro
Dorado Montero (Madrid, 1927), pp. xix–xx.
33 Francisco Giner de los Rios, "Principios de derecho natural" (with Alfredo Calderón),
Obras completas (Madrid, 1916), Vol. I, pp. 124–125, and "A propos de la fonction de
la loi," *Revue Internationale de Sociologie,* Vol. 16, pp. 561–572, in particular pp. 570–
571.
34 De Quirós, *Modern Theories,* p. 127n.
35 Fernando Cadalzo, *Instituciones penitenciarias y similares en España* (Madrid, 1922), p.
128; de Quirós, Preface to *Naturaleza e función del derecho,* p. xliv.

was Pedro Dorado Montero, professor of criminal law in Salamanca, although he was later to work out a penal philosophy of his own. Through these contributions from various sources Spanish penology at the end of the last century and the beginning of this one acquired its special character of a mixture between metaphysicism and positivism. That a certain influence from Roeder still exists in both Spain and in the Latin American countries (whose prisons were mostly patterned on Spanish models) is evident in the importance that solitary confinement still has in several of these countries, especially in the big central prisons in the capitals.

When trying to get a composite picture of Roeder's work and importance, it is perhaps best to start with his contemporaries. For some reason he never found any special following in Germany, but his theories became rather important in several other countries. Besides Giner and others in Spain, among his disciples were Gabba in Italy, Moddermann in Holland, and Vargha in Austria.[36] Many of his German colleagues did not mention his work at all, to his great chagrin. On the other hand he encountered his sharpest critique during his lifetime from two Italian authors, Carrara and Buccellati, in an article in *Rivista penale* in 1875, to which he answered with a spirited defense.[37]

Among those legal scientists who have evaluated Roeder, one, Heinze, has criticized his theory of reformation as a mixture of penal and moral philosophy which is not appropriate for a great number of persons who have committed criminal acts. This number includes both those who act through a conflict of duties and those who have already reformed during the period from the criminal act to the sentence. Furthermore, the theory can only be used to justify medium or long prison sentences.[38]

Another German author in the field was Ludwig Laistner, a private scholar and man of science. His assertions are that the whole basic concept of legal and moral incapacity is only a fiction which leads the observer to the conclusion that all criminals are children; moreover, the need of a possible after-education of criminals cannot be compared with education of children.[39]

A man of probably greater importance than these two, Karl

---

[36] Giner, "Carlos Roeder," p. 152.

[37] Karl Roeder, "Sul fondamento e sullo scopo della pena in riguardo alla teoria critica delle opinioni di Carrara ed Ellero," *Rivista penale di Dottrina, Legislazione e Giurisprudenza,* Vol. 2, pp. 273–286.

[38] Franz von Holtzendorff (ed.), *Handbuch des deutschen Strafrechts* (Berlin, 1871), Vol. I, pp. 264, 269.

[39] Ludwig Laistner, *Das Recht in der Strafe* (Munich, 1872), pp. 162–165.

Ludwig von Bar, who was professor of criminal law in Göttingen, has also had his say on the question. He offers a new argument, namely that the reformative theory offers the prisoners goods that perhaps are unavailable to the great mass of the population; he also calls the whole theory an exclusive cult of the individual.[40]

Another author in the German language is Julius Vargha, an adherent of Roeder and professor of criminal law in Austria. He limits himself to praising Roeder's contributions as a reformer and stressing the importance of continuing his fight for the future.[41]

Von Lilienthal in his biographical evaluation mentions that Roeder was lacking in the fields of philosophy and criminal law, and that his interest in the fight against the conservative penological schools led him to specialize in the practical aspects of prison reform. The resistance that he met and the difficulties he experienced during this fight made him concentrate his theories so much upon the reformative aspect of the criminal that his theory became virtually impossible to realize.[42]

Finally De Quirós, who *a priori* was on Roeder's side, speaks of his importance in contributing to the transformation of the character of punishment into a new concept with non-punitive aspects.[43]

In attempting a personal evaluation of Roeder it should be pointed out that he is mentioned neither in Gabriel Tarde's *Penal Philosophy* nor in Barnes and Teeters' *New Horizons in Criminology*, although both of these basic works otherwise seem to include practically everyone who has had any influence on penal or penological theories. As Teeters has pointed out in another connection,[44] many persons who are well known in European writings seem to be unknown in the United States.

It is impossible to judge Roeder without setting him in relation to that prison system of solitary confinement that he fought so strenuously to introduce. Seen in retrospect, its obvious disadvantages are perhaps too distinct, but compared with the conditions at the time when the system broke through, it must be considered a definite progress and its importance is still far from extinct.[45]

Besides his contributions in the field of practical penology it is

[40] Karl Ludwig von Bar, *Geschichte des deutschen Strafrechts und der Strafrechtstheorien* (Berlin, 1882), pp. 264–265, and *A History of Continental Criminal Law* (Boston, 1916), pp. 446–447.
[41] Julius Vargha, *Die Abschaffung der Strafknechtschaft* (Graz, 1896), Vol. I, p. 130n.
[42] *Allgemeine deutsche Biographie*, Vol. LV, p. 590.
[43] De Quirós, *Modern Theories*, p. 127.
[44] Vernon C. Branham and Samuel B. Kutash (eds.), *Encyclopedia of Criminology* (New York, 1949), p. 517.
[45] Grünhut, *Penal Reform*, p. 62.

also important that Roeder, in many connections, pointed to the legal character of the relation between the State and a person serving a sentence in one of its prisons. In this way he has contributed to the improvement of the legal position of prisoners. That Roeder's theory of the guardianship character of the punishment is not wholly extinct is indicated in a recent book by a noted American psychiatrist, who expresses the same attitude in a totally modern setting.[46]

From all these reasons it would seem unjust if criminology and especially penology were completely to forget Karl Roeder. He should be entitled to at least a niche in the gallery of those who have contributed in advancing criminology in different ways and towards varying goals.

KLAS LITHNER.

BIBLIOGRAPHY

By Roeder

Besserungsstrafe und Besserungsstrafanstalten als Rechtsforderung. Leipzig and Heidelberg, 1864.
Die herrschenden Grundlehren von Verbrechen und Strafe in ihren inneren Widersprüchen. Wiesbaden, 1867.
Grundzüge des Naturrechts oder der Rechtsphilosophie. 2nd ed. Leipzig and Heidelberg, 1860–1863.
Der Strafvollzug im Geist des Rechts. Leipzig and Heidelberg, 1863.
Die Verbesserung des Gefängniswesens mittelst der Einzelhaft. Prague, 1856.
"Zur Verständigung über das Verhältnis der Einzelhaft zur Strafgesetzgebung." *Archiv des Kriminalrechts* 1850: pp. 412–453.
Las doctrinas fundamentales reinantes sobre el delito y la pena en sus interiores contradicciones. 3rd ed. Madrid, 1877.
La idea del derecho. Madrid, 1885.
Necesaria reforma del sistema penal español mediante al establecimiento del régimen celular. Madrid, 1873.
"Sul fondamento e sullo scopo della pena in riguardo alla teoria critica delle opinioni di Carrara ed Ellero." *Rivista penale di Dottrina, Legislazione e Giurisprudenza,* Vol. 2 (1875), pp. 273–286.

General

BARNES, HARRY ELMER. *The Evolution of Penology in Pennsylvania.* 1927; reprinted Montclair, N.J., 1968.
—— *The Repression of Crime.* 1926; reprinted Montclair, N.J., 1969.

[46] Philip Q. Roche, *The Criminal Mind* (New York, 1958), p. 66.

BEAUMONT, GUSTAVE DE, and TOCQUEVILLE, ALEXIS DE. *Du système péniten-tiaire aux Etats-Unis,* (3rd ed.) *augmentée du rapport de M. de Tocque-ville sur le projet de réforme des prisons etc.* Paris, 1845.

BERNALDO DE QUIRÓS, CONSTANCIO. *Modern Theories of Criminality.* Boston, 1911.

CADALZO, FERNANDO. *Instituciones penitenciarias y similares en España.* Madrid, 1922.

Congrès International de Bienfaisance de Francfort-sur-le-Mein, session de 1857. Frankfurt, 1858.

Débats du Congrès Pénitentiaire de Bruxelles, sessions de 1847. Brussels, 1847.

Débats du Congrès Pénitentiaire de Francfort-sur-le-Mein, 28–30 septembre 1846. Paris, 1847.

DORADO MONTERO, PEDRO. *Naturaleza e función del derecho.* Edited with an introduction by C. Bernaldo de Quirós. Madrid, 1927.

FREIDEL, FRANK. *Francis Lieber, Nineteenth Century Liberal.* Baton Rouge, 1947.

GINER DE LOS RIOS, FRANCISCO. "A propos de la fonction de la loi." *Revue Internationale de Sociologie,* Vol. 16 (1908), pp. 561–572.

—— "Carlos Roeder." *Revista General de Legislación y Jurisprudencia,* Vol. 56 (1880), pp. 129–153.

GINER DE LOS RIOS, FRANCISCO, and CALDERÓN, ALFREDO. "Principios de de-recho natural." *Obras completas,* Vol. I. Madrid, 1916.

GRÜNHUT, MAX. *Penal Reform.* 1948; reprinted Montclair, N.J., 1972.

HAYNER, N. C. "Notes on the Spanish Correctional System." *Federal Proba-tion,* Vol. 19 (1955), pp. 48–51.

JULIUS, NICOLAUS HEINRICH. "Das amerikanische Besserungssystem." *Jahr-bücher der Straf- und Besserungsanstalten, Erziehungshäuser, Armen-fürsorge etc.* 1833: pp. 151–159.

—— *Leçons sur les prisons.* Paris, 1831.

—— *Nordamerikas sittliche Zustände.* Leipzig, 1839.

—— *Vorlesungen über die Gefängniskunde oder über die Verbesserung der Gefängnisse und sittliche Besserung der Gefangenen, entlassenen Sträflinge usw.* Berlin, 1828.

KRAUSE, KARL CHRISTIAN FRIEDRICH. *Das System der Rechtsphilosophie.* Edited by Karl Roeder. Leipzig, 1874.

LEWIS, ORLANDO F. *The Development of American Prisons and Prison Cus-toms 1776–1845.* 1922; reprinted Montclair, N.J., 1967.

LIEBER, FRANCIS. *Miscellaneous Writings,* Vol. II. Philadelphia, 1881.

—— *A Popular Essay on subjects of penal law and on uninterrupted solitary confinement at labor, as contradistinguished to solitary confinement at night and joint labor by day, in a letter to John Bacon, Esquire.* Phila-delphia, 1838.

OBERMAIER, G. M. *Die amerikanischen Poenitentiarsysteme in Vergleichung mit der im Zentralgefängnisse zu Kaiserslautern eingeführten Besserungs-weise und ihre gegenseitigen Folgen.* Kaiserslautern, 1837.

—— *Anleitung zur vollkommenen Besserung der Verbrecher in den Strafan-stalten.* Kaiserslautern, 1835.

PERRY, THOMAS SERGEANT (ed.). *The Life and Letters of Francis Lieber.* Boston, 1882.

QUINTANO RIPOLLES, ANTONIO. "Les Aspects modernes des institutions pénitentiaires ibéro-américaines." *Revue Internationale de Droit Pénal,* Vol. 23 (1952), pp. 259–292.

Reports of the Prison Discipline Society of Boston. 1855; reprinted Montclair, N.J., 1972.

TEETERS, NEGLEY K. *Deliberations of the International Penal and Penitentiary Congresses.* Philadelphia, 1949.

—— "The First International Penitentiary Congresses: 1846, 1847, 1857." *The Prison Journal,* Vol. 26 (1946), pp. 190–211.

—— *Penology from Panama to Cape Horn.* Philadelphia, 1946.

VARGHA, JULIUS. *Die Abschaffung der Strafknechtschaft.* Graz, 1896.

Verhandlungen der ersten Versammlung für Gefängnisreform, zusammengetreten im September 1846 in Frankfurt a.M. Frankfurt, 1847.

NOTE ON THE CONTRIBUTOR

KLAS LITHNER is a public prosecutor (state attorney) in Karlskrona, Sweden. He received his law degree from the University of Lund in 1947, and from 1952 to 1957 pursued part-time studies in sociology and criminology at the University of Gothenburg. In 1959–60 he did graduate work at the University of Pennsylvania. He has written extensively in the fields of law enforcement, criminal law, criminology, and legal sociology.

10

ISAAC RAY
1807–1881

By far the most influential American writer on forensic psychiatry during the whole nineteenth century was Isaac Ray.[1] Ray was a man of wide interests, a gifted linguist, and an effective writer on whatever subject he treated. His chief interest throughout his entire lifetime was in the closer application of the principles of psychiatry to the law. Although he wrote a book on mental hygiene and one on mental pathology, together with innumerable articles in various legal and medical journals dealing with various phases of mental disorder, he is principally remembered as the author of *The Medical Jurisprudence of Insanity*, which first appeared in 1838, ran through at least five American editions, and one or two in London, and is still referred to by courts of last resort as the authoritative work on the subject. To deal adequately with a man of these protean interests and gigantic abilities could not be done in the space of less than a full volume. An attempt will be made in this note, however, to point out some of the accomplishments and views of this great American physician.

Isaac Ray was born in Beverly, Massachusetts, January 18, 1807. He came from an old New England family; his English ancestor, Daniel, purchased land in Plymouth in 1630 and removed to Salem the following year. He attended Phillips Andover Academy, studied for a time with Dr. George Shattuck of Boston, and then entered the Medical School of Maine at Bowdoin College. He received the degree of Doctor of Medicine in 1827, and the following

* Reproduced from *The Journal of Criminal Law, Criminology and Police Science*, Vol. 45, No. 3, September–October 1954.

[1] In the preparation of this biographical sketch, the author has been greatly aided by Dr. Louis E. Reik, of Princeton University, who has made available the results of his extended studies of Ray's life and work; by Dr. Henry N. Babcock, Superintendent of Butler Hospital, Providence, for the use of material from the Isaac Ray Library; by Dr. Benjamin Pasamanick of Johns Hopkins University, for permission to use his article on Ray's phrenological interests; and the Librarian of the Houghton Library of Harvard University, who gave authority to quote from Ray's letters to Charles Sumner. For their assistance he expresses herewith his deep gratitude.

September he opened an office in Portland, Maine. While in Portland he gave several series of lectures on botany and natural history and published a volume entitled *Conversations on the Animal Economy*, a presentation in dialogue form of the principles of physiology.

From phrenology to psychiatry

In 1831 he removed to Eastport, Maine, which was then a thriving seaport, with frequent ocean communication with Boston and with a good bit of international trade as well. An English officer travelling in America at about this period commented on the extent and the quality of the stock in Favour's Bookstore, which he visited while passing through Eastport. Certainly, from his many references to French and German writings it is clear that Ray was in touch with a vast amount of foreign as well as domestic literature. Something of the quality of his mind is found in an extract from a lecture delivered by him in Eastport in 1832: " The first obstacle to the reception of truth . . . is a fear of inquiry, and it is one which has always been and still continues to be among the most impregnable strongholds of error. . . . Surely if our opinions are wrong, the sooner they become unsettled the better, and if right, the inquiry by making us acquainted with their foundations and bearings, will strengthen our belief."

Dr. Ray's first article on medical jurisprudence appeared in the *Boston Medical Magazine*[2] under the title " A Review of the Medical Testimony in a case of Alleged Murder." He made a scathing attack upon the lack of fundamental knowledge of pathological anatomy (the subject of his graduation thesis at Bowdoin) exhibited by one of the principal witnesses. " His testimony opens with a flourish of trumpets the like of which for asinine tones was never before heard, we will venture to say, since the world began." He concluded: " The truth is, that medical jurisprudence is too much neglected in this country, and while this neglect continues, errors as unpardonable, though perhaps not quite so gross, will be frequently occurring. Though involving questions of the deepest interest both to the physician and lawyer, it must be confessed that it has received little attention from either. . . . It is strange . . . that physicians should be so deficient in a branch of their science,

[2] Vol. 2, p. 18 (July 1833).

which gives them the best chance in the world of distinguishing themselves either to their credit or their shame."

During his stay in Eastport he became much interested, among other things, in the then prevalent tenets of phrenology. For example, his review of Combe's book on phrenology appeared in 1834.[3] There is, he says, " an original and distinct power for every special end and object of our existence " and the theory, as he says, " lends a powerful support to morality and religion." As shown by this and other even earlier articles, he had completely accepted the phrenological theory at that time. In the same period also he translated two volumes, the fourth and the sixth, of Gall's *Fonctions du Cerveau*. In this venture he was apparently acting as a " ghost writer " for one Winslow Lewis, Jr., M.D. of Boston, whose translation of the works of Gall was published in Boston by Marsh, Capen and Lyon in 1835. This activity of Ray's has been recently explored by Dr. Benjamin Pasamanick of the Johns Hopkins University School of Hygiene and Public Health, who has kindly given me permission to refer to his article (to appear later in the *American* graphy of Isaac Ray."[4] Ray's interest in phrenology continued at *Journal of Psychiatry*) entitled " An Obscure Item in the Biblio- least to some extent during his entire lifetime, although it was considerably attenuated in his later years. Even as late as 1879, for example, he wrote to Nahum Capen, the Boston publisher of Gall, " No storybook was ever devoured with such an abandon of every other thought as was Gall's great work *Sur Les Fonctions*." A large portion of phrenology is today looked upon as a passing fad in the history of thought. Nevertheless, despite its doctrines of " bumps and dents," its notions of organs of " inhabitiveness," " philoprogenitiveness," " combativeness," " love of approbation," " veneration," " conscientiousness," and so on, it made distinct contributions to the knowledge of the structure of the brain, and gave impetus to what later was known as the " German School " of neurology. It was Gall and Spurzheim, for example, who showed first that the white substance of the brain is fibrous. Phrenology was an attempt at a scientific approach to psychiatry, and for a time at least it attracted the best medical minds both in England

---

[3] 16 *The Christian Examiner*, 221 (May 1834).
[4] Since this article was set up the contribution by Dr. Pasamanick has been published in 111 Am.J.Psychiat. 164.

and in this country.[5] It is greatly to the credit of Ray that he was ready to investigate this new approach to the problems of behaviour.

Ray's first essay in the field of psychiatric jurisprudence is found in the form of a Lecture on the Criminal Law of Insanity [6] in 1835. This was a comprehensive discussion in which he took up particularly the questions of lucid intervals and what was then known as moral insanity. He cast doubt upon the legal doctrine of lucid intervals, saying, for example, " Lucid intervals are nothing more than intermissions of the cerebral disease and depend upon the same pathological conditions as other intermittent diseases." In this discussion he referred to a large number of writers, including Pinel, Haslam, Esquirol, Georget, Hoffbauer, Combe, and Gall and Spurzheim. He attacked particularly what may be termed " the intellectual approach " to the problem of criminal responsibility. " The error," he says, " arises from considering the reason, or to speak more definitely, the intellectual faculties, as exclusively liable to derangement, and entirely overlooking the passions or affective faculties. . . . While the reason may be unimpaired, the passions may be in a state of insanity, impelling a man . . . to the commission of horrible crimes in spite of all his efforts to resist. . . . The whole mind is seldom affected; it is only one or more faculties, sentiments, or propensities, whose action is increased, diminished or perverted, while the rest enjoy their customary soundness and vigour. . . . True philosophy and strict justice require that the action of the insane should be considered in reference . . . to the faculties that are diseased." An interesting comment in this essay concerns what he refers to as the " unparalleled frequency " of insanity in the United States. He adds: " The frequency and freedom of elections are constantly influencing the hopes and the passions, and the general accessibility to office diverts the mind from the even tenor of its way, and fills it with vague and insatiable cravings, to an extent that renders the common phrase ' political fever ' something more than a figure of speech."

---

5 See John F. Fulton, "Early Phrenological Societies and their journals," 196 Boston Med.and Surg.J. 398 (March 1927), and Byron Stookey, " A Note on the Early History of Cerebral Localization," 30 Bull.N.Y.Acad.of Med. (second series), 559 (July 1954).

6 14 *The American Jurist*, 253 (October 1835). The reader should appreciate that the word " insanity," shunned today by psychiatrists and now exclusively a legal term, was used in Ray's time with the same meaning and connotation as our modern words and phrases, " mental disease," " mental disorder " and " psychosis."

In a criticism of this article " G.T.C." [7] speaks of a " crusade, the object of which is to rescue bleeding humanity from its imaginary tyrant, precedent." Following this criticism was an editorial note evidently written by Charles Sumner, one of the editors, criticising the critic as misunderstanding Ray. " Doctor Ray has adopted the phrenological theory of insanity of Dr. Andrew Combe, that is, that the brain is not a single organ but a congeries of separate but united organs, each of which has its appropriate function. . . . That science is now receiving the support of so many enlightened and scientific men that it needs no defence at our hand." Doctor Ray made a vigorous rejoinder to " G.T.C.," [8] remarking *inter alia* : " Neither can we object to the law's attempting a definition of insanity, if it be anxious to add another to the thousand and one failures, to define a condition of mind, that never was and never can be thoroughly understood."

Following this there started a series of letters to Charles Sumner from Doctor Ray, now preserved in the Houghton Library in Harvard, which has kindly consented to their use. Under date of May 5, 1836, he wrote to Sumner : " The principle of law, or more properly speaking, of common sense, that insanity excuses crime, of course, no one would blame, but the moment the question of what conditions of mind insanity may be predicated [*sic*], comes up, the law forthwith lays down certain principles to guide our judgment. . . . Now these principles are erroneous, being based on imperfect notions of insanity, and therefore I attacked them." This passage is an interesting adumbration of the much later correspondence between Judge Doe and Doctor Ray which resulted in the enunciation of the so-called New Hampshire Rule. Later in the letter Doctor Ray said : " Your profession needs light on the subject and so does mine, nearly if not quite as much, but there are no works in the language calculated to furnish it. The idea of translating some of the German or French treatises first suggested itself to my mind, but the more carefully I examine them, the less suitable do they appear to answer, in fact, the purpose I thought necessary, and the more strongly I felt obliged to prepare work myself, which should answer fully the idea of what I considered such a work should be. Accordingly, I began one and have written a considerable portion of it."

[7] 15 *ibid*. (April 1836).
[8] 16 *ibid*. 43.

Ray's magnum opus

Thus was *The Medical Jurisprudence of Insanity* born—a book
which John Minson Galt, another of the "Original Thirteen"
founders of the American Psychiatric Association, declared in
1865 [9] "does more credit to America than aught in relation to
insanity that has been produced on this side of the Atlantic."

In his next letter, of May 18, 1836, he said: "The legal relations
of insanity have excited an extraordinary interest in Paris for the
last ten years, and they are beginning to take it up in England. I
trust our own country will not be behind Europe in a matter so
closely connected with the cause of humanity, science, and legislation, and as the influence of authority is less here, perhaps, I think,
it will not. All that is wanted is light." In a later letter to Sumner,
dated October 4, 1837, he asked for Sumner's impartial opinion of
the manuscript of the book on medical jurisprudence and suggested
that perhaps some such person as Judge Story or Professor Greenleaf
might be willing to express an opinion as well. It would be interesting to know the sequel. At any rate, the book when it appeared in
1838 was dedicated not to Sumner or to Story or to Greenleaf, but
to Horace Mann! Friendly relations certainly continued between
Ray and Sumner; the dedication was *not* due to strained relations
with Sumner. In 1844, for example, Sumner wrote a very cordial
letter to Ray, and Ray wrote at least two letters to Sumner in the
fifties, when the latter was United States Senator from Massachusetts.

The Medical Jurisprudence of Insanity is not alone remarkable
because it was produced by a country practitioner in a small town
or that it was to become a classic widely quoted and highly influential. More than all these, it was with the exception of two relatively
minor exceptions the *first* treatment of the relations of law and
psychiatry to appear in the United States. In 1819 in Philadelphia
had appeared the volume entitled *Tracts on Medical Jurisprudence*,
with a preface by Thomas Cooper, M.D., and the *Elements of
Medical Jurisprudence* by Theodric Romeyn Beck, published in
Albany in 1823, contained in Chapter 13 a section on mental alienation. Neither of these volumes, however, was as comprehensive or
as original in any respect as Ray's masterpiece.

The volume was entitled: *A Treatise on the Medical Jurisprudence of Insanity*, by I. Ray, M.D., and was published in Boston

[9] 12 Am.J.Insan. 239.

in 1838 by Charles C. Little and James Brown. The first edition ran to 480 pages. The preface begins: " Few probably, whose attention has not been particularly directed to the subject, are aware how far the condition of the law relative to insanity is behind the present state of our knowledge concerning that disease. . . . In general treatises on legal medicine, this branch of it has always received a share of attention; but the space allotted to it is altogether too limited to admit of those details, which can alone be of any useful service; and it is one of those branches on which the author is usually the least qualified by his own experience to throw any additional light. Insanity itself is an affection so obscure and perplexing, and the occasions have now become so frequent and important when its legal relation should be properly understood, that an ampler field of illustration and discussion is required for this purpose than is accorded by a solitary chapter in works of this description."

The first chapter, including sixty-seven pages, is entitled " Preliminary Views," and presents a summary of Ray's examination of existing rules, with his proposals for improvement. He reviews the doctrines of insanity " dogmatically " laid down by Lord Hale with such effect on his successors. He suggests in a footnote that one reason why the criminal law of insanity has undergone so little improvement in England is probably that the accused, not being allowed counsel, the " officers of government have always been at liberty to put their own construction on the law." " Thus," he says, " the old maxims have been repeated year after year, and not being questioned, their correctness has remained undoubted." He makes a long attack upon the " right and wrong test " as well as upon the " delusion test " laid down in the *Hadfield* case. He then proceeds to an extensive discussion of " moral insanity," a disorder which had been described by Pinel and more recently in English by Prichard. " Insanity is a disease, and as is the case with all diseases, the fact of its existence is never established by a single diagnostic symptom, but by the whole body of symptoms, no particular one of which is present in every case." He reviews the law of insanity in Great Britain and in this country, too, as " loose, vacillating and greatly behind the present knowledge of the disease." He suggests that it would be wiser to permit the jury to decide whether or not the mental unsoundness, if it existed, embraced the criminal act within its sphere of influence. In this connection he recommends court experts in the French manner as a means of giving the jury sound advice. Further, if insanity is pleaded a commission should be appointed, consisting of men well experienced in the study of mental disorder, who will proceed to the examination of the accused " with coolness and impartiality." The chapter concludes with a panegyric of phrenology,[10] although the word phrenology is not mentioned. He says that those who refuse to take the dominant philosophy on trust and seriously inquire into its foundations " are stigmatised as visionaries and over-whelmed with ridicule and censure." [11] This eulogy, it may be added parenthetically, is found in each of the first four editions, but was omitted in the fifth edition of the work, which appeared in 1870.

Ray then proceeds to discuss Mental Disease in General, Idiocy, Imbecility, the Legal Consequences of Mental Deficiency, the Pathology and Symptoms of Mania, and what he terms Intellectual Mania, both general and partial. An original part of his contribution is Chapter 7 on Moral Mania. " Thus far," he says, " Mania has been considered as affecting the intellectual faculties only. . . . It will not be denied that the propensities and sentiments are also integral portions of our mental constitution and . . . dependent on the cerebral organism. . . . We were bound to believe that [the brain] is liable to disease and consequently, that the affective, as well as the intellectual faculties are subject to derangement." Previously to Pinel, he says, it was a matter of universal belief that insanity is always accompanied by derangement of the reasoning powers. Pinel found, however, that " many maniacs have betrayed no lesion whatever the understanding, but were under the dominion of instinctive and abstract fury. This form of mental disorder he designated as *manie sans délire*." [12]

He quotes Prichard as defining this condition as " consisting in a morbid perversion of the natural feelings, affections, inclinations, temper, habits, and moral disposition without any notable lesion of the intellect or knowing and reasoning faculties, and particularly without any maniacal hallucinations." In defending moral insanity Ray recognised the importance of the affective as distinguished from the cognitive life, a fact which was emphasised by the researches of

[10] The word " phrenology " appears in the index of the third edition only.
[11] *A Treatise on the Medical Jurisprudence of Insanity* (Boston, 1838), p. 66.
[12] *Op. cit.* p. 169.

Freud and which is an integral part of the modern concepts of psychiatry. Under Moral Insanity he includes the compulsive acts such as kleptomania, fire-setting, what is now termed sexual psychopathy, and homicidal insanity; in general, that is, some of the neuroses and " psychopathic ['sociopathic'] personality."

He writes later [13] as follows: " In medical science, it is dangerous to reason against facts. Now we have an immense mass of cases related by men of unquestionable competence and veracity, where people are *irresistibly* impelled to the commission of criminal acts while fully conscious of their nature and consequences. . . . They are not fictions invented by medical men for the purpose of puzzling juries and defeating the ends of justice, but plain, unvarnished facts as they occurred in nature; and to set them aside without a thorough investigation, as unworthy of influencing our decisions, indicates anything rather than that spirit of sober and indefatigable inquiry which should characterise the science of jurisprudence. We need have no fear that the truth on this subject will not finally prevail, but the interests of humanity require that this event should take place speedily." It is interesting that the British Royal Commission on Capital Punishment in 1953 was still discussing this very point!

In discussing Lucid Intervals [14] Ray cautions against mistaking the disappearance of symptoms for the cure of disease, citing malaria and epilepsy as examples. " That the intermissions of mania are ever so complete, that the mind is restored to its original integrity, would seem scarcely probable, from the fact, that the very seat of the pathological changes is the material organ on which the manifestations of mental phenomena depend." [15] We should, he says, exercise far greater caution in applying the doctrine in criminal cases than in civil, as the momentary excitement caused by sudden provocation may easily end the " temporary cure." He concludes [16]: " Burdened as the criminal law is with false principles on the subject of insanity, the time has gone by when juries will return a verdict of *guilty* against one who is admitted to have been insane, within a short period of time before the criminal act with which he is charged."

The remaining of the twenty-five chapters are discussions of Dementia, Delirium, the Duration and Curability of Madness,

---

[13] *Op. cit.* p. 263.
[15] *Op. cit.* p. 321.
[16] *Op. cit.* p. 337.

[14] *Op. cit.* Chap. 14.

Simulated Insanity and Concealed Insanity, Suicide, Somnambulism, the Effect of Insanity on Evidence, Drunkenness and finally Interdiction. In this last chapter he discusses, to some extent, matters of guardianship and conservatorship, as well as confinement of the mentally ill. This is a topic which he developed in great detail in later works, as we shall see.

The fourth [17] and subsequent editions contained another chapter on the duties of medical witnesses and referred to the first American case [18] in which it was required that an expert should give his opinion on an hypothesis rather than on the evidence he had heard. Ray referred to the hypothetical question as " a fiction, an acknowledged creation of fancy," which is supposed " to serve the ends of truth and justice better than the actual facts." This chapter was largely based on an article by Ray [19] in which he commented on the fact that although Lord Hale must have made himself familiar with all the learning of his time, the doctrines of physicians on the subject of mental disorder have been treated " as the speculations of visionary men, used by ingenious counsel for the purpose of screening their clients from the consequences of their crimes." The common law, he added, must welcome the teachings of science if it is to deserve the merit its advocates claim for it. In this, as in so many other respects, Ray proved himself far ahead of his time.

The book was enthusiastically reviewed [20] in the *American Jurist* by Luther S. Cushing (later a judge and a reporter of Massachusetts decisions) who, with George Hillard, was a co-editor of the *American Jurist* with Charles Sumner. Emphasising the debt which Ray owed to phrenology, Cushing mentioned his division of the " organs " of the brain into those of the affective powers and the intellectual powers, adding that if this classification be true " it furnishes an intelligible rule for ascertaining the civil rights, as well as the criminal responsibilities, of the insane." Cushing also emphasised the importance of Ray's concept of moral mania.

Superintendent of two mental hospitals

Ray did not remain long in Eastport after the appearance of his *magnum opus*. In 1841 he was appointed the Superintendent of

[17] The fourth edition was published in 1860.
[18] *U.S.* v. *McGlue*, 26 Fed.Cas. 1093 (1851).
[19] 22 *Monthly Law Reporter*, 129 (July 1859).
[20] See 19 *The American Jurist*, 363 (July 1838).

the new Maine Insane Hospital at Augusta, where he remained until 1845. His reports as Superintendent are carefully written and discuss at considerable length his concepts of the proper treatment of the mentally ill. He was opposed to depletion, the method which had been used extensively by Benjamin Rush, and stated that he preferred to depend largely on moral means, that is, treatment which is addressed directly to the mind itself, or as we would say today, psychotherapy. He spoke of amusements and games, reading, walks, religious services and occupation of various sorts. He was somewhat opposed to the English doctrine of non-restraint, considering that on the whole a moderate amount of physical restraint for disturbed patients was beneficial rather than harmful. Apparently he looked on the British method, which of course is now generally accepted throughout Western Europe and the United States, as a form of what he termed " ultra-ism."

It was during his incumbency of the office of Superintendent of Augusta that he became in 1844 one of the " Original Thirteen," the founders of the Association of Medical Superintendents of American Institutions for the Insane, now known as the American Psychiatric Association, the oldest national medical organisation in the United States. Aside from bringing out a second edition of *The Medical Jurisprudence* in 1843 and writing a review of the account of the famous trial of Abner Rogers,[21] in Massachusetts, he did very little other writing in this period.

In 1845, on the recommendation of a number of prominent psychiatrists, the group who were planning to build and operate a private mental hospital in Providence, Rhode Island, appointed him Superintendent of the Butler Hospital. He suggested visiting the European hospitals first, and characteristically insisted on paying his own expenses rather than having them defrayed by the trustees. He spent a number of months in Europe,[22] and on his return

---

[21] 7 Metcalf 500.

[22] This was in all probability Ray's first and only trip to Europe. In an article on Ray in *One Hundred Years of American Psychiatry* (Col.Univ.Press, 1944), p. 67, the present author stated that Ray " interrupted his practice to spend almost a year in England and France (1828–29)," and quoted at length from a diary (unsigned) in the possession of Butler Hospital which was attributed to Ray. That attribution is almost certainly incorrect; rather, the diary appears to have been written by Amariah Brigham, a friend of Ray, who is known to have been in Europe at that time!

Notices in the *Eastern Argus*, of Portland, Maine, recently located by Dr. Louis E. Reik, indicate that in June 1828 Ray advertised to give a two months' course in Botany, and that in November of the same year he proposed to " repeat his course of Lectures on Natural History." The preface of his " conversations on the Animal Economy " was dated May 11, 1829. Thus an " alibi " is established for Ray—he

reported under the title " Observations on Foreign Hospitals for the Insane," in the April 1846 issue of the *American Journal of Insanity* (2: 289). On his return to Providence in the spring of 1846 he engaged in planning and constructing the buildings of the Butler Hospital; he remained as the Superintendent from May 1846 to January 1867, despite his original intention, as stated in his letter of acceptance, not to " continue in the office more than three or four years."

During the period of his superintendency at Butler Hospital Ray spent nearly all of his time at the hospital, travelling very little except on the occasions when he was called as an expert witness. That he did much writing and thinking on medico-legal problems as well as on other matters is quite clear from his bibliography. He wrote, for example, on Shakespeare's delineations of insanity, on education in relation to the health of the brain, on the popular feeling towards hospitals for the insane, etherisation in the treatment of insanity, the insanity of George III, cerebral dynamics and on legislation for the insane in Maine. In the latter article [23] he refers particularly to an Act of 1847 (c. 33) forbidding the care of the mentally ill in gaols, and providing for simpler commitment, and for an observation commitment until further order of the court to a state hospital if a plea of insanity is entered in a criminal case. This latter course, he adds, " is unknown to the forms of the English common law, and this, we suspect, is the first attempt to incorporate it with these forms." He refers also to a " recent New York case " (further details not given) in which doctors who were sent to the gaol to examine a defendant were refused admission on the orders of the District Attorney !

In 1850 he proposed a Project of a Law for Regulating the Legal Relations of the Insane.[24] The insane, he holds, should be held liable in tort and trespass actions, and if a question of mental fitness

certainly was not away from Portland for " almost a year " in 1828 or 1829. Further, Ray himself wrote in the *American Journal of Insanity* for April 1846 (2: 289): " An interval of professional leisure, during the last summer, enabled me to gratify a long-cherished wish of seeing a little of the Old World "—hardly the words of a repeater! Finally, as corroboration may be added the fact that a *Biographical Sketch of Dr. Amariah Brigham* by E. K. Hunt (Utica, 1858) contains lengthy quotations from Brigham's diary which correspond exactly with the handwritten pages of the manuscript diary at Butler Hospital. To those of his colleagues who may have referred to this passage in his article, the author offers his apologies; to Dr. Reik, who made the identification of the diaries as Brigham's, he extends his thanks.

[23] 4 Am.J.Insan. 211.

[24] 13 *The Monthly Law Reporter*, N.S. 3, p. 217, and 7 Amer.J.Insan. 215.

for trial arises the defendant should be preferably committed to a mental hospital for observation. Insane persons should not be held responsible for criminal acts unless such acts are proved not to be the direct or indirect results of insanity. He also recommended a commission for the commitment of the mentally ill. He later expanded the ideas in this article into a comprehensive " project " which will be mentioned below.

Aside from the third and fourth editions of *The Medical Jurisprudence*, the only other book which appeared from Ray's pen during the Butler period was entitled *Mental Hygiene* (1863). This phrase, which seems very familiar and modern to us, actually had been used by Sweetser twenty years earlier (1843). Mental hygiene he defines as " the art of preserving the health of the mind against all the incidents and influences calculated to deteriorate its qualities, impair its energies, or derange its movement." In discussing the influence of the times upon mental disorder, Ray takes the position that mental disease is on the increase and adds: " Every advance in civilisation implies cerebral effort." He speaks of the atmosphere of excitement in which people are living at the present time, " an atmosphere," he says, " which without the most prudent management is calculated to impair the vigour of the mind and facilitate the invasion of disease." Among the factors operating adversely, he comments on the increase of newspapers and books, imaginative books and especially juvenile books, as well as the failing influence of the home in education—a modern ring indeed!

Ray's stay at Butler Hospital was an active and fruitful one. Beside managing the affairs of the hospital closely and writing the annual report, he wrote frequently for the legal and medical journals and presented numerous papers at the meetings of the Association of Medical Superintendents of American Institutions for the Insane. Mention has been made of his presentation at a meeting of the Association in 1850 of a project of a law relative to the legal relations of the insane. This was a matter which occupied much of his thought, and which culminated in 1864 with a proposal adopted by the Association, entitled: " A Project of a General Law for Determining the Legal Relations of the Insane." [25] The article was a comprehensive one, dealing with the principles of commitment and of other relations of the mentally ill, including such matters as

[25] 21 Am.J.Insan. 21–62.

liability in tort and trespass, guardianship, wills and criminal responsibility. For commitment, he recommended a commission which would report to a justice of the court in the case of any person alleged to be in need of care, and recommended authorising a similar commission to report in the event that it was alleged that a person in confinement was not in further need of hospitalisation.

Paragraphs 12 to 16 inclusive are of particular interest as dealing with criminal cases. It is provided: that insane persons shall not be made responsible for criminal acts in a criminal suit, unless such acts shall be proved not to have been the result, directly or indirectly, of insanity; that there be delay of the trial in the event that insanity is alleged, until such time as the insanity shall be cured. In the events of such an allegation the commission shall examine the prisoner, and if he is found to be mentally ill he is to be confined "in some hospital or in some other place favourable for a scientific observation of his mental condition." Commitment is provided in the event of acquittal by reason of insanity, the prisoner to be discharged, however, in the event that the "paroxysm of insanity" is found by the judge to be the first and only one ever experienced, in which case he should be unconditionally discharged. Other sections provide for the responsibility of insane persons in civil suits for injury to person or property, and for the invalidity of contracts and wills of the insane.

Two other items of biography may be mentioned during the Butler Hospital period; he was given the honorary degree of Master of Arts by Bowdoin College in 1846 and in 1855 he was elected president of the Rhode Island Medical Society and what is now the American Psychiatric Association, serving in the latter capacity for four years.

Further articles and books

In January 1867 Doctor Ray resigned as Superintendent of the Butler Hospital, partly at least on account of failing health, and removed to Philadelphia. He immediately became interested in the public affairs of the city and the state, lectured for a time in one of the medical colleges in Philadelphia, testified frequently in medico-legal cases, and continued to write vigorously and effectively on medico-legal matters. During this period two volumes appeared from his pen, both in 1873. One of them, a small booklet entitled

Ideal Characters of the Officers of a Hospital for the Insane, was probably inspired by a tractate of Thomas Fuller, the author of *The Holy War*. It discusses, for example, The Good Superintendent, The Good Steward, The Good Wife of the Superintendent and The Good Attendant. The other volume was entitled *Contributions to Mental Pathology*. This was largely a reprinting of selected articles which had already appeared. The volume shows the wide range of Ray's interests and his forceful way of presenting matters. He deals with such varied topics as causes of insanity, statistics of insanity, objections to moral insanity considered, delusions and hallucinations, confinement of the insane, the law of insanity in criminal cases, medical experts and the reports of a number of interesting trials both of will cases and of crimes.

His article on the confinement of the insane [26] is so timely that an excerpt from it was used in the introduction of the Model Draft Act Governing the Hospitalisation of the Mentally Ill, which was prepared by the Federal Security Agency in 1950. In citing the purposes of a law concerning the confinement of the mentally ill he says: " In the first place the law should put no hindrance in the way to the prompt use of those instrumentalities which are regarded as most effectual in promoting the comfort and restoration of the patient. Secondly, it should spare all unnecessary exposure of private troubles, and all unnecessary conflict with popular prejudices. Thirdly, it should protect individuals from wrongful imprisonment. It would be objection enough to any legal provision, that it failed to secure these objects in the completest possible manner." He criticised the jury system for commitment then in vogue in Illinois, saying that it is " shocking to every notion of domestic propriety." He denied, as did and does everyone familiar with the actual situation, that improper confinement in mental hospitals was more than extremely rare. To him, admission should be as simple as possible, although he added that some sort of legislation is essential. He concludes: "that such legislation would prevent all popular clamour now so loud and wrathful, we do not believe. . . . As long as men are swift to believe any plausible story of wrongdoing, without inquiry or hesitation; as long as newspapers can find in such stories the materials of a great sensation; as long as there is a prevalent belief that no one is insane who is not furiously

---

[26] *Contributions to Mental Pathology*, p. 168.   Also 3 Amer.L.Rev. 193 (1869).

mad—so long will the confinement of the insane in establishments expressly designed for the purpose be viewed with feelings of distrust, whatever may be the legal provisions by which it is regulated."

The chapter on the evidence of medical experts [27] is a trenchant and penetrating critique of a problem which still plagues us today. It is objected, he says, that experts disagree; very little evidence of any sort, he retorts, is completely harmonious. If it be said that expert testimony confuses the jury, so does other testimony. " This objection to the testimony of experts comes with ill grace from lawyers, in view of the fact that it is regarded as sound law to admit, in questions of mental condition, the opinions of ordinary witnesses." He denies that experts are venal—" Because a man's opinions are worth money, it does not follow that they are corruptly bought." He doubts if appointment of neutral experts by the governor could be expected to remedy the situation " before some distant millenial period." He would adopt the Continental system of expertise, or provide, as in Maine, for observation commitment in criminal cases where insanity is alleged. He objects to the hypothetical question, and urges that the judge keep the cross-examination within its proper limits. In the last analysis, " We must look for improvement not so much to any devices of legislation, as to broader views and a firmer spirit on the part of those who administer the laws, to a higher sense of professional honour, both in the lawyer and the physician, and to a healthier public sentiment."

In a much later article on this topic [28] he phrased the proper ethics of the expert thus: " Doctors in testifying are bound by more than the Hippocratic Oath, to serve as faithful ministers of science, casting aside every ignoble prepossession born of the time or the place, and laying upon her altar the offering of an intelligent investigation and an honest purpose."

Two other articles may be mentioned briefly. In a review of a discussion of moral insanity [29] held in Paris in 1866 and attended by Falret, de Boismont, Morel, Baillarger, Moreau and others, he discussed, *inter alia*, hysteria. " The term hysteria is much used to signify whatever is obscure or strange in the disorders, mental and

[27] *Op. cit.* p. 409.
[28] " The Duncan Will Case," 31 Am.J.Insan. 277 (1875).
[29] 57 A.J.Med.Sci. 139 (1869).

bodily, of the fair sex. That it is an expression of ignorance rather than of knowledge can scarcely be denied. . . . None of the substitute names is less liable to objection." (Ray accepted in this article the then general belief that hysteria is confined to the female sex.) The other article [30] asked for a scientific study of occult phenomena in order to save from the " pernicious doctrines of spiritualism, and from our insane asylums thousands who are now hopelessly drifting in that direction." He expressed his belief that " such phenomena will be as satisfactorily explained as are now the wonders of electricity."

The New Hampshire Rule

Probably the most significant event of the Philadelphia period of Ray's life, something which has left its mark upon American jurisprudence, was the adoption of the so-called New Hampshire Rule in the case of criminal charges to which insanity is pleaded as a defence. Recently Dr. Louis E. Reik of Princeton has unearthed a considerable amount of correspondence which took place between Judge Charles Doe of the New Hampshire Supreme Court and Doctor Ray from 1866 to 1872.[31] As we have seen, Ray had long taken the position that the criteria of intellectual comprehension of right and wrong laid down in the M'Naghten Rules are wholly inadequate, and that, indeed, no legal definition or universally applicable test of criminal irresponsibility by reason of insanity can be devised. Judge Doe was thoroughly convinced that Ray was right, although he hesitated to quote Ray as his authority, preferring to confine his arguments to purely legal grounds. He concluded that " the great masters of our law " never made the distinction between law and fact in cases of insanity, and that by setting up various theoretical criteria for legal responsibility they not only invaded the realm of science but also betrayed the spirit of the common law. In 1865 Doe had dissented,[32] but by 1868 he had convinced Chief Justice Perley, so that the latter followed what is now called the New Hampshire Rule in charging.[33] This charge was upheld on appeal and again in the following year the Rule

[30] 22 Atl.Mo. 129 (1868).
[31] " The Doe-Ray Correspondence: A Pioneer Collaboration in the Jurisprudence of Mental Disease," 63 Yale L.J. 183 (December 1953).
[32] *Boardman* v. *Boardman*, 47 N.H. 120.
[33] *State* v. *Pike*, 49 N.H. 399.

was reaffirmed.[34] Judge Doe in his letters insisted that credit be given to his colleagues and that he be left out as much as possible. In a letter of May 24, 1869, Ray, for example, wrote: " I shall substitute Chief Justice Perley for Mr. Justice Doe because you so earnestly wish it, but I shall do it under a kind of mental protest."

In an article entitled " The Law of Insanity "[35] Ray discussed Judge Edmond's charge[36] in the first of three cases, all of which, he thought, paved the way for further advance. He proceeds: " A far greater advance of judicial opinion on this subject—one, indeed, that may be regarded as final—has been made in two cases recently adjudicated in New Hampshire." He then goes on to discuss the cases of *Boardman* v. *Woodman* and *State* v. *Pike.*[37] He adds: " We talk about the law of insanity. Properly speaking, there can be no law on this subject other than the facts themselves. Courts cannot rightfully say that insanity under certain forms destroys no element of responsibility. It may, or it may not; it is simply a question of fact." Commenting on the traditional " tests," he remarks that the older definitions show the state of medical science, then existing, and that only by hearsay. " We might as well," he adds, " go back to Galen and Hippocrates as to Hale's time." And again, " A new truth may be deprived of half its power by being mixed up with old formulas and venerable fallacies." He concludes: " The cases to which we have called the reader's attention, show both the prevailing dissatisfaction with the law of insanity as usually expounded, and the progress that has been making, during the last thirty years, towards that triumphant solution of doubts and difficulties which we have had the pleasure to record. The friends of humanity may now rejoice in the well-grounded faith that the day is not far distant when we shall cease to take the lives of the insane on the strength of a metaphysical subtlety."

Little remains to tell of the Philadelphia period. In 1879 Dr. Ray was honoured by Brown University with the degree of Doctor of Laws. In the same year his only son, Dr. B. Lincoln Ray, died suddenly. Doctor Isaac Ray died in his sleep in Philadelphia on March 31, 1881, his wife, whom he had married in Portland in 1831, surviving him. He was buried in Providence, Rhode Island.

[34] *State* v. *Jones,* 50 N.H. 369.
[35] 4 Amer.L.Rev. 236 (1870).
[36] *People* v. *Kleim,* 1 Edm.Sel.Cas. 13 N.Y.; *Common. ex rel Haskell* v. *Haskell,* 2 Brewster 491, Pa.; *Common.* v. *Rogers,* 7 Metcalf 500, Mass.
[37] Above, notes 32 and 33.

Ray in mid-twentieth century

Isaac Ray has been dead for over seventy years, but his influence and his memory are still strong. Recently, the Butler Hospital at Providence established an Isaac Ray Library, which houses Doctor Ray's personal library. In 1951 the American Psychiatric Association, of which he was one of the founders, established the Isaac Ray Award, to be given annually to a psychiatrist or member of the legal profession who has promoted closer relations between law and medicine. The first lecturer under this award was the author of the present article. The second was Dr. Gregory Zilboorg, the eminent psychiatrist of New York; and the lectures under the third award were given by the Honourable John Biggs, Jr., Chief Judge of the Third Circuit of the United States Court of Appeals. The latest recognition of the influence of Isaac Ray could hardly be more apropos. On July 1, 1954, the United States Court of Appeals for the District of Columbia (Bazelon J., with Edgerton and Washington JJ.), quoting Isaac Ray as one of its authorities, decided as follows[38]: "We find that as an exclusive criterion the right-wrong test is inadequate in that (a) it does not take sufficient account of psychic realities and scientific knowledge, and (b) it is based upon one symptom and so cannot validly be applied in all circumstances. We find that the irresistible impulse test is also inadequate and that it gives no recognition to mental illness characterised by brooding and reflection, and so relegates acts caused by such illness to the application of the inadequate right-wrong test. We conclude that a broader test should be adopted. . . . The rule we now hold must be applied on the retrial of this case and in future cases is not unlike that followed by the New Hampshire court since 1870. It is simply that an accused is not criminally responsible if his unlawful act was the product of mental disease or defect. . . . The legal and moral traditions of the Western world require that those who, of their own free will and with evil intent, commit acts which violate the law shall be criminally responsible for those acts. Our traditions also require that where such acts stem from and are the product of a mental disease or defect as those terms are used herein moral blame shall not attach and hence there will not be criminal responsibility. The rule we state in this opinion is designed to meet these requirements."

[38] See *Monte W. Durham* v. *United States*, 214 Fed. (2d) 862.

Epilogue

A gentleman of wide culture and reading, learned in various languages and a master of English style, a public-spirited citizen, an able hospital administrator, a thoughtful student of law and of medicine, Isaac Ray believed throughly that it was both desirable and possible that science should make further contributions to law. As he said in the conclusion of one of his last addresses—that given before the Medico-Legal Society of New York in 1877: "The administration of justice . . . must often be imperfect until the light of medical science is freely admitted and used; not the light that has travelled down to us from the times of Coke and Hale, but that which we owe to the progress of knowledge during the present century, greater, far greater indeed than that of all centuries together."

WINFRED OVERHOLSER.

BIBLIOGRAPHY

By Ray

A Treatise on the Medical Jurisprudence of Insanity. (3rd ed., 1855.)
Contributions to Mental Pathology. (Boston, 1873, Little, Brown & Co.)

On Ray

FINK, ARTHUR E. *Causes of Crime. Biological Theories in the United States 1800–1915.* (Philadelphia: University of Pennsylvania Press; London: Oxford University Press, 1938.)
WEIHOFEN, HENRY. *The Urge to Punish.* (New York: Farrar Straus & Cudahy, 1956; London: Victor Gollancz, 1957.)

General

ABRAHAMSEN, D. *Crime and the Human Mind.* (1944; reprinted Montclair, N.J., 1969, Patterson Smith.)
ASCHAFFENBURG, G. *Handbuch d. Gerichtlichen Psychiatrie.* (2. Aufl., Berlin, 1909, A. Hirschwald.)
BIGGS, J., Jr. *The Guilty Mind.* (Isaac Ray Award Lectures.) (N.Y. 1955, Harcourt Brace.)
BIRNBAUM, K. *Die Psychopathischen Verbrecher.* (Berlin, 1914, P. Langenscheidt.)
BROMBERG, W. *Crime and the Mind.* (N.Y. 1948, J. B. Lippincott & Co.)
CHAILLÉ, S. E. "Origin and Progress of Medical Jurisprudence, 1776–1876." Reprinted *J.of Crim.Law and Criminology,* 40: 397–444, Nov.–Dec. 1949.

COHEN, LOUIS H. *Murder, Madness and the Law.* (Cleveland, 1952, World Pub.Co.)

DAVIDSON, HENRY M. *Forensic Psychiatry.* (N.Y. 1952, Ronald Press.)

DE SAUSSURE, R. "Influence of the Concept of Monomania on French Medico-Legal Psychiatry" (from 1825 to 1840). J.Hist.Med. 1:365 (1946).

EAST, W. N. *Medical Aspects of Crime.* (London, 1936, Churchill.)

GLUECK, BERNARD. *Studies in Forensic Psychiatry.* (Boston, 1916, Little, Brown & Co.)

GLUECK, S. *Mental Disorder and the Criminal Law.* (Boston, 1925, Little, Brown & Co.)

GRASSET, J. (tr. JELLIFFE). *The Semi Insane and the Semi Responsible.* (N.Y. and London, 1907, Funk & Wagnalls Co.)

GUTTMACHER, M. S. and WEIHOFEN H. *Psychiatry and the Law.* (N.Y. 1952, W. W. Norton.)

HALL, J. K. and ZILBOORG, G. (eds.). *One Hundred Years of American Psychiatry.* (N.Y. 1944, Col.Univ.Press. Chapter on "Legal Aspects of Psychiatry," by Zilboorg, pp. 507-584.)

HOCH, P. and ZUBIN, J. (eds.). *Psychiatry and the Law.* (N.Y. 1955, Grune & Stratton.)

MAUDSLEY, H. *Responsibility in Mental Disease.* (London, 1874, H. S. King.)

MERCIER, CHARLES. *Crime and Insanity.* (London, 1911, Williams and Norgate.)

NEUSTATTER, W. L. *Psychological Disorder and Crime.* (London, 1953, C. Johnson.)

ORENSTEIN, LEO. "Examination of the Complaining Witness in a Criminal Court." Am.J.Psychiat. 107:684 (1951).

OVERHOLSER, W. *The Psychiatrist and the Law.* (Isaac Ray Award Lectures.) (N.Y. 1953, Harcourt Brace.)

RADZINOWICZ, L. (ed.). *Mental Abnormality and Crime.* (London, 1944, Macmillan.)

RAY, I. *Contributions to Mental Pathology.* (Boston, 1873, Little, Brown & Co.)

Report of Royal Commission on Capital Punishment. (1953) Cmd. 8932. H.M. Stationery Office.

SMITH, H. W. (ed.). "Scientific Proof and Relations of Law and Medicine." 29 Va.L.R. 697 (1943).

SOBELOFF, S. "From McNaghten to Durham and Beyond." *Psychiatric Quarterly* 29: 357-371 (1955).

WEIHOFEN, H. *Mental Disorder as a Criminal Defense.* (Buffalo, N.Y. 1954, Dennis & Co.)

WEIHOFEN, H. and OVERHOLSER, W. "Mental Disorder Affecting the Degree of a Crime." 56 Yale L.J. 959 (1947).

WHITE, WM. A. *Crime and Criminals.* (N.Y. 1933, Farrar.)

—— *Insanity and the Criminal Law.* (N.Y. 1923, Macmillan.)

ZILBOORG, G. *The Psychology of the Criminal Act and Punishment.* (Isaac Ray Award Lectures.) (N.Y. 1954, Harcourt Brace.)

NOTE ON THE CONTRIBUTOR

Dr. WINFRED OVERHOLSER was Professor of Psychiatry at Boston University (which awarded him an honorary Sc.D. in 1940) and Commissioner of Mental Diseases for the Commonwealth of Massachusetts. In 1937 he was appointed Superintendent of St. Elizabeth's Hospital in Washington, D.C. He was President of the American Psychiatric Association in 1947–48, and Vice-President of the First World Congress of Psychiatry in 1950. The U.S. Department of Health, Education and Welfare awarded him its Distinguished Service Award; his foreign decorations included the French Legion of Honour; in 1952 he received the first Isaac Ray Award of the American Psychiatric Association. Dr. Overholser was Editor-in-Chief of the *Quarterly Review of Psychiatry and Neurology* and author of *The Psychiatrist and the Law* and (with W. V. Richmond) *A Handbook of Psychiatry*. He died in 1964.

11

CHARLES DOE
1830–1896

THE tides of judicial history sometimes exhibit a strange faculty of ignoring their chief benefactors.[1] A classical example is Charles Doe who, at the age of twenty-nine, was appointed Associate Justice of the Supreme Court of New Hampshire and served in that capacity from 1859 to 1874, and as Chief Justice from 1876 until his death on March 9, 1896.[2] Probably not more than six judges in the United States and England have had a longer judicial career and none of them contributed as much to the advancement and improvement of the administration of justice and the judicial machinery to accomplish it expeditiously.[3]

While Doe's contributions are frequently overlooked, it is significant that those most qualified to judge his work have recognised that he was " one of the great judges of the last century,"[4] " a great name in American Law "[5] and one of " the ten judges who must be ranked first in American judicial history."[6] Wigmore's monumental *Treatise on Evidence* was dedicated to Charles Doe and James Bradley Thayer, " Two Masters in the Law of Evidence,"[7] and Jeremiah Smith has written convincingly of Doe's ability to decide cases on their merits and not permit justice to be " strangled in the net of form."[8] A more recent note has concluded that although Doe had " left a permanent impression on American jurisprudence . . . surprisingly little has been written

---

* Reproduced from *The Journal of Criminal Law, Criminology and Police Science*, Vol. 47, No. 3, September–October 1956.
[1] *Cf.* Abraham, " John Marshall Harlan; A Justice Neglected," 41 Va.L.Rev. 871, 872, 890 (1955).
[2] Elmer E. Doe, *The Descendants of Nicholas Doe*, 230–250 (1918); " Charles Doe," 5 *Dictionary Am.Biog.* 354 (1930).
[3] Hening, " Charles Doe," in 8 *Great American Lawyers*, 241, 243, 317 (Lewis ed., 1909).
[4] Roscoe Pound, *Interpretations of Legal History*, 108 (1923).
[5] Charles Fairman, " Does the Fourteenth Amendment Incorporate the Bill of Rights? " 2 Stan.L.Rev. 5, 86 (1949).
[6] Pound, *Formative Era of American Law*, 4 and note 2, 30–31 (1938).
[7] 1 Wigmore, *Evidence* V (1904).
[8] J. Smith, " Memoir of Charles Doe," 2 Proc.So.N.H.Bar Assn. 125, 144 (1899); Note, 9 Harv.L.R. 534 (1896).

about Doe either during his lifetime or since his death in 1896." [9]
Wigmore had no hesitation in expressing his opinion that Doe was
"one of the greatest of American judges." [10]   Nor is modern
authority from a respected source lacking since Professor Edmund
M. Morgan, an indefatigable leader in the field of reform in the
law of evidence, refers to the classic opinions of "the great Justice
Doe of New Hampshire." [11]

Within the limits of the few pages allotted to the title of this
comment, it is possible only to take a bird's-eye view of Doe the
man, and his contributions as a judge to a more enlightened consideration of insanity and the criminal law. While Doe's substantial
accomplishments in the field of evidence and procedure are the ones
that may be remembered today, [12] it is the purpose of this comment
to consider his single-handed and original contribution in making
medical science the handmaiden of criminal law in its application to
mental disorder. It is believed that Doe's early efforts prior to
1872 in that direction are just beginning to receive modern
consideration. [13]   It may well be he is the only judge, excluding
contemporaries, [14] who can truly be denominated a pioneer in
criminology.

Doe the man

Charles Doe was born in Derry, New Hampshire, on April 11,
1830.   His father, a large landowner and well known in the community, sent his son to the academies of South Berwick, Exeter and

[9] Note, "Doe of New Hampshire: Reflections on a Nineteenth Century Judge," 63
Harv.L.R. 513 (1950).   In addition to the references cited in this note, see also 53
Albany L.J. 161 (1896); 27 Am.L.Rev. 71 (1893); 30 Am.L.Rev. 286 (1896); 3 Parker,
Courts and Lawyers of New England, 573 (1931); Weihofen, "The Flowering of New
Hampshire," in *Symposium on Insanity and the Criminal Law*, 22 U.Chi.L.Rev. 356,
363 (1955).
[10] 2 Wigmore, *Evidence* (3rd ed., 1940), § 445, p. 433.
[11] 1 *Basic Problems of Evidence*, pp. 26, 172 (1954).
[12] "There can scarcely be a single Harvard Law School man here who has not heard of
the great Chief Justice commonly known as 'C. Doe of New Hampshire.' He died as
long ago as 1896, but he had the fire and he had the learning and the practical common
sense which made him, wholly without aid from the legislature of New Hampshire,
the great leader in the improvement of the administration of justice in that state. Full
of whimsies and sometimes as eccentric as a March Hare, he was imbued with the
spirit of justice and fought for it all his life, fought for it in the hard, practical, matter-
of-fact way that one would expect from a native of New Hampshire." Quoted from
an address by Judge Harold R. Medina to the members of the Pennsylvania Bar,
appearing in 36 Jour.of the Amer.Jud.Soc. 8 (June 1952).
[13] *Durham* v. *United States* (D.C.Cir.), 214 F. 2d 862 (1954).
[14] The series of articles under the general title, "Pioneers in Criminology," specifically
eliminates consideration of contemporary criminologists.   "We confess to having been
arbitrary in that we have selected no contemporary criminologist for inclusion in this
series." 45 J.Crim.L., C.& P.S. 1 (1954).

Andover, and one term at Harvard College from which he transferred to Dartmouth where he graduated in 1849. After one term
at the Harvard Law School he returned to New Hampshire to
become county solicitor for Strafford county. From 1854 until his
appointment as an associate justice of the Supreme Court of New
Hampshire on September 23, 1859, he was engaged in a substantial
trial practice, both criminal and civil.[15] During this period he took
an active interest in politics, first as a Democrat and later as a
Republican, and made many friends and acquired an equal number
of enemies.

Although Doe was financially independent, he lived simply,
dressed as a country storekeeper or farmer rather than a judge of
his era and was a thorough believer in fresh air.[16] A typical comment was that he " was a man of simple tastes and eccentric
manners, but of genuine legal talents and clear and impartial
mind." [17] There is not the slightest doubt that Doe was individualistic in thought and action, but there is reason to believe that
references to his eccentricities have been exaggerated. He was stern
with cant, impatient with ceremony unless he conceived it fulfilled
some essential function [18] and was unawed by precedent unless it
appeared to have a logical basis.[19] It remains for someone to make
a more adequate study of his life before we can say with certainty
whether his thoughts were unique or whether their expression may
be classed as eccentric.[20] However, the most recent evaluation of
Doe confirms earlier opinions that his " treatment of substantive
problems sometimes showed an almost unique originality." [21] Doe's
originality did not go unnoticed and it was inevitable that in
addition to criticism there would also be parody. In a humorous

[15] See Hening, above, note 3, at 245: " ' We have been over the dockets again very
carefully, and we feel sure that Charles Doe's name appeared as counsel in 223 different
cases up to the time of his appointment to the bench.' Letter to writer from W. H.
Roberts, clerk of Superior Court, 1906."
[16] " Judge Doe was eccentric in manner, dress and mode of living and was a confirmed
believer in fresh air. . . . Lawyers declare that to attend court in winter, when the
Chief Justice presided, was equal to a trip to the Arctic regions." 53 Albany L.J. 161
(1896).
[17] 20 *Granite Monthly*, 275 (1896).
[18] Eastman, " Chief Justice Doe," 9 *Green Bag*, 245, 250 (1897).
[19] *Metcalf* v. *Gilmore*, 59 N.H. 417, 433 (1879): " As there was a time when there were
no common-law precedents, everything that can be done with them could be done
without them."
[20] John Reid, Esq. of Dover N.H., is presently engaged in a careful and exhaustive study
of all the existing material on Doe. In view of the inadequate material which exists
today, students of Doe will welcome Reid's work as filling a void in American judicial
biography.
[21] 63 Harv.L.R. 513, 518 (1950), above, note 9.

sketch before a Bar Association Doe C.J. is pictured as rendering a certain decision and giving as his sole reason " that the law has hitherto always been understood to be otherwise." [22]

Doe the judge

Doe first gave serious thought to the problem of mental disorder in his dissenting opinion [23] in *Boardman* v. *Woodman*. This was a will case in which the majority held that witnesses who were not experts and were not witnesses to the will could not testify as to the sanity of the testator. Doe objected to the majority ruling which affirmed instructions that delusions were the test of insanity. It was his view that this was a question of fact for the jury and not a question of law for the court to instruct the jury. A summary of some " of his most forcible sentences " [24] appear at p. 150 of the opinion: " If it is necessary that the law should entertain a single medical opinion concerning a single disease, it is not necessary that that opinion should be a cast-off theory of physicians of a former generation. That cannot be a fact in law, which is not a fact in science; that cannot be health in law, which is disease in fact. And it is unfortunate that courts should maintain a contest with science and the laws of nature, upon a question of fact which is within the province of science and outside the domain of our law. All inconsistencies and difficulties are avoided by adhering to the spirit and elementary principles of the law, which declare that a will cannot be produced by any form of mental disease, and that the indications and tests of mental disease are matters of fact."

In *State* v. *Pike* Doe's views prevailed and the decision affirmed the following instructions to the jury [25]: " that whether there is such a mental disease as dipsomania, and whether defendant had that disease, and whether the killing of Brown was the product of such disease, were questions of fact for the jury." In amplification of his criticism of the prevailing right and wrong test, Doe contended that it was an unsuccessful attempt " to instal old exploded medical theories in the place of facts established in the progress of scientific knowledge." [26] " If our precedents practically established

[22] J. Smith, "Memoir of Charles Doe," 2 Proc.So.N.H.Bar Assn. 125, 149 (1897).
[23] N.H. 47, 120, 140 (1866).
[24] 9 Harv.L.R. 534, 535 (1896).
[25] 49 N.H. 399, 407–408 (1869).
[26] *Ibid.* p. 438.

old medical theories which science has rejected, and absolutely rejected those which science has established, they might at least claim the merit of formal consistency. But the precedents require the jury to be instructed in the new medical theories by experts, and in the old medical theories by the judge " [27] (pp. 438–439).

In *State* v. *Jones*, 50 N.H. 369, 398 (1871), a unanimous court rejected the M'Naghten Rules [28] and adopted Doe's theory that criminal responsibility was a question of fact for the jury. If the defendant had a mental disease and the criminal act was a product of that mental disease, the jury was to acquit the defendant. The jury in the *Jones* case was given the same instructions that were used in *State* v. *Pike* and these instructions were upheld as correct: " If the defendant killed his wife in a manner that would be criminal and unlawful if the defendant were sane, the verdict should be ' not guilty by reason of insanity,' if the killing was the offspring or product of mental disease in the defendant." Under the New Hampshire rule there is no legal test of insanity and the issue of criminal responsibility is a question of fact to be decided by the jury upon all the evidence presented to them, including that of the experts. [29] " Whether the defendant had a mental disease, as before remarked, seems to be as much a question of fact as whether he had a bodily disease; and whether the killing of his wife was the product of that disease was also as clearly a matter of fact as whether thirst and a quickened pulse are the product of fever. That it is a difficult question does not change the matter at all."

The New Hampshire rule and the M'Naghten Rules

For many years it has been well known in New Hampshire that Doe not only inspired many decisions but in some cases actually wrote decisions, although they appeared under the name of another judge. [30] Dr. Reik has demonstrated clearly Judge Doe's part in the opinion by Judge Ladd in *State* v. *Jones*, and Doe's attempt to give credit to his colleagues rather than himself in establishing the New Hampshire rule on insanity. [31] Judge Doe owed a great debt to

[27] *Ibid.* pp. 438–439.
[28] *M'Naghten's Case*, 10 Cl.& Fin. 200, 210; 8 Eng.Rep. 718, 722 (H.L., 1843).
[29] A summary of the New Hampshire rule including the authorities that support it and criticise it may be found in Weihofen, *Mental Disorder as a Criminal Defence*, pp. 113–119 (1954).
[30] See Hening, above, note 3, at 304; 63 Harv.L.R. 513, 514, above, note 9.
[31] Reik, " The Doe-Ray Correspondence: A Pioneer Collaboration in the Jurisprudence of Mental Disease," 63 Yale L.J. 145 (1953).

Dr. Isaac Ray, who is generally regarded as an American pioneer in forensic psychiatry.[32] "As we have seen, Ray had long taken the position that the criteria of intellectual comprehension of right and wrong laid down in the M'Naghten Rules are wholly inadequate, and that, indeed, no legal definition or universally applicable test of criminal irresponsibility by reason of insanity can be devised. Judge Doe was thoroughly convinced that Ray was right, although he hesitated to quote Ray as his authority, preferring to confine his arguments to purely legal grounds. He concluded that 'the great masters of our law' never made the distinction between law and fact in cases of insanity, and that by setting up various theoretical criteria for legal responsibility they not only invaded the realm of science but also betrayed the spirit of the common law." [33]

Long before Cardozo [34] and Pound had made forceful pleas for the necessity of integrating law and science, Doe was the first judge to insist that the law should collaborate with science and particularly in the field of criminal responsibility.[35] Even able commentators who think that the M'Naghten Rules should be retained with some modification would agree with Doe that we should continue to find a way to integrate the progress of medical science with the development of the law of mental disorder.[36]

In 1953 the British Royal Commission on Capital Punishment issued its report after a five-year study. It recommended that the present legal tests of insanity be abolished and that the jury be allowed to decide whether the defendant was suffering from such a mental disease or deficiency that "he ought not to be held responsible." [37] At long last the voice of Doe, the first judge who was a pioneer in criminology, at least received modern consideration for the views which he had expressed almost a century ago.[38] In 1954

[32] See above, p. 129. [33] See note 32, above.
[34] Cardozo, *What Medicine Can Do for the Law*, 32 (1930).
[35] See Reik, above, note 31, at 196: "As to the New Hampshire rule itself, we can only conclude from the correspondence here presented that if it deals with matters too complicated for juries to decide unassisted, it nevertheless seeks to open the way for scientific progress in the jurisprudence of mental disease, and marks a step toward true collaboration between science and the law in the spirit of Judge Doe and Dr. Ray."
[36] Hall, "Psychiatry and Criminal Responsibility," 65 Yale L.J. 761, 768–785 (May 1956).
[37] *Report of the Royal Commission on Capital Punishment* (1949–53) (1953), Cmd. 8932, at 116.
[38] Stockly, "Mental Disorders and Criminal Responsibility: the Recommendations of the Royal Commission on Capital Punishment," 33 Tex.L.Rev. 482, 485–486 (1955): "Nearly a hundred years ago, under the leadership of Judge Doe, the New Hampshire Supreme Court, believing that then-used tests of responsibility (the M'Naghten Rules and the irresistible impulse test) were ineffectual, held that the question of an accused's responsibility was for the jury without reference to any test other than an inquiry whether he had acted with a criminal intent."

the *Durham* case[39] decided " that an accused is not criminally responsible if his unlawful act was the product of mental disease or mental defect." While it did not give credit to Doe's pioneer efforts in this field, it did state that the " rule we now hold . . . is not unlike that followed by the New Hampshire court since 1870." Both the *Durham* case and the New Hampshire rule have been defended[40] as well as criticised.[41] " What is the reason for the sudden attention now being shown to Judge Doe's octogenarian wallflower? Is the happening of the *Durham* case and the Royal Commission's report within a year of each other mere coincidence? I am inclined to think not. Rather, these developments seem to me a vindication of Professor George Dession's prophecy made in 1938, that ' the infiltration of psychiatry—and all psychiatrists into the administration of criminal law ' will one day be recognised as ' overshadowing all other contemporary phenomena ' in its influence on the evolution of criminal justice." [42]

The American Law Institute is preparing a Model Penal Code, and while it does not adopt the New Hampshire rule it is at least encouraging to note that the M'Naghten Rules are undergoing reconsideration in the light of modern medical science.[43] Whether one favours the New Hampshire rule, the *Durham* rule or whether one believes that greater progress would be made by the recommendations of the British Royal Commission or the American Law Institute is not material in achieving the real objective of integrating law and medicine in the light of modern knowledge. Improvements will be made even if we follow those psychiatrists who believe there is much merit in the M'Naghten Rules providing that they can be brought up to date in the light of modern scientific developments.[44]

Conclusion

Doe recognised that the legal profession would not adopt medical science as law and that the only solution was to adopt " the venerable principle of the common law " that questions of medical

[39] *Durham* v. *United States*, 214 F. 2d 862, 874–875 (D.C.Cir., 1954).
[40] Sobeloff, " Insanity and the Criminal Law: from McNaghten to Durham, and beyond," 41 A.B.A.J. 793 (1955).
[41] Hall, above, note 36.
[42] Dession, " Psychiatry and the Conditions of Criminal Justice," 47 Yale L.J. 319 (1938).
  Weihofen, " The Flowering of New Hampshire," 22 U.Chi.L.Rev. 356, 363 (1955).
[43] American Law Institute, Model Penal Code, tentative draft No. 4 Sec. 4.01 (1955).
[44] Wertham, " Psychoauthoritarianism and the Law," 22 U.Chi.L.Rev. 336 (1955).

science be left to the jury as questions of fact.[45]   While Doe was convinced that the antagonism between medical science and law could be removed, " my fear is very strong that it can be done within 100 years on no other basis than the principle which I have undertaken to establish. . . ."[46]   Perhaps in 1969 Doe's prophecy may come true but in any event he would be the first to admit that any improvement on the traditional tests for insanity would be a major gain in criminal law even if his method was not adopted. We have already alluded to the fact that Doe was particularly impatient with sham and cant and he would probably agree with Mr. Justice Frankfurter's statements before the British Royal Commission on Capital Punishment: " I am a great believer in being as candid as possible about my institutions.   They are in a large measure abandoned in practice, and therefore I think the M'Naghten Rules are in a large measure shams. . . .   I dare to believe that we ought not to rest content with the difficulty of finding an improvement in the M'Naghten Rules." [47]   While Doe's contribution to the difficult problem of criminal responsibility is not *the* only solution, at least it was " *a* tangible solution in an area where the law has long been criticised for inertia." [48]

One may not agree with Doe's views on criminal responsibility and yet concede that he was the first judge in America who can be rated as a pioneer in criminology.

FRANK R. KENISON.

BIBLIOGRAPHY

REID, JOHN.   "Understanding the New Hampshire Doctrine of Criminal Insanity," *The Yale Law Journal*, Vol. 69, No. 3 (January 1960), pp. 367–420.
—— *Chief Justice: The Judicial World of Charles Doe* (Cambridge, Mass., 1967, Harvard University Press).

45 Reik, above, note 31, at 193.
46 See Doe's letter of March 23, 1869, to Dr. Ray, quoted in Reik, above, note 31, at 194.
47 Note 37, above, at 102.
48 " Criminal Responsibility and Mental Disorder: New Approaches to an Old Problem," 30 Ind.L.J. 194, 217 (1955).   While the quoted statement was made with reference to the Durham decision it is equally applicable to the New Hampshire rule.

NOTE ON THE CONTRIBUTOR

The Hon. FRANK R. KENISON was a Justice of the Supreme Court of New Hampshire from 1946 to 1952 and has been Chief Justice since that time. He had served successively as a County Attorney in his state, as Assistant Attorney-General, and as Attorney-General for the State of New Hampshire, before assuming the office of Justice of the Supreme Court. He is a member of the American and New Hampshire Bar Associations, the American Judicature Society and the American Law Institute.

12

HENRY MAUDSLEY
1835–1918

THERE must be some misgivings as to what Henry Maudsley would have thought of this attempt to evaluate his contribution to criminology. In his view the historian of an eminent person " is very apt, if not pretty sure, to misjudge." In defensive mood he stated that " it is obvious ingratitude and folly . . ." to despise the knowledge of the past as worthless and its errors as contemptible . . ." for " these very errors had their place and value to promote the evolutional process of which it is the outcome." He deplored a proud and sympathetically self-interested generation which shall count invaluable the treasures, records, portraits and relics of its prominent members, for this would be " certainly egotistic egoism in excelsis." Furthermore, though it was inevitable that Maudsley's erudite and wide-ranging mind should have inquired into matters criminological, this was not his primary interest nor the direction in which his contribution was greatest. " Let it be our prayer," he wrote, " that when . . . this generation comes up for critical judgment as a historical study before the tribunal of posterity, it may be said justly of it, that it has done as much for the progress of mankind as some of the generations upon which the wisest of us are apt to look back with indulgent compassion, and the unwise among us with foolish scorn." Surveying the progress in this field since his day, we must surely adopt a more humble judgment than he had feared; we have indeed small grounds for mightily magnifying our own superiority.

Henry Maudsley was born near Settle in Yorkshire in 1835 at a farmhouse called Rome in the parish of Giggleswick. He seems to have had a drab childhood; his memories of his mother, soon to die, were chiefly of a suffering invalid. His father, naturally silent and much affected by the loss of his wife, had hardly a word for

* Reproduced from *The Journal of Criminal Law, Criminology and Police Science*, Vol. 46, No. 6, March–April 1956.

his sons " except when absolutely necessary." Maudsley writes of this time as a succession of sombre and dreary years.

In the year of his birth, and in the same county, Hughlings Jackson was born. Darwin was in the " Beagle," Pritchard published his *Treatise on Insanity*; at about this time, too, Lombroso was born. Gardiner Hill might have been preparing his lectures on the total abolition of restraint in the treatment of the insane, Malthus would be planning his book on the principle of population, Isaac Ray his *Medical Jurisprudence of Insanity*, and Mayo proposing the establishment of a hospital-prison, while Elliotson would be disturbing University College Hospital by his introduction of " mesmerism."

Maudsley proceeded through a formal and unimaginative education to a brilliant medical career. In 1856 at the age of twenty-one, he graduated, M.D., at London and was honoured as " University Medical Scholar " of his year. In later years he exchanged the ten gold medals of his studentship for a watch " which I leave behind me to tick when my heart shall cease to tick." At only twenty-three he was appointed Medical Superintendent of the Manchester Royal Lunatic Asylum. At twenty-seven he was editing the *Journal of Mental Science*, and at twenty-nine and thirty-four respectively he was appointed Physician to the West London Hospital and Professor of Medical Jurisprudence at University College.

The period between Maudsley's twentieth and twenty-fifth years was a stimulating one. He must have been thrilled by the physiological work of Helmholtz and Fechner, and by Darwin's *Origin of Species*. Bain produced his handbook on *Emotions and Will* at this time, and Bucknill and Tuke their famous *Manual of Psychological Medicine*. While Broca was initiating the Anthropological Society of Paris (1859) we know that Lombroso was conceiving his *L'Uomo Delinquente*. Another book which influenced him much was Morel's *Des Dégénéresences*, and, of course, Maudsley's future sparring partner, the M'Naghten Rules, had just appeared. Matthew Davenport Hill, the famous Recorder and reformer in Birmingham, published his *Practical Suggestions to Founders of Reformatory Schools*. The Industrial Schools Act (1857) was passed, and in the same year the penal colony at Point Puer in Tasmania was closed.

Maudsley's considerable influence in forensic matters, with the exception of his *Responsibility in Mental Disease* (1874), was as much through his general works, and especially through translations of them into many different languages, as through works specifically devoted to the subject.   Of the latter, his articles of 1863 and 1864 on " Homicidal Insanity " and " Insanity and Crime " were the first.   In the 1870s, besides his major work on responsibility, he published an article on stealing as a symptom of general paralysis as well as his book in French, *Le Crime et la Folie*, which was reprinted six times.   In those days, book reviews offered an opportunity to the reviewer to voice his own opinions and Maudsley's review of *Female Life in Prison* runs to eighteen pages.   The discussions of learned society meetings were more lively then, and some of those in which Maudsley took part make racy reading.

As to style, Maudsley frequently inveighed against " ventosities of inflated verbiage," yet himself was hardly concise.   His contemporary, Havelock Ellis, wrote: " An artist as much as a man of science, master of a sombre and weighty style, illuminated by vivid flashes of imagination, Maudsley by his numerous works popularised the new ideas, and is justly regarded abroad as a pioneer of criminal anthropology."   Maudsley loved to use metaphors which, he considered, bespeak a deeper unity with nature and more vital value than science can formulate; within the space of one book, besides various plants and flowers, he uses metaphorically no less than forty-four different kinds of animals, from protozoa to pachyderms, from the parsimonious emmet to the nautilus.   Though fully aware of the value of detailed case studies, he happily does not burden his books with them.   While his style is pleasing, his learning admirable and his ideas stimulating, his inconsistency is bewildering.   He himself held that " consistency signifies prejudice and stagnation."   To be sure, only a humbug would deny the inevitable inconsistency of his feelings toward criminals, so that it is not surprising to find the forthright Maudsley more inconsistent in his writings on this subject than on any other.   The policy adopted in this paper is to sample his hottest and coldest rather than to concoct a lukewarm compromise which would reveal nothing of the man.

His attitude toward crime and criminals

" Criminals are extremely unlovable beings . . ." he wrote, not they but " the honest workman who prefers partial starvation to the yielding to temptation" deserves our zealous expression of sympathy. But, in general, his attitude is a tolerant one, not senti-mental but seeking for causes. He agrees with Plato "that the wicked owe their wickedness to their organisation and education, so that not they, but their parents and instructors should be blamed." Criminals "go criminal, as the insane go mad, because they cannot help it." In such generalisations he is handicapped, as we are, by the lack of any adequate classification of criminals, and tends to assume too readily at times that there is a valid entity—the criminal. Sometimes his tolerance seems to overreach itself—" Vice, crime, disease and death are just as natural and necessary events as virtue, health, growth and life." " I can conceive a murderer being a nobler animal than a saint of the Pecksniffian sort. The murderer on a big enough scale, big enough to despise the fools whom he uses and sacrifices for his ambitious ends—what is he? Why, he is a hero! "

His occasional evident identification with the underdog perhaps helped him in his outspoken criticisms of the forensic practice of his day. " In the delays, prolongations, complications and techni-calities of legal proceedings, the great criminal has always a fair chance of escape which the perpetrator of simpler crimes has not." In attacking alike judges, barristers and solicitors, he does not pull his punches. The most eminent advocates, he says, provided the fees are available, will defend most fraudulent doings, " special deceits are sanctioned as legitimate customs " and " the poor man must suffer without remedy." A large proportion of crimes, he held, were not prosecuted " because the injured party will not be at the pains, cost and worry of a prosecution likely to end in a compassionate acquittal or a nominal conviction "—how often do we hear just this criticism of our juvenile courts! He particularly loathed the " foul and unwholesome atmosphere of the Divorce Court " where he found perjury to be a daily practice, " tacitly accepted as normal, if not natural, sometimes even treated as excusable."

In prophetic and balanced vein he wrote: " With a better knowledge of crime we may not come to the practice of treating criminals as we now treat insane persons, but it is probable that we shall come to other and more tolerant sentiments, and that a less hostile feeling towards them, derived from a better knowledge of their defective organisation, will beget an indulgence at any rate towards all doubtful cases inhabiting the borderland between insanity and crime."

Relationship of crime and insanity

His attention to this borderland between insanity and crime stands much to his credit. Certain cases " may be reckoned insane or criminal according to the standpoint from which they are looked at." In the following he seems to anticipate the " predisposition," " susceptibility " and " earlier emotional dissatisfactions " of modern writers. " Now it is only a question of degree and kind of fault how far antisocial feeling, thought and conduct, passing through their divers forms of degeneracy, must go before it becomes madness or crime." " Crime is a sort of outlet in which their unsound tendencies are discharged; they would go mad if they were not criminals, and they do not go mad because they are criminals." He not only visualises some as hovering " between crime and insanity, near one boundary of which we meet with something of madness but more of sin, and near the other boundary of which something of sin but more of madness," but also as sometimes frankly alternating between crime and madness, especially epileptic madness.

Crime and epilepsy

Maudsley's keen observation and capacity to apply knowledge from other fields to that which engaged his interest, shows to advantage in his writings on crime and epilepsy. He spoke of some individuals, " impatient of restraint " " exploding " into a criminal act. " The convulsive energy of the homicidal impulse is sometimes preceded by a strange morbid sensation, beginning in some part of the body and mounting to the brain, very like that which, when preceding an attack of epilepsy, is known in medicine as the *Aura epileptica*." He observed, too, that " the epileptic convulsions may cease to occur in one who has been subject to them, and that in their place attacks of moral derangement with more or less maniacal excitement may appear." Parallel with Hughlings Jackson, Maudsley understood that there may be convulsion of ideas instead of convulsion of muscles. Such knowledge makes his well-known dictum on the legal responsibility of epileptics rather surprising: " at the outset we may declare unhesitatingly that an epileptic person may be quite as sane as one who is not so affected, and, in the event of his doing murder, quite as responsible." In children Maudsley stated that night terrors sometimes develop into epilepsy and that " frenzied children " who take subtle advantage of a sympathetic audience and develop what would now be called temper tantrums at the least opposition may have a kinship with epilepsy.

Some habitual offenders he noted to be epileptic or from families in which epilepsy, insanity or " other neurosis " existed. Perhaps influenced by Lombrosian theory or by Grohmann, who, long before Lombroso was born, had described criminals with defective development, prominent ears, projecting cheek-bones, large lower jaws, deeply placed eyes or a shifty, animal-like gaze, Maudsley, too, tended to link epilepsy with physical stigmata of degeneration and thus with crime.

" Degeneracy "

In general Maudsley developed and stated his ideas remarkably early in his career, subsequently restating them in his various books and being decreasingly influenced by the work of others. His views on degeneracy in relation to crime offer something of an exception to this rule. In his day criminal anthropology was all the rage, and carried to excessive lengths by the Italian school. It must have seemed that the tape and rule were replacing the tawse and rod as the primary criminological tools. An opinion on degeneracy would be essential for one in his position. At first, perhaps following Mayo's concepts, he regarded the criminal as " branded by the hand of nature," as having an original deficiency of moral sense. Later he seemed clearly influenced by Morel's conception of crime as one of the manifestations of individual or family degeneration. Morel's definition of degeneration was loose enough in all conscience—" a morbid deviation from the normal type of humanity " caused by intoxications, famines, social environment, industries, unhealthy occupations, poverty, heredity, pathological transformations, moral causes, but at least it escapes from the rigidity and hopelessness of the strict " anthropological " school. In this sense he wrote that crime and madness were both antisocial products of degeneracy. By 1895, perhaps in response to Lombroso's extreme views, he rather uncertainly modified his opinions : " To say that there is a criminal nature which is degenerate is one thing, a true thing; but to go on to say that all criminals are degenerate and bear on them the stigmata of degeneracy is another and, I believe, quite false thing. I do not see for myself why crime should necessarily be degeneracy." But he clung to his picture of the extreme of degeneracy presenting " a precocious prodigy of evil proclivities," a description which is rather reminiscent of a very recent writer's " poor protoplasm poorly put together," and about as useful a concept.

Environmental causes

Maudsley repeats over and over again (yet not too often) in almost identical words, that " the external factors and circumstances count for much in the causation of crime. Time and chance happen to all men, and no criminal, to my mind, is really explicable except by a full and exact appreciation of his circumstances and nature and of their mutual interaction." He appreciated clearly the double handicap of nature and nurture—" To add to their misfortunes, many criminals are not only begotten, and conceived, and bred in crime, but they are instructed in it from their youth upwards, so that their original criminal instincts acquire a power which no subsequent efforts to produce reformation will ever counteract." This is pessimistic perhaps, but no more so than many writers on " psychopathic personalities " (a term which mercifully had not then arisen) of the present day. And again, " it is exactly in those persons who show the stigmata of morbid heredity that the most serious damage is done "—the larger proportion, if handicapped only in one of these two directions, escapes. Maudsley did not labour, as many subsequent writers did, under a starry-eyed belief that correcting immediate faults necessarily puts all to rights. In his recognition of extensity as well as intensity he was, in this field, ahead of his time. " The effects which are in existence cannot, it is evident, be done away with by removing the causes, for they have become causes and will go on working through successive effects; but by removing the causes in present operation, the production of future effects of a like kind will be prevented."

Maudsley was aware of Quételet's work and quoted his dictum that society prepares the crime for the criminal to carry out. He emphasised society's responsibility in these words: " It is open to the present generation by the institution of systematic education, by bringing classes more closely together, by a general system of moral and physical hygiene . . . to change the character of the society of coming generations." As to cultural factors in the aetiology of crime he indicts the steady drift of the Western world to socialism, the rude abolition of a nation's customs with consequent loss of cohesion and stability in families, tribes and nations. Advancing civilisation, he claimed, has disrupted the " potent and useful " fictions and superstitions which formerly held antisocial impulses in check. " Heaven and Hell " he seems regretfully to say " are not the vivid realities that they were."

Inheritance

With typical Shakespearean flavour Maudsley writes: " There is a destiny made for a man by his ancestors, and no one can elude, were he able to attempt it, the tyranny of his organisation." This was his basic belief, but he appreciated that hereditary factors do not operate *in vacuo*—" a single case . . . thoroughly well observed and described, would be of more value than ten thousand general observations going no further than to establish the existence of hereditary influence."

A great believer in the essential inequality of man and in the concept of bad stock " which counts more than environment in the personal struggle of life," Maudsley seeks eugenically to shed society's encumbrances: " If it does not want them because they are detrimental, it must contrive to forgo their production." Yet he sees with admirable clarity the difficulties of eugenic action. " Qualities which on first sight look bad are no wise always the unmitigated and uncompensated evils which they appear to be in their day and generation "; they may work well in different circumstances or " in the constitutions of persons in the next generation." " Eugenic rules of breeding, if put into force, might . . . not turn out to be entirely eugenic in their consequences; to get rid of all the qualities in the species which are thought bad might be to pluck up the very tap-roots of its vitality and effectually emasculate it."

Psychological causes

It has been said that the only psychological causes which Maudsley recognised were overwork and over-exertion, and that he favoured a " physiological rather than a psychological point of view." Yet Maudsley, in this respect rather ahead of his time,

wrote: " it is the wear and tear of emotions, not of work, that is
the real hurt." At various places in his works Maudsley mentions
the following psychological motivations of crime—frustration, being
teased and irritated, imitation, instigation and coercion (the " cat's
paw "), provocation of circumstances, illegitimacy, bodily abnormalities and oddities. If he visualises these " moral commotions
and mental overstrains " as acting organically, in his favoured
phrase " by breaking the molecular ties of the nerve structure and
so injuring or destroying its vital elasticity," this does not detract
from the credit due for his recognition of and attention to environmental and emotional factors.

The following description of stealing as a symptom of general
paralysis, however, rather suggests that Maudsley did not grasp the
many ways in which psychologically motivated crime may resemble
that occurring in organically damaged individuals, in other words
the extent to which (borrowing a neurological term) a crime may be
the final common path of widely differing disturbances. " The
stealing (of the general paralytic) is often done in a stupid way,
without any adequate motive or without the outlook of any gain
thereby, apparently in obedience to an impulse to possess springing
up in a mind in which the sense of right and wrong has been
weakened or extinguished. In some cases the patient makes no
attempt at concealment; but in other cases there lingers a remnant
of the sense of right and wrong which, too feeble to contend with
the stealing impulse, leads to bungling attempts to hide the petty
larceny."

At moments Maudsley's acceptance of the criminal's motivation
by forces of which he was not aware seems to anticipate the
Freudian concept of the Unconscious. He writes of the criminal
" who has such a strong interest in deceiving himself "; " The
genuine criminal is not thoroughly conscious of his crime." Out of
the " unlit depths " of the individual's nature " from time to time
come faint airs and floating echoes of an infinite past . . . which
determine present moods and, more often than we think, present
acts." But his distrust of introspection does not allow him to
progress far: to judge mental processes by the exclusive study of
their partially conscious manifestations, without taking notice of
their necessary physiological antecedents and mostly subconscious
workings, is, he says, much like what a policeman might do who
should think to watch what is going on at night in a whole town

while scrupulously keeping himself within range of a particular gas-lamp's light. Whence, he asked, do criminal impulses, so forgetful of self-interest, despite the remembrance of retribution for past sin, come? "One thing is certain, that moral philosophy cannot penetrate the hidden springs of feeling and impulse; they lie deeper than it can reach, for they lie in the physical constitution of the individual, and, going still further back, perhaps in his organic antecedents."

Punishment

Maudsley often seemed opposed to the harsh punishment of criminals—"The makers and administrators of law ought really to have some pity for these defective beings suffering, as they do, under an irremediably bad organisation; but so far are they from showing compassion for them that they punish them angrily, not with the hope of reforming them, seeing that experience has shown that to be impossible, nor with the hope of warning or improving others like them . . . but in retaliation for what they have made society suffer by their wrong doings." He understood, too, that beyond certain limits the infliction of punishment actually provokes "more unreason and violence." "Why," he continues rather naïvely, "should a lame mind provoke any more anger than a lame body?"

At times, however, he expressed views so diametrically opposed to such tolerance and forbearance as to make the nonplussed reader cast about (alas unsuccessfully) for evidence of sarcasm or irony. "The public punishment of the whipping post, the stocks, and the shameful exposure on the pillory to public scorn and abuse, and still more the terror of the scaffold when executions were public, were primitive measures effectively employed formerly to teach social responsibility. The open disgrace of them appealed directly and forcibly to the understanding and feeling of the offender and the lookers-on, which more humane methods yet fail to do. To use flogging now as a proper punishment for a particular crime is to deprive it of much of its educational value as a preventive when the flogging is done in secret: the public gives the criminal the painful benefit of it, but does not give him or itself the instructive social benefit which might be obtained from its edifying exhibition." What would Steinmetz, and other opposers of punishment as an effective measure for criminals, have had to say to that?

Even with children he could be very hard. Writing of the thoroughly antisocial children who resist " admonitions, persuasion, appeal, example, entreaties, threats and punishments," he held that they must be " allowed to suffer the uttermost pains and penalties of their misdeeds: so long as they are again and again saved from the just penal consequences by the solicitous affection of fond parents or the more anxious dread of a public exposure of the family disgrace, they will go on sinning; but if they are allowed to touch the bottom of misery the sharp lesson may here and there teach one of them self-control. . . ." Again, his attitude to childish masturbation was surprising: for this he recommended " stigmatisation of it as ' bad form,' dirty, base and degrading, which will not fail, if continued, to betray itself in the face and manners," favouring appeals to vanity rather than moral strictures and giving no evidence that he knew of any alternative to these two approaches. Yet elsewhere he writes: " . . . it is certain that a more open dealing with a natural (sexual) function would dispel much hurtful ignorance, do away with a great deal of enforced hypocrisy, and prevent an incalculable amount of secret and anxious suffering at the critical period of adolescence. . . ."

He sums up the matter as follows: " Punishment, therefore, is properly inflicted, not out of revenge for the wrong done, which would benefit nobody, nor many times with any reasonable expectation of reforming the wrongdoer whose radically unsound nature would often need to regenerate, but as a stern admonition to others not to do wrong and incur a similar fate; for which purpose the severities and cruelties of past punishments may not have been entirely unnecessary and useless, inhumane or inhuman as they are called now." Justice, he said, must be prompt, stern and summary, inspiring " a wholesome fear " in the criminal. " The good of society is a larger interest than the good of the individual . . . it is he who must suffer in the larger interests of society."

His argument suffers through his inability to differentiate control from punishment, his clinging to the unreal concept of " the criminal," and his failure to grasp that even though society may first have to be served yet there is still a duty to help the offender to regain a position of self-respect.

In reading his works one is forced to recognise and allow for his obvious failure to reach a reasonable balance in certain matters, especially love and hate, good and bad, and in his consideration of punishment. Love he disparaged—" at bottom . . . there is nothing particularly holy about it." Yet elsewhere he wrote " love can never be extolled enough by human beings nor ever sufficiently revered as divine." But he is only able to revere it if it is first " spiritualised in its most refined expressions, embellished with all the graces imaginable." " How then is love to live and thrive with no store of hate to sustain it, no resistance for it to react against? " Concerning goodness and badness he wrote: " It was plainly well for the human race in the divine order of things that moral goodness did not prevail in the past seeing how much human progress has owed to its lower nature: avarice, ambition, emulation, envy and other selfish passions, along with the grosser animal appetites and desires, having been as necessary and useful factors in its progress as its higher moral qualities." Bearing this in mind we know from his autobiography that he was a tormenting critic of himself and that " I have always thought and said that the paternal and maternal were never vitally *welded* in me, but only *rivetted*." According to his famous contemporary, G. H. Savage, Maudsley had himself claimed to be " a man of two temperaments, two distinct and original differences." It seems reasonable to suppose, therefore, that his inconsistent views on punishment were at least to some extent symptomatic of his personal difficulties.

Responsibility

In April 1874 Maudsley published his book, *Responsibility in Mental Disease*, which ran to second and third editions in the two succeeding years. This subject was as much or more debated then as it is today. In 1864 a Royal Commission had been set up " to inquire into the provisions and operation of the laws under which the punishment of death is now inflicted in the United Kingdom, and the manner in which it is inflicted, and to report whether it is desirable to make any alteration therein." Maudsley, who had the preceding year demonstrated his interest in the subject through an article, published in the *Journal of Mental Science*, entitled " Homicidal Insanity," may have taken part in the arguments thrashed out by the Association of Medical Officers of Hospitals and Asylums for the Insane which body, through Dr. Harrington Tuke, reported to the Commission.

In the ten years before the publication of his book, three Bills had been introduced to Parliament with the intent to gain recognition of degrees of murder. The M'Naghten Rules had been formulated some thirty years previously and were still being hotly argued. Daniel M'Naghten, to quote from the clinical records of Bethlem Hospital (now linked to the hospital which bears Maudsley's name), at the age of twenty-nine, was admitted from Newgate on March 13, 1843, having been found to be insane at the Central Criminal Court. "His crime created great commotion at the time. In mistake for the late Sir Robert Peel he shot Mr. Drummond as he was going into the Treasury or some other government office, and that time imagined that the Tories were his enemies and annoyed him." M'Naghten remained at Bethlem, solitary, retiring and averse to conversation, deluded, sometimes requiring to be fed with the stomach pump, until his transfer to Broadmoor twenty-one years later.

Of the early authorities, Hale, in the seventeenth century, believed in a total insanity and a partial insanity. Those suffering from the latter " are not wholly destitute of reason, and this partial insanity seems not to excuse them in the committing of any offence for its matter capital, for doubtless most persons that are felons of themselves and others, are under a degree of partial insanity, when they commit these offences: it is very difficult to define the indivisible line that divides perfect and partial insanity." Hale held that the judge and jury must consider the circumstances of each case, and " the best measure that I can think of is this—such a person as labouring under melancholy distempers hath yet ordinarily as great understanding, as ordinarily a child of fourteen years hath, is such a person as may be guilty of treason or felony. . . ." Hale wrestled hard to classify mental disorders; he writes of accidental dementia, whether total or partial, which may be distinguished into that which is permanent or fixed (phrenesis), and that showing certain periods, vicissitudes or lucid intervals (lunacy). Certain famous trials (usually trials in which the victim was a man of high station) such as that of Arnold in 1724 for shooting at Lord Onslow, show that, well into the eighteenth century, the view was held that mental illness should not excuse a criminal from responsibility unless he is " totally deprived of his understanding and memory, and doth not know what he is doing no more than an infant, than a brute or wild beast." At best the test was the ability " to distinguish whether he was doing good or evil, and understood what he did." It was the French alienists, Pinel, Georget and Esquirol, who, championing their forensically awkward concept of monomania, led the revolt against the legal preoccupation with insanity as an intellectual matter.

Before Erskine's famous speech at the trial of James Hadfield for shooting at George III, in which he demolished Hale's test and introduced the concept that " delusion . . . where there is no frenzy or raving madness, is the true character of insanity," despite some capacity to reason, and long before Prichard's work (1842) " On the different forms of insanity in relation to jurisprudence," John Johnstone (apparently not known to Maudsley) had written his admirable and too little recognised *Medical Jurisprudence* (1800). In it Johnstone ridiculed Hale's perfect and partial insanity. He wrote that " it is necessary to have recourse to a chain of evidence to do full and impartial justice "; the findings " before and soon after the commission of any action of consequence may offer a link in the chain of the accused's insanity." This might be compared with the wording of part of the Summary of Conclusions and Recommendations of the recent (Gowers) Commission on Capital Punishment (p. 276) on the subject of diminished responsibility— " . . . the underlying abnormality of the brain may have provided a link in the chain of causation which led to the crime." Johnstone continues with remarkably advanced understanding: " madness is not always distinguishable from manner—for it assumes the form of the character, whatsoever that may be." And in the following passage he seems to realise the importance of the early environment in forming character: " For by reiterated imitation, by slow yet certain steps, we acquire habits, which not only fix the moral character of man, but frequently produce the most pernicious and incorrigible diseases, both of body and mind." And then with admirable honesty he states his belief that " cases exist, in which there is such an obscure disease of understanding, as will not appear in common life, or in common observation, yet under the influence of which great crimes may be committed. But on this insanity, human agents are not competent to decide, and in such cases the law must take its course. Unless indeed in some future stage of the progression of science, the matter may be made so obvious . . . as entirely to clear up all doubts. . . . Of this stage of human knowledge, the dawn is at present so obscure, that hope alone can tinge the dark clouds that hang over the future, with any of her golden hues." In style and directness this might almost have been written by Maudsley himself.

This was the state of knowledge and opinion on matters of criminal responsibility when Maudsley considered the subject—all the main arguments and tests, especially the equation of delusion and insanity, were already on the scene so that he was historically and prophetically correct in stating " there is little to be said that has not been said over and over again; for, notwithstanding that the legal test has been considered by eminent judges and that it has no foundation in science, it still flourishes in full vigour." Nearly all the main arguments which appear in the Gowers Report are in his pages also. He might have said, were he able to read that report today, what he said in quite another connection to the students of University College: " Good Heavens! . . . have you in all that time gained no new experience? " His function was to marshal the facts and put forward his views forcibly, fearlessly and strikingly. " Consciousness of, is deemed to be the same thing as power to, control the impulses of a disordered mind. . . . The (M'Naghten test is based on wrong observation and bad psychology, upon self-observation by sane minds." The test assumes that reason not feeling is the motive force of human action. " The psychology which finds the motive force of action in reason, is very much like a science which should find the active propelling force of a steam boat not in the engine room, but in the captain's orders or in the steersman's arm "; . . . " reason without feeling is impotent to act, feeling without reason being tyrannical in act."

As to the effect on the jury he claims that the juryman will inevitably understand the test in broad and ready fashion to mean that he (the criminal) knew what he was about and that therefore he ought to be punished. " Why, then, maintain a test which is so hard to understand, so easy to misunderstand, so false in science and so uncertain in application, so often interpreted by different judges in different ways, so seldom, I was going to say, interpreted twice in the same way by the same judge? Why bias wrongly the minds of the jury by a prejudgment of facts all of which ought to be left impartially to them? " " What right has the judge to lay down a particular test of disabling mental disease? . . . A particular test of disabling insanity is no more a matter of law than the test of a particular poison."

It might be said that in these views Maudsley leans towards idealism and overestimates not only the abilities and consistency of juries, but also the public willingness to forgo its beloved concept of the avenging agency of the law. Maudsley, like many reformers, is perhaps preoccupied with the goal to the detriment of the steps by which it may be achieved. But in the following none can deny that his recommendation is highly practicable: " Abolish capital punishment, and the dispute between lawyers and doctors ceases to be of practical importance "; this obvious solution is at last in sight.

During the fifty years before 1949, 45·7 per cent. of death sentences in England and Wales were commuted or respited and this has been taken as evidence of community disapproval of the sentences of the court. Maudsley also considered that the conscience of the community tacitly rebels against the present system, " For when a person whose insanity is suspected is condemned to death . . . competent medical skill is then called in to give competent and impartial help which ought to have been given at the time of the trial, and, in fact, to undo quietly in private what has been done, with all the pomp and parade of justice, wrongly in public." He blamed the rules, too, for the fact that sometimes an insane person accused of crime is not tried at all, and therefore deprived of his " most blessed privilege." He illustrates nicely the impasse to which the rules may lead, by quoting the case of Buton, aged eighteen years, who killed a boy and was tried at Maidstone in 1863. Buton had stated " . . . I had made up my mind to murder somebody " and that he did it because he wished to be hanged. His counsel said that his vehement wish to be hanged was the strongest proof of insanity. Counsel for the prosecution said that his having done murder in order to be hanged, showed clearly that he knew quite well the consequences of his act, and that he was therefore criminally responsible !

He demolished the popular notion that a really insane person acts without motive: he observed in " homicidal mania " the most careful planning of crime and noted " exceeding danger of recurrence of the attacks; . . . a person does not, when he becomes insane, take leave of his human passions nor cease to be affected by ordinary motives, and when he acts from one of these motives he does not, by doing so, take leave of his insanity; . . . at the most, we must admit an insane responsibility, such as is recognised in the management of asylums, where the insane are worked upon by ordinary motives, but are not punished as fully responsible agents when these motives fail to hold them in check. . . ." Maudsley thus tended towards supporting a diminished responsibility.

As to the giving of evidence he writes of the " popular suspicion " which the psychiatric witness draws upon himself and, rather bitterly, adds that " it is not difficult for ignorance, appealing to the prejudices of ignorance, to raise an empty laugh against a truth of which there is not the least comprehension." He thought that the medical witness should be allowed to instruct the jury " fully and truly concerning the particular form of mental disease in question, the nature of it, the bearings of it, and its damaging effects on the mind." The court might obtain such evidence in one of two ways, both of which have their proponents today. It might be called by the court itself, or by appointing a competent medical authority to act as assessor; in either case the ignominious spectacle of medical witnesses opposing one another would thus be avoided. " Some, though urgently asked, refuse to give evidence so that those who ' press forward to give evidence ' are heard. Psychiatric evidence is, I am afraid, the most discredited of any kind of evidence given in courts of justice." Presuming that he means " expert " evidence this statement is without doubt equally true today.

In 1895 Maudsley as an old but intellectually active man, was, as Dr. Nicolson then said, " drawn from his privacy " to give the results of his accumulated experience and thought on this matter of responsibility. At that time he said: " to me it seems that the conflict between law and medicine might soon end if words and theories were swept aside, and the facts dealt with on their merits. Let the lawyers renounce unreservedly their discredited test of disabling mental disease, and submit all the facts in a particular case impartially to the jury. Medical men on their side should discard the notion of insanity in the abstract, and leave off talking of it as if it were something definite or constant which annulled all responsibility. To place before the court as plainly as possible all the facts of the particular form of mental derangement in the case; to explain what they mean according to the best scientific information, and how far they affect the mind; and to leave it to judge; that is our proper function."

Children

Maudsley's attitude to children was certainly not sentimental; he rather looked upon them as little animals whose natural tendency to develop into big animals, rather than into responsible human beings, must be countered by an active process of education. "The thoughts, feelings and habits of boys and girls when they are together and not under suspicion of supervision are hardly such as a prudent person would care to discover in order to exhibit proof of the innate innocence though he might watch them curiously as evidence of innate animality of human nature. Only by a patient, systematic and constant culture begun from the beginning of life, infused by the social atmosphere, enforced by social usages, instilled in the language slowly learnt, and applied deliberately in the long and tedious process of education, are the lower tendencies repressed and the higher faculties developed and fixed." Applying these methods, we are not surprised that he finds that advances are "gained with difficulty and lost with ease." Although he does, occasionally, show a rather more enlightened view of education, bearing in mind that Pestalozzi and Froebel had long preceded him, Maudsley's views on this subject were better matched with his times than with his reputation as a thinker.

In common with his generation he had little conception of the importance of the parent-child relationship, especially in the early years of a child's life. He writes at one point of the over-attentive affection of an anxious and fidgety mother as the cause of disturbed behaviour in her child and he realised the "impossibility of teaching her insulted affection," preferring rather to remove the child from home to the care of some calm and sensible person. This is as far as he pursues the intricacies of the parent-child relationships and, furthermore, he seemed positively to turn away from such inquiries —"Especially repugnant is any positive research into the early origin and nature of the moral sense which the scientific inquirer cannot choose but make."

What would Maudsley have had to say about our large problem of juvenile delinquency? He would not have approved the term and would have been sceptical of our approach. "Why 'delinquency,' why not 'crime'?" he might have said, and actually did write: "polite feeling stubbornly ignores the truth, shrinks from plain speaking and gladly uses some decent euphemism or circumlocution to designate the ugly fact. . . . By robbing crime of its proper name they rob it of its ugly horror."

He might have said that much juvenile crime is comparable to the vast amount of minor undetected but concealed immorality practised by adults in most walks of life, for he was much aware of the magnitude of " common trade morality which is actually an immorality."

He might, were he here today, point again to " the more complex and luxurious conditions of present civilised life, which for the most part mean greater physical comforts and conveniences, less patient endurance and self-denial, more desires and indulgencies," a self-conservative instinct tending to become more and more self-gratifying, an individual self-regard prevailing selfishly over the interests of the species. He might even have pointed to our social ills as similar to those " infecting corruptions which accompanied and hastened the ruin of former civilisations (and which) are plainly not lacking in modern civilised nations," for he seemed to enjoy a good sonorous prophecy of death and destruction.

And if, in 1916, he decried " the growing tendency to put the burden of supporting the children of the poorer classes on the state, in stolid disregard of sapping parental self-reliance and of the possible peril to the family and injury to society which may be the consequence," he would surely have been alarmed and despondent at the trend of our modern welfare state. His phrase " the state is not a self-replenishing and inexhaustible source of wealth to be drawn on perpetually " might have come from a recent copy of *Hansard*.

The gentle art of " child-saving " had of course been strongly established long before Maudsley's birth; he might have been acquainted with the work of Jacob Doepler, August Demetz, John Wickern and his mother, Auguste Frank, John Falke, Mary Carpenter, Captain Brenton and many others, but he does not actually indicate that he was so acquainted. " Some benevolent persons," he writes, " it is true, who have conducted the appropriate experiments, assert that decent citizens can be made of children of degraded parents living in squalid surroundings if only the young creatures be caught soon enough and trained aright, although others who have made similar experiments in the same social medium are not equally confident."

He makes some specific observations upon juvenile offenders—

" the child (who) cannot be trusted always to distinguish between facts and fancies, may be accused of inventing the story which it tells and perhaps punished as a liar. The truth is that it does not distinguish between the very vivid images of real things which its intense imaginations are, and the perhaps less vivid images which realities appear to it." " The children who become juvenile criminals, do not evince the aptitude of the higher industrial classes; they are deficient in the power of attention and application, have bad memories and make slow progress in learning. . . ." He notices rare cases of children " born into good circumstances and having every advantage of education but cannot be trained or made to learn, display no affection whatever for parents or siblings, have no real appreciation of the difference between right and wrong, are inherently vicious, steal and lie with a skill hard to believe, cunning and self-gratifying, hopeless pupils, bound to be expelled." All eventually, he says, are constrained to admit defect to what at first seemed simple badness. In such cases inquiry shows " that they come of families in which insanity or some allied neurosis prevails."

While appreciating the importance of family solidarity, the childless Maudsley directs his most devastating and impotent criticism in that direction—" Family feeling, in fact, like individual feeling, can be so keenly self-regarding as to be antisocial. . . . Even the refined joys of parents in their children are self-gratification, though the selfishness be called divine; the protection they give to appealing and confiding weakness pleases their sense of power, exalts their sense of self, and projects a like affection outwardly to that which they feel inwardly. The renunciations, anxieties, sacrifices, cares and pains they undergo for their sakes are pleasing because undergone for those who, sprung from the rapturous fusion of their dear selves and being renewals and memories of themselves, are still united to them by impalpable rhythms of subtilest feeling. . . . Were it not that love of offspring is the vital principle of the family, which hitherto has been the solid base and cement of society—the real social unit—it would be positively antisocial, almost ferocious sometimes, in its exclusive selfishness. . . . When all is said parents do not ask themselves any more than animals do whether they do their offspring a service by begetting them; they gratify a present lust without the least regard to possible consequences."

Treatment

With characteristic breadth of vision Maudsley did not neglect simple social measures in the treatment and prevention of crime. How many persons in a large city, he rather cynically asked, are moral (act morally) simply because of the strong ally which gaslight is to morality? "Human nature needs the support of good social conditions to hinder it from running back to barbarism. . . ." Not for him was the equation of all criminality with mental illness; he had no impractical visions of a vast army of "soul-physicians" treating criminals.

"Crime is not (however) . . . always a simple affair of yielding to an evil impulse or a vicious passion, which may be checked were ordinary control exercised; it is clearly sometimes the result of an actual neurosis which has close relations of nature and descent to other neuroses, especially the epileptic and the insane neuroses; and this neurosis is the physical result of physiological laws of production and evolution." Would he then in the many criminals in which no such "actual neurosis" can be demonstrated or suspected wash his hands of the problem as purely a social one? It would seem rather that he would prefer the physician to co-operate with those working in the social field and that he would have been disappointed, had he viewed the scene today, to observe those who study criminals gathered into several independent camps; the insignia of one group may mean little to the others, nor are they organised under a common leadership or professorship. Maudsley gave £30,000 towards the establishment of a hospital for the treatment of mental disorders; in that hospital, today, there coexist in fruitful amity widely varying psychiatric opinions and practices. We clearly need another to do for criminology what Henry Maudsley did for psychiatry.

Maudsley was very pessimistic about the prospect of treating criminals successfully. "How can that which has been forming through generations be reformed within the term of a single life? Can the Ethiopian change his skin, or the leopard his spots?" So impressed was he by the intractability of criminals that his logical mind naturally sought the remedy along three lines which may be summarised as further investigation, isolation and education. Among these, psychotherapy was not envisaged, nor was there a place in his scheme for the advice, assistance and friendship of the probation officer or supportive clinic.

Over and over again he stresses that only by full investigation of the criminal and his background can we hope to make advances in treatment. "The time is come when we ought to use our prisons, as we do our hospitals, not for the cure and treatment of their inmates only, but for the advancement of knowledge and the improvement of man's estate." He evidently gave considerable thought to the position of the prison in the scheme of things. "Prison officials who perceive them (habitual criminals) to be mentally weak and irreclaimable, and know how surely they will resort to their criminal ways when they are free, would gladly see a way to some means of detaining them in a special establishment at the end of their terms of punishment or immediately after conviction, but as they cannot certify them to be actually insane or imbecile in the legal sense, no such protection is given."

This question of "protection" is carried a stage further in his expressed wish to get rid of the problem of the chronic offender "altogether by excretion or to render it harmless by isolation in a morbid capsule or in a special morbid area," a solution which today is receiving increasing attention under the term "special communities for the handicapped," not so much with the intention of banishment or of dissociating from an uncomfortable problem, as in the realisation that some individuals cannot compete unless in a simpler type of society—a policy which would aim not so much at changing skin and spots as sending Ethiopians to a hot dry climate and leopards to forests.

Relinquishing the hope of dramatic cures for chronic offenders, and knowing the futility of advice (for he found that the criminal invariably rejected it if it ran "counter to his affinities") he relied upon a long and patient course of re-education; whether this could be held to bear any resemblance to what has since been called "relationship therapy" seems very doubtful. He recommended what was in effect his own philosophy of life—a gradual education and continued exercise of the will in relation to the circumstances of life. He clearly placed less hope in education as a curative than as a preventative measure, for "whosoever would transform a character must undo a life history."

Strength of will, he believed, can overcome hardship—what is controllable with its aid is otherwise expressed as insanity or crime. But "a man can no more will than he can speak without having learned to do so," and the best education is one that will "teach man to understand himself, and to understand the nature which surrounds him. . . ." " The formation of a character in which the thoughts, feelings and actions are under the habitual guidance of a well-fashioned will, is perhaps the hardest task in the world, being, when accomplished, the highest effort of self-development." He presented this pursuit of self-culture as an aim in life—a hard, long, weary way of counteracting the causes of insanity and crime. Will, he held to be the supreme function of mental organisation, " the most determined event in all the wide world, the last consummate issue of its long organic travail . . . nature come to self-consciousness in man, striving with deliberate purpose to better itself."

Is this the conclusion of a man strongly influenced by his own long, hard and successful struggle against great personality difficulties, of a man who called himself a " lame minded sceptic," or is it the balanced conclusión of an exceptionally clear-sighted individual? There is enough of the former to justify a most careful examination of his opinions (and to which writer does this not apply?) and enough of the latter, even after so many years, to make it valuable and stimulating to read his work.

Though his prophetic abilities led him to foresee so many advances, for examples, the rationale of leucotomy, convulsive therapy, the elective affinities of different nervous centres for particular poisons, the utilisation of the condensed energies of the " quietly unlocked atom," yet, apart from foreseeing a greater tolerance towards criminals, he made no forecasts in relation to forensic psychiatry. Perhaps a little affected by his pessimism, we may believe that there was no positive prophecy to make, and that there will be no spectacular advance in treating the main mass of criminals as we know them today. Should we not, therefore, as he suggested, be turning our attention to the building of character, " the sincere and thorough development of the intellectual and moral nature," and to the prevention which this implies, by all the means that the scientists of child development, the psychologists, psychiatrists, sociologists and pedagogues have put at our disposal?

PETER SCOTT.

BIBLIOGRAPHY

By Maudsley

Review of *Female Life in Prison* by a Prison Matron, Hurst & Blackett, 1862, in J.Ment.Sci., Vol. 9 (1863), pp. 69–87.

"Homicidal Insanity," J.Ment.Sci., Vol. 9 (October 1863), p. 327.

The Physiology of Mind, London, 1867, Macmillan & Co.

The Pathology of Mind, London, 1867, Macmillan & Co.

Body and Mind, London, 1870, Macmillan & Co.

Responsibility in Mental Disease, London, 1874, Macmillan & Co.

"Stealing as a Symptom of General Paralysis," *Lancet*, November 13, 1875.

Body and Will, London, 1883, Kegan Paul, Trench & Co.

Natural Causes and Supernatural Seemings, London, 1886, Macmillan & Co.

"Remarks on Crime and Criminals," J.Ment.Sci. (July 1888).

"A discussion on Insanity in Relation to Criminal Responsibility," Brit.Med. J. (September 28, 1895); reprinted in J.Ment.Sci., Vol. 41 (1895).

Organic to Human : Psychological and Sociological, London, 1916, Macmillan & Co.

About Maudsley

LEWIS, AUBREY J. "Henry Maudsley: His Work and Influence," 25th Maudsley Lecture, J.Ment.Sci. (April 1951).

NOTE ON THE CONTRIBUTOR

PETER SCOTT, M.A., M.D., F.R.C.P., D.P.M., is a consultant physician to the Maudsley Hospital in London, with which he has been connected since 1948. He is also Psychiatrist to the U.K. Home Office, a senior editor of the *British Journal of Criminology,* and a member of the standing advisory council of the Home Office on the penal system.

13

CESARE LOMBROSO

1835–1909

In the history of criminology probably no name has been eulogised or attacked so much as that of Cesare Lombroso. By the time of his death in 1909 his ideas had gained wide attention among critics and friends engaged in the study of criminal behaviour both in Europe and in America. More has been written by and about Lombroso than any other criminologist, a fact that makes doubly difficult the task of summarising the life, work and influence of one who has been called "the father of modern criminology." The depth and breadth of his investigations permit a post-Lombrosian contemporary approach to the etiology of crime to proceed in Europe without suffering from a unilateral perspective. On the other hand, his emphasis on certain biological traits of criminal identification has provided sufficient fuel for continuous attacks from many critics who no longer take the time to read his works. The biological orientation in continental Europe and the predominant environmental approach in America represent not only two different perspectives on the same fundamental problem of the scientific analysis of the regularities, uniformities and patterns of causative factors in criminal behaviour, but reflect as well two different historical results of Lombroso's writings. As we shall see, the spirit of Lombroso is very much alive in some European contemporary research, especially in Italy, while in America generally Lombroso has been used as a straw man for attack on biological analyses of criminal behaviour. It is important, therefore, that a half century after his death we pause to re-examine the life and contributions of Cesare Lombroso and his position in contemporary criminology.

* Reproduced from *The Journal of Criminal Law, Criminology and Police Science*, Vol. 52, No. 4, November–December 1961.

The man, his works, and influence of others [1]

On November 6, 1835, the second of five children was born to Aron and Zefira Levi Lombroso.[2] As a Jew born in Verona, then under Austrian rule, Cesare Lombroso had the benefit both of a mother who was highly ambitious that her children receive a good education, and of living in one of the few cities under the control of the Hapsburg Kingdom of Lombardy and Venice in which Jewish boys were allowed to attend the Gymnasium, or public school, controlled by the Jesuits. While still at school his interest in history was revealed in two serious papers written when he was but fifteen years old: " Essay on the History of the Roman Republic " and " Sketches of Ancient Agriculture in Italy." [3] His review of the first volume of Paolo Marzolo's *An Introduction to Historical Monuments Revealed by Analysis of Words* greatly impressed Marzolo, who was a well-known philosopher and physician. Marzolo requested an interview with the unknown but learned reviewer and was amazed to find him only sixteen years of age. (The relationship that developed between them is revealed by the fact that much later Lombroso named his first daughter Paola Marzola.) Under Marzolo's influence, as well as that of prior readings, Lombroso was led at age eighteen to begin the study of medicine. He enrolled as a student at the University of Pavia during 1852–54, at the University of Padova in 1854–55, the University of Vienna in 1855–56, and received his degree in medicine from

---

[1] The author wishes to express his gratitude to Professor Richard Snodgrasse of Temple University for ideas he contributed to this section; to Klas Lithner and Thomas Dow, for their reviews of the Congresses of Criminal Anthropology and some of Lombroso's considerations of social factors in crime causation; and to Professor Thorsten Sellin for use of his excellent library on Lombroso.

[2] There appears to be a difference of opinion about the date of his birth. Gina Lombroso-Ferrero (*Cesare Lombroso, Storia della vita e delle opere*, 2nd ed., Bologna, 1921, Zanichelli, p. 1) explicitly states that he was born at 11 p.m. on November 6, 1835. Hans Kurella, lifelong friend of Lombroso, gives the same date (*Cesare Lombroso, A Modern Man of Science*, trans. M. Eden Paul, New York, 1910, Rebman Co., p. 1). The *Enciclopedia Italiana* refers to this date; but the *Encyclopaedia Britannica* offers November 18, 1836, as do a variety of other English sources. Hermann Mannheim refers to this divergence of opinion and mentions that Brockhaus' *Konversations Lexikon* gives November 18, 1836, and that Aschaffenburg in *Handwörterbuch der Kriminologie*, I, p. 833, even gives 1832 (Mannheim, " Lombroso and His Place in Modern Criminology," *The Sociological Review*, XXVIII (1936), 31–49, reprinted in *Group Problems in Crime and Punishment*, 1955, reprinted 1971, Chap. 4). Pinatel says that Lombroso was born on January 10, 1836 ("La vie et l'œuvre de César Lombroso," *Bulletin, Société Internationale de Criminologie*, Année 1959, 2e semestre, pp. 217–222). The present author agrees with Mannheim that the first date, November 6, 1835, is the correct one.

[3] These works were published a little later, however: " Saggio sulla Storia della Repubblica romana," estratto di pag. 57, *Collettore dell'Adige*, Verona, 1852, Antonelli; and " Schizzi di un quadro storico dell'antica agricoltura in Italia," *ibid.* 1853.

the University of Pavia in 1858 and his degree in surgery from the University of Genoa in 1859.

As an ardent student at the University of Pavia he was greatly influenced by Bartolomeo Panizza,[4] a widely known teratologist and comparative anatomist. At Vienna, Lombroso came under the sway of the eminent specialist in internal medicine, Skoda (1805–81), and the writings of the great pathologist, Rokitanski [5] (1804–78). Lombroso's early interest in psychology also occurred during his year at the University of Vienna, and this interest evolved into an abiding professional concern with psychiatry that was sustained by close study of the anatomy and physiology of the brain. Although not clinically trained in psychiatry, he was acquainted with the writings of men whose works undoubtedly loomed large in the emergence of his later writings both in medical and criminal treatises. During his student days Lombroso found himself increasingly in disagreement with the free-will philosophy then current in Italian academic circles, and correspondingly his thinking was shaped in large measure by the French positivists, the German materialists, and the English evolutionists. Auguste Comte (1798–1853), who introduced the term " sociology " but who based many of his ideas on biology and even found reason to support Gall (1758–1824), had published his *Positive Philosophy* (1830–42) and *Positive Polity* (1851–54) during Lombroso's formative years and played no small role in the latter's scientific orientation.[6]

In 1858, the year he received his medical degree, Lombroso became increasingly concerned with cretinism and pellagra, which for two centuries or more had been endemic in Upper Italy. In 1859 the results of his first research on cretinism, which constituted his doctoral thesis, were published.[7] In that same year he volunteered for medical service in the army and served in various posts, including an interesting period in Calabria as an army physician through 1863. During peacetime he began systemative measurement and observation of 3,000 soldiers, seeking to analyse and to

---

[4] Emphasised by Kurella, *op. cit.* p. 7. Elliot Smith claims that Panizza suggested the true localisation of the visual centre in the brain (Elliot Smith, *The Evolution of Man*, 2nd ed., London, 1927, Oxford University Press).

[5] Rokitanski was best known for his *Pathologische Anatomie*, Wien, 1855.

[6] Godwin has probably gone too far in saying that Comte was Lombroso's " scientific godfather " (George Godwin, *Criminal Man*, New York, 1957, G. Braziller, Inc., p. 6).

[7] *Ricerche sul cretinismo in Lombardia* (*Gazzetta Medica Italiana Lombarda*, N. 31, etc.), Milano, 1859.

express metrically the physical differences which he had noted among the inhabitants of the various regions of Italy. From this experience were derived his observations on tattooing, particularly the more obscene designs which he felt distinguished infractious soldiers. This practice of tattooing he subsequently identified as characteristic of criminals.

While being quartered during peacetime in Pavia, he had ample opportunity to pursue his interests in clinical psychiatry. He received permission to study clinically the mental patients in the hospital of St. Euphemia. In 1862 he presented a series of lectures in psychiatry and anthropology in that institution. His *Introduction to the Clinical Course on Mental Diseases*[8] was published in 1863 and was the first time that he had written about pellagra, genius and crime examined in relationship to insanity. The next year saw the publication of another lecture entitled *Genius and Insanity*,[9] the germ for which had appeared in his essay *On the Insanity of Cardano*,[10] written as early as 1855, during his student days. This lecture was also the forerunner of his *L'Uomo di genio*, the sixth edition of which appeared in 1894, and of its sequel, *Genio e degenerazione*, which was issued in 1897.

At one time or another during the years from 1863 to 1872 Lombroso was in charge of the insane at hospitals in Pavia, Pesaro and Reggio Emilia. In 1876 he received his first appointment in legal medicine and public hygiene at the University of Turin where he later was made professor of psychiatry and clinical psychiatry (1896) and of criminal anthropology (1906), the last of which occurred during the same year that he received the rank of Commandeur de la Légion d'Honneur by the French Government and in which he founded the Museum of Criminal Anthropology. Together with Mantegazza, his colleague and experimental pathologist, Lombroso was instrumental in establishing in Italy the meaning of anthropology in the modern sense.[11] That is, as opposed to the Kantian emphasis on descriptive psychology, Lombroso insisted on the use of the experimental method in legal

8 "Prelezione al Corso di Clinica di malattie mentali," *Gazzetta Medica Italiana Lombarda*, Milano, 1863.
9 *Genio e follia*, Prelezione al corso di clinica-psichiatrica, Milano, 1864, Chiusi.
10 "Sulla pazzia di Cardano," *Gazzetta Medica Italiana Lombarda*, Milano, 1855. Girolamo Cardano (1501–75) was a physician and natural philosopher.
11 Physical anthropology, it should be noted, is synonymous with anthropometry, and is an integral part of biometrics, for its data generally are to be understood only through the use of statistics.

medicine, expressing these views strongly in 1865 in a paper [12] that has been considered an important contribution to forensic medicine.[13] Similarly, in *Legal Medicine of the Corpse* [14] (1877) his contributions to the methods of identifying the dead body should warrant his being ranked among the innovators of scientific methods in pathology and police work.[15] The year 1880 was a significant one, for it was then that with the assistance of Ferri and Garofalo he founded the *Archivio di Psichiatria e Antropologia criminale*.

Lombroso's interest in criminology stemmed from his work on cretinism and pellagra as well as from his professional psychiatric studies. During the years before his appointment as professor of medicine at the University of Turin he had been writing serious studies on pellagra [16] that were later to affect his income and relationship with the landed aristocracy in northern Italy. The deficiency diseases of cretinism and pellagra, he felt, more or less retarded or inhibited normal growth and development of the physical and mental faculties.[17] Moreover, pellagra (" Lombardy erysipelas ") in its most severe form often produces, he noted, profound mental changes which may result in violence such as homicide. His early attention to brain pathology is shown in *Some Cases of Lesions of the Central Nervous System* (1861); *Memoir on a Tumour of the Cerebellum* (1863); *Supernumerary Cerebral Convolutions in a Murderer and Satyrist* (1871); and *Existence of a Median Fossette in the Cranium of a Criminal* (1871). The psychiatric aspect of his concern with criminology obviously antedates his paper entitled *On the Criminally Insane in Italy in '68, '69, and '70* (1871). These last two papers, together with the *Anthropometry of 400 Venetian Criminals* (1872) and *Emotions and Passions of*

---

[12] *La medicina legale nelle alienazioni mentali studiata col metodo experimentale*, Padova, 1865, Prosperini; also, " La médecine légale des aliénations mentales étudiée par la méthode expérimentale," Report to the Société de Marseille in *Bulletin des Travaux de la Société Impériale de Médecine de Marseille*, 1865.

[13] See Arturo Castiglioni, *A History of Medicine*, 2nd ed., New York, 1947, Alfred A. Knopf.

[14] *Sulla medicina legale del cadavere*, Torino, 1877, Baglione.

[15] Cf. Castiglioni, *op. cit.*

[16] For example, we might especially point to his *Studi clinici sperimentali sulle cause e terapia della pellagra*, Bologna, 1869, Fave e Garagnani; and *Studi clinici sulla natura, causa e terapia della pellagra*, Milano, 1870, Bernardoni.

[17] Cf. H. F. Harris, *Pellagra*, New York, 1919, Macmillan & Co.; J. D. Spillane, *Nutritional Disorders of the Nervous System*, Baltimore, 1947, Williams and Wilkins; T. D. Spies, " The Control of Pellagra," *Rhode Island Medical Journal* (1949), Vol. 22; T. D. Spies, C. D. Aring, J. Gelperin and W. B. Bean, " The Mental Symptoms of Pellagra, their Relief with Nicotinic Acid," *American Journal of Medical Science*, 196: 461–475.

Criminals (1874) are claimed [18] to have been the nucleus for his most important book *L'Uomo delinquente*, first published in 1876. This major work, which we shall later discuss in more detail, went through five editions in Italy, and translations were published in various European languages, although never into English. The second edition of 1878 established his reputation beyond Italy. An ideologically expanded version, *Le Crime: causes et remèdes*, appeared in 1899 and gave more attention to socio-economic factors in crime causation.

In a posthumous publication,[19] Lombroso indicated the sequence of his interest and activity in criminology as: (1) the background behaviour of the tattooed soldiers whom he observed while a physician in the Italian Army; (2) the application of physical measurements in his studies of the mentally alienated because of his dissatisfaction with current psychiatric procedures, plus his own recent conclusion that the patient, and not the disease, should be the focus of investigation; (3) the extension of these physical and physiological techniques to the study of criminals, *i.e.*, to the differentiation of criminals from lunatics; and (4) the direct analytical study of the criminal compared with normal individuals and the insane.

Lombroso's personal and domestic life was apparently tranquil. In 1869, when he was thirty-four years old, he married a young twenty-two-year-old Jewish girl from Alexandria who later presented him with two daughters, Paola and Gina. We are told that both because of their bringing into their father's orbit of relationships important socially conscious women, and because of their marriages to professionally related men (Gina to G. Ferrero and Paola to M. Carrara) they " brought fresh worlds of ideas into contact with that of their father."[20] It was with Gina's husband that Lombroso spent many long hours in his laboratory examining the skulls of criminals and with whom he wrote *The Female Offender*.[21] During

---

[18] These two works were papers that appeared in the Proceedings of the Royal Lombardian Institute of Science and Letters: "Antropometria di 400 delinquenti veneti," *Rendiconti dell'Istituto Lombardo*, V, Fasc. xii, 1872; and *Affetti e passioni dei delinquenti*, read at the Istituto Lombardo, 1874. Relative to the claim that these two papers constituted the nucleus of *L'Uomo delinquente*, see Gina Lombroso, *op. cit.* pp. 456-457; also Kurella, *op. cit.* p. 18.

[19] Introduction to *Criminal Man According to the Classification of Cesare Lombroso*, 1911, reprinted Montclair, N.J., 1972, Patterson Smith.

[20] Kurella, *op. cit.* p. 81.

[21] *La donna delinquente, la prostituta e la donna normale* (in collaboration with G. Ferrero), Torino, 1893, Roux. Ferrero is also known for his history of Rome.

Lombroso's later life and their maturity, his daughters performed many tasks for him in his Turin home—reading and answering much of his correspondence and literature in the growing field of criminal anthropology, translating and unofficially editing his writings and the *Archivio di Psichiatria*. Many visitors from Italy and abroad came to talk, listen and learn from him as he sat surrounded by the music of Beethoven and Wagner, drawings, sketches, sculpture, prison items, skulls of ancient Peruvians and of modern criminals, his many books, and, perhaps, the model of the famous penitentiary at Philadelphia, which he kept in his museum.[22]

Although he was selected as municipal councillor by one of the working-class quarters of Turin and sat in that capacity for several years, Lombroso was never a regular party worker. He ardently believed in the democratic processes, although he thought that parliamentary procedures offered elected representatives too many opportunities to escape responsibility and become " occasional criminals." [23] He favoured the socialists' efforts at social reform and was no doubt influenced by Loria's affinity to Marxian political philosophy. But he was opposed to revolution and class war, even excessive control by the common man over the upper classes. The common people, he thought, should have " only so much power as may be necessary to wring from the upper classes the concessions needful for the good of the commonalty." [24] During his younger years he was much concerned with agrarian problems because of his study of pellagra and his finding that the disease was caused (so he contended) by the poor quality of maize; he therefore was a passionate opponent of the traditional tariff policy of Italy, the high land taxes and town dues that offered nothing in return to the tenant farmers or agricultural labourers. His investigations into the causes of pellagra led him to speak frankly and openly about economic interests that produced a maldistribution of quality maize. As a consequence, the powerful agrarian interests of Lombardy and Venice boycotted his consulting practice among the upper middle classes that previously had brought him a sizeable income. His theory regarding the cause of pellagra, like that of his *delinquente-nato*, is no longer accepted, but the peasant classes of

[22] Gina Lombroso, *Cesare Lombroso, Storia della vita e delle opere, passim*.
[23] Lombroso, *Il delitto politico e le rivoluzioni* (in collaboration with Laschi), Torino, 1890, Bocca, p. 531; cited by Kurella, *op. cit.* pp. 125–126.
[24] Cited by Kurella, *op. cit.* p. 126n.

Italy gained his support and sympathy, and his descriptions of the symptoms of pellagra were added to the annals of medical literature.

Among the cultural factors that contributed to the making of the scholar must be mentioned the collection of official vital statistics and numerous inquiries and parliamentary investigations that occurred in Italy during the last three decades of the nineteenth century. Agrarian investigations made possible his researches into the causes of pellagra; his anthropometrical researches while an army surgeon in Calabria in 1862 were partially dependent upon the available recruiting statistics that made possible a determination of the ethnic composition of the Italian people; and as he expanded his horizon of investigation, he could make use of good statistics elsewhere, such as those in France that had been instigated in the 1830s by M. de Guerry de Champneuf.[25] Without these nineteenth-century innovations Lombroso's writings would have lacked many of the abundant facts of which he was so proud. The same may be said regarding the opportunities he had as prison physician at Turin to examine clinically thousands of prisoners, for Lombroso was fortunate that the head of the Italian prison administration was an interested scholar and a diligent historian. Beltrani-Scalia [26] put at Lombroso's disposal the entire body of official criminal and penal material and opened all Italian prisons to him and his pupils.

The younger men who surrounded the maestro after his growing reputation from the publication of *L'Uomo delinquente* were not only influenced by him but also had an influence on him. The most prominent of these was Enrico Ferri (1856–1929). When only twenty-four, Ferri went to Turin in 1880 to study with Lombroso, to gather the facts that he felt should precede the theories. This was the year that Lombroso started to edit his periodical, the *Archivio di Psichiatria*, and Ferri contributed to the first volume. It was Ferri who coined the term " born criminal " to refer to the atavistic type which Lombroso believed he had identified. " Between Ferri and the twenty years older Lombroso," says Sellin, " there began a deep and lasting friendship marked by mutual respect and profit to both, for while Ferri owed much of his system of ideas to the stimulation of Lombroso, he also became the catalyst who

[25] See M. C. Elmer, " Century-Old Ecological Studies in France," *American Journal of Sociology*, XXXIX (July 1933), 63–70.

[26] One of the best monographs on the history of Italian prisons was written by this capable prison inspector: Martino Beltrani-Scalia, *Sul Governo e sulla riforma delle carceri in Italia*, Torino, 1867, G. Favale e comp.

synthesised the latter's concepts with those of the sociologist and had no little influence on Lombroso's thinking." [27]

Lombroso's last work, published the year of his death, is a reflection of the interests he pursued during his last years of life.[28] We need not dwell here on his excursions into the world of Eusapia Paladino, the medium who had a strong influence on him during this period, and who helped him to " see," and to " hear " the voice of, his mother during one of the more successful séances.[29] Ferri, Kurella and other friends of Lombroso experienced some of these sessions with him, and it must have been disheartening for them to see the great seeker of facts being emotionally seduced.[30] Again we must remember the times and recall that the period from about 1885 to the end of the nineteenth century was a happy one for mediums and the time for extensive hypnotic experiments. He had opposed spiritualism previously, but after his first sittings with Eusapia Paladino, he wrote in a letter to his friend, Dr. Ciolfi: " I am ashamed and sorrowful that with so much obstinacy I have contested the possibility of the so-called spiritualistic facts. I say the *facts*, for I am inclined to reject the spiritualistic *theory*; but the facts exist, and as regards facts I glory in saying that I am their slave." [31] His friends tried to dissuade him from this interest, " but all this talk did not make me hesitate for a single moment. I thought it my predestined end and way and my duty to crown my life passed in the struggle for great ideas by entering the lists for this desperate cause. . . ." [32]

Lombroso was eulogised by his daughters and disciples, by students and scholars throughout the Continent and in America, at the Congresses of Criminal Anthropology, and in subsequent writings of members of the Italian School he had started. He was also widely and bitterly attacked, however, as we shall later note; but as late as May 1908 Professor John Wigmore, first president of the American Institute of Criminal Law and Criminology, visited

---

[27] Thorsten Sellin, *infra,* Chap. 18.

[28] *Ricerche sui fenomeni ipnotici e spiritici*, Torino, 1910, Unione. The English version of his studies in spiritualism is entitled *After Death—What?* Boston, 1909, Small, Maynard & Company (trans. by William Sloane Kennedy).

[29] *After Death—What?* pp. 68–69.

[30] Kurella was certainly not taken in by the work of the medium Eusapia Paladino, for he tells us that one of the séances he attended with Lombroso " was indeed, a ' miracle ' —*i.e.*, a miracle of adroitness, false bonhomie, well-simulated candour, naïveté, and artistic command of all the symptoms of hystero-epilepsy ": *op. cit.* p. 169.

[31] *Ibid.* p. 175.

[32] *After Death—What?* p. v.

Lombroso and offered him the nomination as Harris Lecturer at
Northwestern University for the year 1909–10. Lombroso was
interested but could not make the trip because of his advanced age.[33]
A few months later, during the early morning of October 19, 1909,
the life of the " father of the Italian School " silently passed away,
" *calma come un fiume che alla sua foce si perde nel mare.*" [34]

It is, of course, impossible to recount all the writers who antedated Lombroso, who were precursors of many of his ideas, or who
directly or indirectly influenced his own intuitive insights and
investigations. In *I Precursori di Lombroso*, Antinori [35] performs
an admirable service in reviewing the growing body of knowledge
that provided a cultural base from Aristotle to Della Porta (1536–
1615), and Lavater (1741–1801) to Morel (1809–73), upon which
Lombroso could build his own ideas. Havelock Ellis, in *The
Criminal*,[36] gives a brief history of the precursors of Lombroso, and
in the second chapter, Ellis mentions no less than twenty-two
scholars in Europe who had anticipated Lombroso in pointing out
the relationship between the criminal's physical and mental characteristics and his behaviour. Despite his prevailing theoretical
opposition to Lombroso, W. A. Bonger's [37] *An Introduction to
Criminology* is also a good source for a review of Lombroso's predecessors, both known and unknown to Lombroso at the time of
his early criminological investigations. Lombroso [38] himself gives
passing attention, not so much to influences on him as to the men
and ideas that preceded him, in " *I precursori dell'Antropologia
criminale* " (1898). Also quite useful are Morselli's [39] article on
" Cesare Lombroso e l'antropologia generale," Marro's [40] chapter

[33] Maurice Parmelee's " Introduction " to the English translation of Lombroso's *Crime :
Its Causes and Remedies*, Boston, 1912, Little, Brown & Co., p. xiii.
[34] Gina Lombroso, *Cesare Lombroso, Storia della vita e delle opere*, p. 425. A victim of
cardiac complications, he lost consciousness around 2 a.m. and died at 5 a.m. on
October 19, 1909. According to his will, his body was taken to the laboratory of legal
medicine, and an autopsy was performed (by Professor Tovo instead of Lombroso's
son-in-law, M. Carrara). His brain was placed in the Institute of Anatomy.
[35] G. Antinori, *I Precursori di Lombroso*, Torino, 1900.
[36] Havelock Ellis, *The Criminal*, 4th ed., London and New York, 1913, Walter Scott Co.
and Charles Scribner's Sons. This book had a wide sale both abroad and in America,
and makes clear the fact that Lombroso, inspired by the evolutionary theories of
Darwin, was only following out lines of thought suggested by European scholars long
before.
[37] W. A. Bonger, *An Introduction to Criminology*, trans. Emil van Loo, London, 1936,
Methuen & Co., Ltd.
[38] " I precursori dell'Antropologia criminale," *Archivio di Psichiatria*, 1898.
[39] E. Morselli, " Cesare Lombroso e l'antropologia generale," *L'opera di Cesare Lombroso
nella scienza e nelle sue applicazioni*, Torino, 1908, Bocca, pp. 1–31.
[40] A. Marro, " Precursori e primordi dell'antropologia criminale," *ibid.* pp. 175–192.

entitled, "Precursori e primordi dell'antropologia criminale," the work of de Quirós,[41] Sellin,[42] Vold[43] and others.[44]

Lombroso knew the works of Esquirol (1772–1840), the outstanding French psychiatrist whose *Traité des Maladies Mentales* first appeared in 1838 and who attempted to distinguish between mental defect and mental disease in his elaboration of Pinel's (1745–1826) *manie sans délire*. Lombroso knew also the works of prominent psychiatrists trained by Esquirol. He was acquainted, *inter alia*, with the writings of Griesinger (1817–68), who influenced German psychiatry toward anatomico-pathological hypotheses, and the Florentine Chiarugi (1759–1820), a leader in the advocacy of more humane treatment of the insane. These two latter writers regarded mental illness as essentially the result of disease or injury of the brain, thus amplifying Morgagni's concept of 1760 that insanity is an organic disturbance.[45]

The French alienist, B. A. Morel (1809–73), was an important influence on Lombroso. A theory of degeneracy was published by Morel in his voluminous *Treatise on Degeneracy* in 1857, in which he tried to explain the social phenomena of degeneracy and to classify them empirically by type. Degeneracy, he found, was expressed in epilepsy, insanity, mental deficiency, crime and similar conditions. He assumed degeneracy to be a pathological phenomenon caused by the interaction of hereditary and environmental factors manifested in both physical and mental deviations from the normal. That a variety of pathological human types exists is clearly pronounced by Morel in his small monograph *On the Formation of Types*, published in 1864 and which contains many of the ideas later developed by the criminal anthropologists. It was Morel who suggested that the new science of human pathology be called "morbid anthropology." There is no doubt, says Sellin, that Morel's ideas had great influence on the thinking of Lombroso. Such belief is confirmed by Lombroso's reference[46] to Morel that some anatomical anomalies of the criminal are indicative of degeneration.

[41] C. Bernaldo de Quirós, *Modern Theories of Criminality*, trans. Alfonso de Salvio, Boston, 1911, Little, Brown & Co., pp. 1–79.
[42] Thorsten Sellin, "En historik aterblick," Chap. I of Ivar Agge *et al.*, *Kriminologi*, Stockholm, 1955, Wehlström & Widstrand.
[43] George B. Vold, *Theoretical Criminology*, New York, 1958, Oxford University Press.
[44] *Infra* under subsequent section.
[45] See the work by Castiglioni, *op. cit.*
[46] *L'Homme criminel*, Paris, Alcan, p. 542, as a good example.

Among the currents of thought that contributed to the thinking and writing of Lombroso must be mentioned, in addition to Comte's positivism and biological basis for his sociology, Darwin's epochal *Origin of Species* (1859), published at the beginning of Lombroso's professional career. *The Descent of Man* appeared in 1871, and the *Expression of Emotion in Man and Animals* in 1872. *The Descent* contains, besides Darwin's observations, information from medicine, philology, sociology and anthropology. *The Expression* extends the comparisons of *The Descent* further into the emotional and mental life of animals and man. Together with publications which criticised or expounded the hypotheses of these two books, Darwin's theories exerted a deep and far-reaching influence on the writings of Lombroso.[47] Meantime, T. H. Huxley was basing his inferences on extensive comparative studies of embryology, the skeletal system, the brain, other viscera, and general bodily structure and concluded in *Man's Place in Nature* (1863): " Thus, whatever system of organs be studied, the comparison of their modifications in the ape series leads to one and the same result—that the structural differences which separate Man from the Gorilla and the Chimpanzee are not so great as those which separate the Gorilla from the lower apes. . . ." Slightly earlier, Schaafflhausen (1858) inferred, after studying the newly discovered skeleton of Neanderthal Man, that its morphologic peculiarities indicated it belonged to a " barbarous and savage race " and represented the earliest inhabitants of Europe. Virchow, the renowned German pathologist who displaced Rokitanski, considered the specimen to be that of an idiot and the result of a pathologic process.

There is no doubt that Rudolf Virchow (1821–1902) had an important influence on Lombroso. Virchow, who coined the aphorism, " every cell from a cell," published his *Cellular Pathology* in 1856 and analysed disease and diseased tissues from the viewpoint of cell formation and cell structure. He spoke of the evolution of man from lower animals, of organic regression, and of the fact that the individual may revert on the moral level to standards of lower animals, or at least to the stage of man's prehistory. Virchow's reference to theromorphism, a term he used to denote the presence in man of certain bodily peculiarities of one of the lower animals, played a significant role in Lombroso's belief

[47] Kurella, *op. cit.* p. 116.

that he had discovered such a condition in the skulls of certain criminals. Lombroso also adhered to, and made use of, the " fundamental biogenetic law," the law of recapitulation, which was formulated by Haeckel (1834–1919) ten years before the appearance of *L'Uomo delinquente*. Haeckel maintained that ontogeny recapitulates phylogeny, and this idea was incorporated by Lombroso into his parallelism between the criminal and the child.

It was Paul Broca (1824–80), the French neurologist and pathologist, who defined anthropology as the " natural history of man " as elucidated by the " zoological method," and who founded the *Société d'anthropologie de Paris* in 1859 and the *Revue d'anthropologie* (1872). He had earlier gained fame with his announcement that he had discovered and localised the centre for articulate speech found in that region of the brain since known as " Broca's speech area." Moreover, Broca had originated methods of classifying hair and skin colour, and of establishing the ratio of brain to skull— information that was to be of use to Lombroso later.

It is difficult to determine the degree to which predecessors of Lombroso affected his thinking regarding the physiognomic, physiologic or psychologic aspects of the criminal. In his investigations as prison physician at Turin, Lombroso minutely examined as many as 200 prisoners a year and subjected many more to ordinary clinical observation. It was *in the course of these investigations*, we are told,[48] that Lombroso first became acquainted with the work of his predecessors. Although he should not be denied credit for his originality and insight, there can be little argument with the fact that the intellectual stage was established for his probing inquiries into criminal behaviour. F. J. Gall (1758–1828), under joint authorship with G. Spurzheim (1776–1832), had written *Anatomie et physiologie du système nerveux en général et du cerveau en particulier* (1810–20), and Spurzheim had authored *Phrenology in Connection with the Study of Physiognomy* (1826). According to the theory of phrenology (craniology) each function has its organic seat in the brain, and the external signs of these mental functions are observable on the skull, as, for instance, the " bump " of theft, that of alcoholism, etc. It should be noted, however, that Lombroso, along with other critics of phrenology, had correctly evaluated Gall's ideas as early as 1853 when he was only eighteen years of age

[48] *Ibid.* p. 13.

and had written a brief work on the relationship between sexual and cerebral development.[49]

Although his early investigations may have been performed without the benefit of knowledge about all his predecessors, Lombroso could hardly help becoming aware of important works like those of H. Lauvergne (1797–1859), who worked at the prison of Toulon and was the author of *Les forçats considérés sous la rapport physiologique, moral et intellectuel* (1841); J. C. Prichard (1786–1846), author of *A Treatise on Insanity* (1835) and the English anthropologist who elaborated on the meaning of " moral insanity "; P. Lucas (1805–85) in his *Traité philosophique et physiologique de l'hérédité naturelle* (1847), who contended that some kind of criminal tendency is present from the moment of birth, and that this tendency is hereditary; E. Dally (1833–87), who pointed out in *Considérations sur les criminels au point de vue de la responsibilité* (1863) that crime and insanity are two forms of organic and mental decay; G. Wilson, to whose paper in England (1869) on *The Moral Imbecility of Habitual Criminals as Exemplified by Cranial Measurements*, Lombroso gives much credit; J. Bruce Thomson (1810–73), the Scottish alienist, whose summary of observations on over 5,000 prisoners was published in the *Journal of Mental Science* and entitled " On the Hereditary Nature of Crime " (1870); H. Maudsley (1835–1918), widely known for his *Crime and Insanity* (1872), and his *Responsibility in Mental Disease* (1874); P. Despine (1812–92), often referred to as the founder of criminal psychology and whose chief work, *Psychologie naturelle* (1868), refers to moral anomalies that stem from an organic cause; Herbert Spencer (1820–1904), whose *First Principles* appeared in 1862, and who was largely responsible for the development of evolutionary theory in social thought; and many others that space prevents our listing here.[50]

It should be noted that Lombroso seems not to have been acquainted with—or at least, not directly affected by—the writings of the Philadelphia physician, Benjamin Rush (1745–1813), which include an essay on *The Influence of Physical Causes upon the Moral Faculty* (1786) and his significant *Diseases of the Mind* (1812).

---

[49] " Di un fenomeno fisiologico comune ad alcuni neurottiere ed imenotteri," *Collettore dell'Adige*, Verona, 1853, Antonelli, cited by Kurella, *op. cit.* p. 17.

[50] Most of these cursory references to Lombroso's predecessors and contemporaries who expressed similar or related ideas have been gleaned from works previously mentioned, such as: Gina Lombroso, *Cesare Lombroso, Storia della vita e delle opere*; Ellis, *The Criminal*; Bonger, *An Introduction to Criminology*; de Quirós, *Modern Theories of Criminality*; Antinori, *I Precursori di Lombroso*.

In the essay Rush suggested that the total absence of a moral sense be called *anomia*, and then proceeded to discuss the effect of climate, diet, alcoholic drinks, hunger, diseases, etc., on the moral faculty. Moreover, although Lombroso made some use of the work of Guerry (1802–66) and of Quételet (1796–1874), there is no trace of a line of historical continuity between the " cartographic " or " geographic " method of analysis that Guerry introduced in his *Essai sur la statistique morale de la France* (1833) and the writings of Lombroso. Nor can we find evidence of any real effect that Quételet's " social physics," in his *Essai de physique sociale* (1835), may have had upon Lombroso, although he does make three minor references to Quételet in *Crime : Its Causes and Remedies*.[51]

In summary, then, we may say that Lombroso was primarily influenced by a German materialism that increasingly sought objective fact in opposition to the " natural philosophy " that had characterised the two preceding generations; by a Comtian positivism that demanded *positive* facts in abundance (regardless of the extent of their immediate relatedness to one another) and that saw the importance of biological factors underlying social phenomena; and by a Darwinian biological evolutionary theory that was eloquently extended into social evolution by Spencer. Within the intellectual climate established by these movements, Lombroso studied, practised, investigated and taught. He fell heir to the growing body of medical, clinical, psychiatric literature that dealt directly and peripherally with the criminal. *From* this knowledge he gained a perspective and theoretical orientation : *to* this knowledge he added new, exciting and controversial dimensions.

Atavism and the classification of criminals

The ideas, investigations and detailed voluminous analyses of Lombroso have been reviewed so often in criminological literature that it is both unnecessary and impossible to present all of this material here in abridged form. We shall discuss only highlights of his ideas regarding the criminal and shall refer to sources for further details. Our task is not to point out the abundant fallacies of his reasoning, but to review his theories and arguments.

His general theory suggested that criminals are distinguished

[51] See Cesare Lombroso, *Crime : Its Causes and Remedies*, trans. Henry P. Horton, 1912, reprinted Montclair, N.J., 1968, Patterson Smith, pp. 179, 182, 185.

from non-criminals by the manifestation of multiple physical anomalies which are of atavistic or degenerative origin. The concept of atavism (from Latin: *atavus*, ancestor, great-great-grandfather's father; from *avus*, grandfather) postulated a reversion to a primitive or subhuman type of man, characterised physically by a variety of inferior morphological features reminiscent of apes and lower primates, occurring in the more simian fossil men and to some extent preserved in modern " savages." It is additionally implied that the mentality of atavistic individuals is that of primitive man, that these are biological " throwbacks " to an earlier stage of evolution and that the behaviour of these " throwbacks " will inevitably be contrary to the rules and expectations of modern civilised society. Lombroso later added to this conceptualism the theory of degeneration, which included a pathological condition in the criminal. The degenerate was a product of diseased ancestral elements which ceased to evolve progressively and give evidence of the process of devolution, so that pathological individuals manifest rudimentary physical and mental attributes of primitive man.

We have previously seen how the general intellectual climate of Europe and the accumulated body of knowledge from physiology, biology, outdated physiognomy and phrenology, and even psychiatry converged in the training and experience of Lombroso to give birth to his emerging insights regarding the nature and causes of criminal behaviour. The idea of atavism, of a reversion to an earlier phylogenetic level of development, was expressed by Darwin when he said: " With mankind some of the worst dispositions which occasionally without any assignable cause make their appearance in families, may perhaps be reversions to a savage state, from which we are not removed by very many generations. This view seems indeed recognised in the common expression that such are the black sheep of the family." [52] But specifically, the notion occurred to Lombroso earlier: " The first idea came to me in 1864, when, as an army doctor, I beguiled my ample leisure with a series of studies on the Italian soldier. From the very beginning I was struck by a characteristic that distinguished the honest soldier from his vicious comrade: the extent to which the latter was tattooed and the indecency of the designs that covered his body." [53]

[52] Darwin, *Descent of Man*, 2nd ed., 1881, p. 137.
[53] Cesare Lombroso, " Introduction " to Gina Lombroso-Ferrero, *Criminal Man According to the Classification of Cesare Lombroso*, p. xxii.

Dissatisfied with abstract judicial methods of studying crime, and desirous of applying the experimental method to a study of differences between lunatics, criminals and normal individuals, he began examining criminals in Italian prisons. He became acquainted with the famous brigand, Vilella, and found him to be a man of extraordinary agility, cynicism and exceptional braggadocio. On the death of this brigand, Lombroso was appointed to make the post-mortem examination, and on opening the skull he found on the interior of the lower back part a distinct depression which he named the *median occipital fossa*, a characteristic found in inferior animals, and a depression correlated with an over-development of the *vermis*, known in birds as the middle cerebellum. In reviewing this and similar moments in his life he says [54]:

> This was not merely an idea, but a revelation. At the sight of that skull, I seemed to see all of a sudden, lighted up as a vast plain under a flaming sky, the problem of the nature of the criminal—an atavistic being who reproduces in his person the ferocious instincts of primitive humanity and the inferior animals. Thus were explained anatomically the enormous jaws, high cheek-bones, prominent superciliary arches, solitary lines in the palms, extreme size of the orbits, handle-shaped or sessile ears found in criminals, savages, and apes, insensibility to pain, extremely acute sight, tattooing, excessive idleness, love of orgies, and the irresistible craving for evil for its own sake, the desire not only to extinguish life in the victim, but to mutilate the corpse, tear its flesh, and drink its blood.
>
> I was further encouraged in this bold hypothesis by the results of my studies on Verzeni, a criminal convicted of sadism and rape, who showed the cannibalistic instincts of primitive anthropophagists and the ferocity of beasts of prey.
>
> The various parts of the extremely complex problem of criminality were, however, not all solved hereby. The final key was given by another case, that of Misdea, a young soldier of about twenty-one, unintelligent but not vicious. Although subject to epileptic fits, he had served for some years in the army when suddenly, for some trivial cause, he attacked and killed eight of his superior officers and comrades. His horrible work accomplished, he fell into a deep slumber, which lasted twelve hours, and on awaking appeared to have no recollection of what had happened. Misdea, while representing the most ferocious type of animal, manifested, in addition, all the phenomena

[54] *Ibid.* pp. xiv–xvi. The description of this same episode was made by Lombroso in his opening speech at the Sixth Congress of Criminal Anthropology at Turin in April 1906. In this speech the month is changed from November to December for the time when he examined Vilella, and the declaration of his having resolved the problem of the origin of the criminal is more pronounced: " At the sight of these strange anomalies I saw, as on a large plain under a red horizon, the solution of the problem of the nature and of the origin of the delinquent; the characteristics of the primitive man and of the animals reproduced in our day " (*Opening Address. Comptes-rendus du VIe Congrès International d'Anthropologie Criminelle*, Turin, Bocca, pp. xxxii–xxxvi).

of epilepsy, which appeared to be hereditary in all the members of his family. It flashed across my mind that many criminal characteristics not attributable to atavism, such as facial asymmetry, cerebral sclerosis, impulsiveness, instantaneousness, the periodicity of criminal acts, the desire of evil for evil's sake, were morbid characteristics common to epilepsy, mingled with others due to atavism.

As we have noted, his early ideas of a theory of the criminal man were published in proceedings of the Royal Lombardian Institute of Science and Letters in 1872 and 1874.[55] In 1876 a full discussion of atavism and the criminal man appeared in the first edition of *L'Uomo delinquente*, which was published in Milan by Hoepli, comprised only 252 pages, in one volume, and received relatively little attention. The second edition gained him a wide reputation, was published in 1878, but increased in size to 740 pages, still within one volume. In 1887 the French edition, *L'Homme criminel*, and the German edition, *Der Verbrecher*, appeared and disseminated his ideas abroad. By 1889, and with the accumulation of many new measurements of criminal skulls, etc., *L'Uomo delinquente* appeared in two volumes comprising 1,241 pages (Vol. I, 660 pages; Vol. II, 581 pages). And in the fifth and final edition, published in 1896 (Vol. I, 650; II, 576) and 1897 (Vol. III, 677), the three volumes totalled 1,903 pages. To these was added *Le crime: causes et remèdes* (527 pages) in 1899. More than the addition of thousands of new measurements appeared in the last edition; for, as would be expected, changes occurred in his thinking to modify his original pronouncements of the atavistic criminal type. These modifications principally took the form of increasingly emphasising the element of degeneration and the commonality between the criminal, the insane and the epileptic. He came to designate the epileptic criminal, the insane criminal and the born criminal as separate types, all stemming from an epileptoid base. Critics and friends alike, particularly Ferri, were later to suggest to him that " the congenital epileptoid criminal did not form a single species, and that if this class was irretrievably doomed to perdition, crime in others was only a brief spell of insanity, determined by circumstances, passion or illness."[56]

[55] See *supra*, note 18. For a good discussion of the first edition of *L'Uomo delinquente*, see the article by A. Marro, " L'opera di Cesare Lombroso nell'antropologia criminale," *op. cit.* pp. 193–203.
[56] Cesare Lombroso, " Introduction " to Gina Lombroso-Ferrero, *Criminal Man According to the Classification of Cesare Lombroso*, p. xxvii.

Lombroso had spent many long years assembling his material, making literally thousands of post-mortem examinations or anthropometric studies of criminals, of the insane and of normal individuals. In order to find the origin of the atavistic phenomenon he studied what he believed to be the evolution of crime in the animal kingdom, among uncivilised races and finally—by using Haeckel's concept of recapitulation—in the child. Lombroso became convinced that the criminal was not a variation from a norm but practically a special species, a subspecies, of man, having distinct physical and mental characteristics. Among these physical stigmata are included the following [57]:

deviation in head size and shape from the type common to the race and religion from which the criminal came; asymmetry of the face; excessive dimensions of the jaw and cheek bones; eye defects and peculiarities; ears of unusual size, or occasionally very small, or standing out from the head as do those of the chimpanzee; nose twisted, upturned, or flattened in thieves, or aquiline or beaklike in murderers, or with a tip rising like a peak from swollen nostrils; lips fleshy, swollen, and protruding; pouches in the cheek like those of some animals; peculiarities of the palate, such as a large central ridge, a series of cavities and protuberances such as are found in some reptiles, and cleft palate; abnormal dentition; chin receding, or excessively long or short and flat, as in apes; abundance, variety, and precocity of wrinkles, anomalies of the hair, marked by characteristics of the hair of the opposite sex; defects of the thorax, such as too many or too few ribs, or supernumerary nipples; inversion of sex characteristics in the pelvic organs; excessive length of arms; supernumerary fingers and toes; imbalance of the hemispheres of the brain (asymmetry of cranium).

In summarising the anatomical study of the criminal he pointed out that his studies show " new analogies between the insane, savages and criminals. The prognathism, the hair abundant, black and frizzled, the sparse beard, the skin very often brown, the oxycephaly, the oblique eyes; the small skull, the developed jaw and sygomas, the retreating forehead, the voluminous ears, the analogy between the sexes, a greater reach, are new characteristics added to the characteristics observed in the dead which bring the European criminals nearer to the Australian and Mongolian type. . . ." [58] He

---

[57] This summarised list is adequate for our purposes and is a partial listing adapted from the basic work of Gina Lombroso's *Criminal Man* . . . , pp. 10–24; is summarised by John L. Gillin, *Criminology and Penology*, 3rd ed., New York, 1945, Appleton-Century, p. 79; and appears in George Vold, *Theoretical Criminology*, New York, 1958, Oxford University Press, pp. 50–51.

[58] *L'Homme criminel*, Paris, 1895, Vol. I, p. 222, cited by Maurice Parmelee, "Introduction," *Crime : Its Causes and Remedies*.

even believed that it was possible to distinguish special types of delinquents, and as early as 1874, two years before publication of *L'Uomo delinquente*, he said that

as a rule, the *thieves* have mobile hands and face; small, mobile, restless, frequently oblique eyes; thick and closely set eyebrows; flat or twisted nose; thin beard; hair frequently thin; almost a receding brow. Both they and those committing *rape* frequently have ears *ad ansa.* The latter often have brilliant eyes, delicate faces, and tumid lips and eyelids; as a rule they are of delicate structure and sometimes hunchbacked. . . . The *habitual homicides* have cold, glassy eyes, immobile and sometimes sanguine and inflamed; the nose, always large, is frequently acquiline or, rather, hooked; the jaws are strong, the cheekbones large, the hair curly, dark, and abundant; the beard is frequently thin, the canine teeth well developed and the lips delicate; frequent nystagmus and unilateral facial contractions, with a baring of the teeth and a contraction of the jaws. . . . In general, *all criminals* have ears *ad ansa,* abundant hair, thin beard, prominent frontal sinuses, protruding chin, large cheekbones, etc.[59]

In addition to physical stigmata, Lombroso noted in the born criminal (a term, as we have mentioned, coined by Ferri) such factors as: (1) sensory and functional peculiarities, including greater insensibility to pain and touch, more acute sight, less than average acuteness of hearing, smell and taste, greater agility, more ambidexterity, greater strength in the left limbs; (2) a lack of moral sense, including an absence of repentance and remorse, or only from hypocritical motives, the presence of cynicism, treachery, vanity, impulsiveness, vindictiveness, cruelty, idleness, participation in orgies, possessing a passion for gambling; and (3) other manifestations, such as a special criminal argot, or slang, the tendency to express ideas pictorially, and the extensive use of tattooing.[60]

As his analyses continued, Lombroso came to believe that the moral imbecile and the criminal were fundamentally alike in physical constitution and mental characteristics. His atavistic theory had been subjected to wide criticism and to further accumulation of more facts. Many of the anomalies that he had found in the

[59] *Della fossetta cerebellare mediana in un criminale*, R. Ist. Lombardo di Scienza e Lettere—Rendiconti, 1872, pp. 1058–1065; cited and translated by Thorsten Sellin, " A New Phase of Criminal Anthropology in Italy," *The Annals of the American Academy of Political and Social Science, Modern Crime*, CXXV (May 1926), 234.

[60] These traits of the born criminal may be found in most of the editions of *L'Uomo delinquente, passim*; see, especially, the 5th ed., 1897, Vol. I, pp. 388–568; and in the English summary by Gina Lombroso-Ferrero in *Criminal Man* . . . , pp. 24–48. See also, and in summary, Lombroso's description of atavism in *Crime: Its Causes and Remedies*, pp. 365–369. However, it must be kept in mind that by the time of this last writing he had modified his ideas to include other types of criminals and had reduced his emphasis on the *delinquente-nato.*

criminal could not be explained by atavism, and he searched for some other pathological condition that caused the arrested development of certain organs, particularly the nerve centres. He finally identified this condition with epilepsy, as he points out in the last edition of his work: " The fusion of criminality with epilepsy and with moral insanity alone could explain the purely pathological and non-atavistic phenomena in the delinquent." [61] Epilepsy becomes the " uniting bond," the morbid condition " that unites and bases the moral imbecile and the born criminal in the same natural family." [62] Although all born criminals are epileptics, not all epileptics are necessarily born criminals. By this time in his writings, he no longer saw the born criminal only in terms of an atavistic return to the savage; he spoke also of arrested development and disease, and combined both atavism and degeneration in his analysis of the etiology of the born criminal [63]—a combination that many scholars, including E. A. Hooton, were to take issue with later.

In addition to the epileptic criminal, the insane criminal and the born criminal, Lombroso refers, in his later editions, to a large corps of occasional criminals.[64] These criminals " are those who do not seek the occasion for the crime but are almost drawn into it, or fall into the meshes of the code for very insignificant reasons. These are the only ones who escape all connection with atavism and epilepsy. . . ." [65] Although the first part of this statement that comes from his last major work (which considers environmental factors in some detail) is consistent with earlier remarks about the occasional criminal, the last part does not conform to his summary diagram in the fifth edition of *L'Uomo delinquente* that tries to show the relationship among his various criminal types. At any rate, the first group of occasional criminals is that of the pseudo-criminals, or those who commit crimes involuntarily, whose acts are not perverse or prejudicial to society but which are crimes so defined by law, committed in defence of the person, of honour, or of family. These crimes do not cause societal fear nor do they disturb the moral sense of the community.

The next and largest group of occasional criminals are the

---

[61] *L'Uomo delinquente*, 5th ed., Vol. I, p. 59.
[62] *L'Homme criminel*, Vol. II, p. 50, as cited.
[63] *L'Uomo delinquente*, 5th ed., 1897, Vol. I, pp. 62–68.
[64] " Delinquente d'occasione," *ibid.* Parte VIII, pp. 482–564.
[65] *Crime : Its Causes and Remedies*, p. 376.

criminaloids. In their case precipitating factors in the environment, or opportunities to commit crimes, constitute the most important elements in their etiology. Opportunities offered for fraud, the associate of the prison and other unfavourable exogamous factors lead this group to crime. The criminaloid, nonetheless, possesses innate traits that tend to cause him to be only slightly less predisposed to criminality. His organic tendency is less intense than that of the born criminal, and he has only a touch of degeneracy. " In the biology of the criminaloid we observe a smaller number of anomalies in touch, sensibility to pain, psychometry, and especially less early baldness and grayness, and less tattooing. . . . Criminaloids, then, differ from born criminals in degree, not in kind. This is so true that the greater number of them, having become habitual criminals, thanks to a long sojourn in prison, can no longer be distinguished from born criminals except by the slight character of their physical marks of criminality." [66]

The habitual criminal constitutes the third group of occasional criminals, and it is this group that seems to come closest to a " normal " criminal in all his writings, for the habitual criminal was born without serious anomalies or tendencies in his constitution that would predispose him to crime. Poor education and training from parents, the school and community at an early age causes these individuals " to fall continually lower into the primitive tendency towards evil." Associations of criminals such as the *Mafia* and *Camorra* in Italy contain members drawn into crime by association.[67] Finally, among the *delinquente d'occasione* Lombroso mentions briefly a class of epileptoids in whom a trace of epilepsy may form the basis for the development of their criminal tendencies.

There is another category of criminals, one that lies outside the general base of epilepsy. Crimes of violence based not upon conditions arising from the nature of the organism but often from " anger, platonic or filial love, offended honour, which are usually generous passions and often sublime," characterise the " irresistible force " manifested by the " *delinquente d'impeto o passione*." Political criminals are included under this classification, and characteristics such as a powerful intellect, exaggerated sensibility, great altruism, patriotic, religious or even scientific ideals, are described

[66] *Ibid.* p. 374.
[67] Is there not here the suggestion of Sutherland's concept of " differential association "? *Cf.* Edwin H. Sutherland, *Principles of Criminology*, Philadelphia, 1947, Lippincott (4th ed.).

as significant factors. Finally, the high frequency of suicide among criminals of passion indicates, he felt, a pathological state of mind.[68]

In order to show the relationship between these groups, Lombroso presented a diagram in which all the delinquents, regardless of type, were placed on an " epileptoid " basis.

Criminal Epileptic
_____
        Criminal
        Moral Imbecile
        _____

               Born Criminal
               _____
                         Criminaloids
                         Occasional Criminals

    E   P   I   L   E   P   T   O   I   D   S   Criminal by
                                                 Passion

(From *L'Uomo delinquente*, 5th ed., 1896, Vol. II, p. 60.)

Lombroso considered the female offender in virtually the same terms used in his analyses of males. His first edition of *La donna delinquente, la prostituta e la donna normale*, written in collaboration with his son-in-law, G. Ferrero, appeared in 1893, after which a new edition was published in 1903 and translated into several languages.[69] He emphasised that anatomically there is much less variability among women in general and that deviations from type are more significant than similar deviations occurring in men. Moreover, he noted that there was less general sensibility and less sensibility to pain among women compared to men.

Women are very much like children in many respects, he suggests, and by use of historical and some ethnological materials he proceeds to show that prostitutes and prostitution represent reversionary or atavistic phenomena. The intimate descriptions he gives of the psychical life of the prostitute led him to conclude that among prostitutes the born criminal type is found more frequently than among other female offenders. The prostitute, even more than the homicidal robber, is the genuine typical representative of criminality. With his usual detailed descriptions of Darwin's tubercle, sessile ears, alveolar prognathism and many case studies, he attempts

[68] *L'Uomo delinquente*, 5th ed., 1897, Vol. II, pp. 204–265.
[69] The English version, *The Female Offender*, with an Introduction by W. Douglas Morrison, was first published in 1895 (New York, D. Appleton & Co.). In 1958 the Wisdom Library (Philosophical Library, Inc., New York) reissued the edition.

to show that genuine women criminals are endowed with the same fundamental peculiarities found in male criminals, and that prostitutes and other genuine criminal feminine types (*rea nata*) are characterised by a lack of the " mother-sense." By the time he had written the fifth edition of *L'Uomo delinquente*, he could still say, however, that " an extensive study of criminal women has shown us that all the degenerative signs, such as functional anomalies, are lessened in them (among the dead as among the living), and are closer to the normal type of women. They seem to escape, therefore, from the atavistic laws of degeneration." [70]

Consideration is given in *The Female Offender* to pathological anomalies, investigations of female brains, anthropometry, facial and cephalic anomalies, atavistic origins, tattooing, the born criminal, occasional criminals, hysterical offenders, crimes of passion, suicides, criminal lunatics, epileptic delinquents and moral insanity. Although he asserts that female born criminals are fewer in number than the males, he contends that the former are much more ferocious. His explanation for their " greater ferocity," although not acceptable today, is succinct [71]:

We have seen that the normal woman is naturally less sensitive to pain than a man, and compassion is the offspring of sensitiveness. If the one be wanting, so will the other be.

We also saw that women have many traits in common with children; that their moral sense is deficient; that they are revengeful, jealous, inclined to vengeances of a refined cruelty.

In ordinary cases these defects are neutralised by piety, maternity, want of passion, sexual coldness, by weakness and an undeveloped intelligence. But when a morbid activity of the psychical centres intensifies the bad qualities of women, and induces them to seek relief in evil deeds; when piety and maternal sentiments are wanting, and in their place are strong passions and intensely erotic tendencies, much muscular strength and a superior intelligence for the conception and execution of evil, it is clear that the innocuous semi-criminal present in the normal woman must be transformed into a born criminal more terrible than any man.

What terrific criminals would children be if they had strong passions, muscular strength, and sufficient intelligence; and if, moreover, their evil tendencies were exasperated by a morbid psychical activity! And women are big children; their evil tendencies are more numerous and more varied than men's, but generally remain latent. When they are awakened and excited they produce results proportionately greater.

Moreover, the born female criminal is, so to speak, doubly exceptional,

[70] *L'Uomo delinquente*, 5th ed., 1897, Vol. II, p. 69.
[71] *The Female Offender*, pp. 150–152.

as a woman and as a criminal. For criminals are an exception among civilised people, and women are an exception among criminals, the natural form of retrogression in women being prostitution and not crime. The primitive woman was impure rather than criminal.

As a double exception, the criminal woman is consequently a monster. Her normal sister is kept in the paths of virtue by many causes, such as maternity, piety, weakness, and when these counter influences fail, and a woman commits a crime, we may conclude that her wickedness must have been enormous before it could triumph over so many obstacles.

Finally, with respect to female crime, he was aware of the common sex differentials reported in criminal statistics. After referring to data collected from England, France, Spain and other European countries showing much lower percentages of female participation in officially recorded crime, he noted that " aside from these facts many other grave reasons make us suspect that the criminality of women is greater than the statistics show." [72] Furthermore, he was convinced that " if cases of prostitution are included in the criminal statistics the two sexes are at once placed on an equality, or the preponderance may even be thrown on the side of women." [73]

In sum, it is obvious that Lombroso experienced a change of ideas regarding his criminal typology. The excessive emphasis in his first edition on anatomical and anthropometric data was the result of a single framework of orientation. Consequently, by focusing attention on skull measurements, facial asymmetries, etc., he distinguished but one type of criminal—the born criminal—and this type led to a unilateral theory of atavism. But by the time later editions were published he had expanded his theory as well as his investigations so that now he could adopt the concept of degeneracy as one of the causes of criminality. Pathological similarities between the born criminal, the moral imbecile and the epileptic broadened his base and added the insane criminal and the epileptic criminal; the criminaloid, by a quantitative difference from the born criminal, and resulting more from precipitating factors than from predisposing ones, became another category; and the pseudo-criminal, the habitual criminal and the criminal by passion lifted Lombroso considerably beyond his original monistic descriptions of the atavistic offender. He considered atavism as a

[72] *Crime : Its Causes and Remedies*, p. 187.
[73] *Ibid.* p. 186. Relative to this contention by Lombroso, see Otto Pollak, *The Criminality of Women*, Philadelphia, 1950, The University of Pennsylvania Press.

possible form of degeneracy, and although biologists have challenged the theoretical marriage of atavism and degeneracy, we see here evidence of his trying to produce a more catholic conceptualism than the delimited rigidity of the *reo nato*, the latter of which is usually the basis of attack by most contemporary critics.

Despite his abundant use of reported precision of anthropometric details and statistical descriptions, Lombroso usually gave only general figures for the proportions and diffusions of anomalies among criminal types and only an approximation of the proportion that born criminals constituted among all criminals. In his last edition of *L'Uomo delinquente* he speaks of 40 per cent. of criminals falling into his category of the born criminal type; and further reduces this proportion to 33 per cent. in *Crime : Its Causes and Remedies*.[74] Whether Lombroso believed that all criminal behaviour had some organic origin will be discussed briefly later, but there is no doubt that he never completely relinquished his belief in the existence of a born criminal type, albeit the proportion of this type among all criminals was reduced in his latest discussion.

His research methods

It is difficult to find a description of the methods of investigation or analysis that Lombroso used without encountering personalised praise by his contemporaries or supercilious, contemptuous disdain by later environmentalists who either failed to read his writings or simply refused to give cognisance to any of his efforts to employ good research habits. Many of his contemporaries had to examine his material with virtually the same level of statistical training as he possessed, and which some commentators contend was relatively low, even for this period.[75] Critics of today, of course, can enjoy the kind of statistical sophistication that has continued since the writings of Karl Pearson, whose benefit Charles Goring possessed at the time he engaged in his study of *The English Convict*.

This section makes no pretence of a detailed examination of Lombroso's procedures, his anthropometry, his deductive thought patterns, nor his statistical tables. We are interested only in reviewing briefly typical comments made about his methods, and in

---

[74] *L'Uomo delinquente*, 5th ed., 1897, Vol. II, pp. 68–69; and *Crime : Its Causes and Remedies*, p. 365. In Chapter 1 of his daughter's summary, *Criminal Man . . .* , there is the statement that "Born criminals form about one third of the mass of offenders . . . " (p. 8).

[75] Bonger, *An Introduction to Criminology*, p. 69.

demonstrating by way of illustration a few of his obvious faults
and some of his virtuous attempts at a valid scientific approach to
the understanding of criminal behaviour. Without need of much
comment errors in method, merely by their presentation, become
obvious.

In general terms it may be said that Lombroso used both clinical
and historical methods in the collection of factual data from which
emerged deductively his theories of atavism and degeneration.
Historical references abound in his many articles and books that
seek to provide illustrative material in support of theory. But it is
essentially the minute and detailed examination of the individual
that characterises his most basic tool of investigation and of gathering data. Not crime in the abstract, but a study of the criminal
himself was the starting-point in 1864 of his criminological career.
" I began dimly to realise," he says in retrospect, " that the *a priori*
studies on crime in the abstract, hitherto pursued by jurists,
especially in Italy, with singular acumen, should be superseded by
the direct analytical study of the criminal, compared with normal
individuals and the insane." [76]   His analysis of the individual
offender was, however, of a static, not a processual or dynamic
phenomenon. His criminal anthropological approach was surely
more comprehensive than that of Virchow, Broca or Mantegazza,
but less experimental and more descriptive. He assumed that congenital and physical characteristics were always ready for observation
and could be subjected to statistical treatment. He had, says
Kurella, " Little inclination for the clinical observation of transient,
morbid processes." [77]   The anomalies and stigmata were for Lombroso permanent documents and primary sources of information.
He was interested in psychical processes but felt them too elusive for
direct observation; hence his emphasis was on a typology based
upon organic factors. He sought some kind of invariable uniformity, a principle of universal law among the phenomena that he
noted always recurring in the same manner. Such a goal could be
achieved, he felt, by a thorough search for facts—empiric data.
It was as if the philosophic sophistry of Italian legalists and German
intellectuals provided the historical moment for a negative reaction,
a search for raw, naked empiricism. [78]   And it was optimistically

[76] " Introduction " to Gina Lombroso-Ferrero, *Criminal Man* . . . , p. xxiv.
[77] Kurella, *op. cit.* p. 136.
[78] This generalisation is in the same spirit with which Talcott Parsons reviews the
    development of sociology. After the grand theorists and theoretical speculators of the

believed that the facts, regardless of their apparent unrelatedness at the moment, would eventually accumulate into an emergent theory of universal applicability.

There are, of course, many doubts that could be registered about Lombroso's anthropometry, but we are not prepared to examine this aspect of his methods. Earnest Hooton, certainly no enemy to Lombroso, and who was one of the world's highly reputed physical anthropologists despite his fleeting failure with his venture into criminology, raised serious questions about the validity of the procedural tools of criminal anthropology in its early years. " Lombroso and subsequent investigators," he says when discussing cranial and facial asymmetry, " have, almost without exception, contented themselves with a mere subjective description of the presence or absence, and the degree of, such asymmetry, and have not developed any quantitative method of appraising it. . . . Consequently, the validity of Lombroso's conclusions as to the prevalence of cranial and facial asymmetry in the criminal skull is impaired. . . . Anyone who has attempted to master the method of grading nonmensurable morphological development is well aware of the great personal equation which affects such estimates, even of a skilled observer who is not obsessed by a theory." [79] Although Ferri did not refer specifically to his elder colleague, he spoke of the defects of some of the anthropological data being collected during his day. A careful reading of Lombroso leads one to suspect that Ferri's comments may apply: " One of these defects is the measuring of skulls in order to determine the cranial capacity of criminals without knowing anything of the stature and respective ages of the subjects, whereas there is a settled connection between the different anthropological characteristics, the capacity of the skull, for instance, being definitely related to the age and especially to the stature." [80] If this criticism of metric methods does not apply directly to Lombroso it surely could apply to the many measurements made by

Spencer era had produced little useful knowledge that could be applied to social situations, a reaction, both negative and crudely empirical, occurred in America during the 1920s and 1930s. See Talcott Parsons, " The Present Position and Prospects of Systematic Theory in Sociology," *Essays in Sociological Theory*, rev. ed., Glencoe, Ill., The Free Press, pp. 212–237; " Some Problems Confronting Sociology as a Profession," *American Sociological Review* (August 1959), 24 : 547–559.

[79] E. A. Hooton, *The American Criminal, An Anthropological Study*, Vol. I, Cambridge, Mass., 1939, Harvard University Press, pp. 12–13.

[80] Enrico Ferri, *Criminal Sociology*, trans. Joseph I. Kelly and John Lisle, Boston, 1917, Little, Brown & Co., p. 63. For details on the method of criminal anthropological research, see Ferri, *L'Omicidio nell'antropologia criminale*, Torino, 1895, Bocca, p. 97 *et seq.*

students throughout Europe and which he seems to have used with inadequate discrimination as supporting evidence.

In his primary concern with the biological principle in personality, Lombroso did not make much use of the *analytique morale* of Guerry nor of the *physique sociale* of Quételet, although references in Lombroso's writings to both of these early statisticians may be found, especially in his later works that reflect his having been criticised for neglecting such data. However, in view of Lombroso's remarks that he could only examine one type of phenomenon at a time, and in the light of his intellectual integrity to recognise deficiencies and to change his approach at times, the comments by Lindesmith and Levin seem unjust: " What Lombroso did was to reverse the method of explanation that had been current since the time of Guerry and Quételet and, instead of maintaining that institutions and traditions determined the nature of the criminal, he held that the nature of the criminal determined the character of institutions and traditions." [81] On this point Lombroso seems to be interpreted correctly by Kurella who said: " It was quite inevitable that Lombroso's sociological thought should be powerfully stimulated by the view of his opponents that law is a product of the intellectual, not of the organic life of mankind, and that therefore it was not nature that produced criminals, but social and national processes. Thus it became necessary for him to prove . . . that nature makes the criminal, but that society provides the conditions in which the criminal commits crimes. . . ." [82] He viewed it [behaviour] in its dependence upon numerous external and internal factors, in part belonging to the organisation of the individual and in part to his environment." [83]

The collection of the positive facts—this above all constituted Lombroso's abiding orientation. From facts emerge theory; but the collector of facts even with an embracing hypothesis is usually faced with an *a posteriori* dilemma of interpretation. It is at this level that Lombroso has so frequently been challenged that it would be

[81] Alfred Lindesmith and Yale Levin, " The Lombrosian Myth in Criminology," *The American Journal of Sociology* (March 1937), 42:661. There is some contradiction in the words these authors use when they refer to institutions and traditions determining the " nature " of the criminal and then criticise Lombroso for holding that the nature (biology) of the criminal determines the character of institutions and traditions. Surely the authors do not mean to say that social institutions are primary factors affecting the individual's biology, heredity, or, more loosely, his nature.

[82] Kurella, *op. cit.* p. 117.

[83] *Ibid.* p. 161.

impossible to document. As the late John Gillin,[84] one of the more diligent and historically-oriented American textbook writers, has observed, Lombroso's explanation of criminality on the basis of atavism, which his demonstrated abnormalities were made to prove, was a philosophical deduction the facts do not warrant. Even the friendly Kurella said that " he knew, also, how to demonstrate his results forcibly and vividly; but was less richly endowed with the faculty of sifting his data, and of grouping them in accordance with a natural, and not merely superficial criterion." [85] Lombroso, we are repeatedly told, was a " slave to facts "; yet, it was under this same slavery that he spoke of the facts of spiritualism with credulity. After his first sittings with Eusapia Paladino he said that he was inclined to reject the spiritualistic theory, " but the facts exist, and as regards facts I glory in saying that I am their slave." [86] If his acceptance of these " facts " was not the result of senility, it is not difficult to understand why some doubt has been cast upon his definition and interpretation of facts concerned with criminals and criminal behaviour. Rash and easy generalisations about atavism and degeneracy deduced from biological anomalies left a vulnerable hiatus between theory and fact. As Merton and Montagu[87] suggested in their review of Hooton's criminological research, " To insinuate an axiom is not to demonstrate a fact."

Even some of the most ardent advocates of Lombroso complained of his " obvious neglect of critical examination of his sources of information." [88] His reliance upon cranium measurements and other anthropometric data compiled by students over whom he had no control compounded the types of errors Hooton refers to in his discussion of " the personal equation " in such matters. Perhaps, however, critics and zealots alike have been most disturbed by his use of the anecdotal method and the method of analogy in presenting his material. Although providing piquancy and reading interest, they constitute doubtful methodology. Hooton expresses his dissatisfaction explicitly: " One of the greatest defects of Lombrosian presentation of criminal anthropological data is the sensational anecdotal method which is utilised to clinch arguments.

[84] John L. Gillin, *Criminology and Penology*, 3rd ed., New York, 1945, D. Appleton-Century Co., p. 79.
[85] Kurella, *op. cit.* p. 98.   [86] *Ibid.* p. 175.
[87] Robert Merton and M. F. Ashley-Montagu, " Crime and The Anthropologist," *American Anthropologist* (July–Sept. 1940), 42:384–408.
[88] Kurella, *op. cit.* p. 56.

Individual case descriptions are still copiously spread over the pages of most works on criminology. Although these are absolutely essential as the primary sources from which general deductions may be drawn, they are quite useless and misleading when introduced singly into discussions, since it is perfectly evident that they are not random selections or illustrations, but rather special cases chosen to bolster up some particular argument. Generalisation from a single case, which is often encouraged by the use of such anecdotes, is wholly unscientific." [89]

The same general remarks may be made about Lombroso's use of analogy. As he compares the criminal type with the insane, and both of these with epileptics, he approaches identification on the basis of similarities in the number and kinds of anomalies. " Thus it happened often enough that, perceiving intuitive analogies, his lively imagination led him falsely to regard them as identities." [90] In his statistical statement of genius, which appears in *L'Uomo di genio* (1888), he derives an " index of genius " by use of analogy and shows his index for every department in France, according to which index the departments are arranged in groups corresponding to department groupings based upon their republican or monarchical character. In additional diagrams, charts and tables he arranges the French departments according to certain geographical configurations, such as mountains, hills, plains and the nature of the soil. Then for each group the predominant political affiliations and the " index of genius " are determined. In this questionable fashion he deduces a virtual identity between genius and republicanism.

The use of " laymen's hypotheses " as guides to scientific research may sometimes be fruitful, if for no other reason than dispelling their traditional tendency to persist, although data collected to test a lay hypothesis may sometimes confirm it.[91] Not only was Lombroso heir to an abundance of old Italian proverbs that implied physiognomic correlations to criminality, but it seems as if he was to some extent influenced by them as he sought to find physical stigmata that would identify the criminal type. To suggest this is not to indict his methods, but merely to indicate the probable role of provincial thought on his intuitions and insights—an element of

[89] Hooton, *op. cit.* pp. 16–17.
[90] Kurella, *op. cit.* p. 98.
[91] With respect to the use of laymen's hypotheses in sociological research, see Alvin Gouldner, " Theoretical Requirements of the Applied Social Sciences," *American Sociological Review* (Feb. 1957), 22:92–102.

methodology that is, after all, as much artistry as science. Creative work in music, poetry or painting may make use of regional legends, myths and proverbs; these same sources appear in Lombroso's writings and seem to have contributed to his thinking.[92] Surely something of this sort must have occurred in the thoughts he expressed at the Fifth Congress of Criminal Anthropology in Amsterdam (1901) when he delivered his paper on *Why Criminals of Genius do not Manifest the Criminal Type*, and in which he suggested that " the habit of thinking elevated thoughts gives certain characteristics to the physiognomy, such as a straight brow and a voluminous cranium." [93]

Probably the most persistent and valid criticism of Lombroso's methods pertains to his use of statistics. It is generally agreed that the chief refutation of Lombroso's work was Charles Goring's *The English Convict*, published in 1913. In this study the author praises Lombroso for his humanitarianism but makes a vitriolic attack upon his research methods. The time that separated *L'Uomo delinquente* and *The English Convict* was not long, but the development of standard deviations around the mean, regression lines, and probable errors constituted a wide difference indeed. The Biometric Laboratory in London and the prison at Turin were more than kilometres apart. This distance permitted Goring to state that " since this belief of Lombroso's was arrived at, not by methods of disinterested investigation, but, rather, by a leap of the imagination, the notion thus reached then forming the basis upon which he conducted his researches, and constructed his theory—the whole fabric of the Lombrosian doctrine, judged by the standards of science, is fundamentally unsound." [94] Few researchers are without their critics, and Goring's work in turn was blasted because it " bristles with . . . logical fallacies and . . . statistical sophistries, all devoted to his

---

[92] In Gina Lombroso, *Criminal Man*, pp. 49–51, Cesare Lombroso refers to some of these proverbial statements: " There is nothing worse under Heaven than a scanty beard and a colourless face " (Rome); " An ashen face is worse than the itch " (Piedmont); " Greet from afar the red-haired man and the bearded woman " (Venice); " Beware of him who looks away when he speaks to you, and of him who keeps his eyes cast down and takes mincing steps " (Venice); " The squint-eyed are on all sides accursed " (Venice); " Better sell a field and a house than take a wife with a turned-up nose " (Venice). His use of these proverbs was to indicate that they express universal distrust of the criminal type. See also Arthur MacDonald, *Criminology*, New York, 1893, Funk and Wagnalls Co., p. 43.

[93] *Congrès International d'Anthropologie Criminelle. Compte Rendu des Travaux de la Cinquième Session*, Amsterdam, 1901, De Bussy, p. 215.

[94] Charles Goring, *The English Convict: A Statistical Study,* 1913, reprinted Montclair, N.J., 1972, Patterson Smith, p. 15.

purpose of proving that criminals are not different from non-criminals. . . ." [95]

The absence of adequate control groups, which was recognised even in Lombroso's day, is the most basic and damaging criticism made in any contemporary evaluation of his methods. Even if he can be excused for his anecdotal approach, or for his use of analogies, philosophical deductions based on unrelated facts, and subjectivism in his anatomico-pathological method, the lack of a good sample, or of a control group of normals that meets the demands of statistical procedures, causes the whole superstructure of analysis to crumble. Durkheim,[96] in his study of suicide in 1897, followed closely in the steps of historical continuity that can be traced from Guerry and Quételet; consequently, he needed only data from human ecology, frequency distributions, rates per unit of population, etc. Durkheim suffered principally from the lack of test statistics, but Lombroso and his fellow criminal anthropologists established the tradition of looking for differences between criminals and non-criminals. Hence, extreme importance must be placed on the representativeness of the sample, or on the variables controlled in an individual or group matching of a " normal " population with the criminal one. Moreover, when reviewing Lombroso's writings, one is impressed with the lack of definition regarding the criminal. He sometimes refers to individuals who are not " legal criminals," but who are " anthropologically criminal." For purposes of analysis, homogeneity of the criminal and non-criminal groups is a basic requirement. Such statements, of course, are easier to make than to accomplish in a research design, and many contemporary researches still suffer, although in a lesser degree than did Lombroso's, from the same deficiencies.

There is both error and truth in the statement by Lindesmith and Levin regarding this point: " The assumption of the Lombrosians that the weighing and measuring of criminals was the only scientific method of studying criminals was particularly ironical in view of the notoriously slipshod methods of the father of criminal anthropology and in view of the neglect of control groups which has characterised the movement to the present day." [97] We agree

[95] Hooton, *op. cit.* p. 23. See the entire section devoted to a criticism of Goring, pp. 18–31; also, " Charles Goring's *The English Convict:* A Symposium," *Journal of Criminal Law and Criminology* (1914–15), 5:207–240; 348–363.
[96] Emile Durkheim, *Le Suicide*, 1897.
[97] Lindesmith and Levin, *op. cit.* p. 664.

with Sellin [98] that the Lombrosians did not assume that " the weighing and measuring of criminals was the only scientific method of studying criminals." That there was a " neglect of control groups " can hardly be denied, but it must be remembered that the sociological studies of the nineteenth century were " in most instances just as poor in method and execution as anything done by the adherents of the biological approach." [99] Lombroso had no adequate basis for a comparison with the general population of the same economic and social class and of the same general level of intelligence; there was numerical inadequacy of the ethnic and racial heterogeneity of the material, and there was a lack of any scientific statistical analysis of the data assembled by a wide variety of students. In some cases thousands of cranial and other types of measurements are reported, but mere magnitude of a sample does not guarantee its representative character; and unless there is some adequate statistical method of appraising the amount of fortuitous divergence in comparing the characteristics of two or more samples, conclusions drawn from such differences cannot be considered valid.

Lombroso crudely correlated a host of factors with crime without much questioning of the presence or absence of the underlying cause-and-effect relationship. Perhaps one of his most indictable instances of this fallacy may be seen in his analysis of the relationship between the use of tobacco and crime. After using questionable data from other countries regarding the proportion of prisoners who smoke, his conclusion begins with an unwarranted dogmatic assertion followed by an interesting ambiguity: " It is clearly to be seen, then, that there is a causal connection between tobacco and crime, like that which exists in the case of alcohol. But, as in the case of alcohol, it is a curious fact that the countries where the consumption of tobacco is greatest have a lower criminality. This contradiction is frequently met in our researches; but it soon disappears, because the abuse of these stimulating substances, as in the case of alcohol, takes place especially among civilised people, who learn to control themselves." [1]

However obvious the limitations and errors of Lombroso's statistical procedures may be to the contemporary criminologist (who cannot afford to be too self-righteous), there is evidence of his

[98] Thorsten Sellin, " The Lombrosian Myth in Criminology " (Letter to the Editor), *The American Journal of Sociology* (May 1937), 42:897-899.
[99] *Ibid.* p. 898.
[1] *Crime : Its Causes and Remedies*, p. 102. *Cf.* Bonger, *op. cit.* p. 77.

having been cognisant of the importance of a control group. In numerous instances he attempts, however crudely, to compare prisoner groups with normals. The median occipital fossa, which he first described, was found, for example, to be present in 4·1 per cent. of the skulls examined for student demonstration, in 14·3 per cent. of prehistoric skulls, in 15 per cent. of ancient Peruvian skulls, in 28 per cent. of Australian aborigines and in 20 per cent. of criminal skulls.[2] As a crude test of his belief that the criminal could be identified on sight Lombroso once asked a school teacher to show her thirty-two young girls twenty portraits of thieves and twenty of great men. We are told that 80 per cent. of the children correctly identified the subjects.[3]

Especially in *The Female Offender* (which Kurella believes is the book in which Lombroso used the best methods) does Lombroso seem to exercise caution and make attempts frequently to compare a group of prostitutes and other female criminals with a control group of " normal " women. For example, after describing his own observations added to those of Tarnowsky and Ottolenghi, he says: " This constitutes a total of 1,033 observations on female criminals, 176 observations on the skulls of female criminals, 685 on the skulls of prostitutes, 225 on normal women in hospitals, and thirty other also normal."[4] Criminal women are compared with normals relative to height and age, weight and age, span of arms, average height of the body seated, the hand, neck, thigh, leg, foot, hair, eye colour and a variety of other physical traits. He relies again upon measurements taken by many other persons whose instruments of analysis he could not control, and whose " normals " were selected without the characteristic of representativeness. Still, one is impressed with his *attempt*, even in the case of examining wrinkles among women, to provide valid comparisons and to use control groups. With a classification of eight major wrinkle types (deep frontal, horizontal; deep frontal, vertical; crow's feet; wrinkles under the eyelids; naso-labial wrinkles; zygomatic wrinkles; goniomental wrinkles; labial wrinkles) he divides three age-groups (14–24 years; 25–49 years; 50 years and over) into normal and criminal populations. The approach to acceptable comparison is present and his caution is noted when he says: " Taking into

---

[2] Reported in Kurella, *op. cit.* p. 32.
[3] Gina Lombroso, *Criminal Man*, pp. 50–51; also, Ellis, *The Criminal*, p. 86.
[4] *The Female Offender*, p. 47.

account only the deeper wrinkles, I concluded, after examining 158 normals (working women and peasantry) and seventy criminals, that among the latter class wrinkles are not more common than among the former. Nevertheless, certain wrinkles, such as the fronto-vertical, the wrinkles on the cheek-bones, crow's feet and labial wrinkles are more frequent and deeply marked in criminal women of mature age." [5] We are not told how the 158 normals were chosen or even where and how he obtained the criminal women, but there is an implicit attempt to hold constant socio-economic class by use of normals from " working women and peasantry." The same awareness is evident elsewhere in his discussion of crime among Jews: " The statistics of many countries show a lower degree of criminality for the Jews than for their Gentile fellow citizens. This is the more remarkable since, because of their usual occupations, they should in fairness be compared, not with the population in general, but with the merchants and petty tradespeople." [6]

He frequently allows himself the luxury of much too free an interpretation or speculation based on meagre data, as in the case of his observation of the bust of an old woman from Palermo (*Vecchia dell'Aceto*) whom he had never seen but which he describes as " so full of virile angularities, and above all so deeply wrinkled, with its Satanic leer, that it *suffices of itself* to prove that the woman in question was *born to do evil*, and that, if one occasion to commit it had failed, she would have found another." [7] But in the summary statement on the anthropometry of female criminals he again tempers his earlier licence: " It must be confessed that these accumulated figures do not amount to much, but this result is only natural. For if external differentiations between criminal and normal subjects in general are few, they are still fewer in the female than in the male." [8]

References to tattooing demonstrate both his attempt to compare criminals with normals and his hasty theoretical deduction from the observed facts. Using statistics of 13,566 individuals of which 4,376 were " honest," 6,347 criminal and 2,943 insane, he shows that tattooing is quite common among criminals. " It may be said that,

[5] *Ibid.* pp. 71–72.
[6] *Crime : Its Causes and Remedies,* p. 37.
[7] *Ibid.* pp. 72–73. Italics added.
[8] *Ibid.* p. 74.

for these last," he suggests, "it constitutes on account of its frequency a specific and entirely new anatomico-legal characteristic." [9] He mentions several "causes" for tattooing, such as religion, carnal love, imitation, idleness, vanity and above all atavism: "But the first, the principal cause which has spread this custom among us, is, in my opinion, atavism, or this other kind of historic atavism called tradition. Tattooing is in fact one of the essential characteristics of primitive man and of the man who is still living in a savage state." [10]

Lombroso seems to have had trouble deciding the proportionate number of anomalies necessary to apply to his designation of the born criminal. In an early examination of a group of 383 criminals, he found 21 per cent. who had only one physical anomaly and 43 per cent. with five or more anomalies. He concluded that as many as five in any individual should be taken as the minimum indication of physical criminal type. (The same inability to objectify and quantify the number or intensity of personality and behavioural traits needed to designate a psychopath still plague the psychologist and psychiatrist.[11]) Although he never seemed to consider all criminals of the born criminal type, he first estimated that the *delinquente-nato* comprised 65 or 70 per cent. It was Ferri, in his review [12] of Lombroso's *L'Uomo delinquente* in 1878, who convinced himself and influenced Lombroso to believe that anthropological postulates do not apply in their complete and characteristic entirety to all those who commit crime: "As to the results of the researches of criminal anthropology, they show that in the mass of delinquents, there are from 50 to 60 per cent. who have only a few organic and psychic anomalies, while about a third show an extraordinary number and a tenth show none at all." [13] We have seen that in his last work Lombroso reduces the proportion of the born criminal type to one-third.

Although far from providing convincing and valid statistical proof of his contentions, some of Lombroso's tables represent the character of his scientific research in criminal anthropology. By way of illustration, let us examine one of these tables.

[9] *L'Homme criminel*, Vol. I, p. 266, as cited.
[10] *Ibid.* p. 295.
[11] See, for example, Karl Schuessler and Donald Cressey, "Personality Characteristics of Criminals," *The American Journal of Sociology* (March 1950), 55:476–484.
[12] Enrico Ferri, "Studi critici sull'Uomo delinquente di Lombroso," *Rivista europea* (1878); cited by Ferri, *Criminal Sociology*, p. 129.
[13] *Ibid.*

Conditions as to anomalies of skull	Criminals guilty of homicide and sentenced to :		Non-criminal Italian soldiers
	Penal servitude	Imprisonment	
	N = 346	N = 363	N = 711
No anomalies of skull	11·9%	8·2%	37·2%
One or two anomalies	47·2%	56·6%	51·8%
Three or four anomalies	33·9%	32·6%	11·0%
Five or six anomalies	6·7%	2·3%	0·0%
Seven or more anomalies	0·3%	0·3%	0·0%
	100·0%	100·0%	100·0%

As Vold suggests, "Lombroso deserves respectful credit for utilising the method of control group comparisons in the application of statistical methods to his problem" although "it remained for others to make more exact and careful application of more adequate statistical methodology to the problem of physical differences between criminals and non-criminals." [15] We have previously raised serious questions about Lombroso's anthropometry, his determination of specific anomalies and their dimensions, as well as his use of representative control groups. If, however, we assume validity of these measurements and of the sample of "non-criminal Italian soldiers," and then apply the non-parametric tool of chi-square to test for significance of difference between observed and theoretical distributions, we may note that there is: (a) a significant difference between the distribution of anomaly categories found among criminals sentenced to penal servitude compared to Italian soldiers ($x^2 = 119·74$; df = 4; P<·001); (b) a significant difference between criminals sentenced to imprisonment and the Italian soldiers ($x^2 = 148·9$; df = 4; P<·001); (c) less of a difference between criminals sentenced to servitude and those sentenced to imprisonment ($x^2 = 15·0$; df = 4; P<·02). We have not taken time to test significance of difference between proportions within each of the anomaly categories, but inspection indicates obvious differences and, combined with the tests computed from this table, support the point Lombroso is trying to demonstrate.

We are not defending this table, nor Lombroso's theoretical deductions from it, nor even the desirability of applying test statistics to it. We are merely trying to show that he applied a scientific approach to his data; that he obviously possessed intellectual

---

[14] Cesare Lombroso, *L'Uomo delinquente*, 4th ed., 1889, p. 273; cited by Ferri, *Criminal Sociology*, p. 12; also used by Vold, *Theoretical Criminology*, p. 52.
[15] Vold, *op. cit.* p. 52.

integrity in his pursuit of understanding; that many contemporary researches use data that have little more validity than his; and that with statistical tables similar to his, conclusions purporting wide applicability have appeared in present-day research. We must remember that Lombroso could not make use of the probable error, the significance of differences between means, the standard deviation, the coefficient of variation, the coefficient of correlation, the chi-square, the coefficient of mean square contingency, etc., etc. These tools, sometimes used today to camouflage dubious research design, were not available to him. Nonetheless, he possessed a methodological insight that should not be denied him.

In referring to his conception of the criminal type he speaks of the type in general and with awareness of a mental construct not in direct correspondence to individual empiric reality: " In my opinion, one should receive the *type* with the same reserve that one uses in estimating the value of *averages* in statistics. When one says that the average life is thirty-two years and that the most fatal month is December, no one understands by that that everybody must die at thirty-two and in the month of December." [16]

Often unnoticed in contemporary quick dismissals of Lombroso's life and contribution is the fact that he challenged his opponents to test his ideas by a controlled investigation of criminals and non-criminals. He felt that such a study would vindicate him from the criticisms made previously and principally by French scholars. The Second International Congress of Criminal Anthropology at Paris (1889) followed a proposal from Garofalo and had appointed a commission of seven members to make a series of comparisons between 100 criminals (one-third murderers, one-third violent criminals and one-third thieves) and 100 " honest " persons. The commission consisted of Lacassagne, Benedikt, Lombroso, Manouvrier, Magnan, Semal and Bertillon. The report was to be submitted to the Third Congress, but was not made; the only result of the commission's work was Manouvrier's private report examining the " basic questions for the comparative study of criminals and honest people." [17] As a result, except for Ferri, the important Italians stayed away from the Third Congress in Brussels (1892) and informed the Congress in a letter sent from forty-nine scientists headed by Lombroso,

---

[16] *L'Homme criminel*, Vol. I, p. ix, as cited.
[17] *Actes du Troisième Congrès International d'Anthropologie Criminelle. Biologie et Sociologie*, Brussels, 1893, Hayez, p. 171.

Garofalo, Ferrero, Ottolenghi and Sighele.[18]   Thus, nothing came of Lombroso's request until 1913 when Charles Goring published *The English Convict* as a direct result of that challenge.

In sum, Lombroso investigated the etiology of crime with procedures in which he had been trained and felt competent.   He used clinical and historical methods, anthropometric and statistical techniques, the tools of analogy and anecdotal illustration.   His ill-defined measurements, unwarranted deductions and inadequate control groups constitute serious deficiencies of his research.   But he also manifested imaginative insight, good intuitive judgment, intellectual honesty, awareness of some of his limitations, attempts to use control groups and a desire to have his theories tested impartially. Many researchers of today fare little better than this.

Social factors

Although the name of Lombroso is most closely associated with terms like atavism, arrested development, degeneracy and the born criminal, his positive approach also included a concern for factors in the physical and social environment of the offender.   It would be incorrect to assert, of course, that he gave attention to social factors equal in space or import to the biological ones.   Nonetheless, induced by his critics and friends as well as by new opportunities to make more expansive inquiries than purely anthropometric, Lombroso came to write *Le crime : causes et remèdes* in 1899. Generally, he was intent upon showing that political and economic developments of civilised nations have given rise to the appearance of abnormalities which induce social reactions.   Throughout his discussions of socio-economic factors there is emphasised a mutual interactive relationship between heredity and environment.   Nature makes the raw material, society provides the circumstances within which the biological structure operates; but the social circumstances may be partially responsible for encouraging or calling forth a variety of transmissible biological anomalies that in turn function within and affect the social structure.   The emphasis is on the biological, it is true, but it would be fallacious to deny Lombroso's recognition of environmental, precipitating factors that lie outside the individual and contribute to the etiology of crime.

Both in the definition of crime and in the determination of

[18] *Ibid*. p. xvi.

penalties, he was aware of cultural relativity and could not always accept purely legal classifications. As Mannheim points out, " Not even Lombroso failed to recognise that crime in the sociological sense changes its content just as much as does the legal conception." [19]   And as early as 1875 Lombroso published an article on the causes of crime, in which he stated:

> There is no crime which does not have its roots in numerous causes. If these often merge or are interdependent, we should, nevertheless, obedient to a scholastic as well as to a linguistic necessity, consider them one by one, as is done with all other human phenomena, to which practically never a single cause can be assigned.[20]

Moreover, in the second edition of *L'Uomo delinquente* (1878) and twenty years before *Le Crime : causes et remèdes*, Lombroso gives attention to several environmental conditions that cause or that have an effect on criminality. He makes use of London data found in Mayhew's *Criminal Life* (1860) and of American descriptions from Brace's *Dangerous Classes of New York* (1874).[21]   In this early edition he discusses the influences of poverty [22]; the relationship between prices of wheat, rye, potatoes, other food products and minor violations, arson, crimes against property and crimes against the person [23]; the influence of alcohol [24]; emigration [25]; the evils of criminal gangs and corruption of police [26]; and the deleterious effects caused by criminal association in prisons that are not constructed on the cellular system.[27]   While it is unfortunate that most of these items were omitted in the fourth edition which was used as the basis for several translations, Lombroso deserves credit for his having early given cognisance to a variety of social factors.

It is not possible to discuss in detail Lombroso's *Crime : Its Causes and Remedies*. Such a discussion would not necessarily be very fruitful of generalisation other than the fact that he modifies

[19] Hermann Mannheim, " Lombroso and His Place in Modern Criminology," *The Sociological Review* (1936), 28:40, *Group Problems in Crime and Punishment*, p. 77. Mannheim refers to Lombroso's *Crime : Its Causes and Remedies*, where the latter remarks: " Civilisation introduces every day new crimes, less atrocious perhaps than the old ones but nonetheless injurious " (p. 57); " Is it possible to believe in an eternal and absolute principle of justice among men when we see this pretended justice vary so greatly within a brief interval of space or time? . . ." (p. 34).
[20] *Etiologia del delitto : Memorie del laboratorio di psichiatria e medicina legale della R. Università di Pavia*, Bologna, 1875; quoted by Thorsten Sellin, " A New Phase of Criminal Anthropology in Italy," *op. cit.* p. 235.
[21] *L'Uomo delinquente*, 2nd ed., 1878, pp. 118, 120, 156, 374, are good examples of his use of these sources in connection with socio-economic factors.
[22] *Ibid.* pp. 363–365.   [23] *Ibid.* pp. 260–262.
[24] *Ibid.* pp. 263–265.   [25] *Ibid.* pp. 368–370
[26] *Ibid.* pp. 373–374.   [27] *Ibid.* pp. 370–371

some original perspectives found in earlier editions of *L'Uomo delinquente*. There are in the work interesting statements and amusing deductions, but no theoretical framework of sociological relevance that emerges from the plethora of facts, save that of a mutual interrelationship between the organic and the environmental. A few summary statements and illustrations will suffice to demonstrate his social perception, on the one hand, and his consistent clinging to the early concept of the born criminal, on the other.

He begins with examination of meteorological and climatic influences and suggests that extremes of temperature, hot or cold, sap the individual's energy and leave little time or enthusiasm for deviations such as crime. His discussion of the influence of race leads to the conclusion that certain groups in every culture are responsible for most criminality, and he gives details of various robber tribes in India and elsewhere. The conclusion minimises the social factors, however, for he suggests that hereditary predispositions seem to function in the case of crime among Jews and gypsies. The influence of civilisation, density of population, alcohol, education, economic conditions, religion, prisons, criminal associations and political crimes constitute the remaining portions of the first part of the book, while " Prophylaxis and Therapeusis of Crime," and " Synthesis and Application " comprise the last 100 pages. In the third part of the book he recapitulates his position on atavism, epilepsy and the classification of other types.

Some provocative, imaginative and insightful statements appear in the first section of *Crime: Its Causes and Remedies*. The examples that follow were specifically selected to show these traits.

Civilisation, wealth and crime : " The progress of civilisation, by endlessly multiplying needs and desires, and by encouraging sensually through the accumulation of wealth, brings a flood of alcoholics and general paralytics into the insane asylums, and crowds the prisons with offenders against property and against decency " (p. 51).

Urban congestion of population : " This unfortunate concentration of crime is to be explained by the greater profits or the greater security which the large cities offer to criminals. But this, perhaps, is not the only reason, for if in cities vigilance is more relaxed, prosecution is more active and systematic; and if temptations and inducements to crime are more numerous, so are the opportunities for honest labour. . . . The very congestion of population by itself gives an irresistible impulse toward crime and immorality " (p. 53).

" We see, therefore, that homicide decreases as the density [of population] increases, especially in the great cities. . . . Theft, rape and resistance to the officers of the law also diminish with the increase in density, to rise again rapidly, however, with the excessive density of the great cities " (p. 61).

" We see that theft becomes more and more frequent as the density increases. Homicides and rapes, on the contrary, show the highest proportion with the minimum or the maximum of the density. This contradiction is explained by the fact that where the population is most compact occur the great industrial and political centres, and ports of immigration, where the *opportunities for conflict* are more frequent; and where there is the minimum density there is the maximum of barbarism, and we have seen that assaults and assassination are there often regarded more as necessities than as crimes " (p. 62, emphasis added).

Women and urban crime: " . . . women are more criminal in the more civilised countries. They are almost always drawn into crime by a false pride about their poverty, by a desire for luxury, and by masculine occupations and education, which give them the means and opportunity to commit crimes against the laws of the Press, and swindling " (p. 54).

Immigration and emigration: " . . . when the tide moving men to emigrate is weak it draws the stronger and more intelligent, but when it becomes too violent it sweeps along good and bad alike. In fact, the greater part of the criminality of the immigrants is furnished by the border provinces, where emigration is easy. . . . On the other hand, the less stable the immigration is the more crimes it furnishes. The Belgians, who became naturalised Frenchmen, commit fewer crimes than the Spaniards, who are nearly always merely temporary residents " (p. 66).

" The emigration from the country to the cities is such that the rural emigrants constitute a fifth part of the urban population; and it is the better and more intelligent who emigrate, thus lowering the level of the country and in return bringing back to it the vices and customs of the city " (pp. 72–73).

Food prices: " But of all studies of the influences at work in the different kinds of crime in Italy, the most conclusive is that of the hours of labour necessary to obtain the equivalent of a kilogram of wheat or bread. In this way the price of food is corrected for variations in wages (Fornasari di Verce, *La Criminalita e le Viconde Economiche in Italia*, Turin, 1895, Bocca). . . . We see here that all crimes against property (except where contradictory factors come too powerfully into play) run with great fidelity parallel to the curve of the hours of work necessary to procure the equivalent of a kilogram of bread or grain. . . . Crimes against morality increase as the necessary hours of labour diminish " (p. 79).

" The effect of the price of provisions upon murder is uncertain or negligible, the latter being also true of assaults. The influence upon theft is very great, as is also the inverse effect upon crimes against good morals, which increase with the falling off in the price of food. Famine lessens sexual vigour, and abundance excites it; and while the need of food drives men to theft, the abundance of it leads to sexual crimes " (p. 81).

We have previously mentioned his awareness of class differences and the necessity to hold the occupational variable constant in an analysis of crimes among Jews. At several points in his writings, Lombroso comes close to admitting that there are normal criminals, although he never totally departs from his original concept of atavism. There are two forms of criminality, he suggests, which consist of " atavistic criminality " and " evolutive criminality ": " Into the first class of criminals fall only a few individuals, fatally predisposed to crime; into the second any one may come who has not a character strong enough to resist the evil influences in his environment." [28] He means that the second group are criminals by legal definition but not from the point of view of criminal anthropology; the real criminals could always be identified by physical and psychological traits. Thus, as Sellin contends, although Lombroso " appreciated the exciting and the restraining effect of the environment, he never brought himself to admit the existence of a normal delinquent, one that is ' provoked and not revealed ' by social conditions." [29] Lombroso's occasional criminals and criminals by passion were conceptually close to borderline normality, and the false or " pseudo-criminals " were " not criminals either in the eyes of society or of anthropology." This last group included those who unintentionally committed crimes or who broke laws enacted " by a dominant opinion or prejudice," poachers, smugglers, real political criminals, etc.[30]

Lindesmith and Levin,[31] in their unwarranted denouncement of Lombroso, claim that *Crime : Its Causes and Remedies* " was in no sense a contribution to criminology." Van Kan [32] argues that Lombroso's discussion of social factors in crime was chaotic and confused, comprised of heterogeneous unrelated facts imperfectly subjected to critical examination of sources by the author who tries to cover too much territory in his preoccupation to arrive at a hasty conclusion. Van Kan is probably correct in asserting that despite all of the socio-economic causes upon which Lombroso reflects, organic factors remain the primary cause even in this last important work.

---

[28] *Crime : Its Causes and Remedies*, p. 45.
[29] Sellin, " A New Phase in Criminal Anthropology in Italy," *op. cit.* p. 235. See also Sellin, " En historik aterblick," *op. cit.* p. 12.
[30] *L'Uomo delinquente*, 5th ed., Vol. II, p. 491; also cited by Sellin, " A New Phase of Criminal Anthropology in Italy," *op. cit.* p. 236.
[31] Lindesmith and Levin, *op. cit.* p. 666, note 21.
[32] Joseph van Kan, *Les Causes économiques de la criminalité*, Paris, 1903, Maloine, pp. 57-58.

In the final analysis, external causes themselves become organic according to Lombroso: "Finally, we have seen that certain circumstances have so strong an action upon criminaloids that they are equivalent to organic causes, and we may even say that they become organic." [33] Even while recognising social class differences when discussing Sighele's division of "collective criminality" into crimes of the upper and lower classes, he still refers to atavistic causes:

> Confronted by these two forms of collective criminality it is natural to ask ourselves, "Why does the criminality of the rich take the form of cunning, while that of the poor is based upon violence?" The answer is easy. The upper classes represent what is really modern, while the lower still belong in thought and feeling to a relatively distant past. It is, then, logical and natural that the former should show the result of modern development in their collective criminality, and that the latter should remain, on the contrary, still violent, not to say absolutely atavistic.[34]

At the First Congress of Criminal Anthropology in Rome (1885), Lombroso gave little or no attention to social and economic factors, and he proposed only the pure doctrine of the born criminal. In his attempt to oppose Lombroso, Lacassagne was quickly rebuked by Fioretto (called the *alter ego* of Ferri) who remarked that "the criminal type is a fact definitely acquired by science. Discussion does not seem appropriate on this point." [35] Only after the Second Congress in Paris (1889), says van Kan, did Lombroso begin to introduce social factors into his writing as a result of the criticism his ideas encountered at that meeting. At the Fourth Congress in Geneva (1896) there was recognition of Lombroso's modifications, for Dallemagne announced: "Lombroso himself seems to be affected by the objections raised, and his writings depart from unilateral formulae by their extended horizons." [36]

Regardless of increasing emphasis that Lombroso may have put on environmental factors, we are inclined to accept Sellin's judgment that "Lombroso, in spite of the very great modifications in his theories, never departed from a monogenetic concept of crime," and we must agree with van Kan, who concluded that "c'était en

---

[33] *Crime : Its Causes and Remedies*, p. 376.
[34] *Ibid*. p. 52.
[35] *Actes du Premier Congrès International d'Anthropologie Criminelle*, Turin, 1886–87, Bocca, pp. 165, 169; cited by van Kan, *op. cit.* p. 54.
[36] *Congrès International d'Anthropologie Criminelle. Compte Rendu des Travaux de la Quatrième Session*, Geneva, 1897, Georg & Co., p. 201. Dallemagne was not happy with this concession: "Voilà qu'aujourd'hui Lombroso fait surgir à nouveau sa théorie dans sa forme la moins acceptable" (*ibid*.).

effet le cas [that Lombroso had abandoned his unilateral theory],
mais non sans le maintien inébranable du type criminel et du
criminel-né." [37]

Punishment and correction

Lombroso's determinism did not lead him to indecision regarding a theory of punishment. There were some negative but
certainly not sterile proposals that his position on the born criminal
were bound to produce; but in general he emphasised sound views
regarding the fundamental principles of reformatory treatment of
all prisoners except born criminals. Accepting the basic theory of
Beccaria, Lombroso contended that only natural necessity and the
right of social defence constituted a sound basis for any theory of
punishment.[38] Hence, both crime and punishment were of natural
necessity. Critics were quick to point out that one could hardly
punish a person unless assumptions were made about moral responsibility. But Lombroso did not mean to suggest that crime was a
social need; crime was simply an inevitable consequence of social
life. Similarly, the law was inevitable for the protection of society,
and since society has the right to defend itself against aggressors, it
has an equal right to punish. This relationship constitutes justice
in Lombroso's terms. Only that amount of punishment is justifiable
that is compatible with social defence. Retribution and vengeance
are excluded, while Beccaria's emphasis on deterrence is embodied
within a more embracing theory of protection.

If the first object of punishment should be the protection of
society, the second is the improvement of the criminal. The fundamental principle, he consistently repeats, is that we ought to study
and to treat not so much the abstract crime as the criminal.
Resulting from this emphasis was his demand for individualisation
of treatment, " which consists in applying special methods of repression and occupation adapted to each individual, as a physician does
in prescribing dietary rules and special remedies according to the
various illnesses." [39] These were ideas, we should note, expressed as
early as his second edition of *L'Uomo delinquente* (1878); and
because this was the edition in which he also discussed a variety of

[37] Van Kan, *op. cit.* p. 55, note 2.
[38] *L'Uomo delinquente*, 2nd ed., 1878, p. 382 *et seq.*; *Crime: Its Causes and Remedies*, pp. 379, 381.
[39] *L'Uomo delinquente*, 2nd ed., p. 429.

social factors in the etiology of crime, individualisation of treatment meant the social necessity to consider the particular type of criminal beyond that of the original atavistic category. Consistency of penological views was maintained throughout his life, for a few months before his death in 1909 he could write to Professor John Wigmore about apportioning penalties to fit the special type of offender rather than the crime, in the same fashion in which he had written about these ideas thirty years earlier. In his final work he was still saying that " the penalty should be indeterminate and should be subdivided according to the principle of Cicero: ' A natura hominis discenda est natura juris.' We must make a difference according to whether we have under our eyes a born criminal, an occasional criminal, or a criminal by passion." [40] As modern and progressive a statement as he makes anywhere is the following:

> In the case of every criminal in whose case the crime itself and the personal conditions show that reparation of the damage is not a sufficient social sanction, the judge should give sentence of imprisonment for an indeterminate time in a criminal asylum, or in the institutions (agricultural colonies or prisons) for occasional criminals, adults or minors. The carrying out of the sentence should be regarded as the logical and natural continuation of the work of the judge, as a function of practical protection on the part of special organs. The commission for carrying out penal sentences should include expert criminal anthropologists, representing the judge, the defence, and the prosecution. These men, together with administrative officers, would stand, not for neglecting and forgetting the prisoner as soon as sentence is pronounced, as happens now, but for a humanitarian work which would be efficacious for the protection, now of the individual against the execution of a sentence which, in his case, has been proved to be excessive. It is apparent, then, that conditional liberation is bound up with the principle of the indeterminate sentence. [41]

The pessimistic note in his penological views concerned the incorrigible and born criminal type. His recommendations for indeterminate sentences, use of fines and probation and his proud connection with influencing Z. R. Brockway and the Elmira Reformatory, [42] were all related to offenders other than the born criminal. " It would be a mistake," he says, " to imagine that measures which have been shown to be effective with other criminals could be successfully applied to born criminals; for these are, for the most part, refractory to all treatment, even to the most affectionate care

---

[40] *Crime : Its Causes and Remedies*, p. 386.   [41] *Ibid*. pp. 386–387.
[42] *Ibid*. pp. 393–394. *Cf.* Zebulon R. Brockway, *Fifty Years of Prison Service*, 1912, reprinted Montclair, N.J., 1969, Patterson Smith, p. 215.

begun at the very cradle. . . ." [43] He also expressed fear that better education of the prisoner in prison would merely produce more educated recidivists, principally because of increased criminal associations in the institution. Based on this same kind of apprehension, he favoured the cellular prison, although he was aware of its psychological disadvantages.

He favoured retention of the death penalty as the only recourse left to a society seeking to protect itself against irreformable elements. The inadequate powers of natural selection should be supplemented by deliberate social selection (presumably excluding, however, positive eugenics) aimed at the elimination of extremely anti-social individuals. With this perspective, the death penalty becomes for him " estrema selezione." Not going so far as Garofalo, but disagreeing with Ferri,[44] who basically opposed the death penalty, and believed it ineffectual because of its little usage, Lombroso felt that " it should remain suspended, like the sword of Damocles, over the head of the more terrible criminals." For the born criminal, " organically fitted for evil," capital punishment was still unfortunately necessary.

After having admitted the utilitarian application of the death penalty for this criminal type, he seems sorry and suggests additionally a " doctrine of symbiosis " by which the criminal could be utilised to accomplish socially useful purposes. " But we shall attain this end completely only upon the basis of the new science of anthropology, which, by individualising its work, can give us powerful aid in discovering the special tendencies of criminals, in order to direct them and utilise the less anti-social of them." [45] This substitute for repressive measures would seek " to direct to great altruistic works that energy, that passion for good " which he believed exists particularly in the criminal by passion and in the political criminal, but even in some cases in the born criminal.

Along with Ferri and Garofalo he believed that the victim of a crime should be properly compensated for injury. This would not only be an ideal punishment, but would benefit the victim as well, he thought. He recognised the difficulties of administering such a

---

[43] *Ibid*. p. 432.
[44] Ferri, *Criminal Sociology*, pp. 530–532. Pinatel suggests that the position of Lombroso on this matter is situated somewhere between the totalitarian social defence of Garofalo and the humane social defence of Ferri. (Jean Pinatel, " La vie et l'oeuvre de César Lombroso," *Bulletin, Société Internationale de Criminologie*, 1959, 2e semestre, pp. 217–222.)
[45] *Crime : Its Causes and Remedies*, p. 448.

proposal, but like a recent suggestion presented to Parliament in England, Lombroso's idea was that " the victim should be legally entitled to receive a part of the proceeds from work done by the culprit during detention." [46]

Despite some pessimistic expressions, Lombroso was more concerned with preventive measures than punitive ones, and when he discusses any criminal type except that of the born criminal, he sees opportunities for prevention. Society has progressed to the point, he felt, where " it has already found means of treating the diseases it has produced, with its asylums for the criminal insane, its system of separate confinement in the penitentiaries, its industrial institutions, its savings banks and especially its societies for the protection of children, which prevent crime almost from the cradle." [47]

It remained for Ferri and other followers of the Positive School to expand and implement some of the basic suggestions introduced by Lombroso, who was less of a legal and penal reformer than were his colleagues and disciples.

Reaction and influence

Space precludes a detailed treatment of the reaction to or influence of Lombroso's work in criminology. His immediate and direct influence on Italian scholars such as Ferrero, Ferri, Garofalo and others is well known, and out of this personal contact arose the Positive, or Italian, School. Particularly after publication of the second edition of *L'Uomo delinquente*, and as a result of the Congresses of Criminal Anthropology, friends and critics of Lombroso became more clearly demarcated and vociferous. Tarde's attack in *Criminalité comparée* (1886) consisted in showing a lack of agreement on what stigmata to use to identify the criminal; and this demonstration of inconsistency among the anthropologists convinced many of his French colleagues. Lacassagne, Manouvrier, Joly and Topinard (successor of Broca and director of the *Archives d'Anthropologie*) wrote articles opposing Lombroso's ideas. At the Second

---

[46] In Gina Lombroso, *Criminal Man*, pp. 191–192. *Cf.* Ferri, *Criminal Sociology*, pp. 511–512; Raffaele Garofalo, *Criminology,* trans. R.W. Millar, 1914, reprinted Montclair, N.J., 1968, Patterson Smith, pp. 434–435. At the First Congress (1885), a resolution was passed which essentially followed the suggestions of Ferri and Garofalo. The Third International Juridical Congress at Florence (1891) recommended the institution of a Compensation Fund. Relative to contemporary England, see *Penal Practice in a Changing Society,* a Paper presented to Parliament by the Secretary of State for the Home Department, London, Feb. 1959, Her Majesty's Stationery Office.

[47] *Crime : Its Causes and Remedies*, p. 58.

Congress in Paris in 1889, says Gina Lombroso,[48] these men "vomitarono fuoco contro Lombroso." Defenders came to his side, including Ferri, Garofalo, Laschi, Van Hamel, Moleschott and many lesser-known followers. Anthropological societies concerned with criminal behaviour and based at least in part on Lombroso's theories were founded in Buenos Aires, Petrograd, Rio de Janeiro and elsewhere. Kurella became the leading defender of Lombroso in Germany with the publication of the former's *Naturgeschichte des Verbrechers* (1893), and in England Ellis disseminated many of Lombroso's ideas through the publication of *The Criminal* (1890). But independent investigations reported by Baer in *Der Verbrecher in anthropologischer Beziehung* (1893) and Goring in *The English Convict* (1913) were extremely damaging blows to concepts of the born criminal, and the voices of highly respected scholars, such as Hans Gross, von Oettingen, Aschaffenburg, van Kan and Bonger, were added to the opposition.

There were many students of criminology who followed directly or indirectly in the theoretical or methodological footsteps of Lombroso. Winkler and Aletrino were evidence of the interest in criminal anthropology in the Netherlands. But it was principally in Italy, as might be expected, where the influence of Lombroso was most deeply felt and continues to be a force. Although there was considerable opposition by Italian lawyers from the beginning, both legislation and research (as much through the reform efforts of Ferri as from the ideas of Lombroso) became explicit results of the Positive School. In the first quarter of the twentieth century Italian research in endocrinology, psychology and forensic psychiatry had greatly extended the horizons of Lombroso beyond the contributions he had made. The work of Morselli, Pende, Lugaro, Vidoni, Clerici, Ottolenghi and others added convincing data regarding the interrelationship between morphological and psychological characteristics.[49] Research since the 1920s has been led by Ottolenghi, Saporito, DeSanctis, Pende, Niceforo, Ceni, Grispigni and Di Tullio.[50] The chain of lombrosian continuity can be traced through

---

[48] See Gina Lombroso's descriptions of these battles in *Cesare Lombroso, storia della vita e delle opere*, p. 279 *et seq.*

[49] For specific details of these researches and a good bibliography for this period, see Sellin, " A New Phase of Criminal Anthropology in Italy," *op. cit.*

[50] For details of this later period in Italy, see Elio D. Monachesi, " Trends in Criminological Research in Italy," *American Sociological Review* (1936), 1 : 396–406; also, Howard Becker and Harry E. Barnes, *Social Thought From Lore to Science*, 2nd ed., Washington, D.C., 1952, Harren Press, pp. 1004–1007.

these scholars to the present status of research in Italy, best reflected in the competent work of Benigno di Tullio, who is the most outspoken heir of clinical criminology and forensic psychiatry. The results of his work have appeared in numerous publications and were early summarised in his book, *Manuale di Antropologia e Psicologia Criminale*, published in 1931. His latest edition of *Principi di Criminologia Clinica e Psichiatria Forense* (1960) makes abundantly clear the comprehensive clinical approach of the contemporary Italian School, which emphasises the individual, pragmatic, eclectic, treatment-oriented approach.

In his studies Di Tullio has support from schools of forensic medicine and from the present Italian correctional administration. The present Commissioner, Nicola Reale, provides governmental recognition of the Italian clinical approach, and through his support the Institute at Rebibbia (Rome) has become one of the important centres for clinical criminology, which Di Tullio designates as the new phase in the evolution of lombrosian doctrine and criminal anthropology. Together with his two capable assistants, Ferracuti and Fontanesi, Di Tullio has both continued a positivist lombrosian tradition and expanded earlier emphases on the psycho-physiological clinical examinations of criminals. These examinations are deemed essential for understanding the motivational dynamics of criminal behaviour and are to be used as an integral basis for treatment programmes.[51] Instead of the static approach of Lombroso, this " biotypological-constitutionalist " method, as Di Tullio calls it, seeks to study the dynamic processes of personality formation, whether that personality be normal, abnormal or sick. References are made in his writings to the psychologically underdeveloped; the constitutional psychopath is compared to the constitutional delinquent; and in some delinquents, traits similar to the epileptic are still noted.[52]

[51] For further details on the contemporary Italian School, see the following as examples: Benigno di Tullio, *Principi di criminologia clinica e psichiatria forense*, Roma, 1960, Istituto di Medicina Sociale; Di Tullio, *Antropologia criminale*, Roma, 1940, Pozzi; Di Tullio, *Manuel d'Anthropologie criminelle*, Paris, 1951, Payot; Di Tullio, " L'Endocrinologia e la morfologia costituzionale in antropologia criminale," *Zacchia* (July–Oct. 1923), pp. 1–30; G. Di Gennaro, F. Ferracuti, M. Fontanesi, " L'Esame della personalità del condannato nell'Istituto di Osservazione di Rebibbia," *Atti del Primo Convegno Internazionale di Criminologia Clinica*, Roma (April 1958), published in *Rassegna di Studi Penitenziari* (May–June 1958), pp. 371–393.
[52] Benigno di Tullio, " Cesare Lombroso," *Scientia Medica Italica* (1955), 4:133–135. See also Di Tullio, *Principi di criminologia clinica*, 1954, pp. 14, 17, 67, 73–74, 78, as examples.

To the list of those who have continued the post-lombrosian framework of reference in their research and writings should be added Vervaeck in Belgium, Saldaña in Madrid and Berardinelli in Rio de Janeiro. But Germany and Austria, probably more than other countries outside of Italy, have reflected the influence of this tradition. From the work of Kretschmer's psychiatric clinic and his famous *Körperbau und Charakter* (1921), scholars had a new and more firm basis for asserting the significance of the relationship between crime, character and constitution. The Bavarian investigations of the period prior to the Second World War included studies by Lenz, in charge of the crimino-biological station at Graz and who spoke of the criminal as a unified system of biological dispositions; Viernstein, director; and Lange, who is best known for his study of twins and concordant criminal behaviour. The crimino-biologists in Germany, says Cantor [53] in his review of research in that country during the 1930s, assumed that while no one is born predetermined to a life of crime, heredity plays the more important role in determining the manner in which one's social experience will be undergone and assimilated. The series of studies under the editorship of F. Exner at the University of Munich was largely devoted to psychological and statistical studies undertaken by lawyers and dealt with particular offences or particular classes of criminals, but publication of his *Kriminalbiologie* (1939), in which he refers to biologically " delinquent dispositions," places him in the camp of the post-lombrosian tradition.

Lombroso received little attention in the United States before the 1890s, largely because his major works remained untranslated into English. Never has any full edition of *L'Uomo delinquente* been translated into English even to this day. However, both the abridged, summary and sketchy version written by his daughter, Gina, which was available in 1911, and *Crime : Its Causes and Remedies*, published in 1912 under the auspices of the American Institute of Criminal Law and Criminology, increased the publicity given to his theories. Before this time, Fletcher, then president of the Anthropological Society of Washington, D.C., wrote on " The New School of Criminal Anthropology " in the *American Anthropologist* (July 1891), and after his recital of European works declared that nothing had yet been done in the United States. William

[53] Nathaniel Cantor, " Recent Tendencies in Criminological Research in Germany," *American Sociological Review* (1936), 1 : 407–418.

Noyes had uncritically adopted the lombrosian position in his 1888 article on " The Criminal Type," and Hamilton Wey (1890) and James Weir (1891) had summarised criminal anthropology.[54] August Drähms, chaplain of San Quentin prison at the time, asked Lombroso to write the introduction to his book, *The Criminal* (1900), in which Lombroso said: " I have not had the good fortune for some time to find an author who so thoroughly understands my ideas and is able to express them with so much clearness, as the author of this book." [55] Arthur MacDonald's *Criminology* had been dedicated to Lombroso as early as 1893, and while Lombroso's ideas were not unknown to American students even before this time, it was probably Drähms' book that most fully and fairly presented these ideas in America. Thereafter, a number of lesser-known persons, mostly physicians, wrote about degeneration, the criminal brain, the criminal cranium and other anatomical deviations.

About the time that an increase in endocrinological research was taking place in Italy, Schlapp and Smith produced their " consideration of the chemical causation of abnormal behaviour " in *The New Criminology* (1928). These authors sought to show that children born malformed through chemical imbalance due to disturbances of the ductless glands show gross defects and " are typical criminals of Lombroso. They exhibit the physical stigmata to which he attached so great an importance." [56] The major study of morphology and crime in the United States was *The American Criminal* by Hooton (1939), whose focus has been called " neo-lombrosian " and who became associated with the constitutional school in biology and psychology. Within a theoretical frame of reference which

[54] Robert Fletcher, "The New School of Criminal Anthropology," *American Anthropologist* (July 1891), 4:201–236; William Noyes, "The Criminal Type," *Journal of Social Science* (April 1888), 24:31–42; Hamilton D. Wey, "Criminal Anthropology," *Proceedings of the National Prison Association*, 1890, pp. 274–291; James Weir, Jr., "Criminal Anthropology," *Medical Record* (Jan. 1894), 45:42–45. All of these references and a description of the first influences of Lombroso in America may be found in Arthur Fink, *Causes of Crime: Biological Theories in the United States*, Philadelphia, 1938, University of Pennsylvania Press, especially pp. 99–133.

[55] Cesare Lombroso, in the Introduction to August Drähms, *The Criminal*, 1900, reprinted Montclair, N.J., 1971, Patterson Smith.

[56] Max Schlapp and E. H. Smith, *The New Criminology*, New York, 1928, Boni and Liveright, pp. 72–73. For good reviews of endocrinological literature relative to crime, see Olof Kinberg, *Basic Problems of Criminology*, Copenhagen, 1935, Levin and Munkgaard; Stephan Hurwitz, *Criminology*, Copenhagen, 1952, G. E. C. Gad. See also Louis Berman, "Crime and the Endocrine Glands," *American Journal of Psychiatry* (Sept. 1932), 12:226 *et seq.*; Edward Podolsky, "The Chemical Brew of Criminal Behavior," *Journal of Criminal Law, Criminology and Police Science* (March–April 1955), 45:675–678.

assumed that constitutional (hereditary) differences denoted superiority or inferiority of basic organisms, his empiric data, based upon a highly inadequate control group, led him to conclude that criminals were the result of environment operating upon inferior biological organisms. The methodological faults of this study were widely discussed and further dissuaded overtures to investigate criminal behaviour from the lombrosian or neo-lombrosian perspective.

Earlier attempts by Mohr and Gundlach [57] to apply Kretschmer's theory and typology to the native-born white male inmate population in Illinois had failed to supply convincing evidence of a relationship between offence, type of body-build and temperament, although the authors were themselves satisfied with their findings. A more recent report on crime and constitution is William Sheldon's study [58] of the relationship between delinquency and somatotypes. He claims that three temperamental types and three psychiatric types are closely related with three basic somatotypes and that in an analysis of delinquents compared with non-delinquents significant differences emerge with respect to these various components. His general approval of Hooton's work is explicit and his observations of delinquents convinced him that " where essential inadequacy is present the inadequacy is well reflected in the observable structure of the organism." The damaging critique by Sutherland [59] probably reflects the thinking of most American criminologists regarding Sheldon's study. Sutherland remarks: " His data, in fact, do not justify any of these conclusions, either that the delinquents are different from the non-delinquents in general, or that the difference if it exists indicates inferiority, or that the inferiority if it exists is inherited."

Sheldon's somatotypes have been used in Sheldon and Eleanor Glueck's *Unraveling Juvenile Delinquency* (1950).[60] *Physique and*

[57] George J. Mohr and Ralph H. Gundlach, " The Relation Between Physique and Performance," *Journal of Experimental Psychology* (1927), 10:117-157; by the same authors: " A Further Study of the Relation Between Physique and Performance in Criminals," *Journal of Abnormal Psychology* (1929-30), 24:91-103.
[58] William H. Sheldon, *Varieties of Delinquent Youth*, New York, 1949, Harper.
[59] Edwin H. Sutherland, " Critique of Sheldon's *Varieties of Delinquent Youth*," *American Sociological Review* (Feb. 1951), 16:10-14.
  A detailed review of the methods and research dealing with crime and constitution may be found in Richard M. Snodgrasse, " Crime and The Constitution Human. A Survey," *Journal of Criminal Law, Criminology and Police Science* (May-June 1951), 42:18-52.
[60] Sheldon and Eleanor Glueck, *Unraveling Juvenile Delinquency*, New York, 1950, The Commonwealth Fund; also, their *Physique and Delinquency*, New York, 1956, Harper.

Delinquency (1956) proceeds under the hypothesis that if bodily structure is relevant to delinquency, then a number of (mainly) personality traits and sociocultural factors should be found to vary among the physique types. In all, sixty-seven personality traits and forty-two sociocultural factors are analysed in relation to body structure. The study is in the positivist, eclectic and multidimensional tradition and certainly can be considered an historic heir of Lombroso. However, the Gluecks are cautious in their interpretations, are supported by sophisticated statistical manipulations, and are quite explicit in their wishing to be absolved from a unilateral approach when they remark that " the present work is not animated by any notion of respectful reawakening of the somnolent lombrosian theory that ' *the* criminal ' is a distinct hereditary species of ' atavistic ' or of degenerative nature. Nor is it begun with any preconception that bodily structure is the most weighty etiologic factor, or matrix of influence, in criminogenesis. It is merely found to be a promising focus of attention. . . ." [61] This statement is probably a valid reflection of whatever vestige of Lombroso's etiologic ideas of the criminal type may remain in American criminology.

A contemporary perspective

A review of the life, research and continuing influence of Lombroso cannot fail in making obvious the relationship he bears to contemporary criminology. The institutional and general sociological approach to an analysis of crime and the criminal predominates in American criminology, and with its emphasis on culture-conflict, subcultures, anomie and social deviance may appear far removed from the anthropometry of Lombroso. Nonetheless, even this approach is indebted to Lombroso for shifting focus from metaphysical, legal and juristic abstraction as a basis for penology to a scientific study of the criminal and the conditions under which he commits crime. Research anywhere that continues to examine differences between a delinquent and non-delinquent population, or that seeks to analyse differences within the criminal group can find its framework antedated by Lombroso. Contemporary endocrinological and biotypological studies are direct outgrowths of his most pervasive and consistent thinking. The clinical, psychological and

[61] Sheldon and Eleanor Glueck, *Physique and Delinquency*, p. 2.

psychiatric analyses of today that report data on personality traits (some of which are dependent upon organic structure and function) are similar to, but much more refined and sophisticated than many of the findings reported by Lombroso. The constitutional psychopath, or sociopath, is a psychiatric category only a little less nebulous and amorphous in conceptualisation than terms and ideas used by Lombroso to designate similar individuals and specific forms of criminal behaviour. The common multiple-factor analysis is related to his search for all kinds of positive facts. The wide diffusion of the deterministic (in lieu of the free-will) approach to an understanding of crime and the most appropriate means for treatment should be credited to Lombroso. In penology, his emphasis on the importance of understanding personality traits of the offender and on individualisation of treatment has long been academically accepted and is increasingly employed in the administration of diagnostic centres, probation, parole and classification systems. We now hold that the evolution of man has not been along the simple lines followed by Lombroso, and the theory that the criminal is physically atavistic has been abandoned. But his later concern with psychological differences among criminals has been the basis for much contemporary research.

By his supporters Lombroso has been referred to as a scientific Columbus who opened up a new field for exploration, and his insight into human nature has been compared to that of Shakespeare and Dostoevsky. Perhaps these encomia are exaggerations, but also from the man generally believed most responsible for refuting Lombroso we are told that " all thinking people today, legislators and judges, as well as the general public, the morality of the age, as well as the voice of science, attest the truth which Lombroso was the first to enunciate as the fundamental principle of criminology and penology: the principle that it is the criminal and not the crime we should study and consider; that it is the criminal and not the crime we ought to penalise." [62] Even Bonger remarked that " Lombroso's merits in the field of criminal law are exceptionally great. He has, indeed, given the impulse to a revolutionary movement the effects of which cannot, as yet, be estimated." [63] And van Kan says: " Cesare Lombroso has the glorious merit of having been the great instigator of ideas in criminology, he created systems

[62] Goring, *op. cit.* p. 12.
[63] Bonger, *op. cit.* p. 76.

and conceived of ingenious and bold hypotheses." [64]   In his treatise
on penitentiary science and social defence, Pinatel [65] in France gives
credit to the positivist doctrine that developed from Lombroso and
that has substituted for punishment, responsibility and equality the
notions of social defence, *témibilité* (the danger the individual
presents to society) and individualisation.

This review of Lombroso's work should dispel the contention of
some contemporary authors that Lombroso and his school " delayed
for fifty years the work which was in progress at the time of its
origin and in addition made no lasting contribution of its own." [66]
The fear of these critics that Lombroso diverted attention from
social to individual phenomena reveal their basic misunderstanding
of his work and its effect; for, as has been indicated, Lombroso
served to redirect emphasis from the crime to the criminal, not from
social to individual factors.   The reciprocal interrelation between
the individual and his society was a phenomenon he did not fail to
consider.   In any case, as Sellin has well said : " Whether Lombroso
was right or wrong is perhaps in the last analysis not so important
as the unquestionable fact that his ideas proved so challenging that
they gave an unprecedented impetus to the study of the offender.
Any scholar who succeeds in driving hundreds of fellow students
to search for the truth, and whose ideas after half a century possess
vitality, merits an honourable place in the history of thought." [67]
Living up to the etymology of his name, Lombroso illuminated the
scientific study of criminal behaviour with many provocative ideas
and deserves a place of honour in his own field.

[64] Van Kan, *op. cit.* p. 59. Even Benedikt, who had often criticised Lombroso's theories,
said at the Third Congress at Brussels (1892): " If Lombroso had created nothing more
than the phrase Uomo delinquente, which contains a great idea and a great programme,
and had discovered nothing else than Enrico Ferri, he still would have done enough for
Science to be immortal." (*Actes du Troisième Congrès International d'Anthropologie
Criminelle*, p. 276.)

[65] Jean Pinatel, *Traité élémentaire de science pénitentiare et de défense sociale*, Paris, 1950.
Pinatel agrees with Vervaeck (" La théorie lombrosienne et l'évolution de l'anthropologie criminelle," *Archives d'anthropologie*, 1910, p. 561 *et seq.*) that Lombroso was
" the first worker of the reform of our judicial and superannuated penitentiary system."
(See Pinatel, " La vie et l'oeuvre de César Lombroso," *op. cit.*)

[66] E. H. Sutherland and Donald Cressey, *Principles of Criminology*, 5th ed., Philadelphia,
1955, Lippincott, p. 55. See also, Lindesmith and Levin, *op. cit.*, who express similar
views.   In answer to the charge that Lombroso set back research in criminology fifty
years, Sellin has said : " The fact that he succeeded in getting many psychiatrists and
others with a natural science training to concentrate on the study of the offender could
hardly have caused sociologists or others interested in environmental theories to fold
their tents, nor is there the slightest reason to suppose that had Lombroso never existed,
the social science approaches to the problem of crime would have enjoyed any greater
prosperity." (" En historik aterblick," *op. cit.*)

[67] Sellin, " The Lombrosian Myth in Criminology " (Letter to the Editor). *The American
Journal of Sociology* (May 1937), 42 : 898–899.

Lombroso's statements at the opening and closing sessions of the Sixth International Congress at Turin in 1906 provide a fitting close to this review of his life and work: "As the oldest soldier of Criminal Anthropology I have the honour of opening this Sixth Congress, which will be the last one for me, but for all of you will be only a step towards greater exploits. . . . Your energy more than reassures me for the toils, spent in thirty years of this work. The idea that it represents, developed, strengthened and handed down to posterity by you will not die—*quasi cursores vitae lampada tradunt.*" [68]

MARVIN E. WOLFGANG.

SELECTED BIBLIOGRAPHY

By Lombroso

Most of the writings of Lombroso have not been translated from the original Italian, and the books listed below constitute only a selected group of his major writings in criminology that are generally available outside Italy. For a detailed bibliography of his writings in book, article or other form, see Gina Lombroso, *Cesare Lombroso, storia della vita e delle opere*, 2nd ed., Bologna, 1921, Zanichelli, pp. 447–476; also, the *Festschrift* in his honour, *L'Opera di Cesare Lombroso nella scienza e nelle sue applicazioni*, Torino, 1908, Bocca, pp. 385–414.

"Antropometria di 400 delinquenti veneti," *Rendiconti dell'Istituto Lombardo*, Vol. V, fasc. xii. (Nucleus of *L'Uomo delinquente*.) (1872.)

Affetti e passioni dei delinquenti. (Paper read at the Istituto Lombardo; the second nucleus of *L'Uomo delinquente*.) (1874.)

L'Uomo delinquente, 1st ed. Milano, 1876, Hoepli.

L'Uomo delinquente, 2nd ed. Torino, 1878, Bocca.

L'Homme criminel, Paris, 1887, Alcan.

Der Verbrecher, Hamburg, 1887, Richter.

L'Homme criminel, 2nd ed. Paris, 1888, Alcan.

Palimsesti del carcere, Torino, 1888, Bocca.

L'Uomo delinquente, 4th ed. Torino, 1889, Bocca.

Il delitto politico e le rivoluzioni (with Laschi), Torino, 1890, Bocca.

L'Anthropologie criminelle et ses récents progrès, Paris, 1891, Alcan.

Le più recenti scoperte ed applicazioni della Psichiatria ed Antropologia criminale, Torino, 1893, Bocca.

La donna delinquente, la prostituta e la donna normale (with G. Ferrero), Torino, 1893, Roux.

[68] *Comptes Rendus de VIe Congrès International d'Anthropologie Criminelle*, Turin, 1908, Bocca, pp. xxxi, xxxvi.

L'Homme criminel, 3rd ed. Paris, 1895, Alcan.
The Female Offender (with G. Ferrero), London, 1895, Unwin.
L'Uomo delinquente, 5th ed. Torino, 1896–97, Bocca.
Le crime, causes et remèdes, Paris, 1899, Schleicher et C.
Delitti vecchi e delitti nuovi, Torino, 1902, Bocca.
Crime. Causes et remèdes, 2nd ed. Paris, 1906, Alcan.
La femme criminelle (with G. Ferrero), 2nd ed. Paris, 1906, Alcan.
Genio e degenerazione, 2nd ed. (with many additions) Palermo, 1908, R. Sandron.
La donna delinquente e la prostituta (new edition, revised and with additions) Torino, 1911, Bocca.
Crime: Its Causes and Remedies, 1912; reprinted Montclair, N.J., 1968, Patterson Smith.

About Lombroso

There is an abundance of material about Lombroso in all major encyclopedias, in special sections of textbooks and in portions of many articles. Most of the items listed below were available to the author and concentrate on Lombroso or have especially provocative discussions about him.

ANTINORI, G. *I Precursori di Lombroso,* Torino, 1900.
BONGER, W. A. *An Introduction to Criminology,* London, 1936, Methuen & Co., Ltd.
DE QUIRÓS, C. BERNALDO. *Modern Theories of Criminality,* Boston, 1911, Little, Brown & Co.
DI TULLIO, BENIGNO. "Cesare Lombroso," *Scientia Medica Italica* (1955), 4:133–135.
—— "Cesare Lombroso e la politica criminale moderna," *La Scuola Positiva* (1959), Serie IV, Fasc. 4, pp. 495–508.
ELLIS, HAVELOCK. *The Criminal,* 4th ed. London, 1913, Walter Scott Co.
GORING, CHARLES. *The English Convict: A Statistical Study,* 1913; reprinted Montclair, N.J., 1972, Patterson Smith.
HOOTON, E. A. *The American Criminal, An Anthropological Study,* Vol. I, Cambridge, Mass., 1939, Harvard University Press.
KURELLA, HANS. *Cesare Lombroso, A Modern Man of Science,* New York, 1910, Rebman Co.
LACASSAGNE, A. "Cesare Lombroso," *Archives d'anthropologie criminelle,* 1909.
LINDESMITH, ALFRED and LEVIN, YALE. "The Lombrosian Myth in Criminology," *The American Journal of Sociology* (March 1937), 42:653–671.
LOMBROSO-FERRERO, GINA. *Criminal Man, According to the Classification of Cesare Lombroso,* 1911; reprinted Montclair, N.J., 1972, Patterson Smith.
LOMBROSO, GINA. *Cesare Lombroso, storia della vita e delle opere,* 2nd ed. Bologna, 1921, Zanichelli.
—— *L'Opera di Cesare Lombroso nella scienza e nelle sue applicazioni,* new ed. Torino, 1908, Bocca.

MANNHEIM, HERMANN. "Lombroso and His Place in Modern Criminology," *The Sociological Review* (1936), 28:31–49. Also in *Group Problems in Crime and Punishment*, Chapter 4, pp. 69–84, 2nd ed., Montclair, N.J., 1971, Patterson Smith.

PINATEL, JEAN. "La vie e l'oeuvre de César Lombroso," *Bulletin. Société Internationale de Criminologie* (1959), 2 semestre: 217–222.

SELLIN, THORSTEN. "A New Phase of Criminal Anthropology in Italy," *The Annals of the American Academy of Political and Social Science, Modern Crime* (May 1936), 125:233–242.

—— "En historik aterblick," Chapter I in Ivar Agge *et al.*, *Kriminologi*, Stockholm, 1955, Wehlström and Widstrand.

—— "The Lombrosian Myth in Criminology" (Letter to the Editor), *The American Journal of Sociology* (May 1937), 42:897–899. (Rebuttal to Lindesmith and Levin.)

VAN KAN, JOSEPH. *Les Causes economiques de la criminalité*, Paris, 1903, A. Maloine. (Especially pp. 55–77.)

VERVAECK, L. "La théorie lombrosienne et l'evolution de l'anthropologie criminelle," *Archives d'anthropologie criminelle*, 1910.

VOLD, GEORGE. *Theoretical Criminology*, New York, 1958, Oxford University Press.

NOTE ON THE CONTRIBUTOR

Dr. MARVIN E. WOLFGANG is Professor and former Chairman of the Department of Sociology at the University of Pennsylvania. He is a former President of the American Society of Criminology, President of the American Academy of Political and Social Science, and a consultant to the President's Commission on Law Enforcement and Administration of Justice. He was a member of the President's Commission on Obscenity and Pornography, of the Advisory Committee on Reform of the Federal Criminal Law, and of the Panel of Social Indicators; and Director of Research of the Commission on the Causes and Prevention of Violence, and Associate Secretary General of the International Society of Criminology. Dr. Wolfgang's publications include *Patterns in Criminal Homicide* (1958), *The Measurement of Delinquency* (with T. Sellin, 1964), *Crime and Race* (1964), *The Subculture of Violence* (with F. Ferracuti, 1967), *Violence in Sardinia* (with F. Ferracuti, 1970), and, as editor, *The Sociology of Crime* (1962, 2d edition 1970), *Studies in Homicide* (1967), *Crime and Culture* (1968), *Delinquency: Selected Studies* (1969), *The Sociology of Punishment and Correction* (1970), and *Crime and Justice* (1971).

14

GABRIEL TARDE
1843–1904

GABRIEL TARDE is an example of men who attain intellectual eminence without leading wholly the scholar's life. For fifteen years he was a provincial magistrate in the small village of Sarlat, his birthplace and home. In this apparently restricted sphere, he obtained a fund of human experience from which to develop his philosophical theories. Later he was called to Paris to direct the Bureau of Statistics in the Department of Justice, and this adventure provided him with a wealth of criminal statistics to buttress his ideas on criminology. He is distinguished as a philosopher, psychologist and sociologist as well as a criminologist of international repute. This paper is concerned with his lasting contributions to criminal and penal philosophy. His emphasis on the social origins of crime is a cornerstone of present American criminological theories. His devastating attack on the Lombrosian theory undermined the influence of that School in Europe. In the field of penology, Tarde furnished us with a theory of moral responsibility which is original and capable of practical demonstration. His logical applications of this theory have been realised in recent innovations of the criminal court system.

The body of Tarde's criminological theories is found in two of his books: *La Criminalité comparée* (1886) and *La Philosophie pénale* (1890). The former is a forceful expression of the view that social factors should be emphasised in studying the criminal instead of the physical and other characteristics of the offender. The latter book developed these views further and became available to the English-speaking public when it was translated by the American Institute of Criminal Law and Criminology in 1912. It thus became one of several important volumes in the Modern Criminal Science Series. In 1891 Tarde published *Etudes pénales et sociales*, another

* Reproduced from *The Journal of Criminal Law, Criminology and Police Science*, Vol. 45, No. 1, June 1954.

book dealing specifically with crime. This was a collection of previously published articles and included an analysis of criminal statistics, explanations of a number of sensational murders of the period and criticism of the current works on crime. During his lifetime he contributed numerous articles to the *Archives d'Anthropologie criminelle*, *Revue philosophique* and other journals. Also, he directed the publication of twelve volumes of criminal statistics when he was in the Department of Justice.

Causes of crime

Tarde examined the prevailing theories of crime causation and rejected the biological and physical ones as inadequate. After a thorough consideration of all the aspects, he arrived at his own theory, a happy marriage of psychology and sociology. Crime, he concluded, has predominantly social origins. To express it in Tarde's own words:

> The majority of murderers and notorious thieves began as children who have been abandoned, and the true seminary of crime must be sought for upon each public square or each crossroad of our towns, whether they be small or large, in those flocks of pillaging street urchins, who, like bands of sparrows, associate together, at first for marauding, and then for theft, because of a lack of education and food in their homes.[1]

Tarde conceded that biological and physical factors might play a part in creating a criminal, but by his analysis of crime in parts of Europe and by citations from other specialists, he showed that the influence of the social environment was most significant in moulding criminal behaviour. It is a short step from this to the prevailing mode of opinion today among American sociologists. Sutherland's theory of differential association,[2] for example, is reminiscent of Tarde.

The importance of the social environment in producing criminals was emphasised by Tarde. Yet he is far from being a sociological determinist. In a vivid passage, he showed the importance of individual choice in a criminal career:

> One could, without any great difficulty, write a treatise upon the art of becoming an assassin. Keep bad company; allow pride, vanity, envy and hatred to grow in you out of all proportions; close your heart to tender feelings, and open it only to keen sensations; suffer also—harden yourself

1 Gabriel Tarde, *Penal Philosophy*, translated by R. Howell (1912; reprinted Montclair, N.J., 1968, Patterson Smith), p. 252.
2 E. H. Sutherland, *Principles of Criminology* (Philadelphia, 1939, J. B. Lippincott), p. 5.

from childhood to blows, to intemperateness, to physical torments, grow hardened to evil, and insensible, and you will not be long in becoming devoid of pity; become irascible and vengeful, and you will be lucky if you do not kill anyone during the course of your life.[3]

Tarde recognised that both the element of individual choice and the factor of chance operate in a criminal career. It is difficult to ascertain which of these he considered the more important. While he insisted that choice operates in every career and that the moral responsibility for each person's acts rests upon that basis, he realised that the slums, the underworld and even the prisons themselves condition the criminal to a life of crime. Such American works as Frederick Thrasher, *The Gang* (1927); Clifford Shaw, *Brothers in Crime* (1938), *The Jack-Roller* (1930) and *The Natural History of a Delinquent Career* (1931); and Clifford Shaw and Henry McKay, *Juvenile Delinquency in Urban Areas* (1942), are proof that Tarde's criminal theories are sound.

Tarde's conception of the criminal as a professional type is of particular interest.[4] He saw murderers, pickpockets, swindlers and thieves as individuals who had gone through a long period of apprenticeship, just as doctors, lawyers, farmers or skilled workmen. It was that the accident of birth placed them in an atmosphere of crime. Without any natural predisposition on their part, their fate was often decided by the influence of their comrades. The idea of a professional criminal who is skilled in special techniques, has a special language known only to his associates and a code of ethics in his relations with other criminals was further developed by E. H. Sutherland in his book, *The Professional Thief* (1937).

It is a tribute to Tarde's originality and foresight that seventy years ago he expounded the ideas on crime causation that are the working hypotheses of American criminologists today. They are accumulating empirical studies to substantiate the pervading influence of the social environment, especially that of close friendships, and examining crime as a profession. Their methods are more exact; yet none have stated these ideas so vividly and succinctly.

[3] Tarde, *op. cit.* p. 256.
[4] This idea was elaborated in his book, *La Criminalité comparée* (1886), and in his paper, "La Criminalité professionnelle," given at the Congress of Criminal Anthropology at Geneva in 1896.

Laws of imitation

The laws of imitation which apply in crime as well as in all other aspects of social life are basic to Tarde's theories. In his studies of criminal behaviour, Tarde noted three types of repetitive patterns. This led him to formulate three laws of imitation.

The first and most obvious law is that men imitate one another in proportion as they are in close contact. In crowds or cities where contact is close and life is active and exciting, imitation is most frequent and changes often. Tarde defined this phenomenon as fashion. In stable groups, family and country, where contact is less close and activity is less, there is less imitation and it seldom changes. Tarde defined this phenomenon as custom. To a greater and less degree, the two forms of imitation, fashion and custom operate in every society and in certain irregular rhythms. Fashion spreads a certain action, which eventually becomes rooted as a custom; but custom is subsequently uprooted by a new fashion which in its turn becomes a custom.

The second law concerns the direction in which imitations are spread. Usually the superior is imitated by the inferior. From the annals of crimes, Tarde traced such crimes as vagabondage, drunkenness, death by poisoning and murder. These crimes originally were the prerogative only of royalty, but by Tarde's lifetime, the latter part of the nineteenth century, they occurred in all social levels. After the royalty disappeared, capital cities became the innovators of crimes. Indecent assault on children was first found only in the great cities, but later occurred in surrounding areas. Such fashions as cutting corpses into pieces began in Paris in 1876 and vitriol-throwing (a woman disfiguring her lover's face) first occurred in that city in 1875. Both of these fashions soon spread to other parts of France.

The last law of imitation Tarde called the law of insertion. When two mutually exclusive fashions come together, one can be substituted for the other. When this happens, there is a decline in the older method and an increase in the newer method. An example of this would be murder by knifing and murder by the gun. Tarde found that the former method had decreased while the latter had increased. He noted exceptions in special cases. If the new fashion increased a demand for the activity, there might be an increase in both. As example, Tarde cited work and stealing.

The purpose of both is to acquire money so that, if one works, one would not steal and if one steals, one would not work. This was not borne out in the case of industrial work for an increase in industrial development creates a need for more money; so thefts, in that instance, increase instead of diminish. The madness for luxury outstrips the salaries and wages of the people. The progress of industrialism gives rise to an increasing number of offences because of the mercantile sentiment, the worship of gold and its immediate enjoyment to the exclusion of everything else. Tarde is implying that the increasing material levels of living which accompany industrialism stimulate crimes, rather than reduce them.

Tarde's explanation of crime was simply the application of the general laws governing social relations, as he conceived them,[5] to the phenomena of crime. All science, in his view, rested upon the recognition of certain similarities in the world of phenomena or of repetitions of movement or being. Periodic movement is the form of repetition in the physical world, and heredity is that shown by life in the world. Correlative and equivalent to these is imitation in the world of social relations. Crime, like any other social phenomenon, starts as a fashion and becomes a custom. Its intensity varies directly in proportion to the contacts of persons. Its spread is in the direction of the superior to the inferior. Every imitation or imitative ray, in the language of Tarde, tends to spread and enlarge itself indefinitely, whence arise interferences between these rays of imitation, thus producing contradictions or oppositions. When two mutually exclusive fashions come together, one tends to be substituted for the other. When two fashions which are not mutually exclusive come together, the distinct rays of imitation combine or complement each other and so by adaptation organise themselves into a larger scheme.

Classification of criminals

Tarde applied his theories in a logical fashion to the classification of criminals, a subject in which he and the other Classical criminologists were interested. As he conceived of crime resulting from social environment and of the criminal as a professional type, he was dissatisfied with previous classifications. He suggested his own on a psychological basis, but he never developed this idea in concrete

---

[5] Tarde, *op. cit.* Editorial Preface by Edward Lindsey, p. xxii.

form. His analysis of rural and urban crime could, if carried one step further, serve as a basis for the classification of criminals. Rural and urban criminal statistics of the various departments of France were used for specified periods. He displayed remarkable acumen for his times in recognising the shortcomings of his figures. He acknowledged that convictions were an inadequate measure of the extent of crime and proposed "crimes known to have been committed" as a better index. After the necessary reservations for the inadequacies of the statistics, he found that in urban crime there had been "a slow substitution of greedy, crafty and voluptuous violence for the vindictive and brutal violence found in the country." [6] City crime was more often acts of burglary, fraud and swindling while the country crime was violent and brutal murder or assault. This distinction is similar to the statistical classification of crimes so widely accepted today: crimes against the person and crimes against property. It suggests to the writer that Tarde had the basis of a classification of criminals: rural and urban, which is social and psychological, and might possibly prove a valuable classification if some enterprising criminologist were willing to experiment along these lines.

Criticism of Lombroso

Tarde's attack on Lombroso and, in fact, on the entire Positivist School, is one of the most significant and convincing.[7] By means of numerous statistical studies, mostly compiled by criminal anthropologists themselves, Tarde showed in his *La Criminalité comparée* (1886) that there was no support for the theory of the born criminal. He cited particularly the study of 4,000 offenders by Marro. Marro had found that atavisms and physical anomalies such as size of frontal cavity of brain, receding forehead and oblique eyes, were as common among non-criminals as among criminals. A comparison of Marro's results with studies of other European criminal anthropologists (Bordier, Heger, Dallemagne, Ferri, Benedikt, Thompson, Virgilio and Lacassagne) led Tarde to conclude that there was no agreement on what stigmata to use to identify the criminal. By the time he had exhausted the list of physical anomalies and showed the inconsistency between anthropologists or the lack of difference

[6] *Ibid*. p. 359.
[7] *Ibid*. Editorial Preface by Edward Lindsey, p. xxi.

between criminals and non-criminals, Tarde had shattered the criminal-type theory.

Tarde gave his attention to Lombroso's elaboration of his theory of the born criminal. First Lombroso considered the born criminal as atavistic; a " throwback " who was really a savage. Later he conceived of the born criminal as a madman. Finally he considered him an epileptic. Tarde destroyed these ideas, one by one, with contradicting evidence. The criminal could not be a savage for anthropological evidence showed that some savages were law-abiding and moral. The slang of criminals was not at all like primitive language. Even tattooing was not found in some tribes so it could not be considered a primitive characteristic. The criminal could not be a madman for he is logical and the madman is not. The criminal could not be an epileptic for fewer than 5 per cent. of prisoners were reported to be epileptic. Tarde did agree with Lombroso that the prisoner's mind was like that of an epileptic for both indulged in exaggerated thoughts and actions. Tarde recognised, however, that exaggerated thoughts and actions are characteristic of the normal personality as well as the criminal. This manifestation could be marshalled in the direction of good as well as of evil.

Tarde's criticism of the Lombrosian criminal type undermined the popularity of Lombroso on the Continent, particularly in France. However, the reputation of the latter was undamaged in England and the United States until the famed Goring study,[8] which showed conclusively by an exhaustive statistical study of English criminals with non-criminals that there was no proof of a born criminal type. It is unfortunate that Tarde's works did not become available in English until 1912, approximately the same time that the Goring work appeared. Since Tarde's influence in the United States and England was hampered by the language barrier and the lack of communication between French and English-speaking criminologists, he has never received the credit due to him in this connection.

Theory of moral responsibility

The crux of penal philosophy, according to Tarde, is the problem of moral responsibility.[9] Again one finds the blend of

[8] Charles Goring, *The English Convict* (1913; reprinted Montclair, N.J., 1972).
[9] *Ibid.* Introduction to the English Version by Robert H. Gault, p. ix.

psychology and sociology so characteristic of Tarde. He considered two factors essential to determine the responsibility of the criminal. The first, individual identity, is the concept of the self, and memory is the most important aspect of the self in relation to responsibility. Each person has some memory of his moral training and social obligations. This makes each person responsible for his acts. But, if memory is impaired, a person is not responsible for his crime. A person during an epileptic fit, hypnotised, suffering from a loss of memory or from a severe mental illness would not be held responsible for his acts because his memory is distorted. The other factor, social similarity, means familiarity with the society in which one lives, and is essential for responsibility. Thus, an Eskimo unfamiliar with French life who commits a crime soon after his arrival in Paris would not be held responsible for it. Social similarity implies that the person has been brought up in the society, experienced common education, prevailing customs and been conditioned to have the interests and desires of that group. The society has recast that individual in its own image. It further implies that this society has unanimous judgments of blame or of approbation and that the group conforms. Tarde emphasised the fact that he considered social similarity the less important of the two factors in determination of moral responsibility. He thought of personal identity as a permanent and all-important determinant and of social similarity as an accessory which in the future would be less important as civilisation progressed and communications improved until finally, among superior civilised beings, it would end by not being demanded at all. In that sense his theory is mainly a psychological standard. He did not exclude other factors, biological and physical, which might influence individuals, but he contended that these are only partially important and did not prevent an offender from being held responsible for his crime.

Tarde's point of view is refreshing as it avoids the dilemma of the philosopher's concept of free will opposing the scientist's viewpoint of determinism. His factors of personal identity and social similarity are more logical and discernible than free will; but, as Robert H. Gault so aptly pointed out,[10] the determination of moral responsibility from these factors presents problems of limit that are not easy to solve. How successful these criteria would be in a

---

[10] *Ibid.* pp. ix–xviii.

criminal court is a hypothetical question at the present time, but
Tarde should be commended for an original and more concrete
theory which circumvents the usual divergent views of the
philosopher and the scientist.

Reforms in criminal procedure

Tarde carried his theory to a logical conclusion when he proposed
that the court's function should be confined merely to the decision
on guilt or innocence of the accused. He suggested that a committee of experts (doctors and psychologists) should be set up in
courts to determine the responsibility of the accused. Once that is
decided, the punishments should be resolved on a psychological
basis. Tarde maintained that a punishment for a specific crime
should not be the same for all offenders since such uniformity would
not represent an equivalent deprivation for each criminal. He
argued that it was unfair to give the same punishment to a country
thief as to a city one. The city thief would feel much more
deprived by the punishment than the country thief since he would
be deprived of many more satisfying activities. An attempt should
be made to balance deprivations. For example, rural criminals
should be given more physical punishments since they commit more
crimes of violence.

Tarde criticised other aspects of criminal procedure. The jury
he distrusted as he was convinced that its members lacked ability
and training to make intelligent and correct decisions. He deplored
the fact that judges acted as both civil and criminal magistrates and
suggested that the two forms be clearly distinguished so that judges
could serve in only one field. He saw the necessity for a special
school for criminal magistrates to insure better administration of
criminal law. Because he believed strongly in the efficiency of
punishment to deter crime, he recommended that the death penalty
be extended as a measure to reduce crime.

Tarde examined the prevailing prison systems and in his own
recommendations he was consistent with his ideas on crime causation. The cell system he deemed useful as it kept prisoners from
contaminating each other or exchanging their criminal techniques.
However, he thought it should be combined with a stream of
kindly disposed visitors whose good influence would be brought to
bear on the criminal. He greeted with favour the introduction of

" conditioned liberty," an intermediary step from the cell to absolute liberty, which was first used in France around 1830. This allowed to prisoners who had a record of good behaviour in prison an earlier release with limited freedom at first. This practice sounds like the beginnings of a modern parole system.

Throughout his work, he treated crime as a social phenomenon but at the same time an anti-social one. He likened it to cancer which participates in the life of an organ but brings its death. Crime, to Tarde, was an industry, but a negative one and every effort should be taken by society to combat it.

Evaluation

Tarde's recognition of the importance of social factors in the causation of crime and his conception of the professional criminal are his two most important contributions to criminological theory. His logical mind and his application of statistics prevented him from taking the dogmatic stand of a social determinist. Other parts of his theory are in disrepute today. His laws of imitation have been largely discredited because they represent an over-simplification of social causation. Modern theorists recognise imitation as a factor in crime as in all social life, but rank it a factor of less importance. Perhaps the reason for the present neglect of Tarde's laws of imitation lies in his serious omissions. Michael Davis who has made the most comprehensive and critical analysis of Tarde's theories to date listed the following research which Tarde had overlooked [11]:

1. The contributions of Baldwin and other genetic psychologists had much to offer Tarde. Their studies concerning the innate (biological) tendencies and physical conditions interplaying inextricably with stimuli from the social surroundings to produce adaptive reactions would have enabled Tarde to give a more satisfactory analysis of the mental processes making up imitation and might have given him the opportunity to approach sociology from the standpoint of the individual as well as from that of the group.

2. The work of Emile Durkheim who stressed the factor of " social constraint," demonstrated that society is in a real sense a

[11] Michael Davis, *Psychological Interpretations of Society* (New York, 1909, Columbia University Studies in History, Economics and Public Law, Vol. XXXIII, No. 2), pp. 132–137.

psychical unity. Traditions, ideals and standards which are commonly accepted by the group do mould the members of the group to conformity; yet Tarde failed to grasp this important point. The two men, contemporaries, were pet antagonists for years and possibly their differences in views and personalities made it impossible for Tarde to appreciate Durkheim's contribution.

3. Tarde did not pay sufficient attention to the work of the biological school of sociology. He did not, therefore, take advantage of the laws of heredity and the work of Quételet, Galton and Karl Pearson.

4. The working principle of selection in society is a topic to which Tarde paid little attention. Every environment not only influences those who are within it, but draws selectively a certain type of man or mind to be within it. If he had considered the work of Lapouge, Hansen or Weber, he might have pushed further his law of imitation from the " superior " to the " inferior " to a specifically applicable principle, illuminated by the concrete motor forces which are its social basis.

5. Tarde considered race a biological factor so he did not allow it to affect his theory. Yet he might have profited by considering the factors of racial and cultural groups, which are significant forces in society.

6. His neglect to analyse the influence of special human motives, particularly the economic, leaves large gaps in his work.

These six omissions explain the inadequacy and one-sidedness of his laws of imitation whether applied to crime or to any other aspect of society.

Tarde's penal philosophy, like that of Lombroso, Ferri and Garofalo, furthered the idea of the criminal as an individual. His penetrating analysis of moral responsibility and his suggested changes in court procedure and the treatment of criminals have much to offer today's penal theorists. Such inroads in court and prison methods as the juvenile courts, testimony of psychiatrists and other experts at trials, Youth Authority Act, the lessened use of the jury trial and the classification and differential treatment of prisoners are concrete evidence of the application of Tardeian philosophy. One may not agree with Tarde's views concerning the extension of the death penalty, or even his suspicion of the jury system, but his discussions of these topics are still stimulating and suggestive three-fourths of a century later and should not be ignored. His vivid language and his frequent resort to analogies make it a delight to read his works and a welcome change from the ponderous and abstruse tomes of many theorists. Artist by temperament, at least as much as scientist, he puzzles and perturbs those who approach his work with the intellect alone. It is well to remember that he was blessed with a literary touch and a Frenchman's sense for the piquant. And what is more significant, he was an independent thinker as well as an original one who left an indelible mark on criminology and penology.

MARGARET S. WILSON VINE.

BIBLIOGRAPHY

By Tarde

La Criminalité comparée (Paris, 1886, Alcan).
Etudes pénales et sociales (Paris, 1892).
La Philosophie pénale (2nd ed., Paris, 1891).
Penal Philosophy, translated by R. Howell (1912; reprinted Montclair, N.J., 1968, Patterson Smith).
" Le Type criminel," *Revue Philosophique* (Vol. 19, 1885).
" Le Crime et l'Epilepsie," *Revue Philosophique* (Vol. 28, 1889).
" La Misère et la Criminalité," *Revue Philosophique* (Vol. 29, 1890).
" Le Délit politique," *Revue Philosophique* (Vol. 30, 1890).
" Criminalité et Santé social," *Revue Philosophique* (Vol. 39, 1895).
" La Criminalité professionnelle," *Archives d'Anthropologie criminelle* (Vol. 11, 1896).
" La Criminalité et les Phénomènes économiques," *Archives d'Anthropologie criminelle* (Vol. 16, 1901).

About Tarde

BONGER, W. *Criminality and Economic Conditions,* translated by H. Horton (Boston, 1916, Little, Brown & Co.).
DAVIS, MICHAEL. *Psychological Interpretations of Society* (New York, 1909, Columbia University Studies in History, Economics and Public Law, Vol. XXXIII, No. 2).
GIDDINGS, F. Introduction to Tarde's life in *G. Tarde's Laws of Imitation,* translated by E. Parsons (New York, 1903, Henry Holt).
LACASSAGNE, A. " Gabriel Tarde (his life and works)," *Archives d'Anthropologie criminelle* (Vol. 19, 1904).

NOTE ON THE CONTRIBUTOR

Dr. MARGARET S. WILSON VINE received her doctorate from the University of Pennsylvania in 1952. There she began research on Gabriel Tarde in a criminology and penal philosophy seminar under Dr. Thorsten Sellin. She has taught at the University of Maine, the University of Pennsylvania, Mount Holyoke College, and Keuka College. Currently she is Lecturer in Sociology at Corning Community College.

15

HANS GROSS
1847–1915

Gross, the Examining Justice

Only about 100 miles south of Vienna, surrounded by the green hills of the Eastern Alps, you find Graz, the capital of Styria, a province in the south-east of today's Austria. There, on December 26, 1847, Hans Gross, the son of an Army Administration Officer, was born. On concluding his studies at the law faculty he took up court practice in 1869.

In the following year this tall, emotional young man, who was full of ideas, was graduated a doctor juris at his home-town university. The chief object of his further life was practical activity. Thus he became an Examining Justice, first in the industrial area of Upper Styria, the centre of the Austrian iron and steel output, then in a merely agricultural district near the Hungarian and Croatian border.

In those days well-trained criminal investigators were not available in the Austrian small towns and in the country. The police forces in both town and country were composed of ex-soldiers who had proved their moral reliability and physical vigour. Without the aid of any technical apparatus they knew very well how to keep up peace and order by merely applying mother-wit and common sense supported by the authority of the Imperial uniform.

The difficult task of crime detection was to the greatest extent in the hands of specially appointed judges (Examining Justices). These had to solve any criminal case to the best of their ability without those technical aids and appliances which nowadays appear to be indispensable; all they could use was the juridical knowledge obtained at the university and the advice of experienced policemen who had got to know human nature during their service and had also gained sufficient worldly wisdom.

* Reproduced from *The Journal of Criminal Law, Criminology and Police Science*, Vol. 47, No. 4, November–December 1956.

So far Hans Gross had only known the criminals by the few
types of juridical abstraction, but now in the small towns and
villages he found a life rich in individual varieties he had never
thought of. On one occasion he had to expose an impostor who
by pretending to be a respectable nobleman had fraudulently
obtained a loan and some jewellery from the daughter of a well-
to-do citizen; at another time he had to reveal the tricks of a gipsy
who acted as a fortune-teller. Using the secret signs left by her
accomplices she told a poor farmer's wife what she had to expect
from future life and tricked her into giving her the money she had
just received for selling a calf in return for her false prediction.
Some other day he might have even had to solve a murder case or—
what is much more difficult than that—to find out by whom or by
what a fire had been caused.

In view of the great number of these problems offered by the
practice Hans Gross was shocked to realise that during all the years
he spent at the university he had learned almost nothing about how
to establish the facts on which he had to base his legal judgment.
Even so it is much easier for the judge to qualify a certain criminal
conduct as larceny, murder, etc., than to establish the facts from
which the criteria for larceny, murder, etc., result and which lead
to the person guilty of the offence.

Being aware of the insufficient practical training the student
had received at the university Hans Gross, owing to his industrious
character, immediately began to work hard on filling this gap of
education. In doing so he was greatly assisted by his capability for
concrete reasoning and careful description. From the very beginning he was convinced that the purpose of this task was not only
to obtain the necessary knowledge for himself, but to make up a
deficiency concerning every law student once for all.

During many years of devoted spadework he checked each case
he had to investigate on its aptitude for supplying results of general
importance. With the same zeal he made each interrogation of a
witness or an accused person the subject of a delicate psychological
study. At first the attitude of the interrogated person towards his
environment and his psychic structure ought to be comprehended,
so that the most suitable treatment could be applied in order to obtain
the greatest possible amount of useful statements as a result of the
interrogation. Generalising the experience gained from the individual case it was furthermore necessary to find out what psychic

influence resulted for any interrogated person from the present significance of the part he took within the legal proceedings. In connection with this he referred to the fact well known to every practitioner that, *e.g.*, a policeman questioning an offender arrested by him shows a conduct which is entirely different from the one he adopts when being questioned himself as a witness in court.

During many fertile years of intensive practical activity as an Examining Justice and later as a Public Prosecutor at Graz Hans Gross collected an enormous amount of experience. He very eagerly studied a great number of treatises on physics, psychology, medicine and science in general. He occupied himself with microscopy and photography and took great interest in the development of the X-rays which at that time was in its earliest stage. By studying all these subjects of physical and technical science he tried to find out to what extent they could assist the investigation of crime. Thus Hans Gross founded the " Criminalistics " as a special police science.

His " Manual for the Examining Justice "

As a result of his thirteen-year activity along this line his *Manual for the Examining Justice* was published in 1883. It surpassed all at that time existing works by Pitaval (1735–43), Jagemann (1841), Avé Lallemant (1860) and Lombroso (1878) in respect of number and nature of problems dealt with and in practical usefulness. This was closely connected with the ideas Hans Gross had about the functions fulfilled by the administration of justice.

In his opinion criminalistic activity was pure research work. He regarded a criminal case as a scientific problem which was to be solved by a judge who apart from having attained the highest possible standard of accomplishments had the very best technical aids and appliances at his disposal, the adopted methods being those of the research without suppositions.

The required knowledge could only be obtained from subject literature in the various fields of science which in practice was almost out of the law student's reach. Sometimes a judge may have taken pains to avail himself of such literature, but even so he was hardly in the position to make use of it as the scientific wording was far beyond easy comprehension. The manual was supposed to help in this respect. The language used by Hans Gross was easily intelligible to anyone of average education.

Offering subject knowledge of particular kind he most elaborately found the right limits to protect the reader from dangerous smattering. With regard to all matters in which it was possible for the judge and police investigator to consult experts, he only made statements of general importance which in spite of their brevity gave full explanation about possibility and extent of the assistance rendered by the expert. With regard to problems of general investigation tactics or activities belonging to the immediate sphere of the investigator he worked out all the details. This fundamental idea commands the whole book.

His Manual begins with a minute explanation of personal and material conditions essential to any criminal investigation activity. Objectiveness, diligence, perseverance, knowledge of human nature and love for veracity are the main points of this explanation. After this the two factors taking the most important part in the procedure of securing the evidence are described in detail. In a chapter with a prevalently psychological trend the interrogation is dealt with as the art of utilising personal evidence. The following paragraphs relate to the inspection which is the base for any positive material evidence.

The foundation for a successful investigation activity thus being laid, the first half of the Special Part deals with the assistance to be expected from experts. Apart from forensic medicine it comprises the subjects microscopy, chemistry, physics, mineralogy, zoology, botany, anthropometry and finger-printing. How open-minded Hans Gross was can be concluded from the fact that more than sixty years ago he dedicates a special chapter to the co-operation with the Press and its use in crime detection.

The second half of the Special Part describes the individual abilities and accomplishments which the successful Examining Justice ought to possess. It ends with the phenomenology of crime. For Hans Gross it goes without saying that only he can be a successful investigator who is well informed about the criminals' habits, means of communication and methods of operation. He thinks it necessary for the judge to be in the position to recognise the methods used by the criminal for disguising his identity as well as the simulation and the secret means of communication. He does not only introduce the reader to the cant and the so-called

" Zinken " (graphic signs of information which were of great importance to the comparatively great number of illiterate persons of those days), but he also demands that investigators and judges should know the elements of ciphering and deciphering codes.

It is of historic interest that with regard to firearms he was still unable to mention a particular branch of experts whom the investigators could consult. Therefore in his opinion a judge's general education was to include the field of ballistics which should be as well known to him as drawing, photography, moulding and explaining foot- or tool-prints or detecting and securing blood traces.

The systematic clearness was at first hampered by the huge amount of presented material. Gradually Hans Gross worked out the term " Criminalistics," using it for the first time as a subheading in the third edition of his manual which he called the " System of Criminalistic." The term " Criminalistics " comprised two fields of science which are nowadays considered to be different from each other. It included phenomenology of crime on one hand, on the other police science. Within the latter he differentiated between Criminal Tactics and Criminalistic Technology.

How far Hans Gross had answered an extremely urgent deficiency by founding this science was proved by the fast spreading of his book. When he died in 1915 the book had been published in seven editions and had been translated into a number of foreign languages.

His theories of " Criminalistics "

While Hans Gross had originally presumed that the scientific treatment of crime was, itself, a rounded-off subject including criminal phenomenology, police science and criminal psychology, he began to realise as soon as the first edition of his work had been published that the psychological problems needed special attention. As the second great result of his scientific work aiming at the improvement of crime detection, a *Criminal Psychology* was published in 1897. It was supposed to become a separate field within the science of the facts of criminal law and should help to get to know the human being and his nature who in Hans Gross's opinion was the most important object of the criminal proceedings.

Even here his basis was not a certain theory. He tried to comprehend the human being's nature without prejudice. He therefore defined the criminal psychology from a merely teleological point of view as a summary of all subjects of psychology that are necessary for the criminal investigator's work. However much the treatise deals with the psychic nature of the criminal, *i.e.*, the psychic motives leading to crime, it is in the first line dedicated to the psychic facts which are quite generally essential to the criminal proceedings.

The author approaches the problem in question from a rather general point of view. First of all he tries to outline the human being with all his good and bad qualities and anticipating the conceptions of the modern science of expression he dedicates particular paragraphs to dress, physiognomy and expressional power of gestures, especially those of the hand. Then he examines the wide field of perception and the phenomena of will and feeling which take a decisive part in the development of the psychic powers. Reflecting his rich worldly experience the final chapter is a study on the types of reaction within the circle of interrogated persons as obtained by considering sex, age, occupation and habit. In between there are essay-like contemplations on lies, sleep, dream and intoxication which may help to make abnormal conduct comprehensible.

Hans Gross is of the opinion that the same general procedure must be applied to studies in Criminal Psychology as to Criminalistics in the strict sense. The criterion of any progress is careful observation and description of facts and not a daring interpretation of them. He founded many new methods of material evidence, but nevertheless he did not underestimate the great importance which would even in future have to be attached to the evidence given by witnesses. He did not intend to eliminate this prevailing kind of evidence of his time from modern proceedings, but he tried to display its limits and weaknesses clearly.

The Inquisition with its rules of evidence had maintained its position up to those days. The corroboration of a witness's statement by a second witness was thought to be the absolute guarantee for truth. Hans Gross tried to explain that even the honest witness often made untrue statements. Owing to Hans Gross and the studies which were on his initiative made along this line it is today known to any layman that the statements of witnesses must only be used with very great care. Nowadays witnesses are not blindly trusted.

Furthermore, the advance to the psychic background of any manifestation and its explanation by a neutral person should provide the basis for the maximum value of the personal evidence. Again and again he points out that the failure of a witness is very often not due to his inability but to unskilful questioning.

Beside an abundant psychology of questioning the book contains an equally careful psychologic treatment of the finding of sentences by judges.

The more Hans Gross was convinced by his many surveys of the various fields of science how helpful the sources were for the detection of crimes, the more he realised that it was impossible for the individual to dig out these unused treasures. The problem could not be solved by accumulating knowledge on the individual which would exceed his powers. A favourable change of fundamental importance could only be expected from a well-schemed teamwork of experts.

In the eyes of Hans Gross one of the most important conditions for creating such a co-operation was the existence of an organ for publication with the only purpose of cultivating the scientific studies of crime and the methods of its suppression. This organ was not at all supposed to serve only his favourite subject " Criminalistics " by which he understood at that time criminal phenomenology, police science and criminal psychology, but it should also make the criminal person as a phenomenon of society and an object of penitentiary treatment the main topic of discussion. It would be wrong to say that Hans Gross deserved the exclusive merit of having developed the science of real facts within the criminal proceedings. Applying scientific perceptions to the judgment of phenomena which had so far merely been considered from juridical aspects, was a feature of those days.

There were the revolutionary theories of Cesare Lombroso in Italy, removing the criminal from the exclusive juridical judgment of that time, and submitting him as a biological fact to a scientific examination. Within the German criminal jurisprudence Franz von Liszt founded a sociological school which demands that when inflicting a punishment more regard should be paid to the person committing an offence than to the offence itself. In his eyes the offender was a phenomenon formed by the environment.

Like Hans Gross he comes from Austria. He was born in Vienna in 1851, his father being Attorney-General. As a young lecturer he worked in Graz from 1876–78. Since that time the two pioneers of modern criminal law and justice continued co-operating successfully, each contributing decisively to the reorganisation of law and its administration according to his individual aptitude.

To whatever extent Hans Gross missed systematic clearness it was supplied by the great scholar of criminal law Franz von Liszt. For the first time he worked out a rounded-off system of the entire criminal jurisprudence. Criminalistics in the wide sense as founded by Hans Gross took a firm position as an exact science within Liszt's system.

A new journal

Hans Gross for his part did not restrict himself to criminalistics and criminal psychology, but he also supplied valuable building-stones for the edifice of criminal aetiology erected by Franz von Liszt which equally considers personal traits and environment. During the time of Adolf Lenz, his successor on the professor's chair in Graz, modern criminal biology resulted from its synthesis.

In the criminal law attention had been drawn away from mere juridical judgment to the human being, unrolling all the relevant problems. It was therefore obvious that also in the course of criminal proceedings greater importance should be attached to the acting person than to the mere juridical procedure. Like Franz von Liszt who had founded a suitable organ named *Zeitschrift für die gesamte Strafrechtswissenschaft* (*Journal for the Entire Criminal Jurisprudence*) in 1880, which he himself and his collaborators of the " Union internationale de droit pénal " used as their mouthpiece about two decades later, in September 1898, Hans Gross introduced his *Archiv für Kriminalanthropologie und Kriminalistik* (*Archives for Criminal anthropology and Criminalistics*).

In the introduction he stated that one of the most important tasks of this new journal was to report on observations with regard to both criminal anthropology and criminalistics, also to collect material, sort it out and check it if and how far it could be utilised for the criminal law. Referring to the disillusionment following Lombroso's theories which had first been accepted as revelation, he said that these two fields of science were too recent to draw conclusions from the collected material and to deduct incontestable results.

With regard to criminal psychology the most important task of this new journal was to find out the reasons why out of a number of witnesses, experts and judges each got a different notion of one and the same event. Above all he wished to display the importance of a preconceived opinion and the deception by memory and organ of sense. Last, not least, it was necessary to get to know and recognise the different kinds of deliberate and morbid lying.

In the field of criminalistics the possibilities of employing experts, such as physicians, analytical chemists, physicists, zoologists, botanists, mineralogists, microscopists, photographers, handwriting and ballistic experts or artisans, were to be pointed out. But also the lawyer should get a hearing. He was to inform the experts about problems occurring in practice and to report about possibilities of improved crime detection resulting from the interchange of experience with representatives of other branches of science.

By the time of his death in 1915 sixty-five volumes of the *Archives* had been published. At the present time the journal is being edited by Robert Heindl and amounts to 117 volumes. Since the death of Hans Gross it has simply been called *Archives for Criminology*.

All this scientific pioneer work of unique standard was achieved by Hans Gross while performing his duties as a judge and public prosecutor. He did not retire until he was fifty-one years old. After this he wholly devoted himself to his scientific research work.

Gross, the Professor

Although never having taught at universities before, he was in 1898 appointed a Professor in Ordinary for Criminal Law and Justice Administration at the University of Czernowitz which at that time was Austrian, but is today situated in the Soviet Union. Five years later he was called to the University of Prague where he worked in the same capacity for two years. In 1905 he returned to Graz to hold the chair in his home-town university. His scientific activity here was of such a successful nature that his name became well known far beyond the borders of his home country.

In those days his greatest wish was to elaborate the *Archives for Criminal Anthropology and Criminalistics* which had quickly spread beyond the frontiers of the German-speaking countries,

Owing to his teaching duties he paid increased attention to Criminal Law and Justice Administration.

His mind being occupied with dogmatic and criminalistic problems as well as with criminal policy the book on *Rarity Fraud* [1] which was published in 1901 must be called a peculiar result of this combination of thoughts. Here he had a chance to prove himself a great judge of arts. This book was also supposed to show what impulses the criminal policy was able to gain from a deep-seated knowledge of the facts which were to be ruled by the law.

His last fundamental treatise was dedicated to the medical expert. A volume of almost 1,000 pages was published in 1908 with the heading *Criminalistic Activity and Position of the Physician*. He informed the medical expert about the aid he could get from modern criminalistics and psychology when working out his diagnosis. Whilst the Manual was meant for the Examining Justice to draw the lawyer's attention to the expert's work, the purpose of this book was vice versa. The expert should learn what aid he could possibly expect from the lawyer and to what extent the lawyer counted on him.

The new Criminalistic Institute

Owing to the open-mindedness of the Austrian education authorities his lifelong work was somehow crowned when he succeeded in opening a Criminalistic Institute at the University of Graz in 1912. For the first time a university centre for teaching and research purposes had thus been founded at which all problems raised by the crime and the necessity for its prosecution were scientifically administered. The new Institute was a full success.

Primarily it served the cultivation of those auxiliary fields of science which are in direct connection with the Criminal Law. Propaedeutic lectures were held there for law students within their general course of studies at the law faculty. They dealt with individual and social causes of crime, *i.e.*, criminal biology in today's terminology; further subjects were psychology of criminal proceedings, criminal statistics and criminalistics as phenomenology of crime and police science. In addition, periodic courses were held with the purpose of promoting the practical training of all police and court personnel being employed in the prosecution of crime.

[1] *Der Raritätenbetrug.*

At the seat of the Institute an instructive collection of criminologically important objects was established. It comprised the criminals' secret means of communication, the signs of their superstition, the tools of their criminal activity, the traces of their presence and the signs of their occupation in prison. Thus the collected material was of great visual aid for criminological research work and instruction.

Attached to the Institute was a department of evidence which soon was regarded as a model by all institutes for investigation dealing with modern criminal technique. It soon became an important aid in all problems of tracing science especially with regard to comparison of writings, forgery and identification of arms and burglary tools. In this way a bridge was spanned from science to practice as a result of which both spheres of interest and activity took alternate advantage.

The plea made by Franz von Liszt and Hans Gross for adding the science of the facts of crime and punishment to the university law studies soon became a common part of the Austrian criminal jurisprudence. The law faculties of the Austrian universities, especially the University Institutes of Criminology at Graz and Vienna, deal with criminal phenomenology, criminal tactics, psychology of criminal proceedings, police science and with all those subjects which are summed up by the term " Criminology " in America.

The development started by Hans Gross was to some extent of basic importance to Austria as the Examining Justice was kept in office by our legislation in respect of felonies and, besides, in the large towns where special police forces were organised, lawyers were put in charge of all affairs of criminal investigation. In this way there are, *e.g.*, within the boundaries of the Vienna Police Headquarters about 150 lawyers, apart from about 1,000 C.I.D. men, employed in the prosecution and prevention of crime. They all owe their elementary preparation for criminalistic practice to the fundamental ideas of Hans Gross.

Conclusion

The particular gift of Hans Gross was to find out with astonishing reliability if and how far his practical and theoretical experience was of general use to the detection of crime and treatment of human

. beings. Any walk, any talk with a neighbour, no matter how senior or junior in rank, workman or fellow traveller, and any production of fine arts or literature was a useful impulse to him. In all his books there is no sign of boring theory, but a constant flow of immediate experience.

Hans Gross depended on self-instruction. He never tried to achieve a rounded-off system of his science, but was primarily busy collecting experience which should help him and his learned friends to master the difficulties resulting from insufficient training for criminalistic practice. During thirty years of his occupation as a judge, which he concluded as the chairman of a Senate at the Appellation Court in Graz, he introduced a full generation of young judges to his science of facts. To them he was less a teacher than a fatherly friend. His books are not written by a pedantic school-master, but are at every possible opportunity illustrated by interesting examples. Whoever reads them is in the happy position of gaining a generous insight into the treasures which a successful collector assembled in the course of his life.

When Hans Gross died on December 9, 1915, he left his science to us as a firmly established edifice. It resisted all the tempests of time, and today, forty years after his death, criminalistics is undividedly recognised in theory and practice. It is the hope of any wrongfully suspected person and it is feared by any offender conscious of guilt.

ROLAND GRASSBERGER.

BIBLIOGRAPHY

By Hans Gross

Handbuch für Untersuchungsrichter (Manual for the Examining Justice); 1st ed. 1893; 2nd ed. 1894; from 3rd ed. onwards: *System of Criminalistics*, 1899; 4th ed. 1904; 5th ed. 1908; 6th ed. 1914; 7th ed., issued by E. Höpler, 1922; 8th ed., by E. Seelig, 1943.
Lehrbuch für den Ausforschungsdienst der Gendarmerie (Textbook for the Investigation Branch of the Country Police), 1894.
Kriminalpsychologie (Criminal Psychology), 1st ed. 1898; 2nd ed. 1905.
Enzyclopädie der Kriminalistik (Encyclopedia of Criminalistics), 1901.
Die Erforschung des Sachverhaltes strafbarer Handlungen (The Investigation of the Facts of Criminal Actions), 1st ed. 1902; 3rd ed. 1909; 5th ed. 1919.

Der Raritätenbetrug (*The Rarity Fraud*), 1901.

Kriminalistische Tätigkeit und Stellung des Arztes (*Criminalistic Activity and Position of the Physician*), 1908.

Gesammelte Kriminalistische Aufsätze (*Collected Criminalistic Essays*), 1902–1908.

Archiv für Kriminalanthropologie und Kriminalistik (*Archives for Criminal Anthropology and Criminalistics*), since 1899. Now published under the name of *Archiv für Kriminologie* (*Archives for Criminology*).

About Hans Gross

GLEISPACH, WENZEL. "Hans Gross," *Österreichische Zeitschrift für Strafrecht*, 6th annual.

GRASSBERGER, ROLAND. "Hans Gross, Fondateur de la Criminalistique, son oeuvre, ses émules et ses continuateurs," *Revue Internationale de Criminologie et de Police Technique*, Vol. VII, p. 194 *et seq.*

LENZ, ADOLF. "Hans Gross," *Zeitschrift für die gesamte Strafrechtswissenschaft*, Vol. 37, p. 595 *et seq.*

SEELIG, ERNST. "Hans Gross, His Life and Work," *Zeitschrift des historischen Vereins für Steiermark*, 36th annual, p. 1.

STRAFELLA, GEORG and ZAFITA, HERMANN. "Hans Gross, Necrolog," *Archiv für Kriminalanthropologie und Kriminalistik*, Vol. 65, p. 1.

NOTE ON THE CONTRIBUTOR

Dr. ROLAND GRASSBERGER is Professor of Criminal Law and Criminology at the University of Vienna and Director of the Vienna University Institute of Criminology. He has been working as an expert in criminology, especially in the fields of handwriting, questioned documents and the investigation of fires. His most important publications are: *The Criminality of Arson, Sentencing Policy, Habitual and Professional Criminals in the United States, The Solution of Problems of Criminal Policy by Mechanical Statistics* and *Psychology of Criminal Proceedings* (all in German).

16

RAFFAELE GAROFALO
1852-1934

FOR good reason it is customary to identify Raffaele Garofalo as one of the three leading exponents of the Italian school of criminology, which came into being during the closing years of the nineteenth century. The relationship with Lombroso and Ferri is clear, but it ought not to obscure the distinctive quality of Garofalo's thought or the particular range of his major interests.[1] No doubt the emphasis of his work was in large measure the product of his distinguished professional career. Born a member of the Italian nobility at Naples in 1852, he served in his mature years as a lawyer, prosecutor and magistrate. In addition, he performed the duties of professor of criminal law and procedure in the university of his native city. But from whatever cause, there is exhibited in Garofalo's writings a consistent concern with practical reform of the criminal law and legal institutions associated with the administration of criminal justice. This, of course, is not to say that Garofalo's inquiries failed to encompass matters of theoretical scientific interest. But even as he deals with such topics, he displays a continuing effort to relate the fruits of such investigation to the legal context and to gain insights which may be useful in the practical business of legislation and administration. This note is struck in the first paragraph of his *Criminology*. Speaking of the then-recent efforts at scientific study of criminality, he observes: "But when we come to consider how this theory may be applied to legislation, serious difficulties are encountered."[2] Later,

---

* Reproduced from *The Journal of Criminal Law, Criminology and Police Science*, Vol. 45, No. 4, November–December 1954.

[1] *Cf.* De Quiros, *Modern Theories of Criminality* (De Salvio trans. 1911), 28: "With the anthropologist, Lombroso, the sociologist Ferri and the jurisconsult Garofalo, the school of criminal anthropology can be considered as fully established. Hence, one of its critics has called these three men *evangelists* and their works *gospels*. From that time on they are always mentioned in a kind of trinity, a little divided at times only by Garofalo's political and penal conservatism."

[2] Garofalo, *Criminology* (Millar trans. 1914, reprinted 1968), 3. The work will be cited hereinafter as *Crim*.

discussing Ferri's classification of criminal types, he concludes: " Being of no avail to legislation it is consequently without practical interest." [3] It is perhaps not too much to say that this detailed concern with the concrete problems of legal and institutional reform provides a chief source of interest in Garofalo's writings for most modern readers. [4]

Although Garofalo enjoyed a long and productive scholarly career, he is known principally in this country through his major work, *Criminology*. The first edition of the book appeared in 1885 when Garofalo was only thirty-three years of age. A second Italian edition was published six years later and a French version, prepared personally by Garofalo, received a sufficiently wide response to justify several subsequent editions. The excellent English translation, completed in 1914 by Professor Robert W. Millar of the Northwestern University School of Law, is based largely on the French edition of 1905. [5]

In approaching a study of his *Criminology* it is well that several general considerations be kept in mind. The work in its original version appeared some seventy years ago. Inevitably time has taken its toll. Many of the assumptions and the data upon which these assumptions are based have been placed in serious doubt by subsequent investigations. More fundamentally, *Criminology* is in considerable degree a product of certain important intellectual currents which profoundly affected social thought during the last half of the nineteenth century and which have lost much of their power to impress the modern mind and to stir the modern imagination. The pervasive influence of social Darwinism and the speculations of Herbert Spencer are, for example, clearly discernible at almost every

---

[3] *Ibid.* at 134.

[4] No doubt this element in Garofalo's work explains in part the highly favourable response to the English translation of *Criminology* in American legal periodicals. See 48 Am.L.Rev. 945 (1914); 14 Col.L.Rev. 545 (1914); 28 Harv.L.R. 221 (1914); 10 Ill.L.Rev. 455 (1916); 63 U.of Pa.L.Rev. 148 (1914); 23 Yale L.J. 554 (1914). The following comment appeared in the above-cited discussion in the Harv.L.R. at 222: " Its moderate tone and practical nature make a good preparation for the audacious theorising of Lombroso and the brilliant ingenuity of Tarde."

[5] In the translator's preface to the English version, Professor Millar states at p. xiii: " The translator, however, has kept the second Italian edition constantly before him, and has found it of much service. Indeed, the interests of the English version have at times seemed to require that the Italian edition be laid under direct contribution. It is thus responsible for verbal deviations, here and there, from the French text, for some amplification of statements of fact in relation to criminal cases referred to by the author (containing, as a rule, a fuller account of such cases), and for slight additions to the footnotes. So, also, it has considerably influenced the matter of quotations from Italian writers."

stage of Garofalo's argument. For modern tastes there is perhaps a too-easy assumption of the inevitability of moral progress and the beneficence of political power.[6]

But this is far from denying the continuing interest of the work and its considerable relevance to contemporary issues. For his *Criminology* contributes a full measure of significant insights which are often largely independent of the theoretical superstructure on which Garofalo built. Moreover, the essential honesty of his methods and eagerness to discipline his conclusions by a constant reference to fact does much to bridge the years. There is pleasure, too, in following his lively and often closely reasoned argument. It is perilous to attempt evaluation of a writer's literary style in translation, but the bite of his language emerges clearly enough. Thus, commenting on certain of Lombroso's work, he states: " In his later writing the same writer contended that epilepsy is always to be found in the born criminal. This theory I shall not stop to discuss since the fact is far from being established. Moreover, it is flatly contradictory of the theory of atavism, despite Lombroso's efforts to reconcile the two theories. It seems hardly possible to conceive our first parents as unhappy epileptics." [7]

His concept of " Natural Crime "

The starting-point of any criminological system is the delimitation and definition of its subject-matter. Even with the passing of the years, these basic and primary issues remain in agitation and controversy. Garofalo rightly saw, with a clarity not matched by many who came before and after him, that the prior questions to be resolved centre about the proper formulation of the concept of crime—the " criminal " presupposes " crime." [8] Thus, at the outset he observes that " . . . although the naturalists speak of the *criminal*,

---

[6] Another difficulty might well be mentioned. Many of Garofalo's illustrations and much of his data relate to patterns of criminality then prevailing in southern Italy, Sicily and Corsica. These patterns, while perhaps not entirely unique, are sufficiently atypical to increase the difficulties of critical evaluation.

[7] *Crim*. 105–106.

[8] *Cf.* Ferri, *Criminal Sociology* (Kelly and Lisle trans. 1917), 77–78: " Garofalo's definition was, however, an original and happy attempt, although for my part, as Fioretti had already remarked and as I have said elsewhere, I do not feel the antecedent necessity for such a definition. In my opinion, a definition with which metaphysicians and classical jurists ever love to begin, can on the contrary only be the ultimate synthesis. It should, therefore, come at the end and not at the beginning of the researches of criminal sociology. And this is not only because the general reasons of the positive method require it; but also because the difficulty raised by opponents and combated by Garofalo is not serious."

they have omitted to tell us what they understand by the word *crime.*" [9]

Perhaps partly in reaction to the excesses of the Austinian school, Garofalo sharply rejected as inadequate for scientific purposes the notion that crime may properly be defined as that conduct for which the law has provided penalties and has denominated criminal.[10] This " juridical " conception, it is urged, fails in that it both includes and excludes behaviour properly encompassed in a " sociologic notion of crime." For Garofalo only the latter is of concern to the scientific investigator; and in giving content to this sociologic notion he formulates one of his most important concepts, the idea of " natural crime." " Natural " he defines as that " . . . which is not conventional, . . . which exists in human society inde-dependently of the circumstances and exigencies of a given epoch or the particular views of the law-maker." [11] In short, " natural crime " consists of that conduct which offends the basic moral sentiments of pity (revulsion against the voluntary infliction of suffering on others) [12] and probity (respect for property rights of others).[13] The basic moral sensibilities appear in more or less advanced form in all civilised societies and are, indeed, essential to the coexistence of individuals in society. Hence, the true criminal against whom society must make defence is he who has revealed the absence or deficiency of either or both these essential moral capacities.

In further refining the concept, Garofalo makes clear that he is speaking only of the sentiments of pity and probity as manifested by the average moral sense of the community, which may fall con-siderably below the level of moral perception attained by the exceptional and superior members of the group. Moreover, the truly criminal act must be harmful to society.[14] At first blush, Garofalo's idea of natural crime may appear as a latter-day revival

---

[9] *Crim*. at 3.
[10] See especially Chap. II, " The Legal Notion of Crime," *ibid*. at 54 *et seq*.
[11] *Ibid*. at 4.
[12] *Ibid*. at 23 *et seq*.   [13] *Ibid*. at 31 *et seq*.
[14] Garofalo summarises his position in the following manner: " From what has been said . . . , we may conclude that the element of immorality requisite before a harmful act can be regarded as criminal by public opinion, is the injury to so much of the moral sense as is represented by one or the other of the elementary altruistic sentiments of *pity* and *probity*. Moreover, the injury must wound these sentiments not in their superior and finer degrees, but in the average measure in which they are possessed by a community—a measure which is indispensable for the adaptation of the individual to society. Given such a violation of either of these sentiments, and we have what may properly be called *natural crime*." *Ibid*. at 33-34.

of the *jus gentium*. And, indeed, he believed that for the western European countries, which had arrived at near the same level of cultural development, a true " law of nations " might be formulated in the penal area, as evidenced by his draft of suggested principles for an international penal code.[15] Nevertheless, as he makes clear, the concept of natural crime does not consist of a catalogue of acts which are universally or widely conceived to be criminal. History, chance and the varying levels of social development have produced great differences in the kinds of overt behaviour characterised as crime at various times and places. The uniformity lies rather in the basic altruistic sentiments of mankind; and true crime is that conduct which, upon evaluation by the average moral sense of the particular society under consideration, is deemed offensive to those sentiments.[16]

One further point of clarification needs to be stated. Garofalo does not intend to limit offences recognised by any government to those included in the category of natural crime. He assumes that a great variety of other offences will be defined and punished. Indeed, he makes the rather extraordinary assertion that " Beyond question, every disobedience to law should be attended with a penal sanction. . . ." [17] In this connection, however, he advances the interesting suggestion that in the statutes such " police offences " might better be included in a code separate from that dealing with natural criminality.[18] But for Garofalo, the chief function of the natural crime concept is to delimit the area of conduct of major, perhaps exclusive, concern to the scientific criminologist.[19]

Garofalo's concept of natural crime has, as might be expected, produced its critics and its qualified disciples.[20] It is based fundamentally on the idea that, for scientific purposes, the concept of crime cannot be accepted as a legal category since the factors which produce the legal definitions of crime are contingent and capricious and display no consistent, unifying principle.[21] The motivation is

[15] See Part IV: " Outline of Principles Suggested as a Basis for an International Penal Code." *Ibid.* at 405 *et seq.*
[16] *Ibid.* at 6–10.
[17] *Ibid.* at 34.
[18] *Ibid.* at 59.
[19] This is perhaps stated most clearly in *ibid.* at 47.
[20] See, *e.g.*, De Quiros, *op. cit. supra*, note 1 at 28; Ferri, *op. cit. supra*, note 8 at 80; Tarde, *Penal Philosophy* (Howell trans. 1912, reprinted 1968), 69 *et seq.* And see Hall, *General Principles of Criminal Law* (1947), 547 *et seq.;* Tappan, "Who is the Criminal?" 12 Am.Soc.Rev. 96 (1947).
[21] See, *e.g.*, *Crim.* at 4. And note the comment of Tarde, *op. cit. supra*, note 20 at 72: " The most striking thing to be here observed is the sight of an evolutionist making

clear; and yet, it may be doubted that so complete an elimination of the legal content of the concept has well served the development of criminological theory.[22] Certainly, the efforts to obtain agreement on a definition of crime in purely naturalistic terms have not proven conspicuously successful, as the controversies which continue to agitate theory demonstrate.[23] The condemnation of conduct through the political agencies is a relevant social fact of the greatest importance. Any theoretical system which ignores or unduly minimises considerations of such relevance and importance is likely to produce results which are partial and unsatisfactory. Moreover, this tendency may produce positive dangers in its practical applications. For a consideration of measures which impose stringent disabilities on individuals cannot safely be isolated from the legal and political values. Even within the assumptions of his concept of natural crime, Garofalo cannot escape legitimate criticism. Thus, it is probably true that an analysis which attaches the idea of criminality only to violations of the moral " sentiments " of pity and probity is incomplete [24] and insufficiently sophisticated. One doubts, for example, whether the particular horror often associated with certain kinds of sexual offences can be completely or adequately explained as a manifestation of pity for the victim.[25] Nor do these categories comfortably encompass serious political crime, particularly in a period of intense political conformity when conceptions of morality are identified in significant measure with patriotic sentiments.[26]

Nevertheless, Garofalo's concern with actual problems of legislation and administration, already noted, tends to counterbalance many of the more dubious tendencies of his theory. Furthermore,

this desperate effort to attach himself to some fixed point in this unfathomable flood of phenomena and cast anchor exactly in what is the most fluid and evasive thing in the world, that is to say, feeling.''
[22] See Llewellyn, " Law and the Social Sciences—Especially Sociology," 62 Harv.L.R. 1286, 1287 (1949).
[23] See Tappan, *op. cit. supra*, note 20.
[24] Ferri, *op. cit. supra*, note 8 at 80.
[25] *Cf.* " In other words, a failure to punish a criminal is a kind of threat to the repressions which each person places upon his own *id*." Griffith, *An Introduction to Applied Psychology* (1934), 265, quoted in Harno, " Rationale of a Criminal Code," 85 U.of Pa.L.Rev. 549 (1937). An interesting account of public reaction in early nineteenth-century England to prisoners condemned to the pillory for the crime of homosexuality may be found in Armitage, *History of the Bow Street Runners* (1933), 175–180.
[26] Garofalo deals at some length with political crimes and notes that " . . . the act which is normally a political crime may become a natural crime when a society suddenly returns to a condition in which the collective existence is threatened." Writing in a happier time he optimistically observes: " But at the present day the state of war is a crisis of short duration. As pacific activity succeeds to predatory activity, the morality of the state of peace succeeds to that of war, . . ." *Crim.* at 39.

in emphasising the relevance of " moral sentiment " to the problem of defining criminal behaviour, the concept of " natural crime " has a continuing relevance, even though probably not precisely that which Garofalo intended. Certainly, the modern legislator, with Garofalo, can gain little solace or assistance from the shibboleth that crime is whatever the legislature says it is. For the legislator, particularly at a time when governmental power invades more and more aspects of social life, there are few problems of policy more pressing than identifying and reconciling the social interests to be protected by political power, determining which of these interests can sensibly be defended by criminal sanctions, and designing such sanctions in the form most likely to attain the desired ends.[27] No perceptive legislator believes that he is completely at large in this area. There are certain regularities of social and individual behaviour which can be ignored only at peril. Garofalo's identification of serious criminality with immorality suggests one of these limiting factors.[28] His distinction between the " natural " crimes and the " police offences " points to one of the most serious problems confronting the expanding welfare state,[29] however imperfectly he may have understood the complexities of policy in the latter category of offences.[30] Finally, his insistence that there are problems here which demand systematic investigation of the underlying facts of social and individual behaviour produces an emphasis of a value which has not diminished with the passing of the years.

Characteristics of the criminal

In Garofalo's theoretical system, the concept of natural crime serves the primary end of identifying the true criminal against

[27] See Michael and Adler, *Crime, Law and Social Science* (1933, reprinted 1971), 23–26, 352–361.
[28] Garofalo's fellow countryman, Beccaria, had written perceptively on these matters a century and a quarter earlier. See especially Chap. XXXIII of the latter's *Crimes and Punishments* (1764; Eng. printing, 1872), 126–129, the opening sentences of which observe: " Smuggling is a real offence against the sovereign and the nation; but the punishment should not brand the offender with infamy, because this crime is not infamous in the public opinion. By inflicting infamous punishments, for crimes that are not reputed so, we destroy the idea where it may be useful. If the same punishment be decreed for killing a pheasant as for killing a man, or for forgery, all difference between those crimes will shortly vanish. It is thus that moral sentiments are destroyed in the heart of man; . . ."
[29] Clinard, *The Black Market* (1952, reprinted 1969); Hall, *op. cit.* note 20 at 279; Jackson, "Absolute Prohibition in Statutory Offences." 6 C.L.J. 83 (1936): Lee. "The Enforcement Provisions of the Food, Drug, and Cosmetic Act," 6 L.& Cont.Prob. 70 (1939); Perkins, " The Civil Offence," 100 U.of Pa.L.Rev. 832 (1952); Sayre, " Public Welfare Offences," 33 Col.L.Rev. 55 (1933).
[30] See note 17, *supra*.

whom measures of social defence must be taken. Natural crime is behaviour which violates certain basic moral sentiments. The true criminal is he whose altruistic sensibilities are lacking or are in a deficient state of development. The concepts of crime and the criminal are thus integrally related. Garofalo, to be sure, makes clear his conviction that " our knowledge of the criminal is not limited to his acts." [31] But it is perhaps this joining of the ideas of crime and criminal which leads to the frequent emphasis on the act as a primary index of criminality. In this respect Garofalo's assumptions often tend to approach those of classical criminology, however much they may diverge in other particulars.[32]

It is not surprising that in his efforts to delineate the characteristics of the true criminal, Garofalo should turn first to the views of the criminal anthropologists, particularly those of Lombroso. It is clear that Garofalo approached with great interest and considerable sympathy the then-current efforts to demonstrate the association of criminality with certain anatomical and physiological characteristics.[33] He finds, for example, that the undue size of the mandibles is " an unmistakable sign of brutality or violence " [34] and that it is " generally admitted that in criminals, the occipital region exhibits a much greater development than the frontal region." [35] Nevertheless, on the whole, his treatment of these matters reveals commendable caution and a healthy detachment. His ultimate conclusion was that the theories describing the criminal as a distinct anthropological type had not yet been proved. " But what criminal anthropology really lacks," he asserts, ". . . is convincing proof that a given character of the skull or skeleton is found more often among criminals than among persons presumably honest." [36] After reporting the frequency of striking degenerative or regressive characteristics in murderers under his observation, he

[31] *Crim.* at 66.

[32] See, *e.g.*, Beccaria, *op. cit. supra*, note 28. This parallelism is most clear in Garofalo's discussion of the murderer and violent offender, less clear in his treatment of the offender against property rights. Thus, as to the latter, he writes: " ' What! ' someone may exclaim, ' Would you make no distinction in punishment between the man who has stolen twenty francs and the man who has stolen but twenty centimes? '

" My answer is that I do not know, for the question is one which cannot be decided abstractly. The thing important here to determine is—which one of these two thieves has the greater criminal aptitude, and is thus the greater danger to society? It may well be the former, but it may quite as well be the latter." *Crim.* at 299.

[33] A survey of modern work in this area is presented in Snodgrasse, " Crime and the Constitution Human: A Survey," 42 J.Crim.L.& Criminology 18 (1951).

[34] *Crim.* at 71.

[35] *Ibid.* at 67.

[36] *Ibid.* at 74.

adds: " Still, these characteristics are not always the same: sometimes it is one which is present, sometimes another. The murderer
type cannot be described anthropologically." [37] He was aware, also,
of the difficulties inherent in validating hypotheses in this area, for
he notes the problem of accurately identifying the criminal and
non-criminal " pair " for the purposes of trustworthy comparison.[38]

Having found the emphasis of Lombroso's theories inadequate
for his purposes, Garofalo advances his second major concept, the
idea of psychic or moral " anomaly." The true criminal lacks a
proper development of the altruistic sensibilities. This lack or
deficiency is not simply the product of circumstance or environmental conditioning but has an organic basis. For Garofalo
" There is no such thing as the casual offender—if by the use of
this term we grant the possibility of a morally well-organised man
committing a crime solely by the force of external circumstances." [39]
Moreover, the moral anomaly is to be carefully distinguished from
insanity or mental disease. The former is not a pathological condition but rather a " psychic variation " appearing much more
frequently among members of " certain inferior races " than in
modern civilised societies.[40] That the moral anomaly is hereditarily
transmissible he finds " established by unimpeachable evidence." [41]
But the precise physical basis of the moral anomaly he is unable to
describe.[42] At times he refers to it as the product of " some
mysterious atavism." [43] At others, as the result of moral degeneracy
of more recent origin.[44] Ultimately, he says, " The only safe conclusion which we are justified in forming is that criminals have

[37] *Ibid*. at 77.
[38] *Ibid*. at 75.
[39] *Ibid*. at 95–96. And see: " Hardly anything could be more inaccurate, in my opinion,
than the adage: ' Occasion makes the thief.' To be true, the phrase should be:
' Occasion enables the thief to steal.' " *Ibid*. at 226.
[40] *Ibid*. at 99–105.
[41] *Ibid*. at 92. For the modern reader, the evidence for the hereditary transmissibility of
criminal propensities adduced by Garofalo often seems particularly inconclusive and the
conclusions derived therefrom at times naïve and unsophisticated. Certainly, these
conclusions often appear to ignore alternative explanations which in the absence of conclusive evidence are at least equally persuasive. Thus, after noting the allegedly higher
frequency of criminality among children of elderly parents, he seems to attribute this
phenomenon exclusively to the hereditary transmission of psychic traits attributable to
old age. *Ibid*. at 93.
[42] " We shall therefore leave the anatomic aspect of the subject and direct our attention to
the criminal's psychic anomaly, without admitting or denying that this latter may have
a purely physical source." And in a footnote he quotes with approval a statement
attributed to Benedikt: " We are very far from possessing an anatomy of molecules."
Ibid. at 79.
[43] *Ibid*. at 99–102, 105–111.
[44] *Ibid*.

regressive characteristics—characteristics which indicate a degree of
advancement lower than that of their neighbours." [45]

It is apparent that these ideas tend to relegate the social and
environmental factors of criminality to positions of secondary importance. Clearly, too, such assumptions profoundly affected
Garofalo's conclusions as to practical measures of crime prevention
and repression. He regarded education as chiefly determinative of
the kinds of crime committed rather than as an agency for elimination of crime.[46] He was sceptical of economic distress as a cause of
crime though, again, he did not deny that economic conditions may
affect the form in which crime is manifested.[47] To sound family
environment and religious instruction, especially when directed to
the child of tender years, he attributed more significance as preventive factors.[48] But even the latter elements were hardly conceived
as of first importance. "Without doubt," Garofalo writes, "external causes such as tradition, prejudices, bad examples, climate,
alcoholic liquors, and the like are not without important influence.
But in our opinion, there is always present in the instincts of the
true criminal, a specific element which is congenital or inherited,
or else acquired in early infancy and become inseparable from his
psychic organism." [49] Nevertheless, these "external factors," even
if of secondary importance, must be taken into account. He did not
doubt that the manifestation of even the innate criminal propensities can often be repressed by "a favourable concurrence" of
external circumstances.[50] The devising of appropriate measures of
repression thus becomes the practical problem of central concern.

But in Garofalo's view, the organic deficiency in moral sensibilities, characteristic of true criminality, varies in significant degree
from one criminal to another. These variations make necessary a
more particular classification of criminal types before intelligent
consideration of repressive measures is possible; for differences in
the types require differences in the measures to be applied. Garofalo identifies four basic criminal classes which, though distinct, are

[45] *Ibid.* at 109. [46] *Ibid.* at 137–140.
[47] *Ibid.* at 142–165. From what has been said up to this point, the two following conclusions may be drawn: "(1) The present economic order, that is to say, the distribution
of wealth, as it exists today, is not a cause of criminality in general. (2) The fluctuations which are wont to occur in the economic order may bring about the increase of
one form of criminality, but this increase is compensated by the limitation of another
form. These fluctuations are, therefore, possible causes of *specific criminality*." *Ibid.*
at 164.
[48] *Ibid.* at 140–141. [49] *Ibid.* at 95.
[50] *Ibid.* at 97.

yet related in that each is characterised by a deficiency in the basic altruistic sentiments of pity and probity. These four classes are those of (1) the murderer, (2) the violent criminal, (3) the thief, and (4) the lascivious criminal.[51]

The murderer is the man in whom altruism is wholly lacking.[52] The sentiments of both pity and probity are absent, and such a criminal will steal or kill as the occasion arises. This extreme form of the moral anomaly is frequently revealed in the very circumstances of the crime committed. The lesser criminals, on the other hand, may be more difficult to identify; and here psychologic and anthropologic examination may be required to assist in his proper classification. These lesser offenders fall into two major groups: violent criminals, characterised by the lack of pity, and thieves, indicated by lack of probity. The violent criminal may often be guilty of offences against the person of the type particularly characteristic of a given locality. Such crimes Garofalo terms endemic offences.[53] Admittedly, these patterns of criminal behaviour are strongly influenced by environmental factors. But though imitation plays a significant part in such acts, the offender is an abnormal man, as evidenced by the fact that even where endemic criminality is rampant, such offences are committed by a small minority of the population. The violent criminal may also commit crimes of passion, sometimes under the influence of alcohol. For Garofalo, such crimes, committed in a fit of anger, are indicative of inferior innate moral capacities. "Moreover," he adds, "it has been my uniform experience as a criminal magistrate that men who have taken life under the influence of liquor are nearly always persons who had sustained a previous bad character or had been formerly convicted of similar offences."[54]

Garofalo recognises that the thieves, his second major subdivision of lesser criminals, may be more the product of social factors than the criminals in other classes.[55] Certain environments, particularly, contribute to crimes against property. "The limits of such an environment need not be wide," he writes, "two or three evil companions, sometimes a single intimate friend, are sufficient to lead a youth into this sort of crime."[56] Nevertheless, many manifestations of such behaviour can only be attributed to "a

[51] *Ibid.* at 111–134.
[53] *Ibid.* at 112–115.
[55] *Ibid.* at 125–130.

[52] *Ibid.* at 111–112.
[54] *Ibid.* at 117.
[56] *Ibid.* at 127.

remote atavism " and, in other cases, to a general deficiency in " moral energy." Finally, there is the rather amorphous category of lascivious criminals.[57] Many sexual offenders, he recognises, must be classified among the violent criminals. The behaviour of others is the result of mental disorder. But fitting comfortably in neither category is a group of sexual offenders, requiring separate classification, whose conduct is characterised less by the absence of the sentiment of pity than by a low level of moral energy and deficient moral perception.

Theories and measures of social defence

In a sense, all of Garofalo's major concepts relating to crime and the criminal may be taken as providing the preliminary ground-work for his consideration of social defence against criminality. Almost the entire second half of his *Criminology* is devoted to a study of the theories and measures of crime prevention and repression. For the modern reader, this portion of the work contains some of Garofalo's most interesting and perceptive pages.

Garofalo's starting-point in considering the problems of intelligent community response to crime is revealing, for he founds his thought on one of those analogies characteristic of the social Darwinism of his day. In nature, through the processes of natural selection, the penalty for lack of adaptation is elimination. The true criminal by the absence or deficiency of the basic altruistic sentiments similarly demonstrates his " unfitness " or lack of adaptation to his social environment. Elimination from the social circle is thus the penalty indicated. " In this way, the social power will effect an artificial selection similar to that which nature effects by the death of individuals inassimilable to the particular conditions of the environment in which they are born or to which they have been removed. Herein the state will be simply following the example of nature." [58]

Whatever may be said concerning the integrity of the analogy so drawn, it clearly produces assumptions of the greatest importance in Garofalo's thought. In the first place, the emphasis on elimination results in a theory of penalties or treatment which makes incapacitation of the criminal the consideration of central importance. Thus, at the outset, deterrence of potential offenders and

---

[57] *Ibid.* at 130–131.   [58] *Ibid.* at 219–220.

reformation of the criminal are relegated to positions of secondary or incidental significance. Secondly, the analogy relating criminal penalties to " natural selection " is suggestive of the types of penalties which may properly be imposed and, perhaps, serves as a kind of moral justification for criminal punishment by identifying it with the scheme of the natural universe.

It is upon these basic assumptions that Garofalo constructs his programme of criminal sanctions. Although his proposals are elaborated at considerable length,[59] they can be stated in their essence rather succinctly. The fundamental purpose to be sought is the elimination from society of those who because of moral anomaly are incapable of social adaptation. The surest and most efficient form of elimination is death. And death is the sanction clearly indicated when the offender has demonstrated his complete absence of moral sensibilities and who is hence " forever incapable of social life." [60] While there should be no hesitation to apply the death penalty in such cases, the moral sentiments of the community will not permit its imposition on offenders in whom the psychic anomaly appears in less extreme form. For, as Garofalo observes, " the death penalty has always excited public indignation when inflicted for offences not seriously violating the moral sense." [61] For these lesser offenders some measure of adaptation is always possible, and the practical problem is to find the environment which will make adaptation probable. Here, again, the question is one of degree, and elimination may be relative as well as absolute. There are some who, like certain types of violent criminals, professional thieves and habitual criminals in general, are incompatible with any civilised environment. Elimination in these cases must take the form of life imprisonment or overseas transportation. The latter, where available, is much to be preferred on the grounds both of security and humanity.[62] In dealing with young offenders and those whose behaviour has been strongly influenced by environmental factors, commitment for indefinite periods in penal agricultural colonies may be indicated.[63] There are also cases where elimination need go no further than expulsion of the offender from

---

[59] *Ibid.* at 220–229. And see the final chapter of the work entitled " The Rational System of Punishment," *ibid.* at 372 *et seq.*
[60] *Ibid.* at 224.
[61] *Ibid.* at 223.
[62] *Ibid.* at 224–225.
[63] *Ibid.* at 225.

his particular social situation which may accordingly involve the permanent loss of rights to practise a given profession (where those rights have been abused) and the denial of certain civil and legal privileges.[64] Finally, there are offenders who have committed true crimes but in whom the moral anomaly has revealed itself much less clearly. Here the appropriate sanction is enforced reparation. Damages are to be assessed in sufficient amount not only adequate for complete indemnification of the injured party but to cover the expenses incurred by the state as a result of the offender's dereliction. If the offender's means are inadequate, his labour must be devoted to the required reparation.[65]

Even this brief recital of Garofalo's programme of repressive measures casts considerable light on his purposes and assumptions. There is revealed, for example, his conviction that the legal sanctions ought to be modelled upon consideration of the psychic characteristics of the particular offender, as well as his dissatisfaction with the conventional penal measures in this respect. As disclosed by his advocacy of the completely indeterminate sentence and particularly the expansion of capital punishment, stern penalties were for him an essential ingredient of a rational criminal code. That he desired as broad a use of the death penalty as has sometimes been supposed is less clear, however; for he does not estimate the fraction of the total criminal population consisting of those totally bereft of altruistic sentiments which make up the class eligible for capital punishment.

But a satisfactory appraisal of Garofalo's thought on these matters requires a more particular examination of his theories of punishment and his analysis of competing penal philosophies. A comparison of his position with certain of the postulates of classical criminology may be particularly instructive. Garofalo at the outset reveals fundamental theoretical differences with the classical school in his unequivocal rejection of the idea of moral responsibility as a

---

[64] *Ibid.*
[65] Garofalo's idea of "enforced reparation" is one of his most interesting contributions. Included as an appendix to the English translation is a paper on the subject submitted by him to the International Penitentiary Congress of Brussels in 1900. *Ibid.* at 419–435. *Cf.* Lex, "Restitution *or* Compensation and the Criminal Law," 34 Law Mag.& Rev. 286 (1909); Bates, *Prisons and Beyond* (1938), 292–294; Michael and Wechsler, *Criminal Law and Its Administration* (1940), 537–540. The views of Bentham on "pecuniary satisfaction" also provide an interesting comparison. See Bentham, *Theory of Legislation* (Eng.ed., 1871), 282 *et seq.* It should be noted that Bentham receives only one rather disparaging reference in *Criminology* (at p. 55), and Garofalo demonstrates no great familiarity with his work.

basis for criminal liability. Consistently with the positivist position,[66] he rejects the notion of freedom of the will and accepts a
thorough-going determinism.[67]   To Garofalo the idea of moral
responsibility is basically inconsistent with the objective of social
defence, for it is the offender least capable of making and acting
upon moral judgments who is most dangerous to social interests.
". . . [W]hen we undertake to ascertain whether a man is really
responsible for what he does," he writes, " we always end by
discovering that he is not.   It is to the fallacy which pervades the
entire system that the present ineffectiveness of repression is due.
The whole blame rests upon the two principles of moral responsibility and penal proportion." [68]

Since Garofalo's day the concept of responsibility has proved a
persistent source of acrimony and controversy.[69]   Without agitating
these issues further, it may be relevant to suggest that the explicit
rejection of the idea of moral responsibility presented Garofalo with
certain theoretical difficulties and to question whether he succeeded
in consistently maintaining the determinism he asserted.   Given the
important role of the " moral sentiments " in his conceptions of
both crime and the criminal, Garofalo's determinism produced for
him the formidable task of separating the idea of morality from
that of moral responsibility.   He approaches this task by advancing
what might be termed an aesthetic theory of moral values.   We feel
admiration for physical virtues such as beauty, strength and grace,
and are repelled by the absence of these qualities quite independently of whether the individual possessing any of these traits is
free to have other virtues or defects.   This is equally true of the
moral qualities.   " The praise of virtuous and the blame for vicious
acts really presents the same case. . . . ' Merit ' and ' demerit ' have
always relation to acts dependent upon moral qualities.   The words

---

[66] *Cf.* the statement of Ferri in his chapter entitled " The Positive School of Criminology ": " Positive psychology has demonstrated that the pretended free will is a purely
subjective illusion." Ferri, *op. cit. supra,* note 8 at 38.

[67] *Crim.* at 273–287.   Compare the statement of one of the leading Italian exponents of
the classical school in Carrara, *Programma del Curso de Derecho* (Span. ed., 1925), 31,
quoted in Amadeo, *Schools of Penal Thought Reflected in Modern Penal Legislation* 5:
" I do not waste my time in philosophical questions, I presuppose the existence of the
free will and the moral culpability of man, because without it is impossible to build a
criminal science."

[68] *Crim.* at 337.

[69] The enormous literature in this field is familiar and requires no citation.   Attention may
be called, however, to a recent discussion: " Criminal Responsibility and Psychiatric
Expert Testimony," Comm. on Psych. and Law of the Group for the Advancement
of Psychiatry (May 1954).

themselves require no change. All that is needed is a correct understanding of their meaning." [70] An interesting test of Garofalo's
position relates to the treatment of the insane criminal. Garofalo
emphatically insists that although the insane offender is a criminal [71]
and may be quite as dangerous as any other offender, capital
punishment must not be imposed upon him. This withholding of
the death penalty, completely consistent with the classical conception of responsibility, would appear, at least initially, to involve
Garofalo in contradiction. But Garofalo denies any inconsistency.
A necessary requirement for the imposition of capital punishment,
he says, " is that sympathy for the criminal has ceased to exist." [72]
What is the source of this sympathy for the insane man which persists despite the danger of his acts? Garofalo first replies that we
recognise in him a potential capacity for social life: " Insanity does
not engender a permanent moral character: the perversity in this
case is transient and capable of change." [73] But surely, many insane
offenders, under the present state of knowledge, display at least as
unfavourable a prognosis as those whom he would consign to the
death penalty. Garofalo's ultimate refuge seems to lie in the almost
metaphysical distinction " between the natural instincts innate in
the individual, the instincts which go to make up his real or irre-
ducible character, and [in the case of the insane] the adventitious
instincts resulting from physical deterioration." [74]

. In turning to the explicit consideration of competing penal
philosophies, the modern reader will discover some of Garofalo's
most interesting insights. Naturally enough, he rejects the idea of
vengeance or moral expiation as a sufficient theoretical basis for
penal sanctions.[75] The idea that punishment will produce a moral
regeneration of the offender through remorse and repentance fails
because, by his very nature, the true criminal lacks the moral
capacities the theory assumes. Nevertheless, he finds sound historical basis for the notion that criminal penalties represent in some

[70] *Crim.* at 304–305.
[71] In discussing the criminal accountability of the insane, Garofalo distinguishes between those whose mental illness has completely destroyed the capacity for ideation and those in whom " the faculties of ideation " are not altogether destroyed. The idea of criminality would not attach to the former: " For unless act corresponds with intention, crime does not exist." *Ibid.* at 280. Even as to the latter who would be labelled criminal, special methods of treatment would be applied. *Cf.* Ferri, *op. cit. supra,* note 8 at 356–363.
[72] *Crim.* at 282.
[73] *Ibid.* at 283.
[74] *Ibid.* at 284.
[75] *Ibid.* at 230–239.

measure a manifestation of socialised vengeance. Nor is he at all hostile to the sense of outrage and repugnance produced in honest men by the true criminal. For the feeling of outrage provides the social mechanism through which the rational goal of elimination is reached, however imperfectly this may be understood by the public at large.[76]

Garofalo's conception of criminality as something organic and innate in the offender leads, as might be expected, to a considerable scepticism of the possibilities of reformation through education or other modes of treatment.[77] Actually, some of his proposals, already noted, for handling offenders whose crimes reveal a considerable environmental influence are perhaps more in accord with the reformative ideal than he himself suspected.[78] Moreover, his emphasis on the individualisation of punishment has probably placed his influence, in the long run, on the side of the correctionalist goals. Nevertheless, his criticism of the reformative theory is an essential part of his thought, and his observations on this subject even yet supply a useful antidote for the more Utopian and irresponsible assertions of some of the correctionalists. At the outset he avoids the error, too often committed, of conceiving that any system of enforced treatment, whatever its motives and purposes, can be stripped of punitive aspects. "The mere deprivation of liberty, however benign the administration of the place of confinement, is undeniably punishment."[79] He notes, furthermore, that the existence of other social goals and values places limits on what may be done in the interest of reformation, assuming that the latter can be accomplished.[80] Nor should the prosaic problems of the

---

[76] "Public sentiment thus coincides with the rational method of social reaction and, perhaps unconsciously, has no other tendency than that of bringing about the same effect. It is important, however, to notice that this tendency is not the direct result of any process of reasoning by which is demonstrated the social utility of elimination. . . ." *Ibid.* at 234.

[77] *Ibid.* at 255–269.

[78] It should be noted, also, that, to a degree not often fully appreciated, the reformative goal was given recognition by the classical criminologists. In this connection, see Bentham, *op. cit. supra*, note 65 at 338–339: "It is a great merit in a punishment to contribute to the *reformation of the offender*, not only through the fear of being punished again, but by a change in his character and habits. This end may be attained by studying the motive which produced the offence, and by applying a punishment which tends to weaken that motive. A house of correction to fulfil this object ought to admit a separation of delinquents, in order that different means of treatment may be adapted to the diversity of their moral condition." (Italics in the original.)

[79] *Crim.* at 256.

[80] "All this no doubt is very admirable. It is based, however, upon an utterly false notion of state omnipotence. It completely ignores the fact that society, like any natural organism, undergoes a development which is slow and gradual, a development in which

public purse or the matter of personnel be ignored. " Where are
we to find a sufficient number of these soul-physicians? " he asks.
" And what of the expense of such an undertaking? " And would
the cure effected by this " moral therapy " survive the offender's
return to his old haunts? Fundamentally, however, Garofalo's
objections are based on his conviction of the fixity of character types.
His hopes for substantial progress were largely confined to reformative programmes of the Elmira type directed to the very young
offender.[81]

But perhaps most interesting and significant is Garofalo's
analysis and criticism of the classical theories of deterrence.[82]
Although he ultimately rejects the deterrence of potential offenders
as an adequate theoretical basis for criminal penalties, he reveals a
more perceptive understanding of the theory than often displayed
by its critics. He recognises, at the outset, that justification for the
deterrent theory need not be rested solely on the direct intimidatory
effect produced on potential offenders by the threat of penal sanctions. Rather, in more subtle fashion the criminal penalties may
regulate behaviour by producing and reinforcing general moral
attitudes toward certain forms of conduct. Thus the law, by
making such behaviour unrespectable, subjects the individual to
powerful extra-legal sanctions. " No doubt for many persons, the
consciousness of the evil involved would destroy any pleasure which
the criminal act might afford and is therefore sufficient to cause
abstention from crime. But even these persons involuntarily think
of the extra-legal social reaction attendant upon the offence, namely,
by their honest neighbours; and this thought is continually
strengthening their resolution to abstain from the acts in question." [83] Without the stimulus of these sanctions, the moral

the law-maker is a minimum factor. But what of the practical side of the question?
Has this, at least, been approached? For if crime is a symptom and its cause is recognisable, it is the business of a good system of social therapeutics to deal with this cause,
provided that it is capable of yielding to treatment. In this lies the whole question:
What are the means? " *Ibid.* at 179. Speaking of Ferri's programme of " penal
substitutes," Garofalo states: " His plan involves nothing less than the complete making
over of a whole system of social and economic legislation." *Ibid.* at 182. And compare Dession, " Psychiatry and the Conditioning of Criminal Justice," 47 Yale L.J. 319,
339–340 (1938).

[81] *Crim.* at 266–267.   [82] *Ibid.* at 239–251.

[83] *Ibid.* at 241. Compare the statement of Stephen quoted in Andcnaes, " General Prevention—Illusion or Reality? " 43 J.Crim.L.& Criminology 176, 189 (1952): " Some men,
probably, abstain from murder because they fear that if they committed murder they
would be hanged. Hundreds of thousands abstain from it because they regard it with
horror. One great reason why they regard it with horror is that murderers are hanged
with the hearty approbation of all reasonable men."

sentiments " would tend to weaken and even, in the course of time, might altogether disappear." [84]

It is apparent, therefore, that in this regard Garofalo's rejection of the position of classical criminology was by no means complete. Indeed, an important part of his justification for the use of the death penalty in proper cases is the assumed intimidatory result.[85] Nevertheless, deterrence, while an important and desirable effect of criminal penalties, cannot be accepted by Garofalo as the proper criterion of punishment. This conclusion is reached on the interesting ground that the deterrent theory offers no clear standards by which either the kind or amount of punishment can be determined.[86] How is the legislature to measure in advance the quantum of punishment necessary to prevent a given form of conduct in the various social circumstances in which it may appear?[87] How is the danger to social interests of such behaviour to be reflected proportionately in the penalties applied? This inherent uncertainty may result either in an excess or a deficiency of punishment. In times of stress and insecurity the effort to deter may result in draconian measures with consequent injury to individual and social interests. On the other hand, the stipulation of the quantum of punishment in advance often requires the release of still-dangerous offenders to the community. For Garofalo, the only rational criterion is that which measures the penalty by reference to the characteristics of the particular offender.

Certainly, Garofalo's analysis of deterrence has point and relevance. The difficulties he suggests are real. Although the assumptions of the deterrent theory continue to dominate most criminal legislation, there has been little systematic effort to test and validate these assumptions through empirical study.[88] Few today would assert that considerations of deterrence are in themselves adequate for the construction of a modern system of criminal justice. Nevertheless, it may properly be asked whether in some measure these uncertainties, which Garofalo deplores, are not inherent in any programme of action and whether he adequately

[84] *Crim.* at 242.   [85] *Ibid.* at 377–378.

[86] *Ibid.* at 245 *et seq.*

[87] These difficulties did not escape the classical writers. See, *e.g.*, Beccaria, *op. cit. supra*, note 28 at 30: " If mathematical calculation could be applied to the obscure and infinite combinations of human actions, there might be a corresponding scale of punishments, descending from the greatest to the least; but it will be sufficient that the wise legislator mark the principal divisions, without disturbing the order, lest crimes of the *first* degree, be assigned punishments of the *last*." (Italics in the original.)

[88] See Andenaes, *op. cit. supra*, note 83.

appreciated the difficulties of his own position. In the first place, it should be noted that for the vast area of penal regulation falling outside the confines of " natural crime," Garofalo fully embraces the deterrent theory with all its infirmities.[89] Secondly, it seems clear that Garofalo never fully appreciates the problematical nature of identifying and evaluating those criminal characteristics in the individual which make him a threat to the community. As already noted, Garofalo would identify the extreme criminal primarily by consideration of the criminal act; and in this respect he approaches the position of classical criminology.[90] The lesser criminal, however, is to be identified, at least in part, through anthropologic and psychologic examination. But little effort is made to demonstrate the adequacy of existing scientific knowledge and techniques for these purposes. The reader is confidently assured that " criminology is quite capable of " making these discriminations.[91] At another point, Garofalo refers to " what might be called the queen of proofs—an hereditary history of vice, madness or crime," as indicating something of the method he contemplates.[92] It is difficult to escape the conclusion that his assurances are based on incomplete demonstration. One need not deny the relevance of scientific knowledge and methodology to the treatment of the criminal or the prevention of crime to recognise that the real utility of such knowledge is dependent upon a critical appraisal of its limitations. Nor is it necessary to labour the point that a penal system can place basic values in jeopardy by assuming the existence of non-existent or institutionally unavailable techniques.[93] That Garofalo was less than sensitive to these dangers can hardly be denied.

Conclusion

Although one of the conscious and explicit purposes of Garofalo's *Criminology* was to challenge certain basic assumptions of classical penal theory, a full consideration of his thought reveals much less than a complete rejection of the classical position. This is

---

[89] " For the stamping out of these non-criminal offences, it will employ punishments of greater or less severity as necessity dictates, *keeping principally in mind their intimidatory effect*—their influence as an example and warning to would-be wrongdoers." (Italics added.) *Crim.* at 217.

[90] See note 32, *supra*, and accompanying text.

[91] *Crim.* at 228.

[92] *Ibid.* at 388. See also *ibid.* at 66, 112.

[93] *Cf.* Tappan, " Sentences for Sex Criminals," 42 J.Crim.L.& Criminology 332 (1951).

indicated by his close identification of the concepts of crime and the criminal with attendant emphasis on the act as an index of criminality, by his qualified recognition of the deterrent effect of penal sanctions, and by his attention to the necessity for some ordering of penalties. These correspondences may suggest that when emphasis is directed to the real and recurring problems of criminal administration, there are wider possibilities for attaining practical reconciliation of diverging theoretical viewpoints than is sometimes assumed.

Nevertheless, Garofalo's differences with the classical writers, such as his fellow countryman, Beccaria, are frequent and important. Two of general significance should be noted. First, there is in Garofalo's work a recognition of the relevance of the scientific method which rarely receives a comparable emphasis in classical criminology. This is not to deny that Garofalo's thought is pervaded by certain untested, *a priori* assumptions and that many of his views so based have not survived the passing of the years. Yet his devotion to the ideal of empirical investigation provides a mechanism for the adjustment of hypothesis and theory to new knowledge as it is acquired.

Secondly, in contrast to the classical writers, there is in Garofalo's thought a persistent tendency toward the exaltation of social interests and a devaluation of individual rights. Both Beccaria and Garofalo, interestingly enough, accept the concept of necessity as the justification for criminal penalties.[94] But necessity means something quite different for each. Beccaria assumes the dominance of individual rights and accepts penal restraints only to the extent required for social coexistence, which, in turn, leads to a fuller realisation of individual rights. But Garofalo reveals scant sympathy for any view which accords priority to interests other than those of the group. "Metaphorically speaking," he writes, "the individual represents but a cell of the social body."[95] Nowhere does this tendency appear more clearly than in his discussion of criminal procedures.[96] Recognising that the procedures he discusses are founded on a very different tradition from our own and that criticism by one foreign to that experience is perilous, one cannot help but be struck by the fact that Garofalo's whole attention is directed to the more efficient apprehension and conviction of

[94] Compare Beccaria, *op. cit. supra*, note 28 at 17–19 with *Crim.* at 270–273, 299–308.
[95] *Crim.* at 224. See also *ibid.* at 302, 306–308, 368.   [96] *Ibid.* at 338 *et seq.*

offenders. Mistake or the malevolent use of state power as possibilities demanding safeguards plays no part in his analysis. This faith in the beneficence of political authority no doubt reveals Garofalo as a child of his times.[97] But in a less happy day we are not free to make the same easy assumption. Accordingly, the sense of political realities which pervades the thought of Beccaria and his school has a relevance for the present which it obviously lacked for Garofalo.

A full appreciation of Garofalo's contribution requires a more extensive consideration than can be given here of a number of specifically legal topics. His discussion of criminal attempt, for example, remains one of the classic treatments of that difficult subject.[98] His perceptive criticism of the idea of premeditation and his efforts to incorporate a more specific reference to motive in criminal legislation are notable and require attention in any modern effort to restate the penal law.[99]

Admittedly, an appraisal of the continuing significance of Garofalo's *Criminology* must recognise that, despite the value of its insights, many of the assumptions and a great deal of the theoretical apparatus have lost much of their relevance for modern thought. But in addition to its very real contributions, the work retains its power to stimulate; for the issues it raises are real and persistent. Perhaps this is enough to require of any book.

FRANCIS A. ALLEN.

BIBLIOGRAPHY

By Garofalo

Criminology (first Italian ed., Naples, 1885; second Italian ed., Turin, 1891; French ed., trans. by the author, 1905; Spanish ed., trans. by P. Dorado y Montero, ——; Portuguese ed., trans. by J. De Mattos, ——; English ed., trans. by Robert W. Millar, 1914, reprinted Montclair, N.J., 1968).

---

[97] It is worth noting, however, that Garofalo took vigorous exception to the socialism of certain members of the Italian school, particularly Ferri. The latter, for example, wrote: "Sociology will be socialistic or it will not exist." Ferri, *op. cit. supra*, note 8 at 17, note 2. A contemporary account is interesting in this connection: "His [Garofalo's] latest volume, entitled *Socialist Superstitions* has excited much wrath and astonishment in socialistic and anthropological camps, and was severely combated, especially by Ferri, who wrote a pamphlet on purpose to confute the publication. R. Garofolo [*sic*] was born in Naples, in 1852, of an old patrician family, hence perhaps by atavism he is debarred from being a socialist." Zimmern, "Criminal Anthropology in Italy," 10 *Green Bag* 342, 382, 385 (1898).

[98] *Crim.* at 308–321.

[99] *Ibid.* at 373–382.

Di un criterio positivo della penalità (Naples, 1880).
Il tentativo criminoso con mezzi inidonei (Turin, 1882, Loescher).
Ciò che dovrebbe essere un giudizio penale (Turin, 1882, Loescher).
Riparazione alle vittime del delitto (Turin, 1887, Bocca).
La Superstition socialiste (Paris, 1895, F. Alcan).
De la solidarité des nations dans la lutte contre la criminalité (Paris, 1909, Giard et Brière).

About Garofalo

ZIMMERN. "Criminal Anthropology in Italy," 10 *Green Bag* 342, 382 (1898).
H. B. E. "Review of Garofalo, *Criminology*," 28 Harv.L.R. 221 (1914).

NOTE ON THE CONTRIBUTOR

Dr. FRANCIS A. ALLEN is Edson R. Sunderland Professor of Law at the University of Michigan. He has served on the faculties of Northwestern University, Harvard University, and the University of Chicago. From 1966 to 1971 he was Dean of the Law School at the University of Michigan. He is a graduate of Cornell College and Northwestern University School of Law. He served as Law Clerk to Mr. Chief Justice Fred M. Vinson of the U.S. Supreme Court from 1946 to 1948, as Chairman of the Attorney General's Committee on Poverty and Federal Criminal Justice in 1961–62, and in various other capacities in the federal and state and local governments. He is author of *The Borderland of Criminal Justice* (1964) and of numerous articles on criminal law, criminology, and constitutional law.

17

WILLIAM DOUGLAS MORRISON
1852–1943

IT is perhaps the dearth of information concerning the life of the
Rev. William Douglas Morrison and his professional position as religious leader rather than as man of science that have rendered his
name as an early criminologist rather obscure. Aside from a brief
statement in *The Times* noting his death and a short paragraph
in *Who Was Who*,[1] little is known of Morrison's biography. His
demise was not even mentioned in *The Journal of the Royal Statistical Society,* an organization to which he had belonged since 1891
and to which he had delivered a paper that was presented as the
opening article in the 1897 publication of the *Journal*.[2]

Born in 1852, the son of R. Morrison of Newton, New Brunswick,
W. D. Morrison was educated at Glen Almond, a well-known boys'
school in Scotland, and at the University of St. Andrews (which was
to confer upon him the honorary degree of LL.D. in 1898). A few
years after his ordainment by Bishop Ripon, he became a chaplain
in Her Majesty's Prison Service, a position which he occupied from
1883 until 1898. His two books on crime, *Crime and Its Causes* and
Juvenile Offenders, had their genesis in this early prison experience.[3]
Morrison was said to be one of those modernists who are also Board
Churchmen, meaning that he was willing to live and let live. This
attitude, however, should not be interpreted as an acceptance of the
status quo on the part of Morrison; any such disposition, in addition
to being incongruous with his formal station in the social order, was
also belied in his criminological writings. In 1908 Morrison became
Rector of St. Marylebone in London—a position which he held until
the age of 91, when he died from the effects of an accident.

---

* Reproduced from *The Journal of Criminal Law, Criminology and Police Science,* Vol. 55,
No. 1, March 1964.
[1] *The Times* (London), 15 December 1943, p. 7; *Who Was Who,* Vol. IV (1941–1950),
p. 818.
[2] W. D. Morrison, "The Interpretation of Criminal Statistics," *Journal of the Royal Statistical Society,* Vol. 60, p. 1.
[3] *The Times* (London), 15 December 1943, p. 7.

Editor, letter-writer, and author

In addition to preparing a number of religious works, Morrison was the editor of Fisher Unwin's Criminology Series,[4] in which his *Juvenile Offenders* appeared. Morrison was apparently well acquainted with the work of Lombroso, having written the introduction to *The Female Offender*. In his foreword, Morrison's treatment of Lombroso's theory of atavism and physical degeneracy is cursory in comparison with his own comments on the functioning of the criminal law and penal administration. Neither, he asserts, is fulfilling its purpose of protecting society; in support of this position Morrison refers to the increase in criminal expenditures and to the growth of the habitual criminal population among all civilized communities. Great Britain herself was incurring a bill of £10 million annually in connection with crime. This huge expenditure could be somewhat justified if the people of England were getting their money's worth in terms of a decreasing criminal class. Unfortunately this was not the case.[5]

Morrison recognized that the ordinary man could be deterred from crime on critical occasions by fear of punishment and public indignation. But the criminal population, he maintained, is not composed of ordinary men. Consequently the purely punitive principle on which the penal law rests is not applicable to them: ". . . a high percentage of them [criminals] live under anomalous biological and social conditions. And it is these anomalous conditions acting upon the offender either independently or, as is more often the case, in combination which make him what he is." It is because the criminal laws are not constructed to cope with the social and individual conditions which distinguish the bulk of the criminal population that they are so helpless in their contest with crime. An almost inevitable extension of this reasoning—and one that Morrison does not fail to note—is that the criminal law errs in demanding equal sentences for the same or equal offenses. "The duration and nature of sentences, as well as the duration and nature of prison treatment, must be adjusted to the character of the offender as well as to the character of the offence." This would require, at the most, classification of institutions and, at the least, classification within institu-

---

[4] The Criminology Series comprised Cesare Lombroso and Guglielmo Ferrero, *The Female Offender* (1895); Enrico Ferri, *Criminal Sociology* (1895); W. D. Morrison, *Juvenile Offenders* (1896); and Louis Proal, *Political Crime* (1898). Each title was published in New York by Appleton shortly after it appeared in London.
[5] W. D. Morrison, Foreword to *The Female Offender*, by Cesare Lombroso and Guglielmo Ferrero (New York, 1895), pp. v–vi.

tions. For it is useless to apply the same method of penal treatment to a number of different classes of offenders. The penal law, if it is to be effective, must cope with the conditions which produce the criminal. Once this is accomplished and enlightened principles of penal treatment are applied, Morrison insisted, it is certain that society will enjoy a greater immunity from crime.[6]

Having written the preface and having provided a partial translation of Enrico Ferri's *Criminal Sociology,* Morrison could not have been less familiar with Ferri's contributions to criminology than with Lombroso's. In this preface, Morrison touched upon the superficial interpretations so often placed upon returns relating to crime and the futility of resorting to increasingly severe punishments.[7] It is interesting to note that in translating *Criminal Sociology* Morrison omitted the entire first section of the book because it was too heterodox.[8]

Morrison's periodical commentaries on crime found their way into such scholarly publications as the *Journal of the Royal Statistical Society,* the *Sociological Review,* the *Journal of Mental Science, Mind,* and others. But Morrison could not be accused of restricting his thoughts on crime to esoteric audiences. By any standard Morrison would have to be considered an avid civic-minded correspondent: from 1891 to 1938 no less than 28 communications of his, ten of which dealt with criminal problems, had appeared among the "Letters to the Editor" in *The Times.*[9]

Despite the wide circulation of Morrison's reflections on crime which appeared in newspaper and journal articles, his major contributions to the field of criminology are to be found in his two books: *Crime and Its Causes,* published in 1891, and *Juvenile Offenders,* which came on the scene nine years later.

"Crime and Its Causes"

Shortly after its appearance *Crime and Its Causes* was reviewed in the *Political Science Quarterly,* the *Annals of the American Academy of Political and Social Science,* and *The Nation.* The two

[6] *Ibid.,* pp. viii–xi, xviii, xx.

[7] W. D. Morrison, Preface to *Criminal Sociology,* by Enrico Ferri (New York, 1897), pp. v–viii.

[8] Thorsten Sellin, *infra,* p. 371n.

[9] When he was 79 years of age, Morrison contributed an article to *The Times* titled "Aids to Longevity." Judging from his own life-span it would seem that Morrison was eminently qualified to write on this subject. *The Times* (London), 11 February 1931, p. 8.

latter journals commented favorably on the book, using such expressions as "thoughtful and thought-suggesting book" and "a sociological investigation . . . distinguished for its thoroughly scientific
spirit." [10]   The *Political Science Quarterly* summarized Morrison's
main findings without commenting on their quality; it did however
suggest that Morrison had omitted an important factor in crime
causation, namely, the offender's lack of any settled trade or occupation.[11]   This criticism of Morrison, though, does not seem entirely
justified.   While Morrison did not discuss the relationship between
productive employment and crime at great length in *Crime and Its
Causes,* he did not fail to consider it.

> The closeness of the connection between degeneracy and crime is, to a con-
> siderable extent, determined by social conditions. A degenerate person, who
> has to earn his own livelihood, is much more likely to become a criminal than
> another degenerate person who has not. Almost all forms of degeneracy
> render a man more or less unsuited for the common work of life; it is not easy
> for such a man to obtain employment. . . . A person in this unfortunate posi-
> tion often becomes a criminal, not because he has strong anti-social instincts,
> but because he cannot get work. Physically, he is unfit for work, and he
> takes to crime as an alternative.[12]

Be this as it may, the *Quarterly*'s review of Morrison's work could
not by any means be described as disapproving; it was simply non-
committal.

The first chapter of *Crime and Its Causes* takes up the statistics
of crime. To be exhaustive, Morrison says, criminal statistics should
include more than the age, sex, and occupation of the offender and
the amount of crime, basic as such information is. These data need
to be supplemented by the personal and social history of the criminal.
The methods to be employed in deterring criminals can be ascertained only after the most searching preliminary inquiries into all
the main facts of crime; accordingly, the life-history technique of
data collection is strongly recommended.[13]   In the same chapter
Morrison divides the factors which are responsible for crime into
three main categories—cosmical, social, and individual. The cosmical factors are climate and the variations in temperature; the social
factors refer to the political, economic, and moral conditions of man
as a member of society; while the individual factors are attributes

[10] Book Review, *Annals of the American Academy of Political and Social Science,* Vol. 2, p. 125; Book Review, *The Nation,* Vol. 53, p. 128.
[11] Book Review, *Political Science Quarterly,* Vol. 6, p. 355.
[12] W. D. Morrison, *Crime and Its Causes* (London, 1891), p. 199.
[13] *Ibid.,* pp. 3–4.

which are inherent in the person, such as sex, age, mental characteristics, etc. Though Morrison readily admits that these categories
can be reduced to two—the organism and the environment—he feels
that this three-fold division is more convenient for purposes of analysis.[14] The following chapters of the book, with the exception of the
last, examine the facts of crime as expressions of these three general
factors. The main conclusions reached by Morrison are as follows.

(a) *Climate and Crime.* Crimes against property preponderate
in cold climates and during the winter months, while crimes against
the person are more prevalent in warm regions and high tempera-
tures. Crimes of a violent nature, in particular, tend to be committed more frequently in warm climates and seasons than in cold.
There are two reasons for this: a rise in temperature serves to
diminish a sense of human responsibility, and good weather, multiplying the occasions for human interaction, necessarily increases the
opportunities for criminal conduct.[15] And yet, Morrison contends,
the adverse influence of climate should not be regarded as irrevocable.
Innumerable methods and devices exist which can protect man
against the hostility of the elements. In this connection Morrison
refers to the society of India whose caste structure is such as to neu-
tralize the effect of climate in producing crimes of blood. Although
the average temperature of the Indian peninsula is about 30 degrees
higher than that of the British Isles, India has fewer crimes against
the person than the most highly civilized countries of Europe. Morrison's explanation of India's low homicide rate is strongly Durk-
heimian, suggesting that the caste status of the masses binds them
effectively to social groups with an established way of life from
which deviation is neither permitted nor desired.[16]

(b) *Destitution and Crime.* Morrison defines a destitute person
as one who is without a home and, though able and willing to
work, without a job and thus facing starvation. The essential question is whether any appreciable amount of crime is due to the despera-
tion of such individuals. To answer this query, decides Morrison, it
is first necessary to analyze the type of crimes these persons would be
most likely to commit, namely, begging and theft. He then proceeds to determine the proportion of the total volume of crime that
is represented by these two offenses and, secondly, the extent to which

[14] *Ibid.,* p. 21.
[15] *Ibid.,* pp. 28, 43–46, 66, 77.
[16] *Ibid.,* pp. 46–48, 57–58.

they are the result of destitution. Cases of this type were found to constitute 15 percent of all cases tried in England and Wales during 1887, 8 percent consisting of offenses against property and 7 percent offenses against the Vagrancy Acts. However, half of the offenders against property, far from being destitute, were earning wages at the time of their arrest.[17] Of the remaining 4 percent of property offenders, 2 percent were habitual criminals and therefore not "destitute" as defined above. So only 2 percent of the property offenders could have been driven to crime by destitution. With respect to offenders against the Vagrancy Acts in the year 1888, less than half were charged with begging; the other offenses were unlikely *a priori* to be motivated by destitution.[18] Finally, by a careful process of exclusion, Morrison reaches the conclusion that of the beggars, again not more than 2 percent were made criminals by destitution.[19] Consequently, the destitute class does not account for more than 4 percent of the criminal population. In further support of his position that destitution is not a significant cause of crime, Morrison refers to statistics collected by M. Monad of the Ministry of the Interior in France. According to Monad, a benevolent citizen, anxious to test the truth of statements of sturdy beggars that they were willing to work if given a chance, offered employment at four francs a day to every able beggar who presented himself. During the course of eight months 727 beggars came to this citizen's attention, all complaining that they had no work. Each was asked to come the following day to receive a letter of introduction which would enable him to obtain employment at the above-specified wage. More than half of them (415) never came for the letter; 138 returned for the letter but never used it; only 18 were found at work at the end of the third day.[20]

(c) *Poverty and Crime.* If actual destitution did not contribute appreciably to crime, perhaps poverty did. Unfortunately Morrison provides no explicit definition of poverty, but he does make it clear that this class of people, while being in a more favorable position than the destitute, are nevertheless in a state of economic distress. Morrison relies upon international statistics to throw some light on the relation between poverty and crime. The offense those in a state of poverty are most likely to commit is theft. Putting together all

[17] *Ibid.*, pp. 82–84.
[18] These other offenses consisted principally of prostitution, possessing implements of housebreaking, frequenting places of public resort to commit a felony, and being found on enclosed premises for unlawful purposes. *Ibid.*, p. 91.
[19] *Ibid.*, p. 119.
[20] *Ibid.*, pp. 104–105.

the offenses against property under the common heading of "theft," Morrison finds that although England is six times as wealthy as Italy, more thefts per 100,000 of the population are committed in England than in Italy. Similarly, though the wealth of France is much greater than that of Ireland, the French commit more property offenses than the Irish. These comparisons are, of course, subject to criticism on the basis of the variation in the collection and presentation of criminal returns among different countries. A comparison between England and Ireland, however, would be especially valid since both of these countries gather their statistics on very much the same principles; they are also very similar in the administration of their law. Such a comparison reveals that the Irish, despite their poverty, are not one-half so addicted to property offenses as the English with all their wealth.[21] Morrison presents additional evidence on this topic, but perhaps enough has been said to indicate that all his facts "instead of pointing to poverty as the main cause of crime, point the other way. . . . It has been reserved for this generation to propagate the absurdity that the want of money is the root of all evil; all the wisest teachers of mankind have hitherto been disposed to think differently, and criminal statistics are far from demonstrating that they are wrong." [22] Thus economic adversity, expressed in destitution and poverty, is rejected as the explanation of criminal behavior.

(d) *Crime in Relation to Age and Sex.* Although females commit considerably fewer crimes than males, asserts Morrison, the offenses they do commit are often much more serious than those of males, and female offenders are therefore less reformable than male. English prison statistics, moreover, indicate that women convicts are much more likely to be reconvicted than men. Nevertheless females are generally less criminal than males, and Morrison attributes this fact to (1) their superior moral quality, fostered by their maternal role, (2) their comparative lack of physical power, and (3) the retired and secluded nature of their lives. It is therefore expected that whenever the social status of women approaches that of men, a stronger resemblance will develop between their criminal proclivities. With regard to the age distribution of the criminal population, criminality is at its lowest level from infancy until sixteen; from this point on it steadily increases until it reaches a maximum between

[21] *Ibid.,* pp. 128–132.
[22] *Ibid.,* pp. 145–146.

thirty and forty, whereupon it begins to descend. Women begin their criminal activities later and bring them to a close earlier than men. It is later in starting because of the greater control exercised over girls than over boys, but while it exists it is more persistent because devotion to crime is more intractable in a woman than in a man.[23]

(e) *The Criminal in Body and Mind.* No definite conclusions can be drawn regarding the skull or the brain of criminals.[24] Oddly enough, in discussing the physiognomy of the criminal Morrison posits a rather narrow environmental determinism of facial characteristics.

> It must be borne in mind that a prolonged period of imprisonment will change the face of any man, whether he is a criminal or not. . . . If a man spends a certain number of years sharing the life, the food, the occupations of five or six hundred other men, if he mixes with them and with no one else, he will inevitably come to resemble them in face and feature. . . . The action of unconscious imitation, arising from constant contact, is capable of producing a remarkable change in the features, the acquired expression frequently tending to obliterate inherited family resemblances.[25]

Fortunately, Morrison did not attribute great causal power to physiognomy as a crime-producing agent. He did find that the English criminal population was characterized by a high percentage of disease and degeneracy and that, on the whole, the criminal class was less gifted intellectually than the rest of the community. Concerning the emotions of criminals, Morrison felt safe only in saying that they do not possess the same keenness of feeling as the ordinary man and that their family sentiment is underdeveloped. Despite these findings, Morrison concluded, it cannot be demonstrated that the criminal has any distinct physical conformation; nor can it be proved that there is any necessary connection between anomalies of physical structure and a criminal mode of life.[26]

"Juvenile Offenders"

Juvenile Offenders was published in 1900 and was reviewed by the *Westminster Review, Popular Science Monthly,* and *The Nation.* Only the *Catholic World* was critical of this work, charging that Morrison had ignored the moral control and responsibility which

[23] *Ibid.*, pp. 151–161.
[24] *Ibid.*, pp. 181–182.
[25] *Ibid.*, pp. 185–186.
[26] *Ibid.*, pp. 190–198.

the individual has over his own behavior.[27] Nonetheless, this small book was regarded as the standard work on the subject for many years.[28]

The first part of *Juvenile Offenders* considers the conditions which produce juvenile delinquency. Morrison divides these conditions into two fundamental classes, the individual and the social, thereby omitting the cosmical category which appeared in his earlier volume. The principal individual conditions are the sex, age, and bodily and mental characteristics of the juvenile offender; on the whole the results here are so similar to those expressed in *Crime and Its Causes* that they will not bear repetition. Morrison's comments, however, on the most important social conditions of crime may be briefly presented. Regarding the parental status of juvenile offenders Morrison finds that, other things being equal, illegitimate children are more likely to become offenders than legitimate ones.[29] More than one-half of the inmates of industrial schools are children who are illegitimate, have one or both parents dead, or are the offspring of criminals and parents who have deserted them. It is the task of society, so far as possible, to remove any conditions which are deleterious to the young. Therefore whatever tends to reduce illegitimacy and the death-rate among adults, and to encourage the moral and spiritual elevation of the community, will aid in this task. But it is not the mere fact of being illegitimate, orphaned, or descended from criminal parents which contributes toward delinquency. These circumstances simply express a more general and important factor in juvenile delinquency: the absence of sound parental moral character in directing the children's careers. In the case of deserted or illegitimate children all guidance and direction are lacking, while the criminal parent provides his offspring with the wrong kind of guidance.[30] Parental character, or rather lack of it, then, emerges as one of the most significant causes of juvenile crime.

The economic circumstances of juvenile offenders are, to a large extent, determined by those of their parents. There is, then, a close relationship between parental character and economic position; and the juvenile at a disadvantage regarding the former is, almost of necessity, at a similar disadvantage with respect to the latter. It is

---

[27] Book Review, *Catholic World,* Vol. 65, p. 117.
[28] A. M. Saunders *et al., Young Offenders: An Enquiry into Juvenile Delinquency* (Cambridge, England, 1942), p. 9.
[29] W. D. Morrison, *Juvenile Offenders* (New York, 1900), p. 129.
[30] *Ibid.,* pp. 145–148.

extremely difficult for a juvenile living under these conditions to learn any trade which would make him independent and self-supporting. His lack of apprenticeship, continues Morrison, either makes it impossible to find any employment at all or necessitates his becoming a laborer. Either of these alternatives becomes a fruitful source of crime. This theory is supported by the fact that while the laboring group does not exceed 20 percent in the general community, the proportion of laborers in the male prison population amounts to approximately 70 percent. Irregularity of employment, which itself is the result of parental penury, perpetuates the same condition in the offspring. To be sure, in espousing financial adversity as a prominent cause of delinquency Morrison makes the usual qualifying statements, but his position is nonetheless puzzling when one recalls the considerable lengths to which he went in *Crime and Its Causes* in discounting poverty and destitution as factors leading to crime. *Crime and Its Causes,* however, dealt primarily with adult crime; and Morrison could argue that the inability at the outset of life to obtain regular employment ultimately develops into a distaste for it, so that its causative power on the juvenile level would not have its counterpart on the adult level.[31] Even so, such an explanation is not entirely satisfactory.

Part II of *Juvenile Offenders* is devoted to the repression of juvenile crime and attempts to show how existing methods of dealing with the younger generation may be better adapted to reducing the causes of misbehavior. Methods of repression are divided into three classes —admonitory, punitive, and educational. Admonitory methods simply warn the offender against a repetition of the offense, place him on good behavior, or put him under surveillance; punitive techniques consist of fines, corporal punishment, or imprisonment; the educational measures involve sending the juvenile offender to an industrial, truant, or reformatory school, or to a voluntary home.[32] Morrison is in favor of using admonitions whenever practical, since an actual conviction presents a serious impediment to the future success of the young.[33] Fining also appeals to Morrison because of its effectiveness in handling offenses which require more than admonition but less than deprivation of liberty; at the same time it is the only punitive

[31] *Ibid.,* chap. 8.
[32] *Ibid.,* pp. 180–181.
[33] *Ibid.,* p. 189.

measure which is not irremediable. In this connection the acceptance of installment payments is recommended.[34] Such a practice could do much to protect the juvenile from a prison experience, which so often transforms him into a habitual criminal;[35] it would also be more in keeping with the original intent of the law, which sought not to imprison but to punish financially. Although Morrison is a disbeliever in the deterrent value of capital punishment, he does not support its abolition. It is his firm conviction that as all law rests in the last resort on the sanction of the public, it would first be necessary to convince the people that capital punishment was no longer needed for the protection of society.[36] He sees little value in corporal punishment or imprisonment: the former, in particular, contains nothing of a constructive nature to prevent the repetition of the offenses.[37] He lists as one of the chief defects of imprisonment the fact that the conditions of institutional life are diametrically opposed to those found in the free community. If prison experience is to prepare an individual for appropriate conduct in the world outside, the conditions of prison residence should approximate the conditions of normal existence.[38] In any event, when imprisonment is necessitated, the separation of juveniles from adults, as well as other refinements of treatment, is absolutely necessary. No less essential than the classification of prisoners, however, is the classification of the prison staff, for without trained personnel utilized differentially on the basis of the reformative contributions they can make, classification becomes perfunctory.[39] The more or less conscious recognition of the failure of imprisonment, suggests Morrison, has resulted in the establishment of corrective institutions as an alternative manner of handling juvenile offenders. Reports on the after-conduct of children released from reformatories and industrial schools suggest that these institutions are proving highly effective: three-quarters of the children committed to reformatory schools in England do well after their discharge. On the other hand, it cannot be assumed that all those committed to corrective institutions would have become criminals if they had been sentenced to prison—or had been otherwise dealt with. Admitting these possibilities, Morrison still concludes

---

[34] *Ibid.*, pp. 195, 199.
[35] *Ibid.*, p. 220.
[36] "Executions," *The Times* (London), 22 December 1910, p. 4.
[37] Morrison, *Juvenile Offenders*, p. 220.
[38] *Ibid.*, p. 234.
[39] *Ibid.*, pp. 262–263.

that the work of these schools is highly important and beneficial to their charges.[40]

The preceding should not be interpreted as a complete rejection by Morrison of the punitive value of punishment. Punishment, Morrison maintains, cannot dispense with its punitive character; but, to be effective, it must progress beyond the mere infliction of pain and must offer in addition an experience from which the offender may learn something socially useful.[41]

The interpretation of criminal statistics

Morrison's work in criminology is characterized, above all else, by its empirical orientation. He was careful to avoid an uncritical application of statistics to his material. As excellent example of Morrison's sophistication and analytical perception is to be found in a paper which he read before the Royal Statistical Society on December 15, 1896.[42] He began by dividing criminal statistics into three main branches—police, judicial, and prison statistics; the purpose of this division was to enable him to point out the differential weight to be attached to each of these methods of recording the nature and proportions of crime.

Police statistics are defined as a body of returns relating to the number of offenses annually reported to the police and the number of police apprehensions as a result of these reports. Statistics of this nature, Morrison writes, are the most comprehensive account of the annual dimensions of crime. Neither prison nor judicial statistics merit the same claim to completeness. Prison statistics, in their turn, are less representative of the prevalence of crime than are judicial statistics; as partial proof of this the number of convictions in England and Wales in 1892 amounted to 589,532, but only 172,225 prisoners were committed to local prisons.[43]

Police statistics are the best index of crime simply because large numbers of crimes are regularly reported for which no one is apprehended.[44] The average annual number of indictable crimes

---

[40] *Ibid.*, chap. 13.
[41] Morrison, *Crime and Its Causes*, p. 204.
[42] Morrison, "Interpretation of Criminal Statistics," *op. cit.* note 2.
[43] *Ibid.*, p. 2.
[44] In connection with unapprehended criminals, Morrison suggested a type of legal compensation to those who were convicted. He proposed that punishment be increased in point of magnitude as it fell short in point of certainty. Sentences for a given crime should be graduated in the various counties of England according to the local apprehension-rate of criminals. For example, in the metropolis 34 persons were apprehended for

known to the police for the period 1890–1894 was 83,777; whereas the average annual number of prosecutions for indictable offenses for the same period was 56,070. It would, of course, be a mistake to suppose that even the police statistics were complete, for the actual number of offenses committed annually is always in excess of the amount of officially recorded crime.[45]

With this as the essence of his paper, Morrison proceeds to elaborate upon the disadvantages and compensations of each of the sources of criminal statistics. In developing the topic, it is of interest to note that he discusses a phenomenon which recently has been called the categoric risk of offenses, one expression of which is the relation between the accuracy of statistics and the gravity of the offense. Morrison demonstrates this relationship by referring to the rate of drunkenness from 1874 to 1894, which according to the official statistics was decreasing, despite the fact that the 53d annual report of the Registrar-General stated that "the deaths attributed to intemperance have increased year by year since 1884 and in 1890 were both absolutely and relatively to the population more numerous than in any previous year." It is clear to Morrison that the decrease in intemperance is illusory and to be explained by the more tolerant attitude of the police toward the drinking class.[46]

The increase in crime

Morrison's almost obsessive concern with the interpretation of criminal statistics was not without direction. His analysis of the procedural aspects of data collection, his attention to attitudinal changes on the part of the police and public, his consideration of shifts in judicial policy—in a word, his intensive examination of the *meaning* of criminal statistics—are all utilized to substantiate an unshakable conviction that is central to his entire system of thought and consequently permeated all of his writing: crime is increasing in England and Wales.[47] Although Morrison discusses the movement of crime in the first chapters of his two books, it is in an article

every 100 crimes. In the south and southwestern counties 73 were apprehended for every 100 crimes committed. Morrison held that since the person who was convicted in the south and southwest had chances of detection that were 39% better than one living in the metropolis, this person should have his sentence shortened by 39% of what it would otherwise be. W. D. Morrison, "Excessive Sentences," *The Times* (London), 2 February 1892, p. 12.

45 Morrison, "Interpretation of Criminal Statistics," p. 3.
46 *Ibid.*, pp. 8–9. For a complete statement of categoric risks in crime, see Walter C. Reckless, *The Crime Problem* (New York, 1961), chap. 3.
47 Morrison discusses the increase of crime in Liverpool in "Excessive Sentences."

published in the *Nineteenth Century* in 1892 that this subject is covered most pointedly and systematically. In it the movement of crime in England and Wales was tested by an investigation of the statistics of cases tried, both summarily and on indictment, during the three decades from 1860 to 1889. The yearly average of cases tried in the decade 1860–1869 was 466,687; in 1870–1879 it was 628,027; and in 1880–1889 the number reached 701,060. "The most superficial glance at these figures is enough to show that the total volume of crime has increased very materially within the period to which they refer." Although the creation of new offenses, especially the Elementary Education Acts of 1870, had fostered the growth of crime in the last two decades, this was counterbalanced by the abolition in recent years of several old penal laws, as well as by the greater reluctance of the police to set the law in motion against trivial offenders. In any case, the fact remained that in the last three decades crime had steadily increased. Morrison shows that this was not only an absolute but a relative increase: in 1860–1869 one case was tried annually for every 44 citizens of England and Wales; in 1880–1889 one case was tried for every 38 inhabitants.[48]

To test whether crime was increasing in severity along with its expansion in absolute volume, Morrison presented figures on the yearly average of indictable offenses tried: in 1860–1869 there were 19,149 such cases, in the second decade there were 15,817, and in the last decade 14,058. Although at first glance these figures would seem to indicate a decrease in serious crime, certain preliminary observations were forthcoming. In the last two decades, as a result of the passage of the Summary Jurisdiction Act, a large number of offenses which previously (1860–1869) were indictable could now be disposed of summarily. In order to arrive at an accurate estimate of serious crime committed in the first decade as compared with the following two decades, Morrison selected murder as representative of a serious offense[49] unaffected by changes of public feeling or judicial procedure within the period under study. Accordingly, he

[48] W. D. Morrison, "The Increase of Crime," *Nineteenth Century*, Vol. 31, pp. 950–952.
[49] Undoubtedly Morrison's most articulate detractor was E. F. Du Cane, whose article "The Decrease of Crime" appeared in the *Nineteenth Century* (Vol. 33, p. 480) less than a year after Morrison's "The Increase of Crime." Du Cane takes Morrison to task for the way in which he determined the increase in juvenile crime, for interpreting an enlargement of the police force as indicative of a growth in the criminal class, and for relying upon "the most serious of crimes" as representative of serious crime in general. By utilizing police testimony and by a careful critical analysis of Morrison's statistical presentation, Du Cane arrives at conclusions which are in direct opposition to Morrison's. The compelling validity of many of Du Cane's arguments cannot be easily dismissed.

found that in 1860–1869 the yearly average of murders reported to the police was 126 [50] as contrasted with 160 reported in 1880–1889. He concludes, therefore, that the decrease in the number of indictable offenses from 1860–1889 cannot be attributed to an actual decrease in serious crime. In passing on to examine the movement of juvenile crime, he discovered a steady upward trend: the yearly average committed to prison in the decade 1860–1869 was 127,690 as compared with 170,827 in 1880-1889; the annual average of juveniles in reformatory and industrial schools in the first ten-year period was 6,834 and rose to 25,505 in the last decade. This despite the enormous expansion of philanthropic enterprise in the form of homes for the young and assistance to the destitute.[51]

Prison and prisoners

Morrison had little confidence in the effectiveness of imprisonment.

> We are sometimes told that the existing English prison system is the best in the world. And if the value of a prison system is to be measured by its uniformity of discipline, its attention to cleanliness, its machine-like methods of dealing with convicted men, no doubt our prisons need not shrink from comparison with other institutions of a similar kind abroad.[52]

He was never at a loss in answering his critics who pointed to the decrease in the prison population in very recent years (which Morrison never denied) as evidence that crime was not increasing and that imprisonment was exerting some deterrent effect. This method of reasoning, he argued, was fallacious because the rise and fall of the prison population depends upon many circumstances besides the amount of crime.[53] An increasing proportion of those who are convicted of crime are not sentenced to prison but are nonetheless criminal. In 1868 the number of summary convictions was 372,707 and the number imprisoned 95,263. The number convicted summarily in 1887 had risen to 538,930, but the number sentenced to

---

[50] It is curious that Morrison, having decided to use cases tried as the criterion of the movement of crime, suddenly switches to police statistics when referring to the offense of murder.

[51] Morrison, "Increase of Crime," pp. 952–955. Morrison apparently overlooks or discounts the possibility that the rising number of juveniles in reformatory and industrial schools reflects a greater social consciousness expressed in the concern for the young, rather than an increase in juvenile crime.

[52] W. D. Morrison, "Are Our Prisons a Failure?" *Fortnightly Review*, Vol. 61, p. 460.

[53] W. D. Morrison, "The Study of Crime," *Mind: Quarterly Review of Psychology and Philosophy*, Vol. 1, p. 493.

prison had fallen to 78,438.   In other words, the number of convicted
persons sentenced to prison had decreased from 25 percent in 1868
to 14 percent in 1887.   Similar results are found in the case of serious
offenses.[54]   Hence, the diminution of the English prison population
of late is accounted for by the imposition of shorter sentences and
the substitution of other forms of repression.[55]

But what does the prison do psychologically and socially to its
inhabitants?

> Imprisonment so far from serving the purpose of protecting society adds
> considerably to its dangers. The casual offender is the person to whom crime
> is merely an isolated incident in an otherwise law-abiding life. The habitual
> criminal is a person to whom crime has become a trade; he is a person who
> makes his living by preying on the community. The prison is the breeding
> ground of the habitual criminal. The habitual offender is the casual of-
> fender to begin with. But the prison deteriorates him, debases him mentally
> and morally, reduces him to a condition of apathy, unfits and indisposes him
> for the tasks and duties of life; and when liberated he is infinitely more dan-
> gerous to society than when he entered it. It is not sufficiently recognized
> that punishment may be of a character which defeats the ends of justice.[56]

Morrison reasoned that the increase in annual expenditures in
connection with crime was due primarily to the augmentation of the
habitual criminal class.

> Is it to be supposed that the borough and county authorities . . . are con-
> tinually adding to the dimensions of the police force for the mere pleasure of
> seeing a larger proportion of the adult male population walking about in blue
> uniforms? The idea will not bear a moment's examination. . . . The in-
> crease in the police force will go on, and the growth of expenditure on crime
> will go on, until we can succeed in reducing the dimensions of recidivism.[57]

Though Morrison disparaged imprisonment, he did feel there
were certain advantages to be gained from locally controlled and
operated prisons in contrast to the system of centralized prison administration which was currently in existence. Morrison's inquiries
revealed that during the last five years of local prison administration
(1873–1877) the number of offenders recommitted to prison after
one or more convictions amounted to 40 percent of the prison population. During the last five years of the new system (1888–1892) the
number of recommittals increased to 48 percent. Moreover, the rate

[54] Morrison, "Excessive Sentences."
[55] Morrison, "Interpretation of Criminal Statistics," p. 13.
[56] W. D. Morrison, "Prison Reform: Prisons and Prisoners," *Fortnightly Review*, Vol. 69,
p. 782.
[57] Morrison, "Are Our Prisons a Failure?" p. 467.

of insanity among prisoners under the centralized system was twice that under local prison administration. And individualized treatment was more likely to occur under local prison authority.[58] For these reasons Morrison supported a Prisons Bill, the object of which was to "decentralize an over-centralized system, to distribute responsibility, to establish a healthy balance of power within the administration, to make accurate information accessible to the Home Secretary, and through him to the public at large." On the more specific level of the daily life of the prisoner, the bill proposed (1) to shorten the offender's stay in prison by making the duration of his sentence dependent on the proportion of the fine he is able to pay, and (2) to allow prisoners sentenced to nine months and over to earn a remission of their sentence equivalent to one-quarter of its duration.[59] Apparently this bill never became law, since it was not again alluded to in print.

Density of population

Although Morrison consistently held that the causes of crime were multiple and were to be found in the interaction of the social and individual factors previously discussed, he did isolate one factor which he considered essentially responsible for the increase in crime.

With respect to the growth of crime in general, my opinion is that the increasing density of population is to a large extent accountable for it. It may be set down as a tolerably accurate axiom that the more dense a community is, the more offenses it commits in proportion to its members. . . . The following statistics for the 20 years 1857–76 will explain the intimate connection between density of population and crime. In 1871 Wiltshire, Dorset, Devon, Cornwall, and Somerset contained 238 persons to the square mile and had .59 indictable offenses per 1,000 inhabitants; Yorkshire had 402 persons to the square mile and .79 indictable offenses; Cheshire and Lancashire had 1,131 persons to the square mile and 1.22 indictable crimes. Crime, therefore, tends to grow in consequence, to a considerable extent, of the greater concentration of the population.[60]

In turn, the increasing density of population is caused by a growing tendency of the community to congregate in large cities: "A highly concentrated population fosters lawless and immoral instincts in such a multitude of ways that it is only an expression of literal exactitude to call the great cities of today the nurseries of modern

[58] *Ibid.*, pp. 463, 468, 461.
[59] Morrison, "Prison Reform," pp. 786–787.
[60] Morrison, "Excessive Sentences."

crime." All statistics point in this direction, but it can be understood, contends Morrison, without the aid of figures. The aggregation of large multitudes within restricted areas heightens the chances of conflict and thereby promotes opportunities for crime. Moreover, a population in this crowded state has to be restrained and controlled on all sides by a formidable network of laws; and as every new law forbids something previously permitted, a multiplication of laws is necessarily followed by an increase of crime. Besides these evils, Morrison goes on, the immense concentration of property within such areas generates a host of temptations, and a thieving class is developed which possesses unlimited opportunities for theft.[61]

Contemporary in all but time

The essential content of Morrison's thought-system in criminology was developed and reached maturity in the late nineteenth and early twentieth century. He was nonetheless remarkably advanced in the pursuit and substance of his subject. He shared with present-day social scientists a calm commitment to social reform. He looked at the society of his time and saw in it social miseries from which it had to be liberated, if higher forms of civilized life were to be attained. These problems—unemployment, pauperism, insanity, crime —may have differed in external appearance. But at a deeper level they were strongly united: each was intimately connected with the other and collectively they constituted the Social Problem. Morrison hoped that in his own way he could contribute to the solution of the Great Problem by studying a small part of it.

The work of William Douglas Morrison was characterized by the demand for cautious interpretation of criminal statistics, the insistence on understanding the conditions surrounding the data before drawing inferences from them, the reliance upon empirical confirmation whenever possible, the emphasis placed upon the study of the offender as well as the offense, the enunciation of what was tantamount to a theory of differential association, disapproval of capital punishment and dissatisfaction with imprisonment as a solution to the problem, the stress upon classification of offenders in an effort to individualize treatment, the rejection of intemperance and economic conditions as the primary causes of crime, and the analysis of criminal behavior as the result of certain major individual and

[61] Morrison, "Increase of Crime," p. 956.

social factors working interdependently relatively free of free-will. The validity of his ideas is attested to by the fact that they have become an integral part of the contemporary criminological scene.

GERALD D. ROBIN.

BIBLIOGRAPHY

By Morrison

Crime and Its Causes. London, 1891.
Juvenile Offenders. London, 1896; New York, 1897.
"Reflections on the Theories of Criminality." *Journal of Mental Science,* Vol. 35 (1889), p. 14.
"The Increase of Crime." *Nineteenth Century,* Vol. 31 (1892), p. 950.
"The Problem of Crime." *Mind: Quarterly Review of Psychology and Philosophy,* Vol. 1 (1892), p. 489.
"Are Our Prisons a Failure?" *Fortnightly Review,* Vol. 61 (1894), p. 459.
"The Interpretation of Criminal Statistics." *Journal of the Royal Statistical Society,* Vol. 60 (1897), p. 1.
"Prison Reform: Prisons and Prisoners." *Fortnightly Review,* Vol. 63 (1898), p. 781.
"The Criminal Problem." *Sociological Review,* Vol. 1 (1908), p. 34.

General

CARR-SAUNDERS, SIR ALEXANDER MORRIS; MANNHEIM, HERMANN; and RHODES, E. C. *Young Offenders: An Enquiry into Juvenile Delinquency.* Cambridge, England, 1942.
DU CANE, E. F. "The Decrease of Crime." *Nineteenth Century,* Vol. 33 (1893), p. 480.
FERRI, ENRICO. *Criminal Sociology.* London, 1895; New York, 1896.
LOMBROSO, CESARE, and FERRERO, GUGLIELMO. *The Female Offender.* London, 1895; New York, 1895.
"Is Crime Increasing?" *Popular Science Monthly,* Vol. 43 (1893), p. 399.

NOTE ON THE CONTRIBUTOR

Dr. GERALD D. ROBIN was Director of the Evaluation and Research Unit, Philadelphia Regional Office of the Pennsylvania Governor's Justice Commission. He was previously Director of Social Science Research at National Analysts, Inc., a survey research organization.

Dr. Robin served as a consultant to the President's Commission on Law Enforcement and Administration of Justice, and has taught at the University of Pennsylvania and at La Salle College. Several of his research contributions have appeared in the professional literature. He is currently Associate Professor, Division of Criminal Justice, at the University of New Haven.

18

ENRICO FERRI

1856–1929

WHEN Enrico Ferri died, April 12, 1929, one of the most colourful and influential figures in the history of criminology disappeared. Born at San Benedetto Po in the province of Mantua, February 25, 1856, his active life spanned more than half a century, beginning with the publication of his dissertation in 1878 and ending with the fifth edition of his *Criminal Sociology*, which was being printed when he died. During the intervening five decades he became the acknowledged leader of the so-called positive school of criminal science, a highly successful trial lawyer and Italy's perhaps greatest contemporary forensic orator, Member of Parliament, editor of the socialist newspaper *Avanti*, indefatigable public lecturer, university professor, author of highly esteemed scholarly works, founder of a great legal journal, and a tireless polemicist in defence of his ideas. His was a rich and varied life, to which no brief article can do justice.

In the book which Ferri published in 1928 on the *Principles of Criminal Law*,[1] a work which contained the systematic presentation of the legal principles of the positive school, he listed what he himself regarded as his most important contributions. They were the demonstration that the concept of freedom of will has no place in criminal law; that social defence is the purpose of criminal justice; the three types of factors in crime causation; the classification of criminals in five classes; penal substitutes as means of indirect social defence; motivation, rather than the objective nature of the crime, as the basis for sanctions; the demand that farm colonies be substituted for cellular isolation of prisoners by day; the indeterminate sentence instead of the dosage by fixed terms of institutionalisation; the demand that hospitals for the criminal insane be

---

* Reproduced from *The Journal of Criminal Law, Criminology and Police Science*, Vol. 48, No. 5, January–February 1958.
[1] *Principii di diritto criminale* (xvi, 848 pp., Torino, 1928, UTET).

established; the abolition of the jury; the stress on the use of indemnification as a sanction in public law; and the principle that the crime must be studied in the offender.

Other observers have been inclined to add to this list his invention of the term the "born criminal," the introduction of the concept of legal rather than moral responsibility, his pioneer work in establishing criminal sociology and his propaganda for the scientific training of judges and correctional personnel.

One manner (usually chosen for a brief biography) of dealing with the work of Enrico Ferri would be to pass quickly over his personal life and systematically indicate the nature of his scientific and philosophical contributions in their final form. But anyone who has immersed himself in the writings of Ferri and about him would agree that Ferri, the man, is as fascinating as Ferri, the scholar. In this article I shall therefore attempt both to tell the story of his life and to show the gradual development of his thinking on criminological and criminal law problems, especially during his youth and early manhood.

Ferri's early life

Ferri was the son of a poor salt and tobacco shop keeper.[2] His early education was somewhat perturbed—private tutoring for two years, then two years at a school in Mantua where he "learned nothing," failure in an examination when he tried to jump a school year, transfer to another school where he was almost expelled for truancy (he had become a bicycle enthusiast), taken out of school by his father who threatened to put him to manual labour, repentance after a week and return to the *ginnasio*, where shortly he took a successful final examination qualifying him to enter the *Liceo Virgilio* in Mantua.

At the Liceo, he made a beginning at finding himself. Not yet sixteen, he fell under the influence of a great teacher, Roberto Ardigò, who had just published a book, *Psychology as a Positive Science*, and had left his clerical robe to devote himself to independent philosophical study. The adolescent Ferri found in Ardigò's lectures a brain food " which decided my scientific

---

[2] Biographical details have been garnered from the book of his disciple and co-worker Bruno Franchi, entitled *Enrico Ferri, il noto, il mal noto, e l'ignorato* (183 pp., Torino, 1908, Bocca) and from autobiographical notes frequently found scattered in Ferri's writings.

orientation for the rest of my life." [3]   Among other subjects, he made a fine record in mathematics and showed an interest in Latin; he simply ignored the requirement in Greek and was forced to " cheat " in his final examination for the diploma. [4]

Ferri now enrolled at the University of Bologna where he was to spend three years. The first two of them were evidently much devoted to extra-curricular student activities. He attended the lectures in legal medicine and in criminal law, the latter given by Pietro Ellero, a prominent representative of the so-called " classical school." The third year he settled down to serious study. It was then he conceived a thesis in which he tried to demonstrate that the concept of free will, implicit in the current criminal law, was a fiction, and that the pretended moral responsibility of a criminal based on that fiction should give way to the concept of social or legal responsibility, almost every person, regardless of his nature, being " socially accountable " for his actions by the fact that he was a member of society and not because he was capable of willing the illegal act. The thesis was brilliantly defended in 1877 and won him a scholarship.

He had struck his first blow at the theories of the classical school and proceeded promptly to spend the next academic year at the University of Pisa, where the acknowledged master and leader of the traditional philosophy of criminal law, Francesco Carrara, held the chair in that subject. Ferri attended lectures, argued with everybody about his ideas (he was nicknamed " free will Ferri ") and practised his own system of elocution in preparation for a teaching career. Later he referred to these exercises in the following words: " At Pisa I did not as yet think of the bar, being all immersed in the thought of gaining a university chair in spite of my scientific heterodoxy. But in the interest of this future chair I felt

---

[3] Ferri often acknowledged Ardigò's influence, especially in a brief article, " Ricordi liceali," which he contributed to a volume in honour of his teacher in 1898 and reprinted in his *Studi sulla criminalità ed altri saggi* (viii, 542 pp., Torino, 1901, Bocca), pp. 474–477. See also his commemorative article, " Roberto Ardigò," published after Ardigò's suicide in 1920 in *La Scuola Positiva*, ser. 3, Vol. 11, pp. 289–294 (1920).

[4] His stratagem apparently evoked no moral indignation, for in later life Ferri told the story publicly. In a defence speech in a forgery case in 1923, while discussing signatures, he mentioned how he invented his own characteristic one. " During the examination for the liceal diploma, I made a show of writing the paper in Greek, which I did not know and which was written by my very dear fellow student Achille Loria. To distract the professor's attention, I began writing my name in various ways and finally in the manner I have since repeated for fifty years." See his *Difese penali* (3 vols., 3rd ed., Milano, 1925, UTET), Vol. 2, p. 686. Ferri had reciprocated by writing Loria's examination in mathematics.

a need to engage in pulmonary gymnastics, make speaking easy
and acquire the habit of order and clarity of exposition. I forced
myself daily—at spots removed from the traffic on the beaches,
along the Arno outside the city—to talk aloud for an hour at a
stretch, improvising on some topic which I picked at random from
a number of cards that I had prepared and put into my pocket
before leaving home." [5]

Part of the year was spent in revising his dissertation and preparing it for the printer. Before the end of the term, Carrara, who
must have regarded his twenty-year-old opponent with a mixture of
amusement and irritation, and once exclaimed that " instead of
learning from us Ferri has come to teach us," permitted him to
deliver a lecture on criminal attempts from the point of view of the
" newer ideas." It was to be the first of many, for three years
before his death, he estimated that he had by then delivered some
2,300 university lectures and over 600 public lectures of a scientific
nature (on some forty topics), not counting addresses in court and
thousands of political speeches.[6]

Lombroso on Ferri and Ferri on Lombroso

When he published his dissertation in the summer of 1878,[7] he
sent a copy to Lombroso who had just brought out the second
edition of his *Criminal Man*. Years later, Ferri reported that
Lombroso " responded in an encouraging and congratulatory manner, but . . . gave our mutual friend Filippo Turati . . . the
following appraisal of my book, in which I explicitly affirmed my
intention to apply the positive method to the science of criminal
law: ' Ferri isn't positivist enough! ' I remember that at that time,
burdened as I was by a remnant of scholastic and metaphysical
concepts (because of which, as Garofalo said, and as I have since
declared and demonstrated in successive publications, my theory of
imputability was little in harmony with the preceding negation of
free will and with the beginning renovation of the criminal law)
Lombroso's opinion seemed to me inexact and exaggerated. And I
wrote to Turati: ' What! Does Lombroso suggest that I, a lawyer,

---

[5] *Difese penali*, Vol. III, p. 5.

[6] Cited by Teresa Labriola in an article on " Enrico Ferri," in *Scritti in onore di Enrico
Ferri per il cinquantesimo anno di suo insegnamento universitario* (526 pp., Torino,
1929, UTET), p. 265.

[7] *La negazione del libero arbitrio e la teorica dell'imputabilità* (476 pp.).

should go and measure the heads of criminals in order to be positivist enough?!'"[8]

Ferri would, within a few years, answer that question of his in the affirmative, but at the moment he was getting ready to leave for France, having won a travelling fellowship by his dissertation. He was to spend a year in Paris. He had set for himself the task of making a study of the trends and characteristics of criminality in France during half a century, using the data of the judicial criminal statistics which had been appearing since 1826, and which had been little exploited by scholars since the early days of Quételet and Guerry.

The collection of the data for his project absorbed a great deal of his time, but he also studied German at Melzi's institute (he never really learned English), attended the lectures of Laboulaye, political theorist, and Quatrefages, physical anthropologist, and wrote a lengthy review of Lombroso's book. In November 1878 he sent the review to the *Rivista Europea* which published it.[9]

He commended Lombroso for having " gone in search of the characteristics that should reveal to us . . . the habitual, incorrigible criminal, who is such . . . because of the inexorable tyranny of his own organic constitution, inherited from his ancestors; a criminal who persists in evil . . . and who is not reformable by the old spiritualistic systems, according to which man commits a crime or is good, reforms or relapses solely by the fiat of his own will and not due to the necessary effect of the conditions in which he is placed by a given environment." He was especially pleased to see so many case histories in the book, for they provided "a vivid scientific material for anyone who wants to search for general juridical principles, not in abstractions of metaphysical character but in the study of those living beings who, while absent from all ancient and modern treatises of criminal law, encounter us at every step in the courts of assizes and the lower courts. He [*i.e.,* Lombroso] thus offers us a first ray of light to dispel the most serious contradictions at least, which in practice always arise between the conclusions of psychiatry and the so-called eternal verities of an aprioristic criminal science."

[8] Enrico Ferri, " Polemica in difesa della scuola criminale positiva " (1886). Reprinted in *Studi sulla criminalità ed altri saggi*, pp. 234–329; p. 245; extract from a symposium with the same title, of which he, Lombroso, Garofalo and Fioretti were co-authors.
[9] " Studi Critici su *L'Uomo delinquente* del Prof. C. Lombroso." Reprinted in *Studi sulla criminalità ed altri saggi*, pp. 1–12.

As for the statement by Lombroso that crime is a natural necessity—a statement which had caused his critics to point out that one could hardly punish a person unless one assumed his moral responsibility—Ferri simply replied that Lombroso had been grossly misunderstood. Crime is not a social need but it is inevitable in society. But equally inevitable is the law, because society believes that punishments are necessary and inevitable for its protection. Since society has the right to defend itself against aggressors, it has the right to punish. That is all there is to justice. Justice is the will of the majority, which considers a given provision necessary. "When an institution is desired by the majority of the citizens as being necessary for the public welfare, it is—and only because of this—just." Ferri was to be quite consistent in holding this view. Toward the end of his life it helped him to come to terms with fascism and even to accept, within certain limits, the death penalty to which he had been a lifelong opponent.

Studying with Lombroso at the University of Turin

If he had not been a complete positivist when he left Italy, his stay in France completed his education. He later looked upon his study of the French criminal statistics and his attendance at the lectures of Quatrefages as a "healthful naturalistic bath from which I issued a true and convinced positivist." It is not that he accepted the positivistic philosophy *in toto*, but that he would from then on repeatedly declare that the "experimental," *i.e.*, inductive method of investigation, the method of Galileo and Bacon, was the only one that would yield knowledge that would permit a nation to deal intelligently with the problem of crime.

It is not surprising that Ferri went to the University of Turin the following year: Lombroso was professor of legal medicine there. Some time before he left Paris in the spring of 1879, Ferri had asked the Council of Higher Education in Rome for a licence as titular docent in criminal law and had also applied to the University of Turin for a docentship in criminal procedure with the right to hold examinations. To qualify for this latter position he lectured on the jury system before the examining committee. He remained a consistent opponent to jury trials for ordinary crimes, for in a scientifically oriented court procedure, judges trained in the social and psychological sciences would be better able to dispose of offenders properly. The lecture, which won him the docentship, grew into a celebrated monograph published late in 1880.

In the Council of Rome, Ferri's application faced tough opposition. One very influential Council member, averse to his views, nearly defeated his application, but finally he received his licence and promptly afterward gave his introductory lecture at the University on " Penal Substitutes." [10] By this term he meant all the social measures, including non-criminal legislation, which a nation might take in order to prevent crime and thereby reduce the need for using criminal sanctions. It was in this lecture that he stated what he called his law of criminal saturation, according to which the level of a country's criminality is determined by factors in the social environment and changes when they change.

Ferri completed his analysis of the French data and prepared a manuscript for publication while he was in Turin.[11] He had begun that research because he recognised that Lombroso's studies, which had been largely limited to habitual and insane prisoners, dealt only with a narrow aspect of the problem of criminality. " Crime," he said, " like every other human action, is the effect of multiple causes, which, although always interlaced in an indissoluble net, can nevertheless be separated for research purposes. The factors of crime are anthropological or individual, physical or telluric, and social. Anthropological factors are: the offender's age, sex, civil status, occupation, residence, social class, degree of training and education, organic and mental constitution. Physical factors are: race, climate, fertility and distribution of soil, the daily cycle, the seasons, the meteorological factors, the annual temperature. Social factors are: increase or decrease of population, migration, public opinion, customs and religion, the nature of the family; political, financial and commercial life; agricultural and industrial production and distribution; public administration of safety, education and welfare; penal and civil legislation, in general." [12]

He chose the social factors for investigation for two good reasons: the scope of the investigation of the " phenomenon of crime " needed to be widened, and these factors had a more direct

---

[10] " Dei sostitutivi penali," *Arch. di psichiatria*, Vol. 1, 1880.
[11] *Studi sulla criminalità in Francia del 1826 al 1878, secondo i dati contenuti nei* " Comptes generaux de L'administration de la Justice criminelle." *Annali di statistica*, serl. 2, Vol. 21, 1881; reprinted in *Studi sulla criminalità ed altri saggi*, pp. 17-59. Citations are to the reprint.
[12] *Ibid*. p. 18.

relationship with sociology and legislative practice. Even when the legislator in this area of " social pathology " had some understanding of the importance of anthropological and physical factors there was little he could do to modify them; social factors could be influenced because they were more tractable. His findings convinced him of the wisdom of his judgment, for he arrived at the conclusion that criminality had shown an enormous increase (*i.e.*, total criminality, divided into offences against persons, property and public order) in France, and at the conviction that since both physical and anthropological factors undergo relatively minor changes in time, changes in the social environment must have been responsible for the increase.[13]

This first empirical study of Ferri's, begun in a positivistic spirit and pursued with great skill, was very well received. He was soon after (1882) appointed by the Minister of Justice, Zanardelli, a member of the Commission on Judicial and Notarial Statistics and remained as such for a dozen years.

Ferri had gone to Turin, because of his belief that " in order to formulate principles concerning crimes, penalties and criminals, it is first necessary to study . . . criminals and prisons, since facts should precede theories. I therefore went for a year to Turin to study with Lombroso and, as his student, visited prisons, mental hospitals and laboratories." [14] It was the year in which Lombroso started to edit his periodical, the *Archivio di psichiatria*. Ferri contributed to its first volume not only his lecture on penal substitutes but also a paper on the relationship of criminal anthropology and criminal law,[15] which contained what he always regarded as one of his basic ideas, a scientific classification of criminals, which would serve as the basis for a rational system of sanctions. In presenting this classification, consisting of five classes, he coined the term " born criminal " to designate the atavistic type which Lombroso believed he had identified. The classification included " (1) the born or

[13] Two decades later, Ferri added a footnote to the reprinted study, in which he congratulated himself on having stressed the importance of social factors as early as in 1880. This, he said, proved that Italian and French critics, who claimed that the positive school dealt only with anthropological factors, were wrong. It also served " to explain the logical evolution of my thinking, which has gradually, but on the basis of scientific research in the field of both general and of criminal sociology, arrived at the ultimate consequences of socialistic doctrines." *Ibid.* p. 19.
[14] " Polemica in difesa della scuola criminale positiva," *loc. cit.*
[15] " Dei limiti fra diritto penale ed antropologia criminale," Arch.di psich. I, p. 444 *et seq.*, 1880–81.

instinctive criminal, who carries from birth, through unfortunate heredity from his progenitors (criminals, alcoholics, syphilitics, subnormals, insane, neuropathics, etc.), a reduced resistance to criminal stimuli and also an evident and precocious propensity to crime; (2) the insane criminal, affected by a clinically identified mental disease or by a neuropsychopathic condition which groups him with the mentally diseased; (3) the passional criminal, who, in two varieties, the criminal through passion (a prolonged and chronic mental state) or through emotion (explosive and unexpected mental state), represents a type at the opposite pole from the criminal due to congenital tendencies and, besides having good personal antecedents, has a normal moral character, even though he is nervously very excitable; (4) the occasional criminal who constitutes the majority of lawbreakers and is the product of family and social milieu more than of abnormal personal physico-mental conditions, and therefore has psychological traits less deviating from those of the social class to which he belongs; (5) the habitual criminal, or rather, the criminal by acquired habit, who is mostly a product of the social environment in which, due to abandonment by his family, lack of education, poverty, bad companions in urban centres, already in his childhood begins as an occasional offender; add to this his moral deformation, caused or not hindered by contemporary prison systems where he enters into contacts with other and worse criminals in the prisons, as well as the difficulties of social readaptation once he has served his term, and he will acquire the habit of criminality and, besides constant recidivism, may actually come to make crime a trade." [16]

Ferri did not believe that every criminal always fitted completely into his classification. Classes do not exist in nature, he said, but they are a necessary instrument by which the human mind can better understand the multiform reality of things. In daily life, criminals would often not appear so well defined as the classification suggested. Rather, a judge would find that the defendant would present mixed characteristics. This realisation was to cause Ferri, in a near future, to study the murderer with greater care in order to acquire knowledge about aggressive dangerous criminals that would aid judges in identifying them as such.

[16] As elaborated in his *L'Omicida nella psicologia e nella psicopatologia criminale*, 2nd ed. —*L'Omicidio-Suicidio. Responsabilità giuridica*, 5th ed. (xii, 768 pp., Torino, 1925, UTET), pp. 54–55.

The classification remained unchanged in Ferri's mind for most
of his life. In fact, his addition of a sixth class in the fifth edition
of his *Sociologia Criminale* (1929–30) appears to have been a kind
of afterthought which, although clear, was so poorly integrated that
he forgot or had no time to revise other sections of his book that
still mentioned only five classes. Even his co-worker, Arturo Santoro, who had seen his book through the press, later mentions only
the five classes in his biography of Ferri. Yet, in the work just mentioned, Ferri said: " To these five categories of voluntary criminals
it is necessary to add a class, which is becoming more and more
numerous in our mechanical age and in the vertiginous speed of
modern life, namely, the involuntary criminals. . . . They are
pseudo-criminals who cause damage and peril by their lack of foresight, imprudence, negligence or disobedience of regulations rather
than through malice, and they represent various degrees of
dangerousness." Some of them have a weak sense of moral sensi-
tivity, some lack technical knowledge, some are inattentive, and
others are exhausted.[17]

Between Ferri and the twenty years older Lombroso there began
a deep and lasting friendship marked by mutual respect and profit
to both, for while Ferri owed much of his system of ideas to the
stimulation of Lombroso, he also became the catalyst who synthesised the latter's concepts with those of the sociologist and had no
little influence on Lombroso's thinking.

Ferri the teacher

Ferri stayed but a year in Turin. Pietro Ellero had been
appointed a justice of the Supreme Court and before he left his chair
at Bologna he expressed the desire that Ferri be appointed as his
successor. Ferri thus returned to his Alma Mater as professor of
criminal law three years after receiving his degree. In December
1880, before he was twenty-five years old, he held his introductory
lecture on the subject of " the new horizons in criminal law and
procedure." One present described it as one of those events " that
are epoch-making in university annals." The young professor
" spoke impassionately for two hours, with growing enthusiasm,
irresistibly. Borne upon impetuous waves of eloquence were the

---

[17] *Sociologia criminale*, 5th ed., Vol. II, pp. 295–296.

daring, magnificent and original ideas dressed in a limpid, imaginative, exact and always challenging prose." [18]   It was this lecture which grew into his best-known work, the *Criminal Sociology*.[19]

Ferri was a born and imaginative teacher.   He began at Bologna a plan which he continued to follow later in teaching criminal law —he took his students on a tour of penal institutions and mental hospitals, true to his belief that the future system of criminal justice must be administered by people who have a knowledge of the criminal.

In the fall of 1881 he began a study of 699 prisoners in the prisons of Castelfranco Emilia and Pesaro, 301 insane in the mental hospital of Bologna and 711 soldiers in the military barracks of Bologna, the soldiers being a control group so selected that they would belong to the same sections of Italy from which the experimental groups came.   The research was based on individual case studies.   He assembled as much information about each individual as possible from the institution's records, observed each prisoner discretely in his cell or in the prison yard, interviewed him and examined him for about half an hour, on the average, one part of the examination being somatic, the other psychological.   Out of this research, which occupied him intensively for three years, grew his

---

[18] Quoted in Franchi, *op. cit.* p. 94.

[19] The first and second editions of 1881 and 1884 carried the title *I nuovi orrizonti del diritto e della procedura penale*.   The third edition, with the title of *Sociologia criminale* was issued in 1892.   (He had defined the term criminal sociology in an article published in 1882.)   In the preface Ferri observed that the new title was more in harmony with the content of the book and he characterised the opus as " a work of propaganda and an elementary guide for anyone who intends to dedicate himself to the scientific study of offenders and of the means of prevention and social defence against them.   Hence the almost superabundant citations and the voluminous bibliography."   The fourth edition came in 1900 and he claimed that he had examined all the literature of the previous decade to complete his documentation.   The fifth and final edition was published in two volumes in 1929 (Vol. I) and 1930, posthumously.   Arturo Santoro, who had been assisting Ferri, and who had been asked to complete the footnotes, wrote the preface and saw the work through to publication.   It seems clear that in the nearly three decades between the last two editions, Ferri had found less and less time to keep up with the literature, except that of his own country.   Of the *circa* 4,700 footnote references in the fifth edition less than 1,100 date from this century and 75 per cent. of these are to Italian sources, compared with 48 per cent. of the references to works published before 1900.   Ferri used to say during his later years that he found nothing written of such importance that it had caused him to change his views.

Translations of this or that edition were published in different countries.   A partial translation into English of the third edition appeared in a " Criminology Series," edited by a British clergyman, W. Douglas Morrison (*Criminal Sociology*, xx, 284 pp., London and New York, 1896, Appleton), who, according to Ferri, omitted the entire first section of the work, because it was too heterodox.   The American Institute of Criminal Law and Criminology sponsored a translation of the fourth edition (*Criminal Sociology*, xiv, 577 pp., Boston, 1917, Little, Brown & Co.).

monograph on homicide-suicide and his work on homicide, both of them important.[20]

And so he finally also " measured the heads of criminals! " A few years later, 1886, he was to write: " Having digested and assimilated some kilograms of criminal statistics and added some anthropological researches, I believed that I had gained an adequate enough concept of reality to be able to undertake the construction of a truly positive legal system. That is what I am now doing with the monograph on homicide, studied both naturalistically and juridically, at which I have been working for three years (because positivistic studies are slower and more difficult than the construction of fantastic syllogisms) and which will be, I hope, an eloquent response, for my part, to the minute criticisms now being directed at us even though the scientific edifice of the new school is unfinished (we have worked at it only seven years). . . . Then I also understood clearly what Lombroso meant by his opinion of my first book and therefore I now understand the psychological state of mind and the intellectual phase in which our critics find themselves, for at that time, I too did not have that scientific attitude, which can only be acquired by the methodical examination of facts." [21]

He had already left Bologna, before the works just mentioned were seen in print. In 1882 he accepted a chair at the University of Siena, where he remained for four years. This was a fruitful period of teaching and study. Papers on " the right to punish as a social function " (in which his concept of legal responsibility took final form); " the positive school of criminal law "; " collective property and the class struggle " and " socialism and criminality " were written. The book on homicide-suicide was published and a second edition of his *New Horizons*. The International Prison Congress, in 1885, and the simultaneous first Congress of Criminal Anthropology gave him an opportunity to present his views on prison reform in an address on the cellular (*i.e.*, Pennsylvanian) system

---

[20] Already cited. The monograph on homicide-suicide appeared first serially in 1883–84 in the *Archivio di psich. e scienze penali* and in book form in later editions in 1884, 1892 and 1925. The monograph on homicide was not published until 1895; the second edition of 1925 omitted all the anthropological and statistical data which occupied 216 pages in the first edition, together with several hundred pages of graphic material. The second edition was entirely devoted to the psychology and psychopathology of the homicide and was frankly addressed to judges, prosecutors and defence attorneys. For a comment on the first edition, see H. Zimmern, " Enrico Ferri on Homicide," Pop. Sci.Mo. 49: 678–684, 828–837, September–October 1896.

[21] " Polemica in difesa della scuola criminale positiva," *loc. cit.*

and the labour of prisoners, in which he condemned the cellular system as the greatest mistake of the century.

Ferri the Marxist and " people's orator "

But he was soon to leave, for a long time, the calm atmosphere of the university. In the province of Mantua a large group of peasants were being prosecuted for incitement to civil war, the case having grown out of certain troubles between them and their land-lords. Ferri was engaged as one of their defence attorneys. His brilliant socio-economic address to the court secured their acquittal.[22] Two months later, in May 1886, Mantua elected him a deputy to the national Parliament, where he was to sit, through eleven re-elections, until 1924, representing various boroughs of the country.

The election was a personal victory, because Ferri carried no party label. His studies had brought him close to socialism, but the brand of naïve Utopian socialism current in Italy did not appeal to his rational mind. He had at various times pointed out to those who claimed that a socialist society would eliminate crime that crime is an inevitable phenomenon and that every society, whatever its nature, had its own forms of criminality. Where in a feudal society crimes against the person dominated; in a capitalistic society, crimes of theft and fraud prevailed; in a socialist society, new forms would arise. His Mantuan defence speech revealed how far he had progressed toward a consistent Marxism. At least, it revealed it to Ferri himself who, after re-reading it in 1925, said that doing so made him realise " that already then, in 1886, I was a Marxist without knowing it. The speech is, in fact, completely oriented toward historical materialism (which I have called economic deter-minism) by means of which it can be demonstrated that historical individual and social facts are the direct or indirect product of the underlying and determining economic conditions of the individual and the collectivity." [23]

And so the Ferris moved to Rome. He had married a Florentine woman in 1884, Camilla Guarnieri, a marriage which proved most successful from all points of view and was to give him two sons and a daughter. In Parliament Ferri attached himself to the radical liberals. He had given up his chair at Siena but continued to teach in Rome as " libero docente," wrote about the positive school and

[22] " I contadini Mantovani al processo di Venezia imputati di ' eccitamento alla guerra civile.' " *Difese penali*, Vol. I, pp. 85–156.   [23] *Ibid.* p. 8.

its mission, began to increase his fame as a trial lawyer and started to organise labour co-operatives among the poverty-stricken agricultural workers of Mantua. In 1890 he was—miracle of miracles—called to succeed Francesco Carrara at the University of Pisa, but he was to hold the chair only three years, because Marxian doctrines were becoming known in Italy and he was led, partly by his philosophy of economic determinism and partly by his loyalty to his constituents who were being drawn into the newly organised (1892) Italian Socialist Labour Party, to join the Party in 1893. This act led to the loss of his professorship.

The family now moved to San Dominico, near Fiesole, where he was to live for several years. Life was becoming more and more hectic. Ferri soon discovered the weakness of the Party in Parliament and threw himself into the task of educating the masses. Franchi claims that during twenty years Ferri spent 200 out of 365 nights in a Pullman sleeper. He became the people's orator *par excellence*, lecturing on some forty topics of scientific, historical, economic and sociological character. There was no village in Italy where he had not been at least once; the urbanites heard him more often. In 1896 when the National Socialist Congress decided to start a party newspaper, it was Ferri who went out on a three-weeks' lecture tour to collect the necessary 10,000 lire, and later, during a brief period, he edited the *Avanti*.

In the Parliament he achieved nation-wide attention on more than one occasion, but especially when he led a filibuster against the government in 1899 and particularly when he campaigned for an investigation of graft in the Navy Department. That experience, 1903–06, involved him in law suits. He was even sentenced to eleven months in prison in a criminal libel suit brought by the Minister of the Navy, but finally Parliament set up an investigating commission, which discovered that the charges made by Ferri were true. He was openly praised in Parliament, the sentence against him was dropped and he was called, in 1906,[24] to succeed Impallomeni as professor of criminal law at the University of Rome. He had been a candidate for this chair and for professorships at other universities several times during the previous decade, but had always been by-passed because of his political views and the government's

[24] It was during this period that portraits of Ferri appeared in American magazines. See *Munsey's*, 26:829, March 1902; *World Today*, 9:876, August 1905; *Outlook*, 85:692, May 23, 1907.

preference for more traditional ideas on criminal law, although he had, as already mentioned, been lecturing as " libero docente." He had also given lecture courses at the University of Brussels every other year from 1895 to 1903, and at the School of Advanced Social Studies in Paris in 1889 and 1901, not to mention a lecture tour at Dutch and Flemish universities.

His campaign for the reform of the criminal law had suffered nothing in the meanwhile. In 1892, Ferri had founded a legal journal, *La Scuola Positiva*. This gave the positivists an organ of their own, where they could propagate their ideas. The journal became a worthy opponent to Luigi Lucchini's *Rivista Penale*, chief organ of the classicists, and complemented Lombroso's *Archivio*. He remained editor, or chief of the editorial board, until his death, though he had many collaborators and associates.

In 1908 Ferri went to South America on a lecture tour, giving eighty lectures in 110 days. The tour was evidently handled by some impresario and the topics were chosen to appeal to a lay public. His success was phenomenal. Two years later he returned there at the invitation of universities, when he lectured to professional audiences. He died before he could realise his ambition to lecture in the United States.[25]

His views also became well known abroad due to his participation in nearly all international congresses of criminal anthropology and in many similar congresses of the International Criminalistic Society (now the International Association of Criminal Law); of the International Prison Congresses he attended only the one in Rome, 1885, and the one in London, 1925.

The positive school's projected reforms

The positive school placed great emphasis on trained judges and the professionalisation of all who dealt with crime or criminals. In

---

[25] In addition to his *Criminal Sociology*, translated into English in 1896 and 1917, a few books and articles by Ferri appeared in the United States. The books were *Socialism and Modern Science (Darwin—Spencer—Marx)* (213 pp., *New York*, 1900, Intern.Libr. Publ. Co.) and *The Positive School of Criminology* (125 pp., Chicago, 1913, Charles H. Kerr & Co.). An article of his on " The Delinquent in Art and Literature " appeared in the *Atlantic*, Vol. 60, pp. 233–240, August 1897, and the following appeared in the *Journal of Criminal Law and Criminology*: " Present Movement in Criminal Anthropology " (Part 2 of a symposium on Charles Goring's *The English Convict*), Vol. 5, pp. 224–227, July 1914; " Nomination of a Commission for the Positivist Reform of the Italian Criminal Code," Vol. 11, pp. 67–76, May 1920; " Reform of Penal Law in Italy," Vol. 12, pp. 178–198, August 1921; " A Character Study and Life History of Violet Gibson, who attempted the life of Benito Mussolini on the 7th of April, 1926," Vol. 19, pp. 11–19, August 1928.

1912 Ferri founded, in Rome, a School for Applied Criminal Law and Procedure (*Scuola di applicazione giuridico-criminale*) which drew many students, even from abroad.

Finally, at the end of the First World War, it seemed that the time of harvest had arrived for the positivists. In 1919 the Minister of Justice, Ludovico Mortara, one of Ferri's schoolmates in the Liceo at Mantua, invited him to take the presidency of a commission that would prepare a project of a criminal code to replace the one of 1889. The commission was to have a membership drawn from all the various " schools " of thinking on such matters, but in the end, as a result of resignations, it came to represent mostly a positivistic orientation. The resulting project was presented in 1921 and is the greatest achievement of the positivists, even though it contained some compromises. It was translated into several languages, including English, and was widely distributed.[26] John H. Wigmore, to cite but one example, wrote Ferri on April 17, 1921 : " I am happy to have received the Italian project. It is a masterpiece, even judging from a cursory examination. What a marvellous reward for your patient, brilliant apostolate, which has permitted you to translate your ideas into a code! I hope that the Parliament will approve this project."

This hope was not fulfilled. Post-war Italy became more and more unsettled. The Fascist revolution succeeded because the government was unable to cope with the country's economic and social problems. Ferri had left the Socialist Party before the war and in 1924 he was to close his parliamentary career by refusing re-election. His attempts to save his project failed; the need for a new code was to be filled by one drafted by the new government. Ferri was made a member of the commission which, in 1927, presented a project which was adopted in 1930. In the fifth edition of his *Criminal Sociology*, in connection with a discussion on the need for social reforms that would eliminate poverty and other social evils, he wrote in a footnote: " While in the fourth edition (1900) I alluded hopefully to socialist trends—to which I have given my fervid enthusiasm, especially by the propaganda I have carried on for the moral and social education of the Italian masses—now in the fifth edition (1929) I have to note with regard to Italy that since the influence of the Socialist Party disappeared after the war, because it

---

[26] " Relazione sul Progetto preliminare di Codice Penale Italiano " (Libro I), *La Scuola Positiva*, N.S. I, pp. 1–130, 1921. The project itself follows on pp. 131–156.

neither knew how to make a revolution nor wanted to assume the responsibility of power, the task of the social prevention of criminality was assumed and has begun to be realised by the Fascist Government, which both in the Rocco Project of a Penal Code and in many special statutes has accepted and is putting into effect some of the principles and the most characteristic practical proposals of the positive school." [27]   In theory, he objected to many concepts in the Rocco project, which carried the stamp of the middle of the road school of thinking of the neo-classicists, but as a practical man he viewed it as a step in the right direction and as a partial victory for his idea.   As for Fascism, he saw something of value in it, so far as criminal justice was concerned, because it represented to him a systematic reaffirmation of the authority of the state against the excesses of individualism, which he had always criticised.

His last years were devoted chiefly to the work which was to contain the entire legal formulation of positivistic thought in the field of criminal law.   He had for nearly fifty years taught this subject and out of this teaching grew his *Principles of Criminal Law*, which he sent to the printer the summer before he died.   He was also working on the final revision of his *Criminal Sociology* and had just completed it at his death.   A month before that event he had been nominated Senator, but his confirmation never took place.

Ferri's life and system of ideas

An activity as varied and rich as Ferri's could be exercised only by a man whose life was well organised.   He reserved his mornings from seven to half past twelve for his authorship—the preparation of books, articles, briefs, etc.   In the afternoon he read professional literature, made notes for future use, and took care of his correspondence.   He never worked after eight in the evening and went to bed after his evening meal.   He was abstemious, never smoked, believed in physical exercise and manual labour, which he took some opportunity to engage in during his vacations.   In the summer he usually took his family to different parts of Italy so that his children would become acquainted with them.   During these periods he rested from all work as much as possible.   In August and

[27] *Sociologia criminale*, Vol. I, pp. 11–12. See also his " Fascismo e Scuola Positiva nella difesa sociale contro la criminalità," *La Scuola Positiva*, N.S. 6, pp. 241–274, 1926.

September he travelled to international congresses.   He was no theatre or concert goer; it interfered with his sleep.

As he became more and more famous as a lawyer, he learned more and more about the practice of advocacy.   The lengthy prefaces to the editions of his *Difese penali*, a veritable casebook for the aspiring trial lawyer, are a manual on the art of the advocate, not only how to prepare and develop an oration but on the personal hygiene of the orator.

Ferri's system of ideas has been, at least partially, evoked in the preceding pages.   A remarkable fact is that his basic philosophy of criminal justice and most of his fundamental concepts had been formulated and stated in various publications by the time he was twenty-six years old.   Looking backward, he was able to say, in the preface to his collected essays in 1901, that he was fortunate in that his " early theoretical and practical conclusions were firm, for while their integration has inevitably evolved and been completed and corrected in some details, they have remained basically unchanged."

Ferri was essentially a legal reformer.   His solid contributions to the study of the etiology of criminal conduct were incidental means for achieving a greater understanding of the course which the reformation of criminal justice should take.   A broad vein of practicality ran through all his work; a desire to achieve a demonstrably effective criminal justice, which would afford maximum protection or defence of society against the criminal.

The " positive school " of which Ferri was the chief architect stood in clear opposition to traditional, " classical " criminal jurisprudence.   Historically, the principal reason for the rise of a positivistic view of criminal justice was the necessity . . . to put a stop to the exaggerated individualism in favour of the criminal in order to obtain a greater respect for the rights of honest people who constitute the great majority.[28]   Practically, " the positive school consists of the following: study first the natural origin of crime and then its social and legal consequences in order to provide, by social and legal means, the various remedies which will have the greatest effect on the various causes that produce it.   This is our assumption, this the innovation we have made, not so much in our particular conclusions as in our research method." [29]   Ferri repeatedly contrasted this mode of thinking with that of the " classical

[28] Preface to the Spanish edition of the *New Horizons* . . . , reprinted in *Studi sulla criminalità ed altri saggi*, pp. 320–333; p. 324.   [29] *Ibid.* p. 323.

school." In 1886, he said, in a polemic against the critics of that persuasion, who were attacking the new movement: "Very well, what can we positivists do against such critics? Frankly speaking, nothing. We speak two different languages. For us, the experimental [*i.e.*, inductive] method is the key to all knowledge; to them everything derives from logical deductions and traditional opinion. For them, facts should give place to syllogisms; for us the fact governs and no reasoning can occur without starting with facts, for them science needs only paper, pen and ink and the rest comes from a brain stuffed with more or less abundant reading of books made with the same ingredients. For us science requires spending a long time in examining facts one by one, evaluating them, reducing them to a common denominator, extracting the central idea from them. For them a syllogism or an anecdote suffices to demolish a myriad of facts gathered through years of observation and analysis; for us the reverse is true." [30]

The positive school cultivated a "science of criminality and of social defence against it." As Ferri conceived it, this discipline consisted (1) of the scientific study of the crime as an individual fact (somato-psychological condition of the offender) by anthropology, psychology and criminal psychopathology; and (2) as a social fact (physical and social environmental conditions) by criminal statistics, monographic studies and comparative ethnographic studies —for the purpose of systematising social defence measures (a) of a preventive nature, either indirect or remote (through "penal substitutes") or direct or proximate (by the police); or (b) of a repressive nature through criminal law and procedure, techniques of prison treatment, and after-care. This science Ferri called criminal sociology. (His subordination of criminal law irritated his antagonists immensely; they preferred to look on the social and biological sciences as "auxiliary disciplines" of the criminal law.) Outside of criminal sociology lay certain other essential disciplines: criminal policy, *i.e.*, the art of the legislator in adapting the defensive and repressive defence measures proposed by criminal sociology in a way to meet the exigencies of a given people; legislative technique, *i.e.*, the actual drafting and adoption of legislation; penal jurisprudence, *i.e.*, the art of judges and attorneys in using scientific ideas, such as biosocial data and juridical doctrines, in the

---

[30] "Polemica in difesa della scuola criminale positiva," *op. cit.* p. 244.

interpretation of the criminal law and its application to the individual case.[31]

We have already noted that Ferri made original contributions both to the study of the crime as an "individual fact" by his researches on prisoners, leading to his works on homicide and suicide, and to the study of crime as a "social fact" by his studies of French criminal statistics, in particular. His most important and lasting contribution was, however, his ideas concerning the reformation of the system of criminal justice, some of the most important of which will be mentioned here.

First, it would be necessary to abolish the concept of moral responsibility and replace it by one of legal or social responsibility. "The positive theory says: every man is always responsible to society for any crime he commits. Whether he is a juvenile, insane, drunk or a sleepwalker, he should always be held responsible, *i.e.*, subject to the consequences of his criminal act, when that act is contrary to public safety and forbidden by the criminal law. . . . There is no more or less of criminal responsibility; either one is responsible or not responsible (for legally justifiable reasons)."[32] Moral responsibility was to Ferri a metaphysical concept; it designated something which no one could adequately measure and led to the acquittal or the failure of prosecution of offenders who often were extremely dangerous to social safety. For him, social defence against the criminal required a system based on legal responsibility.

Moral responsibility having been eliminated, the consequences of crime for the convicted offender would no longer be retributive punishments (*pena-castigo*), but scientifically determined sanctions (*pena-difesa*) based on the degree of danger which the offender constituted for society and the degree to which his motives were blameworthy, rather than on the objective nature of his act. The function of the court would be to select the proper sanction for the convicted offender. To do so would require a great deal of understanding and knowledge on the part of the judges and prosecutors. In 1896 Ferri said: "The criminal justice of the future, administered by judges who have sufficient knowledge, not of Roman or civil law, but of psychology, anthropology and psychiatry, will have for its sole task to determine if the defendant is the material author of the

31 *Sociologia criminale*, 5th ed., Vol. II, pp. 554–555.
32 "Il dolo criminoso," *Difese penali*, 3rd ed., Vol. III, p. 177.

established crime; and instead of brilliant logomachies by the prosecution and the defence in an effort to trick one another, there will be a scientific discussion on the personal and social condition of the offender in order to classify him in one or another anthropological class to which one or another form of indeterminate segregation will apply." [33]

Any attempt at real individualisation of sentences by courts should be discouraged. He believed it Utopian to think that any judge could make minute studies of every convicted offender. The judge should have enough scientific knowledge to permit him to place the offender in the proper class (*i.e.*, in one of Ferri's five or six classes) and then assign the sanction proper to each class whether this would be merely a warning (judicial pardon), the payment of reparations (which Ferri believed to be adequate for a number of offenders); compulsory labour in freedom (the worker's wages being attached); or indeterminate commitment to a mental hospital for the criminal insane, a reformatory, an institution for alcoholics, an agricultural colony, etc. Individualisation, beyond this point, should be left to those who execute sentences, but even then he was inclined to think that, considering the numbers involved, real individualisation of treatment would remain an incompletely realisable hope. In the treatment of offenders after sentence the greatest effort should be made in the case of the occasional criminal; it was not really worth spending much effort on the mentally abnormal or the congenital offender.

As for those committed on indeterminate sentences to some form of institutionalisation, a periodic revision of the sentence should occur. The criminal justice of the future would see the setting up of " permanent committees in which judges, prosecutors, defenders (who would also be public officials because it is absurd to consider the defence of a suspect as a private affair like the interpretation of a contract) and with them psychiatrists and anthropologists would examine periodically those committed with the guarantee of publicity, to determine if the term should be prolonged or not." [34]

The state should also provide for after-care and supervision.

---

[33] See " Il Congresso d'Antropologia Criminale a Ginevra," in *La Scuola Positiva*, September 1896, reprinted in *Studi sulla criminalità ed altri saggi*, 1901, pp. 216–233; p. 229.
[34] *Ibid*.

Epilogue

The influence of the positive school has been felt in Italy and throughout the world. The reforms made in the criminal law in all civilised nations in the last half-century have resulted in the adoption of many of the proposals of the positivists. The entire European movement to provide so-called " security measures " parallel with or subsequent to " punishments " as means of dealing with habitual offenders, abnormal offenders, vagrants, etc., derives from the positivists, and the " social defence school " which has arisen in Europe since the last war owes its stimulus and many of its basic ideas to Ferri and his co-workers.[35]

Ferri remained until his death completely certain that regardless of what compromises might have to be made with more traditional views of criminal justice, his ideas would in the end be accepted as the most logical basis for social defence against crime. At the end of his preface to his treatise on the *Principles of Criminal Law* (1928), he wrote: " Thus I close my scientific life, showing the juridical application of these doctrines, originally and obviously Italian, which in the last fifty years I have seen, after the early fearful anathemas, progressively adopted in all countries; this gives me a serene certainty that they will finally be completely realised."

A few months ago I drove along the Viale Ferri at Rocca di Papa, the picturesque hill town some twenty miles from Rome, where Ferri had a large villa, from which he had a magnificent view to the west over the Roman campagna, Lake Albano and Castelgandolfo. I first met him there more than three decades ago and still remember the courtesy and kindness he showed a young student. Some days later I heard him give the introductory lecture —in November 1925 at the University of Rome—a report on the International Penal and Penitentiary Congress, which he had just attended in London. Slender of build, a head taller than most Italians, with a shock of white curly hair and a white beard, he was an imposing figure and still possessed, at seventy, the clarity of exposition and the manner of the great orator. The labours of a lifetime preceded that address, a lifetime devoted to battling for an idea. In his introductory lecture in 1921, Ferri told his students: " In your life as students and later in your fight for existence in your profession, remember that science and life teach us the lesson

[35] Marc Ancel, *La défense sociale nouvelle* (183 pp., Paris, 1954, Editions Cujas).

to be tolerant with people, because all men of good faith should be respected, whatever may be the philosophy, religion or political belief they profess; but be inflexible and tenacious defenders of your own ideas. . . . If the idea is wrong, no amount of ability or propaganda will save it from extinction, but if the idea is true, neither academic fear of novelty nor legal persecution can stop its final triumph "; and in an address on " human justice " delivered in 1924 in Naples at the Congress for the Advancement of Science, he said: " By temperament I am an idealist because I have always believed—and my life is an example—that life without an ideal, whatever it may be—in art or in science, in politics or in religion— is not worth living."

THORSTEN SELLIN.

BIBLIOGRAPHY

By Ferri

" Dei limiti fra diritto penale ed antropologia criminale," *Archivio di psichia-tria*, Vol. I, 1880–81.
" Dei sostitutivi penali," *ibid.*
Difese penali. 3 vols. Milano, 1925, UTET.
" Fascismo e scuola positiva nella difesa sociale contro la criminalità," *La Scuola Positiva*, N.S. 6 : 241–274, 1926.
L'omicida nella psicologia e nella psicopatologia criminale, 2nd ed. *L'omi-cidio-suicidio. Responsabilità giuridica*, 5th ed., xii, 768 pp., Torino, 1925, UTET.
Principii di diritto penale, xv, 848 pp., Torino, 1928, UTET.
" Relazione sul Progetto preliminare di Codice Penale italiano," *La Scuola Positiva*, N.S. 1 : 1–130, 1921.
Sociologia criminale, 2 vols. Torino, 1929–30, UTET.
Studi sulla criminalità ed altri saggi, viii, 542 pp., Torino, 1901, Bocca.
" A character study and life history of Violet Gibson, who attempted the life of Benito Mussolini," *Journal of the American Institute of Criminal Law and Criminology*, 19 : 11–19, August 1928.
Criminal Sociology, xiv, 577 pp., Boston, 1917, Little, Brown & Co.
" Nomination of a commission for the positivist reform of the Italian criminal code," *Journal . . . of Criminal Law and Criminology*, 11 : 67–76, May 1920.
" Present movement in criminal anthropology," *ibid.* 5 : 224–227, July 1914.
" Reform of penal law in Italy," *ibid.* 12 : 178–198, August 1921.
Socialism and Modern Science (Darwin—Spencer—Marx), 213 pp., New York, 1900, Intern. Library Publ. Co.

"The delinquent in art and literature," *Atlantic*, 60:233–240, August 1897.
The Positive School of Criminology, 125 pp., Chicago, 1913, Charles H. Kerr
& Co.

About Ferri

ANCEL, M. *La défense sociale nouvelle*, 183 pp., Paris, 1954, Ed. Cujas.
FRANCHI, BRUNO. *Enrico Ferri, il noto, il mal noto e l'ignorato*, 183 pp.,
Torino, 1908, Bocca.
*Scritti in onore di Enrico Ferri per il cinquantesimo anno di suo insegna-
mento universitario*, 526 pp., Torino, 1929, UTET.
ZIMMERN, H. "Enrico Ferri on homicide," *Popular Science Monthly*, 49:678–
684, 828–837, September, October 1896.

NOTE ON THE CONTRIBUTOR

Dr. THORSTEN SELLIN, Gilmanton, New Hampshire, is Emeritus
Professor of Sociology at the University of Pennsylvania.

19

EMILE DURKHEIM
1858–1917

THE year 1958 marked the 100th anniversary of the birth of Emile Durkheim, one of the most outstanding European scholars of the late nineteenth century. Contemporary writers not only in the social sciences but in related fields have come to recognise the unique and far-reaching contributions he has made to the understanding of anti-social behaviour. Few, if any, scholars in the West have formulated such a keen theoretical analysis of the basic problems confronting society as he presented in his concept of " Anomie." His meaningful exposition of the desocialisation and fragmentation of society has enabled men to understand the true effects of social isolation and the " collective sadness " in present-day society. Even a number of literary persons have utilised his referential construct of society as but the " disorganised dust of individuals."

Emile Durkheim was *L'avant Garde* for the present " age of loneliness," the " rootlessness," " the cut offness " of living and the insecurity of contemporary urban life. Trigant Burrows has revealed the ravages of " Atomisation," " fragmentation " and " separative factors " of the present presaged by Durkheim.[1]

Even the poet T. S. Eliot reflects the thinking of Durkheim when he has Celia, in one of his poems, describe our dissociated culture by saying:

" Do you know
It no longer seems worthwhile to speak to any one!
No—it isn't that I want to be alone
But that everyone's alone—or so it seems to me they make noises, and think
　　they are talking to each other:
They make faces, and think they understand each other,
And I'm sure that they don't." [2]

* Reproduced from *The Journal of Criminal Law, Criminology and Police Science*, Vol. 49, No. 1, May–June 1958.
[1] Trigant Burrows, *The Social Basis of Conscience*, London, 1927.
[2] T. S. Eliot, *The Cocktail Party*, London, 1949, p. 118.

More recently Paul Halmos followed Durkheim when he indicated that man's social reconstruction lies " in the transcendence of his loneliness." [3] If he understand that a " pioneer is one who goes before preparing the way for others—exploring in advance " it can be rightly said that Durkheim was a pioneer in criminology.

The man and his times

Emile Durkheim was born in Epinal, the Department of Vosges, a city in Eastern France, on April 15, 1858. His ancestors came from one of the cultured Rabbinical families, long residents of the province. Durkheim's natal city was one of those ancient French cities which had its origins in the tenth century dating back to Theodoric, the Bishop of Metz. As early as 1860, the city had been built as part of a thirty-mile-long fortification along the Moselle River guarding the frontiers of France against an invasion from the East. At the end of the nineteenth century Epinal had a population of about 20,000 inhabitants. In spite of its nearness to Strasbourg, Epinal had a technical school, a training college and a well-equipped library. Significant in the life of young Durkheim is the fact that his native city was invaded and occupied by a German army on October 12, 1870, when he was twelve years of age. Years later in 1875, the citizens erected a monument commemorating the victims who had died in those early days of the war. Thus, at an early age Durkheim came to experience in his own city the ravages of war, a fact which may explain his fervent nationalism to the degree that M. M. Mitchell once described him as a " fiery jingoist " at the outbreak of the First World War in 1914.[4]

Durkheim received his early education in the college of his native city and later at the *Lycée Louis de Grand* and *École Normale Supérieure* in Paris. In 1882, at the age of twenty-four, he completed his formal education and became a professor of philosophy at various academic institutions in France. Five years later in 1887, at twenty-nine years of age, he joined the faculty at the University of Bordeaux where he taught the first course in sociology to be offered in a French university. In 1902 (at forty-four years of age) he became a professor of philosophy and education at the

[3] P. Halmos, *Solitude and Privacy*, A study of Social Isolation, London, 1952, p. xv. Halmos describes three kinds of loneliness: Communal, National and Cosmic.

[4] M. M. Mitchell, " E. Durkheim and the Philosophy of Nationalism," Polit.Sci.Quart., Vol. 46, 1931.

University of Paris where he had earned his doctorate ten years earlier. His thesis dealt with " The Division of Labour " which later became one of his outstanding works.

Some authorities have been concerned about the lateness at which Durkheim arrived at the professorship in the University of Paris. A few have indicated that the competitive nature of academic life made advancement slow. Others have contended that certain prejudices and vested interests may have been involved. It will be recalled that it was not until 1895 that Captain A. Dreyfus (1858–1935) finally obtained reinstatement into the French Army after years of civil and military litigation. Apart from this, the French academic life had its normal amount of intellectual rivalry. G. Tarde, the champion of the " Laws of Imitation," was a contemporary of Durkheim who played a very important part in the penal philosophy of France. These two men sat on opposite sides of the academic household and never were able to reconcile their divergent views about society. Tarde spoke of Durkheim as an " ontologist," " scholastic " and a " medieval realist."

Intellectual background

Anyone who attempts to delineate the work of a scholar is always confronted with the query—how much of the man's work was original and how much was merely the replication of other men's efforts? This question is especially important when dealing with pioneers. In order to answer the problem it may prove valuable to outline very briefly the intellectual landscape in which Durkheim lived. It is a well-known fact that his life paralleled the lives of a number of leading social scientists in Europe. To begin with, it should be pointed out that Durkheim was born a year after the death of A. Comte (1798–1857), the founder of sociology. At the very outset the mantle of Comte, therefore, hung in the academic halls of France waiting for someone to don it. Comte's " Positivism " was, therefore, a point of departure for Durkheim. There were other countrymen of stature within France. Gustav Le Bon (1841–1931) best known for his *The Crowd* (1897) and G. Tarde (1843–1909) better known for his *Penal Philosophy* (1890) and *Laws of Imitation* (1890), were a part of the intellectual life of Paris. Before these there was F. Le Play who had already published his *European Working Men* in 1855 and *Social Reform* in 1864 in which he advocated Social Solidarity. Across the Alps C. Lombroso (1835–1909) had completed his great works in criminology and created an Italian School of Penology. Across the Rhine in Germany were a number of social economists sometimes called " socialists of the chair." By 1890 George Simmel (1858–1918) had published his *Ueber Soziale Differenzierung* and F. Tonnies (1855–1939) his *Gemeinschaft und Gesellschaft* in 1887. In addition, W. M. Wundt (1832–1920) had been engaged in his *Folk Psychology* before the Franco-Prussian War. Farther to the east beyond the Oder there was already a group of Russian sociologists. P. Lilienfeld (1829–1903) completed his *Gedanken ueber die Sozialwissenschaft der Zukunft* in five volumes during 1873–81. Professor E. De Roberty (1843–1915) had written his *Sociology* in 1876 which was translated into French in 1886, the same year that he visited France. Across the Channel in England, Herbert Spencer (1820–82) had already been at work on his *Sociology* and *Psychology* and other works and B. Kidd (1858–1916) had published his *Social Evolution* in 1894. Further, James A. Frazer (1854–1941) had published his well-known works on primitive religions and totemism. In America H. C. Carey (1793–1879) had completed his *Principles of Social Science* (1858), the year Durkheim was born, and L. F. Ward had completed his *Dynamic Sociology* in 1883 and *Outline of Sociology* in 1898.

There is no question that Durkheim knew these men or their works for he mentions them, and many others, in his writings. The ultimate answer to the question of originality may be made clear by a statement which Durkheim himself made in one of the issues of his journal, *L'Année Sociologique*, No. XII. He denies any claim to the originality of his ideas " except the claim to having been the first to introduce these views into France and into French thought." [5]

From all evidence at hand it appears that there are three main sources upon which Durkheim drew for his works. First, from his own predecessors and contemporaries in France. Secondly, from a number of social economists in Germany, and, thirdly, from the Russian scholars. It is also possible that he found the American Carey useful in his treatment of solidarity and the division of labour, for he refers to his books.

[5] C. C. Gehlke, *Emile Durkheim's Contribution to Social Theory*, Columbia University Studies, New York, 1915, footnote on p. 84.

There is no doubt that Durkheim acquired his " Social Realism " and " positivism " from A. Comte. In a sense he continued Comte's work although he was critical of him at various points. Also he knew Le Bon personally and G. Tarde was a colleague in his own university. In addition, Durkheim, in a number of places, indicates his indebtedness to the French philosopher C. B. Renouvier (1815–1903) who had attempted to combine the positivism of Comte with the theories of E. Kant. Furthermore, Durkheim states that he derived much benefit from A. Espinas, one of the French Neo-positivists. F. de Coulanges (1830–89) is a French historian known to Durkheim, from whom he gained his theories of religion. What Durkheim owes to De Roberty, the Russian, is a matter of conjecture. It is known that De Roberty did spend some time in France and that his works had been published in French in 1886.

It is evident that Durkheim was influenced by a number of German scholars, for some time between 1885 and 1886 he visited a number of their universities. There he came to know W. M. Wundt, the founder of folk psychology who established the first laboratory in experimental psychology. Some maintain that Durkheim's explanation of religion as a factor in social control came from G. Simmel but he says they are from his former teacher Boutroux. Durkheim's fundamental postulates of reality he gained from three German scholars. Albert Schäffle (1831–1903) at Tübingen and Vienna had already developed certain organic analogies in his effort to interpret Comte and Darwin. A. H. G. Wagner (1835–1917) who taught economics at Göttingen and Heidelberg had explained how the expansion of government encompassed an increase in social welfare. Finally, Durkheim attributes much of his historical economics to G. Schmoller (1838–1917).[6]

These are but a few of the important scholars Durkheim knew personally or indirectly through their publications. Whatever he may have owed to each, should not detract from the great contribution he made to sociology and to criminology in the nineteenth century and after. Through his logical and careful analysis of

---

[6] To the above list could be added many others such as A. Coste who in his works (1899) attempted to measure by " sociometrika " the sociality of a population. Also V. La Pouge had published his *Social Selection* in 1896. Whether Durkheim knew of the socio-legal works of the Russian scholar, L. Petrajizsky is not known but it is clear that there is close similarity in such areas as " motivation of human behaviour," " forms of conduct " and " the laws' influence on people." C. H. C. Wright in his *History of French Literature* maintains that Durkheim had much in common with Bergson because both had studied under Boutroux at the École Normale Supérieure, this, however, is mere conjecture.

human behaviour he gained the undisputed leadership among the French social scientists. Prior to our present mechanical devices such as IBM machines, prior to vast research funds committed to " basic research " and prior to the huge staffs of workers in academic institutions with their co-operative research programmes, Durkheim accomplished more in his lifetime than a score of " programmatic " or committed researchers.

Theory of criminality

Durkheim's eminence in the field of criminology rests upon his broad approach to anti-social behaviour. Scholars before and after him have attempted to find *the* " cause " for crime in external factors as in natural forces, climate, economic conditions, density of population or certain ecological areas. In contrast to these Durkheim maintained that if an explanation is to be found " it is necessary to look for an explanation " in the very nature of society. In this respect he agrees with A. Lacassagne who said: " Le milieu est le bouillon de culture de la criminalité." From this it follows that the " individual is rather a product than an author of society " (Espinas). In other words, the individual is but a small image of the world in which he lives. For Durkheim crime is immanent in society and results from social interaction. This is the view expressed by A. Prins, " Criminality proceeds from the very nature of humanity itself, it is not transcendent, but immanent." [7]

The normality of crime

To present-day social scientists it may seem strange that Durkheim should maintain that criminality is a " normal " factor rather than a pathological one. He indicates that crime is found in all societies, " Crime is normal because a society exempt from it is utterly impossible." The " fundamental conditions of social organisation—logically imply it." Crime is not due to any imperfection of human nature or society any more than birth or death may be considered abnormal or pathological. It is all a part of the totality of society. " A society exempt from it [crime] would necessitate a standardisation of the moral concepts of all individuals which is neither possible nor desirable." [8]

---

[7] A. Prins, *Criminalité et Repression*, Bruxelles, 1886.
[8] E. Durkheim, *The Rules of Sociological Method*, ed. by G. E. G. Catlin, 1938, p. xxxviii.

In reality crime can disappear only when the " collective sentiments " in a community reach such an intensity that all persons
concur in the same common values and when " the horror of
bloodshed becomes widespread and deep in those social strata from
which murderers are recruited." [9]
Durkheim maintains that crime is not only normal for society
but that it is necessary. Without crime there could be no evolution
in law. If society is to progress each person must be able to express
himself. " The opportunity for the genius to carry out his work
affords the criminal his originality at a lower level." " Aside from
this indirect utility, it happens that crime itself plays a useful role."
" According to Athenian law, Socrates was a criminal, and his
condemnation was no more than just. However, his crime, namely,
the independence of his thought, rendered a service not only to
humanity but to his country." [10] Crime, therefore, " must no
longer be conceived as an evil that cannot be too much repressed."
This, however, does not lead Durkheim to condone crime or " to
present an apology for crime." When he stated that crime is
merely a normal element he viewed the whole of society as reality.

Penological theory

Durkheim maintained that the kind and the degree of punishment and the rationale behind sanctions have varied according to
the organisational structure of a society. In a homogeneous un-
differentiated society anti-social acts offend the strong cohesive
conscience of the people. Punishment in such a society is only to
the degree that it sustains and reinforces the collective conscience.
Punishment, therefore, is a mechanical reaction to preserve solidarity. Individuals are but the instruments of society who " strike
back " at the offender without any sense of justice or immediate
utility.[11] There is no thought of correction or of reformation of the
offender. In some instances the punishment becomes so passionate
as to reach other persons related to the wrongdoer. Some may view
this " aimless emotional reaction as a useless vengeance," as
extreme cruelty, but to this Durkheim does not agree. In spite of

---

[9] Durkheim does, however, point out that if or when crime increases to undue proportions such as an increase of 300 per cent. in France, then it may be considered
pathological and abnormal. He further indicates that while crime is normal this does
not mean that the criminal is normal.
[10] *Rules, ibid.* p. 71.
[11] E. Durkheim, *The Division of Labour*, trans. by G. Simpson, 1933, p. 86.

the crudeness of the method it is a " veritable act of defence " to destroy that which appears to be a menace. Punishment " is a defence weapon which has its worth." The wrongdoer is punished in order to make certain that the act may be considered as abhorrent to the minds of all men. In turn, this preserves the moral ideal of the people. Without punishment no man would know whether acts were " good or bad."

In contrast to this immediate and non-rational reaction to crime the advanced and differentiated urban society develops another type of penal principles. In such a society the law is not concerned with the preservation of social solidarity but merely with restitution and reinstatement. Hence, the punishment becomes evaluated in terms of the amount of harm done to the victim. The law, the court and the judge act as arbiter between the offender and the victim and the state. At this point legal concepts and practices " operate outside the collective conscience," because the wrong done is not considered a threat to social cohesion because men are little aware of it. The wrong is measured only in terms of the damage or injury done to the victim. This change of the penal thinking is the result of the advance in the division of labour and the greater segmentation in the society. The amount of the injury in time is measured in terms of a certain " occupational morality " rather than a common conscience. The complexity of life, therefore, demands certain conformity to rules not to protect society but to give protection to other individuals in society. The sacrosanct nature of sanctions gives way to mere man-to-man requirements. This develops into a kind of co-operative morality in which duties are imposed by others.

In such a society crimes are thought of as acts which offend others and not the collective conscience. This, in turn, causes a lessening of the law norms and decreases the amount of punishment. The punishment is evaluated in terms of a satisfactory settlement with the victim. Such adjudication takes the form of the breaking of a contract in which a fine or some type of restitution satisfies " justice." Under such a condition punishment may be applied to the wrongdoer in order to reform him. Punishment in order to preserve the common conscience and social solidarity is changed to what is good or proper for the individual. When this point has been reached the entire rationale of punishment for crime disappears and prisons are thought of as hospital or curative devices to correct aberrations.

This series of transformations of punishment to protect social solidarity, to punishment which is centred upon the individual is but the end-result of the changes in the division of labour in society. In a sense punishment is but the function of the type of division of labour. This is Durkheim's answer to the changes in punishment in society. Ultimately it creates a number of problems which he hoped would be solved when a new type of " organic solidarity " arose from the increased segmentation of society by the increase of the division of labour. However, the problem still remains. If or when there is no rationale for punishment, if there is no social force behind efforts to keep the criminal from doing wrong how can the social order be preserved? This is a condition which " organic solidarity " has not solved. Durkheim answered this by saying that the division of labour produces a solidarity because men become " exchangist." In doing this an entire system of right and wrong develops, and a new code of behaviour will arise.[12]

Durkheim on " Anomie "

Of the many contributions which Durkheim has made to the field of criminology his advancement of the theory of " Anomie " stands out above all others.[13] Social scientists have found this theoretical construct the most valuable means of explaining the etiology of crime. The theory of " Anomie " is the one fundamental principle which follows consistently from the entire schematic structure of society. For Durkheim the elemental factors which give solidarity and cohesiveness to society are exteriority and constraint arising from the compulsive force of a common conscience. Individuals are a part of the total integrated bond of oneness. This inner compulsion to conformity arises from a number of social factors such as authority, respect, fear and the sacred. Men

[12] Durkheim, however, was too much of a realist to hold that society had reached a new state of equilibrium. " Our faith has been troubled; tradition has lost its way; individual judgment has been freed from collective conscience. . . . The new life which has emerged so suddenly has not been able to be completely organised, and above all it has not been organised in a way to satisfy the need for justice which has grown more ardent in our hearts. . . . What we must do to relieve this anomy is to discover the means for making the organs which are still wasting themselves in discordant movements harmoniously concur by introducing into their relations more justice. . . . Our illness is not, then, as often has been believed, of the intellectual sort; it has more profound causes . . . morality is irremediably shattered, and what is necessary to us is only in process of formation." *The Division of Labour*, pp. 408–409.

[13] The word " Anomie " comes from the Greek, *Anomia*, which originally meant lawlessness. In the seventeenth century the term meant disregard for divine law. The present use implies lawlessness or lack of conformity. Durkheim first used the term in 1893 in his *Division of Labour*.

have an inner sense of a conscience superior to themselves which is outside and above the individual. This does not imply a reality apart from the totality of individuals in a society but merely a collective mindedness. This does not imply a " thought substance " but a " continuous succession of representation " growing out of social interaction. It is not separated from the group but a part of it. This is what Wundt may have called the folk-psychology. In a sense " society sees farther and better than the individual." All this brings about a certain moral discipline in a population. Under this condition of concordance crime is at a minimum.

In the process of social change (evolution) in society due to increased division of labour and heterogeneity the unifying forces of society tend to weaken. The standards and norms which had regulated society in the past become obsolete and inoperative or meaningless. When this occurs the restraints on passions no longer hold and a condition of " deregulation or anomy " arises. The absences of restraints soon bring disorder and " social chaos." The end result is a smashing of the norms and society becomes " atomised," fragmented and a " disorganised dust of individuals."

As a result of this fragmentation and atomisation another serious condition arises in society—social isolation which brings about a decrease in social participation. People become but individuals living in proximity but in a social vacuum. The end result is a social emptiness, or what Durkheim calls " Collective sadness," in which people have lost their identity either to place, to group or to tradition. In such a formless and fragmented society there is no solidarity, no sharing of life or experiences, no obligations to anyone or anything. This separativeness becomes intensified by an increase in mobility and with the growth of great metropolitan centres which become " Citadels of Loneliness." The Persian proverb of " death or a friend " takes on a new meaning. In time this inner longing expresses itself in the arts and the music. Urbanites try to forget their isolation by " Cocktails " while they listen to some " Blues Singer " in a night club. The earlier songs of " Home on the Range," " Dixie " or " The Eyes of Texas Are Upon You " are replaced by " We are little black sheep who have lost our way," " Why was I born? " or " I'm a stranger in Heaven." People develop " a restless movement, a planless self-development, an aim of living which has no criterion of value and in which happiness lies always in the future, and not in any present achievement."

This is the milieu which produces crime and anti-social disorders. There are no constraints and the cult of individualism cuts away all inhibitions. This breaks down the cohesive forces and each man becomes a " law unto himself." This is " Anomie "—the dead end of meaningless living. " The Citadels of Loneliness " become " Grand Central Stations " where people come and go with a ticket to some " Island in the Sun," " Bali Hai," " Shangri-la " or " Over the Rainbow."

If social scientists desire an explanation of crime in high or low places the real explanation lies in Durkheim's " Anomie." It is a qualitative non-scorable factor that cannot be entered as an item on a punch card. This cut-offness creates a " Terror " for which the best psychoanalysts with the softest couches have not been able to find a solution. It is just such loneliness which drives prisoners to try to find companionship among animals, mice, birds or rats. This loneliness causes some men to try to find an escape in a " Seven Storey Mountain " while others search for " The Blue Bird." Such is " Anomie."

A recent monograph by Bernard Lander has taken Durkheim's construct of " Anomie " and applied it to a given city in his study of delinquency.[14] After making a thorough analysis of " surface associations " such as poverty, bad housing conditions, density, etc., Lander comes to the conclusion that these factors do not reach the crux of the problem and fail to take into account " the direct motivation of behaviour." He indicates that the explanation of delinquency may be found in the degree that " Anomie " is present in a given area. " Delinquency is a function of the stability and acceptance of the group norms with legal sanctions and the consequent effectiveness of the social controls in securing conforming juvenile behaviour." " The factor analysis indicates, that the delinquency rate is fundamentally related only to ' Anomie ' " (p. 89). In essence Lander confirms what Durkheim found much earlier that where cohesion breaks down, where isolation is great, where social controls no longer exist, there crime rises to a high rate.

Durkheim on suicide

Of the many scholars who have attempted to deal with the problem of suicide only Durkheim has given the most satisfactory

---

[14] B. Lander, *Juvenile Delinquency*, A study of 8,464 cases of Juvenile Delinquency in Baltimore, Columbia University Press, 1954.

and understandable explanation.   The hypothesis which he advanced in his *Suicide* follows logically from his theory of social cohesion and social isolation.   He postulates that in a society where there is a high degree of social cohesion, a strong sense of identity and group integration and a sense of " belonging " where people are not " cut off " there will be little or no suicide.   The total integration of each person into a collective whole supported by strong sacrosanct sanctions discourages suicide.   Contrariwise, as social cohesion decreases, the society becomes segmented, and men feel a sense of separateness and psycho-social isolation, to that degree suicide increases.   " Anomy, therefore, is a regular and specific factor in a suicide in our modern society; one of the springs from which the annual contingent feeds."   Durkheim calls this the " Egotistical type " of suicide and by giving it a type name establishes an analysis.   This, the egotistical, explains the high rate of suicide among divorced persons, urban dwellers, groups where the family structure is weak, the heterodox religious individuals and the " free souls " who are no longer oriented to society.   The " Deadend " meaninglessness of life and the extreme isolation from others around them drives them to the Persian proverb " a friend or death."   Without a friend, without identification and without group support life ends in a meaningless nothingness.

By using the opposite pole of social relationships of strong cohesion Durkheim establishes his second type and analysis of suicide. In a culture where the individual is submerged, where custom and tradition are rigid and strong, people become so firmly bound to customs or group conscienceness that choices are made for them. Cases of self-sacrifice illustrate such a condition whether to duty, to a deity or tribal custom.   The primitive leaps into a volcano or over a cliff because it is the rule of a god.   In some areas a wife takes her own life at the death of her husband because tradition dictates such an act.   This is what Durkheim calls the " Altruistic type " of suicide.

The third type of suicide Durkheim explains is due to the sudden shattering of the customary bonds of relationships which normally give an individual a sense of security.   " Man kills himself because of the loss of cohesion."   This he calls the " anomique " type of suicide or a condition of sudden and far-reaching changes which shatter the social shell of solidarity in which people live.   Such a shattering may be due to a crisis brought about by economic losses, a break in the stock market, loss of prestige, loss of " face " or a quick drop from a high to a low position in society. This explains the rise in suicides when the " stock market crashes " or when persons in high command positions are faced with defeat or when an Oriental " loses face in the eyes of his ancestors."

To these three types and explanations of suicide Durkheim suggests the possibility of a fourth type which he names the " fatalistic type." The individual who is driven by excessive domination in which all the normal passions and wants of a person are " blocked and thwarted " such as a prisoner " choked by oppressive discipline " or confronted with extreme punishment may take his own life rather than live. This type of suicide has some of the characteristics of the " anomique " but circumstances are somewhat different. Had Durkheim lived through the days of the Second World War, with all the cruelty of the concentration camps, he may have found material to expand this type of suicide. As it was, he stated this type " has so little contemporary importance and samples are hard to find aside from the cases just mentioned that it seems useless to dwell upon it." [15]

Epilogue

Death came to Durkheim on November 15 during the third year of the First World War at the age of fifty-nine years, but his spirit lived on in his students and contemporaries. After the war these men continued the work Durkheim had initiated. The journal, *L'Année Sociologique*, which he had begun earlier but which ceased publication during the war, reappeared in 1924. The next year a group formed the French Institute of Sociology with M. Mauss, a nephew of Durkheim, as president.[16] In due time these men published a number of Durkheim's lectures and manuscripts. The *Revue Philosophique* published his " Introduction à la Morale." In 1925 his well-known lecture on " The Conjugal Family " appeared in *Annals de la Faculté des Lettres de Bordeaux*. In the same year appeared " L'Éducation Morale " and three years later " Le Socialisme." Earlier in 1919 George Davy, who later became Dean at the Sorbonne, published *Durkheim, Choix de*

---

[15] *Suicide : A Study in Sociology*, from a footnote on p. 276.

[16] Among these men were: Maxine David, Antone Bianconi, Jean Regnier, R. Gelly, Paul Fauconnet, Theodor Ribot, Marcel Grant, Joseph E. Wilbors, M. Halbwachs and others.

textes and *Emile Durkheim, L'homme et L'oeuvre*. In 1924 M. Halbwachs published *Origines du sentiment religieux d'après Durkheim*. A year before Albert Bayet produced *Le Suicide et la suicide*. These efforts represent some of the publications of Durkheim's followers and the impact he had made upon the intellectual life of France. In the third decade of the present century Durkheim came to be known in America where his influence has played an important part in social theory and research.

In a day of nuclear fission, social atomisation, social fragmentation, hot and cold wars, " Murder Inc." and " Blackboard Jungles " it may be that Durkheim's contribution toward a better understanding of society will become more significant. It may be that there will be " nothing left but little fishes " unless we come to appreciate what Durkheim said more than a half-century ago. " Man's characteristic privilege is that the bond he accepts is not physical but moral: that is, social. He is governed not by material environment brutally imposed on him, but a conscience superior to his own." [17] This may be the solution to the present " collective sadness " and a means of bringing order out of the " disorganised dust of individuals."

WALTER A. LUNDEN.

BIBLIOGRAPHY

By Durkheim

De la Division du travail social, Étude sur l'organisation des sociétés supérieures, Paris, 1893. Translated as *Division of Labour in Society* by George Simpson in 1933, published by Macmillan & Co.

Les Règles de la Méthode, Paris, 1895 (Parts had appeared in Rev.Phil., Vols. 37 and 38). Translated by S. A. Solovay and John H. Mueller and edited by G. E. G. Catlin as *The Rules of Sociological Method* in 1938 by The Free Press.

Le Suicide; Étude de Sociologie, Paris, 1897. Translated by J. A. Spaulding and George Simpson in 1951, by The Free Press.

Les Formes élémentaires de la vie religieuse, Paris, 1912. Translated by J. U. Swain as *The Elementary Forms of the Religious Life* in 1915, George Allen & Unwin, Ltd., London.

L'Année Sociologique, Publiée sous la Direction de Emile Durkheim.

[17] *Suicide*, p. 252.

About Durkheim

BARNES, H. E. "Durkheim's contribution to the Reconstruction of Political Theory," Polit.Sci.Quart., Vol. 35, 1920, pp. 236–254.

GEHLKE, C. E. "E. Durkheim's Contributions to Social Theory," *Studies in History, etc.*, Vol. LXIII, No. 1, Columbia University, 1915. (This study contains a list of Durkheim's papers and publications in various journals.)

GRAZIA, S. DE. *The Political Community, A study in Anomie*, Chicago, 1948.

PARSONS, T. *The Structure of Social Action*, New York, 1937, pp. 301–472.

SOREL, G. "Les Théories de E. Durkheim," *Le Devenir social*, 1895.

SOROKIN, P. A. *Contemporary Sociological Theories*, New York, 1927, pp. 160–162, 215–217, 463–480 and 491–493.

STOETZEL, JEAN. "Sociology in France," in *Modern Sociological Theory*, edited by H. Becker and A. Boskoff, New York, 1957.

TOSTI, G. "Durkheim's Sociological Objectivism," A.J.S., Vol. IV, 1898–99.

NOTE ON THE CONTRIBUTOR

Dr. WALTER A. LUNDEN was Professor of Sociology at Iowa State College from 1947 until his retirement in 1969. During and after the Second World War he served as a prison officer in the British and U.S. Armies in England, France and Germany. He is the author of *Systematic Source Book in Juvenile Delinquency* (1938), *Statistics on Crime and Criminals* (1940), *Basic Social Problems* (1950), *Offenders in Court and Prison* (1955), *Courts and Criminal Justice in Iowa* (1957), *War and Delinquency* (1963), *Statistics on Delinquents and Delinquency* (1964), *Crimes and Criminals* (1967), and numerous articles in periodical literature.

20

PEDRO DORADO MONTERO

1861–1919

Among the Spanish-speaking reformers advocating a new criminal law and criminology, Pedro Dorado Montero [1] has always been considered as one of the most important pioneers who, as we shall see, advocated one of the most radical and interesting criminological theories of the late nineteenth century. [2]

Although some of his conclusions raised and still raise serious objections, and by some are considered as Utopian, it cannot be denied that in many aspects he was very much ahead of his time, and in fact still is in some respects.

As very often happens with reformers, Dorado's ideas have been once in a while misunderstood or even distorted by self-appointed followers and critics. They have attributed to him ideas which he never expressed or have identified them with some of the theories held by certain penal schools of his time. While it is true that even the most contradictory theories may have certain features in common the fact remains that it would be extremely difficult to identify Dorado with any other school of thought than that known in Spanish-speaking countries as " Escuela correccionalista." [3]

The man and his ideas

Dorado Montero was born of parents in modest circumstances in an isolated hamlet near Béjar, Salamanca, in 1861. As a boy he had to walk every day to Béjar in order to attend school. His assiduity and interest rewarded the efforts of his parents who, like many other Spanish farmers, wanted to send their son to the university.

---

* Reproduced from *The Journal of Criminal Law, Criminology and Police Science*, Vol. 46, No. 5, January–February 1956.
[1] His full name was Pedro García Dorado Montero.
[2] The term " criminological " is used here in its broader sense.
[3] Although there is much in common between the terms " correccionalismo " and " correction " they are not interchangeable. " Correctionalism " would give a better idea of what the Spanish term means.

An accident—a fall from a cart—left him lame and with a crippled right arm for life. Only his strong character enabled him to overcome the handicap—then greater than now—inherent in such disabilities. Being a cripple undoubtedly influenced Dorado's character which was already reserved, austere and not very sociable. He was a hard worker and very fond of the country, where he went as often as possible. His life was a twofold struggle: he fought first against traditional criminological ideas and systems, and secondly, against his physical handicap.

Although as a professor he spent most of his life in Salamanca, Dorado remained fundamentally a countryman. The city never conquered him. The influence of Nature, very understandable if we remember his origin, remained strong in every respect and can be seen in his ideas, occasionally expressed with examples in which Nature plays a part.

Dorado and Unamuno were at a certain moment the most interesting personalities of the University of Salamanca. They contrasted strongly in their characteristics and it is no wonder that what was at the beginning a promising friendship ended in a rather distant and cold academic relationship. The varied activities of Unamuno, his wit and philosophy were very probably not the best means to impress Dorado, with his somewhat introvert personality and his devotion to a single question: Criminology.

What is remarkable is that a man like Dorado, crippled for life, having a rather difficult character, leading an isolated and financially hard life should have postulated one of the most humanitarian and generous criminological theories, the theory that the purpose of criminal law is not to punish but to afford effective moral and social protection to offenders. Such is what actually means his theory of *El Derecho protector de los criminales*, in which even the adjective " criminal " as applied to law has been suppressed.

In connection with his theory Dorado has occasionally been labelled a radical advocating a society in which the state as a political entity is unnecessary. Without denying that in some of his essays there are passages which might lead the superficial reader to such a conclusion, the fact is that although he advocated a total change of the administration of justice in criminal matters the basis of which would be a new kind of society, he never considered himself as a revolutionary, but always regarded peaceful political evolution as far more desirable than political revolution. Natural evolution of ideas and systems was the only way through which he envisaged the adoption of his theory, and for that, a great deal of time was needed.[4]

Although sceptical about the existing judicial machinery,[5] he maintained the necessity of the state, of a judicial system, and of a penal function. The latter should have as a basis a total identification of the interests of the individual and of society. In view of this identification of interests Dorado cannot be classified with the abolitionists of penal law like Soloview, Kropotkin and others, or as an adherent of the Italian Positive School which actually is based on the fundamental distinction between the interest of the individual and of society. The fact that Dorado accepted some of the ideas of the Italian Positive School does not make him a member or supporter of that School. In fact, Dorado opposed on several occasions some of the most important postulates of the Italian Positive School, namely, those concerning the theories of " criminal nato " and " delito naturale." Such point of view did not prevent Dorado from going, in certain aspects of his own theory, far beyond the Italian Positive School, but such an extreme position should be considered as the result of his extreme " correccionalismo " influenced by the philosophical system of Comte rather than by the ideas or principles of Lombroso, Ferri and Garofalo. After all, it was possible for Dorado to be influenced by Comte's philosophy without necessarily being influenced at the same time by the founders of the Italian Positive School. Such a distinction has not always been taken into account in the evolution of Dorado's theory which tried to reconcile two very different things: Comte's positivistic ideas with some of the principles of the old Spanish School of thought aiming at the moral " enmienda " (moral correction) of the offender. The term " enmienda " must be understood meaning for more than the term " correction." Literally, its equivalent would be " moral emendation," *i.e.*, all previous errors or faults should be removed from the offender and he should be protected against new errors or faults. Briefly, Dorado is a reformer and a pioneer firmly rooted in the Christian ideas so prevalent among the Spanish penologists. Although it is true that at a certain moment—when he was in Italy

[4] See *El Derecho y sus sacerdotes*; *Valor social de leyes y autoridades*; *Problemas de Sociología política* and several passages of some of his papers in *El Derecho protector de los criminales*.

[5] See *El Derecho protector de los criminales*, where he stated that justice is what three out of five want.

and was about twenty-five years old—and after a deep spiritual struggle he decided to abandon Catholicism, the effects of such a decision should be considered in the light of this question: to what extent did Catholicism abandon him? In this respect it should not be forgotten that until then he had been a fervent and active Catholic and that his family, his professors and environment were Catholic too. Without denying that a change took place in him after he took his firm decision in Italy, the fact remains that although a man may abandon certain ideas, these ideas, especially when they are firmly rooted in him, do not always abandon him entirely, *i.e.*, without leaving an impact. This seems to be evident in Dorado. His theory, therefore, is not the expression of a particular faith but the expression of a Christian spiritualism in which other elements than those strictly orthodox from a Catholic point of view play a role. This seems to be confirmed by the frequent references made by him to the importance of religion in the treatment of offenders. Even more, in one of his most significant papers he maintains, even terminologically, a striking parallelism between the religious concepts of sin, confession and penitential sanction and the juridical terms of offence, confession and criminal procedure.[6] Briefly, Dorado is the pioneer of the penal sanction as a pure spiritual function.

Dorado devoted all his life and efforts to his university and to the dissemination of his theory and ideas. He published a considerable number of books and an impressive number of essays and articles.[7] His knowledge of several languages allowed him not only to translate into Spanish important publications, not all of them directly related to criminological matters, but also to be familiar with the current ideas in criminology and penology. He took an active part in some of the existing controversies and contributed interesting papers to several international conferences or gatherings on criminological and penal matters.

After a long and prostrating illness, Dorado died in Salamanca on February 26, 1919.

The main characteristics of Dorado's theory may be briefly stated as follows:

---

[6] See " La función penal cura de almas " in *El Derecho protector de los criminales*. It should be noted that one of his most significant books has as a title *El Derecho y sus sacerdotes* (The Law and its Priests).

[7] See his papers, *El Derecho protector de los criminales* and *La sentencia indeterminada*.

Identification between Individual and Society

Such identification should be considered as the point of departure of Dorado's theory. According to him all the evils and therefore failures of the existing penal systems have their origin in the sharp distinction and even antagonism between Individual and Society. Such distinction leads necessarily to a legal duel between judge and offender in criminal matters. Both become enemies during the criminal proceedings in which the judge as a representative of Society takes practically only into account what can be used against the offender while the latter reacts in an opposite way and refers only to what is in his favour. Such divergent attitudes are re-inforced by the general belief that any penalty in itself is an evil and as such should be imposed by the judge for the wrong he considers has been done and should be avoided in the eyes of the offender. The result of such controversy very seldom leads to the correction of the offender.

Such attitudes and poor results would completely change if Individual and Society considered themselves as having identical aims and interests. The most important corollary of such identification would be the amalgamation of the principles " pro reo " and " pro societate " in a single principle representing the common interests of both elements. With respect to the process through which the identification of interests should take place, Dorado never had in mind any revolutionary methods or processes. He thought that such identification could be achieved by a process of social evolution, resulting from the progress of the sciences, especially of Psychology, which according to him will eventually absorb Sociology and Anthropology.

Penal system

The compatibility and even identity of interests already mentioned would, in his opinion, lead to a new penal system having the following characteristics :

(a) The principle " nullum crimen, nulla poena, sine previa lege " would disappear, as in the new penal system the historical and political antagonism between the Individual and Society would become a thing of the past.

(b) In the application of penal treatments, the individual rights should be considered as subordinated to the effectiveness of such treatment aimed at the moral correction of the offender.

(c) Eventually no definition of criminal offences would be needed. Criminal codes would be used rather as flexible terms of reference and not as binding legal provisions. In fact, criminal codes would be replaced by the " moral and scientific conscience " of the judge.

(d) There would no longer be any distinction between criminal law for adults and special legislation for juvenile offenders, as the principles and methods applicable to the latter would also apply to the former.

Judicial function

On the basis of the foregoing the characteristics of the judicial function would be as follows :

(a) Criminology would become more and more psychologically oriented. Although Anthropology and Sociology are important, both of them would be eventually absorbed by Psychology and Correctional Pedagogy. This broad conception of Psychology is repeatedly put forward by Dorado who accordingly considers the judicial function as a " cure of souls." To quote one of his statements, " the judicial function should be something having a psychological character, and should be applied in a way corresponding to what I have called on several occasions, the progressive spiritualisation of the penal function." [7] According to Dorado such spiritualisation, making the judicial function more and more humane, has a parallel in other fields of human knowledge. It is a general trend pervading all aspects of contemporary life.

(b) Logically the judicial function would be essentially preventive in character so that not only offenders but especially pre-delinquent and even potentially delinquent people would be submitted to a treatment. In other words, all people constituting a social danger should be treated. As a first step, the judicial function aims at a social diagnosis but this diagnosis can be only provisional and can therefore be modified according to circumstances and to the changeable characteristics of human nature.

(c) No solicitors, attorneys and other legal officers would be needed. Judges should be especially selected and trained in anthropology, sociology and psychology in order to be able to prevent offences and to cure offenders. They would be assisted by specialists.

(d) The existing criminal procedure would be replaced by a flexible one, adaptable to the circumstances of each case, and having as its only aim the cure of the offender or potential offender.

(e) Owing to its protective nature the treatment would be applied as long as circumstances demanded it. Consequently, a judicial decision would be retractable. On the other hand, the fact that a protective measure has been applied and the person concerned seems to be cured need not prevent the judge from applying new protective measures to that person if circumstances warranted. On this point, Dorado is emphatic and rejects the principle of " *res judicata.*" The traditional conception that the offender has paid his debt to Society as soon as he has completed his sentence has no place in Dorado's protective system.

The delinquent

To the question what is a delinquent? Dorado's answer is briefly as follows: There is no such thing as a criminal type, any more than there is the born criminal. For Dorado the term type is merely conceptual and does not represent any entity. His reasoning is quite simple and effective; if it is recognised that ontologically there are no criminal offences because such offences are man-made definitions based on prevailing systems of values, then how can one admit the existence of individuals possessing criminal characteristics or tendencies? [8]

According to Dorado the delinquent is only morally inferior and as a result of such inferiority he is placed in an unfavourable condition in which he needs the protection of the " criminal " law. His moral disintegration should be prevented, he should be made morally better through a psychological treatment. If such a change is not possible his individual tendencies should be diverted into a different channel and be given an appropriate application. [9] According to Dorado, the fact that the offender is a man in need of a moral and psychological treatment does not imply that he should be considered as a sick person. This important distinction has been

---

[8] See the paper, *El Derecho protector de los criminales.*
[9] *Ibid.*

occasionally overlooked by some of the so-called Dorado's followers in spite of the fact that he cautioned against identifying the two cases.[10]

Dorado seems to consider the offender as suffering from a moral deterioration that eventually affects his will and self-determination. In combining free will and determinism, *i.e.*, in admitting both of them, Dorado goes further than the old Spanish penologists, to whom the free will was the basic element of any penal treatment. On the other hand, in admitting a determinism mitigated by free will, he did not go as far as the supporters of the Italian Positive School. Briefly, for Dorado, offenders are morally weak persons in need of protection.

Treatment

According to Dorado, the treatment of offenders should be essentially psychological because crime is nothing else than a moral-psychological problem. Owing to its protective nature the treatment should be applied not only to those who have already committed an offence but also to those from whom it is reasonable to expect that they will commit one. Crime and tendency to crime are the points of departure for the application of a treatment the main characteristics of which are educational, correctional and tutelar. This protective aim is the prevailing one and should guide and inspire the treatment. The increasing importance of psychological factors in the treatment is the result of the increasing spiritualisation of human life. Dorado constantly refers to this spiritual evolution as the foundation of his theory, though what he exactly understands by it is not always clear. Apparently, when speaking of spiritualisation, he had in mind the increasing importance that psychological factors and therefore Psychology play in modern human life as a result of evolution and progress. The conclusion would be that the human mind is becoming more affected by progress and at the same time more in need of spiritual protection. Be that as it may the aim of the treatment is the reform of the offender's soul. Only when a new and sound soul has replaced the previous one can the offender be considered as cured.[11] In spite of his positivism and determinism, Dorado is here, like in other important aspects of his

[10] See, especially, *Problemas jurídicos contemporáneos.*
[11] See especially, *La sentencia indeterminada.*

theory, under the evident influence of the old Spanish School of Penology.

By its own nature and purpose the treatment is indeterminate and can be changed when necessary. Such flexibility presupposes the non-existence of a formal sentence and that the decision taken at a certain moment has only a provisional character. Accordingly, all available means and techniques, including penal sanctions, should be used for the moral correction of offenders and potential offenders. All treatments should be based as far as possible upon an accurate diagnosis for which the knowledge of the aetiology of the particular offence is essential. The application in certain cases of penal sanctions as part of the treatment does not minimise the individual protective character of that treatment because such penal sanctions are applied not for the protection of society but for the protection of the individual. It is this difference in the spirit in which the sanctions are applied that makes it possible to correct the individual.

The person determining the treatment would be the judge assisted by the necessary specialists. In order to ascertain the nature and extent of the treatment, the judge would direct as many inquiries as he deems necessary. Such inquiries would not be conducted according to existing criminal procedure and lawyers, solicitors and attorneys would be excluded from them. Everything would be concentrated in the judge's hands and he would be the only one who could direct, change or end the treatment.

As a result of its protective-curative nature, the treatment would exclude the use of amnesty, judicial pardon and similar practices. Adequate establishments should be maintained for the application of the treatment. Prisons would not be totally excluded but they should be used in accordance with the protective nature assigned to criminal law. Finally, Dorado does not exclude the possibility of using penal colonies.

Conclusions

Although influenced by the Italian Positive School, Dorado represents fundamentally a continuation of the " correccionalista " Spanish Penological School of thought whose origin can be traced to Seneca. On several occasions Dorado tried to relate his theory with some of the points of view already expressed by Spanish penologists from the sixteenth to the nineteenth centuries, namely, Cerdán de Tallada, Juan Eusebio, Lardizabal y Uribe and Marcos Gutierrez. For all of them the protection of the offender and his moral correction are the main purposes of the penal sanction and treatment. In Dorado's theory, that protective and correctional aim assumes an enlarged and occasionally Utopian term. His influence, however, among Spanish-speaking writers especially in Spain, has been considerable although none of his followers has ever maintained his extreme points of view. On the other hand, and as very often happens, his theory has been misinterpreted and used to support conclusions completely foreign to his own.

It may be said in conclusion that Dorado was an important pioneer of modern Criminology in that he laid such great stress on the exclusively protective character of the penal sanction without advocating its suppression. The idealism, however, led him to advocate principles which if applied would have eventually denied the human rights which he would have been the first to defend. The protection of such rights implies the protection of everybody, offenders included.

Manuel Lopez-Rey.

BIBLIOGRAPHY

Dorado's bibliography, especially as far as essays and papers are concerned, is considerable. We shall, therefore, mention only his most significant publications.

Problemas jurídicos contemporáneos, 1893.
Problemas de Derecho penal, 1895.
Estudios de Derecho penal preventivo, 1901.
La Psicología criminal en nuestro Derecho legislado, 1910.
El Derecho y sus sacerdotes, 1911.
El Derecho protector de los criminales, 1916.

The last one is by far the most important. Actually it is a considerably enlarged and revised edition of the *Estudios de Derecho penal preventivo*. The two volumes—about 1,300 pages—include twenty-nine papers of a varied nature and purpose. The first one—180 pages—is the basic one and its title was used as the title for the two volumes.

NOTE ON THE CONTRIBUTOR

Dr. MANUEL LOPEZ-REY was until 1965 Chief of the United Nations Section of Social Defence. His career includes professorships at the University of Madrid and in Venezuela, Peru, Chile, Argentina, Uruguay and Bolivia. He was Director-General of the Spanish Ministry of Justice in 1936 and Minister Plenipotentiary to Bucharest from 1937 to 1939. He has been Delegate or Legal Adviser to many international conferences and Director of numerous international seminars. In 1955 he represented the Secretary-General of the United Nations in the First United Nations Congress on the Prevention of Crime and the Treatment of Offenders. Since his retirement he has been lecturing in America and Europe and has held regular seminars at the Institute of Criminology in Cambridge, England. Dr. Lopez-Rey's more recent publications (in English) include *International Co-operation by the U.N. in the Prevention of Crime and the Treatment of Offenders* (1953), *Considerations on the Institutional Treatment of Juvenile Offenders* (1954), and *Crime: An Analytical Appraisal* (1970).

21

JOHN HENRY WIGMORE
1863-1943

"THINK of a genius not born in every country, or every time; a man gifted by nature with a penetrating, aquiline eye; with a judgment prepared with the most extensive erudition; with a herculean robustness of mind, and nerves not to be broken with labour; a man who could spend twenty years in one pursuit." Thus Edmund Burke, speaking of Montesquieu.[1] So far as they go, these words fitly apply to John Henry Wigmore, though yielding him less than justice in failing to reckon with the rich immensity, technical accuracy and wide-ranging sweep of his scholarship. Author of what is undeniably the greatest legal treatise on a specific subject which the Anglo-American law has ever produced—that majestic ten-volume *Treatise on the Anglo-American System of Evidence,* applauded alike by scholars on the one hand and the active ministrants of the law on the other—a work whose historical research, exploration of theory and practice and fealty to literary excellence has made it a household word in the habitations of the law and a *vade mecum* of the lawyer in full practice,—such nevertheless have been his catholicity of interest and versatility of accomplishment that countless other fields of the law and its allied provinces have been the beneficiaries of his achievements.

And not least of these is the high place that he has won in the annals of criminal science, his entitlement to rank as an American pioneer in that field. It had come to him, as to many others, that our institutions and methods directed to the protection of society against crime were not adequately fulfilling their function, either in respect of society itself or those who thus were assailing it. But to this was added the realization, acquired in the course of his extended investigations of comparative law and comparative institutions, that

* Reproduced from *The Journal of Criminal Law, Criminology and Police Science,* Vol. 46, No. 1, May–June 1955.
[1] Edmund Burke, "An Appeal from the New to the Old Whigs," *Works,* ed. F. W. Raffety (London, 1925–1930), Vol. V, p. 132.

on the continent of Europe scientific thought had been conspicuously addressing itself to the study of crime and the criminal, as a matter distinct from the consideration of the technical criminal law. These studies, he conceived, were something which so far almost altogether lay outside our cognizance, but which offered us effective aid in solving our own problems. Detached articles and studies had appeared from time to time in our own publications, and many minds had interested themselves in various phases of the questions involved. Tentative steps had already been taken in a number of our jurisdictions looking toward individualization of punishment in the direction of probation and parole, the indeterminate sentence and the special treatment of juvenile offenders. But any consideration of the collective problem on a comprehensive scale awaited further investigation and discussion. To bring together those interested in the relative questions, to learn and compare the results of their inquiries and experiences, to enlist the aid of the European studies, to give cohesion to the scattered efforts at betterment, and to organize a nation-wide movement for reform of methods, constituted an imperative need. And Wigmore's talent lent itself to meeting precisely that need.

Architect of the National Conference on Criminal Law and Criminology

In 1909 he was the prime mover and architect in the organization of the National Conference on Criminal Law and Criminology, which met at Chicago. To quote from the editorial of Professor James W. Garner appearing in the journal to which it was to give birth,[2] this "was composed of about one hundred and fifty delegates, representing the various professions and occupations concerned directly or indirectly with the administration of the criminal law and the punishment of criminals, and included members of the bench and bar, professors of law in the universities, alienists, criminologists, penologists, superintendents of penal and reformatory institutions, psychologists, police officials, probation officers and the like. Delegates attended from every section of the country, and the conference was a very representative gathering of those either actually concerned with the administration of the criminal law or interested in its problems as students and scientists. In character and purpose the con-

---

[2] *Journal of the American Institute of Criminal Law and Criminology,* Vol. 1, p. 3.

ference was entirely without precedent in the history of the United States. It represented the first instance of co-operative effort among those interested in a better system of criminal justice, and marks, we venture to assert, the beginning of a new era in the history of American criminal jurisprudence." One hundred and thirty-five topics were submitted to the conference for discussion, but it was determined to confine attention to a smaller number to be made the subject of committee investigation and report. A committee was appointed, consisting of Professors John D. Lawson and Edwin R. Keedy, to study the administration of criminal justice in England. Provision was made for the translation into English and publication of the more important of the European studies above mentioned. "Finally, impressed with the advantage of uniting the efforts of lawyers, criminologists, sociologists and all others in the cause of a better criminal law, the conference resolved to effect a permanent national organization to be known as the American Institute of Criminal Law and Criminology, whose purpose shall be to advance the scientific study of crime, criminal law and procedure, to formulate and present measures for solving the problems connected therewith, and to coordinate the efforts of individuals and of organizations interested in the administration of certain and speedy justice." [3] And, appropriately, Wigmore was made president of the Institute thus set on foot.

As one of its first steps the Institute, recognizing the new interest in the problem of the repression of crime, and "believing that an organ should be provided for promoting the new spirit of research and investigation," proceeded forthwith to the establishment of such an organ. Thus came into existence the *Journal of the American Institute of Criminal Law and Criminology,* which, as editorially stated, "will aim to arouse and extend a wider interest in the administration of the criminal law, including the cause and prevention of crime, methods of criminal procedure and the treatment of criminals, to provide a common medium for recording the results of the best scientific thought and professional practice in this and foreign countries concerning the larger problems of criminal science," as well as to record the progress of legislation and administration in its chosen field, advocate the introduction of proper reforms in the matter of criminal justice, and particularly with respect to criminal statistics, and furnish reviews of current scientific literature, foreign and do-

[3] *Ibid.,* p. 5.

mestic, dealing with crime and the criminal.[4]   Under the brilliant
editorship of Professor Garner, the Journal embarked upon the program thus outlined.   In 1911 he was succeeded as editor-in-chief by
Professor Robert H. Gault, under whose patient attention, indefatigable labor and skill of administration, the editorship of the Journal
has since been carried on.   In 1932, on the occasion of the completion of twenty-one years of service on his part, it was well said that
"rarely has more zeal and a sustained ability been freely given to any
publication" than by Dr. Gault [5]—a judgment which his subsequent
editorial career has strikingly confirmed.   And as to the Journal itself no one can doubt that its program as originally outlined has
been abundantly fulfilled.   It is to be added that in the same year,
1932, the *American Journal of Police Science* which had been edited
by Lieutenant Colonel Calvin H. Goddard and published by the Scientific Crime Detection Laboratory of Northwestern University—an
institution whose conception was Wigmore's—became fused with the
Journal, and thenceforward was conducted as a section of the latter.[6]

The Modern Criminal Science Series

The committee work originated in the National Conference was
carried on by the Institute.   The reports made from time to time by
the various committees appear in the Journal, and represent a contribution of signal value to the cause in which all were engaged.   More
than ordinary significance attaches to the work of two of these committees.   The first is that of the committee, consisting of Professors
Lawson and Keedy, charged with visiting the English courts, which
superlatively executed its mandate in a report of two parts, affording
such a descriptive commentary on criminal justice in England as to
become a virtual classic.[7]   The other committee function of especial
moment was that relating to the translation and publication of European treatises.   The result of its labors was the Modern Criminal
Science Series, consisting of nine volumes, carefully selected from the
writings of European scholars in the field.   These volumes are:
Modern Theories of Criminality, by C. Bernaldo de Quirós, translated from the second Spanish edition by Professor Alphonso de

---

[4] *Ibid.,* p. 6.
[5] Andrew A. Bruce, "Editorial," *Journal of the American Institute of Criminal Law and Criminology,* Vol. 23, p. 5.
[6] Calvin Goddard, "Editorial," *ibid.,* p. 166.
[7] This report appears in *Journal of the American Institute of Criminal Law and Criminology,* Vol. 1, pp. 595, 748.

Salvio; *Criminal Psychology,* by Hans Gross, translated from the fourth German edition by Dr. Horace M. Kallen; *Crime, Its Causes and Remedies,* by Cesare Lombroso, translated from the French and German editions by the Rev. Henry P. Horton; *The Individualization of Punishment,* by Raymond Saleilles, translated from the second French edition by Rachel Szold Jastrow; *Penal Philosophy,* by Gabriel Tarde, translated from the fourth French edition by Rapelje Howell; *Crime and Its Repression,* by Gustav Aschaffenburg, translated from the second German edition by Adalbert Albrecht; *Criminology,* by Raffaele Garofalo, translated from the first Italian and fifth French editions by Robert W. Millar; *Criminality and Economic Conditions,* by Dr. Willem A. Bonger, translated from the French by the Rev. Henry P. Horton; and *Criminal Sociology,* by Enrico Ferri, translated from the fifth Italian and second French editions by Joseph I. Kelly and John Lisle.[8] The selection thus made amply justified the statement of the committee that

the effort . . . has been made to select those works which best represent the various schools of thought in criminal science, the general results reached, the points of contact or of controversy, and the contrasts of method—having always in view that class of works which have more than local value and could best be serviceable to criminal science in our country. As the science has various aspects and emphases—the anthropological, sociological, legal, statistical, pathological—due regard was paid in the selection, to a representation of all these aspects.[9]

It was a particularly happy thought to include in the Series de Quirós' book, *Modern Theories of Criminality.* For this gave the reader essentially a bird's-eye view of the corpus of studies looking to diagnosis of the causes of crime. As said in the introduction by William Smithers, it "reveals all the shades of thought which have marked the development of the science and constitutes a compendium that no student of the subject can ignore without disadvantage."[10] On the basis of this introductory study the reader is prepared intelligently to understand and appreciate, for example, the

---

[8] See the Report of the Committee on Translations, Bulletin No. 3 of the Institute, April 1910, *Journal of the American Institute of Criminal Law and Criminology,* Vol. 1, pp. 450–455, and the list appearing opposite the title page in the published volumes. Translation of the Ferri volume was interrupted by the death of Joseph I. Kelly when a little more than half finished, and was completed by John Lisle. Owing to the death in turn of Mr. Lisle, the text was revised and seen through the press by George F. Deiser and Dr. John A. Forst. W. W. Smithers, "Editorial Preface," in *Criminal Sociology* by Enrico Ferri (Boston, 1917), pp. xxiv–xxv.

[9] Report of the Committee on Translations, p. 452.

[10] W. W. Smithers, "Introduction to the English version," in *Modern Theories of Criminality,* by C. Bernaldo de Quirós (Boston, 1911), p. xvi.

ideas of Lombroso, Ferri and Garofalo, with the differentiation and diversification of stress coming from the pens of the several authors. In such wise there came to pass the dream of Wigmore that there should be available to the English-speaking reader the quintessence of authoritative Continental thought regarding a matter of such high social concern.

On this point it is interesting to quote Wigmore's own words, written in 1938. "In 1909," he said, "we knew and cared nothing about Criminology—the very name was unknown. But from 1910 to 1917 my Committee published the Modern Criminal Science Series; it was eaten up by all groups of persons concerned with crime repression. Its volumes still pay a royalty to some of the European authors . . . and Criminology is now an established field of study all over our country." [11]

We have dwelt on the work of the Conference and of the Institute because Wigmore was essentially its heart and soul. His was the idea which gave it birth, his the organizing ability which brought the movement into activity and endowed it with vitality of function. Not only does the work everywhere bear the mark of his personal accomplishment, but he possessed and exercised the precious faculty of imbuing others with his enthusiasms and attracting their aid and support, by means of which he was enabled to enlist and bring to bear upon the tasks in hand the talent and wisdom of many other outstanding men of science and scholarship. No work of the kind would be possible without financial support, and it was his ability to find sources for such support that permitted the movement to proceed. He it was who had the principal voice in the selection of the volumes of the Modern Criminal Science Series, who carried on correspondence with the authors, made arrangements for publication of the books, and determined in fine upon the persons to serve as translators and introducers. For the Journal his advice was constantly sought, and its original shaping came substantially from his hands. That advice was ever at its command, and his influence upon the character and contents of the Journal continued until the end of his life. In no exaggerated sense he was the founder of the new movement of which the Conference, the Institute and the Journal are the tangible attestation.

[11] Wigmore to Frederic R. Coudert, March 4, 1938.

His other work

But his services to criminal science in no whit abated his interest in the technical side of criminal law. It was exemplified not only by articles and addresses, but particularly by scores of case notes, appearing for the most part in the *Illinois Law Review,* in which he took occasion to analyze and comment upon the judicial result, especially in cases decided by the Supreme Court of Illinois. He never hesitated to criticize where the occasion demanded; his views were always sharp and decisive; always impatient of looseness of thinking, he never permitted anything to disturb his fidelity to what he conceived to be the correct application of the legal rule. His criticisms sometimes were not relished by the courts involved, but they did much toward building up a more sensible attitude in decision and yielding a better appreciation of the true rôle of criminal justice.

But important and far-reaching in effect as were the things done by John Henry Wigmore in the realm of criminal science and criminal law, it stands out that these represent but a single panel of the tapestry upon which is spread the rich record of his scholarly achievements and his labors in the public weal.

That record, unfortunately, has never been fully committed to print. Something of its contents may be glimpsed in the editorial tributes paid to him in 1941 in the "Honoring John Henry Wigmore" number of the Journal,[12] as also in the memorial addresses appearing in the volume of the Journal for 1943.[13] But anything like an adequate account of these contents is a task awaiting a future biographer—a task which in view of Wigmore's ramified intellectual quests, wideness of learning and surpassing energy can never be aught but an extensive one. Pressing closely upon the attention, however, are his services in the cause of legal education, to which he yielded a measureless contribution. All know the indebtedness which the Law School of Northwestern University owes to his efforts. First as a professor, and then for years as dean, he gave it the high character and international repute it now enjoys, gave it also through patient and unremitting endeavor the beautiful building which is its habitation. His efforts, too, brought into being the Gary Library of Law, with its rich collections, notably of Continental and other foreign law. Throughout the country, with repercussions beyond its

[12] *Journal of Criminal Law and Criminology,* Vol. 32, pp. 263–296.
[13] *Ibid.,* Vol. 34, pp. 75–92. These appear also in *Illinois Law Review,* Vol. 38, pp. 1–15.

borders, his influence in the field of legal education was conspicuously marked and widely accepted. Incident to this field, through his instrumentality and leading participation, operating under the auspices of the Association of American Law Schools, the literature of the law in its less technical aspects was enriched by three important series, namely, Select Essays in Anglo-American Legal History, in three volumes; the Modern Legal Philosophy Series, in twelve volumes, and the Continental Legal History Series, in ten volumes. His was in the main the selection of authors, and in the case of foreign material, that of translators; his likewise was largely the editorial work, the arrangements for printing, and the activities of publication. He also compiled, jointly with his colleague, Professor Albert Kocourek, the three volumes of *Evolution of Law*.

We referred at the outset to his transcendent *Treatise on the Anglo-American System of Evidence*. Around this work Wigmore produced a cluster of satellites, for which the reader is referred to the Bibliography. In rather different domains of the law are his *Select Cases on the Law of Torts* (a field which bears the impress of his talent for analysis and systematization), and three particularly noteworthy works, *A Panorama of the World's Legal Systems, A Kaleidoscope of Justice,* and *A Guide to American International Law and Practice*. In these and other fields there came from his pen, besides lesser books and works of individual editorship, a multitude of articles, comments, addresses, lectures, reviews, and introductions to books of other writers, always enriching the subject in hand from his well-balanced thinking and wealth of learning.

In other regards the roll of his undertakings necessarily encompasses his notable career as an officer of the Judge Advocate's Department in World War I, in which, indelibly associated with Selective Service, he was the stalwart support and counsellor of the Provost Marshal General; his services to the reform of civil procedure, marked by his active participation in the establishment and labors of the American Judicature Society; his furtherance of legal aid to the poor, through the Law School and otherwise; his services for years as a member of the National Commission on Uniform State Laws; his work on behalf of Japanese legal history—a sentimental heritage from the days when he commenced his teaching career as professor of Anglo-American law at Keio University, Tokyo; his participation in the work of the international congresses of comparative law; his labors on behalf of radio and air law, including his service to the Government in the formulation of air law regulations and his instrumentality in founding the *Journal of Air Law*. To name these is but sparsely to indicate the cardinal activities which drew him outside the main lines of his endeavor.

Fame was his portion, both at home and abroad. His name will always be one "fast anchored in the deep abyss of time." But with every homage to the magnificence of his intellectual achievement, his memory as a man will be devotedly cherished by all who knew him. His personal charm, the graciousness of his manners, his genuine interest in the studies of others and the encouragement of their efforts, all elicited their love and admiration. For those coming into close association with him as fellow teachers or otherwise, that association was a gladdening and rewarding thing. Well might each of them say with Cicero's Laelius that its recollection is such *"ut beate vixisse videar, quia cum Scipione vixerim."*

ROBERT WYNESS MILLAR.

BIBLIOGRAPHY

By Wigmore

A Digest of the Reported Decisions, Precedents and General Principles Enunciated by the Board of Railroad Commissioners of the Commonwealth of Massachusetts from 1870 to 1888, inclusive. Boston, 1888.

The Australian Ballot System as Embodied in the Legislation of Various Countries. Boston, 1889; 2nd ed., revised, 1889.

A Treatise on the System of Evidence in Trials at Common Law, including the Statutes and Judicial Decisions of All Jurisdictions of the United States. 4 volumes. Boston, 1904–1905. Republished in a 2nd ed., 5 volumes, 1923, and a 3rd ed., 10 volumes, 1940, as *A Treatise on the Anglo-American System of Evidence in Trials at Common Law* . . .

A List of Legal Novels. Chicago, 1908. Wigmore also contributed "One Hundred Legal Novels" to *Library Journal*, Vol. 52 (1927), pp. 189–190.

A Preliminary Bibliography of Modern Criminal Law and Criminology. Chicago, 1909.

A Pocket Code of the Rules of Evidence in Trials at Law. Boston, 1910. Republished in a 2nd ed., 1935, and a 3rd ed., 1942, as *Wigmore's Code of the Rules of Evidence in Trials at Law.*

Select Cases on the Law of Torts. 2 volumes. Boston, 1910–1912.

The Principles of Judicial Proof as Given by Logic, Psychology, and General Experience. Boston, 1913. Republished in a 2nd ed., 1931, as *The Principles of Judicial Proof; or, The Process of Proof as Given* . . . and in 1937 as *The Science of Judicial Proof, as Given* . . .

Military Justice during the War. Washington, D.C., 1919.

Problems of Law, Its Past, Present, and Future. Three lectures. New York, 1920.

A Panorama of the World's Legal Systems. Illustrated, 3 volumes, St. Paul, 1928; combined into one volume and expanded, Washington, D.C., 1936.

A Students' Textbook of the Law of Evidence. New York and Chicago, 1935.

A Kaleidoscope of Justice. Washington, D.C., 1941.

To Popularize for Lawyers the Study of American International Law; A Syllabus of American International Law for American Practitioners. Chicago, 1941.

A Guide to American International Law and Practice. Albany, 1943.

Wigmore as Editor

Materials for the Study of Private Law in Old Japan. 4 volumes. Tokyo, 1892.

Examinations in Law. Chicago, 1899.

A Selection of Cases on Evidence, for the Use of Students of Law. Boston, 1906. Republished in a 2nd ed., 1913, and a 3rd ed., 1932, as *Select Cases on the Law of Evidence.*

Select Essays in Anglo-American Legal History. With E. Freund and W. E. Mikell. 3 volumes. Boston, 1907–1909.

Military Source Book. St. Paul, 1919.

Rational Basis of Legal Institutions. With Albert Kocourek. New York, 1923.

Evolution of Law. With Albert Kocourek. 3 volumes. Boston, 1915–1918.

Law and Justice in Tokugawa Japan. Tokyo, 1941.

Wigmore was a co-editor of the Modern Criminal Science Series (9 volumes, Boston, 1910–1915); the Modern Legal Philosophy Series (12 volumes, New York, 1911–1921); and the Continental Legal History Series (10 volumes, Boston, 1912–1920). He also contributed introductions to many other books, and numerous articles to journals.

NOTE ON THE CONTRIBUTOR

ROBERT WYNESS MILLAR was Professor of Law at Northwestern University from 1915 until his retirement in 1942, and Professor Emeritus there until his death in 1959. From 1897 to 1915 he had been a practicing lawyer. He was a Judge Advocate in the U.S. Army in the First World War, and in 1945 he received the Navy Department's Distinguished Civilian Service Award. Professor Millar is the author of *Common Law Pleading* (1912), *Formative Principles of Civil Procedure* (1923), and *Civil Procedure of the Trial Court in Historical Perspective* (1952). He translated and edited the *History of Continental Civil Procedure* (1927), and has contributed numerous articles and essays to the literature of Comparative Civil Procedure.

22

GUSTAV ASCHAFFENBURG
1866–1944

THREE names—Henry Maudsley, Cesare Lombroso and Gustav Aschaffenburg—suggest the tremendous impetus that criminology has experienced from medical science—mainly from psychiatry. Maudsley lived before my time. I was no longer young when Lombroso's daughter conducted me through the shrine-like study in Turin of the eminent Italian who has been " buried " so many times and is not dead yet. But Aschaffenburg—I knew him well. We were fighters on the same battlefield for many years. Fate fell on him like a thunderbolt; an unjust and an undeserved fate. He came to the hospitable shores of the United States broken in heart and broken in health. His hope to find a publisher came to naught. He who had played a prominent part at all international meetings in Rome, in Prague, in· London died in oblivion. The writer is performing a long-postponed duty in reviving the memory of the man and his work.

A great man should be sized up by two different individuals or groups. Those who happened to be on intimate terms with him, liked him, loved him or hated him. Ten or twenty years later, when the silent effect of his work has become visible, when opinion and judgment have grown unemotional, a second critic should review the essence of what he strove for and what he achieved. But we are not yet as far away from Aschaffenburg as that.

A portrait of Aschaffenburg

It may seem curious to find a criminologist trying to sketch a " portrait parlé " of another criminologist. When the writer first met Aschaffenburg a few years after the First World War he saw a small, stocky man enter the bungalow he was occupying in the

* Reproduced from *The Journal of Criminal Law, Criminology and Police Science*, Vol. 45, No. 2, July–August 1954.

charming surroundings of Munich. He moved with the uncertainty
of a very short-sighted man and, at the same time, with the directness of a doctor who is accustomed to giving orders and to being
obeyed. One would have thought that he was slightly uneasy; but
his breathlessness was not of emotional origin, just the attitude of a
person suffering from asthma and highly sensitive to atmospheric
conditions. Aschaffenburg's greatest assets were not his looks, but
his delightful personality, his penetrating eyes, his never-tiring
interest, his cheering vivacity and an unhesitating helpfulness which
was not always reciprocated. With profound scholarship he combined the heart of a child. It always struck me that he who had
seen all the depths of human degradation and misery had still
preserved a certain prudishness. I still remember the story he told
me with a certain embarrassment. There was a meeting in the
small university town of Greifswald. Before going to bed he went
for a short walk in the deserted streets. A young girl came out of
the darkness and accosted him, using one of those eternal and
well-known phrases. He asked her in bewilderment what she
wanted. And she enlightened the famous psychiatrist by saying:
" I am the night-life here." He fled to his hotel.

I mentioned this episode because it shows the delicate fibre of the
unusual man. He was well aware of his personal magnetism. That
is why he made every effort to break through the barriers of spatial
distance and to reach the region of human contact. When he
entered a big hall, attention turned away from the more or less
fascinating paper which was being delivered and was directed
toward this short man, his unusual face and his good-natured smile,
and tardily returned to the speaker. Many meetings in the capitals
of Europe seemed to lack something—somewhat like a blank cheque
—when he was not attending. But he liked meetings, discussion
and contradiction, notwithstanding his peaceful character, and he
was present as often as he could be.

One of the main traits in the mental make-up of Aschaffenburg
was his startling mental activity. Whenever he came to see me and
we went for long walks through the woods, he used to stand still
from time to time to discuss a problem which was on his mind.
He liked to be stimulated by other people's opposite opinions and he
carried with him a tremendous amount of clinical and judicial
experience. Being rather reserved and prudent himself, he was fond
of listening to daring ideas and inventive interpretations. At times,

with all his critical powers, he yielded to one of his finest qualities: his wish to help and to save. We disagreed, for instance, on the guilt of that supposed American lawyer, Karl Hau, who, disguised by a false beard, had come to Baden-Baden to shoot his wealthy mother-in-law. Hau got a death sentence and was a lifer in the penitentiary at Bruchsal (Baden), maintaining his innocence to the last. He wrote a suggestive prison book and committed a dramatic suicide after his parole in the ruins of Rome. Aschaffenburg's conviction was never shaken that Hau had not been the murderer of the mother-in-law. At a big official dinner party Aschaffenburg had been seated by chance near the Minister of Justice. Some years before this man had been one of the judges who sentenced Hau. A hot dispute started, everyone in the large hall grew silent and for a while the old judicial duel was fought all over again. In such a moment the calm scholar changed, to everybody's surprise, to a pugnacious and stubborn opponent; the less prepared he was the more forcible and convincing he was, and in this outburst of his temper hardly to be convinced.

Aschaffenburg had a few enemies and many friends. I would have liked to watch him as a prison doctor and to keep an eye on reactions toward him. But this period of his life lay behind him when we first met. He was now the big boss, head of the Psychopathic Clinic of Cologne (one of the richest cities of Germany at that time), internationally known, a much sought after psychiatric expert all over Germany. He was tired of fame and work and recognition. At that time he came to see me in my retreat at Wessling and asked me whether I would not like to help him edit the *Monatsschrift für Kriminalpsychologie*. I was struck by his trust in me and said "Yes." A co-operation started at that time which was unique in its complete accord, and I must admit that this conformity was maintained much more by Aschaffenburg's peaceful and tolerant disposition than by my own temperament. I was rash, impatient and adverse to compromise, especially twenty years ago. Aschaffenburg was calm; balanced to a degree that could be described as wise. Our opposite natures fitted marvellously together. There was a natural consonance and a cheerful concurrence which the readers of the *Monatsschrift* must have appreciated, since they started flocking in from all parts of the world. A glance at the contributors from 1925–34 will show that the most distinguished criminologists, in the United States, Japan, Russia, Italy, France, Spain, Belgium,

Holland, Scandinavia and South America sent us their papers. It was " One World " in criminology.

Destiny brought about one last disagreement. After the Nazi régime had lasted one year, I saw clearly that honest science could not live in the atmosphere of *Gleichschaltung* or thinking on order. The publisher was fearful and urged a change in tone or greater caution. I was not ready to yield and tendered my resignation. Aschaffenburg thought I had been too impetuous. He hoped that conditions might improve and revert to the normal. He wrote a paper in answer to the attacks of Professor Dahm, the leader of the Nazi school of criminal law, and offered quiet discussion and a settlement on common ground. He continued publishing the *Monatsschrift* in 1935. In 1936, when he should have celebrated his seventieth birthday, the régime took the *Monatsschrift* away from him, appointed a new publisher and asked new editors—uncorrupted and unspoilt—to take over. One comfort was left. The famous old appellation was changed to *Kriminalbiologie*. I crossed the ocean and Professor Aschaffenburg followed two years later. He went to Baltimore; I lived in the Rocky Mountains. The old close friendship had long been restored and letters went to and fro. We thought of the future and drafted our plans. Like all refugees, we underrated the duration of the German imbroglio. Then, when hostilities were drawing to their end, death took away the remarkable man. His name will not vanish from our textbooks. Three psychiatrists left their impression upon the last century: Maudsley, Lombroso and Aschaffenburg.

His life and his work

Gustav Aschaffenburg was born in Zweibruecken, west of the Rhine, on April 23, 1866. His father was a business man. After his medical studies in Heidelberg, Wuerzburg, Freiburg, Berlin and Strassburg, and after having served as an interne under Professor Krafft-Ebing in Vienna and under Professors Ball, Charcot and Pierre Marie in Paris, he became assistant to the great Kraepelin in Heidelberg. The vogue in Heidelberg was experimental psychology at that time and Aschaffenburg eagerly joined the group of young scholars. It may be that his life-long aversion to alcohol dated from his experiments with that poison. According to Professor Wilmanns, who succeeded Kraepelin when the latter went to

Munich, this eminent psychiatrist led Aschaffenburg's interest towards criminology. Kraepelin is also said to have encouraged his promising assistant to write the book which made him famous: *Das Verbrechen und seine Bekaempfung*, published first in 1903. But at this time Aschaffenburg had already moved away from Heidelberg and had accepted a position as head of the medical service at the prison in Halle.

Heidelberg offers more opportunities for the study of crime than other German universities. Three penal institutions are sending their difficult cases to the Heidelberg clinic. The population is partly urban (Mannheim), partly rural (the Neckar valley). The whole Palatinate on the left bank of the Rhine has no university and is bound to make use of the medical facilities of Heidelberg. This Palatinate has the highest rate of crimes of violence in Germany. All these experiences could be enlarged in Halle and in Cologne where Aschaffenburg started teaching psychiatry in 1904 at the Academy of Medicine. When Cologne restored its ancient university in 1919 he became Professor of Psychiatry and Director of the Clinic. Aschaffenburg has often depicted the careless, somewhat autocratic way in which Konrad Adenauer, then mayor of Cologne, called him in and told him that he had appointed him to this great position. In Cologne he stayed till the train took him to Bremerhaven and to the transatlantic liner, never to see Germany again. He loved his country more than he knew himself. Professor Ruffin in Freiburg has told me of a significant episode. When Aschaffenburg was about to leave Germany in 1938 a great Swiss publishing house approached him and asked him to write a textbook of psychiatry. He declined and told Ruffin that he would not be able to do so without seeing German students before him whilst writing the book, and this had become impossible now and for all times.

The reader is not so much interested in the *Handbuch der Psychiatrie* published before the First World War and Aschaffenburg's *Handbuch der gerichtlichen Medizin*, edited jointly with Professor Hoche in Freiburg. Our attention is focused on the book which caused the editors of the *Modern Criminal Science Series* to lay it before the American public in an excellent translation which made his fame. The *Monatsschrift* is too well known to dwell upon it at length, but the book deserves a few remarks. When it appeared fifty years ago and was reprinted in three large editions the approach was refreshingly new and original. The first part, called the general causes of crime, is essentially sociological. Aschaffenburg has tried to forget the medical side of the problem by making use of extensive statistical material and a very happy selection of literature. Some opinions may be contradicted or have been discarded by later studies. On the whole it is a most readable and most stimulating book. I have been requested more than once by Aschaffenburg to join him in writing a fourth and enlarged edition, but I always thought that the book should remain as it was with all its foibles and all its high qualities. If we have moved forward since—and it cannot be said that we have done so in every respect—we could not have done it without standing on his shoulders.

Lombroso died in 1909. The objections Aschaffenburg raised against the great Italian, his praise and his criticism, could be levelled against himself and will be aimed probably at each of us by those who come after us. Yet they will know so much better than they would otherwise know because we endeavoured in our time to gather new material, found new interpretations and ventured into new hypotheses which may be approved or disapproved by facts we were not aware of, because they were not available in our time.

There were very good reasons why scientific meetings all over the world listened with intense attention when Aschaffenburg rose to speak. Professor Ruffin has pointed at Aschaffenburg's artistic nature. That is why so many painters, musicians and actors came to seek relief and support in his optimistic attitude and his understanding compassion. The poor were sure of his care as well as those who could not be cured. Professor Gruhle has a story to tell. He had it from Aschaffenburg himself. He had been asked by the court to present his opinion on a pseudological personality; a few years later this same confidence man made him a sucker. Such things happened all the time. He had one of those salons where he and the cultivated Mrs. Aschaffenburg used to receive distinguished guests who happened to live in Cologne, or to come through the city and were the famous professor's patients. One evening a well-known actress who had been cured from a drug habit came in and said goodbye. She left the same night for Berlin to be back on her job. About midnight the telephone rang and continued to ring. It was the police calling from a station halfway between Cologne and Berlin. The cured patient had taken cocaine again and had left the sleeping car in a minimum of clothing. Where should she be brought for further medical attendance? We thought it funny, but Aschaffenburg was plunged into thought. Could psychiatry still be perfected?

It was a mark of honour to be invited to Mrs. Aschaffenburg's salon. Honorary degrees had been showered on her husband. No scholar of distinction came to Cologne without trying to see him. Then came the landslide of 1933. It came with a fury no one expected; no generation in civilised Western Europe had experienced the like since the French Revolution. To Aschaffenburg's inner decency it seemed not only a political change, but the collapse of a world. It was as if this earth and a meteor had collided. Something unbelievable, quite contrary to the order of the moral planetary system had happened. He never accepted it, nor believed, nor overcame it. The shock first stunned, then killed him. Posterity, if it wants to maintain its nimbus as the incorruptible judge of men and times, owes Gustav Aschaffenburg more than the usual share of reparation.

Epilogue

An eminent American friend has put me on the spot by asking whether Aschaffenburg would have followed new lines of thought if he had been able to write a revised edition in 1930. We used to discuss the fundamental issues for hours on long walks through the Bavarian woods. I cannot say that Aschaffenburg had changed, yet tentative steps on the way of a compromise were more palpable to an old friend than visible to the outsider. Aschaffenburg saw the whole rising generation get up in arms against us, the " supernumerary " old set. They were of one mind. We were split into the classical school and the modern group, left leaderless after the death of von Liszt. The mob was raging in the streets. Millions of unemployed were in terror of the future and were turning their ears and their faint-hearted hopes towards the man who was promising everyone everything. A new world seemed to be in travail. Aschaffenburg, a social being *par excellence*, who wanted to like and be liked, was afraid of ostracism and loneliness although you could see him fight bravely against what he himself recognised to be a weakness. It is one of the hardest things in the world not to yield to the majority after having been taught that it is the essence of good democracy to submit to its will and command.

But these were only undercurrents in Aschaffenburg's mind. They never succeeded in getting the upper hand. They may have emerged to the surface in one or two articles in which he expressed the hope of an armistice between the two hostile camps. Yet we were defeated and no quarter was given. You cannot offer a fair settlement to the victor in the midst of his triumph, and—besides— scientific convictions do not admit mutual concessions. When Aschaffenburg had realised the cruel finality of the situation, he did not speak of it any more to me or to others. He died from an overdose of disappointment. The new edition remained unwritten, but the old book is living on.

HANS VON HENTIG.

SELECTED BIBLIOGRAPHY

Das Verbrechen und seine Bekämpfung (first German ed. 1903); English translation, *Crime and its Repression* (1913; reprinted Montclair, N.J., 1968).
Die Stimmungsschwankungen der Epileptiker (1906).
Die Sicherung der Gesellschaft gegen gemeingefährliche Geisteskranke (1913).
Handbuch der Psychiatrie, edited by Aschaffenburg (1911–23).
Founder of the *Monatsschrift für Kriminalpsychologie* which he edited from 1904–35.

NOTE ON THE CONTRIBUTOR

Dr. HANS VON HENTIG, formerly Professor of Criminal Law at the University of Bonn and Dean of the Bonn Law School, was for ten years co-editor of the *Monatsschrift für Kriminalpsychologie und Strafrechtsreform*, founded by Professor Aschaffenburg. He was dismissed by Hitler in 1935, went to America in 1936, taught at Yale and the State Universities of California, Oregon, Iowa, Colorado and Kansas City, and was Research Assistant to the Attorney General in Washington, D.C., and Director of the Colorado Crime Survey. After the war he was called back to assume the chair of Criminology at the University of Bonn. He is now retired. Dr. von Hentig has written *Crime, Causes and Conditions* (1947), *The Criminal and His Victim* (1948), *Die Strafe* (translated into English as *Punishment* (1937)), several volumes of *Zur Psychologie der Einzeldelikte*, and smaller works entitled *Der Gangster, Der Schiffsmord, Die Besiegten, Der jugendliche Vandalismus, Der Muttermord*, and *Über den Zusammenhang von kosmischen, biologischen und sozialen Krisen*.

23

CHARLES BUCKMAN GORING
1870–1919

A BUDDING science periodically requires a sceptic who, being erudite both in the data of the science and in logic, is motivated to assess its alleged theories and to vitalise theory construction. Charles Goring, English psychiatrist and philosopher, possessed this unusual stature in criminology.

Goring was educated at the University of London. He received the B.SC. in 1895 and the M.D. in 1903. In 1893, he was awarded the John Stuart Mill Studentship in Philosophy of Mind and Logic, and four years later was elected a Fellow of University College. From 1902 until his death in 1919 he was employed as a medical officer in various English prisons.

Under the sponsorship of the British Government, Goring, assisted by other prison medical officers, as well as Karl Pearson and his staff at the Biometrica Laboratory, collected and organised data bearing upon ninety-six traits of each of over 3,000 English convicts. By a statistical comparison of the distribution of these traits among classes of criminals, and among criminals and non-criminals, he tested and partly refuted the propositions of the Positive and Correctionist Schools of criminology. He also laid the foundation from which a scientific criminology might be constructed. His findings, which are the result of twelve years of diligent study, were published in 1913 under the title, *The English Convict*. This work is still the classic example of the application of biometrics to the study of the criminal.[1]

This writer, in presenting a résumé of Goring's major contributions to criminology, does so with a reservation: a just appraisal of his ideas requires that each reader personally probe *The English*

* Reproduced from *The Journal of Criminal Law, Criminology and Police Science*, Vol. 47, No. 5, January–February 1957.
[1] Thorsten Sellin, "Charles Buckman Goring," *Encyclopedia of the Social Sciences*, edited by E. R. A. Seligman and A. Johnson, New York, 1931, Macmillan, Vol. VI, p. 703.

Convict. Several of his contributions are today of interest to sociologists. The use of the statistical method, which Goring emphasised,
to discern etiological elements in human behaviour is currently
fashionable in sociological research. Recent discussions of the conceptions of the criminal [2] and the relation of these conceptions to
theories of criminality [3] serve to point up his originality. Goring's
discussion of the role of age in the genesis of crime antecedes but
closely parallels that of the Gluecks.[4] The recent work of Clemmer [5]
substantiates Goring's finding that imprisonment is inadequate as a
method of reforming the offender. Two other contributions require
consideration. His data on the vital statistics and fertility of
criminals are interesting *per se* and as a means of bolstering his
theory of criminality. Lastly, Goring provides a programme of
crime control that is logically consistent with his etiological proposition. The reader who follows Goring through the development
of these topics is impressed with his scientific imagination, logic and
excellent prose. The comment of Karl Pearson is apropos:

> The world has yet to realise that achievement in every field is the product
> of trained imagination alone. Truth in science as in art is not the product of
> mere computation or careful observation, but of these guided by fertility of
> imagination. The creative mind has the potentiality of poet, artist and
> scientist within its grasp, and Goring's friends were never very certain in
> which category to place him. Perhaps the specification was as difficult and
> would be as unprofitable as it must ever be in the case of the Florentine, the
> master spirit of this type of mind.[6]

The statistical method

Modern criminologists have generally acclaimed Goring for his
critique of Lombroso's conception of the " born criminal type."
Yet Goring was quick to stress that he was not opposed so much to
Lombroso's findings as to his method of arriving at them. This

[2] Paul F. Tappan, " Who is the Criminal? " Amer.Sociol.Rev., Vol. XII: 96–102, 1947;
Frank E. Hartung, " White-Collar Offences in the Wholesale Meat Industry in Detroit,"
Amer.Jour.of Sociol., Vol. LVI: 25–34, 1950; E. W. Burgess, " Discussion of Frank E.
Hartung: White-Collar Offences in the Wholesale Meat Industry in Detroit," Amer.
Jour.of Sociol., Vol. LVI: 32–34, 1950.

[3] Daniel Glaser, " Criminality Theories and Behavioural Images," Amer.Jour.of Sociol.,
Vol. LXI 5: 433–444, March 1956.

[4] Sheldon and Eleanor Glueck, *Juvenile Delinquents Grown Up*, New York, 1940, The
Commonwealth Fund, pp. 90–106.

[5] Donald Clemmer, " Imprisonment as a Source of Criminality," Jour.Crim.Law,
Criminol.and Pol.Sci., Vol. XLI: 311–319, 1950.

[6] " Charles Goring, 1870–1919, Obituary Notice and Appreciation," *Biometrika*, Vol.
XII: 298, November 1918–December 1919.

method—the anatomico-pathological—simply consisted of direct observations by the senses, without the use of measuring instruments, of supposedly abnormal anatomical traits in man. Lombroso defined any marked deviation from the mean value of any trait as an abnormality, or anomaly, and presumed that the degree of moral alienation in men could be inferred from the anomalies stigmatising them. Goring rejected this method on three grounds. First, a science requires precise measurement, and this is not obtained by sense impressions. He admirably demonstrated this by revealing the marked contrast between a composite drawing of thirty imaginative portraits of criminals and that of thirty photographic portraits of criminals. Secondly, Lombroso had, contrary to statistical science, erected differences of kind in treating deviations from the mean value as abnormal rather than unusual phenomena. Lastly, the roughness of the measuring technique provided results that had a low rate of reproducibility. This may account for Tarde's observation that the physical anthropologists were not in agreement with respect to the stigmata of the criminal.[7]

The statistical technique, argued Goring, is the method *par excellence* for the scientific study of the criminal. It permits us to build our knowledge of human beings on foundations as solid and reliable as those of the physical sciences. The conclusions reached by this method are based on steps which are rooted in logic and explicitly stated, and are independent of the preconceptions of the investigator. However, he was quick to note that the use of this technique necessitates two assumptions.[8] First, we must assume that the distribution of human traits is not fortuitous but according to the Gauss-Laplacian curve. He felt that this assumption was valid in view of the findings of Quételet, Galton and Pearson. Secondly, it must be assumed that criminals and non-criminals are qualitatively comparable. The reasonableness of this assumption depends upon whether one accepts the legal or ethical conception of the criminal. The latter, making no distinction between sin and crime, views the criminal as being innately pathological, *i.e.*, an incarnation of original sin. In rejecting this conception, Goring

---

[7] Margaret S. Wilson Vine, *supra*. Chap. 14.·

[8] A general discussion of this topic is provided by L. Festinger, " Assumptions Underlying the Use of Statistical Techniques," *Research Methods in Social Relations*, by M. Jahoda, M. Deutsch and S. W. Cook, New York, 1951, Dryden Press, Part II, pp. 713–726.

argued that a fine distinction between the immorality of the criminal
and the morality of the non-criminal had no basis in fact: the non-
criminal also commits breaches of the normative order. Unless,
then, there is some specific quality distinguishing crime from other
antisocial acts, the difference between criminals and non-criminals
is one of degree only. Criminals differ in the fact that their anti-
social acts are so grave as to result eventually in conviction and
imprisonment by legal authority.

The criminal diathesis

In regarding the criminal as a legal fact and crime as merely an
extreme degree of antisocial conduct, Goring did not accept the still
current presupposition that constitutional factors play no part in a
criminal career. He observed that acceptance of this presumption
and its corollary, that innately all normal men are mentally and
morally equal, resulted by deduction in one of the following propositions: (1) that criminality depends upon the deliberate choice
of an individual between good and evil—the classical idea; or (2) the
criminal is not a normal man, and his criminality is a product of
disease—the Lombrosian notion; or (3) criminality is a traditional
moral acquisition, produced solely and entirely by misdirected education—the modern deduction. To broaden the range of possible
explanations, Goring deemed it mandatory to assume that constitutional as well as environmental factors may be instrumental in
criminality:

> In other words, we are forced to an hypothesis of the possible existence of
> a character in all men which, in the absence of a better term, we call the
> "criminal diathesis"— . . . a constitutional proclivity either mental, moral
> or physical, present to some degree in all men, but so potent in some as to
> determine for them, eventually, the fate of imprisonment.[9]

Therefore, Goring set out to ascertain the association between the
criminal diathesis and the environment, training, stock and attributes of the criminal. However, the diathesis, being hypothetical,
could not be measured directly. Variations in its presence among
men must be inferred from differences among them in the tendency
to be convicted and imprisoned for crime. This tendency ranges
from non-conviction to frequent and/or prolonged imprisonment.

---

[9] Charles Goring, *The English Convict: A Statistical Study*, 1913, reprinted Montclair, N.J.,
1972, Patterson Smith, p. 26.

Unfortunately, Goring was unable to compare with respect to every trait individuals occupying the extreme positions because of a paucity of data pertaining to the non-convict population. As an alternative procedure, he compared criminals, grouped according to both their kinds and degrees of criminality. It was assumed that there should be significant differences between criminals convicted of such different offences as: violence to the person (assault), damage to property (mainly arson), stealing and burglary, sexual offences and fraud. Two scales were employed to express degrees of criminality. One was based upon the frequency of conviction during the total life span, and the other, which was to portray the gravity of the offender's acts, was based upon the ratio of years of imprisonment to years of freedom for an offender after his first conviction. Striking here, as elsewhere in his work, is the lucid manner in which Goring makes explicit the basis for this procedure:

> Assuming that conviction and reconviction for crime are not purely circum-stantial occurrences, and constitutional factors play some part in this eventuality, it is a reasonable presumption that, whatever may be the ultimate nature of the criminal diathesis, increasing frequency of conviction to, and increasing periods of detention in, prison, should vary directly with increasing intensities of this diathesis, and, consequently, if this inward potentiality for committing, and being apprehended and convicted of crime, which we call the criminal diathesis, were reflected by outward signs, it is reasonable to suppose that progressive changes in physical attributes would be associated with progressive changes in frequency of conviction to, and length of confinement in, prison.[10]

Physical and mental traits to criminality

Goring's examination of the relations of thirty-seven physical and six mental traits to criminality led him to reject the claims of Lombroso and other criminal anthropologists that there are specific stigmata characterising the criminal.

Of the thirty-seven physical traits, only six of them, when corre-lated with type of crime, yielded coefficients above 0·15. Further, the mean value (0·107) of the coefficients for the whole series of traits differed only slightly from the value of a pure chance relation-ship (0·075). As far as degree of criminality was concerned, Goring found that it was independent of the few traits considered: stature, distance between the eyes, head circumference, weight and cephalic index. One significant difference was found in the distributions of

---

[10] *Ibid.* p. 123.

cephaly, hair and eye colour, defective hearing, nose conformation and left-handedness among criminals and non-criminals (consisting of such diverse groups as: Cambridge, Oxford and Scottish students; British and Scottish schoolboys; University of London professors; Scottish insane; German army recruits; and British Royal Engineers). The criminals differed from the Engineers in having slightly smaller horizontal contours (of the head), and in the tendency of their contours to decrease with increasing age. Throughout his examinations, Goring corrected for differences between his groups in age, stature and intelligence-factors which were positively correlated with physiognomy.

The correlation of physical attributes with physique rather than criminality did not lead Goring to deduce that criminals and non-criminals were co-equals in physique. However, he felt that a valid comparison of their physiques required that class and occupational differences be controlled.

> The mean stature of the criminal, like that of the non-criminal sections of the community, depends greatly upon the social class from which individuals belonging to particular sections have been drawn, and is also determined by the extent to which they have been selected by stature, for the occupancy of any section. Thus, the mean stature of policemen is greater than that of citizens generally, because citizens of small stature are not eligible for the police force; and commissioned army officers are taller on the average than non-commissioned officers, because of the different social classes from which these two types of soldiers are respectively selected; and, again, the labourer is taller than the artisan, probably because only individuals with good physical development can earn a livelihood by performing heavy manual labour.[11]

Consequently, the physique and constitution of the groups were compared after they had been arranged in four social classes and seven occupational classes. Goring found criminals, with the exception of those convicted of fraud, to be inferior to the general population in stature and weight. With respect to health and constitution (determined by the degrees of muscularity and obesity), violent offenders were stronger and more sound constitutionally, and thieves and burglars (90 per cent. of the total criminal group) were puny in build as compared with both the total criminal group and the general population. Except for these relationships, neither type of crime nor degree of criminality was found associated with stature, weight, health, muscularity or obesity. These, stated

[11] *Ibid.* p. 175.

Goring, " are the facts: and according to our inquiry, the sole facts at the basis of *criminal anthropology*; they are the only elements of truth out of which have been constructed the elaborate, extravagant and ludicrously uncritical criminal doctrines of the great protagonist of the ' criminal type ' theory." [12]

In explaining the physical inferiority of the criminal, Goring stressed the dual selective processes, previously mentioned. Physique is a factor in that the physically unfit would have less chance of escaping the clutches of the law. It is not, however, the sole factor. If it were, for example, that only short men can function as pickpockets, then everywhere the stature of the criminal would be the same. This is not the case as shown by the marked contrast between English criminals and those of Scotland and New South Wales (Australia). Therefore, selection by class is also a factor.

> Convicted parents, selected from the general community, as already explained, by inferior stature, have sons, who, while tending to be similarly convicted, inherit the diminutive stature of their fathers. Here, we have the conditions which in the course of generations would lead to an inbred physical differentiation of the criminal classes.[13]

In order to determine the role of mental stigmata in criminality, Goring measured the associations of kinds and degrees of criminality with the factors of: temperament, temper, facility, conduct (behaviour while imprisoned), suicidal tendency (measured by number of attempted suicides) and insane diathesis (determined by previous confinements in an asylum). It was found that fraudulent offenders were somewhat egotistic, and violent offenders were marked by hot and violent temper, lack of facility, and insane and suicidal tendencies. Any other differences between the convicts depended entirely upon their differences in general intelligence.

It is with respect to intelligence that criminals are most differentiated from the general community. On the basis of his data and a report of a Royal Commission survey in 1908, Goring discovered a high association ($r = 0.6553$) between criminality and defective intelligence. Thus, he concluded, " English criminals are selected by a physical constitution, and a mental constitution, which are independent of each other [14]—that the one significant physical association with criminality is a generally defective physique; and

---

[12] *Ibid*. pp. 200–201.   [13] *Ibid*. p. 200.

[14] By Goring's computation, the correlation coefficient for physique and intelligence is 0.02 ± 0.03, *ibid*. p. 263.

that the one vital mental constitutional factor in the etiology of crime is defective intelligence." [15]   Later, Goring added moral defectiveness as the third constitutional factor in order to account for the conduct of some serious offenders who were neither physically nor mentally inferior.

Age and criminality

To buttress his argument that defective intelligence is one of the primary sources of criminality, Goring pointed to the age structure of criminals.   Star-class (non-habitual) criminals, whom he considered as only one step removed from the general community in terms of the diathesis, were very similar to the general community in age structure.   On the other hand, habituals had a mean age of twenty-two years (S.D. nine years) at the time of first conviction, whereas in the general community the mean was thirty-seven years (S.D. seventeen years).   He dismissed the ideas that the tendency of habituals to be convicted at young age was due: to a tendency in society to more severely punish young persons; or to young persons being more criminally disposed; or to special environmental factors associated with age.   Rather, an " individual's selection for conviction by age must be sought in the particular conjuncture of opportunity to commit crime with the intensity of the criminal predisposition—a conjuncture which obviously is highly correlated with age." [16]

By the analogy of the onset of scarlet and enteric fevers, he attempted to prove this point.   Both fevers are of environmental and constitutional origin.   The onset of either results when there is the invasion of the body by infectious agents (the environmental factor) plus the presence of bodily tissues which favour its development. The infectious agents of scarlet fever are omnipresent but those of enteric are more easily avoided.   From the point of birth, the individual is susceptible to either.   The age structures of the fevers show that those who succumb do so at an early age.   The mean and mode of scarlet fever are 5·26 years and 8·61 years, respectively; they are 13·39 and 18·97 for enteric.   Goring attributed the difference in age structures to variations in the environmental stimulus, and considered the youth of victims of both diseases as evidence that constitutional traits manifest themselves at the earliest possible moment. The mean and mode of criminality (from the point that conviction for crime was possible in England—twelve years of age) were 10·07 years and 13·31 years. His " conclusion, upon the age distribution of first offenders, is that some mental constitutional proclivity is . . . the primary source of the habitual criminal's career." [17]

Social factors and criminality

Goring dismissed the claims of Lacassagne, Ferri and others that the genesis of criminality lay in social factors. He found that type and degree of criminality had no positive association with the factors of: nationality; education, as measured by either the length of schooling or achievement in school; regularity of employment prior to first conviction; order of birth in the family; and the broken home. Alcoholism was correlated only with crimes of personal violence ($r = 0.20$).

He did observe that types of crime appeared to be related to certain occupations and social classes. For example, people convicted of damage to property and sexual offences were most often agricultural labourers, miners and seamen, whereas those convicted of acquisitive crimes were usually from the commercial and artisan groups. However, Goring felt that type of occupation did not induce criminality but rather different occupations present dissimilar opportunities for committing a particular crime. Among the social classes there was a predominance of: crimes of violence, stealing and burglary in the lower class; sexual offences in the poor and destitute classes; and fraud in the middle and upper classes. However, when stealing, burglary and fraud were grouped together as acquisitive crimes, the association of class position with crime almost completely disappeared. The upper class, constituting 4 per cent. of the general community, was responsible for 3 per cent. of these offences. In view of this and the fact that 95 per cent. of all convictions were due to acquisitive crimes, Goring felt that poverty was of minor importance in criminal conduct.

Vital statistics and marital condition of criminals

The vital statistics of the criminal are important *per se* and in relation to Goring's theoretical position. If criminality was due to

[17] *Ibid.* p. 214.

the inheritance of a defective constitution, then, provided that there were no abrupt changes in the social structure, the size of the prison population in this generation should approximate the fertility rate of criminals during the past generation. He substantiated this proposition by pointing out that the prison population of England had remained constant from 1882 to 1901 (despite an increase of 20 per cent. in the general population), and that criminals had just about replaced themselves. Out of 1,000 male offenders, 629 married and had an average of 3·50 offspring.

There were slight variations in the marriage rates of offenders, convicted of different kinds of crimes, from the rate in the general community (621/1,000 males). In his explanations of two of these variations one finds ideas that have been confirmed, in part, by recent studies.[18] " An excess in the marriage rate of fraudulents is attributed to the stress of marriage in inducing fraud; an excess of 7·6 per cent. in the marriage rate of violent crimes represents the extent to which criminals committing this crime are indicted for committing violence upon their wives. . . ." [19]

An examination of the morbidity and mortality rates of criminals convinced Goring that there was no substance in Lombroso's claim that disease was a factor in criminality. Comparing the sickness rate of the general community with that of convicts, he found that criminals were slightly less affected by illness. Certain types of disability were, however, differently distributed among the two populations. Strong, positive associations exist between criminality and insanity ($r = 0.44$), epilepsy ($r = 0.26$), and syphilis and venereal diseases ($r = 0.31$). On the other hand, as shown by their correlation coefficients, chronic diseases militate against the commission of crime: chronic heart disease ($r = -0.13$), cancer ($r = -0.11$), and chronic bronchitis ($r = -0.12$). In similar manner the mortality of criminals and non-criminals from these conditions differed. But their general mortality rates were approximately equal.

Heredity v. intimate association

Goring presented an exceedingly cogent rebuttal of the theory that " intimate association " accounts for the close resemblance

[18] V. Peterson, "Why Honest People Steal," Jour.Crim.Law and Criminol., Vol. XXXVIII: 94–103, July–August 1947; Kaare Svalastoga, "Homicide and Social Contact in Denmark," Amer.Jour.of Sociol., Vol. LXII, I: 37–41, July 1956.
[19] Goring, *op. cit.* p. 334.

between individuals and their parents (r = 0·60) and their brothers (r = 0·45) in criminality. If the high correlations were the result of individuals having associated with a corrupting influence, then, " we would expect in certain circumstances the prevalency of crime to be increased by marital condition." [20] On the surface, the correlation of 0·6378, representing the association of criminality in one parent with criminality in the other, seemed to bear this out. However, he argued, in view of the fact that the modal age of criminality was about six years lower than that of marriage, the correlation was to a considerable extent the result of assortative mating. Further, if contagion were the factor, we would have to presume that criminal wives are four times as infective as criminal husbands to explain why every other female criminal had a criminal husband but only one out of eight criminal males had a criminal spouse. He felt, therefore, that the correlation indicated assortative mating augmented by the restrictions imposed upon the criminal female in choosing a husband.

Other evidence convinced Goring that criminality was more bred in the home than inoculated there. There was not much greater similarity between parents and their offspring in the types of the crimes where learning should be most necessary than in those where it should be least important. The parental correlations for professional crimes (stealing, burglary and fraud) ranged from 0·48 to 0·58, and those for damage to property and sexual offences were 0·45 to 0·50, respectively. He deduced that the influence of criminal contagion was from 0·05 to 0·1. Goring computed in another way the influence of contagion. " Assuming the influence of paternal and maternal inheritance to be equal, an excess in the correlation coefficient (in crime) of one parent over the other, should express the minimum value for the influence of contagion. The difference, averaging about 0·05, corresponds to the minimum value, given above." [21] Lastly, he found that early removal of a delinquent child from his home did not increase the probability of his reformation.

Control of criminality

Goring felt that criminality could be drastically reduced through legislative enactments that gave appropriate consideration to the

[20] *Ibid*. p. 365.
[21] *Ibid*. p. 367.

importance of constitution, opportunity and reproduction in criminality. He argued that the inherited tendency to commit crime might be modified by educational measures. This tendency, like others, must be nurtured; therefore, despite the low correlation of education with criminality, there was no reason for presuming that the general standard of morality could not be raised by training. The opportunity to commit crime might be modified by segregation and supervision of the unfit. He felt, however, that confinement was purely ameliorative because recidivism was not lessened by imprisoning rather than fining first offenders. The real cure, as he saw it, lay in the regulation of the reproduction of those traits associated with the diathesis, namely, feeble-mindedness, epilepsy, insanity and defective social instinct.

Evaluation

Soon after its publication, Goring's work aroused heated controversy. Its supporters argued that it dealt the lethal blow to Lombrosian doctrine whereas its opponents saw in it a vindication of Lombroso. The former view is that which predominates today among United States criminologists. Unfortunately, in their preoccupation with Lombroso and by their intellectual predisposition to reject biological explanations of criminality, they have glossed over two aspects of Goring's work. First, Goring, like Lombroso, stressed the role of biological factors. Secondly, some of the shortcomings of *The English Convict* make moot the proposition that it constitutes a refutation of Lombroso's peculiar biological theory.

The following criticisms are presented by several investigators [22]:

1. Use of the statistical method.
    (a) Low and insignificant correlations are frequently used as a basis for prediction.
    (b) Real differences between classes of criminals or between criminals and non-criminals are reduced to alleged insignificance by correcting the coefficients to remove the influence of irrelevant sociological and physical features.
    (c) The validity of the original data is impugned when differences, which Goring did not desire to obtain, were irreducible by statistical correction.

[22] "Charles Goring's *The English Convict: A Symposium*," Jour.of Crim.Law and Criminol., Vol. V: 207–240, 348–363, 1914–15; Bryan Donkin, "Notes on Mental Defect in Criminals," Jour.of Ment.Sci., Vol. LXIII: 16–37, 1917; E. Hooton, *The American Criminal*, Cambridge, Mass., 1939, Harvard University Press, pp. 18–31.

(d) Certain characters were roughly rather than precisely measured. For example, the intelligence of criminals was determined not by the use of the Simon-Binet metrical scale, which was available, but by the investigator's impression of whether the criminal was intelligent, slightly intelligent, mentally weak, or imbecilic.

(e) Only in a very few instances were non-criminals compared with criminals; and, when they were, they were not legitimately comparable because they represented sections of the general community from which criminals do not usually come. Further, non-criminals were measured by different techniques.

(f) The statistical technique is not an adequate device for laying bare all of the characteristics of the criminal. Lombroso had stated that many are internal and microscopic and that only a competent anthropologist can discover them. Lombroso in 1889 proved this to Manouvrier and Topinard by pointing to anomalies that Magnan, the famous alienist, had failed to detect.

2. Definitions.

(a) The distinction between the "abnormal" and the "unusual" is too arbitrary. It is simply a verbal preference to hold out for the use of the statistician's "unusual" rather than the pathologist's "abnormal" when speaking of forms of infantilism, gigantism, disgenitalism, etc.

(b) The concept "environment" is narrowly construed.

(c) The consideration of insanity and epilepsy as strictly constitutional in origin is questionable.

3. The diathesis.

(a) Goring, by assuming the diathesis to be present in all men, exempted himself from explaining the act of crime and examined only the why of conviction and imprisonment.

(b) In order to account for the diathesis in strictly constitutional terms, it was necessary to introduce the element of moral defectiveness and assume it to be constitutional.

Goring anticipated criticisms of his work but hoped that they would motivate others to extend and surpass his findings. He states: " Our tables of figures speak for themselves, we have said: but we do not claim that they utter the last word. The finality of any verdict of ours depends, of course, upon the accuracy and representativeness of the statistics from which it has been gathered. . . .

" We believe that our results do give the general drift of the facts. If these results serve as a stimulus to a more extended inquiry, we shall have achieved our principal object." [23]

EDWIN D. DRIVER.

[23] Goring, *op. cit.* p. 373.

BIBLIOGRAPHY

"Charles B. Goring, 1870–1919. Obituary Notice and Appreciation," *Biometrika*, XII: 297–307, November 1918–December 1919.

"Charles Buckman Goring," *The Lancet*, CXCVI: 914, 1919.

DONKIN, BRYAN. "Notes on Mental Defect in Criminals," Jour.of Ment.Sci., LXIII: 16–37, 1917.

—— "The Factors of Criminal Actions," Jour.of Ment.Sci., XLV: 87–96, 1919.

GORING, CHARLES. *The English Convict: A Statistical Study,* 1913; reprinted Montclair, N.J., 1972, Patterson Smith, with the *Schedule of Measurements and General Anthropological Data.*

—— "The Etiology of Crime," Jour.of Ment.Sci., LXIV: 129–146, 1918.

HARRIS, J. ARTHUR. "Charles Buckman Goring," SCI. n.s., LI: 133–134, January–June 1920.

HOOTON, E. *The American Criminal,* 1939, Harvard University Press, pp. 18–31.

LOMBROSO FERRERO, GINA; FERRI, ENRICO; SANCTIS, SANTE DE; WHITE, WILLIAM A.; NEWKIRK, H. D. and BOWERS, PAUL. "Charles Goring's *The English Convict: A Symposium*," Jour.of Crim.Law and Criminol., V: 207–240, 348–363, 1914–15.

PARMALEE, MAURICE. *Criminology,* 1920, Macmillan.

SELLIN, THORSTEN. "Charles Buckman Goring," *Encyclopedia of Social Sciences,* edited by Edwin R. A. Seligman and Alvin Johnson, 1931, Macmillan, VI, p. 703.

NOTE ON THE CONTRIBUTOR

Dr. EDWIN D. DRIVER is Professor of Sociology at the University of Massachusetts at Amherst, with which he has been connected since 1948. Among his publications are "Interaction and Criminal Homicide in India," "A Critique of Typologies in Criminology," and "Confessions and the Social Psychology of Coercion."

24

WILLEM ADRIAAN BONGER

1876–1940

OFTEN criminologists have asked for, sought after, and perhaps found the causes which make men criminal. Seldom or never have these criminologists put the question of why a man becomes a criminologist. Nevertheless, both questions are equally interesting. It is true that there are far fewer criminologists than criminals. In numbers, therefore, the criminals are of much greater importance. Further, there must be criminals before there can be criminologists. But without the criminologists we would have no scientific study of crime and its treatment.

Why did Bonger become a criminologist ?

Does the life of Willem Adriaan Bonger, the Dutch criminologist, or do his writings give an answer to the question: Why does a man become a criminologist? Hardly! Almost nothing in his youth or family circumstances gives any indication that he was to become a world-famous criminologist. His father, Hendrik C. Bonger, was active in an insurance firm in Amsterdam, and is described to us as a sound-minded, quiet, always equanimous and amiable man, who, notwithstanding his overcrowded business life and the care of a large family (Willem was the youngest of ten children), found great pleasure in his music.[1] In the Bonger household a rather liberal atmosphere reigned. Father Bonger was a Remonstrant-Protestant. There was harmony between the parents and the children. Mother Bonger, Hermine Louise Weissman,

---

* Reproduced from *The Journal of Criminal Law, Criminology and Police Science*, Vol. 46, No. 3, September–October 1955.

[1] Short sketch of the life of Professor Dr. W. A. Bonger by his son H. Bonger, published in the *Collected Papers of Bonger*, Amsterdam, 1950, N. V. De Arbeiderspers (in Dutch). For details of the life of Bonger, I made ample use of parts of this sketch, as well as of the article which Professor Dr. J. Valkhoff wrote about the works of Bonger, which appears in these same *Collected Papers*. About the criminological work of Bonger, Professor B. V. A. Röling wrote an article in the Dutch *Tydschrift voor Strafrecht*, L II (1942).

showed a mild humour and great solicitude for her children. She was nearly illiterate, without any special interests, but spiritual and original. Why then did a son of this family, that in itself was just like hundreds of other households of good citizens, become a criminologist? In the first place, there must have been some hidden hereditary factor that drove him to scientific work, instead of the practical work in the branch of insurance law which his father had wished him to follow. This hereditary trait we find also in one of Bonger's sisters, " Jo," born in 1862, who became the wife of Theo van Gogh, the brother of the famous Dutch painter, Vincent. It was she who did so much to collect the correspondence between the van Gogh brothers, to get these letters translated and edited and who succeeded in bringing world fame to Vincent after his death.[2]

An elder brother of Willem, Andries, was also a gifted man. He went as a young man of nineteen to Paris without having studied at a university, but he had a great love of art, literature and painting and a rather universal knowledge.[3] He was a great friend of Theo and Vincent van Gogh and of Odilon Redon. Andries was the fourth child of his parents and suffered from their rather poor circumstances during the first half of their married life. He became, though he had not studied law, a much sought-after specialist in maritime insurance law. In his biography his wife tells us that he had had a hard youth in which work played the most important role. If Willem had been the fourth child instead of the tenth he, like Andries, probably would have attended the *Handelsschool* (Mercantile School) and not the *Gymnasium* (Classical preparatory school). The *Handelsschool* did not lead to matriculation for the university. The " birth-number " of Willem played an important role, in that he would perhaps never have become a university man if he had not been the youngest of the ten children.

It is very probable that somewhere in the families of Bonger's parents there must have been hereditary factors which gave to him and to his elder brother and sister a predisposition for art and science. But that does not explain why Willem Bonger became a criminologist. Why was his scientific interest directed to crime?

---

[2] A little biography of the life of Johanna Gesina van Gogh-Bonger by her son V. W. van Gogh is published as part of the preface to the collection of the letters of Theo to Vincent, *Wereldbibliotheek*, 1932, and in the English edition of these same letters (London-Boston).

[3] His biography was written by his second wife, Mrs. F. W. M. Bonger-van den Borgh van Verwolde, and published in the *Jaarboek van de Maatschappij der Nederlandse Letterkunde* te Leiden, 1936–37, p. 112.

Is it possible and probable that criminologists become interested in crime as a way of sublimating their own criminal tendencies?

At first sight, this does not seem to be true of Bonger. His son tells us that for Bonger, as well as for his brother Andries, the dark side of life had no attraction. They enjoyed spiritual pleasures much more and had a great sense of moral responsibility and moral norms. Nevertheless, it is not impossible that a certain antagonism to the somewhat stuffy religious atmosphere which reigned in the home of father Bonger caused Willem, even as a schoolboy, to have doubts about the origin of life and particularly about sin. It is not common for so young a boy to study the works of Darwin. In his later life he certainly shows a certain antagonism to religion and to the pretensions of religious people that they can solve the riddles of life and death by faith. He enjoyed, rather, making clear in his article, " Geloof en Misdaad " (Faith and Crime, 1913), that religion and religious conviction are not the panacea for crime they were held to be by authors like Alexander von Oettingen,[4] the Belgian Roman Catholic author De Baets,[5] the Protestant parson Dr. Jaeger[6] and Cathrein.[7] " Bonger himself was absolutely irreligious. He was religious in the Spinozistic sense: ' Everything which exists is in God and God is nature.' He was a Spinozistic pantheist and considered God as immanent and as non-transcendental. He was a Humanist. The Calvinistic creed had no attraction whatever for him and from the Catholic he did not expect much good, for he abhorred the authoritarian character of their church." Thus, he is described by his pupil J. Valkhoff, now Professor in Amsterdam, who wrote a preface for the collected papers of Bonger.[8]

Such an irreligious attitude, and certainly in Holland round about 1900, was in opposition to the conviction of the majority. On the other hand, among the little group of intellectuals it was rather common. In a Remonstrant-Protestant family such as Bonger's there was no reason for the parents to be alarmed at this attitude. The great difference between the Remonstrants and the Calvinists has been since the days of Arminius (1619), and even since the time of Dirk Volkertsz Coornhert (1522–90), that the Arminians or Remonstrants did not believe that sin was something emanating

---

[4] Alexander von Oettingen, *Moralstatistik*.
[5] De Baets, *Les influences de la misère sur la criminalité*.
[6] Jaeger, *Zunahme der Verbrechen und Abhilfe*.
[7] Cathrein, *Moralphilosophie*.
[8] *Collected Papers of Bonger*, I, p. xlv.

from or created by God. It was something purely human. But for one who, like Bonger, following Spinoza, thought that God was in nature, this Remonstrant conviction was not wholly satisfying. The Remonstrants still recognised a free will, but for a Spinozist the human will is not a free cause, but determined by necessity. It is improbable that Willem Bonger was very much interested in these theological questions; on the contrary, even as a young man he must have seen them as insoluble, and therefore he tried to understand as much of human life as was possible through human methods, particularly empirically and as a positivist.[9]

This must have caused some antagonism between Willem and the faith in which his parents lived. Willem Bonger must have felt deeply that the mild and pacific way in which they accepted religion and God, while at the same time crime, misery, illness and poverty existed, did not solve the problem of life. Therefore, one can understand that he was attracted to the great idealistic movement of his time, Socialism, which promised to solve all human ills, in a human way, by changing the economic and social circumstances.

But even this mild antagonism to the faith of his parents, and still more to the other religions prevalent in his country, cannot explain why Bonger became a criminologist. There is more. The hereditary factor in Willem Bonger is largely to be ascribed to the family of his mother, Hermine Louise Weissman. This family came from Neustadt am Berg, in Württemberg, Germany. Here in the eighteenth century lived a vine grower, named Martin Weissman. His son, Andreas, came to Holland in 1780 and married Dirkje Muller. This Andreas Weissman was an educated man of great culture. He had a gift for drawing, was very musical and read Schiller, Koerner, Racine and Voltaire. He had two sons, Gerrit Weissman, who became a vintner, and Adriaan Willem Weissman, who went to South America (at seventeen), and a daughter, Hermine Louise Weissman (the mother of our Bonger).[10] This Weissman family was very gifted. The son of Adriaan Willem Weissman, born March 4, 1858, and named after his father, became a famous architect. In the Bonger family the mother, Hermine Weissman, dominated her sister-in-law in the Weissman family,

---

[9] Valkhoff, *ibid.* p. xxvii.
[10] All these data are to be found in the *Jaarboek*, XLII (1948) of the Genootschap Amstelodamum under the title: *Memories of A. W. Weissman*, published by V. W. van Gogh (the son of Theo van Gogh).

Mrs. Weissman-Stoethaan.[11] Since Willem Bonger was the youngest
of ten children, it is not improbable that there was a strong relationship and tie to the mother. According to Mr. V. W. van Gogh:
" The Bongers were amply gifted, but with the exception of Jo (the
mother of V. W. van Gogh) and Andries, who went to Paris, they
were all difficult people. Willem and his other three sisters had not
achieved their independence in a normal way. The three sisters
remained at home and did not marry."

It is not impossible that this strong tie connecting Willem
Bonger with his mother created feelings of guilt which he suppressed in his subconscious. It may be an indication of this that as
a boy of ten he often stood for long periods at the side of a toy
horse and thrashed it with a little whip,[12] an act which at that age
is nearly pathological. Here perhaps lies one of the origins of
Bonger's interest in criminology. Possibly his unconscious feelings
of guilt required an explanation, and to give this within the limits
which he could accept, he rationalised the origin of all criminal
tendencies by finding the causes of these tendencies in the milieu.
The strong *Mutter-Bindung* probably created protest-feelings against
the authority of the mother which were satisfied by his joining the
Socialist Party. That his protest against the mother played an
important role in his ideas he shows in his Doctor's thesis. There
he considers it a mistake that the education of young children
depends, for the greater part, upon the mothers. This is wrong, in
his opinion, because the mother is only a " dilettante " in questions
of education, and because the character of " the woman " is seriously
damaged by the inferior position she occupied during many centuries. Bonger himself would not have had any sympathy with
such a hypothesis about the origin of his becoming a criminologist.
He was very sceptical about psycho-analysis and liked to ridicule this
sort of psychology.

I think Bonger himself would have explained his choice of
criminology in the same terms in which he discussed the origin and
role of the great men in history.[13] Bonger recognises that there are
always only a few men who combine those talents and qualities
required to make either a great artist, a great scientist, or a great

[11] Information given by V. W. van Gogh.
[12] Information given by V. W. van Gogh.
[13] Bonger, " Over de rol der grote mannen in de geschiedenis " (On the role of great men
in history); a stenogram of a lecture held on December 1, 1928, for the Socialistic
Debating Society in Amsterdam, published in *The Collected Papers*, II, p. 65.

leader. He is in agreement with Quételet that the majority of men (± 85 per cent.) do not even combine in themselves those capacities and qualities which would enable them to go further than a lower-school education and that only 5 per cent. of men are qualified to go to a university. He does not deny the great influence of hereditary qualities and capacities, but states that even the man with great gifts does not become a genius or a talent save under certain social circumstances. "If Darwin," says Bonger,[14] "had not learned how to read or to write he would not have found the theory of evolution." "If Marx had not been born in the nineteenth century during the rise of industrial capitalism he would not have produced his theory of scientific socialism."

To a certain extent—but only that—the same is true for the fact that Bonger became a sociologist and criminologist. In his first years as a law student at the University of Amsterdam, he found a group of students interested in socialism and in social problems. Among these friends was K. H. Bouman, later Professor of Psychiatry in Amsterdam, who subsequently became very much interested in criminological problems.

Perhaps the greatest influence was his teacher of Criminal Law, Professor Dr. G. A. van Hamel, well known to everybody who knows the history of criminal law. Van Hamel had founded the International Association of Penal Law (*Internationale Kriminalistische Vereinigung—Union International de droit pénal*) in 1888, with Fr. von Liszt and Ad. Prins. The principal idea of the members of this society was that the methods and measures to treat and fight crime must be derived not only from a juridical but also from an anthropological and sociological point of view. Without any doubt it was van Hamel's idea that the law faculty of the University of Amsterdam in 1899 proposed offering a prize for an essay entitled, *Un aperçu systématique et critique de la littérature concernant l'influence des conditions économiques sur la criminalité.*[15] Two students of the university, Joseph van Kan and Willem Bonger, submitted papers. Van Kan's received the gold medal.[16] Bonger's was only honourably mentioned. But van Kan afterwards specialised exclusively in Roman and Civil Law and History. Bonger

---

[14] *Ibid.* p. 75.
[15] A systematic and critical review of the literature concerning the influence of economic conditions on criminality.
[16] *Les causes économiques de la criminalité*, A. Malonie, Paris, 1903.

remained a sociologist and criminologist throughout his life. Van Kan had succeeded in what he attempted; for Bonger it must have been a blow that he had not gained the prize.

Bonger was a very emotional man. His emotionality certainly was the most outstanding quality in his whole personality. It must have evoked in him a strong feeling of sympathy with all men who suffered. But at the same time he had some difficulty in his relations with other people. With his brothers and sisters, with the exception of Jo, he had rather many conflicts.[17] His children respected him very much, but were at the same time rather afraid of him.[18] He had a little bit of contempt for those who thought along other lines than he did, and in such a case discussion with him was rather impossible, particularly on subjects about which he was not well informed.

Is it too far-fetched to suppose that the same causes (particularly feelings of guilt and a strong *Mutter-Bindung*, protest against the authority of the parents), which, hidden subconsciously, make a man criminal can, when he has sufficient intellect, emotionality and activity, result in the sublimation of these criminal tendencies and in transforming them into a particular interest in the origin of crime, which is then rationalised in some way or other, either by ascribing them to a certain " degeneration " and " atavism " as did Lombroso, or to the milieu as Bonger did, or to a combination of hereditary and pathological traits and milieu as did Aschaffenburg? In each case the criminologist must have a certain sympathy with crime and criminals, while avoiding himself these sympathies by suppressing them. Bonger certainly was an intelligent and emotional man and a very regular worker. He must have had a great sympathy for all sorts of people whom the world in general did not like: Jews, Negroes, primitive people and the poor. For all of them alike he has tried to prove that it was more the economic and social circumstances than hereditary and racial traits which either caused the greater incidence of criminality among them or at least caused what might seem a greater immorality. For the poor he has given his arguments in his study: *Criminalité et conditions économiques*. The first part of this was his essay for the Amsterdam law faculty, published in 1905 in a more elaborate form as a doctor's thesis. In 1916 it was translated into English and published in the American

---

[17] Information given by V. W. van Gogh.
[18] Information given by his son, Hendrik Bonger.

" Modern Criminal Science Series " under the title: *Criminality and Economic Conditions.* Concerning the Jews in Holland and Germany, he made it clear that their criminality was different from that of other people, and that it certainly was less serious.

Bonger's work and conceptions

In his book, *Race and Crime* (in Dutch in 1939, in English in 1943 with a preface of Professor John H. Wigmore), he explains the greater criminality of the Negroes by environmental influences.[19] These influences are such that " *a priori* it is not necessary to ascribe their criminality to any other influence." Bonger's was a typical one-track mind. Once he had recognised the influence of the milieu, he tried to explain every social phenomenon by it. Primitive man was the subject of his inaugural lecture as Professor at the University of Amsterdam. This lecture, entitled, " The evolution of morality," shows us Bonger in all his force, and, one might say, in all his weakness. His force is demonstrated by his sharp criticism of the modern capitalistic organisation of society, which, according to him, leads to unlimited egoism. For the near future Bonger saw, in 1922, cause for the blackest pessimism. The Second World War has, to a certain extent, proved that he was right in this prediction. For the more remote future he is not so pessimistic.

" The process of growth most clearly points to the continual progress of organisation in society. Through this organisation, the evolution of morality must come into action. To say it with the words of Manouvrier: ' We must act in such a way that every man continually gets more and more interested in being useful to his equals and less and less in damaging them. That is the formula which we have to apply.' "

The direct and immediate effects of organisation on moral feeling Bonger does not rate very highly, but for the more indirect, remote effects he considers this organisation of the utmost interest. According to him between egoism and altruism lies a wide field of activity. When the various interests of all men run strongly parallel, then self-interest requires, not thwarting the interest of others, but

---

[19] In my textbook on *Criminology* (published in Dutch, 3rd ed. 1952, p. 284) I drew attention to the fact that perhaps a greater sensuality and a lower degree of intelligence of the Negro might be racial and hereditary qualities which might not be wholly ascribed to environmental circumstances.

promoting them. One might call this field that of solidarism and mutualism. The wider this field becomes, the less conflicts between men, the more possibility for a real development of the moral factors in the natural ability of mankind. Here we see clearly the weaker part of Bonger. He always saw everything in black and white. This was the result of his strong emotionality. For the near future everything was black. The capitalistic society " leads to unlimited egoism." The more remote future and the life of primitive people are seen in a much rosier light. Organisation will bring forth the field of co-operation and solidarism indicated by Bonger. But why should it do so? And the primitive people had much more fellow-feeling within their little " island of friends amid a sea of strangers and enemies " [20] than ever any society afterwards.

Bonger in this inaugural lecture jumps from primitive society to the modern world of the nineteenth century and denies that a real evolution of morals has taken place. That, perhaps, to suggest a few, the abolition of the ordeals in the Middle Ages, the substitution of prison for the death penalty, the abolition of the death penalty in many countries, the abolition of corporal punishment, the abolition of slavery and serfdom, the increasing recognition of the equality of all men, etc., were so many steps in the evolution of morality—these Bonger does not take into account. Rather grudgingly he admits that law and morality develop very slowly, much slower than technics, and though he does not deny that men themselves contribute to this development, here again his historic-materialistic-Marxist conviction plays a formidable role. He says: " The advancement of the material and spiritual level of the great masses is an event of the first order in world history: at one time they stood on a level on which moral life was scarcely possible, now at least they have attained that level."

But the explanation of the improvement is largely in material terms. " The opinion," he says, " that to act morally for non-moral reasons is without any ethical significance, seems to me untenable. In this way are not only the better characters attracted, but example and custom have their influence. But it is right to say that these are only secondary influences. This is why only slight consequences of a moral kind are connected with the changes in capitalistic practice. . . ." The curious thing in his whole argument is that while

[20] Quoted by Bonger from Hobhouse, *Morals in Evblution*, I, p. 280.

he recognises that some men have better characters than others, he does not attach much value to the influence of these better characters.

The reason for this is that Bonger always paid much more attention to the masses than to the individual. This he did in criminology to such an extent that he never wrote about any individual criminal. All his books and articles treat crime as a mass-phenomenon. And in his sociological work, as well, it is only society as a whole which he describes and tries to explain. He hardly ever wrote about an individual great man. Only to Lombroso, Marx and Adam Smith he devoted articles. Marx and Adam Smith he discussed as sociologists, Lombroso was only a subject for opposition.

In these articles, too, we recognise Bonger's most cherished ideas. He contests Carlyle's concept of great men, *i.e.*, that from their spirit a *generatio spontanea* originates. " Abstractions," says Bonger, " are formed out of reality and not vice versa; the human spirit, that of great men included, does not create out of a vacuum, but from reality." [21]

Bonger does not deny the influence of hereditary traits, but for great men as well as for criminals he denies the existence of " free will," and everything is to be explained by environmental circumstances. Now, even when we agree with him that the influence of a " free will " has always been much exaggerated, even if we recognise that particularly persons with defects in intelligence, character and temperament are for an overwhelming part forced to their acts and crimes by the circumstances under which they live, it certainly goes too far to deny every subjective force which plays a role in men themselves and particularly in great men.

The curious thing is that Bonger does not remain true to his own conception. For example, in his article about Marx he writes, shortly after his statement that the human spirit does not create out of a vacuum, the following sentences:

" Man has always had to fight against the scarcity in nature and its dangers. His very special intellect, his technical abilities and capacities procure to him the weapons for this fight: instruments are invented, division of labour asserts itself. The productive power of mankind rises. The stress of nature never ends, but at a certain

---

[21] " Marx als socioloog " (Marx as a sociologist), *Collected Papers*, II, p. 6.

level still other driving forces originate which put the whip to the creative power of man with a multiplied force. Thus, the speed of social development differs in various periods and has become nowadays *prestissimo*. When the rise in the productivity of labour has reached a certain level, the economic relations between men change. The new relations are detected first by a few (with the finest moral tentacles), afterwards by more, then they are consolidated in rules which begin to push aside the earlier moral code and in the end eliminate it."

We are entitled to ask where do the "special intellect" and "the productive power of mankind," and the "creative power" and the "finest moral tentacles" originate.

Bonger has no answer, and perhaps none of us can give a scientific answer. Here only faith can give an answer. We have already seen that Bonger did not want to mix up science and faith. But then it is not justified to deny that the human spirit creates from a "vacuum" and to contend that it only creates from "reality." At least we must include the human mind and spirit in this reality, a reality which is not wholly consciously known to us.

Bonger, the scientist, criminologist and idealist

Bonger himself was certainly a great man. Not one of the greatest in history, but his publications had great effect. It was due to him that criminology in Holland became a separate field of science. Particularly his small classic, *An Introduction to Criminology* (published for the first time in Dutch in 1932), was a great success. It was translated by Emil van Loo into English in 1936 and published by Methuen & Co., Ltd., London. Even to this day there is no other textbook which gives such a complete survey of criminology so compactly.

Through this little book and his doctor's thesis, *Criminality and Economic Conditions*, Bonger had a great influence on American and English authors. Just because of his one-sided view that economic conditions were of the utmost importance in criminality as a mass-phenomenon, he inspired others to make an elaborate study of these circumstances [22] and he stimulated opponents, particularly psychiatrists and psychologists, to argue that the

---

[22] Reckless, *e.g.*, quotes Bonger seven times in his book on *Criminal Behaviour* (1940), Sutherland in his *Criminology* (1924) three times, Barnes and Teeters in their *New Horizons* (1945) six times.

psychological and pathological causes of crime had their influence too, not only on the individual crime but also on crime as a mass-phenomenon.

Bonger was a very independent scientist. He was never impressed by " the general opinion," by doctrines and dogmata, rather the contrary. On many points he had ideas which were far from generally accepted. This independence did not only show in his professional work in scientific criminology and sociology, but also in his political party (the Socialist Party). Instances of this independence are his argument for a declining birthrate for Holland,[23] his protest against the indignation of society on the subject of homosexuality,[24] his opposition to the disdain which the Socialist Party often showed for intellectuals.[25]

Bonger really deserves a place among the great criminologists and sociologists because he fought against hypocrisy, untruthfulness, dilettantism. He was one of the first who proved that criminology and sociology may be exercised in a scientific way. In all his books and articles he gives a great mass of statistical proof. He was, to a great extent, a perfectionist, but not in his style of language. He wrote just as he spoke; emotionally and personally. But a perfectionist he was in the way he fought for his ideas. Once he had conceived an idea, he tried to make it clear and acceptable to everybody by gathering all the proof he could find for it. He certainly was an idealist. Truthfulness and altruism were for him the principal virtues. Just because of the impossibility for him to find the foundation for these virtues in religion he tried to prove that they were human virtues which mankind had conquered and was still conquering in a long evolution of society. It is always risky to sustain this. One fights in this way against the whole of Christianity, and that must cause for a man, born in Western Europe, and particularly in Holland, a certain feeling of guilt, even if he is convinced, as Bonger certainly was, that he is on the right way. Bonger himself probably would have denied this hidden feeling of guilt. On the contrary, he perhaps felt himself somewhat superior above all people who considered faith as the basis of their science. It was just because of this that he was able to fight for a sociology and

[23] In his article: " De stand van het bevolkingsvraagstuk in Nederland " (The status of the question of population in the Netherlands), 1936, *Collected Papers*, II, p. 55.
[24] Preface written by Bonger to a book of Commutator, on *Homosexuality*, 1927 (in Dutch).
[25] In his article, " Intellectuals and Socialism," 1925, *Collected Papers*, II, p. 192.

criminology as purely human parts of knowledge just like physics, biology, etc.

One may agree with him in this respect or not, but it is certain that he proved that a religious foundation for both these sciences may be deceiving, and that in each case we must never neglect the facts, which might lead into other conclusions.

This same respect for facts made him suspicious to most sorts of philosophy and metaphysical conceptions.

Thus doing, he gave to sociology and criminology the standing of causal sciences.

The First World War was a great shock to Bonger. He saw the war as the biggest crime that could ever be committed, and afterwards he tried in two articles to unravel the intricate question of to whom the guilt for this crime was to be ascribed.[26] Bonger certainly hoped that there would never be a second world war. His son writes: He never was an absolute pacifist; though he loathed violence. He had at the same time a disdain for everything " half-soft." He was convinced that democracy must be defended by weapons. In the years just preceding 1939, many of his publications reflected his concern: " The problems of democracy " (1934), " The lie of antisemitism " (1935) and among others an article, " The danger for Czechoslovakia " (in French) in the Czech *Sociologische Revue*. Shortly before 1939 he went on a secret government mission to the foreign offices of the three Scandinavian countries. Its objective was to stimulate them to give asylum more freely to greater numbers of Jewish refugees.

He was a fervent antagonist of all forms of dictatorship. After September 1939 his name was mentioned several times by the Bremer radio as an arch-enemy of Nazism. He refused to emigrate to America although he knew that an invasion of Holland by Germany would mean the end for him.

When, on May 10, 1940, the German soldiers crossed the Dutch-German frontier he was fully prepared. He wrote to his son: " I don't see any future for myself and I cannot bow to this scum which will now overmaster us."

And in this way he found his death by suicide, the form of death which he himself had written of as the only one in which the human will plays a role.

J. M. van Bemmelen.

---

[26] " War and Guilt " and " Diagnosis and Prognosis," 1917 and 1918, *Collected Papers*, I, pp. 220 and 272.

BIBLIOGRAPHY

*of books and the most important articles
written by W. A. Bonger*

1905 *Criminalité et conditions économiques* (Thesis, Amsterdam University), English translation, 1916, Boston, U.S.A.

1909 " Cesare Lombroso," *Die neue Zeit*, 28 Jahrg. I.

1911 " Crime and socialism," *De nieuwe tijd*, July, August 1911 (in Dutch).

1912 " The social factors of crime and their significance compared with the individual factors," *Tijdschrift voor Strafrecht*, XXXIII (in Dutch).

1913 *Religion and Crime*, Leiden, 1913; Amsterdam, 1917 (in Dutch).

1915 " Crimes committed under the influence of alcohol seen from a criminological point of view," in *De Wegwijzer*, XVIII (in Dutch).

1917 " War and guilt," in *De Socialistische Gids*, July–October 1917 (in Dutch).

1918 " Diagnosis and Prognosis " (continuation to " War and guilt "), in *De Socialistische Gids*, October–November 1918 (in Dutch).

1922 *Evolution of morals* (inaugural lecture, Amsterdam) (in Dutch).

1929 " Suicide as a social phenomenon," *Mens en Maatschappij*, July 1929 (in Dutch).

—— " The role of the great men in history," *Weekblad voor gymnasiaal en middelbaar onderwijs*, September 1929 (in Dutch).

—— " On fanatism," *De Socialistische Gids*, April 1929 (in Dutch).

1930 " War as a sociological phenomenon " *De Socialistische Gids*, August 1930 (in Dutch).

1932 *Introduction to criminology*, Volksuniversiteitsbibliotheek, Haarlem, 1932 (in Dutch; English translation, London, 1936).

1933 " Marx as a sociologist," *De Socialistische Gids*, December 1933 (in Dutch).

—— " Development of the penal law in the Netherlands," *Journal of Criminal Law and Criminology*, XXIV, No. 1, May–June 1933.

1934 *Problems of Democracy*, Groningen-Batavia, 1934; 2nd ed., Amsterdam, 1936 (in Dutch).

1935 " The ' new ' criminal law," *Rechtsgeleerd Magazijn*, LIV, 1935 (in Dutch).

1936 " Le suicide comme phénomène social," *Revue de l'Institut de sociologie*, XVI, 1936.

1937 " History and Sociology," *De Socialistische Gids*, October 1937 (in Dutch).

1938 " On criminal statistics," *Tijdschrift voor Strafrecht*, XL, 1938 (in Dutch).

—— *Lessons from the War-Crisis of September 1938*, publication of the Socialistische Vereniging tot bevordering van maatschappelijke vraagstukken 1938 (in Dutch).

1939 *Race and Crime* (in Dutch, Haarlem, 1939; English translation, 1943, reprinted Montclair, N.J., 1969).

1940 "War as a sociological problem," *Mens en Maatschappij*, XVI, 1940
(in Dutch).
Most of the articles written by Bonger are reprinted in: *Prof. Mr. W. A.
Bonger, Verspreide Geschriften*, Amsterdam, 1950, N.V. De Arbeiderspers.

NOTE ON THE CONTRIBUTOR

Dr. J. M. VAN BEMMELEN was Professor of Criminal Law and Criminology at the University of Leiden from 1931 to 1968. He studied at
the University of Groningen, and was awarded his doctorate in 1923.
He became a lawyer in Rotterdam; from 1932 to 1940 he was also
a police-judge in The Hague; and from 1943 to 1945 he was juridical
adviser to the Commander-in-Chief of the Dutch resistance. In 1951
he taught criminology as a Visiting Professor at the University of
Aberdeen, and in 1969 he taught international criminal law at New
York University. Dr. van Bemmelen has written textbooks on Dutch
Criminal Procedure (1936), on Criminology (1942) and on the Special Part of Criminal Law (1954).

25

THE HISTORICAL DEVELOPMENT
OF CRIMINOLOGY

Introduction

This paper is a summary statement of the contributions made by the pioneers in criminology. Sociologists in general and criminologists in particular have been negligent in their treatment of the historical development of ideas and theories.[1] The Pioneer Series has performed a much-needed service for criminology by reminding us of that history. Criminologists can benefit from a re-evaluation of the major contributions made to criminology and the issues which result therefrom. The Pioneer Series emphasised something that is too often ignored in textbooks; namely, the variety of disciplines which have contributed to the development of criminology: law, medicine, sociology, psychology, psychiatry, chemistry, physics, architecture, history, theology and social work. Many of the issues in criminology are a result of differences in training and orientation in various disciplines.

If we understand the pioneers, then we can better understand the current issues in criminology. Tracing the major strands of thought running throughout the Pioneer Series in terms of theoretical issues, we find at the same time indications of the ways in which these issues have influenced the modern criminologist. Twentieth-century criminology is a product of the theories of the eighteenth and nineteenth centuries. An historical evaluation of criminology is of no value unless we relate it to the things which criminologists are doing today. It is the major thesis of this paper that criminologists today are interested in certain problems because they are involved in the theoretical issues developed by the pioneers. What these issues are and the ways in which they influenced modern criminology are the objectives of this paper.

* Reproduced from *The Journal of Criminal Law, Criminology and Police Science*, Vol. 50, No. 1, June 1959.
[1] Howard Becker and Alvin Boskoff, *Modern Sociological Theory*, New York, 1957, Dryden Press, p. 35 *et seq.*

Criminology involves three different types of problems:

(1) The problem of detecting the law-breaker, which is the work of the detective, the police officer, the medical specialist, the chemist; in other words, the field of criminalistics. The Pioneer Series article on Hans Gross discusses the pioneering work of this man in the field of criminalistics.

(2) The problem of the custody and treatment of the offender once he is detected and legally judged to be guilty, which is the work of the penologist. Social workers, psychiatrists, sociologists, psychologists, juvenile court judges, probation and parole officers and others are engaged in correction work in connection with the prevention and control of delinquency and crime. Pioneer Series articles on Haviland, Maconochie, Doe, Aschaffenburg, Ray and Maudsley deal with one or more aspects of correctional work.

(3) The problem of explaining crime and criminal behaviour, which is the problem of scientifically accounting for the presence of crime and criminals in a society. The legal aspect of crime is of interest to the lawyer and to the sociologist who is studying the sociology of criminal law. The explanation of criminal behaviour is of interest to the sociologist, the psychologist, the psychiatrist, the anthropologist and the biologist. Pioneer Series articles on Bentham, Beccaria, Garofalo, Lombroso, Ferri, Goring, Tarde, Durkheim and Bonger deal with crime and criminals from several different points of view. The problems associated with the detection, treatment and explanation of crime and criminals are mutually interrelated, and there is a great deal of overlapping of fields.

Any attempt to classify the men dealt with in the Pioneer Series would be arbitrary since each pioneer wrote about a number of issues from a number of viewpoints. A classification of the following type is suggested:

Classical School	*Positive School*
Bentham	Garofalo
Beccaria	Lombroso
	Ferri
	Goring

Legal Aspects of Crime	*Psychiatric Aspects of Crime*
Doe	Aschaffenburg
Montero	Ray
	Maudsley

Sociological Aspects	
of Crime	*Prison Architecture*
Tarde	Haviland
Durkheim	
Bonger	
Prison Reform	*Criminalistics*
Maconochie	Gross

Another type of classification, based on whether the pioneer in question was primarily interested in crime or in the individual offender, can be made in this way:

Crime	*Individual Offender*	
Bentham	Lombroso	Doe
Beccaria	Garofalo	Maudsley
Montero	Ferri	Maconochie
Durkheim	Goring	Tarde
Bonger	Aschaffenburg	Gross
	Ray	Haviland

In any historical survey of criminology we must deal with a dilemma. This dilemma is found in the Classical School, founded by Bentham and Beccaria, and the Positive School, founded by Lombroso, Garofalo and Ferri.[2] The Classical School developed in the eighteenth century in an attempt to reform the legal system and to protect the accused against harsh and arbitrary action on the part of the state. The Positive School developed in the nineteenth century as an attempt to apply scientific methods to the study of the criminal.

The Classical School defined crime in legal terms; the Positive School rejected the legal definition of crime. The Classical School focused attention on crime as a legal entity; the Positive School focused attention on the act as a psychological entity. The Classical School emphasised free will; the Positive School emphasised determinism. The Classical School theorised that punishment had a deterrent effect; the Positive School said that punishment should be replaced by a scientific treatment of criminals calculated to protect society.

The Positive School has dominated American criminological thinking.[3] This school finds supporters in biology, psychiatry,

---

[2] See articles on Lombroso, Garofalo, Ferri, Bentham and Beccaria, above.

[3] Jerome Hall, *Criminology, Twentieth Century Sociology*, ed. by Georges Gurvitch and Wilbert E. Moore, New York, 1956, Philosophical Press, p. 346.

psychology, social work, sociology and anthropology, each of whom applies the concepts of his science to the study of the criminal. As a result of this orientation, criminology has been dominated by an interest in the individual offender: his personality, body build, intelligence, family background, the neighbourhood from which he comes, or the groups to which he belongs. The basic assumption since Lombroso's time is that an explanation of human behaviour is an explanation of crime. The criminologist looks for the aetiology of crime in behaviour systems rather than in legal systems.

Definition of crime

The Classical School defined crime within the strict limits of criminal law. Bentham placed emphasis on the crime, not on the criminal. Bentham was much more concerned with the consequences of the act than with the motivation for the act.[4] Beccaria was opposed to the barbaric and arbitrary practices associated with the court system in England during his time. He believed in the social contract theory of government, that is, that sovereignty resided in the people and the law applied equally to all members of society.[5] The Classical School believed in the doctrine of *nullum crimen sine lege*, no crime without a law.

The Positive School attacked the legal definition of crime, and in its place substituted a concept of natural crime. The positivist rejected the juridical concept of crime in favour of the sociological notion of crime.[6] Garofalo notes that the concept of a " criminal " presupposes the concept of " crime." He observed that " although the naturalists speak of the criminal, they have omitted to tell us what they understand by the word crime." [7] The positivist's rejection of the legal definition was based on the idea that for scientific purposes the concept of crime cannot be accepted as a legal category, since the factors which produce the legal definition are contingent and capricious. Garofalo then defined natural crime as an act that offends the moral sentiments of pity and probity in the community. Allen and Hall have pointed out the fact that the positivistic notion of crime is susceptible to corruption in the hands of corrupt political officials. The fact that Ferri became a member of the Fascist movement in Italy is of concern to those who regard civil liberties as a

---

[4] See above, Chap. 3.   [5] See above, Chap. 2.
[6] See above, Chaps. 13, 16, 18.
[7] See above, p. 320 *et seq.*

fundamental aspect of criminal law.[8] Whereas for Beccaria individual rights are supreme, there are no safeguards against abuse of state power in the work of Garofalo and Ferri.[9]

As a result of the rejection of legal categories by the Positive School there is no agreement in criminology today as to " what is crime? " Sutherland, Reckless, Sellin, Clinard and others have either rejected the legal definition of crime or have stated that criminological research should not be limited by such legal definitions.[10] The most common definition of crime by the sociological school is the definition of crime as " anti-social " behaviour. Sellin states that criminologists should study violations of conduct norms rather than legal norms. The eminent British criminologist, Professor Hermann Mannheim, is in agreement with Sellin's position. Mannheim asks the question, " Is criminology concerned exclusively with criminal behaviour in the legal sense or rather with the much wider conception of anti-social behaviour? "[11] He answers the question by noting that criminology tends to become the science of undesirable social behaviour.[12] " It is the object of Criminology to study criminal behaviour and the physical, psychological, and socio-economic factors behind it; how and why people commit crimes. . . ."[13] Mannheim focuses attention on criminal behaviour while at the same time removing the study of law from the field of criminology. " While it is no doubt one of the functions of the Sociology of the Criminal Law to examine the conditions under which criminal laws develop, such an examination cannot be regarded as coming under the scope of Criminology."[14]

Opposition to the definition of crime as anti-social behaviour or undesirable behaviour has come from Jerome Hall, Francis A. Allen, Paul Tappan, George B. Vold, Robert G. Caldwell and the writer.[15] Hall writes, " Criminology is synonymous with Sociology of Criminal Law. . . . The above theory suggests the general boundaries of criminology. It must be concerned, first, with the

---

[8] See above, pp. 376–377; also Hall, *op. cit.* p. 346 *et seq.*
[9] See above, Chaps. 16 and 18.
[10] Clarence Ray Jeffery, " The Structure of American Criminological Thinking," Jour.of Crim.L., Criminol.and Pol.Sci., January–February 1956, p. 658 *et seq.*
[11] Hermann Mannheim. *Group Problems in Crime and Punishment,* 2nd ed., Montclair, N.J., 1971, Patterson Smith, p. 261.
[12] *Ibid.* p. 262.
[13] *Ibid.* p. 261.
[14] *Ibid.* p. 260.
[15] Jeffery, *op. cit.*; Robert G. Caldwell, *Criminology,* New York, 1956, Ronald Press, pp. 112 *et seq.*, 67 *et seq.*; Hall, *op. cit.*; George B. Vold, " Some Basic Problems in Criminological Research," Fed.Prob., March 1953, p. 37.

meaning of the rules of criminal law . . . and this requires investigation of their origins, the legislative history, . . . and accompanying social problems." [16] Hall traced the development of the law of theft from the *Carrier's Case* to the present in order to show how the criminal law has developed in response to social and economic changes brought about by the Industrial Revolution. The interrelations of law and economy in the solution of social problems are highlighted in his book, *Theft, Law and Society*.[17] Francis A. Allen states, " It may be doubted that so complete an elimination of the legal content of the concept has well served the development of criminological theory." [18]

The view that crime is undesirable social behaviour is especially apparent in the field of juvenile delinquency. The broad legal definition of delinquency makes it possible to equate " delinquency " with " problem behaviour." Paul Tappan refers to this situation as " legal nihilism." He notes that a juridical approach to delinquency is uncommon, and in its place we find a casework approach that is non-legal or anti-legal in orientation.[19] Roscoe Pound observed that the discretionary power of the Star Chamber was a trifle compared to that of the juvenile court.[20] A juvenile court hearing is not regarded as a criminal trial; therefore, the usual constitutional guarantees as to life and liberty do not apply. The juvenile is often deprived of legal rights which are available to the adult.[21]

Because there is no standard from which delinquent behaviour can be measured, a subjective evaluation of the behaviour by a judge or caseworker must be relied upon. What constitutes " vulgar language," " idleness," " immorality " or " habitually " is a major problem in the administration of any juvenile court code.[22] The jurisdiction of the juvenile court is often based on the fact that the child has an emotional problem rather than on any act of delinquency.[23] There is some question as to whether the juvenile court should function as a welfare agency. " It is even more pathetic that the very social instrument that was once hailed as a great reform

[16] Jerome Hall, *General Principles of Criminal Law*, Indianapolis, 1947, Bobbs-Merrill Co., p. 559.
[17] Jerome Hall, *Theft, Law and Society*, 2nd ed., Indianapolis, 1952, Bobbs-Merrill Co.
[18] See above, p. 259.
[19] Paul W. Tappan, *Contemporary Survey of Juvenile Delinquency*, New York, 1952, United Nations, pp. 3–9.
[20] Herbert A. Bloch and Frank T. Flynn, *Delinquency*, New York, 1956, Random House, p. 320.
[21] *Ibid.* p. 305 *et seq.*
[22] *Ibid.* p. 313.
[23] *Ibid.* p. 322.

measure now stands as a barrier to progress in meeting their basic needs." [24]

The confusion of crime and criminals is commonplace in criminology. The criminologist seeks the answer to crime in the behaviour of the offender rather than in the criminal law. Ferri stated that "crime must be studied in the offender." [25] The question "why and how people commit crimes" is an important one; however, a theory of behaviour is not a theory of crime. Behaviour is criminal only when judged by some standard of conduct. The term "crime" refers to the act of judging or labelling the behaviour, rather than to the behaviour itself. Why people behave as they do and why the behaviour is regarded as criminal are two separate problems requiring different types of explanation. If we wish to include all anti-social behaviour within the scope of criminology, we must either state that all deviant behaviour is criminal or that criminology is concerned with non-criminal as well as criminal behaviour. What we are concerned with in either case is the sociology of deviant behaviour, not the sociology of crime. Only in the criminal law do we find the distinction between criminal and non-criminal behaviour. People are executed or sent to prison for violating a law; they are not executed or sent to prison for "anti-social" behaviour in general. Sellin points out that man belongs to many different social groups, each with its own system of conduct norms. However, when he states that the criminologist ought to study all norms violations he ignores the fundamental and important differences between state norms, familial norms, religious norms, educational norms, economic norms or voluntary association norms. By placing all conduct norms in a single category he is overlooking certain important characteristics of the norms.

The removal of crime from the realm of legal fact has blurred the distinction between criminal and non-criminal behaviour. In textbooks it is common to observe that 99 per cent. of the population commit acts for which they could be charged with a crime. [26] Less than 4 per cent. of the crimes known to the police result in a prison sentence. [27] These observations place the criminologist in a *cul-de-sac*. If he is to ignore the legal status of crime, he then must study

[24] *Ibid*. p. 337.
[25] See above, p. 362.
[26] Walter C. Reckless, *The Crime Problem*, New York, 1955, Appleton-Century-Croft, Inc., p. 12.
[27] *Ibid*. p. 18.

all deviant behaviour. This is an acceptable procedure if one is interested in explaining behaviour; it is not too helpful if we wish to understand why individual A is in prison and individual B is not. From these statistical observations of non-criminal populations we must conclude that they differ from criminal populations, not in terms of sociological and psychological variables related to the life experiences of the individual offender, but in terms of the process of legal adjudication. The criminal has been caught and convicted in a court of law. The problem shifts from " why and how individuals commit anti-social acts " to " why and how criminal law is administered."

The problem of the " non-adjudicated " criminal concerned Sutherland a great deal, and his research in connection with white-collar crime was an attempt to bring within the scope of criminology the criminal who was not in prison. He defined white-collar crime as " socially injurious acts " whether conviction occurred or not, a concept that has been criticised by Tappan and Caldwell.[28] Sutherland made a valuable contribution to the sociology of law by pointing out the differential treatment of white-collar criminals by our judicial system. However, he did not focus attention on the interaction of economic and legal institutions in the same way that Jerome Hall did, for example, in his study of theft. Sutherland shifted his attention to the question " why do certain individuals commit white-collar crimes? " He entered into a discussion of a shoe salesman who became a white-collar criminal through differential association.[29] The problem of what social changes in the nineteenth century produced government regulation of business is ignored in Sutherland's work. The legal dimension of white-collar crime is slighted in favour of a study of the offender. In Sutherland's work we have a beautiful example of the shift in emphasis from the crime to the criminal. White-collar crime did not exist before certain legal changes occurred. Why these changes occurred can be determined only by a study of law and society, not by a study of the criminal. The progress and development of criminal law has been due to social and economic historical forces. No evaluation of the personality of the individual criminal is going to substitute for a sociological analysis of law.

[28] Caldwell, *op. cit.* p. 67 *et seq.*
[29] Edwin H. Sutherland, *White Collar Crime*, New York, 1949, Dryden Press, p. 235 *et seq.*

The acceptance by many criminologists of the Positive School's position in respect of the definition of crime and the emphasis placed on the study of the individual offender is not surprising if one considers the history of American sociology. The original problem which occupied the attention of sociologists during the period from 1910 to 1939 was the problem of socialisation and personality development. The work of W. I. Thomas, G. H. Mead, John Dewey and C. H. Cooley was in the area of socialisation. These men were interested in the question of how a person comes to be a member of a group. It mattered little whether the social norms involved were legal or non-legal in nature. It was not until the late 1930s that there occurred in American sociology a revival of interest in European sociologists such as Weber, Durkheim, Toennies, Sombart and others.[30] The problem of social structure and social institutions now assumed a more important place in sociological discussions. The sociology of law is a European import, based on the work of such European writers as Weber, Durkheim, Maine, Jhering, Ehrlich, Gurvitch, Sorokin and Timasheff.[31] It is of interest to speculate as to why sociologists in the United States did not develop an interest in the study of law until recently.

One additional observation concerning the definition of crime is in order. If we define crime as the violation of a law, we must then state what we mean by law. This would require us to investigate such topics as the sociology of law and sociological jurisprudence. If we equate law and custom, as some writers do, then the legal definition of crime and the social definition of crime are synonymous. It is beyond the scope of this paper to pursue further the various meanings of the term " law " except to note that the definition of crime, be it legal or sociological, must be based on a study of law and society rather than on a study of the individual offender.

Is criminology a science ?

According to George B. Vold, " the essential point in positivism is the application of a deterministic and scientific method to the study of crime."[32]   This writer would disagree with Vold's

---

[30] Becker and Boskoff, *op. cit.* p. 79 *et seq.*
[31] Becker and Boskoff, *op. cit.* p. 424 *et seq.*; *Twentieth Century Sociology*, *op. cit.* pp. 297–341.
[32] George B. Vold, *Theoretical Criminology*, New York, 1958, Oxford University Press, p. 39.

observation to this extent: the main characteristic of positivism is its attempt to answer the riddle of criminality by means of scientific studies of the individual offender. The use of scientific method is one of the major characteristics of positivism; however, scientific studies can be made of crime and criminal law as well as of the criminal. Because of his orientation the criminologist has not concerned himself with these other theoretical issues.

The reason the criminologist is not interested in studying law and society is his reform orientation. There is no way in which knowledge of law and society can be used to reform the criminal. The criminologist assumes that he must reform the criminal if the science of criminology is to be a success. When this writer recently advocated that greater attention be paid to the study of criminal law he was told by several probation officers, " But this does not help us to deal with the individual offender." Criminology has developed to a great extent as a branch of the penal reform movement in the United States. The major problems in criminology have been derived from the needs of parole boards and prison administrators for tools with which to reform or manage criminals. The interest shown in parole prediction tables and prison research is illustrative of this reform orientation. The development of criminology is limited by this interest in penal reform and prison problems.

Auguste Comte is the father of positivism in sociology. He envisioned a society in which all social problems are solved by scientists using positivistic methods of research. When society reaches the positive stage of development morals and politics will become positivistic sciences. Positivism subordinates questions about what ought to be or what must be to questions of what in fact is. " Positivistic thinkers . . . have wished to see intelligence applied to the alleviation of all pressing human ills." Auguste Comte " was first and foremost a social reformer, and he was interested in science because he thought of it as an instrument for the reorganisation of human life." [33] America has developed a philosophy, which, like Comte's, takes its point of departure from the disparity between the state of natural sciences and the state of social affairs, and which proposes to eliminate this disparity by extending the scientific outlook to all domains of human behaviour.[34]

[33] *A History of Philosophical Systems*, ed. by Vergilius Ferm, New York, 1950, Philosophical Library, pp. 330–331.
[34] *Ibid.* p. 337.

The positivistic view of Comte was offset by the development of a German school of sociology. The German school made a distinction between the *Sein* and the *Sollen*, the *is* and the *ought*. Max Weber regarded sociology as value-free. Sociology is concerned with what is; it does not attempt to determine ethical and moral issues. Weber recognised that values are facts which can be scientifically analysed. He also recognised the fact that sociology does not furnish answers to questions concerning how people ought to behave. Weber made a distinction between natural and social science, a distinction which the positive school has denied.[35] Most American sociologists follow the value-free approach. Robert Bierstedt writes: " Sociology is a categorical, not a normative discipline, that is, it confines itself to statements about what is, not what ought to be." [36] Kingsley Davis writes: " The normative approach (in the sense of analysing norms and institutions, not in the sense of laying down moral imperatives) is used. . . ." [37] Talcott Parsons states: " Existence and values are intimately related and interdependent, and yet . . . conceptually distinct." [38]

The positivistic position established by Comte is found today in such works as George Lundberg's *Can Science Save Us?* In his writings Lundberg argues that, by emulating the physical sciences and by using statistical and quantitative techniques of analysis, sociology can be used as a tool for obtaining social objectives. Lundberg, following John Dewey and the pragmatists, regards science as an instrument of human adjustment and human progress. The final objective of science is the prediction and control of events which is possible when one uses mathematical models. Lundberg agrees with Weber that sociology must be free of values and value-judgments. He feels that science can furnish us with the means to reach the goals or ends which are existent in society. The major tenets of positivism are quantitativism, behaviourism and pragmatism.[39]

[35] John Cuber, *Sociology*, 3rd ed., New York, 1955, Appleton-Century-Croft, Inc., p. 42 *et seq.*; Ralph Ross and Ernest Van Den Haag, *The Fabric of Society*, New York, 1957, Harcourt, Brace & Co., p. 273 *et seq.*
[36] Robert Bierstedt, *The Social Order*, New York, 1957, McGraw-Hill Book Co., p. 11.
[37] Kingsley Davis, *Human Society*, New York, 1949, Macmillan Co., p. 80.
[38] Kenneth S. Carlston, *Law and Structures of Social Action*, London, 1956, Stevens & Sons, p. 20.
[39] Becker and Boskoff, *op. cit.* p. 86; Roscoe and Gisela Hinkle, *The Development of Modern Sociology*, New York, 1954, Doubleday & Co., p. 54 *et seq.*; George Simpson, *Man in Society*, New York, 1955, Doubleday & Co., p. 48 *et seq.*

According to Weber the purpose of sociology is to understand social events; according to Comte and Lundberg the purpose of sociology is to aid in the scientific solution of social problems. Criminologists in general have followed the Positive School. Criminologists are very anxious that criminology be recognised as a science. They believe that the crime problem can be solved if criminology is scientific. That is why the criminologist has been willing to reject the legal definition of crime in favour of " universal categories of behaviour " which he feels is necessary for scientific analysis. The Michael-Adler report concluded that criminology is not a science due to the unscientific nature of sociology and psychology.[40]

Whether or not we regard criminology as a science depends upon the use to which we want to put our knowledge. Scientific studies can be made of crime, criminal law, criminals, prisons and other such topics. In this sense a science of criminology is possible. If we believe, however, that science can determine the policy to be pursued in the treatment of criminals then we are no longer within the realm of science. Punishment and reform are not a means to an end; they represent goals or values. Science cannot determine the ultimate values of society. Even an extreme positivist such as Lundberg feels obliged to make a distinction between science and policy. The advocates of the " New Penology " ignore this issue. Studies of criminals and prisons will never tell us how we ought to treat the criminal any more than studies of the atom will tell us how we ought to use the atomic bomb. In the next several sections of the paper free will, determinism and punishment will be discussed in terms of this distinction between the *is* and the *ought*.

The criminal

Lombroso is generally credited with shifting the criminologist's attention from the crime to the criminal. Since his time the major issue has been " how and why do people commit crimes? " Attention has been focused on the individual offender. The history of criminology is the history of theories of personality development. Whenever a new theory of personality appears, it is immediately applied to the criminal. Textbooks in criminology tell us a great

[40] *The Sutherland Papers*, edited by Albert Cohen, Alfred Lindesmith and Karl Schuessler, Bloomington, 1956, Indiana University Press, p. 229 *et seq.*

deal about the physical, mental, emotional and social characteristics of the criminal.

The biological school was developed by Lombroso, Garofalo, Ferri and Goring. Lombroso started with the concept of the born criminal, but he in his later writings recognised other factors as being important. Ferri emphasised the importance of anthropological and social as well as physical factors. Ferri classified criminals as born, insane, habitual, occasional and passionate. Goring discovered through his measurements of English convicts that the criminal was physically and mentally inferior to the noncriminal. It is of interest to note that Tarde, not Goring, is responsible for the refutation of Lombroso. Edwin Driver in his article points out that the American criminologist has credited Goring with the refutation of Lombroso while ignoring the biological orientation of his work.[41] The interest in heredity and constitutional types is still seen in the writings of Hooton, Sheldon and the Gluecks.

The mental testers attempted to locate the cause of criminal behaviour in mental defectiveness. Henry Goddard is representative of this stage of criminological thinking.

Tarde located the cause of criminal behaviour in imitation, and it is a short step from Tarde to Sutherland. Guerry and Quételet emphasised the importance of criminal statistics in relation to ecological processes, age, sex, climate and other variables. Park, Burgess, Shaw and McKay developed the ecological school in the United States, work which was basic to the formulation of Sutherland's theory. Bonger emphasised poverty and economic conditions as a factor in criminality, and many studies have been made in an attempt to relate crime rates to economic conditions.

The Freudian theory of personality development has been used by psychiatrists as a basis for explaining criminal behaviour. The psychiatric approach is both individualistic and social psychological depending upon the school of psychiatry to which one belongs. Both the sociological and psychiatric schools emphasise the importance of the family in relation to crime. The sociologist emphasises the environmental and associational aspects of family living; the psychiatrist emphasises the emotional aspect of family living. The two major explanations of behaviour today are the sociological,

[41] See above, Chap. 23.

symbolised by Sutherland, and the psychiatric, symbolised by Freud.[42]

The shift from the biological orientation of Lombroso to the social and psychological orientation of the modern criminologist has misled some as to the true influence of the Positive School on modern criminology. If the term " positivist " is applied to Sutherland, for example, someone will object because Sutherland's theory of behaviour is not the same as Lombroso's. The importance of the Positive School is that it focused attention on motivation and on the individual criminal. It sought an explanation of crime in the criminal, not in the criminal law. This is true of every theory of criminal behaviour which is discussed in the textbooks today, even though the explanation is in terms of social and group factors rather than in terms of biological factors. The shift in criminological thinking has been from a biological to a sociological and psychological explanation of behaviour, not in terms of a shift in interest from the criminal to crime. The emphasis is still upon the individual offender, not crime.

When the definition of crime was discussed above, it was noted that the reason the criminologist feels the need to reject legal definitions of crime is that he is seeking a universal category of behaviour that can be explained in terms of a theory of behaviour. If one is attempting to explain motivation and behaviour, one cannot rely upon legal categories for the obvious reason that the same behaviour pattern will be both legal and illegal at different times and in different places.[43] Regardless of whether we accept Lombroso's theory of behaviour, or Sheldon's theory, or Sutherland's theory, or Glueck's theory, we are still dealing with the criminal, not crime. Sutherland's theory of differential association is a theory of behaviour, based on a study of criminals. The only reason the issue of a definition of crime is raised in modern criminology is that the criminologist has to have some device by which to place behaviour in that category before it is studied as such. However, the criminologist is in a real dilemma in this respect, since as soon as he has derived his universal category of behaviour he has lost the very thing he started out to study, namely, crime.

Two major difficulties confront us today in respect to the problem of understanding the criminal. (1) A theory of criminal

[42] Caldwell, *op. cit.* p. 181 *et seq.*
[43] Jeffery, *op. cit.* p. 671 *et seq.*

behaviour is not a theory of crime. It does not explain why the behaviour is criminal or non-criminal. (2) There is no theory of criminal behaviour available which explains all criminal behaviour. The psychiatric theory is inadequate because not all criminals are emotionally disturbed, and few emotionally disturbed individuals are criminals. The sociological explanation is inadequate because not all criminals have a history of prior associations with other criminals, and not all individuals who associate with criminals become criminals. A theory which integrates the legal, sociological and psychological aspects of crime and criminal behaviour is needed.[44]

In his study of the individual criminal the criminologist has confused two distinct and separate sociological processes: institutionalisation and socialisation.

The individual learns group-defined ways of acting and feeling, and he learns many of them so fundamentally that they become a part of his personality. The process of building group values into the individual is called socialisation.[45]

Socialisation is the sociologist's inclusive term for the various processes through which the original nature becomes fashioned into the social being. . . . A major part of a socialisation process consists, of course, of learning.[46]

By institutionalisation we mean the development of orderly, stable, socially integrating forms and structures cut of unstable, loosely patterned, or merely technical types of action.[47]

Sociologists have coined the term institutionalisation to describe the process of formalising interaction in groups. There is a tendency for participation in most groups to become habituated and formalised into increasingly rigid roles. Each person's behaviour becomes laid out for him in specific ways, and elaborate rules and regulations exist prescribing the proper procedure.[48]

The process of learning behaviour expected of a person in the group is socialisation. Sutherland's theory of differential association is a theory of socialisation. Non-sociological theories of behaviour

---

[44] The writer has outlined some of the problems in such an approach to criminological theory in an article entitled, " An Integrated Theory of Crime and Criminal Behaviour," published in the March–April 1959 issue of the *Journal of Criminal Law, Criminology and Police Science.*

[45] Leonard Broom and Philip Selznick, *Sociology*, Evanston, 1955, Row, Peterson & Co., p. 81.

[46] Cuber, *op. cit.* p. 180.

[47] Broom and Selznick, *op. cit.* p. 238.

[48] Cuber, *op. cit.* p. 319.

place little or no emphasis on socialisation processes. On the other hand, the way in which law develops in response to social problems and social change is institutionalisation. Jerome Hall's study of *Theft, Law and Society* or the writer's study of crime and social change in England are examples of studies of institutionalisation.[49] Crime is a product of institutionalisation; behaviour is a product of socialisation. The confusion of crime and behaviour is the confusion of institutionalisation and socialisation.

Free will v. determinism

Whereas the Classical School accepted the doctrine of free will, the Positive School based the study of criminal behaviour on scientific determinism. Every act had a cause. The Pavlovian theory of conditioned response patterns strengthened the deterministic approach to behaviour. John B. Watson made determinism popular in the United States at about the same time that Freud introduced the theory of psychic determinism.

The major argument today concerning determinism occurs in the criminal law. The law assumes the responsibility of the individual for his voluntary conduct. The Neo-Classical School recognised that infants, lunatics and others were not legally responsible for their actions. The legal position has been under attack by psychiatrists for many years.[50] The Pioneer Series articles on Isaac Ray, Charles Doe and Henry Maudsley deal with this issue of legal versus psychological responsibility. The legal test of insanity, the right and wrong test as stated in the *M'Naghten* case, has been criticised by psychiatrists. Ray and Doe were influential in setting aside the M'Naghten rule in the state of New Hampshire. The New Hampshire rule was applied in the case of *United States* v. *Durham*. In the *Durham* case the court said: " The accused is not criminally responsible if his unlawful act was the product of mental disease or mental defect."

Psychiatrists in general are in favour of the Durham rule. Nearly 90 per cent. of the psychiatrists interviewed concerning the test of criminal responsibility indicated that they favoured the Durham

---

[49] Jerome Hall, *Theft, Law and Society, op. cit.*; Clarence Ray Jeffery, " Crime, Law and Social Structure," Jour.of Crim.L., Criminol.and Pol.Sci., November–December 1956, p. 423 *et seq.*; Clarence Ray Jeffery, " The Development of Crime in Early English Society," Jour.of Crim.L., Criminol.and Pol.Sci., March–April 1957, p. 647 *et seq.*
[50] Jerome Hall, " Psychiatry and Criminal Responsibility, Yale L.J., May 1956, p. 761 *et seq.*; Hall, *Principles, op. cit.* p. 477 *et seq.*

test.[51] The Royal Commission on Capital Punishment recommended abrogating the M'Naghten test and leaving it to the jury " to determine whether at the time of the act the accused was suffering from disease of the mind to such a degree that he ought not to be held responsible." [52] The acceptance of the psychiatric position by lawyers and courts is a current trend. The late George Dession stated in 1938 that " the infiltration of psychiatry into the administration of criminal law will one day be recognised as overshadowing all other contemporary phenomena in its influence on the evolution of criminal justice." [53] Fredric Wertham, a psychiatrist, regards this as a dangerous trend in the administration of justice.[54]

In the issue of criminal responsibility we again witness clearly the influence of the Positive School. The criminal rather than the crime is the issue at hand. Scientific determinism replaces volitional conduct. The inner motivation of the act replaces the overt harm or consequence of the act. The innermost aspect of the psyche is explored in an effort to answer the question " how and why do people commit crimes? " The evaluation of behaviour is placed in the hands of experts. Fredric Wertham feels that the M'Naghten rule should be retained, and he refers to the psychiatric position as " psychoauthoritarianism." [55] Robert G. Caldwell refers to the general movement away from judicial procedures as " the tyranny of the expert." [56]

The argument that scientific determinism ought to replace free will is always framed in terms of psychic determinism. When the psychiatrist offers testimony he is doing so in terms of certain concepts he has concerning determinism. An issue which seems to have been systematically ignored is that there are also sociological determinants of behaviour. Why do we allow a defendant the defence that certain psychic factors determined his behaviour, if we do not allow the same defence to the man who has lived in a criminalistic sub-culture and whose behaviour is therefore determined by his environment? Why not have sociologists testifying as to the environmental determinants of the behaviour of a Negro male living in Harlem? Certainly this individual did not will to be born a Negro or to live in Harlem. The writer is not suggesting

[51] *University of Chicago Law Review*, Winter 1955, p. 327.
[52] *Ibid.* p. 356.
[53] *Ibid.* p. 363.   [54] *Ibid.* p. 581.
[55] *Ibid.* p. 336.   [56] Caldwell, *op. cit.* p. 342.

this as a policy, but is asking the question " why has the discussion of determinism been concerned solely with psychic determinism? "

The law is a measure of social, not individual, responsibility. The law assumes that individuals are responsible for their actions, for otherwise a state of social anarchy would exist. The deterministic argument assumes that responsibility and free will are synonymous, and that determinism precludes responsibility.[57] It can be argued that unless a person is conditioned to expect certain consequences for his action he is not aware of the prohibitions and thus is not responsible. Determinism leads to responsibility. It is on the basis of these anticipated consequences of behaviour that society holds the individual responsible. The socialisation process is based on role-taking processes which allow one to anticipate the consequences of his behaviour and thus one orients his behaviour toward the significant other. The late Robert Lindner expressed it in these terms, " Because every act involves other persons, and most if not all actions at the time of their inception include some fore-knowledge of their potential effects, a network of responsibility exists among all members of the species." [58] Kenneth S. Carlston writes, " Responsibility on the part of the members for the effective performance of their roles in accordance with accepted norms is another distinguishing feature of the organisation (of society)." [59] Not only is the concept of responsibility necessary for the function of society but for the understanding of the social psychology of personality development. Coutu has suggested the term " social accountability " in place of responsibility, and perhaps such a term would be preferred by those who think of responsibility in terms of free will.[60] This is similar to the position taken by Enrico Ferri, namely, that a person is legally or socially responsible for his actions by the fact that he is a member of society, not because he is capable of willing an illegal act. Ferri applied the concept of responsibility to the insane, to juveniles and to others now regarded as being incapable of responsibility.[61] Arnold Green has written:

" The first proposition—that the criminal is not responsible for his crimes—is inconsequential, at least from the point of view of

---

[57] Ross and Van Den Haag, *op. cit.* p. 295 *et seq.*
[58] Robert Lindner, *Must You Conform ?* New York, 1956, Rinehart & Co., p. 204.
[59] Kenneth S. Carlston, *Law and Structures of Social Action*, London, 1956, Stevens & Sons, p. 31.
[60] Walter Coutu, *Emergent Human Nature*, New York, 1949, Alfred A. Knopf, p. 412.
[61] See above, p. 380.

maintaining society. Whether or not a man is responsible for what he does, he must be held personally accountable for what he does. Only on the basis of mutual accountability can mutual prediction of behaviour take place, without which all social relationships would be impossible. We know, for example, that an individual will act thus and so in a given situation because deviation from expected behaviour would be to his discredit or disadvantage. He would be punished, either by losing his reputation, ridicule, or in extreme cases, expulsion. Only by accepting responsibility (accountability) for his actions can an individual invoke upon his fellows their common system of moral norms. Only through a mutual assurance that future behaviour can be predicted on the basis of past and present actions can social relationships be preserved. But the person who denies the concept of responsibility (free will) often attempts to relieve the criminal of responsibility (accountability)." [62]

The desire on the part of the psychiatrist to abolish certain basic concepts such as responsibility, guilt and punishment has brought the following reply from Fredric Wertham:

" The ultra-radical proposal has been made to turn most or all offenders over to psychiatry, and to abolish the very concepts of responsibility, crime, punishment and personal guilt. This is not only impracticable, but harmful, for it deflects our attention from the present-day abuses of psychiatric criminology and from the fight against them. Such an abolition of judicial categories would in practice infringe on the safety of society and on the rights of the individual." [63]

Instead of just delving into the minutiae " of doubtful dreams " he should develop a social orientation corresponding to the growing awareness of social responsibility in a changing world. Instead of the currently too-prevalent practice of giving for social ills individualistic and therefore evasive explanations, the psychiatrist should not shirk his duty to determine the point where individual guilt resolves itself into social responsibility. [64]

The association of the terms " conditioned response " and " involuntary action " is due to the fact that Pavlovian or classical conditioning is used as the example. B. F. Skinner and other psychologists interested in learning theory have introduced into

[62] Arnold Green, *Sociology*, 2nd ed., New York, 1956, McGraw-Hill Book Co., p. 36.
[63] Fredric Wertham, *Show of Violence*, New York, 1949, Doubleday & Co., p. 18.
[64] *Ibid*. p. 18.

psychological literature the term " operant " or " instrumental " conditioning, based on self-initiated or voluntary behaviour on the part of the subject. If modern psychologists, using the latest research techniques, can use such terms as " self-initiated " or " voluntary actions," certainly the lawyer is justified in talking about voluntary actions or intent.[65]

Law is both descriptive, the law as it is, and evaluative, the laying down of moral imperatives. The study of law can be descriptive, and thus a member of the social sciences, or it can be evaluative, and thus within the field of ethics and morals. The law regulating adultery exists as a fact, as a code of behaviour; it also represents a moral imperative, namely, people ought not to commit adultery. Confusion arises when law is treated exclusively either as a fact or as a moral imperative. Very often moral imperatives are confused with conventional behaviour. Social norms, legal and otherwise, tell us how people ought to behave, not how they do behave. Statistical norms are confused with norms that establish standards of behaviour. The *ought* can never be derived from the *is*. The distinction between the descriptive and prescriptive aspects of law goes to the very heart of jurisprudence.[66] The descriptive is often confused with the prescriptive.[67] The relationship between science and policy is demonstrated today in the physical sciences. Physicists were able to produce an atomic bomb, but the moral implications of the bomb have driven many scientists into other areas of research. The physicist does not determine how the bomb ought to be used. The programme to produce satellites also illustrates the difference between the scientific knowledge necessary to launch a satellite and the governmental policy which the United States has pursued in an effort to do so. These examples not only point out the gap between science and policy, but they also point out the fact that scientists do not determine policy. They work within the policy framework determined by the power structure of society.

---

[65] Ernest H. Hilgard, *Introduction to Psychology*, 2nd ed., New York, 1957, Harcourt, Brace & Co., p. 29 *et seq.*

[66] Morris R. Cohen, *Reason and Law*, Glencoe, 1950, Free Press, p. 159 *et seq.*

[67] William Seagle, *Quest for Law*, New York, 1941, Alfred A. Knopf, pp. 7–17. The school of philosophical jurisprudence emphasises the ethical aspect of law. The analytical school emphasises the descriptive aspect of law. Sociological and historical jurisprudence attempts to relate law to the social sciences. Jerome Hall has stated that it is a mistake to separate law as fact and law as value. He advocates integrative jurisprudence which combines the descriptive and evaluative aspects of law. See *Interpretations of Modern Legal Philosophies*, New York, 1947, Oxford University Press, p. 313 *et seq.*

If we make a distinction between what is and what ought to be, and if we assign to science questions of what is and to policy makers questions of what ought to be, then this conflict between law and psychiatry takes on a new meaning. Psychiatry is, or wants to be, a science. Law has a policy making function. The psychiatrist has attacked the M'Naghten rule principally on the grounds that it is not scientific. The M'Naghten rule is not a scientific statement; it states a matter of policy. When the psychiatrist argues that the M'Naghten rule is not longer acceptable, he is arguing as a policy maker, not a scientist. The sociologist has decided he could not act as both scientist and policy maker, and perhaps the psychiatrist will find it necessary to make a similar distinction between science and policy. It is no refutation of a legal doctrine to observe that it is not scientific. Law evaluates behaviour and establishes norms of conduct. The criminal is one who has been judged by the group to have violated a conduct code and is deserving of punishment and condemnation. Mental illness is not defined as the violation of a conduct code. There is no scientific approval or disapproval of mental illness, any more than one approves or disapproves of an infected appendix. A man may have syphilis and commit a crime at the same time. We do not ask a lawyer to treat syphilis, and the doctor is not supposed to make a moral issue of syphilis. The fact that doctors treated syphilis as a moral and not as a scientific issue for years illustrates the point. At the same time we do not ask the doctor what punishment ought to be assigned to the man who has contracted syphilis through an illegal act. In the case of crime, however, we assume that the presence of mental disease places in the hands of psychiatrists the moral evaluation of the behaviour. There is a right and wrong in law; there is no right and wrong in science, only what is. This observation does not preclude the possibility that policy decisions may be based on scientific evidence. Gregory Zilboorg, a psychiatrist, makes such a distinction between science and policy.

" If we as scientific contemporaries are to pass judgment on every contemporary social crisis in terms of our civic reactions clothed in the cloak of our scientific training, much of that which is positive, creative and permanent in our science is bound to be tarnished, as so much of the human spirit was tarnished, whenever scientific knowledge was made to serve the immediate ends of social crises. This mistake is a dangerous error which little helps our civic performances and hurts a great deal our scientific performance and capacity. . . ." [68]

" As scientists we cannot exist unless we stand *au dessus de la mêlée*. If we find ourselves unable to stand above the battle, we must give up our scientific position. There is no choice. For there is no socialist physics, or capitalistic algebra, or Soviet astronomy, or Fascist biology; and there is no American psycho-analysis or British psychiatry. Science remains universal and cosmopolitan as it always has been, or it is not science." [68]

Zilboorg goes on to state that criminals are neurotic individuals, and " Such individuals should be treated, of course, instead of punished." [69] Zilboorg fails to realise that when he states we ought to substitute treatment for punishment he is contradicting what he said a few pages earlier about the separation of science and policy and the maintenance of scientific neutrality on social and political issues. He also states that as a psychiatrist he is identified " with the person to be served and not with the disindividualised aggregate called society or history.[70] Here he is stating that he is a positivist, that is, he is interested in the criminal and not in social meaning of crime, guilt and punishment.

The purpose of punishment

The Classical School advocated a definite penalty for each crime. The punishment must fit the crime, *e.g.*, for armed robbery a man would receive five years in prison. The Classical School punished the man for the crime, for what he had done.

The Positive School rejected the doctrine of *nulla poena sine lege*—no punishment without a law. The Positive School emphasised individualised treatment and the protection of society against the criminal. The punishment must fit the criminal. A man was sentenced, not according to the seriousness of the offence, but according to the factor or factors which motivated him to commit a crime. It is foolish, reasoned the positivist, to sentence all men guilty of armed robbery to the same length of time, since the motivational pattern for each man would be different. One man might commit armed robbery because he does not have the vocational

---

[68] Gregory Zilboorg, "On Social Responsibility," *Searchlights on Delinquency*, ed. by K. R. Eissler, New York, 1949, International Universities Press, p. 334.
[69] *Ibid*. p. 335.
[70] *Ibid*. p. 337.

training necessary for him to get a job; another man might commit armed robbery because it served him as a psychological substitute for love which he did not receive from his parents. In the one case the criminal would receive vocational training; in the other case he would receive psychotherapy. Since it is not possible to know at the time of the trial how long a time will be necessary to rehabilitate the criminal, an indefinite sentence is needed, which could theoretically be from one year to life.[71] Each criminal would receive individualised treatment according to his own psychological and sociological needs. The criminal, not the crime, governed the sentence or punishment given. The time a man spent in prison would be determined, not by the crime he had committed, but by the time needed to adjust and rehabilitate him. Whether or not a man was adjusted and ready to return to society would be determined by scientific penology.

Garofalo was sceptical about the possibility of reforming the criminal. He advocated the death penalty, overseas colonies and life imprisonment for those lacking all moral sense. For the young offender he recommended the indeterminate sentence, and for less serious violations he advocated reparations rather than punishment.[72] Garofalo also recognised the value of the deterrence theory, though he also realised its limitations. He also observed that any system of enforced treatment is punitive in nature.[73]

Ferri continued the Positive School's emphasis on social welfare and social defence. The purpose of criminal justice was to afford maximum protection or defence of society against the criminal. The defence of society was placed above the rights of individuals. Ferri recommended penal colonies, indeterminate sentences, hospitals, scientifically trained judges and the abolition of juries. Although he recognised the value of individualised treatment, he also recognised its limitations. Individualised treatment was limited to the five classes of criminals which he developed.[74]

The modern trend in penology has been in the direction of positivism, with such innovations as the indeterminate sentence, parole, probation, suspended sentences and good time laws.[75] " The

[71] Walter C. Reckless states, for example, " The ideal indeterminate sentence law fixes all sentences from one year to life." Walter C. Reckless, *The Crime Problem*, 2nd ed., New York, 1955, Appleton-Century-Croft, Inc., p. 622.
[72] See above, p. 331.
[73] See above, p. 334.
[74] See above, p. 368 *et seq.*
[75] Hall, *Principles, op. cit.* p. 50 *et seq.*

reforms made in the criminal law in all civilised nations in the last half-century have resulted in the adoption of many of the proposals of the positivists." [76] For Bentham a harm or pain must result from the crime before it is punished. The positivist turned attention to motivation, and punishment was related to human motivation rather than to the overt act or consequence of the act. " Motivation rather than the objective nature of crime, is a basis for sanctions." [77] This attitude, again, is illustrative of the positivist's interest in the criminal rather than crime. The social defence position has resulted in such legislation as sexual psychopathic laws and habitual offender laws.

Ferri delivered a lecture entitled, " New Horizons in Criminal Law," which was later published as *Criminal Sociology*. Barnes and Teeters published *New Horizons in Criminology* in which they propose such reform measures as the elimination of prisons, the elimination of punishment, the elimination of the jury system, the elimination of the concept of free will, individualised treatment and the elimination of other aspects of the legal system. Scientists and mental hospitals would replace judges, juries and prisons. [78]

The abandonment of the principle of legality often leaves the accused without the traditional safeguards found in the law. Jerome Hall has been an outspoken critic of this movement. [79] Francis A. Allen asks the question, " What social interests are to be protected by the criminal law? " We must deal with the problem of the expansion of state power into more and more aspects of social life. [80] The late George Dession emphasised the protection of individual rights as an important function of criminal law. Dession deplored the development of such legal proceedings as denaturalisation of naturalised citizens, deportation of aliens, loyalty hearings, anti-trust proceedings and sexual psychopathic laws which allow a man to be committed for an indefinite period even though he has committed no offence. These actions are always taken under the disguise of social welfare. " Should not the safeguards of criminal proceedings be applied in the above situations? " [81] The Pioneer

---

[76] See above, p. 382.
[77] See above, p. 361.
[78] Harry Elmer Barnes and Negley K. Teeters, *New Horizons in Criminology*, New York, 1950, Prentice-Hall, Inc., p. 289 *et seq.*; p. 644 *et seq.*; p. 947 *et seq.*
[79] Hall, *Principles, op. cit.*, p. 19 *et seq.*
[80] See above, Chap. 16.
[81] Richard C. Donnelly, " George Dession," Jour.of Crim.L., Criminol.and Pol.Sci., March–April 1956, p. 773.

Series article on Montero is relevant in this respect because Montero placed emphasis on the protection of individual rights and the limitation of the power of the state.[82]

The positivist has ignored the fact that the criminal law is a double-edged sword. It protects society against the individual, and it protects the individual against the arbitrary actions of the state. The law prescribes the area in which the state can act.

Criminology textbooks pay a great deal of attention to the inhumanity of man to man: the inhumanity of punishment, the brutal methods of torture and punishment, the ineffectiveness of capital punishment, the complicated legal procedure followed by courts of law, the dishonesty of judges and police officials, the injustices of trials and jury decisions, the brutality of police methods, and the unsavoury conditions in all prisons. What is sometimes ignored is the fact that the Classical School developed as a reaction to harsh penal methods where people were executed for minor offences. The principle of legality was a political doctrine designed to protect the accused against such abuses. Bentham and Beccaria led a wave of legal reform in England.[83] The Positive School places us in a major contradiction in this respect. In order to carry out the social defence philosophy it must sacrifice the individual offender. " The Positive School is committed to the thesis that any measure necessary to protect society (the accused and, of course, the convicted person are automatically excluded therefrom) is justifiable." [84]

In the case of the adult offender, as in the case of the juvenile, the issue is sometimes whether the accused has a personality problem which needs treatment, rather than whether or not the defendant has committed an objective harm. The sexual psychopathic laws represent a movement in this direction. " The sexual psychopathic laws have given birth to a bastard class—neither criminal nor insane—whose members are designated ' offenders ' because of their offensive behaviour. These unhappy nonconformists may be punished or treated just as badly as the criminal and the insane, but obtain far less in the way of due process of law." [85] Hermann Mannheim, E. H. Sutherland and Paul Tappan have criticised the sexual psychopathic laws in this country.[86] Harsh

[82] See above, Chap. 20.   [83] See above, Chaps. 3 and 2.
[84] Hall, *Principles, op. cit.* pp. 550–551.
[85] *University of Chicago Law Review*, p. 355.
[86] Mannheim, *op. cit.* p. 205 *et seq.*

penal methods are now appearing under the guise of "reform" and "science."

It is often stated that the purpose of criminal law ought to be treatment and reform. The observation has been made that there is always a punitive aspect to treatment.[87] Whether or not punishment and treatment can be separated is a relevant question. Sheldon Glueck once commented, "A sick person has a right not to be treated; it is only when he becomes contagious that he may be quarantined."[88]

The reform argument assumes that reform is possible, and that we have the knowledge necessary to reform the criminal. This argument assumes we know the cause of crime and therefore the cure. It overworks the analogy between crime and disease.[89] It overlooks the fact that crime is a product of society. In his book, *Must You Conform?* the late Robert Lindner argues that when we classify homosexuality as a disease and not a crime we are not really helping the homosexual but are in fact creating new oppressive measures to use against him. It is control disguised as reform and treatment. The same thing can be said for regarding behaviour of other types as a disease rather than a crime. If crime is the product of society, do we reform the individual or must we reform the society?

The rehabilitative treatment of the offender is the objective most frequently discussed and applauded today. Criminological positivism, with its focus upon the individual offender, was introduced by Lombroso and his followers. An individualised and, more particularly, a therapeutic orientation has developed rather steadily in subsequent years under the impetus of the modern clinical movement. . . . The focus upon mental pathology has resulted in a conception of criminals as "sick people."[90]

The positivist emphasises parole and the indeterminate sentence, yet a determinate sentence has more value than does the indeterminate sentence as a factor in success or failure of parole.[91] Sweating out a parole and observing the political manoeuvres of parole boards is very demoralising to an inmate. Many inmates feel that

---

[87] *University of Chicago Law Review*, p. 350 *et seq.*
[88] Henry Nunberg, "Problems in the Structure of the Juvenile Court," Jour.of Crim.L., Criminol.and Pol.Sci., January–February 1958, p. 507.
[89] Cohen, *op. cit.* p. 55; Hall, *Principles, op. cit.* p. 132.
[90] Paul W. Tappan, *Contemporary Correction*, New York, 1951, McGraw-Hill Book Co., pp. 110–111.
[91] Reckless, *op. cit.* pp. 637–639.

a release on parole automatically lessens one's chances of reforming after release from prison. " Society is not yet fulfilling its responsibility to the implications of parole." [92]   Today the Youth and Adult Authorities are held in high esteem by penologists.   The American Law Institute was instrumental in the establishment of these agencies.   The model Correction Act removed from the courts the power of probation and placed the offender in the hands of the Authority for an indeterminate period for which there is neither a minimum nor a maximum.[93]   " It seems to many that this feature of the model Act is extreme and even dangerous, in view of the possibility of miscarriages of justice, as well as mistakes in judgment." [94]   The arguments against the indeterminate sentence are many and varied.[95]   Alexander Maconochie, the British reformer, emphasised the importance of the indeterminate sentence, but as John Barry noted in his article, " Maconochie would have been surprised at the arbitrary powers entrusted to tribunals such as the Adult and Youth Authorities and Parole Boards." [96]   The emphasis has shifted from a rigid sentencing procedure which did not take into account individual factors, to an indeterminate sentence which does not take into account the rights of individuals.   Perhaps we can find a compromise between such two extremes.   At least it is difficult to justify the indeterminate sentence and parole as " reform measures."

The modern criminologist places little value on the deterrent theory of punishment, though both Lombroso and Garofalo realised the deterrent effect of criminal law.   They placed more emphasis on overseas colonies and capital punishment than on reform.[97]   As Morris R. Cohen points out, we cannot say that law does not deter because some individuals commit crimes.[98]   The notion that law does not deter is fatalistic and this conflicts with the positivist's concept of determinism.[99]

The optimum result in treatment cannot be attained by mere reaffirmations of faith in " individualisation " and " therapy," or

[92] Donald F. Wilson, *My Six Convicts*, New York, 1951, Pocket Books, Inc., p. 281.
[93] Bloch and Flynn, *op. cit.* p. 490.
[94] *Encyclopedia of Criminology*, ed. Vernon C. Branham and Samuel B. Kutash, New York, 1949, Philosophical Library, p. 465.
[95] Caldwell, *op. cit.* p. 644 *et seq.*; Edwin H. Sutherland and Donald R. Cressey, *Principles of Criminology*, 5th ed., New York, 1955, J. P. Lippincott, p. 560 *et seq.*
[96] See above, p. 103.
[97] See above, pp. 279 and 330.
[98] Cohen, *op. cit.* p. 49.
[99] *Ibid.* p. 49.

by the elaboration of case histories. It cannot be achieved, either, by a cavalier rejection of the incapacitative and deterrent objectives of correction in favour of an exclusively rehabilitative goal.[1]

In the case of punishment, as in the case of responsibility, there is a confusion of what is and what ought to be. The question of punishment is a moral issue. The sociologist and psychiatrist do not hesitate in suggesting what ought to be done with the offender. At its conception American sociology was dominated by a philosophy of social reform; however, this aspect of sociological thinking has been modified since that time. In criminology the reform issue still looms large, and the criminologist is more often than not more of a reformer than a scientist. Science can tell us that executing some criminals will not deter others; it cannot tell us that we ought not to execute them. One of the major difficulties encountered in criminology when we deal with ethical issues is that the sociological positivist and the legal positivist divorce fact and ethics.[2] This does not mean that the positivist does not make ethical judgments; it means that he makes ethical judgments without acknowledging that he is making them. Criminology is a science; law is a policy making procedure.

Perhaps the most glaring defect in the sociological analysis of punishment is that it views punishment always in the context of what it means to the individual offender, never in terms of what it means to society. Because the positivist is concerned with the individual offender, it should be expected that he would neglect the sociological meaning of punishment. The social purpose of punishment is to create social solidarity. Emile Durkheim viewed punishment as a reflection of group solidarity. Any act which violated the social code had to be punished in order to restore order and to reaffirm the violated code. In this way group solidarity was maintained.[3]

Since sanctions are not revealed by analysis of the act that they govern, it is apparent that I am not punished simply because I did this or that. It is not the intrinsic nature of my action that produces the sanction which follows, but the fact that the act violates the rule which forbids it. In fact, one and the same act, identically performed with the same material consequences, is blamed or not

[1] Tappan, *Contemporary Correction*, *op. cit.* p. 12.
[2] Hall, *Principles*, *op. cit.* p. 546.
[3] See above, Chap. 19.

blamed according to whether or not there is a rule forbidding it. The existence of the rule and the relation to it of the act determine the sanction. Thus homicide, committed in time of peace, is freed from blame in time of war. An act, intrinsically the same, which is blamed today among Europeans, was not blamed in ancient Greece, since there it violated no pre-established rule.

We have now reached a deeper conception of sanctions. A sanction is the consequence of an act that does not result from the content of the act, but from the violation by that act of a pre-established rule. It is because there is a pre-established rule, and the breach is a rebellion against this rule, that a sanction is entailed.[4]

The purpose of punishment is social disapproval of the act through collective action on the part of the group. Durkheim's analysis of punishment has the advantage of placing attention on the normative structure relating to acts and not on the act itself. The Positive School was opposed to the position taken by Durkheim, that is, it focused attention on the act and not on the meaning of a violation to the social group.

The use of punishment by society is not as important in terms of whether or not it reforms the individual as in terms of what it does for society. Punishment creates social solidarity and re-enforces the social norms.

Conclusions

In the *Pioneers in Criminology* we witness the development of the major issues underlying modern criminological thinking. Whereas the Classical School focused attention on the *crime*, the Positive School shifted the emphasis to the *criminal*. The major characteristic of criminological thinking since Lombroso's time is the preoccupation of criminologists with the problem " why do individuals commit crimes? "

The Positive School gained its name from the positive philosophy of the nineteenth century which applied scientific method to social problems. This school maintained the position that criminology must become scientific, by which they meant that the explanation of criminal behaviour and the treatment of criminals must be accomplished by scientific means. Science is designed to explain why people behave the way they do; it does not tell us how people ought

---

[4] Lewis A. Coser and Bernard Rosenberg, *Sociological Theory*, New York, 1957, Macmillan Co., p. 108.

to behave. The reason we have crime, however, is not because individuals behave the way they do, but because others think they ought not to behave in that way and have it within their power to judge their behaviour. Crime involves an ethical issue.

The biological explanation of behaviour has been seriously challenged by sociologists and psychologists since Lombroso's time. This tenet of positivism has been refuted. However, the criminologist has accepted a theory of behaviour as a theory of crime. Crime and criminal behaviour are confused. Even though in modern criminology the Lombrosian explanation of behaviour is rejected, the positivist's interest in the criminal is maintained.

Because the positivist wanted to study the criminal rather than crime, he was obliged to reject the legal definition of crime. " Anti-social behaviour " is often used in place of a legal definition. There is no agreement among criminologists as to the meaning of the term " crime," though this is presumably the starting-point for any research. Some use a social definition of behaviour; some use a legal definition of behaviour. Some regard the sociology of law as outside the scope of criminology; some regard it as basic to criminological theory.

The scientific approach substituted determinism for volition. The individual criminal is again the centre of attention, since the question is one of individual responsibility. Although Ferri used the concept of legal responsibility in place of moral responsibility, the individualistic approach is gaining headway in law as evidenced in the recent *Durham* decision.

The Positive School regarded the protection of society as the governing factor in punishment. Punishment was designed to fit the criminal, not the crime. Such reform measures as parole, probation and indeterminate sentences furthered the individualistic approach to criminology. The objection to the social defence school comes from those who do not want social welfare placed above individual welfare. Individualised treatment must of necessity place great discretionary power in the hands of the experts.

The Positive School advanced the field of criminology by placing the study of the criminal within a scientific framework. Today, as a result, we know a great deal more about the criminal than we have known heretofore. The criticisms made of the positivist are to be viewed as attempts to raise questions other than those raised by this school, and not as a blanket condemnation of a healthy interest shown in the criminal. The criminologist's attempt to separate criminology and criminal law, and his related attempt to derive criminality from the behaviour of the criminal offer a major obstacle to a theory of crime. More attention needs to be paid to the meaning of crime in terms of criminal law, social structure and social change. A re-evaluation of the theoretical structure of criminology is called for at this period in the development of criminological thinking.

AMERICAN TRENDS IN CRIMINOLOGY
1960–1970

The pioneers, positivism, and the 1960s

When I wrote my conclusion to *Pioneers in Criminology* in 1959, I claimed that the particular problems in which criminologists are interested today derive from the issues developed by the pioneers. The framework of modern criminology was built by the nineteenth-century positivists who rejected the classical position, and it is they who dominated criminology for most of this century. Some changes that have occurred in the past decade suggest that it may now be time to take another look at positivism, before seeing how these changes have affected the positivist framework.

The basic postulates of positivistic criminology are (1) a rejection of legal concepts of crime and criminal procedure, and their replacement with individualised justice based on a therapeutic model, (2) a rejection of punishment and its replacement with correctional treatment, (3) a rejection of free will and its replacement with scientific determinism, and (4) a rejection of the study of criminal law, and its replacement with a study of the individual offender and his medical, psychological, and social characteristics.

The pioneers added to the second edition of *Pioneers in Criminology* reinforce its coverage of the development of positivism in nineteenth-century criminology. With the exception of Wigmore, who advocated a close relationship between criminology and criminal law, these pioneers uniformly took a positivistic position. As individuals and collectively, Livingston, Morrison, Roeder, Lucas, and Bonneville delivered such advice as: study the causes of crime in the character of the offender; look for a lack of education and employment; abolish capital punishment in favor of imprisonment; resocialise the offender by "moving from the crime to the criminal"; make the "punishment fit the criminal and not the crime"; individualise treatment procedures; have reparation made to victims; put prisoners on indeterminate sentences, parole, probation, and work-release projects; and build separate institutional facilities for youths and women.

The chapter on Morrison reads like a present-day textbook in criminology, in the way it discusses the biological and social factors in crime, the use of individualised treatment procedures, and the impact of age, sex, social class, and climate on crime rates. It is fascinating to see how long ago Morrison and Lucas independently concluded, with considerable statistical sophistication, that poverty *does not* cause crime. This makes one wonder what we were doing in the 1960s in the U.S.A. when we undertook a mammoth "War on Poverty" program in an effort to reduce crime and delinquency. The failure of this program has been described by Daniel P. Moynihan as a "Maximum Feasible Misunderstanding." [1] One of the useful purposes the Pioneer Series will serve is that of reminding us how often we have reinvented the wheel. One reflects, after reading of the accomplishments of the pioneers, how little progress has been made in the twentieth century in criminology.

Criminal law and positivism

The impact of positivism on American criminology caused the field of criminology to develop in sociology and psychology quite independent of the influence of criminal law. The criminologist studied the offender with little regard for the legal process by which crimes are created.[2] As a result, we saw the emergence of the juvenile court and a non-criminal definition of delinquency, the use of indeterminate sentences (transferring the power to hold a man in prison from the law to men in administrative posts), and the use of law to force men into treatment settings without the benefit of criminal procedures or safeguards. Potential dangerousness and per-

[1] Daniel P. Moynihan, *Maximum Feasible Misunderstanding* (New York: Free Press, 1969).
[2] C. R. Jeffery, "The Structure of American Criminological Thinking," *Journal of Criminal Law, Criminology, and Police Science*, Vol. 46, No. 5 (January 1956), pp. 658–672; Gerhard O. W. Mueller, *Crime, Law, and the Scholars* (Seattle: University of Washington Press, 1969).

sonality defects replaced overt criminal behavior as grounds for deciding who was to be institutionalized. Under the guise of treatment we place individuals in hospitals "until cured," which may mean a life sentence without due process [3]—a danger referred to in my 1959 conclusion.

The impact of the positivist position can be seen in recent court decisions which support the "criminals are sick and must be treated within a medical model" philosophy: *Durham* v. *U.S.* (mental illness), *Driver* v. *Hinnant* (alcoholism), *California* v. *Robinson* (drug addiction), and *Easter* v. *District of Columbia* (alcoholism).[4]

However, during the 1960s the philosophy of the Classical School, which had not disappeared from criminal law in spite of its apparent submersion at times beneath positivism, suddenly reemerged in court decisions. In *Kent* v. *U.S.*[5] the court held that "there may be grounds for concern that the child receives the worst of both worlds; that he gets neither the protections accorded to adults, nor the solicitous care and regenerative treatment postulated for children." In *The Matter of Gault* [6] Justice Fortas wrote: "Certainly these figures and the high crime rate among juveniles could not lead to the conclusion that . . . the juvenile system is effective to reduce crime or rehabilitate offenders." In the *Gault* case the court applied to juveniles many of the classical ideas that are embodied in the Constitution. In *Rouse* v. *Cameron* [7] the doctrine of the right to treatment of those being held in mental hospitals was upheld because of the *Durham* decision. There is evidence that the doctrine of the right to treatment will be applied to other areas as well.[8] In *Powell* v. *Texas* [9] the court reversed earlier decisions that had declared that alcoholics were sick persons in need of treatment, and declared that placing a sign over a jail calling it an "alcoholic rehabilitation center" did not answer the problem of alcoholism. In the *Powell* case the court restated the failure of treatment programs for alcoholics and reaffirmed a basic doctrine of criminal responsibility.

The extension of positivism into criminal law has created an un-

[3] Thomas Szasz, *Law, Liberty, and Psychiatry* (New York: Macmillan, 1963) and *Psychiatric Justice* (New York: Macmillan, 1965).
[4] *Durham* v. *U.S.*, 214 F. 2nd 862 (1954); *Driver* v. *Hinnant*, 356 F. 2nd 761 (1966); *California* v. *Robinson*, 370 U.S. 660 (1962); *Easter* v. *District of Columbia*, 361 F. 2nd 50 (1966).
[5] *Kent* v. *U.S.*, 383 U.S. 556 (1966).
[6] *In the Matter of Gault*, 87 S. Ct. 1428 (1966).
[7] *Rouse* v. *Cameron*, 373 F. 2nd 451 (1967).
[8] Donald S. Burris (ed.), *The Right to Treatment* (New York: Springer, 1971).
[9] *Powell* v. *Texas*, 392 U.S. 514 (1968).

tenable position wherein the legal rights of juveniles, alcoholics, addicts, and the mentally ill are ignored in the name of treatment while at the same time the defendant is not afforded treatment which can make any claim to effectiveness or impact on future behavior. The criminal law has ignored its deterrence aspect in favor of the rehabilitative ideal,[10] even though there is mounting evidence of the failure of rehabilitation as a means of handling our crime problem. We arrive at a position in history where we do not protect the rights of the accused, rehabilitate the convicted, or protect the public from future criminal acts.

A new theoretical base for criminology and criminal law is badly needed, and it will only come out of interdisciplinary efforts to relate criminal law to the behavioral sciences. The work of Gerhard O. W. Mueller[11] is a good example of a current effort to carry on the work started by Wigmore in relating criminal law to criminology.

The decline of positivism in the 1960s

In 1959 I concluded that the impact of positivism on sociology and psychology had been great, and that the study of the individual offender had dominated academic criminology. Professor Mannheim in his Introduction to the book was critical of this view of positivism. He noted in his historical review the fact that in certain European countries the Lombrosian view of criminals had been rejected—as it has been in the United States, it might be added—and he observed that "the determined efforts of Havelock Ellis to popularise the work of Lombroso had only very limited appeal" (p. 17). I had attempted to show that positivism is a commitment to the study of the individual criminal, not of crime, and that the study of the offender included his physical, psychological, and social characteristics. Ferri considered criminal behavior in terms of anthropological, physical, and social factors. Edwin H. Sutherland was as much of a positivist as was Lombroso, though he did not follow Lombroso's theory of criminal behavior. That a rejection of a biological theory of criminality is not a rejection of a positivist's position was also, I hope, made clear in the 1959 paper.

Mannheim suggests that the "sociological analysis of the law . . .

---

[10] Francis A. Allen, "Criminal Justice, Legal Values and the Rehabilitative Ideal," *Journal of Criminal Law, Criminology, and Police Science*, September 1959, pp. 226–232; Norval Morris and Frank Zimring, "Deterrence and Corrections," *The Annals*, January 1969, pp. 137–146.

[11] Mueller, *op. cit.* note 2.

may be the task of the sociology of the criminal law rather than that of criminology" (p. 33).   While I argued that the sociology of criminal law was an essential and critical part of criminology, he felt that the proper subject-matter of criminology was the criminal. When he states that "the object of Criminology is to study criminal behavior and the physical, psychological, and socio-economic factors behind it," Mannheim sounds very much like the pioneer positivist Ferri, who wrote that "the proper subject of criminal anthropology is the anti-social individual in his tendencies and in his activities." [12] Mannheim writes that "while it is no doubt one of the functions of the Sociology of the Criminal Law to examine the conditions under which criminal laws develop, such an examination cannot be re- garded as coming under the scope of Criminology."   He argues that criminology must be made independent of criminal law.[13]   This position, which is basic to positivism, has been rejected in American criminology in the 1960s.   Whereas in 1959 I was able to conclude that American writers had ignored the classical/positivist argument while maintaining a positivistic position, by 1972 the classical school had become a major focus of criminologists.   Mannheim's conclu- sions about the separation of crime and criminal behavior have not been borne out by the recent history of American criminology.

Matza, in his book *Delinquency and Drift*,[14] attempted to com- promise the hard determinism of positivism and the free-will doctrine of classicism with what he called "soft determinism" or drift between legal values and delinquent values.   Such a position is indefensible within a scientific framework, whereas the major contribution made by the positivists was precisely to place the study of behavior within a scientific framework.   One of the basic difficulties in criminology was pointed out in 1932 by Michael and Adler when they noted that a science of criminology was impossible as long as a science of human behavior was lacking.[15]   In 1967 the President's Crime Commission found that "until the science of human behavior matures far beyond its present confines, an understanding of delinquency is not likely to be forthcoming." [16]   "Many kinds of knowledge about crime," the

[12] Enrico Ferri, *Criminal Sociology* (Boston: Little, Brown, 1917), p. 79.
[13] Hermann Mannheim, *Group Problems in Crime and Punishment* (1955; reprinted Mont- clair, N.J.: Patterson Smith, 1971), pp. 260–263.
[14] David Matza, *Delinquency and Drift* (New York: Wiley, 1964).
[15] Jerome Michael and Mortimer J. Adler, *Crime, Law, and Social Science* (1933; reprinted Montclair, N.J.: Patterson Smith, 1971).
[16] President's Commission on Law Enforcement and Administration of Justice, *Juvenile Delinquency and Youth Crime* (Washington, D.C.: U.S. Government Printing Office, 1967), p. 8.

Commission stated, "must await a better understanding of social behavior." [17] The current revolution in behavioral and genetic biology, experimental and physiological psychology, environmental psychology, and related areas will totally alter our concept of behavior in the next twenty or thirty years. So far, however, the influence of this on criminology has not manifested itself in much more than a few crude behavior-modification projects in institutions.

Another change in sociological criminology is related to the development of the labeling school. The legal definition of crime, as we have seen, used to be rejected by sociologists in favor of a social definition. In recent years there has developed a body of literature stating that "deviance is not a quality of the act the person commits, but rather a consequence of the application by others of rules and sanctions to an offender. The deviant is one to whom the label has successfully been applied; deviant behavior is behavior so labeled." [18] "No behavior is criminal until it has been so defined through recognized procedures of the state. In this sense criminal behavior differs from non-criminal behavior only according to the definition that has been created by others. It is not the quality of the behavior, but the nature of the action taken against the behavior that gives it the character of criminality." [19] The American criminologist in the 1960s returned to the Classical School in this respect, though he did not acknowledge that he was returning to a historic tradition. The "labeling school" emerged as if it were something new. Only Quinney relates his work to the historical development of criminology.[20]

In 1956 and in 1959 I argued that the sociology of criminal law must be a major aspect of criminology. During the 1960s there was an important movement in criminology to develop a sociology of criminal law. "The scope of criminology has broadened in recent years to include the process by which persons and behaviors become defined as criminal. That is, the criminal law—including its formulation and administration—no longer is taken for granted, but serves as a major orientation for the study of crime. Research in the last decade has substantiated the importance of criminal law in crimi-

[17] President's Commission on Law Enforcement and Administration of Justice, *The Challenge of Crime in a Free Society* (Washington, D.C.: U.S. Government Printing Office, 1967), p. 273.
[18] Howard S. Becker, *Outsiders* (New York: Free Press, 1963), p. 9. See also Jack P. Gibbs, "Conceptions of Deviant Behavior: the Old and the New," *Pacific Sociological Review*, Spring 1966, pp. 9–14.
[19] Richard Quinney, *The Social Reality of Crime* (Boston: Little, Brown, 1970), p. 207.
[20] Richard Quinney, *Crime and Justice in Society* (Boston: Little, Brown, 1969), pp. 1–5.

nology."[21] The works of Quinney, Schur, Turk, and Chambliss have been related to the development of a sociology of criminal law in the United States.[22]

The behavioral scientist has been as concerned in the 1960s with the administration of justice as with the criminal. This is reflected in the reports of the President's Commission on Law Enforcement and Administration of Justice, as well as in works by James Q. Wilson,[23] David J. Bordua,[24] and Jerome H. Skolnick.[25] One should also mention the books in the Administration of Criminal Justice Series by Dawson, Newman, Miller, LaFave, and Tiffany *et al.*[26] The decision of the positivists to reject criminal law was seriously questioned in the 1960s, a trend which was inherent in criminology in the 1940s and 1950s in the writings of Allen, Hall, Tappan, Caldwell, and the present writer.[27]

Doubt over the acceptability of our current concepts of crime has increased markedly since 1960. The confusion caused by the positivists over the meaning of crime is today reflected in arguments concerning political criminals. The view (held e.g. by Garofalo) that crime consists of a violation of the moral sentiments of the community, and the view that crime must be defined in other than legal terms, have resulted in an intolerable situation in which criminologists cannot define a crime or argue that a criminal act has been committed. The questions can be answered with either a yes or a no according to one's political and social ideology. If we follow this line of reasoning criminology is reduced to a political ideology rather than a scientific academic discipline, with social protest replacing scientific knowledge.

The positivists argued that the State could define as crimes any behavior it desired in order to protect society, without regard for the principle of legality. That is why Ferri became a member of the Fascist government of Italy. The present-day criminologist often

21 *Ibid.*, p. 30.
22 Edwin M. Schur, *Our Criminal Society* (Englewood Cliffs: Prentice-Hall, 1969); Austin T. Turk, *Criminality and Legal Order* (Chicago: Rand McNally, 1969); William J. Chambliss, *Crime and the Legal Process* (New York: McGraw-Hill, 1969).
23 James Q. Wilson, *Varieties of Police Behavior* (Cambridge: Harvard University Press, 1968).
24 David J. Bordua (ed.), *The Police: Six Sociological Essays* (New York: Wiley, 1967).
25 Jerome H. Skolnick, *Justice Without Trial* (New York: Wiley, 1966).
26 Robert O. Dawson, *Sentencing* (1969); Donald J. Newman, *Conviction* (1966); Frank W. Miller, *Prosecution* (1969); Wayne R. LaFave, *Arrest* (1965); Lawrence P. Tiffany, Donald M. McIntyre, Jr., and Daniel Rotenberg, *Detection of Crime* (1967; all published Boston: Little, Brown).
27 C. R. Jeffery, *op. cit.* note 2, and *supra*, p. 458 *et seq.*

reverses the argument and maintains that the individual must decide for himself whether a law is a just law to be obeyed or an unjust law to be violated and opposed. "The state's power is legitimate only when it is so regarded by the citizens. . . . When the state's use of power to control others does not rest on consent and legal guarantees, the authority of the state is illegitimate and need not be obeyed. In fact, obeying illegitimate authority would be an unprincipled act." [28] If we accept this definition of legitimate and illegitimate, we define crime in terms of the consent of each individual. What is a crime for one person becomes an act of heroism and martyrdom for another. I have grave doubts whether this will suffice for a basic definition of crime and criminals.

Has rehabilitation a future?

The positivists were foremost in their concern for the individualised treatment and rehabilitation of offenders. This view has been around for at least one hundred and fifty years, and yet one still hears present-day criminologists and correctional workers say that they belong to the New School of penology that believes in the treatment of offenders. *Pioneers in Criminology* should dispel the notion that to be treatment-oriented is to be modern. The truth of the situation is that the major stumbling block to reform measures of a significant type in criminology is the fact that we are frozen into a treatment posture and are unwilling to look at alternatives. We assume we have the techniques for rehabilitating offenders, an impression reinforced by the absence of any scientific evaluation of the results of such efforts. A major effort is now under way to find alternatives to imprisonment in halfway houses, community-based treatment programs, and work-release projects.[29]

The few studies that have attempted to show the success of prison programs, community-based programs, probation and parole, psychotherapy, and so forth have not turned up any real evidence of success. We cannot yet say that doing something is better than doing nothing.

Several recent statements summarise the past one hundred and fifty years of treatment philosophy. A recent survey of the California correctional system concluded that

28 Richard Quinney, *op. cit.* note 18, p. 313.
29 John P. Conrad (ed.), "The Future of Corrections," *The Annals*, January 1969.

variations in recidivism rates are for the most part attributable to initial differences among the types of offenders processed and the remaining differences in violation rates between programs may be accounted for by differences in interpreting an event as a violation or designating it as such. No evidence was found to support claims of superior rehabilitative efficacy of one correctional alternative over another.

Group counseling has been one of the most widely applied and recommended prison treatment techniques. . . . There were no differences in parole outcome by treatment status after release. . . . Contrary to the expectations of the treatment theory, there was no significant difference in outcome for those in various treatment programs or between the treatment groups and the control groups.

There is no evidence to support any proposed claim to superior rehabilitative efficacy. The single answer, then, to each of the five questions originally posed—Will the clients act differently if we lock them up, or keep them locked up longer, or do something with them inside, or watch them more closely afterwards, or cut them loose officially—is "Probably Not." [30]

The authors of a current textbook in the field recently wrote,

When measured against this correctional pattern, California and some other states have made enormous steps forward in the field. This progress, however, is toward a more humanistic approach to criminals and delinquents, not necessarily to a truly effective rehabilitation program. [31]

Beker and Hyman have recently evaluated the California Community Treatment project, and they found no evidence to support any claim of success through the use of I level theory and differential treatment of young offenders. [32] A consultant's paper for the President's Crime Commission stated that "There are no demonstrable and proven methods for reducing the incidence of serious delinquent acts through preventive or rehabilitative measures." [33]

If the theory of deterrence is a failure, and punishment cannot be used within the criminal justice structure to control human behavior; and if the theory of rehabilitation is a failure and we are unable to devise a system of treatment to change antisocial behavior; then we must come up with an alternative approach to crime control. The present effort is exemplified by federal policy to implement,

[30] James Robinson and Gerald Smith, "The Effectiveness of Correctional Programs," *Crime and Delinquency*, January 1971, pp. 67, 73–74, 80.
[31] Martin R. Haskell and Lewis Yablonsky, *Crime and Delinquency* (Chicago: Rand McNally, 1970), p. 467.
[32] Jerome Beker and Doris S. Hyman, "A Critical Appraisal of the California Differential Treatment Typology of Adolescent Offenders," *Criminology: An Interdisciplinary Journal*, May 1972.
[33] *Juvenile Delinquency and Youth Crime, op. cit.* note 15, p. 410.

through the Law Enforcement Assistance Administration, the treatment philosophy by means of correctional programs and the deterrence philosophy by means of police action programs, while leaving the courts torn between deterrence and reform.[34]   Our present policy tries to pull in opposite directions at once—on the one hand we are weakening the deterrence aspects of the system when we strengthen the rehabilitative aspects, and on the other hand when we increase the efficiency of the police we add to the already critical load on the courts and the correctional system.

Mannheim writes that the Social Defence movement can be viewed as a potential twentieth-century "Third School" (p. 35). However, Social Defence (as I have written elsewhere), while modifying some of the harsher aspects of positivism, is essentially a neo-positivistic position.[35] According to Marc Ancel the object of social defence is "a rational penal policy which aims at the systematic re-socialization of the offender." [36]   The treatment or rehabilitation of individual offenders is the core policy pursued by the Social Defence school, and this is in no way different from what the positivists were advocating.   What I would advocate is a concept which transcends both the Classical and Positive Schools of criminology.   As presented elsewhere,[37] a new model would replace deterrence and treatment with *prevention,* i.e., rather than waiting for the crime to occur, society would take measures to prevent criminal acts from occurring in the first place; it would replace punishment and treatment of offenders with *environmental design;* it would replace legal and social services to offenders with *research* designed to answer questions concerning the interaction of the organism and the environment.   Such an approach would be interdisciplinary in nature, based on biological engineering, physiological and environmental psychology, urban design and planning, operations research, and systems analysis.   The objects of concern would not be criminals but features of the urban environment that create high crime rate areas —streets, parks, buildings, terminals, expressways.   It starts with the fact that to change behavior we must deal with the environment, not

---

[34] Frank F. Funstenberg, "Political Intrusion and Governmental Confusion: The Case of the National Institute of Law Enforcement and Criminal Justice," *The American Sociologist,* Vol. 6, Supplementary Issue, June 1971, p. 59 *et seq.*

[35] C. R. Jeffery, *Crime Prevention through Environmental Design* (Beverly Hills, California: Sage Publications, 1971), p. 31.

[36] *Ibid.,* pp. 31–33.

[37] *Ibid.*

the individual client. Buckminster Fuller summarised the approach when he stated "reform the environment, not man." [38]

The Classical School said "reform the law." The Positive School said "reform the man." The environmental school would say "reform the environment."

CLARENCE RAY JEFFERY.

NOTE ON THE CONTRIBUTOR

Dr. CLARENCE RAY JEFFERY received his Ph.D. in sociology from Indiana University in 1954. He was an Associate Professor of Sociology at Arizona State University and a Professor of Public Administration at New York University, and currently he is a Professor of Criminology at Florida State University. He was a Senior Fellow in Law and Behavioral Science at the University of Chicago Law School in 1958–59, and a Fellow at the Summer Institute on the Administration of Criminal Justice at the University of Wisconsin in 1960. Professor Jeffery is the co-author of *Society and the Law,* and the author of *Criminal Responsibility and Mental Disease* and *Crime Prevention through Environmental Design.* He served as book review editor for the *Journal of Criminal Law, Criminology, and Police Science* from 1963 to 1969, and he is the present editor of *Criminology: An Interdisciplinary Journal.*

---

[38] R. Buckminster Fuller, *Utopia or Oblivion* (New York: Bantam Books, 1969), p. 320.

SUBJECT INDEX

INDEX OF PERSONS

PATTERSON SMITH SERIES IN
CRIMINOLOGY, LAW ENFORCEMENT, AND SOCIAL PROBLEMS

* new material added

PATTERSON SMITH SERIES IN
CRIMINOLOGY, LAW ENFORCEMENT, AND SOCIAL PROBLEMS

* new material added   † new edition, revised or enlarged

PATTERSON SMITH SERIES IN
CRIMINOLOGY, LAW ENFORCEMENT, AND SOCIAL PROBLEMS

* new material added   † new edition, revised or enlarged

PATTERSON SMITH SERIES IN
CRIMINOLOGY, LAW ENFORCEMENT, AND SOCIAL PROBLEMS

* new material added   † new edition, revised or enlarged